INTERPRETING
THE NEW TESTAMENT

INTERPRETING
THE NEW TESTAMENT

Second Edition

James L. Price
Duke University

Holt, Rinehart and Winston, Inc.

New York   Chicago   San Francisco   Atlanta   Dallas
Montreal   Toronto   London   Sydney

Permission to quote from the following publications is gratefully acknowledged: *The Book of the Acts in History,* by H. J. Cadbury, and *Eschatology and Ethics in the Teaching of Jesus,* published by Harper & Row; *The Quest of The Historical Jesus,* copyright 1953, The Macmillan Company, New York and London; *Jesus and Christian Origins,* by H. Anderson, and *Conversion,* by A. D. Nock, The Oxford University Press; *A New Quest of the Historical Jesus,* by J. M. Robinson, Alec R. Allenson, Inc.; *An Introduction to the New Testament,* by E. Goodspeed, copyright 1937 by the University of Chicago; W. G. Kümmel, *Introduction to the New Testament* (Founded by Paul Feine and Johannes Behm, 14th rev. ed.), Eng. Trans. by A. J. Mattill, Jr., Abingdon Press and the S.C.M. Press, Ltd.; *Invitation to the New Testament,* by W. D. Davies, Doubleday & Co., Inc., and Darton, Longman & Todd, Ltd.; *A New Eusebius,* ed. by J. Stevenson, Society for Promoting Christian Knowledge, London; *Early Christian Fathers,* Vol. I, The Library of Christian Classics, newly translated and edited by Cyril Richardson, published simultaneously in Great Britain by S.C.M. Press, Ltd., London, and in the United States of America by the Westminster Press, Philadelphia, 1953; *History and Hermeneutics,* New Directions in Theology Today, Vol. II, by Carl E. Braaten, copyright © MCMLXVI, W. L. Jenkins, The Westminster Press and the Lutterworth Press; and *Word and Faith,* by G. Ebeling, The Fortress Press.

To Ruth,
in gratitude for the encouragement of her love
and confidence

PREFACE

Ten years have passed since the publication of *Interpreting the New Testament*. The reception accorded the book surpassed the author's fondest hopes. A word of thanks for the many helpful comments he has received. Once it was decided that a revision should be undertaken, readers' suggestions for the improvement of the book were given careful consideration. For these reasons, and others, extensive sections of the text have been rewritten.

A few of the more significant changes may be noted. The chapters on "the historical Jesus" have been revised. Recent efforts to advance research in this important problem area are reported. The development of a method known as "redaction criticism" is applied to the Gospels in order to identify more precisely the theological contributions of the four evangelists. The chapters on the criticism and interpretation of Paul's Letter to the Romans and of the Gospel of John required a thorough revision since this writer's understanding of their authors' intentions has undergone substantial change through the study and teaching of these books during the past decade.

Comparisons of this edition with the earlier text will disclose other modifications. A new introduction describes an interest and a debate which reaches farther afield than New Testament scholarship. "Hermeneutics" is the term currently employed to identify the problem of interpretation, that is, the need for a vital translation of the meaning of a text. With the refinement of critical methodology and the advance of historical knowledge, the value of the tools of research and the applicability of the information obtained through their use have become increasingly problematical. Another critical issue that has emerged is the problem of achieving accurate understanding of the relation of early Christian thought and behavior to the rise of Gnosticism in the Greco-Roman world. In the final section of this book I have attempted to investigate the relation of some gnostic tendencies that have been identified to the various interpretations of the Christian Gospel manifested in the latest books of the New Testament. One's judgments in this area of research must remain somewhat tentative because much obscurity surrounds the sources of Christian and non-Christian Gnosticism and questions concerning their influence.

The new edition preserves features of the book which its first readers found useful as aids to the interpretation of Scripture. Chapter Two presents a reasoned statement of the particular approach to the canonical writings which this edition recommends. The author has found no other approach as satisfactory as this one. Again, the primary purpose of the book remains substantially the same: to discover the uniqueness and particular values of each New Testament writing as a significant literary and theological entity. Some historians view these primitive Christian documents as the exiguous and miscellaneous collection of source materials to be dissected, sorted, and used selectively for historical reconstruction and documentation. This book is designed to discourage fragmentation of the New Testament material and to foster the appreciation of a unity that is integral to each book and to the collection as a whole. To further its primary objective this book contains an outline of each New Testament writing, followed by a descriptive analysis of its contents. The reader is thus encouraged to enter into dialogue with each writer through a perception of the structure of the composition and its writer's inimitable development of ideas. At the same time, this author recognizes that no literature can be understood fully apart from some knowledge of the particular, contemporary influences which shaped its writer's interest, beliefs and modes of expression. Chapters Three and Four, Thirteen, and Eighteen concisely describe the environment of Christianity during the New Testament Era. These descriptions are based upon the principal literary sources for knowledge of the various intellectual perspectives and institutions of Ancient Judaism, and of other peoples, in the Roman society of the Hellenistic Age. Thus while *Interpreting the New Testament* has, as its primary objective, an increase in one's understanding of the intrinsic value of the separate New Testament books, an honest effort is made—for theological as well as historical reasons—to sketch the background of the entire New Testament. This is one means of exhibiting the underlying unity of the diverse books in this early Christian collection.

In revising the text and notes, cognizance has been taken of some of the most significant books and articles written since 1961. No one dare claim comprehensiveness in the burgeoning field of publications, nor presume that nothing of real value has been overlooked. There has been an acceleration in the translation into English of important works written in other languages, especially German. Fortunately, it is now possible to refer to current European literature, as well as to some earlier works excluded in the original edition out of consideration for the majority of its readers.

Several persons have devoted much thought and effort to the preparation of this edition for the press. My special thanks to Stephen Frederick, graduate student in New Testament studies, and to Mrs. Oma Lee Smith, office secretary, Duke University; and to Miss Marie Lonning of the editorial staff and Miss Enid Klass of the Photo Research Department, Holt, Rinehart and Winston.

J. L. P.

Durham, North Carolina
January 1971

CONTENTS

Preface vii
List of Maps and Charts xv

Introduction

1. **Historical Interpretation of the New Testament:** *The Need and the Problem* **3**

Overcoming Initial Resistance 5
How Historical Criticism Functions 6
Literary Criticism 7
Historical Criticism 8
The Search for an Adequate Hermeneutic 9

2. **Methodological Considerations:** *A Point of Departure; The Course of Study; An Overview of the New Testament* **17**

Four Approaches to the New Testament 18
The Early Church and the Literature of the New Testament 21
The Common Faith and Hope of the Early Church 26

Part One   The Recovery of Christian Origins

3. **Reconstructing the Setting of Early Christianity** **31**

Background to New Testament Times 34
The Literary Sources 47

4. **The Beliefs and Practices of Palestinian Jews 59**

Organization of Judaism 62
Influential Parties and Sects 68
The Religion of the Masses 76
Ancient Jewish Eschatologies 78

5. **Narrative of Christian Beginnings: *Acts 1–12* 91**

Acts 1–12: Initial Impressions 95
An Outline of the Acts of the Apostles, 1–12 95
Ancient Church Tradition Concerning Acts 99
Modern Criticism and Acts 1–12 101
The Question of the Sources and the Date of Acts 103
The Purpose of Luke–Acts 107

6. **Beliefs of the First Christians 113**

A Summary of Early Christian Beliefs 117
Christology in the Earliest Church 123
Manifestations of the Holy Spirit 131
The Community Consciousness of the Eschatological Congregation 135

7. **Early Christian Organization, Missions, and Opposition 137**

The Order of the Community 140
Ritual in the Early Church 144
The Scattering of the Brethren 148
Early Conflicts with Jewish Authorities 154

8. **Early Oral and Written Traditions Concerning Jesus 157**

Earliest Traditions 161
The Apostles' Teaching 164
The Method, Values, and Limitations of "Form Criticism" 165
The Beginning of Written Accounts 173
An Outline of the Sayings Source 176

9. **Three Portraits of Jesus: *Matthew, Mark, and Luke* 183**

The Gospel of Mark 187
An Outline of the Gospel According to Mark 192
The Gospel of Matthew 200
Matthew's Use of Mark 201
The Composition of Matthew 13 204
The Composition of Matthew 5–7 205
An Outline of the Gospel According to Matthew 206
The Gospel of Luke 215
"Special Luke" 217
The Passion Narrative in Luke and Mark 219
The Outline of the Gospel According to Luke 222

10. **The Ministry of Jesus: *Prolegomena* 231**

The Quest of the Historical Jesus, Old and New 235
An Outline of Jesus' Ministry 249
The Proclamation of the Kingdom of God 251
The Son of Man in the Synoptic Gospels 261

11. **The Ministry of Jesus:** *In Galilee* 267

Before the Ministry 270
The Galilean Ministry 276

12. **The Ministry of Jesus:** *Beyond Galilee and in Judea* 299

A Momentous Confession and Announcement 302
Forebodings of Death; Intimations of Its Meaning 307
The Ministry in Judea and beyond the Jordan 309
Last Days in Jerusalem 310
The Nativity Traditions in Matthew and Luke 321

Part Two **Early Expansion of Christianity and the Career of Paul**

13. **The Environment of Gentile Christianity** 327

Cults and Mystery Religions 331
The Widespread Belief in Astrology and Magic 340
The Popular "Schools" of Hellenistic Philosophy 340
Mystical Religions of the Greco-Roman World 343
The Rise of Gnosticism 345
Judaism of the Dispersion 348

14. **The Acts Narrative of Paul's Missions** 351

The Composition of Acts 13-28 354
The Witness of Paul from Antioch to Rome 355
The Acts Story of Paul's Conversion and Early Experiences 357
Mission to Cyprus and Galatia 360
The Jerusalem Conference 363
Mission to Macedonia and Achaia 366
Paul in the Roman Province of Asia: The Ephesian Ministry 371
Paul's Last Visit to Jerusalem 374
The Voyage to Rome 378

15. **Paul's Letters to Thessalonica and to Corinth** 381

The Letters to the Thessalonians 385
An Outline of the First Letter of Paul to the Thessalonians 387
An Outline of the Second Letter of Paul to the Thessalonians 390
The Corinthian Correspondence 392
An Outline of the First Letter of Paul to the Corinthians 397
An Outline of the Second Letter of Paul to the Corinthians 405

16. **The Galatian and Roman Letters** 413

The Letter to the Galatians 416
An Outline of the Letter of Paul to the Galatians 416
The Letter to the Romans 426
An Outline of the Letter of Paul to the Romans 430

17. **Letters from Prison** 447

The Letter to the Philippians 450
An Outline of the Letter of Paul to the Philippians 452
The Letter to Philemon 459

An Outline of the Letter of Paul to Philemon 460
The Letter to the Colossians 463
An Outline of the Letter of Paul to the Colossians 466

Part Three Conflict and Consolidation in the Postapostolic Age

18. Christianity in the Postapostolic Age 473

The Position of Christianity in the Empire 477
Jewish–Christianity and the Conflict between the Synagogue and the Church 480
Doctrinal Disputes in Postapostolic Times 482
Moral Problems in the Churches 485
The Development Toward Formal Organization 487

19. Writings from the Pauline Circle 493

Letter to the Ephesians 496
An Outline of the Letter to the Ephesians 500
The Pastoral Letters 505
An Outline of the First Letter of Paul to Timothy 509
An Outline of the Letter of Paul to Titus 511
An Outline of the Second Letter of Paul to Timothy 513

20. Five "Open Letters" to Christians 517

The First Letter of Peter 520
An Outline of the First Letter of Peter 524
The Letter to the Hebrews 527
An Outline of the Letter to the Hebrews 531
The Letter of James 534
An Outline of the Letter of James 535
The Letter of Jude 541
An Outline of the Letter of Jude 542
The Second Letter of Peter 543
An Outline of the Second Letter of Peter 544

21. Writings from the Johannine Circle 549

The Martyrdom Tradition 552
The Revelation to John 553
An Outline of the Revelation to John 558
The Three Letters of John 565
An Outline of the Third Letter of John 565
An Outline of the Second Letter of John 566
An Outline of the First Letter of John 567

22. The Gospel According to John 571

The Problem of Origin 574
An Outline of the Gospel According to John 576
Interpreting the Fourth Gospel 589

Bibliography 601
Index 617

LIST
OF MAPS AND CHARTS

Chronology of the New Testament Era   22
Alexander and the Hellenistic Rulers   36
Hellenistic Empires   38
The Hasmoneans and Herods   42
Herod's Temple Jerusalem   65
Palestine under the Herods   98
Palestine in the Time of Jesus   278
Jerusalem in the Time of Jesus   311
Roman Empire in the Time of Paul   334–335
Greece and Italy   367
Agora in Athens after Hellenistic Remodeling   370
A Sketch of the Area of Ephesus   373
A Sketch of Corinth—Central Area   382
Paul's Christian Interpretation of History   443
Pauline Churches in the Lycus Valley   447
Asia, Macedonia and Achaia   561

INTRODUCTION

chapter one

HISTORICAL INTERPRETATION OF THE NEW TESTAMENT

The Need and the Problem

CHRISTIANITY as a historical movement produced a variety of writings concerning Jesus of Nazareth who is called the Christ. Not all at once but in the course of their expansion and development, Christian churches added to their "scriptures," inherited from Judaism, twenty-seven small books. It was believed that these writings were authentic statements of the Christian faith, representing the Christian communities from the earliest period. By the time agreement was reached concerning the limits of the collection, the word *canon* was being applied to it. This Greek term identified "a stiff reed," and because it was an article often used for measurement or alignment, *canon* came to signify a *rule* or *standard*. Thus the determination of the canon of the New Testament (or New Covenant) was the churches' confession that these writings, as the fulfillment of the earlier "scriptures," provided the authoritative standard or norm defining the religion of people called Christian.

It is not altogether clear what were the factors which contributed to the formation of the Christian canon. Historical investigation of the subject leads one into a study not only of the origin of the various New Testament books, but also of their early dissemination and eventual acceptance as authoritative by Greek, Latin, and Syrian churches. The story of the origin of the canon is related to ecclesiastical decisions concerning doctrine, and the resolution in the ancient Church of the rival claims of various leaders and institutional forms. In the second and third centuries those books which were attributed to the Apostles, or were believed to contain their true witness, were canonized. But the usefulness of other writings in Christian worship and instruction, and in the nurture of piety, afforded additional criteria for canonization.[1] Suffice it here to note the importance of the end result. Common ascription to the canonical status of the New Testament enabled the churches of the Roman Empire to obtain an essential unity in spite of serious schisms within and among them. Veneration of the same scriptures later provided a ground for unity and continuity, as when the Orthodox Eastern and Roman Catholic churches separated in the ninth century, or when the Western Church divided in the sixteenth century following the Reformation. The phenomenon of the modern "ecumenical movement" arises in part from an acknowledgment, by all churches concerned, that the same twenty-seven books possess a unique authority, to which appeal can be made for guidance in all essential matters pertaining to faith and community.[2]

In this fact—the existence and persistence of belief in canonical scriptures—lies the need for historical interpretation if one is to understand the Christian religion. The witness of the New Testament to the appearance in history of Jesus who is called the Christ came to possess (and still possesses) for many persons an abiding, normative significance. But Christianity, thus bound to the record of its unique historical origin has, of course, been subject to the march of time, and each generation has needed to come to terms with the fact of change. In this fact—the existence and persistence of belief in canonical scriptures—lies also, then, a problem endemic to Christianity as a historical religion. The problem,

[1] A. H. McNeile, "The Growth of the New Testament Canon," *An Introduction to the Study of the New Testament*, ed. C. S. C. Williams (rev. ed., 1953), pp. 310ff. [hereafter, *Intro.*]; Paul Feine and Johannes Behm, *Introduction to the New Testament*, ed. W. G. Kümmel, trans. A. J. Mattill, Jr. (14th rev., 1966), pp. 334ff. [hereafter, Feine-Behm-Kümmel, *Intro.*]; for an excellent concise account, see F. W. Beare in *Interpreter's Dictionary of the Bible*, vol. 1, pp. 520ff. [hereafter *IDB*].

[2] *IDB*, p. 520. Exception is taken to this common view by E. Käsemann, who represents a radical Protestant's narrowing of the limits of the canon: *Essays on New Testament Themes*, trans. W. J. Montague (1960), pp. 95ff. [hereafter, *Essays*].

stated as a question, is this: By what means or process do ancient texts, valued for their witness to God's saving action in Christ once-for-all, become proclamation, that is, good news for modern man?

In recent years an old Greek term has been reclaimed to focus this process of deriving meaning from the past for the present, so crucial to Christian knowledge, the term *hermeneia* (interpretation). By this term the Greeks referred to that complex act of bringing to understanding some reality through speech, written statement, exposition, translation. The task of "interpreting the New Testament," in its broadest scope, is one of reaching understanding through its language (i.e., of perceiving with its writers what they intended to say); of translating its archaic words and ideas into the clarity of one's own language; and of explicating obscurity by means of clearer expression.[3] More simply expressed, *hermeneutic* is a shorthand term employed today for that process whereby the understanding of what an ancient text *meant* becomes an understanding of what it *means*.[4] The achievement of the ultimate objective, expressed in this inclusive description of New Testament study, will be considered at the end of this chapter. In the meanwhile, attention is given to the need for a genuinely historical approach to Christian origins. But first one must acknowledge some objections.

OVERCOMING INITIAL RESISTANCE

One often encounters today resistance to the general idea of historical study. In part this is attributable to the strange ambivalence that modern man displays toward the past and its significance for him. On the one hand, it is judged that since men's perceptions of their natures and of human society, as well as of physical reality, have undergone such radical changes in the course of the scientific and technological revolution, a garnering of knowledge of the past is of little importance to the modern world. Ancient men, with their archaic self-evident assumptions, speak out of a past that is dead and might well be forgotten. "History is bunk" was once an anti-intellectual slur spoken, ironically, by an inventive genius who was a major contributor to modern technocracy—and to the problem of air pollution. "History is bunk" is no longer a saying attributed to Henry Ford alone, but a slogan of "the now generation."

On the other hand, modern man is seeking to further his revolutions of thought and action, and justify his angry renunciation of his heritage, by rewriting history. "Revisionist historians" aim to recover the truth about man in his past in order better to understand man's present predicaments. Such men have become acutely aware of the social uses of historical study.[5] For example, many black scholars in modern America seek to enable their people to understand their identity and

[3] *New Frontiers in Theology, The New Hermeneutic,* ed. J. M. Robinson and J. B. Cobb, Jr. (1964), vol. II, pp. 1ff. [hereafter, *New Frontiers*]. The neglect and virtual disappearance of "hermeneutics" as a scholarly discipline in the nineteenth century is illustrated in Robinson's essay, pp. 17ff.

[4] K. Stendahl, *IDB*, vol. 1, pp. 418ff.

[5] *Time Magazine*, Feb. 2, 1970, pp. 14f.

their present objectives in society through a study of Afro-American history, which is seen as a revision of the traditional story of America's past, and of the white historians' account of the Negroes' place in it.

It is unlikely that many persons, unless they are seriously alienated from their intellectual and cultural heritage, can be expected to abandon belief in the importance of the study of history. Historical criticism is an indispensable tool for understanding modern man. Antihistorical movements seem ephemeral, and impotently reactionary, when they are compared with the impact of others which are based upon an interpretation, or a reinterpretation, of man in his history—past and present. Sacrificial commitments to a new future have often arisen out of these analyses.[6]

A more specific kind of resistance is sometimes evoked among Christians when one speaks of the necessity of historical criticism in interpreting the canonical scriptures. The belief that the New Testament is an essential part of "the Holy Bible" has been accompanied by a conviction that this book is quite different in kind from all other religious texts. A corollary of the doctrine of the incarnation, as an event *sui generis*, is the doctrine of a unique and infallible scripture. The New Testament, it is said, should not be expected to yield its truths to the approaches of "scientific" historical research, and will not in fact do so.[7]

The present writer has no wish to make light of this position—sometimes identified as "biblicism," or as a main tenet of "fundamentalism"—least of all to appear contemptuous of it. Surely one can honor insistence upon the need for an adequate *doctrine* of scripture. The point to be made here is that in interpreting the New Testament today the way forward is through the use of those critical tools which sound scholarship employs in seeking to understand all ancient texts, not by resorting to a precritical, ahistorical approach. An appeal to the abuses of particular biblical scholars may lend plausibility to one's objections to criticism, but such errors can be seen as data for improving a valid methodology. The philosophical presuppositions, the research procedures, and the conclusions of all historical critics are subject to the rigorous review of other critics, and by this means much ignorance and presumption have been dispelled.

HOW HISTORICAL CRITICISM FUNCTIONS

The claim that historical criticism is needed in order to understand the New Testament does not answer the question of how it functions. As an essential first step in interpretation, historical criticism, broadly conceived, may be said to be "the means of gaining authentic access to the intention of the text."[8] Various techniques have been employed to achieve this objective. In their development

---

[6]E.g., G. W. F. Hegel; K. Marx. See C. H. Dodd, *The Bible Today* (1947), pp. 122ff.

[7]G. Ebeling's vigorous defense of the positive significance for Christian scholarship of the critical historical method gave rise to an equally vigorous statement of an opposition, more often expressed than articulated: *Word and Faith*, trans. J. W. Leitch (1963), pp. 18ff.

[8]R. W. Funk in *New Frontiers*, ed. Robinson and Cobb, p. 183; R. M. Grant, *A Historical Introduction to the New Testament* (1963), pp. 74ff. [hereafter, *Intro.*].

specialization has been inevitable, and the division of biblical scholarship into supplementary studies has resulted, giving rise to some confusion in nomenclature.

Biblical scholars in the modern period have distinguished two major types of criticism: lower, or textual, criticism; and higher, or documentary, criticism. The former aims to recover the "original" text and to achieve adequate modern language translations. Perhaps one may describe these interests and some others under the rubric "literary criticism."

LITERARY CRITICISM

The student of a painting or a musical composition will wish to know whether he is dealing with an original or with a retouched work or revised version. Just so, the student of great literature desires to read the actual words of an author, or at least to have a reasonably accurate text. New Testament criticism logically begins with a concern for the text itself. It is certainly a legitimate question to ask, let us say, whether a Greek manuscript of Paul's Letter to the Romans contains the actual words written to this church. It is a fact, however, that we do not now have access to the original of the Roman letter, or, for that matter, of any other New Testament book. Since this is so, it is not simply one's curiosity which makes one ask whether an accurate text can be reconstructed from the copies which are known. Moreover, since the New Testament was written in Greek, it is surely a valid question to ask if at any given point the English version faithfully renders the most reliable, reconstructed Greek text.

These are the concerns of textual, or lower, criticism. They are matters which should be handled by persons with specialized training, not by beginners. To become a textual critic, or to be able to evaluate the findings of others, one must know the Greek language, especially at the stage of its development in New Testament times and later. He must know other languages, such as Syriac and Latin, in which some of the valuable early copies were made. He must be proficient in the methods of dating manuscripts. By means of the collation and classification of manuscripts a history of the different text types (or "families") is written, and upon these findings a "critical text" is reconstructed. After this comes the task of achieving an accurate translation. The translator of the New Testament must possess still other capabilities, such as a thorough familiarity with modern language usages.

Several accounts of the history of textual criticism, of the achievements of the modern period, and of the tasks yet to be accomplished have been written for the nonspecialist.[9] The history of the creation of Latin, German, English, and other great versions of the Bible is another chapter in the transmission of its text.[10] Though a lively interest in textual criticism is felt chiefly by specialists, everyone

[9] M. M. Parvis, *IDB*, vol. 4, pp. 594ff.; for more detailed, technical accounts, see Feine-Behm-Kümmel, *Intro.*, pp. 359ff.; B. M. Metzger, *The Text of the New Testament* (1964).

[10] For a description of ancient, medieval, and modern versions, see the illustrated articles in *IDB*, vol. 4, pp. 749ff.

should recognize the importance of such studies for the determination of a correct text of the New Testament and for the securing of adequate translations.

Recent New Testament scholars have stressed the importance of another dimension of research which surely belongs to literary criticism. Special attention is given to such matters as the genre of a given book, word usage, sentence and paragraph structure. Notice is taken of the presence in a text of confessional or hymnic formulae, derived perhaps from traditions possessed by the writer's community, as well as of possible interpolations by later editors or scribes. Observations concerning the composition of a New Testament book shed light upon its author's purpose or intention (and that of his source[s], or redactor[s]).[11] In this regard, "literary criticism" is not easily distinguishable from a special concern of "historical criticism," to be discussed below, which is to define as nearly as possible the circumstances under which a book was composed. Some persons prefer to bracket the aims of literary and historical criticism as an investigation of the origin and composition of the New Testament writings. But the range of interests, specifically those of historical criticism, needs further clarification.

HISTORICAL CRITICISM

Documentary, or higher, criticism explores questions of the authorship, date, and destination of the various New Testament writings. The evidence which is examined by higher criticism is of two types: internal and external. Sometimes a book of the Bible yields direct or indirect information concerning its origin. In evaluating this internal evidence the higher critic is like the person unraveling the "whodunit" or working a jigsaw puzzle. He endeavors to fit the scattered bits together. External evidence consists in references to the origin of Bible books in ancient Church traditions. Sometimes also the influence of a book is reflected in the impress of its language or ideas upon writings contemporaneous (or nearly so) with it. The critic must then ask to what extent such circumstantial evidence can be relied upon. Primary importance is placed upon the internal evidence, which sometimes supports the external evidence but at other times seems to impugn the latter's authenticity.

Textual and documentary studies lead logically to the exploration of the historical setting of a book, in the widest and most inclusive sense of the word. Again it should be stressed that the tasks of the literary critic cannot be separated sharply from those of the historian, but the special importance of the latter needs to be acknowledged. The appreciation of any ancient book depends upon knowledge of the conditions of its period, and, for the recovery of these, all of the historian's techniques are needed. Such sciences, too, as geography and archeology enable the reader of the New Testament to reconstruct partially the backgrounds of its books. They help him to view the central persons of the New Testament more concretely in terms of their life situations, avoiding a modernization of such personalities, yet preventing him from thinking of real people as so many abstractions. The methods of historical criticism are used to study the culture of the

[11] Grant., *Intro.*, pp. 59ff.

period, its possible influence upon the writer and the ideas and practices which he reports. Just as a river is inseparable from its banks and the terrain through which it flows, even so the Christian movement cannot be understood fully apart from its environment. The reader of the New Testament may not have the specific interests of the historian. Nevertheless, he will wish to know what sources are available for a knowledge of New Testament times, and the importance which scholars have attached to these, even though he is not himself in a position to evaluate critically their significance.

It may now be said that historical criticism of the New Testament has as its object a credible narrative of Jesus and the first century of the Church. Building on the work of all other critical specialists, the historian of New Testament times reconstructs "a narrative which reports events in a sequence roughly chronological." Chronology is sometimes disparaged as a thing of little value, yet "without chronicle history cannot be written."[12] No interpretation based on causal relationships is possible without the establishment of a plausible sequence of events and influences. The historian also aims to flesh out this skeleton of history he has reconstructed, to bring to life the persons involved, their motives and their actions, to re-create and relive things as they actually happened insofar as this is possible.

The concerns of the historian of the New Testament lead him to the nebulous boundaries between fact and fiction, but the value of his efforts to reconstruct the past cannot be gainsaid. By this means modern readers of the New Testament are placed in the position of its first readers. In the theater this active audience participation is called empathy. By analogy we may say that historical criticism has the effect of getting the interpreter of the New Testament into the drama itself, quickening and at the same time controlling his thought, imagination, feelings. Thus far-off scenes and events take on an apparent immediacy. The impact of words are felt with a startling directness. At the same time, historical criticism has the opposite effect of making the interpreter aware of the enormous distance separating him from the New Testament times. In seeking to understand the text in its true historical setting—in its pastness, its particularity and uniqueness—the interpreter is often confronted with its strangeness, its lack of connection with his own world and immediate concerns. Thus it would seem that historical criticism has the effect of either modernizing or archaizing the New Testament, of bringing it up to date or pushing it from us into "the long ago and far away" (or of doing both at the same time?). This paradoxical situation leads us to raise again the hermeneutical problem, and to explore briefly some of its theological implications.

THE SEARCH FOR AN ADEQUATE HERMENEUTIC

Consideration is now given to that aspect of New Testament interpretation which carries one beyond the usual concerns of literary and historical criticism. The modern use of the loanword *hermeneutic* focuses, as we have seen, not only

---

[12] Ibid., p. 74.

upon this process of bringing to understanding the content of ancient texts, but also upon appropriating their contemporary meaning and discovering their possible relevance.

Perhaps the problems to be faced in achieving a modern hermeneutic may be recognized if one surveys a few developments in the history of the Church of the West, especially within Protestantism since the Enlightenment.[13]

In ancient and medieval times, Christians do not seem to have been aware of a hermeneutical problem. The world picture of the Bible was believed to be so compatible with the philosophical assumptions of men that it was nearly always possible to apply to life directly the New Testament's teaching. The difficulties in rendering literally some texts were overcome by allegorical interpretations or an eclectic use of the scriptures. The major factor which fostered belief in the continuing contemporaneity of the canonical writings, however, was the prevailing understanding of the nature of the Church and its authority. The revelation of God in Jesus Christ was made present through the contemplative and imitative piety of those persons belonging to monastic orders—who sought to reproduce in their communities the religion of Jesus and the Apostles—and through the participation of all Christians in the mystical body of Christ through the sacraments. The doctrine that the church of Rome existed in episcopal succession unbroken from the days of the Apostles, and that the pope, the vicar of Christ, possessed infallible authority, meant that the events of revelation in the past were continuously re-presented in the Church.

The Protestant Reformation of the sixteenth century threatened to destroy many of these links between the world of the New Testament and the ongoing world of men living in the Church of the West. The radical position was taken that the historic, once-for-all revelation of God in Christ becomes present only through an individual's faith response to the Word of God, interpreted as his gracious offer of salvation. By thus elevating the proclamation of the Word, Reformed theology and preaching became primarily an exposition of scripture.

In principle, therefore, the hermeneutical question acquired fundamental significance at the time of the Reformation. By the exercise of his enlightened critical faculties, the Reformer believed that it was possible to cut through the overlay of ancient Church tradition to the meaning of the text itself. No traditional interpretation must be set alongside of scripture, no infallible teaching office interpret its meaning. In practice, however, neither the Reformers nor the Protestant scholastics after them became aware of the hermeneutical question as a problem. Their expositions of scripture continued to be based on the assumption that the biblical picture of man in the world and in history was self-evidently true. "The general speculative presuppositions, in which the [Christ-event] of revelation had become embedded and anchored in Church tradition," were not questioned. Indeed, one must conclude that the Reformers "gave insufficient recognition to their distance from early Christianity," and consequently did not

---

[13] In what follows the writer acknowledges special indebtedness to Ebeling's *Word and Faith*, pp. 28ff., and Carl E. Braaten's *New Directions in Theology Today: History and Hermeneutics* (1966), vol. II, pp. 33ff., 130ff. [hereafter, *History and Hermeneutics*].

distinguish sufficiently the authority of their own views from the testimony of scripture.[14] All too soon among their followers the belief arose, in contradiction to the Protestant principle of being bound solely to the scriptures, that the time-conditioned confessional statements of the Reformers, inspired by their reading of scripture, were to be preserved indefinitely, and that scripture could be interpreted rightly only *in the light of* the "pure doctrine" of the Reformers. "Protestant orthodoxy lapsed into a harmonistic approach, bringing Bible passages into line with dogmatic truths."[15]

The immediate consequence of the late seventeenth-century Enlightenment was an "age of rationalism" (ca. 1650–1780). Scholars with an interest in Christian scriptures searched them for illustrations of universal laws. The British philosopher David Hume (1711–1776) has been cited as stating clearly the conviction of Enlightenment scholars: "mankind are so much the same, in all times and places, that *history informs us of nothing new or strange* in this particular. Its chief use is only to discover the constant and universal principles of human nature."

During the nineteenth century this perspective changed radically. Historical science "claimed total independence from dogmatic and metaphysical assumptions which imposed an *a priori* web of interpretation upon the facts of history . . . Leopold von Ranke (1795–1886), the great German historian, formulated the ideal of the historian—to discover what actually happened."[16] Guided by naturalistic assumptions or the axioms of philosophical positivism, many nineteenth-century historians took the position that in their reconstructions of the past they "could not presuppose supernatural intervention in the casual nexus." To do so would frustrate their ideal of objectivity, the achievement of that emotional distance from the texts under investigation, so necessary in their research. As a result "scientific historians" sought to explain every event as an unraveling of "the skein of natural, social and psychological causes."[17]

The achievements of these historians failed to measure up to their methodological aims, but confidence in the importance of historical criticism for a true understanding of man's past did not wane. Within Protestant circles in the late nineteenth century, scholars adopted and rigorously applied the critical methods of the secular historian. Although it seemed that "what actually happened" in the time of Jesus and the early Church, according to New Testament scholars, appeared to be quite different from what Church tradition had taught for many centuries, most Protestant institutions embraced the new critical methods and findings as an essential path to Christian knowledge. Paul Tillich (1886–1965) wrote that "the historical approach to Biblical literature is one of the great events in the history of Christianity and even of religion and human culture. . . . It was an expression of Protestant courage when theologians subjected the holy writings of their own church to a critical analysis through the historical method. It appears that no other religion in human history exercised such boldness and took upon

---

[14] Ebeling, *Word and Faith*, p. 40.
[15] Braaten, *History and Hermeneutics*, p. 35.
[16] Ibid., pp. 35f.
[17] Funk in *New Frontiers*, ed. Robinson and Cobb, pp. 185f.

itself the same risk."[18] In view of the risk, and the early, tradition-shattering results, it is no wonder that one encountered serious reservations.

Objections were voiced not only by persons resistant to liberal learning; a leading theologian of the early nineteenth century, Friedrich Schleiermacher (1768–1834), argued that an understanding of the New Testament required something more than literary and historical analysis. The hermeneutical "art" consisted in supplementing objective analysis with an intuitive understanding of the text as the authentic expression of an author's religious consciousness. By an act of imagination, modern interpreters must re-create the perspectives and experiences of each New Testament author.

Other scholars developed further Schleiermacher's psychological hermeneutic, likewise assuming that since both writer and interpreter participated in history they were susceptible to similar perceptions and experiences. The difficulty with all these efforts to bridge the gap between past and present by means of psychological re-creation is that attention was shifted from the content of the New Testament to the process by which a given text arose from its author's consciousness. Certainly there are a very limited number of passages in the New Testament whose principal intention is the expression of inner feelings common to all men.

In the period of Europe's upheaval following World War I, a Swiss theologian, Karl Barth (1886–1968), established a new era in Protestant theology by the publication, among other significant writings, of his commentary on Paul's Letter to the Romans. In prefaces to the successive editions of this work, Barth wrote: "the critical historical method of research into the Bible is right enough: it aims at a preparation for understanding, and that is never superfluous . . . But my attention has been directed to seeing *through* the historical to the Spirit of the Bible, who is the eternal Spirit (1918) . . . I have been called a 'declared enemy of historical criticism' . . . But what I reproach them with is not the historical criticism, the right and necessity of which on the contary I once more explicitly recognize, but the way they stop at an explanation of the text which I cannot call any explanation, but only the first primitive step toward one, namely, at establishing 'what is said'" (1921).[19]

A major contribution to the modern search for a satisfactory hermeneutic was made by Rudolf Bultmann (1884–), and by several scholars who, beginning with Bultmann, sought to modify and extend his positions. In some respects "the new hermeneutic" of the Bultmann circle retains continuity with Schleiermacher and his successors, but the impact of Barth's "dialectical theology" and European existentialist philosophy, as applied by Bultmann to the New Testament, are more direct.[20]

Bultmann affirms that the approach to scripture which justifiably adopts the methodology of the empirical sciences, but which is content to establish how

---

[18] Quoted by Braaten, *History and Hermeneutics*, pp. 33f.

[19] Quoted by Ebeling, *Word and Faith*, p. 309, n. 2.

[20] See Bultmann's "Autobiographical Reflections" in *Theology of Rudolph Bultmann*, ed. C. W. Kegley (1966), pp. xxiii f.

things once were (*Historie*), is inadequate to the task of interpreting scripture, and is circumscribed in its legitimate goals. There is another and more significant dimension of history (*Geschichte*) which can only be understood through the interpreter's personal, existential, involvement with significant historical texts. From this perspective the New Testament writings are no longer viewed as containing inert data, objects of modern man's knowledge, but the testimony of writers—subjects—who proclaim things which concern the interpreter existentially, which require acknowledgment and an active response.[21]

By attributing different meanings to two German words for *history* (in parentheses above), Bultmann distinguishes two modes of historical knowledge: the one eschewing all metaphysical assumptions because of their problematical nature, and insisting upon impartial investigation and objective verification; the other taking fully into account the inevitability of any interpreter's "preunderstanding" and of its importance as either an aid or a hindrance to obtaining historical knowledge.[22] This distinction enables Bultmann to affirm that modern man's understanding of the New Testament's essential proclamation, and his decision respecting it, is in no way dependent upon the ever-changing and uncertain "conclusions" of critical scholarship. But equally important is Bultmann's insistence that an essential part of any interpretation of history (*Geschichte*) is the determination of those particular assumptions and questions which are appropriate. Therefore in seeking to understand the New Testament the interpreter must discover that particular understanding of existence being expressed in the text itself.

Bultmann affirms that what is most relevant in the New Testament is that which can be understood beforehand as a possibility for man's existence, as offering him authentic self-understanding. Bultmann and his successors found in the philosophy of Martin Heidegger a penetrating analysis of the particular assumptions and questions which are the concerns not only of modern man *but of early Christians as well*, so that one may see that the language of the New Testament authors is addressed to the human condition.[23] The texts of the New Testament possess not only a record of man's understanding in the past, but challenge his self-understanding in the present, and proclaim a meaningful option concerning his future existence.

In order to clarify the basic understanding of man's existence set forth in the New Testament, and to remove unnecessary hindrances, Bultmann established a program of demythologizing, claiming that the real intention of the mythical forms and language used by New Testament writers was not to proclaim an objective world view—a cosmology—but to express man's understanding of himself in the world. Accordingly, it is true to the intention of the New Testament

---

[21] Ibid., pp. 6f.; Braaten, *History and Hermeneutics*, pp. 37ff.

[22] R. Bultmann, "Is Exegesis Without Presuppositions Possible?" *Existence and Faith*, trans. S. M. Ogden (1960).

[23] "Heidegger's existentialist analysis of the ontological structure of being would seem to be no more than a secularized, philosophical version of the New Testament view of human life." R. Bultmann, in *Kerygma and Myth*, ed. H. W. Bartsch, trans. R. H. Fuller (1954), p. 24.

to interpret its myths existentially. Instead of discarding the myths as clearly archaic, one must perceive what are the ideas of human existence brought to expression in them.[24]

Bultmann's demythologizing has been the most controversial aspect of his New Testament interpretation, but his bifocal view of "history" (*Historie/Geschichte*) raised more serious theological issues.

Gerhard Ebeling (1912—), a post-Bultmannian, argues that the modern critical historical method "can include in itself the whole hermeneutic process" provided it is "freed from the mistaken curtailment to a mere technical tool . . . The very process of taking the historical source in all its historicity (and that means in its distance from the present) and making it luminous by means of a critical examination . . . and thereby at the same time also critically correcting the prejudices of the expositor . . . that very process creates the necessary basis for a genuine encounter with the text . . . also the possibility of having it speak to us."[25]

Ebeling's position may be termed a radical Protestantism. He insists on "an inner connection between the Reformer's doctrine of justification *sola fide* and the historical method." The critical historical method "shatters all possible assurances which faith might be tempted to find in historical facts." Thus the believer's uncertain knowledge of the constitutive events of the Christian religion is not a liability but an asset; he is thereby driven to live by faith alone.

Other Protestant theologians have also rejected the tenability of Bultmann's dichotomy between *Historie/Geschichte*, and his claim that critical analysis and existentialist interpretation are two distinct modes of understanding the New Testament. Wolfhart Pannenberg (1928—) and Richard R. Niebuhr (1926—) both contend that the theological justification of historical criticism must depend upon liberating it from its present bondage to philosophical positivism.[26] The constructive ground for a new hermeneutic therefore must be "a critique of historical reason." Protestant liberals too easily acceded to a reduction of all historical phenomena to a closed continuum of cause and effect. In consequence the possibilities of historical knowledge were reduced to typical or analogous occurrences. But also the historical basis of faith in the unique, once-for-all, Christ-event was sacrificed. "The hermeneutical difference between New Testament texts and our present time," writes Pannenberg, "would at once be respected and superceded in a concept of the *history* connecting both, if this history can again be regarded as the work of the Biblical God."[27] From this perspective the interpreter of the New Testament views the hermeneutical arch connecting the saving action of God in Christ, past and present, as a continuum made up of events occurring in the history of the Church as well as the world. This position seems to require a rethinking within Protestantism of the relation between scripture and the tradi-

---

[24] Ibid., pp. 1ff. Cf. G. Bornkamm, "Myth and Gospel, "in *Kerygma and History*, ed. C. E. Braaten and R. A. Harrisville (1962), pp. 172ff.

[25] Ebeling, *Word and Faith*, p. 49.

[26] Braaten, *History and Hermeneutics*, pp. 41f.

[27] Ibid., pp. 144ff.

tion-oriented history of the Church, the cultural expressions of its ongoing faith and life in manifold forms.

This sketchy account reports but a few of the solutions, so-called, to the hermeneutical problem. The strengths and weaknesses of the various proposals which have been summarized will be assessed differently by readers of this chapter. Perhaps the search for an adequate hermeneutic today requires an open, nondefensive dialogue between all Christian groups—Roman Catholics, and Protestants, and Orthodox Easterns as well. Already a new era of communication between these churches seems to have begun, marked by seriousness and mutual respect.

Within these discussions some questions need to be pondered. Has the Protestant emphasis on *sola scriptura* too often disparaged tradition, and failed to acknowledge the important role that the historic creeds and confessions play in bringing understanding to the New Testament? Have Roman Catholic and Orthodox Eastern theologians defensively inflated the value of their traditions, sacraments, liturgies, with a resultant disparagement of the once-for-all significance of the canonical scriptures?

Many theologians in the Roman and Greek churches today seem ready to concede that while their traditions serve as an essential linkage between the Christ-event and Christian proclamation in the present time, any authentic bridge must rest upon the firm foundation of scripture. Radical Protestants, as we have seen, insist upon the contrast between scripture and tradition, and embrace historical criticism as a tool for clearing away the rubble of tradition obscuring modern man's understanding of the gospel of Christ. Yet other Protestants, who also recognize "the ambiguity of tradition" and insist upon its "subordination to scripture," consider themselves to be both evangelical and Catholic. Among such today one finds a genuine interest in recovering the value of tradition, as a means both of understanding and of proclaiming the gospel.[28]

A genuinely critical interpretation of the New Testament which seeks understanding not only through its content but also through the historic creeds, confessions, liturgies, and life-styles of Christian churches, can provide an important corrective to any Christian's partial vision. Possibly, also, by means of open dialogue between men of goodwill within these churches, and their consequent mutual enrichment, the muted, often forgotten or ignored, witness of the New Testament may again obtain clarity of expression and become good news for modern men. This book has powerfully sustained the faith and hope of man— even, or one might say especially, in periods of cultural upheaval and radical change such as this present time.

[28] Ibid., p. 149.

chapter two

METHODOLOGICAL CONSIDERATIONS

A Point of Departure
The Course of Study
An Overview of the New Testament

THE previous chapter began with an acknowledgment that the twenty-seven books of the New Testament function as the essential part of Christianity's canonical scripture. With the passage of time the task of interpretation has established the necessity of historical criticism. While the specific values of this criticism remain under discussion, this much is clear: A critical historical analysis of the diverse writings of the New Testament is needed if we are to understand their origins, in relation to the *earliest* Christians—their thought, lives, and activities—and also in relation to the cultural milieu within which this Christianity originated. Having viewed the New Testament as the Church's book, we consider now this collection of writings as the product of the earliest churches.

The arrangement and order of the New Testament canon poses a basic problem of methodology. What point of departure is one to adopt? Among a variety of possible approaches which commends itself? And how is one to proceed, once a beginning is decided?

FOUR APPROACHES TO THE NEW TESTAMENT

From first to last, according to the order of the New Testament: Each book is a significant whole and can be studied profitably as a unit. Many earlier "introductions to the New Testament," recognizing this fact, followed its traditional literary arrangement. Beginning with The Gospel according to Matthew, each book is viewed in terms of its origin and other special problems relating to its content. Such questions as the following carry forward the discussion: Who wrote this book? When and from what place? To whom was it written and for what purpose?

At first sight this plan of study seems logical. Yet a number of difficulties face the reader starting with Matthew and working straight through to Revelation. It is known that the books in the canon nearest the front were not the earliest written. For example, most scholars agree that Mark was written before Matthew, Galatians before Romans, and so on. Moreover, the present arrangement of books does not provide the reader with a consecutive development of events. For example, 1 and 2 Thessalonians, the thirteenth and fourteenth books, reflect situations in the life of Paul and the Church which are earlier than those presupposed by the Apostle's letter to the Romans (the sixth book). Accordingly, in many "introductions," rearrangements are offered. While still viewing each book as a unit for study, the author groups the writings in what he supposes to be their proper sequence.

From first to last, according to dates of composition: Some books introducing the New Testament have been organized on a strictly chronological plan. It is proposed that the students begin with the earliest books, that is, with the letters of the Apostle Paul. The development of the Christian Church is then traced according to its primary documents considered in the order of their writing.

Aside from the fact that there are uncertainties as to the dates of these books, there are serious weaknesses in this approach. This method obscures the obvious truth that Paul's career followed that of Jesus and the establishment of the Christian Church. We know from his own writings that Paul takes for granted his readers' acquaintance with the main facts about Jesus. Also it can easily be shown that Paul's missions presuppose the existence of earlier Christian communities. Paul's gospel rests upon the testimony of Christians before his conversion. This is true whatever we may say about Paul's independence or about his reinterpretation of the traditional faith. It is hazardous, therefore, to overlook Christianity before Paul and to give no consideration to its possible influence upon him. A serious reader ought to fill in the background as clearly as possible before tackling Paul's letters. They are never easy to understand, but they are especially difficult if one starts with them.

From the career of Jesus to the latest book concerning him: It is perhaps the most common practice to introduce a systematic study of the New Testament with the life and teachings of Jesus, as they may be recovered from the Gospels. Obviously there are good reasons for beginning with Jesus. Christianity originated as an interpretation of Jesus' Ministry, and still draws its inspiration from this original source. But this approach, as ordinarily followed, presents some real problems. The fact is that the New Testament contains no biography of Jesus written during his career or even shortly thereafter. At the appropriate place we shall consider how the Gospels came to be written and what their distinguishing characteristics are. It is sufficient now to affirm that they were made up from fragments of the oral and written tradition relating to various aspects of Jesus' work and teachings and were composed by men who selected and treated these materials according to their own theological interests and motives. Before the stories of Jesus were written down they had been employed in the preaching, teaching, worship, and defense of the earliest Christian communities. Thus the Gospels, like all other New Testament writings, are the products of the life and thought of various Christians. They were composed to establish and sustain the ever-widening community of faith, to guide that conduct and inspire that hope which accompanied personal allegiance to Christ. It is Jesus as he is remembered by the earliest Christians and experienced in their fellowship whom we meet in the Gospels.

If the Gospels of the New Testament are interwoven with the life and thought of the earliest Christians, it is important that we consider what is known about these communities responsible for transmitting the stories of Jesus.

From the early Church through the Gospels to Jesus, thence to Paul, his letters, and the remainder of the New Testament books: This fourth alternative approach to the study of the New Testament has been adopted for this text. Consideration will first be given to The Acts of the Apostles, the one New Testament writing which purposes to record the experiences, the faith, and the characteristic activities of the earliest Christians.

Does this seem to the reader to be a case of putting the cart before the horse, to begin with a sketch of primitive Christianity and not with the life of Jesus? At the risk of laboring a point, let it be said again that in spite of its apparent reasonableness, the alternative of beginning with the Ministry of Jesus is beset with grave difficulties, particularly for the nonspecialist. The desire to get back to the "real Jesus," to get behind the testimony of the Gospels, can be a worthwhile endeavor. Indeed, it can be a scientific study and, at the same time, be prompted by the highest religious motives. "The quest for the historical Jesus" has engaged New Testament scholars for over a century. It is unlikely that it will be eclipsed by other interests in the years ahead, at least for very long. But it is questionable whether in an introductory study of this sort the reader should be encouraged to begin with a matter of such very great complexity and importance.

The logic of the approach which is here being adopted has been stated by H. J. Cadbury:

> The recent study of the Gospels is making clear to us how important for our understanding of them it would be to know thoroughly the apostolic age. They are not merely uncolored accounts of Jesus' words and deeds but they have included the interests, motives and ideas of the generation through which the story had already been handed down—largely in a fluid state of oral tradition. They are at once a witness to that early Christianity and they themselves are in need of being corrected or discounted by that Christianity if the facts and the figure behind them are to be surely known. *Now the book of Acts is our principal narrative source for knowledge of that exact period in which these influences on the Gospel material were active.*[1]

The first half of the Acts narrative, chapters 1 through 12, provides a point of departure in tracing the fascinating history of the gospel tradition. Upon a completion of a study of the origin of the earliest Gospels and their distinguishing characteristics, a reconstruction of the Ministry of Jesus will be attempted.

After the study of Jesus we shall return to Acts and follow its narrative from chapter 13 to the end. A narrative of Paul's career would be practically impossible without Acts. A few of Paul's experiences can be gleaned from his letters but no one has satisfactorily ordered these fragments without having recourse to the Acts narrative. After studying the New Testament source for our knowledge of Paul's missionary journeys, we shall then consider the letters of Paul in what appears to be their order of composition.

The concluding section of the text will study the remaining books of the New Testament in their probable sequence. The New Testament provides no narrative setting for these writings. The early Church had no historian to portray its fortunes in the latter part of the first and the early part of the second century. If the writer of Acts ever planned a third volume, as some scholars suppose, there is no evidence that he wrote it. Even the most skeptical critic of the historical value of Luke–Acts will realize the appropriateness of the adage, "You never miss the water till the well runs dry."

The author hopes that the approach of this text will commend itself as a historical one.[2] As we have seen, "historical questions" are preliminary to, or stop short of, the highly personal questions involving faith or unbelief. Nevertheless, the historian's approach to the New Testament is a sound and necessary one for the student seeking to apprehend its spiritual values. It was the dynamic development of a particular religious community, under certain known conditions, in a given period of world history, that produced the books of the New Testament. It is the author's hope that the relevance of these books to the reader's own life and time will be better understood as he studies the vital interplay of life and literature in Christianity's first century. In the words of Albert Schweitzer: "In

[1] H. J. Cadbury, *The Book of Acts in History* (1955), pp. 122f. Italics mine.
[2] "The proper historical approach to the study of the New Testament is . . . by way of church history, viz., in its earliest period." F. C. Grant, *The Gospels: Their Origin and Their Growth* (1957), p. 17 [hereafter, *Gospels*].

spite of all innovations of doctrine, present or future, it will always remain the true ideal that our faith should return to the richness and vitality of the primitive-Christian faith."[3]

THE EARLY CHURCH AND THE
LITERATURE OF THE NEW TESTAMENT

In the first century of its existence Christianity manifested two stages of development: a period of rapid expansion, ca. A.D. 30–65, and a period of conflict and consolidation, ca. A.D. 65–150.

Christianity's first stage of development dates from the death of Jesus at Jerusalem in the reign of the Roman emperor, Tiberius. The year of Jesus' death is usually given as A.D. 30. Within a single generation, Christian communities were established in nearly all of the eastern provinces of the Roman Empire as well as in Italy and in Rome itself.

This early expansion of the Church is partially represented in The *Acts of the Apostles*. The book of Acts was not composed until late in the first century. It is not the earliest New Testament writing. Nevertheless, it is the most primitive narrative source of Christian beginnings. In it we possess a record of the earliest traditions of Christianity, as the succeeding chapters of this book will show.

This period is also reflected in the letters of Paul. These letters are the earliest literary documents of Christianity. According to the great majority of modern scholars, the New Testament contains nine genuine letters of the Apostle Paul. Six of these were almost certainly written between the years A.D. 50 and 60: The First and Second Letters of Paul to the Thessalonians; The First and Second Letters of Paul to the Corinthians; The Letter of Paul to the Galatians; and the Letter of Paul to the Romans. The origin of Galatians, its place of writing, date, and destination, is much disputed by critical scholars. Three other letters of Paul, known as "the Prison (or Captivity) Epistles," are also variously dated and placed: The Letter of Paul to Philemon; The Letter of Paul to the Philippians; and The Letter of Paul to the Colossians. The principal question concerning the origin of these three letters is whether they were composed at Rome in the early 60s, as ancient Church tradition reports, or whether some or all of them were written a decade earlier from Ephesus or Caesarea.

In addition to these letters, there is a tenth book which many hold to be from Paul's hand, The Letter of Paul to the Ephesians. Several competent scholars have pointed to evidence which may indicate that Ephesians was written by a Paulinist and not by Paul himself. A popular judgment is that it was composed by a collector of Paul's letters, but this does not seem to be a satisfactory explanation.

Such questions concern the identification of genuine letters of Paul and problems of origin, questions which will be considered in some detail later. The points to be grasped now are these: In spite of uncertainty as to the precise number

---

[3] A. Schweitzer, *The Mysticism of Paul the Apostle*, trans. W. Montgomery (1931), pp. 383f.

CHRONOLOGY OF NEW TESTAMENT ERA

Dates	Events	Herods	Procurators of Judaea	Roman Emperors
10 B.C.		Herod I The Great 37-4 B.C.		
0	Birth of Jesus	Archelaus 4 B.C.-A.D. 6		Augustus 27 B.C.-A.D. 14
A.D. 10		Philip 4 B.C.-A.D. 34		
20		Herod Antipas 4 B.C.-A.D. 39		
30	Ministry of John the Baptist; Ministry of Jesus; Crucifixion; Paul's conversion		Pontius Pilate 26-36	Tiberius 14-37
40		Herod Agrippa I 37-44		Caligula 37-41
50	Paul's missions	Herod Agrippa II 50-53		Claudius 41-54
60	Paul's arrest; Paul in Rome		Felix 52-60; Festus 60-62	Nero 54-68
70	Destruction of Jerusalem			Galba 68-69 / Otho 69 / Vitellius 69; Vespasian 69-79
80				Titus 79-81
90				Domitian 81-96
100				Nerva 96
110				Trajan 98-117

of and occasion for Paul's genuine letters, the New Testament contains a great treasure in its "Pauline corpus." These books reflect the great Apostle's interpretation of Christianity. From them it is possible to trace the main lines of Paul's theology. Few men in antiquity are known as intimately as Paul is known through his writings. His letters disclose the main lines of the early development of Christianity, the amazingly vigorous thrust and penetration of Christian missions northwest from Jerusalem into Asia Minor, Greece, and Italy within a single generation. They illustrate conditions existing within the young churches in these regions, their internal affairs, and some of the typical attitudes of outsiders.

The end of the first stage may be fixed at the point where the steady advance of Christianity was momentarily halted. In the winter of A.D. 64–65 there was a disastrous fire in Rome. The rumor spread that the Emperor Nero (54–68) had set the city afire in order to further his building plans for a greater capital. According to Tacitus, Nero put the blame for the fire upon the followers of a "mischievous superstition."[4] The emperor turned upon Christians as a minority group within the city and made scapegoats of them. Christianity was outlawed and, as Tacitus reports, those who were thus victimized suffered terrible brutalities.

Just how long Christianity had been established at Rome and what had been the early fortunes of the Church there are subjects for conjecture. The Roman writer Suetonius, in his *Lives of the Caesars*, says that Claudius (41–54) expelled the Jews from Rome for continual rioting "at the instigation of Chrestus."[5] Many scholars take this comment to refer to the troubles between Jews and Christians. If this identification is correct, Christianity had reached Rome and attracted the attention of the government within two decades after Jesus' death.

In the years following A.D. 65, the beginning of the period of conflict and consolidation, Christians in the Empire must have been painfully aware of their hazardous position. There is no evidence that they were continually persecuted by government authorities. Still, the ever-present possibility of persecution must have called for courage and endurance. It should not be supposed that during the years of the rapid expansion of Christianity the followers of Jesus enjoyed an immunity from suffering. Various kinds of opposition and conflict were experienced, mostly arising from the Jewish synagogues and the authorities of the temple in Jerusalem. But the conflict of Christians with the Roman government dates from the period now under review.

The typical mood of the New Testament books written at the close of the apostolic age is one of tension. Christians are being warned to be on the alert, to stand ready to sacrifice themselves. The reader also senses in these books a wistful longing for a better life beyond the crises of the time, and an intensification of hope that the promise of the new age will soon be fulfilled. Ancient Church tradition has it that both Peter and Paul were martyred at Rome during Nero's persecution. These tragedies are not reported in the New Testament but there are no good reasons for doubting that they happened. The thinning of the ranks

---

[4] Tacitus, *Annals*, xv. 44. See below, p. 196.
[5] Suetonius, "Claudius," *Lives of the Caesars*, xxv.

of eyewitnesses to Jesus' historic Ministry aroused the churches to a need for perpetuating their recollections of Jesus.

The first composition of a connected account of the Ministry, so far as is known, was The Gospel according to Mark. The troubled conditions which existed in Nero's Rome loom through this brief narrative. Mark emphasizes the example of Christ's sufferings as the precondition of his glory. Nero's policies may well have fixed in the gospel tradition Jesus' warning that his disciples must take up their crosses. Also, this crisis may have led to an emphasis upon Jesus' sayings concerning the near advent of "the Son of man," and the vindication and victory of those persons who confess him in and through their sufferings.

Within the next two critical decades other Gospels appeared. The one entitled The Gospel according to Matthew has been aptly described as a revised and enlarged edition of Mark. The new material in Matthew includes, among other things, the teachings of Jesus concerning "the higher righteousness of the kingdom of heaven." The Gospel according to Luke is the first part of a two-volume work dedicated to one who is addressed "most excellent Theophilus." The second volume is the book of Acts. These companion books, which may be fittingly designated Luke-Acts, are dominated by a strong missionary aim.

Other writings commonly assigned to the early part of the postapostolic period are The First Letter of Peter; The Letter to the Hebrews; and The Revelation to John. Several scholars have held that these three writings are best understood as relating to three phases of a single crisis growing out of the stiffening opposition of Rome to the Christian movement. The fact is that there are large elements of conjecture with respect to the origin of these books and their relationship, if any, to each other. Anyone seeking to trace the changing fortunes of Christianity in the Roman Empire, the attitudes of various emperors and other authorities toward the Christian religion, enters a darkened tunnel. Not until the turn of the century does one emerge from this darkness and begin to see the problems clearly. But it is probable that during the last three decades of the first century, Christians in various parts of the Roman Empire had faced stern opposition. In some cases they had suffered martyrdom. Other Christians had become indifferent. Some had renounced their faith. A letter from Pliny, the governor of Bithynia, to the Emperor Trajan (ca. A.D. 112) reports that some of the persons he had questioned in his province, who were loyalty risks, had testified that they had abandoned their Christian faith many years before.[6]

The latest writings of the New Testament are dated within the last years of the first century to the middle of the second century. They indicate that there were dangers confronting Christianity at this time which were more insidious than was the open hostility of the Jewish synagogues or Caesar's agents. The "heroic age" had passed in which powerful forces for unity had been felt. For one thing, the hope that Jesus the Messiah would soon return seems to have waned. There is some evidence that the validity of this hope was being denied

---

[6] Pliny, *Letters*, xcvi f. See below, pp. 479f.

by some Christians. At any rate, loyal leadership and efficient organization were needed if the churches were to survive in the indeterminate future. Most important of all, the integrity of the rank-and-file membership had to be secured. Christian literature of this time is much concerned with the promotion of order and discipline and shows an acute sensitivity to irregularity of belief in the Christian churches.[7]

This final stage in the development of the Church of the New Testament has been known as an age of consolidation. The word, through its military usage, suggests the strengthening of a position which has been gained by costly struggle and some losses, through reorganization or retrenchment. The Letter of Paul to Titus, and The First and Second Letters of Paul to Timothy, commonly referred to as "the Pastoral Epistles," were written for this purpose, to consolidate the discipline and doctrine of Christianity. Several letters known as "the General (or Catholic) Epistles" also seem to fit into this period and contribute to our knowledge of it. Among these are The First, Second, and Third Letters of John, and The Letter of Jude. It is probable too that The Letter of James dates from this period. The book called The Second Letter of Peter is probably the last of the New Testament books to have been written.

No mention has been made thus far of The Gospel according to John. There are sufficient reasons for dating this important book within a few years on either side of A.D. 100. The other writings of the New Testament which belong to this time afford some help in understanding the contemporary significance of "John's Gospel." Yet there remain many perplexing problems concerning its origin. Ancient Church tradition and the evidence of the Gospel itself are not decisive. Recently scholars have ransacked non-Christian literature of the period in the hope of uncovering the particular needs which John in his Gospel sought to satisfy. Scholars have hoped in this way also to identify the source of the specific thought-forms which are employed in this Gospel.

The origin and environment of the Fourth Gospel is an exceedingly complex study, more interesting to some readers than to others. But whatever a student's interest in these historical questions, it will be readily acknowledged that the book has had a pervasive influence upon the life and thought of the Church from the late second century to the present time. John presents a fresh interpretation of Jesus and his Ministry, in some ways different from the other three Gospels. It is probable that he told his story in order that the Church might be enabled to bear witness to those Jews and Greeks possessed of a particular type of mentality, to the end that both understand the gospel and believe it. At any rate, whatever his immediate intention, the fourth evangelist created a language for the Church which has spoken to the human situation in every age. For many persons this book mediates the gospel of Jesus Christ with an unparalleled directness and power.

---

[7] "The catchword propounded by the Pastoral [Letters], 'sound doctrine' . . . is something like the common denominator which can be found in most of the New Testament writings of the postapostolic period." E. Käsemann in *Studies in Luke–Acts*, ed. L. E. Keck and J. L. Martyn (1966), p. 290 [hereafter *Luke–Acts*].

THE COMMON FAITH AND HOPE
OF THE EARLY CHURCH

The above sketch provides a temporal or circumstantial setting in the early history of Christianity for all twenty-seven books of the New Testament, and may stand as a prospectus for this text. Some readers will recognize at once the margins of uncertainty with respect to the origin of several of the New Testament books. It is not intended that this preview gloss over these lingering uncertainties as though they are not significant. The origin of each book must be studied as we come to it without preconceived solutions. But the margin of uncertainty should not be exaggerated. Most of the books of the New Testament are more easily understood—their authors' intentions as well as their present applications—through a search for their specific setting in the ongoing development of the witnessing Church.

The above survey may help the reader to appreciate the fundamental unity which underlies the rich variety of the New Testament. It is important that the serious reader not lose sight of the unity of the New Testament, whether the stage of his research be on an introductory level or on more advanced levels. While the analysis of each book must be mainly concerned with its particular circumstances and its distinctive teachings, the process of dividing and dissecting the New Testament can go so far as to obscure the intrinsic unity of the whole. It is hoped that the approach adopted in this book preserves this intrinsic unity. The historical continuity of the witnessing, expanding community of Christians supports and carries forward the oral traditions, as well as the written records, out of which the New Testament was composed. This cavalcade of people and events, marking the rapid expansion, defense, and consolidation of the Christian movement, provides a dynamic and unified background against which one can view the varieties of thought and experience to be found within the New Testament.

The claim has been made that no religion becomes a distinctive phenomenon until it has produced a community, a fellowship of persons bound together by common ideas and experiences. Judged by this standard, Christianity in New Testament times emerges as a distinctive phenomenon in history. Yet Christianity is not so much distinguished by its common ideas as by the attachment of its members to the person of Jesus. As we proceed with this study it will become evident that the New Testament reflects a central and controlling perspective because everything is focused upon this one person. As different as these books are in their form and manner of verbal expression, they all bear witness to Jesus as one who acted, taught, and suffered as the Messiah, as the Christ. Moreover, the writers and the communities they represent stand united in a common loyalty to Jesus; not only to the Christ who had come, but also to One acknowledged to be the living Lord of life. Every book reflects the impact of the person of Jesus upon men in the present, as well as in the recent past. And finally, throughout the New Testament there is also manifested a confidence that the leadership of Jesus Christ as Lord is destined in the future to become worldwide, unto the glory of God and the fulfillment of His purposes for all mankind.

The following statement expresses well this overarching perspective:

> There is a unity in all these early Christian books which is powerful enough to absorb and subdue their differences, and that unity is to be found in common religious relation to Christ, a common debt to Him, a common sense that everything in the relations of God and man must be and is determined by Him.[8]

[8] J. Denney, *Jesus and the Gospel* (1908), p. 101.

part 1

THE RECOVERY OF
CHRISTIAN ORIGINS

RECONSTRUCTING THE SETTING
OF EARLY CHRISTIANITY

a   b   c   d

(a) Silver tetradrachm of Alexander the Great (356–323 B.C.): obverse, the head of Heracles; reverse, Zeus Olympios enthroned. (The American Numismatic Society) (b) A tetradrachm of Ptolemy I of Egypt (305–283 B.C.), founder of the dynasty of kings who ruled Egypt from 323–30 B.C. (The Chase Manhattan Bank Money Museum) (c) A tetradrachm of Seleucus I (312–280 B.C.), Alexander's general, King of Syria: obverse, head of Zeus; reverse, war chariot drawn by elephants. (The Chase Manhattan Bank Money Museum) (d) Silver tetradrachm of Antiochus IV (c.215–163 B.C.): obverse, head of the monarch; reverse, Zeus Olympios surrounded by inscription, "King Antiochus, god manifest, bearer of victory". (The American Numismatic Society)

View from the air of the Herodium, a fortress-palace and tomb monument built and named by Herod the Great about four miles southeast of Bethlehem. (Georg Gerster from Rapho-Guillumette)

Wadi Qumran and ruins of the Jewish sectarian settlement on the southern edge of the marly plateau about $\frac{1}{2}$ mile inland from the Dead Sea. (Georg Gerster from Rapho-Guillumette)

Bust of Octavian (Caesar Augustus) as a youth. (Staatliche Antikensammlungen und Glyptothek, Munich)

THE principal political changes which took place in Palestine in New Testament times will be surveyed in this chapter. The influences of various developments within the Greco–Roman world upon Judaism and upon Christianity will then be described in two installments. In Chapter 3, attention will be focused upon Judaism in Palestine at the time of Jesus and the establishment of the earliest Christian churches. The second installment will be deferred until Chapter 13, where consideration will be given to that broader geographical area and cultural environment beyond Palestine in which communities of Jews and of Christians were established.[1]

BACKGROUND TO NEW TESTAMENT TIMES

The choice of any point of departure in time is arbitrary. Perhaps we are justified in beginning with the conquests in the East of Alexander the Great (356–323 B.C.).

Alexander's Conquests, 334–323 B.C.

The youthful king of the city-states of Greece fought his first battles in the East in the year 334 B.C.[2] Alexander's campaign, the fulfillment of the ambition of his father, Philip of Macedon, may have been provoked by an economic crisis facing Greece at the time. Too, the autonomy of the kingdom which Alexander inherited had been in jeopardy since two Persian offensives in the fifth century B.C. Alexander's armies crossed the Hellespont and within three years pushed through the Cilician Gates into Syria and on into Palestine and Egypt, wresting these territories from the Persians. In many places the Greeks were welcomed as liberators. Flavius Josephus, the Jewish historian, reports that Alexander visited Jerusalem, was impressed by its priests and temple, and offered sacrifices.[3] There may be a kernel of truth in this legendary account, for Alexander is known to have sometimes made votive gifts to the gods of the peoples whose territories he added to his dominions.

[1]The two-installment plan may seem to be an unnecessary fragmentation. Yet a comprehensive survey of the historical setting of the entire New Testament suggests that the environment of Jesus and the earliest Christians was more complex than in fact it was. It is only when one seeks to understand the literature of Christianity after its geographical spread beyond Palestine that the exploration of the wider world becomes necessary.

[2]In reading the following account, see chart on p. 36; also an atlas, e.g., Plates XI-XIII, *The Westminster Historical Atlas to the Bible*, ed. G. E. Wright and F. V. Filson (rev. ed., 1956) [hereafter, *Westminster Atlas*]; *Nelson's Atlas of the Bible*, ed. L. H. Grollenberg (1957).

[3]*Antiquities of the Jews*, XI. viii. 5 [hereafter, *Antiq.*].

Alexander dreamed of one world mastered by Greek culture. No direct attempt was made, however, "to replace the ruling classes and dominant cultures of the Middle East with Greek and Macedonian elements. Instead, he left the Oriental rugs where they were, so to speak, only making sure that he had his feet firmly planted on them."[4] Alexander marched his armies as far east as the region now called Pakistan. Here his troops mutinied and Alexander was forced to turn westward. At Babylon he died of malarial fever, thirty-three years of age, having bequeathed to his countrymen the whole of the far-flung Persian empire.

Alexander's military victories were not long-lasting, but several enduring tendencies were set in motion by them. The numerous Hellenistic cities, established by Alexander and his *diadochi* (successors), became not only administrative and commercial centers, but the bases for the dissemination of the Greek way of life and cultural achievements. The language adopted throughout Alexander's vast empire was a simplified dialect of classical Greek, known as *Koine* (common). This universal language greatly facilitated the exchange of thought, customs, and trade between East and West for generations to come. The intermingling of cultures after Alexander's conquests went far toward destroying the parochialism which had prevailed for many centuries. Strictly speaking, the so-called Hellenistic Age extends from 323 B.C. to the founding of the Roman Empire in 30 B.C. Yet for four or five centuries Greek influences modified and molded almost every culture in the region of the Mediterranean.

The Hellenistic Kingdoms, 323–168 B.C.

After Alexander's death there was no man to succeed him who was his equal. As a result of much squabbling among his generals, several political units were formed. First, Egypt and Palestine came under the domination of Ptolemy Lagi. The dynasty which he founded lost Palestine slightly more than a century later. The Ptolemaic kingdom, however, with its capital at Alexandria at the mouth of the Nile, lasted until 30 B.C., when it fell to the Romans. Second, Asia Minor came under the control of Antigonus, who founded the short-lived Antigonid dynasty. After 301 B.C. this territory was divided among other successors. Third, Seleucus assumed control over Babylon, which was lost to him for a time but regained. Syria was added to his domain with Ptolemy's support. After 312 B.C. the Seleucid kingdom, with its capital at Antioch in Syria, expanded westward and southward, absorbing much of Asia Minor and Palestine. Numerous uprisings and constant dynastic strife during the second century led to the gradual dissolution of the Seleucid kingdom. In 65 B.C. it became a part of the Roman world. Last, minor kingdoms, beyond the interests of this survey, were founded in Macedonia and Thrace.

Inevitably the tiny Persian satrapy Judea was affected by these great changes in the fourth century B.C. The Jewish people found themselves once again between two rival empires, the Seleucid and the Ptolemaic. Yet the impact upon Judea of the world-transforming onslaught of the Greeks was not so great as one might

[4]B. Reicke, *The New Testament Era*, trans. D. E. Green (1968), p. 36.

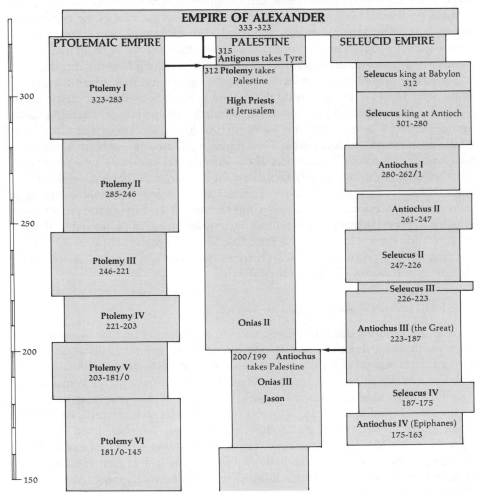

ALEXANDER
AND THE
HELLENISTIC RULERS
(WESTERN AND EASTERN EMPIRES)

suppose. In the century following the edict of Cyrus (538 B.C.), which liberated captive peoples of Persia, Israel had become a self-contained religious community existing within a political order which did not share its own faith. The priests of the second temple in Jerusalem and the scribes of the synagogues encircled the Jews with a wall of the Mosaic tradition.

As has been stated, Palestine came under the nominal control of the Greek–Egyptian Ptolemaic kingdom in the struggles after Alexander's death. Seleucus had an intense interest in this region. It is probable that the strength of the fleets at Alexandria, and the Ptolemies' control and defense of the trade routes and commercial ports of Palestine, both deterred and whetted his ambition for territorial expansion. Throughout the third century B.C. life went on as usual in Jerusalem. The Ptolemies were content to let the Jews retain their customs, institutions, and language so long as the rulers were profiting economically from them and they posed no military threat. What did it matter to devout Jews that there had been an exchange in overlords, so long as there was no interference with their religious observances?

The political and cultural changes wrought by Alexander's conquests had a more far-reaching effect upon the Jews living outside of Judea. For example, by 250 B.C. so many of the Jews living in Egypt spoke only Greek that a translation of the Old Testament was begun. We shall consider later the importance of this Greek version of the Old Testament, known as the Septuagint. During this century many Jews emigrated to the various centers of population studding the shores of the Mediterranean. Greeks also emigrated to Palestine, and their cities were destined to become colonies of the homeland. Later developments will show to what extent Hellenistic influences began almost immediately to seep through the walls of Jewish separatism. It should be noted that during the Ptolemaic rule of Palestine the influence of the office of the high priest in Jerusalem seems to have gradually increased.

The Maccabean Revolution and the Rule of the Hasmoneans, 168–63 B.C.

The Seleucids, under the leadership of the imperialistic Antiochus III, surnamed the Great (223–187 B.C.), finally wrested the political and economic control of Judea from the Ptolemies in 198 B.C. Many in Jerusalem welcomed this change with enthusiasm but their ardor was to show itself premature. With the rise to power in Syria of the usurper Antiochus IV, a great religious crisis emerged. In the year 168 B.C. Antiochus, who dubbed himself "Epiphanes" (God-manifest), decided to destroy Judaism and to Hellenize his Jewish subjects. The religious rites of the temple in Jerusalem were abolished in order that it might become a shrine to the Olympian Zeus. Swine were offered upon the altar. Worship of the pagan gods became compulsory in Palestine. Observance of the Mosaic Law was forbidden; circumcision, Sabbath rest, and the keeping of the festivals were prohibited under the penalty of death.

Historians have been unable to agree as to the reasons for this policy of Antiochus Epiphanes. Was it his desire to destroy once and for all the Jews' stubborn resistance to Hellenization? Did he realize that only a unification of all eastern Mediterranean peoples would deter Rome's conquest of the East? Was he angered by news of a pro-Egyptian rebellious spirit among the Jews? However the motives of Antiochus are analyzed, it is evident that discord among the priestly families at Jerusalem had aggravated the situation. Soon after the accession of Antiochus, Onias III, the high priest, had fled to Egypt. Antiochus established in his stead the brother of Onias, Joshua, although Onias had a son and rightful heir to the office. Joshua adopted the Greek name Jason and became the local promoter of subjection to the Seleucids and of Greek habits of dress, games, and customs. In this Hellenizing program, Joshua–Jason was supported by the Tobiads,

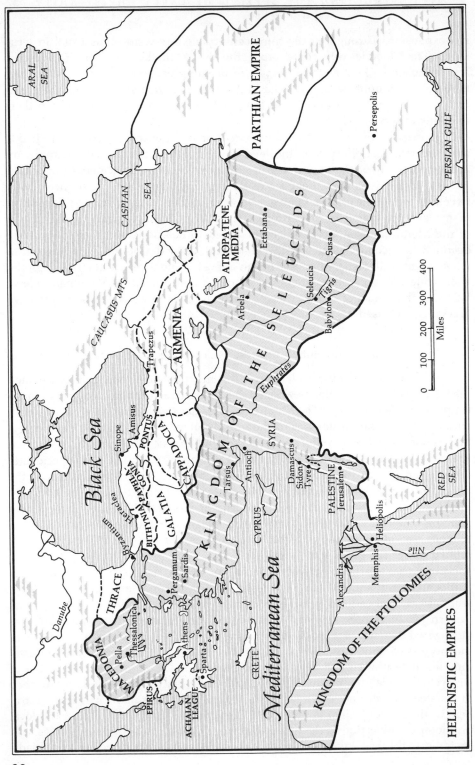

ARAL SEA

PARTHIAN EMPIRE

Persepolis

PERSIAN GULF

CASPIAN SEA

ATROPATENE MEDIA

Ectabana

Seleucia

Susa

Tigris

Arbela

Babylon

K I N G D O M   O F   T H E   S E L E U C I D S

400

300

200

100

Miles

CAUCASUS MTS.

ARMENIA

Euphrates

Trapezus

Sinope

Amisus

PONTUS

Black Sea

PAPHLAGONIA

BITHYNIA

Heraclea

Byzantium

GALATIA

CAPPADOCIA

Tarsus

Antioch

SYRIA

Damascus

Sidon

Tyre

PALESTINE

Jerusalem

Heliopolis

RED SEA

Nile

Pergamum

Sardis

CYPRUS

CRETE

Mediterranean Sea

Memphis

Alexandria

KINGDOM OF THE PTOLOMIES

THRACE

MACEDONIA

Pella

Thessalonica

Athens

Sparta

EPIRUS

ACHAIAN LEAGUE

Danube

HELLENISTIC EMPIRES

a family of wealth descended from Joseph ben Tobias, a Judean tax collector for the Ptolemies. Jason's successor Menelaus, a Tobiad usurper, even permitted Antiochus to plunder the temple.[5] As a result of these shocking actions of the high priests, a group of Jewish loyalists banded together. They became known as the Hasideans (pious ones or loyalists), sometimes rendered Hasidim. Among this group were the fiery patriots who waged the wars of independence against the Seleucids.

When a Syrian officer came to the village of Modein to enforce the royal decrees of Antiochus, a priest named Mattathias killed a renegade Jew and the Syrian and fled with his five sons to the mountains. Mattathias persuaded the Hasideans, who were stunned by the slaughter of over a thousand of their fellow patriots who had refused to defend themselves on the Sabbath, to wage an offensive war against the Syrians. At the time of his death, shortly after this struggle began, the militant priest singled out for leadership one of his sons named Simon. Another son, Judas Maccabee, was appointed commander of the army.[6] The name *Maccabbee*, probably meaning "the Mallet-headed," may have been given Judas because of his physical features or because of his hammerlike blows at the enemy. At any rate, in later Christian circles, the name *Maccabean* was applied to the family and its descendants. The histories of their times were called the Books of the Maccabees. The Maccabean dynasty was designated "Hasmonean"—the sons of Asmoneus. Possibly Asmoneus was an ancestor,[7] but more probably it was a term of honor, signifying "prince" or the like, which was later mistaken for a proper name.

Two Syrian armies were dispatched to deliver a knockout blow to the revolutionary Maccabeans. Judas led forth the Hasideans and routed the Syrians. In 165 B.C. Antiochus dispatched one-half of his military strength, about fifty thousand men, against the Jews. A dawn patrol under Judas' leadership surprised the confident Syrians and gained a decisive victory. On the twenty-fifth day of Chislev (Kislev; November–December) the temple in Jerusalem was rededicated to the worship of God.[8] This occasion has been celebrated ever since by the Jews, under the name of *Hanukkah* (dedication) as a "feast of lights." For about eighteen months peace ensued, the Syrians being needed in Persia to settle a disturbance there. After this Antiochus hastened toward home to vent his wrath upon the Jewish insurgents, but on the way he died.

Religious liberty had been won. Never again did the Syrians attempt to stamp out Judaism; however, the warfare had not ended. The Syrians continued to hold the Acra, the military fortress (hard by the temple area) which Antiochus Epiphanes had commanded to be built, and Syrian armies did not cease to invade Judea.

---

[5]For intrigues of the priests, see 2 Macc. 3:40–5:27; R. H. Pfeiffer, *History of New Testament Times* (1949), pp. 9ff. [hereafter, *New Testament Times*]. S. Zeitlin, *The Rise and Fall of the Judean State* (1962), pp. 73ff. [hereafter, *Rise and Fall*], emphasizes the political and economic motives of the Tobiads and others in courting the favor of Antiochus and in promoting Hellenization of the Jews.

[6]1 Macc. 2:65f.; cf. *Antiq.*, XII. vi. 3.

[7]*Antiq.*, XVI. vii. 1; XX. vii. 2.

[8]1 Macc. 4; *Antiq.*, XII. vii. 4ff.

Moreover, the support of the Syrians was sometimes solicited, first by one and then by another of the Hellenizing, priestly factions in Jerusalem. Many of the Hasideans wished for an end of armed strife after freedom to practice their religion had been won, yet they preferred the leadership of the Maccabeans to that of the ambitious, pro-Syrian priestly families of Jerusalem. It was doubtless difficult for the Hasideans to lay down their arms.

Jonathan, who succeeded his brother Judas as military leader, showed himself to be a wily warrior. He took advantage of Syria's inability to retaliate, resulting from internal struggles for power and warfare with Egypt, in order to gain territory for the Jews, to increase the renown of his own family, and to make possible the economic development and political security of the newly acquired Jewish towns. At the Feast of Booths in the year 152 B.C., Jonathan stood before his people as their high priest. Jonathan's power became a serious threat to Seleucid control. He was taken captive in 143 B.C. by a Syrian commander, and executed.

Simon, his successor, the last survivor of the sons of Mattathias, was a shrewd leader. In the first year of his rule, 143–142 B.C., Simon gained independence for his people, winning for them freedom from tribute, and driving out the Syrian garrison from the Acra. He fortified Jerusalem, laid in stores, and chose the right party among rivals for the Seleucid throne. The conquest of trade routes and coastal cities begun by Jonathan was continued. Thus it is recorded that "the yoke of the Gentiles was lifted from Israel," and the people began to write in their documents and contracts, "in the first year of Simon, the great high priest and commander and leader of the Jews."[9] In the following year Simon was confirmed in these offices and they were made hereditary. The Hasmonean dynasty was established.[10]

The succeeding priest-rulers devoted themselves to the "fashioning of a Jewish Palestine out of Judea."[11] Simon's son, John Hyrcanus, reigned from 135 to 105 B.C.; John's son, Judas Aristobulus, the first to claim the title king, ruled from 105 to 104 B.C.; and the brother of Aristobulus, Alexander Janneus, reigned from 104 to 78 B.C. New territories were conquered by Hyrcanus and his two sons. The inhabitants were forcibly Judaized, and some strategically located villages were repopulated with Jews, therby breaking the commercial monopolies of Greek merchants and Hellenistic officials. Since most of the Hasideans had by then come to see all too clearly the imperial ambitions of the Hasmoneans, mercenaries were needed to accomplish these conquests.

By the time of John Hyrcanus there were movements of disaffection among the Jewish people, spearheaded by a group of quietists known as the Pharisees. Hyrcanus had once called himself a Pharisee but he found cause to be suspicious of the party's loyalty to him, and turned against them. The situation worsened under the rule of his sons. One incident was a symptom. When Alexander Janneus

[9]1 Macc. 13:42; *Antiq.,* XIII. vi. 7.
[10]1 Macc. 14:41ff.
[11]The phrase is J. Klausner's: *Jesus of Nazareth,* trans. H. Danby (1929), pp. 135ff. [hereafter, *Jesus*]. For archeological evidence of these conquests, see J. A. Thompson, *Archeology and the Pre-Christian Centuries* (1958), pp. 95–99.

officiated at the altar, a group of men inspired by the Pharisees pelted him with citrons. During the reign of Hyrcanus and his sons a group of Jews more pious than the Pharisees probably retired to the Judean hills overlooking the shores of the Dead Sea. Recent excavations at Qumran indicate a semimonastic settlement of Jews, zealous students of the Law, from around 100 B.C. onwards. From this community center the Dead Sea sect may have directed the life of small groups or camps in various villages of the realm.

On his deathbed Janneus recognized the seriousness of his subjects' disaffection and counseled his wife, Salome Alexandra, to relinquish some of the powers of the crown and to heed the advice of the Pharisees. The king's counsel was followed. Queen Alexandra ruled from 75 to 69 B.C. Since she could not fulfill the role of the high priest, she appointed to this office her son Hyrcanus II. This favor was resented by his ambitious brother, Aristobulus II. During Alexandra's last illness, Aristobulus gathered together the war cronies of his father, who had been passed over in the quietist-dominated reign of the queen. At Alexandra's death this army of Aristobulus drove Hyrcanus from Jerusalem and moved into the palace. The position of Aristobulus seemed secure.

Herodian and Roman Palestine 63 B.C.–A.D. 135

One man in particular found this turn of events intolerable—Antipater, the military governor of Idumea. More than any other person Antipater was responsible for the downfall of the Hasmonean dynasty. He gained the support of the Nabateans and challenged the rule of Aristobulus II in the name of Hyrcanus II.[12] The strife between the Hasmonean brothers led to the intervention of Rome in 63 B.C. Pompey, the general who had fought to extend Roman rule to the Euphrates, was then in Syria. Pompey reinstated Hyrcanus as high priest. He drastically revised the Jewish territory and government, and made Hyrcanus responsible to the Roman governor of the province of Syria. Jewish independence had come to an end. In the years that followed, the Herods were sometimes called kings but actually they were agents and underlings of Rome.

The situation was ripe for the growth of Antipater's power. The aging Idumean was made a Roman citizen, appointed viceroy of Judea by Julius Caesar, and recognized by him as the real power in Palestine. Antipater used his two sons in administering his territories. One of them, Herod, showed a potential for rule

---

[12] Josephus, *The Jewish War*, I. vi. 2. [hereafter, *War*]; cf. *Antiq.*, XIV. i. 3f. The Nabateans were a nomadic Arab people who began to occupy Edomite territory during the sixth century B.C. Their remarkable civilization was founded upon agriculture and commerce, as shown by modern archeological excavations of a chief city, Petra. Nominally subject to Persian rule, the Nabateans gradually attained independence. From the time of Alexander's conquest they remained free until Trajan annexed their territory (A.D. 106). While there is no direct reference to Nabateans in the NT, Paul writes that King Aretas attempted to arrest him (2 Cor. 11:32; cf. Acts 9:23ff.). Idumea was a region southeast of the Dead Sea settled by Edomite refugees after the Nabatean influx. The political fortunes of the Idumeans fluctuated during the intermittent wars among the Syrians, Jews, and Nabateans. Idumean princes provided the ruling family (Herodian) in Palestine for almost a century and a half. *IDB*, vol. 3, pp. 491ff.

THE HASMONEANS AND HERODS
(with N.T. references)

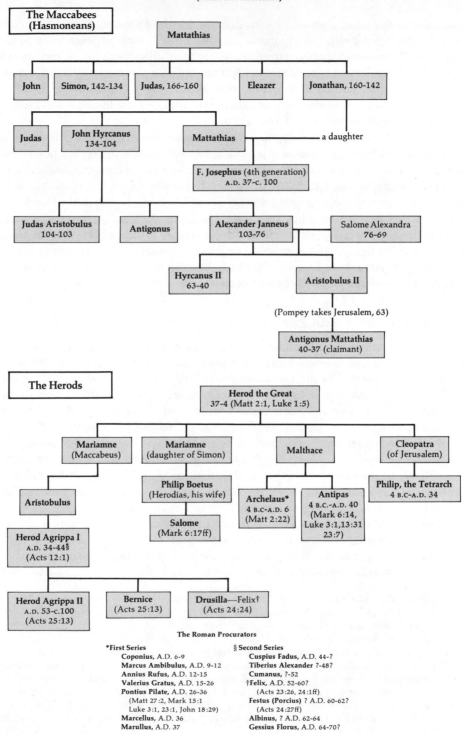

The Maccabees (Hasmoneans)

Mattathias
- John
- Simon, 142-134
- Judas, 166-160
- Eleazer
- Jonathan, 160-142

Judas, 166-160:
- Judas
- John Hyrcanus 134-104
- Mattathias — a daughter
  - F. Josephus (4th generation) A.D. 37-c. 100

John Hyrcanus 134-104:
- Judas Aristobulus 104-103
- Antigonus
- Alexander Janneus 103-76 — Salome Alexandra 76-69

Alexander Janneus:
- Hyrcanus II 63-40
- Aristobulus II

(Pompey takes Jerusalem, 63)

Antigonus Mattathias 40-37 (claimant)

The Herods

Herod the Great 37-4 (Matt 2:1, Luke 1:5)
- Mariamne (Maccabeus)
- Mariamne (daughter of Simon)
- Malthace
- Cleopatra (of Jerusalem)

Mariamne (Maccabeus):
- Aristobulus
  - Herod Agrippa I A.D. 34-44§ (Acts 12:1)
    - Herod Agrippa II A.D. 53-c.100 (Acts 25:13)
    - Bernice (Acts 25:13)
    - Drusilla—Felix† (Acts 24:24)

Mariamne (daughter of Simon):
- Philip Boetus (Herodias, his wife)
  - Salome (Mark 6:17ff)

Malthace:
- Archelaus* 4 B.C.-A.D. 6 (Matt 2:22)
- Antipas 4 B.C.-A.D. 40 (Mark 6:14, Luke 3:1,13:31 23:7)

Cleopatra (of Jerusalem):
- Philip, the Tetrarch 4 B.C.-A.D. 34

The Roman Procurators

*First Series	§ Second Series
Coponius, A.D. 6-9	Cuspius Fadus, A.D. 44-?
Marcus Ambibulus, A.D. 9-12	Tiberius Alexander ?-48?
Annius Rufus, A.D. 12-15	Cumanus, ?-52
Valerius Gratus, A.D. 15-26	†Felix, A.D. 52-60?
Pontius Pilate, A.D. 26-36	(Acts 23:26, 24:1ff)
(Matt 27:2, Mark 15:1	Festus (Porcius) ? A.D. 60-62?
Luke 3:1, 23:1, John 18:29)	(Acts 24:27ff)
Marcellus, A.D. 36	Albinus, ? A.D. 62-64
Marullus, A.D. 37	Gessius Florus, A.D. 64-70?

in his vigorous suppression in Galilee of "bandits" under the leadership of a Jewish patriot named Hezekiah.[13] Through the bloody years of civil war in Rome following Caesar's assassination, Antipater—and after his murder in 43 B.C., his son Herod—managed to appear a friend of the victors. The Hasmonean loyalists recognized in Herod, whom they called "the Idumean slave," a formidable foe. Yet they resisted him and the result was their own undoing. In the year 40 B.C. Herod's loyalty to Rome was rewarded. The title "King of the Jews" was conferred upon him. It took Herod three years to consolidate his realm, but from 37 B.C. until his death in 4 B.C. Herod's territories and prestige increased. Eventually he controlled the entire Hasmonean kingdom, with the exception of the Decapolis.[14]

An unending debate rages around the reign of Herod the Great. Some persons claim that he proved to be Israel's greatest king.[15] Others argue that whereas the Maccabeans had built up a Jewish Palestine, the Herods destroyed it.[16] Doubtless both Christian and Jewish historians have exaggerated the first Herod's cruelty and atrocities. Octavian, who in 31 B.C. triumphed over Antony and Cleopatra to become Caesar Augustus, found Herod to be a dependable man and strengthened his position. To increase his own reputation and to promote Hellenistic civilization, Herod undertook numerous building projects. He began in 20 B.C. to rebuild Jerusalem's temple although this magnificent plan was not fulfilled during his lifetime. Herod's policies have been likened to those of King Solomon. A great builder, his projects, like those of Solomon, became a severe financial burden to his people. Herod's real paragon was Caesar Augustus.[17]

The reaction of the Jewish people to events after 63 B.C. will now be noted. As early as 41 B.C., Jewish delegations had complained to the Romans of the harsh measures of Antipater's sons. Hezekiah's "bandits," whom Herod massacred in Galilee, were in all likelihood hot-headed Jewish patriots of the same type as the guerrilla warriors of Judas Maccabee. The popular reaction to Herod's pogrom was so great that Hyrcanus II was forced to bring Herod before the Sanhedrin, the Jewish court. Herod was condemned, but without the support of the governor of Syria and Hyrcanus, the Jewish council was unable to carry out its sentence.

During Herod's reign the Jewish settlement at Qumran seems to have been abandoned.[18] A terrible earthquake in 31 B.C. was probably responsible for this, but the coexistence of Herod at Jericho and of this "puritanical" sect just seven miles away may have been intolerable. The fierce and bloody wars between Herod and the last Maccabean contender for the throne (40–37 B.C.) increased the Jewish hatred of the Idumean ruler. Many of the quieter Jews acquiesced to the inevitable, but they doubtless stored in their hearts a bitter resentment and contempt because of these bloody purges. Herod attempted, by his marriage with Mariamne, a

---

[13]*War*, I. x. 5.

[14]A league of ten Greek cities situated to the east of Samaria; see Plate XII, *Westminster Atlas*.

[15]M. S. Enslin, *Christian Beginnings* (1938), pp. 53ff. [hereafter, *Beginnings*].

[16]Klausner, *Jesus*, pp. 135ff.

[17]For a description of the reign of Augustus, see *Westminster Atlas*, pp. 85–88.

[18]A group of agricultural buildings at Ain Feskha belonging to a Jewish sect (Essenes?) was also abandoned at this time.

princess of the Hasmonean line, to neutralize his people's hatred, or else to gain their respect. This marriage brought great grief to Herod in the last nine years of his reign. With evident satisfaction, Josephus reports details of the domestic strife, palace intrigues, and bloodshed which crowned Herod's days.[19] As Herod lay dying, an insolent band of rebels made a demonstration. Herod rallied and had forty of the ringleaders killed, as well as his son Antipater who was on probation for earlier misconduct. Shortly before Herod's death there was born in Bethlehem of Judea a baby who was given the name Jesus.

The last of Herod's many wills decreed that his kingdom should be divided among three of his sons: Herod Antipas was to receive Galilee and Perea, and the title "tetrarch"; Philip, the territories northeast of the Sea of Galilee, and the same title; and Archelaus was to be given Samaria, Judea, the northern part of Idumea, and the title "king." Augustus approved these bequests with the exception of reducing the rank of Archelaus from king to ethnarch. In A.D. 6 Archelaus was deposed because of misrule. In his place a Roman procurator, Coponius, was appointed.[20]

Of Philip, very little is known. Herod Antipas seems to have been the most capable of Herod's sons. He became a favorite of the Emperor Tiberius. Like his father, Antipas was a builder. He rebuilt Sepphoris, the ancient capital, a short distance from Nazareth. Later, he had a new capital constructed and named it Tiberias. Both cities became centers of Hellenistic culture. Apparently he did not wish to affront his Jewish subjects, and, since he was able to rule until A.D. 39, he must have been fairly successful.[21]

The downfall of Antipas came in part as a result of the activities of Agrippa, his wife's brother. When Gaius (Caligula), who had earlier befriended Agrippa, became emperor, Agrippa was favored. The fact that Antipas had a large arsenal was used by Agrippa to make it appear that his brother-in-law was plotting revolt. There is some evidence that Antipas, prodded by Herodias, did covet the title and prerogatives of a king. Antipas was banished by the emperor and his territories given to Herod Agrippa I. The latter's frequent visits to Rome stood him in good stead again, for, when Claudius succeeded Caligula (A.D. 41), Agrippa's realm was extended to the southernmost unit of Palestine, including Judea. Agrippa was awarded the title "king"; he ruled over the territories which had belonged to Herod the Great from 41 until his death in 44.[22]

The son of the king, who bore his father's name, was too young at the time to be entrusted with power or to watch over the precarious peace. Procurators were sent a second time to Palestine and they continued to rule in Judea to the end of New Testament times. In the meanwhile, Herod Agrippa II was gradually

---

[19]*Antiq.*, XVI. A clear account of this complicated narrative is given by Enslin in *Beginnings*, pp. 56–60. See also S. Sandmel, "Herod," *IDB*, vol. 2, pp. 588ff.

[20]The political divisions and their rulers during the Ministry of Jesus, with the exception that Pontius Pilate, fifth procurator, ruled Judea.

[21]This is the Herod Jesus referred to as "that fox," Luke 13:32.

[22]This Herod persecuted the earliest Christians, executing James and imprisoning Peter. Acts 12:21ff.; cf. *Antiq.*, XIX. viii. 2.

assigned more and more territory. By 54 his kingdom included the regions northeast of Galilee, and parts of Galilee and Perea. He was more Roman than Jew and assisted Titus in the Roman war against his countrymen.[23] Herod Agrippa II died shortly before or after 100.

Let us consider now some of the chaotic conditions existing under the successors of Herod the Great. Notice has already been taken of the deposition of Archelaus in A.D. 6. The institution of procurator rule did not bring peace to Palestine. Josephus reports that "in those days Judea was filled with bands of marauders."[24] The situation was even more ominous in Galilee. "Judas the Gaulanite" is, in all probability, to be identified with Judah the son of the martyred Hezekiah. This Judas gathered a large group of nationalists and in the critical year A.D. 6 raided the arsenal at Sepphoris, an hour's journey from Jesus' boyhood home, Nazareth.[25] Sepphoris was burned by the Romans in reprisal. Herod Antipas was shortly to rebuild this city as his first capital.

Some claim that these protests and struggles of the Jews against the Herods marked the beginning of the end, and that "the great rebellion," 66–70, really began immediately after the death of Herod the Great in 4 B.C.[26]

A real source of grievance during the rule of the Herods and the Roman procurators was the matter of revenues. All tariffs, with the exception of direct taxation, were farmed out to the highest bidders, known as *publicani* (publicans). This system of collection invited corruption, and many of the publicans, especially the Jews among them, were despised and known as "robbers" or, according to the gospel tradition, classed alongside "sinners and harlots." That this tribute to Rome was galling to the nationalist Jews is shown by the fact that the revolt of Judas in Galilee in A.D. 6 coincided with the census ordered by Quirinius, governor of Syria, to facilitate tax collection.

The constant surveillance of the local rulers by the Romans likewise proved a source of irritation. The procurator could appoint and depose the high priests. Their robes were kept in Roman custody. A Roman army was permanently stationed in Palestine and at the time of the great feasts the procurator, whose residence was at Caesarea, took up residence in Jerusalem. Sentinels and spies were everywhere. The jurisdiction of the Jewish Sanhedrin was largely limited to religious matters. The proceedings of the Sanhedrin were subject to the procurator's review.

It is estimated that more than 200,000 men died in uprisings and pogroms during the rules of the Herods and the procurators. Everyone was dissatisfied with the existing political and social conditions, with the exception of the wealthier families, many of whom were priests, known as the Sadducees. This ruling faction kowtowed to their overlords. Fear, hatred, and bitter resentment were in evidence

---

[23]The Apostle Paul made a defense of himself before this last Herod, Acts 25:13ff.

[24]*Antiq.*, XVII. x. 8.

[25]Acts 5:37; cf. *War*, II. viii. 1; *Antiq.*, XVIII. i. 1.

[26]Klausner, *Jesus*, p. 155. During these days of mounting tension Jesus taught in Galilee and Judea, and was crucified at Jerusalem. From thence the first Christians went forth to bear witness to him in the troubled world of the Jews.

everywhere; and, on top of these things, there was much poverty. In spite of recurrent warfare, the population had increased during these centuries. Declining food supplies and wasteful governments made desperate the plight of all citizens, except for some of the provident and hard-working peasants and artisans. Commercial and maritime trade had greatly increased during the era of the Hasmoneans and the Herods, but this influx of wealth had not improved conditions among the masses. It had tended rather to uproot them from their lands and, in chaotic times, to make them a restless group of homeless malcontents. The number of hirelings must have greatly increased in New Testament times.[27]

The Revolts of the Jews, 66–70 and 132–135

The time of the procurator Felix (51–60) marks the beginning of that open hostility which inevitably led to "the great rebellion." This procurator's summary measures against a group known as the Sicarii (because of their concealed weapons), and sometimes referred to as the Zealots, made martyrs of them and rallied the people to their side. A Jewish prophet from Egypt aroused a mob in the wilderness. These revolutionaries were quickly dispersed by the Romans, who arrested six hundred, killing four hundred.[28] The next procurator, Festus, attempted to keep order by gentle measures, but his two successors, Albinus and Gessius Florus, resorted to strong-arm methods. A rash of rioting broke out, with the Zealots storming Roman strongholds to secure weapons. Late in 66 the Syrian legate laid siege to Jerusalem. His rout united Jewish resistance, but the Emperor Nero dispatched his experienced commander, Vespasian, to bring an end to the revolt. Galilee was the first area to fall to the Romans. Nero's death in 69 halted the fight for the greater part of a year. Vespasian returned to Rome to become emperor, leaving his son Titus in charge.

In the spring of 70 the final siege of Jerusalem began. It ended in a holocaust. The Arch of Titus in Rome symbolizes this defeat; Josephus' *The Jewish War*, Books V–VI, describes the horrors of the siege in unforgettable details. Earlier the Jewish–Christians of the city had fled to Pella. Before the fall of Jerusalem, Johanan ben Zakkai, a Pharisee, had also left the fated city. At Jamnia he established a council of rabbinical scholars. It was this group of Pharisees at Jamnia that was chiefly responsible for preserving the Jewish religion, standardizing its sacred texts and script, and making the study of the ritual law a substitute for the sacrificial system—thus in time rendering obsolete the temple and its priests.

On two other occasions in New Testament times the Jews fought unsuccessfully against Rome. During the reign of Trajan (98–117) rebellions broke out in Egypt, Mesopotamia, and elsewhere. Thousands of Jews were killed. The final revolution occurred in Palestine during the rule of Hadrian (117–138). The emperor, we are told, had forbidden the practice of circumcision, as a part of his general ban against

[27]Ibid., pp. 174ff.; F. C. Grant, *The Economic Background of the Gospels* (1926). Note the frequent mention of "hirelings" in the Gospels.

[28]*War*, II. xiii. 2ff; cf. Acts 21:38. While Paul was imprisoned at Caesarea (58–60?) a race riot broke out there; Acts 23:23ff.

mutilation of the body because of the practices of the various religious cults within his realm. Hadrian also had begun plans for the erection of a temple to Jupiter upon the ruins of "Herod's temple" in Jerusalem. A Jewish rebellion broke out in 132 which lasted for three years. Its leader was Simon ben Kosibah.[29] At the end of this disastrous struggle Jerusalem became a Roman colony, Aelia Capitolina. Jupiter's temple was erected and Jerusalem was declared out of bounds for the Jews. Even as late as the fourth century this ban was not relaxed, except for one day each year, in order that the Jews might come to weep at the site of their temple.

THE LITERARY SOURCES

The three centuries of history which have been sketched may be aptly described as the fight of the Jews to maintain their faith. Certain religious aspects of this struggle have already been considered. In the next chapter an attempt will be made to set forth more explicitly the essential characteristics of the religion of the Jews during these times. Before this is done, however, the student should be introduced to the literary sources for our knowledge of ancient Judaism. The principal sources will be listed below, according to their familiar literary groupings, and briefly described. Then an estimate of their relative value will be attempted.

The Rabbinic Literature

Judaism should certainly be permitted to speak of its history in the New Testament times in its own way. Therefore, first of all, attention should be given to the rabbinic writings. One aspect of the immediate background of early Christianity is the teaching of the Tannaim (Repeaters). This term refers to the principal scribes or rabbis from the time of Herod the Great to the end of the second century. We may be sure that the early Christian understanding of God's revelation in "the law and the prophets" was influenced by the interpretations of the Tannaim.

The teachings of the Tannaim were for the most part expositions of the Torah (a transliteration of the Hebrew word for teaching or instruction, usually rendered

[29]Variously spelled. Manuscripts found in the caves at Murabba'at (1952) establish that the Jewish warrior's self-designation was "Simon ben Kosibah." The name was punned by Rabbi Akiba, who hailed Simon as Messiah (Kochebah = star; cf. Num. 24:17). Later those who condemned Simon as an imposter punned his name again (Kozibah = falsehood). A letter written by Simon was found at Murabba'at:

> From Simon ben Kosibah to Yeshua ben Gilgolah to the men of the stronghold, greeting.
> I call Heaven to witness that unless thou breakest not away from the Galileans whom thou
> hast protected, all of them, I shall fetter
> thy feet as I have done to ben Aphlul.
> Simon ben Kosibah, prince of Israel.

G. Vermes, *Discovery in the Judean Desert* (1956), pp. 20–23, 203f.

in English, "the Law"). It was the presupposition of the Tannaim that the first five books in the Jewish scriptures contained the whole of God's teaching for His people. Interpretations of the Torah were of two different classes. Exposition of its legal precepts was known as *halakah* (rule). Sermonic expansion of the narrative portions of the Torah was referred to as *haggadah* (story). For nearly two centuries the teachings of the Tannaim, like the traditions of the scribes before them, were transmitted orally and taught by rote.

Several types of documents were compiled to embody these oral traditions of the rabbis. Some of the teachings of the Tannaim, and of the earlier scribes whom they honored, were arranged according to subject matter and designated by such titles as "On the Festivals" or "On Women." Topical arrangements of the halakah were known as "orders." A collection of orders was termed a *mishnah* (repetition). One such collection containing six orders, subdivided into sixty-three "texts," or tractates, was compiled by a rabbi named Judah, who became known as Judah the Patriarch. This mishnah attained an almost canonical status and was preserved in two major recensions. The contents of a mishnah may be described as traditional rulings involving the application of the Torah to special cases. For example, the halakah recorded in the Mishnah of Rabbi Judah under "set festivals" gives these two tractates concerning the Sabbath:

SABBATH 9.5
Any [persons are culpable] that take out on the Sabbath wood enough to cook the smallest egg . . . or shells of walnuts or skins of pomegranates . . . to dye a garment small as a hair net. . . . R. Judah says: enough to spread over a stain. 6 . . . or any quantity soever of . . . alter-earth or of worn-out sacred books . . . R. Judah says: or any that take out aught soever pertaining to idols, for it is written, *And there shall cleave nought of the devoted thing to thine hand* (Deut. 13:17).[30]

Another collection of the teachings of the Tannaim is referred to as the *tosephta* (supplement). It is similar in its arrangement to the mishnah but it contains more haggadah. Parts of the tosephta may be earlier than the material in the famous Mishnah of Judah, but the extant collection was edited considerably later. The following tosephta is interesting for its list of some rabbinic principles employed in interpreting the Torah:

TOSEPHTA SANHEDRIN 7.11
Hillel the Elder (about the beginning of the Christian Era) expounded seven principles before the elders of Petherah: light and heavy (i.e., arguments from the less to the greater, or vice versa); analogy; a standard conclusion based on two passages; general and particular—particular and general; analogy with another passage; proof from context. . . .[31]

A second type of rabbinic literature preserving the teachings of the Tannaim is represented by the *midrashim*, or midrashes (expositions). The midrashes are

---

[30]*The Mishnah*, trans. and ed. H. Danby (1933), pp. 108f.
[31]*The New Testament Background: Selected Documents*, ed. C. K. Barrett (1957), pp. 146f. [hereafter, *Background*]. For a selection of rabbinic writings, see pp. 139–172.

anthologies of rabbinic teaching in the form of commentaries on the Scipture. The following passage is an example of haggadah taken from the *Midrash Rabbah,* or "Large Midrash," on the Pentateuch:

EXODUS RABBAH 33.1

A parable. It [the Torah] is like a king who had one only daughter. There came a certain king and took her to wife; and he sought to go to his own land and take his wife with him. The king said: My daughter, whom I have given you, is my only daughter; I cannot be parted from her, but neither can I say to you, Do not take her, for she is your wife. But do me this kindness. Where you go, make a bedroom for me that I may dwell with you, for I cannot let my daughter go. In the same way said the Holy One (blessed be He) to Israel: I have given you the Law, but I cannot be separated from it; nor can I say to you, Do not take it. But wherever you go make me a house in which I may dwell, as it is said, *Let them make me a sanctuary that I may dwell among them* (Exod. 25:8).[32]

A third type of rabbinic literature is the *targum* (translation). The targums were written for Jews who spoke Aramaic, a dialect of the mother tongue, but who were unable to understand the Hebrew script of the sacred scrolls. Translators or interpreters seem to have been present in the synagogues of Judea as early as the second century B.C. We may suppose that for a long time these Aramaic translations were given orally and that they consisted of free paraphrases of the text. After much repetition they became standardized.

There is some evidence that the *Targum of Jonathan* (on the prophets) was largely standardized by the first century B.C., probably a century before it was written down for reading in the synagogues.[33] The Septuagint and the rabbinic sources attest the existence of a written targum on Job in an earlier period.[34] The oldest extant targum of the Torah is known as the *Targum of Onkelos* and dates from the middle of the first century or later.

The importance of the targums consists in the light they throw on popular interpretations of the scripture.

On the basis of the mishnahs, especially the one attributed to Rabbi Judah, discussions of the Torah were carried on by the rabbinic "schools" of Palestine during the third and fourth centuries. This later interpretative material is known as the *gemarah* (completion). In time gemarah was appended to the Mishnah of Judah, which it explains, and a literature came into being which is known as the *Palestine* (or Jerusalem) *Talmud* (learning, teaching). Apparently a similar development occurred in the rabbinic schools of Babylon. During the fifth and sixth centuries this accumulated material was codified and the *Babylonian Talmud* produced.

One other type of literature, in all probability composed by rabbis, may be noted: the benedictions and other liturgical texts. Some of the earlier portions

[32]Ibid., pp. 151f.

[33]W. H. Brownlee, "The Habbakuk Midrash and the Targum of Jonathan," *Journal of Jewish Studies* VII, nos. 3–4 (1956).

[34]A targum of Job was found in Qumran Cave XI; see J. T. Milik, *Ten Years of Discovery in the Wilderness of Judea* (1959), p. 31 [hereafter, *Ten Years*].

of the Jewish "Book of Daily Prayers" for use in the synagogue, especially the "Eighteen Benedictions," may date from New Testament times. Some of the liturgical practices associated with the traditional Passover service also may have been followed in the period of Christian origins, as one may see by comparing these with rabbinic teaching in the Mishnah.[35]

The Septuagint; The Apocrypha and Pseudepigrapha

Since the monumental publication of two huge volumes edited by the British scholar R. H. Charles, it has been customary in English-speaking countries to classify some two dozen late Jewish writings under the title *Apocrypha and Pseudepigrapha of the Old Testament*.[36] Let us begin by identifying the collection of which the Apocrypha are a part, the Septuagint. In commenting on the effects of the penetration of Greeks into the Near East, notice was taken of the need for a Greek translation of the Hebrew scriptures among the Jewish people living at Alexandria. In the third century B.C., this translation was accomplished and was later known as the Septuagint. This Latin title signifies the number of scholars who are reputed to have been at work on the project, seventy (hence the symbol, LXX). The story of the Septuagint's origin is told in a second-century B.C. writing called the *Letter of Aristeas*.[37] This account is legendary, and questions concerning the text of the original Septuagint, additions to it, and various recensions, are exceedingly difficult to answer.

The production of the Greek Old Testament was an event of great significance for Judaism and for the Christian church. The Septuagint was the Bible of the Greek-speaking Jews, a collection which was added to until, by 100 B.C., it contained about a dozen writings not contained in the Hebrew scriptures of the rabbis of Palestine.[38] Without the Septuagint, Judaism could hardly have survived among Jews of the Dispersion, or Diaspora (a technical term, based on the Greek word *diaspora*, referring to the settlement of Jews abroad). The Septuagint aslo served as the Bible of the Christians, for the language of the Church soon became Greek. Accordingly, most of the New Testament writers quote from the Septuagint and reveal by their interpretations of the Old Testament how much their expositions are affected by its text. The Christians' use of the Septuagint led the Jews in time to revise their high estimate of it. Christian teachers constantly pressed upon the Jews proof texts from the Septuagint, texts whose meanings were not identical with those of the Hebrew scrolls. As a result some Jewish apologists in the second century went so far as to pronounce the Septuagint a fraud. Indeed, copies of it would have been lost had not Christian communities preserved them. Of course the need among the Jews for Greek translations of their scriptures continued.

---

[35] *The Mishnah*, Pesahim (Passover) 10:1-7, pp. 150f. For a discussion of first-century texts from the Jewish Prayer Book, see F. C. Grant, *Ancient Judaism and the New Testament* (1959), pp. 44ff.

[36] Oxford: Clarendon Press, 1913, vols. 1 and 2.

[37] Ibid., vol. 2, pp. 83ff.

[38] Some of the books contained in LXX mss. were found in Qumran caves; see below, note 39.

New ones were made which were based on the Palestinian text and canon.[39]

It is now possible to define the Apocrypha as that collection of Jewish writings (in whole or in part) which are in the Septuagint but which are not found in the Hebrew Old Testament.[40] The books of the Apocrypha are (following the RSV) 1 Esdras, 2 Esdras, Tobit, Judith, Additions to Esther, The Wisdom of Solomon, Ecclesiasticus, or the Wisdom of Jesus the Son of Sirach, Baruch, The Letter of Jeremiah, The Prayer of Azariah and the Song of the Three Young Men, Susanna, Bel and the Dragon, The Prayer of Manasseh, 1 Maccabees, and 2 Maccabees.

No classification of the books of the Apocrypha according to their type or their origin is wholly satisfactory. Some may be placed equally well in two or more classes. 1 Maccabees is historical writing of a high order, yet 2 Maccabees must be classed as history and legend. Baruch may be grouped with additions to canonical books, or classified as wisdom literature. The student who wishes to familiarize himself with the varied character of the Apocrypha should make some soundings for himself. No effort need be made here to establish the date or the place of origin of any of these books. All of them were written within the period 200 B.C. to A.D. 100, that is, well within the time to be accounted as sources for our knowledge of ancient Judaism.

The Pseudepigrapha is a collection of books bearing an awkward title. The word is from the term *pseudepigraphon,* used by Jerome to indicate a writing falsely attributed to an ancient personage. The collections vary from fifteen to seventeen books, or fragments of books, which are very largely apocalyptic in character. The R. H. Charles edition of the Pseudepigrapha contains the following books: Jubilees, Letter of Aristeas, Book of Adam and Eve, Martyrdom of Isaiah, 1 Enoch, Testament of the Twelve Patriarchs, Sibylline Oracles, Assumption of Moses, 2 Enoch, 2 Baruch, 3 Baruch, 4 Ezra, Psalms of Solomon, 4 Maccabees, Pirke Aboth (Sayings of the Fathers,[41] Story of Ahikar, and Fragment of a Zadokite Work.

Most of these writings apparently were composed in Palestine during the days of the Maccabees and Herods. To a certain extent after A.D. 60, but more certainly after A.D. 135, writings such as these were disparaged by the Tannaim. Had they not stimulated false hopes and bloody insurrections? Thus these pseudepigraphs, along with many which must have passed into oblivion, were classed as writings "which do not defile the hands" (that is, lacking in holiness) and banned as dangerous and damning.

To what extent should the Apocrypha and Pseudepigrapha be used in describing the essential beliefs of ancient Judaism? The answer to this question will be

---

[39]Fragments of LXX, and Hebrew and Aramaic fragments based upon a text type similar to that used by LXX translators, found at Qumran, reveal that the LXX underwent revision in the late first or early second century. Thus a "missing link" in the history of the Greek translation of the Old Testament is provided by the recent discoveries. Milik, *Ten Years,* pp. 23–27.

[40]A working definition. These qualifications should be noted: Two of the fifteen books in most English editions are absent from oldest mss.—2 Esdras and the Prayer of Manasseh; some LXX mss. contain 4 Macc.

[41]Pirke Aboth is a section of *The Mishnah,* pp. 446–461. R. H. Charles includes 3 Macc. in the Apocrypha.

deferred until we have considered another collection of ancient Jewish writings, the so-called "Dead Sea Scrolls." These documents have gone far to revise the conventional descriptions of the religious situation in Palestine during New Testament times.

The Dead Sea Scrolls

In 1947 an Arab shepherd happened into a cave in a ravine called Qumran located near the northwest corner of the Dead Sea. He discovered there some old leather scrolls.[42] Since that day search parties prompted by a variety of motives have explored the vicinity. Ten other caves were found to contain hidden treasure. Thus far the manuscripts or parts of manuscripts from Qumran Caves One, Four, and Eleven have been considered the most significant by scholars.

The story of the discovery of the Dead Sea Scrolls and the struggle for their possession reads like an exceedingly complex suspense novel. It was not until 1955 that the general public in America became acquainted with these historical discoveries and some of their far-reaching implications.[43] In the meanwhile a vigorous debate had been going on among Jewish and Christian scholars as to the age of these scrolls, the identity of the particular people who composed or copied them, and the time of their abandonment in the caves. By early 1949 archeologists had explored Cave One and begun fresh excavations at Khirbet Qumran, the ruins of a community center situated in the same ravine, about 1200 yards west of the Dead Sea.[44] The chaotic political situation in Palestine, and the fact that manuscripts and artifacts became divided among various national groups, complicated these investigations.

The contents of Qumran Cave One, discovered in 1947 and 1949, were published during the years 1950–1956. Of special significance are the seven scrolls listed below (with the symbols commonly used to identify them): a complete Isaiah scroll (1QIs^a); A Manual of Discipline or "Rule of the Community" (1QS); A Commentary on Habakkuk (1QpHab),[45] War of the Sons of Light against the Sons of Darkness (1QM); Thanksgiving Hymns (1QH); an incomplete Isaiah scroll (1QIs^b); and an Aramaic scroll, only partially published (1956), known as "A

---

[42]W. H. Brownlee, "Mohommad ed-Deeb's Own Story of His Scroll Discovery," *Journal of Near Eastern Studies* XVI, no. 4 (Oct. 1957). The Arab shepherd dates his discovery in the year 1945.

[43]E. Wilson, *The Scrolls from the Dead Sea* (1955); M. Burrows, *The Dead Sea Scrolls* (1955) [hereafter, *D.S.S.*].

[44]See the *National Geographic*, Dec. 1958; Milik, *Ten Years*, pp. 44ff.; K. Schubert, *The Dead Sea Community*, trans. J. W. Doberstein (1959), pp. 21ff.

[45]These three scrolls were published in *The Dead Sea Scrolls of St. Mark's Monastery*, ed. M. Burrows, *American Schools of Oriental Research*, vol. I (1950), vol. II (1951). Meaning of symbols: 1 = cave, Q = Qumran, Hab = Habbakuk, the small "p" designates the type of commentary—*pesher* (explanation). The following excerpt from 1QpHab identifies this form:

> Hab 1:13: *Why do you look on faithless men, but art silent at the swallowing by the wicked man of the more righteous than he?* This means the house of Absalom and the men of their party, who kept silence at the chastisement of the teacher of righteousness, and did not help him against the man of the lie, who rejected the Law in the midst of the whole congregation. Burrows, *D.S.S.*, p. 367.

Genesis Apocryphon." A noteworthy example of the smaller fragments recovered from Cave One is the two-column section of a manual (or rule) of the community related to, but not a part of, 1QS. Indeed, hundreds of fragments of other Old Testament writings and of known and otherwise unknown pseudepigraphs were found in this cave.[46]

The evidence accumulated by all the scholarly disciplines relating to questions of dating ancient manuscripts supports the conclusion that the libraries of the sect living in the region of Qumran were deposited in caves at the time of "the great rebellion" of the Jews, A.D. 66–70. No consensus, however, as to the date of these scrolls and the occasion for their composition is to be expected so soon after their discovery. Moreover, there is an open debate concerning the identity of the people who lived in the vicinity of Khirbet Qumran.

We cannot concern ourselves with the intricacies of these problems, but certain generalizations now seem possible. For one thing, it seems fairly certain that all of the Dead Sea Scrolls thus far unrolled and the fragments examined were written within the period 200 B.C. to A.D. 70. 1QIs[a], sometimes referred to as "the Isaiah scroll of St. Mark's Monastery," may be dated around 100 B.C. 1QS, the Manual of Discipline, is commonly assigned to the early years of the first century B.C., and the Habakkuk commentary, 1QpHab, to its latter half. The military scroll, 1QM, and the second or fragmentary Isaiah scroll, 1QIs[b], were probably written during the period A.D. 1–50. No such agreement has been reached as to the origin of the "Thanksgiving Hymns," 1QH, although many scholars would date them in the first century B.C.

The occasion and date of the composition of these scrolls is determined in part by the historical allusions to be found in them. The Habakkuk commentary and the commentary on Nahum have attracted the most attention in this regard. For example, Habakkuk's "wicked" and "righteous" men refer in the Qumran scroll to "the wicked priest" and "the teacher of righteousness" respectively; the Chaldean invaders in Habakkuk are identified in the scroll as "the Kittim." The writer's methods do not require a circumstantial connection between one verse and another. Once this is recognized, the identity of the Kittim–Romans, which is probable enough, does not necessarily imply that a setting for all of the people and events alluded to in the text must be Roman times. It may be safely concluded, however, that this commentary was written a short while before or after 63 B.C.[47] The five-column scroll, 4QpNahum, contains the first identifiable proper names to come from the Qumran discoveries: "Demetrius, King of Greece," refers most probably to Demetrius III, a commander in the days of Alexander Janneus; and "the lion of wrath" to the Maccabean king himself.[48]

[46]D. Barthelemy and J. T. Milik, *Qumran Cave I: Discoveries in the Judean Desert,* vol. I (1955); T. Gaster, *The Dead Sea Scriptures in English Translation* (1956).

[47]W. H. Brownlee, "The Historical Allusions of the Dead Sea Habakkuk Midrash," *American Schools of Oriental Research,* No. 126 (April 1952), pp. 10–20; cf. Milik, *Ten Years,* pp. 64ff.

[48]J. M. Allegro, "Further Light on the History of the Qumran Sect," *Journal of Biblical Literature* LXXXV (June 1956); 89–95 [hereafter, *JBL*]; Milik, *Ten Years,* pp. 71–73; for "identity" of the sect's "teacher of righteousness" from portions of 1QH, *Ten Years,* pp. 74ff.

Shortly after the discovery of the first Dead Sea Scrolls, it was noticed that in several respects they were reminiscent of a Jewish document which had been found in Cairo late in the nineteenth century. This manuscript fragment was included in R. H. Charles' edition of the Pseudepigrapha and called "Fragments of a Zadokite Work." The document is now frequently designated "the Cairo–Damascus document (CD)." Since the discovery of the Dead Sea Scrolls, scholars have turned to this older manuscript find with renewed interest. Some of the same terms are employed to denote persons. For example, "the teacher of righteousness" and many unusual expressions found in the Habakkuk commentary are present also in the CD document. The Cairo manuscript presupposes a flight of the sect whose views it represents into the wilderness, and perhaps a settlement at Damascus. Is it possible that we possess in it an allusion to the Qumran settlement? Was there a real migration to Damascus which took place at the time of one of the abandonments of the community at Qumran? A discovery of fragments of the Damascus document at Qumran (Caves Four and Six) complicates these questions.[49] It is reasonable to assume, however, that the sect which produced the Damascus document and the people at Qumran adhered to very similar teachings and practices. They were probably the same group, or else they represent different stages in the development of a particular sect.[50]

Who were these people who produced the writings found in the vicinity of Qumran? It is widely held that they belonged to the Essenes, or certainly to a sect of the Essene type. However the question of identification be disposed of, it is obvious that our knowledge of ancient Judaism has been greatly increased. How influential were these persons who produced, or at least popularized, these writings? Did their beliefs and practices influence John the Baptist or Jesus, either directly or indirectly? Were the earliest Christians, or later interpreters of Christianity, acquainted with this sect and their writings? These questions will be considered in the next chapter and will concern us at various stages of this study.

Flavius Josephus

Alongside two books from the Apocrypha, 1 and 2 Maccabees, the writings of Josephus form the principal authority for the history of the Jews in Maccabean and Herodian Palestine. Josephus was born at Jerusalem in A.D. 37–38, the first year of the Emperor Caligula's reign. The time of his death is not known, but he outlived Herod Agrippa, for Josephus records the latter's death in A.D. 100. Josephus was the son of a priest. He claimed descent from the Hasmoneans. As a young man he was attracted by the teachings of various parties and sects in Palestine but eventually he joined the popular party, the Pharisees. During the

[49]F. M. Cross, Jr., *The Ancient Library of Qumran and Modern Biblical Studies*, rev. ed. (1961), pp. 81ff. [hereafter, *Ancient Library*].

[50]Another alternative, suggested by Brownlee, is that the folk of Damascus and of Qumran were both influenced by "the teacher of righteousness." When the Qumran settlement was abandoned in 31 B.C. did the sect take refuge with their "kin" near Damascus, and later return with copies of the Damascus Document?

procuratorship of Felix, Josephus went to Rome to obtain the release of some arrested priests. Shortly after his return the Jewish war began. Perhaps the impressions of Roman power which he had gained led Josephus to attempt to thwart the foolish rebellion in Palestine. But he was swept into the maelstrom as a partisan and for a time held a position of military leadership in Galilee. After the Roman victories in this region and his arrest, Josephus sought to mediate between the warring groups. It was not a popular position for he was suspected by the Romans and hated by the Jews. He was able, nonetheless, to observe much of the war at first hand. Afterwards he witnessed the triumphal procession of Titus at Rome. He lived there, until his death, in order to receive citizenship and various privileges, and to write his "apologies." He assumed the family name of the Emperor Vespasian, Flavius.

Josephus composed four works which survived because of their popularity with early Christian writers: *The Jewish War* (seven books), reporting the history of Jewish nationalism from around 175 B.C. to A.D. 70; *The Antiquities of the Jews* (twenty books), presenting the history of his people from the Creation to the outbreak of the great revolt in A.D. 66; a *Life,* written as a sequel to the Antiquities, and consisting chiefly in a defense of his career and of the historicity of his earlier works; and, finally, a treatise *Against Apion* (two books), a reply to further criticism of himself and of the Jewish people generally.

The character of Josephus and his credibility as an historian, both highly regarded until the modern period, were called into serious doubt by nineteenth-century scholars. The enigma of his personality will not concern us here, nor can the value of his writings as sources be adequately discussed, but the following facts must be taken into account in estimating the latter. The patent apologetic motives, coupled with the patronage of Roman officials, account for some of the distortions and willful omissions in the writings of Josephus. For example, he discusses the various Jewish parties and sects as though they were philosophical schools.[51] He holds that the insurrections against the Romans which he records were instigated by self-seeking "brigands" and secular-minded nationalists. In this way he seeks to exonerate the Jewish people as a whole. He almost eliminates reference to the Messianic expectations and claimants of the period. He is given to gross exaggerations. Yet in spite of these limitations, the works of Josephus must be judged according to the standards of his time and on the basis of the quality of the sources at his disposal. Without the writings of Josephus, a connected narrative of Jewish history in New Testament times would be impossible. Few would deny him a place among the greatest historians of the ancient world.

Philo Judaeus

Philo was born at Alexandria of a Jewish family of high standing during the last decades of the first century B.C. He became a religious philosopher and exerted

---

[51]Possibly Josephus, like the rabbis after A.D. 70, minimized the differences between sects within Judaism.

a considerable influence upon Hellenistic Judaism until the time of his death around A.D. 50. His world view may be described as Neoplatonic, but for Philo the highest philosophy and the revelation of the Hebrew scriptures were in complete accord. Most of his thirty-eight writings are allegorical commentaries on the Torah, or else essays on themes selected from it. For him, Moses was the wisest of all men.

To what extent did Philo's religious philosophy, his methods of scriptural interpretation and apologetic, influence Judaism of the Dispersion? Does a knowledge of Philo's writings throw light upon the interpretation of any of the New Testament books? These questions will arise several times in this study.

Some of Philo's writings refer to events of the Greco–Roman period. One of his works, apparently consisting of five books, narrates the judicial downfall of several Roman rulers who had persecuted the Jews. Only two of these books survive, *Against Flaccus* and *Embassy to Gaius* (Caligula). According to Eusebius, one of the lost books included a description of the Jewish sect, the Essenes.[52] Fortunately, there is still extant another book by Philo which contains a description of the Essenes, *Every Good Man is Free.*[53] Still another treatise of Philo, *The Contemplative Life,* describes an ascetic Jewish sect in Egypt, the Therapeutae.

On Employing the Sources

What critical procedures ought to be followed in reconstructing the principal features of ancient Judaism from these sources? Notice should now be taken of several influential judgments. The thesis of G. F. Moore, set forth in his famous volumes on Judaism, is that the development of the religion of the Jews in this period was fairly uniform.[54] The rabbinic literature reflects the normal religion of the Jews in the age of the Tannaim. The rabbis of the first Christian centuries were conservers of tradition, not reformers. Therefore, the Talmudic sources are valid for the earlier period as well as for the time of their codification. Several writings from the Apocrypha and Pseudepigrapha are taken into account by Professor Moore in his reconstruction. But, the apocalyptic writings are almost excluded from his review of "normative Judaism." These books are estimated to be "extraneous sources," imperfectly Jewish, and therefore of relatively minor importance. Professor Moore's thesis accords with the perspective of many modern Jewish scholars. Jesus, Paul, and the teachings of the New Testament generally, are viewed against the background of the earliest materials of the Talmud.[55]

Early in this century a different thesis was proposed and defended by a distinguished German historian, Wilhelm Bousset. He regarded the Jewish religion of New Testament times as a many-sided movement, one element of which was the teaching of the Tannaim. He insisted that our sources for the views of the Tannaim

[52]Eusebius, *Praeparatio Evangelica*, VIII. 11.

[53]IX. 53–63.

[54]*Judaism in the First Centuries of the Christian Era*, vols. I-III, (1927) [hereafter, *Judaism*].

[55]E.g., S. Sandmel, *A Jewish Understanding of the New Testament* (1956); cf. J. Klausner, *The Messianic Idea in Israel*, trans. W. F. Stinespring (1955), pp. 246f., 273 [hereafter, *Messianic Idea*].

must be carefully sifted by the historian. The Talmudic materials as they stand do not fairly represent the teachings of the Pharisees in the synagogues of the first century. The Judaism which Jesus and the early Palestinian Christians knew was more variegated than the chastened and liberalized Judaism of the "schools" following A.D. 70 and 135.

For two decades or more the views of Moore gained ground in this country. Moore's masterful use of the unsystematic Talmudic materials made his volumes, and others modeled after his, handbooks for the untutored in rabbinic studies.[56] With the discovery of the Dead Sea Scrolls, the old argument has revived. Some of the more outspoken of the scroll experts claim that the conventional picture of normative Judaism needs revision. It is now considered questionable, to say the least, whether there is to be found in Pharisaism the Jewish setting from which Christianity emerged. Some have claimed that the substratum of much of Christianity is to be discovered not in Pharisaism but in Essenism.[57]

This is not the place, nor have many the skill, to take an unequivocal stand on this highly debatable issue. Some critical procedure must be adopted, however, in this introduction. There would seem to be justification for abandoning the conception of a normal or normative Judaism; that is, prior to the second century after Christ. Bousset may have been hypercritical in his use of the Talmudic materials; yet the recent manuscript finds would seem to justify his description of the religion of New Testament times as a variegated Judaism.[58] The presence of Essenes and their toleration can be accounted for only on the ground that no regulative discipline as yet rested in the hands of the Pharisees. This, however, is not to deny that their influence was great. Furthermore, the Qumran documents make it evident that the differences between the Palestinian and Alexandrian canons of scripture were not so distinct as has been commonly supposed. Nor was apocalypticism so "extraneous" to Judaism in the age of Tannaim as it came to be for the Pharisees at Jamnia and thereafter. The later rabbis' disapproval of the Pseudepigrapha ought not to be read back to the days of Jesus and Paul.

Professor Moore justly chided scholars who assume that Christianity marked an epoch in the history of Judaism. Nevertheless, there were events which took place in Palestine in the years leading up to A.D. 70 which made for a wide breach between past and future. In the period of Christian origins there was a greater diversity among the Jews than is suggested by those who draw a straight line of development from the Old Testament to the Talmud.

[56] E.g., Enslin, *Beginnings*, pp. 14–110; cf. B. S. Easton, *Christ in the Gospels* (1930), pp. 83ff.

[57] A. Dupont-Sommer, *The Jewish Sect of Qumran and the Essenes* (1954), pp. 151ff.

[58] R. Marcus, "Pharisees, Essenes, and Gnostics," *JBL* LXXIII (1954): 157–161.; see also, M. Smith, "The Dead Sea Sect in Relation to Ancient Judaism." *New Testament Studies* 7 (1961): 347ff. [hereafter, *NTS*].

chapter four

THE BELIEFS AND PRACTICES
OF PALESTINIAN JEWS

a   b   c   d

(a) John Hyrcanus (135–105 B.C.), probably the first Maccabean to strike coins, although Simon was granted the prerogative. The obverse bears the inscription, "Yehohanan the High Priest and the Community of the Jews" (Note the concept of shared rule). (The American Numismatic Society).   (b) Under Herod I (37–4 B.C.) the Judean state became a Roman client-kingdom. This inscribed "King Herod" bronze coin bears symbols of Apollo on the obverse; a helmet (?) or a censer on the reverse (The Chase Manhattan Bank Money Museum).   (c) Coin of the first Jewish revolt (A.D. 66–70). The inscription encircling a cultic chalice, on the obverse, reads "a shekel of Israel;" on the reverse are symbols of the high priesthood (?) and the inscription "Jerusalem the Holy (City)" (The Chase Manhattan Bank Money Museum).   (d) A denarius with a bunch of grapes on the obverse, and a three-stringed lyre on the reverse, from the second revolt of the Jews (A.D. 132–135) (The Chase Manhattan Bank Money Museum).

Pere de Vaux, principal archaeologist of Khirbet Qumran, standing in front of Cave I where the first Dead Sea Scrolls were found. (Courtesy James Charlesworth, Duke University)

Khirbet Qumran: The fault in steps leading to a large cistern was caused by a great earth tremor in 31 B.C. The steps are particularly interesting to archaeologists in marking a phase in the settlement's occupation and abandonment. (Courtesy James Charlesworth, Duke University)

The Thanksgiving Scroll (1 QH) partially unrolled showing column IV. (American Friends of the Hebrew University)

Ruins of a third century Jewish synagogue at Capernaum marks the site of an older synagogue on the shores of the Sea of Galilee which Jesus visited. (Israel Government Tourist Office)

T H E beliefs of Jesus and the earliest Christians should be understood in close relation to the Judaism they knew. A knowledge of the Old Testament is not sufficient. Of course, the basic tenets of Judaism are set forth in "the Law, the Prophets, and the Writings," but Judaism was a living religion and adapted itself to its changing environment. The reader of the New Testament cannot afford to pass over the historical developments we have just surveyed as though Judaism were unaffected by them. This chapter offers a reconstruction of the essential characteristics of the religion of the Jews known to Jesus and his first followers.

ORGANIZATION OF JUDAISM

During the period of Christian origins the practice of Judaism was related to four basic institutions: the home, the temple, the Sanhedrin, and the synagogue.

The Home

Marriages were arranged by the parents of Jewish youth. It was the duty of the father to get his son a wife or his daughter a husband of his own choosing. The common judgment of rabbis was that a man should be married at eighteen. Postponements were not formally condoned except for the study of the Torah, but the inability of a young man to support wife and family resulted in some delays. The betrothal was more than a legal act. By it a young girl was consecrated to her husband. As much as a year or more might elapse before the marriage was consummated, but in the meanwhile infidelity was counted as adultery, and the relation of a betrothed couple could not be dissolved without a bill of divorce.[1] After the nuptial ceremonies the husband was bound to work for his wife, to support her and provide for her food and clothing; the wife's household duties were to grind meal, bake, wash clothes, nurse her child, and to weave and sew. If a part of her dowry included female slaves she was relieved of some of these occupations, but idleness was frowned upon as a corrupter of morals and as sometimes leading to a form of insanity.

Slavery was practiced in Palestine in the Hasmonean and Roman periods to relieve the burden of labor in the home and in the fields. The Maccabean conquests had augmented the supply of slaves, but it is probable that hired servants provided a more common source of menial labor than slaves. The special need for laborers at harvest times made necessary the recruitment of "hirelings" from

[1]Moore, *Judaism*, vol. II, pp. 121f.

the peasant holders of small lands or the landless population of villages. The Mishnah affirms the right of hired servants to receive their wages at the end of each day, but allows each worker the choice of letting his wages accumulate.[2]

The father of the home was obligated to support his children during their early years. His obligations to a son were clearly defined. He was bound, of course, to circumcise him on the eighth day after birth, and during his boyhood to teach him the Torah as well as a trade. Special emphasis was placed on this duty to teach sons both the Law and a trade. It was believed that unremitting study, even of the Torah, did not incline a young man to a life of piety.

Beyond question, male infants were more welcome in Jewish homes than female.[3] Nevertheless, the training of daughters was not limited to preparation for their domestic duties. Few were taught by their fathers to read the scriptures since knowledge of ancient Hebrew would have been required, but daughters were instructed in the Torah and in the performance of all laws applying to women.[4] The father's instruction of his sons was more thoroughgoing, for the life under the Law was the chief end of man.

"Above all we pride ourselves on the education of our children," wrote Josephus, "and regard as the most essential task in life the observance of our laws and pious practices based thereupon which we have inherited . . . [children] shall be taught to read, and shall learn both the laws and the deeds of their forefathers, in order that they may imitate the latter and be grounded in the former, may neither transgress nor have any excuse for being ignorant of them."[5]

Among all the commandments set forth in Torah and tradition, the "weightiest of the weighty" pertained to filial piety. A child's honor for father and mother was akin to reverence for God.[6]

A principal religious observance of the Jews which centered in the home, like the performance of the rite of circumcision, was the sanctification of the Sabbath. The Sabbath was a day for religious exercises in the synagogues, and when it was joined with the annual festivals the Sabbath became a day of holy convocation. But the keeping of the Sabbath was a household duty as well as a joyful privilege.

The Torah and its traditional interpretation prescribed thirty-nine species of "work" which profaned the Sabbath. In addition to these various species other prohibitions were deduced to make sure that all members of Jewish households kept holy the Sabbath day.[7]

The commemoration of the Sabbath as a festal day was related to the family

[2]Ibid., pp. 135ff. Lev. 19:13; Deut. 24:15. *The Mishnah*, Baba Metzia (Middle Gate), 9:11f., pp. 363f.; Matt. 20:1ff.

[3]Note the many anxieties which daughters caused their fathers, Ecclus. 42:9f.

[4]Moore, *Judaism*, vol. II, pp. 128ff.

[5]*Against Apion*, 1.66, 2.204, *Josephus*, trans. H. St. J. Thackeray, vol. I, pp. 187, 375. For a concise survey of Jewish schooling in New Testament times, see B. Gerhardsson, *Memory and Manuscript* (1961), chap. 4.

[6]Moore, *Judaism*, vol. II, pp. 131f. Ex. 20:12 (cf. Lev. 19:3). Moore cites Philo's comment on the subject.

[7]Moore, *Judaism*, Vol. II, pp. 26ff.

meals, which often included guests. At sundown on Friday a Sabbath lamp was lighted to burn throughout the holy day. The arrival of the Sabbath was marked by the Kiddush (sanctification) ceremony. The head of the house, at the table surrounded by family and guests, took a cup of wine and pronounced over it the usual blessing for meals as well as the Blessing of the Day. The "Cup of Blessing" was then shared by all. After this, another blessing was pronounced over the two loaves of bread on the table, symbolizing the double portion of manna provided Israel on the Sabbath during the wilderness wandering. A note of joy pervaded the mealtime which followed.[8]

The annual Passover festival was observed in the homes by the heads of households who could not make the pilgrimage to Jerusalem. In the holy city the slaughtering of the lambs took place at the temple, and rooms were rented for the Passover meal. In other communities the Passover was celebrated in private homes and provided an outstanding event in the families' experience. The "father" presided at the table and the oldest "son" inquired of him the meaning of this special day. In joyful remembrance of the event whereby God brought his people out of Egypt, the family was bound together—united in a common loyalty to the Torah and its teaching, and in their hope for the future which the Passover portended.

The Temple and the Priests

The authority of the Torah had secured by New Testament times the centrality of the temple and the power of the priestly office. The final editing of the Torah by priests had grounded in antiquity the temple, its sacrifices, and other activities centered there. There was but one temple, the one standing on the sacred site in Jerusalem, which Herod had rebuilt and adorned. It was an effective symbol of God's accessibility to Israel through worship.

The Jerusalem temple attracted thousands of Jewish pilgrims. It held a special fascination for those of the Dispersion. Jewish literature, written in Palestine or elsewhere, glorifies the temple and its ritual.[9] The horror of the Jews at the desecration of the temple or a discontinuance of its sacrifices reveals the central place of the cult in pre-Christian Judaism. The refusal of some pious groups to participate in the temple sacrifices should not be considered a disparagement of these things, but rather their conviction that the priests who officiated were corrupt or otherwise unworthy of their sacred offices.

Two principal classes of temple ceremonies were the daily sacrifices and those offered for the nation at the festivals and during solemn fast days. The daily sacrifices were at dawn and in the midafternoon, but offerings could be made at any time in the name of their sponsors.

The festivals and solemn fasts of the second temple were set according to a lunar-solar calendar. This calendar seems to have been in use since the middle of the fifth century B.C. It was a crystallization of a long process of Israelite time

[8]Ibid., p. 36.
[9]Pfeiffer, *New Testament Times*, p. 48.

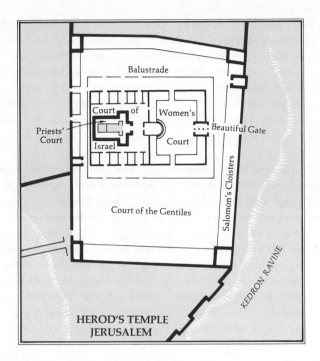

Balustrade

Court of Israel

Priests' Court

Women's Court

Beautiful Gate

Salomon's Cloisters

Court of the Gentiles

KEDRON RAVINE

HEROD'S TEMPLE JERUSALEM

calculation adopted from Canaanite and Babylonian models.[10] The day was reckoned from sunset, rather than from sunrise, to sunset. The lunar year consisted of $354\frac{1}{4}$ days divided into twelve months of, alternately, thirty and twenty-nine days each. A thirteenth month was inserted every two or three years, usually after the twelfth month, to make up for the eleven-day discrepancy between the lunar and solar calendars. While the Herodian temple stood, such adjustments in the calendar were necessary to ensure the regular observance of Israel's feasts and fasts.

The Jewish year began in the Spring with the month called Nisan (March–April). Within this month was celebrated the eight-day festival of Passover and Unleavened Bread. Other important temple ceremonies included the following: The Feast of Weeks (or Pentecost—"fiftieth day"), a harvest festival held seven weeks after the Feast of Unleavened Bread; the Day of Atonement, a solemn day of fasting set for the tenth day of the seventh month, Tishri (September–October); the Feast of Tabernacles, also celebrated in the month of Tishri and a second, popular eight-day festival; and the Feast of Dedication (Hanukkah—"rededication" of the temple after the Maccabean revolt), another eight-day festival beginning on the twenty-fifth of the month of Chislev (November–December).

The authority of the high priest rested upon an assumption of the divinely sanctioned antiquity of the office. It was supposed that the incumbent priest was

[10] Zeitlin, *Rise and Fall*, pp. 213ff. The "official" calendar was not everywhere accepted among Palestinian Jews, e.g., the Qumran sectarians followed another calendar, identical with or approximating the one outlined in Jubilees (6:22ff.) and 1 Enoch (72ff.). See Milik, *Ten Years*, pp. 107ff.

linked with Aaron through an unbroken line of his first-born descendants. It may be recalled that from Solomon's day priests of Zadok's line had officiated at the temple. After the Exile, the Jerusalem priests were identified as "the sons of Aaron," but sixteen of the twenty-four courses into which the priests were divided for the sacrifices were Zadokites. The privileges and keep of a whole retinue of temple attendants of various sorts, descendants from the line of Levi, were provided in the Torah. These Levites functioned alongside the priests in New Testament times. The temple also had its musicians, choristers, doorkeepers, and so on.

During the fourth and third centuries B.C., the high priest became a powerful figure in religious and civil matters. The assumption of the high priesthood by the Maccabean kings was, as we have seen, a mixed blessing. Under the Herods and the Roman procurators, the powers and prestige of the high priest were greatly diminished; yet his influence, and that of the priestly hierarchy in Jerusalem, presisted until A.D. 70. The number of priestly families increased during the days of the Maccabees and the Herods. The hereditary principle was overlooked and some appointments were of short duration. This accounts for the coexistence of several high priests and of numerous "chief priests" referred to in the New Testament. In the time of Herod the Great there were about eighteen thousand priests and Levites. As a whole they may not have been a wealthy class, but a few families had amassed great riches. Support for the priests consisted of payments in kind as prescribed by the Torah, the half-shekel tax paid by Jews from all countries, and various other fees and gifts.

The Sanhedrin

The authority of the high priest rested not alone upon his religious and socially privileged position, but also upon the fact that he was president of the Gerousia (council), or Sanhedrin (court). Josephus mentions the existence of the former in the days of the Seleucids and refers to the latter during the Roman period.[11] It is probable that both references are to the same governing body of the Jews which was influential early in the second century B.C. and continued to be so throughout Roman rule, although Herod the Great sought to curb its powers. The Mishnah's tractate concerning the organization and procedures of the Sanhedrin reflects a late situation. Yet it is probable that the earlier court consisted of seventy-one members, including the incumbent high priest. Doubtless its powers were variously defined at different times, depending on a particular ruler's willingness to delegate authority. Ordinarily, the Sanhedrin exercised both legislative and judicial powers. Under the Roman procurators there were Sanhedrins in several Judean communities, and the authority of the supreme Jerusalem

---

[11] *Antiq.*, XII. iii. 3; Jth. 4:8 (LXX); and *Antiq.*, XIX. ix. 3ff. It is possible that the Sanhedrin was founded upon the precedent of Jehoshaphat, 2 Chron. 19.8f. Or did the Chronicler write against the background of an existing council?

Sanhedrin was very great. Historians seem unable to agree as to the Sanhedrins' authority respecting capital punishment.[12]

The Synagogues and the Scribes

Little is known of the origin and early development of the Jewish synagogue (assembly), but it is supposed that this institution came into being quite spontaneously during the Babylonian exile of the sixth century B.C. or shortly thereafter. During this time the Jews had been bereft of their traditional place of assembly, Solomon's temple, and the people's ignorance of the Torah was keenly felt.[13] In the early years of their existence the synagogues must have been considered an adjunct to the temple; however, the synagogue was destined gradually to supplant the temple as the institutional mainspring of Judaism. By its establishment we may say that the Jews were prepared for being deprived of their temple in A.D. 70.[14]

During New Testament times, synagogues were to be found all over Palestine and in all lands of the Dispersion. The presence of ten Jewish men justified the establishment of a new one. Meetings were held on several weekday evenings and on the Sabbath morning. Outside of Jerusalem the feast days were observed in the synagogues, but there were no animal sacrifices. The synagogue services probably consisted in readings from the Torah and from the Prophets, followed by their exposition, the singing of psalms, and public prayers. A priest might read or interpret these scriptures, but only as a teacher, not in fulfillment of his priestly office. Indeed, anyone who wished to do so might read, translate, or comment on the sacred writings. On numerous occasions, Jesus, and later Paul, exercised this privilege. The management of the synagogues was vested in a council of elders.

As might be expected, the synagogue became a popular platform for a professional class, the students of the Torah. These were known in the early postexilic period as Sopherim, men of the book. Later, the disciples' term of respect, *rabbi* (my master), came to designate respected students of the Torah. The term *scribe* was also used in speaking of these specialists. We must not suppose that they were mere copyists. These men undertook to interpret and apply the commandments of the Torah. The first scribes may have been priests, but with the growth in influence of the second temple and the extension of its activities, priests became involved in their official duties and in politics. Thus the scribe became more and

[12]P. Winter, *On the Trial of Jesus* (1961), pp. 11f. [hereafter, *Trial of Jesus*]. The priests did not always control the Sanhedrin, e.g., in Queen Alexandra's time, but their position on the council and in the temple gave them great power. Enslin, *Beginnings,* p. 130.

[13]The earliest archeological evidence of Palestinian synagogues is A.D. second century. W. O. E. Oesterley. *The Jews and Judaism during the Greek Period* (1941), p. 213 [hereafter, *Judaism during Greek Period*]. Note Ezek. 33:31; Pss. 74:8, 149:1; Mal. 3:16.

[14]Moore, *Judaism,* vol. II, pp. 12ff. For an excellent account of the importance of the Galilean synagogues, see Reicke, *New Testament Era,* pp. 119ff.

more a specialist and a scholar, to be distinguished from the priest. Schools for their training were held in the homes of men who were eminently wise, or in synagogues.[15] In the first century A.D. many priests were scribes, residing in Jerusalem as well as in Essene communities. Nevertheless, the majority of the influential scribes were doubtless laymen identified with the party known as the Pharisees.[16] The Hellenization of many priests during the Seleucid times, and their corruption during the Roman occupation, contributed to the transference from priest to scribe of spiritual authority over the masses. A scribe known as "the Teacher of Righteousness" exerted a tremendous influence upon the group (or groups) represented in the Damascus document and the Qumran scrolls.

Discussions among scribes and before the people were not limited to what the Torah said, but revolved around what it had come to mean, and its contemporary application. Thus there were developed the various kinds of commentary, the halakah, haggadah and pesher midrashes, constituting an unwritten Torah, or oral law.

During the days of the Maccabees the scribal tradition was frequently associated with the names of famous "Pairs"; that is, two colleagues who represented alternative teachings. Shammai and Hillel, the last of the venerable "Pairs," founded two great rival schools in the time of Herod the Great. These two scribes marked the beginning of the age of the Tannaim. Their opposing views were debated in Jesus' day, and Jesus' antagonists attempted, on one occasion at least, to draw him into the controversy. Gamaliel, believed to be a follower of Hillel, was an elder contemporary of the Apostle Paul. During the period when the New Testament books later than Paul's letters were being written, some influential scribes were Johanan ben Zakkai, founder of the "great council" at Jamnia after A.D. 70, and Rabbis Akiba ben Joseph and Ishmael ben Elisha, prominent in the period leading up to the war in Hadrian's time.

INFLUENTIAL PARTIES AND SECTS

There were four parties of the Jews in New Testament times according to Josephus. For his Roman readers, he designated these parties "philosophies." The preservation of contemporary Jewish books by Christians, the Pseudepigrapha, and the discovery of the Cairo-Damascus document in 1896 threw some doubt upon the comprehensive character of Josephus' descriptions. Then with the sensational discovery of the Qumran scrolls (1947–1956) the question concerning the variations within Judaism became a matter of open debate. Many scholars identify the Essenes of Josephus with the sect (or sects) whose teachings are found in the Qumran and Damascus documents. Some few have held that the Qumran community closely resembles the habhuroth (associations) of the Pharisees in the

---

[15]Note Ecclus. 51:23.

[16]Oesterley, *Judaism during Greek Period*, pp. 229f. The student should be careful not to equate scribe and Pharisee. "Scribe" designates the person's profession; "Pharisee," his party. See Mark 2:16; Luke 5:30.

first century B.C., which are described in the Mishnah. The Qumran documents indicate that the description given in Josephus of the number and types of Jewish sects existing in Palestine must now be considered incomplete.[17]

For the sake of convenience, the classification of Josephus will be followed in this text, but his labels will be understood to indicate parties and sect types, not different groups with a "card-carrying" membership. Special notice will be taken of the views of the different groups arising from their interpretations of the scriptures. In short, we shall see how these various groups defined Jewish piety. Of course, such an analysis touches upon their conceptions of patriotism. A final section in this chapter will discuss the varieties of hopes for the future cherished by these groups.

The Pharisees

The origin of the Pharisees is obscure. Most scholars believe that they represent one group which developed from the Hasideans. The name probably means "ones who are separated (or separate)." Whether this implies some break-away from the Maccabean house, or a separation which was the social consequence of their rigorous obedience to the Torah and tradition, is debatable.[18] Josephus mentions the Pharisees as one of three parties existing at the time of Jonathan (ca. 145 B.C.)[19] According to the same writer, the first rift between the Hasmonean dynasty and this party occurred in the reign of John Hyrcanus.[20] Notice has also been taken of the Pharisees' contempt for Alexander Janneus, of his persecution of this party, and of his deathbed repentance. In speaking of the influence of the Pharisees during the time of Queen Alexandra (78–69 B.C.), Josephus gives a classic definition of the Pharisees. He calls them "a body of Jews with the reputation of excelling the rest of their nation in the observance of religion, and as exact exponents of the laws."[21] Throughout the rest of the New Testament era, most Pharisees considered the practice of religion their sole occupation, and adopted a political policy of passive resistance toward the Herods and the Romans. When the national crises of A.D. 66 and 132 arose, political involvement became almost inevitable.[22]

Josephus described several characteristics of the Pharisees. One, they believed in the direction of all things by divine providence, while not denying individual men a freedom of choice, and hence a responsibility for their actions. Two, they

[17]*The Mishnah* and other rabbinic writings are less reliable than Josephus as sources for a knowledge of sectarian Judaism because of the tendency of the rabbis to explain the tenets of all groups in terms of their own ideas. C. Rabin, *Qumran Studies* (1957), pp. 71f.

[18]Moore, *Judaism,* vol. I, pp. 60ff.; cf. T. W. Manson, *Servant-Messiah* (1953), pp. 18ff. Also, Schubert, *Dead Sea Community,* pp. 38ff., who suggests that "Pharisee" originates from a group's "separation" from "the priestly fanatics of the Law at Qumran, and their acute Messianic speculations."

[19]*Antiq.,* XIII. v. 9.

[20]*Antiq.,* XIII. x. 5f.

[21]*War,* I. v. 2. The Pharisees opposed the claims of Hyrcanus II and Aristobulus II before Pompey (63 B.C.), preferring rule by the Sanhedrin.

[22]*Antiq.,* XV. x. 4f.; XVII. ii. 4. Klausner, *Jesus,* p. 202.

believed in the resurrection of the dead, and in postmortem rewards and punishments.[23] Three, they recognized the supreme authority of the Torah and its traditional, oral interpretations.[24] This third tenet of the Pharisees accounts for the other two. The latest writings of the Old Testament and the earliest books of the Apocrypha show that Jewish thought in the postexilic period had moved beyond that of Job's friends concerning the problem of evil, and that belief in a general resurrection had, in some quarters, replaced the old Hebrew conception of an afterlife in Sheol. Thus along with their acceptance of the halakah, the scribal interpretations of the precepts of the Torah, the Pharisees affirmed many other developments in the religious thought of the Jews. Yet we must not suppose that they considered themselves innovators or reformers of Judaism. God's Torah was perfectly adapted to fit every situation which could arise; therefore, they sought by their interpretations to rediscover and reapply the ancient truth. This characteristic openness to late developments also accounts for a fourth tenet of Pharisaism: the belief in angels and demons, or in hierarchies of good and evil spirits.[25]

On the assumption that the above fourfold description fits the Pharisees exclusively, various scholars have identified books of the Apocrypha and Pseudepigrapha as productions of the Pharisees. Then, on the basis of these writings, further characteristics of the party have been given. Such reasoning becomes dangerously circular. Still, it may be that some of these books which the later Pharisees rejected as not being holy enough to "defile the hands" represent the views of independent thinkers. Mention may be made here of the Book of Tobit and its association with the Pharisees. Although a pre-Maccabean date is usually given for Tobit, its author has been called a precursor of the Pharisees in his doctrines and conceptions of piety. Another book of the Apocrypha, Judith, has been called the writing of "a left-wing Pharisee."[26] The writer of Jubilees has also been identified as a Pharisee, although it must be admitted that he "had some original views."[27]

Did the Pharisees form themselves into "associations" with definite rules and officers, with regular times of meeting, as some suppose? Or were they a party united simply by their similar views, yet at the same time sufficiently broad to permit wide diversities of opinion within their ranks, presenting a common front only when occasion demanded it? It is hard to choose between these alternatives. Josephus reported that the Pharisees numbered about six thousand in the time of Herod the Great. Whether or not they were closely organized, they exerted an influence out of proportion to their numbers and position. They gained "a

---

[23]Josephus translates this into a discussion of fate and freedom, of reincarnation and the immortality of the soul, likening the Pharisees to the Stoics. *Antiq.*, XIII. v. 9; XVIII. i. 2ff.; *War*, II. viii. 14.

[24]*Antiq.*, XVIII. i. 2; *War*, II. viii. 14.

[25]E.g., Acts 23:6ff. Acceptance of Daniel as canonical carries with it belief in angels and in the resurrection.

[26]Pfeiffer, *New Testament Times*, p. 65. Judith personified some Pharisaic ideals of piety but her militant nationalism would have repelled many of them. Did Pharisees write Pss. Sol. and XII P?

[27]Ibid., p. 69. The subjectivity of judgments of this sort is illustrated in this case. The interest of the Qumran sect in Jubilees suggests to some that its author was an Essene. See Milik, *Ten Years*, p. 32. Note also the new light of Qumran upon the origins of the XII P.; *Ten Years.*, pp. 34f.

very great influence over the masses," according to Josephus, "and all religious ceremonies, in the matter of prayers and the offering of sacrifices, are performed according to their directions."[28] Some Christian scholars have insisted that Pharisees and hypocrites are synonymous terms, and some Jewish apologists have been uncritical of the Pharisees, in their reaction against "New Testament caricatures" and "slander." These polemics have not contributed to a judicious estimate of the character of the Pharisees as a group. The Pharisees possessed both virtues and failings, as we shall have occasion to observe.

The Sadducees

Who were the Sadducees? The name itself tells us little, if anything. Attempts have been made to derive it from Zadok, the priest in Solomon's time, but these conjectures have been widely contested. Josephus introduced the Sadducees as the party supported by John Hyrcanus after his quarrel with the Pharisees. No mention was made of them again until the time of Archelaus when, Josephus says, they were not numerous.[29] Who were the people who composed the membership of this party? Doubtless there were some priests and Levites among them, drawn from the upper ranks of the temple hierarchy, but the rest seem to have been wealthy, property-owning laymen, who lived in Jerusalem or its environs.[30]

Josephus reported that the Sadducees were "persons of the highest reputation"; yet, with evident satisfaction, he commented that they were "influential only with the wealthy," and that they "had no following among the populace."[31] In their relationship to each other, the Sadducees were "rather boorish in their behavior," and in their relations with their countrymen, "as rude as with aliens."[32] These qualities are likely to be found in persons who are forced to be subservient and compromising, that is, if they are to keep their positions. One could hardly expect religious idealism to flourish among the Sadducees. Theirs was a philosophy of expediency. Driven to make the best of bad bargains, they maintained that human choices are free and responsible. Unlike the Pharisees, they held "that all things lie within our own power."[33] The statement of Josephus that the Sadducees "do away with fate altogether" is probably not to be understood as a denial of belief in providence, nor should his comparison of Sadducees with the Epicureans be pressed. The Sadducees stood for the old dogma of retribution: God is responsible solely for the good, not for the evil—not even for its toleration. Men are responsible for their blessings and bring their misfortunes upon themselves. "As for the persistence of the soul after death, penalties in Hades and rewards," Josephus

[28]*Antiq.*, XIII. x. 6.

[29]*Antiq.*, XIII. x. 5f.; cf. XVIII. 1. 4.

[30]Perhaps "Sadducee" derives from an Aramaic term meaning civic official. Were these men "syndics" who were charged by the Romans to represent their people and be in charge of fiscal affairs? T. W. Manson, *Servant-Messiah*, pp. 12ff.

[31]*Antiq.*, XVIII. i. 4; XIII. x. 6.

[32]*War*, II. viii. 14.

[33]*Antiq.*, XIII. v. 9.

records that the Sadducees "will have none of them."[34] In the New Testament the disbelief of the Sadducees in angels and in demonic spirits is reported. Josephus declared that the Sadducees did not "regard the observation of anything besides what the Law (the written Torah) enjoins them."[35]

In interpreting this last statement the bias of Josephus must be allowed. It would be false to regard the Sadducees as strict literalists. They relied on many unwritten traditions to support their piety, customs, and judicial decisions. In principle they were free to modify these traditions, when occasion demanded, as the Pharisees were not, since only the written authority was binding.

Can anything else be known about the Sadducees? Did the writing of any of their scribes survive? Some scholars believe that "Jesus son of Sirach" was a precursor of the Sadducees. The writer of 1 Maccabees has been identified as a Sadducee since there is no mention in this writing of the mediation of angels or of life after death. This argument from silence is a precarious one. Must all Jews at this time necessarily have belonged to one of the four groups described by Josephus? The scarcity of information concerning the Sadducees is doubtless due to the fact that after A.D. 70 they disappeared from history.[36]

The Essenes

Before the discovery of the Dead Sea Scrolls the debate concerning the origin and nature of the Essenes had reached a stalemate. Almost a dozen proposals for the origin of the term had been suggested. On the basis of the beliefs and practices of this sect, some scholars derived the Essenes from the Hasideans, or from Pharisaism. Others held that non-Jewish influences, Persian or Greek Pythagorean, were responsible for Essenism. Some scholars wavered between these positions deriving the Essenes from Jewish or non-Jewish sources, attempting a mediating view. The principal sources for knowledge of the Essenes had been the Jewish writers, Philo and Josephus. The comment of a first-century A.D. Latin writer, the "Elder Pliny," had not been overlooked, nor references to the Essenes in early Christian literature. A few scholars had attributed one or more Pseudepigrapha to the Essenes.

We have observed that many scholars hold that the scrolls of the Qumran caves and the Damascus document are Essene writings. The significance of this claim, if accepted, is that we now possess extensive primary sources concerning the beliefs and practices of the Essenes. In the account which follows, the Essenes will be described on the basis of secondary sources, following the pattern of description employed in presenting the Pharisees and Sadducees. Similarities and differences between these Essenes and the sect of the Qumran scrolls will then be noted.

According to both Josephus and Philo, there were about four thousand Essenes at the time of Christian origins.[37] Josephus declared that they settled in large numbers in every village. Philo's reference to their self-contained communities

---

[34] *War*, II. viii. 14.
[35] *Antiq.*, XVIII. i. 4.
[36] See Klausner, *Jesus*, pp. 217ff.
[37] *Antiq.*, XVIII. i. 5; Philo, *Every Good Man Is Free*, XII.

and Pliny's comment concerning their settlement on the west side of the Dead Sea imply the establishment of isolated Essene societies.[38] At any rate, wherever ten or more Essenes lived, a form of life existed in which everything was held in common. Such community centers were an asylum for the sick, the aged, and all traveling brothers. Only adults belonged to the Essenes, but children were received at their settlements for training.[39]

Candidates for membership were given a year's probation and after this time, if they were considered worthy, admitted to the "waters of purification." Two additional years of probation were necessary before full admittance into the council of the community. The "tremendous vows" of initiation included an oath of obedience to the standards of piety prescribed by the sect, submission "to their elders, and to the majority," preservation of the secrets and books of the order, and so on.[40] After these solemn oaths no further ones were permitted. Josephus declared that "certain stewards" were appointed to manage the properties and food supplies of the Essene communities.[41]

Were there any women present in the Essene settlements? Philo reported that the Essenes were celibate. Josephus stated that they were distrustful of women and "disdained marriage," although not condemning the institution on principle. But he wrote that members of one order of Essenes did marry, differing from the others only in this respect, that they married not for "self-indulgence but for the procreation of children."[42]

The daily life of the Essene communities was ordered according to the Torah and the traditions of the sect. Josephus declared that "after God" the Essenes "hold most in awe the name of the lawgiver (Moses), any blasphemer of whom is punished with death."[43] He described also several peculiar forms of Essene piety, such as prayers toward the rising sun, the sanctity and silence of meals in the common refectory, the scruple against oil anointing, the modesty of members in disposing of excrement and in the matter of spitting, and so on.

One puzzling reference in Josephus concerns the attitude of the Essenes to the temple: "and when they send what they have dedicated to God into the temple, they do not offer sacrifices, because they have different rites of purification; on which account they are excluded from the common court of the temple, but offer their sacrifices themselves" [at another place?].[44] A comment of Philo throws little light upon the matter: "they [the Essenes] have shown themselves especially devout in the service of God, not by offering sacrifices of animals, but by resolving to sanctify their minds."[45]

[38]Eusebius, *Praeparatio Evangelica*, VIII. 11; excerpts from Philo's work "Apology for the Jews"; Pliny, *Natural History*, V. xv.

[39]*War*, IX. viii. 2ff.

[40]Ibid, II. viii. 7, 9.

[41]*Antiq.*, XVIII. i. 5; *War*, II. viii. 3; cf. Philo; also Eusebius, *Praeparatio Evangelica*, XII.

[42]Philo; Eusebius, *Praeparatio Evangelica.*, XIII: "no one of the Essenes marries a wife"; cf. *Antiq.*, XVIII. i. 5, and *War*, II. viii. 13.

[43]*War*, II. xiii. 9.

[44]*Antiq.*, XVIII. i. 5.

[45]*Every Good Man Is Free*, XII. Did the Qumran sect tend to spiritualize temple and sacrifices as a result of their alienation from the temple hierarchy?

The Essenes studied the scriptures not only to become "athletes of virtue" but in order to foretell the future. Josephus recorded that the Essenes were versed from their early years in the writings of the prophets. "Seldom if ever do they err in their predictions," he adds.[46]

Josephus stressed the fatalism of the Essenes and their doctrine of the future life and its states. Understood in Jewish terms, he reported that the Essenes believed more firmly in the sovereignty of God than did the Pharisees. He likened Essene beliefs in perishable bodies and immortal souls to Greek conceptions, declaring that the Essenes "maintained that for virtuous souls there is reserved an abode beyond the ocean . . . refreshed by the ever gentle breath of the west wind . . . while they relegate base souls to a murky and tempestuous dungeon, big with never-ending punishments."[47]

For the purposes of comparison, let us assume the identity of the groups represented in the Qumran scrolls and the Damascus document, or at least the continuity of the two. Some of the resemblances between the sect of the scrolls and the Essenes described in the secondary sources are as follows:

Both groups were separatist in tendency, being organized into communities composed of persons who had voluntarily dispossessed themselves of personal property, and submitted themselves to the rigorous discipline of an assembly of brothers headed by a superintendent. Both required of prospective members a period of probation and similar initiatory oaths. The form and conduct of the community sessions were very similar; both groups administered discipline by a vote of the assembly and offenders suffered punishments or expulsion. Agreement in such detail as the prohibition against spitting in the midst of their councils is noteworthy.

We have noted the intense interest of the Essenes in the study of the Torah and of the Prophets, their fascination for books of the ancients, and their preservation of the secret writings of the sect. It is obvious that members of the sect disclosed in the new scrolls spent many hours studying the Torah; and the numerous fragments of commentaries on the Prophets which have been found in the vicinity of Qumran reveal their interest in understanding current and future events as related to these scriptures. The rigid predestinarian beliefs of the scroll sect go beyond the teaching of the Pharisees and are reminiscent of Josephus' comment concerning the Essenes.[48]

At the same time, the following differences have been pointed out: It has been judged by many that the attitude of the Essenes to the temple and its animal sacrifices is not compatible with statements found in the scrolls. The absence of any mention in the secondary sources of "the teacher of righteousness," or of the belief that the Essenes constituted the people of the "new covenant," has been considered evidence militating against an identification. Furthermore, some

[46] *War*, II. viii. 12.

[47] *Antiq.*, XVIII. i. 5; *War*, II. viii. 11.

[48] For a discussion of "the views of the brotherhood [Qumran]," arranged topically, e.g., dualism, immortality, etc., see J. van der Ploeg, *The Excavations at Qumran*, trans. Kevin Smyth (1958), pp. 90ff.; Schubert, *Dead Sea Community*, pp. 52ff.

scholars have held that the attitude of the Essenes and of the scroll sect toward war and the weapons of war cannot be reconciled. It is claimed that the militant spirit and organization for war reflected in "the Military Scroll," 1QM, cannot be harmonized with statements of Philo concerning Essene pacifism. Although the Qumran sect taught an eschatology of bliss for the righteous and of doom in an eternal conflagration for the wicked, no counterpart of the paradise of the Essenes has been found in the scrolls.[49]

How is one to assess these similarities and differences? Two points of view have predominated. There is an impressive number of Jewish and Christian scholars who are persuaded that the people of the scrolls belonged to the Essenes. It is claimed that the similarities outweigh the differences and that the latter have seemed to be more serious than they possibly are because of earlier misinterpretations of statements by Josephus and Philo, statements written by outsiders and for Greeks who knew nothing about sectarian Judaism and who were provided with misleading parallels. The scrolls enable the student to see through the Hellenizing veneer which had previously obscured Essene beliefs and practices. Furthermore, some allowance must be made for changes over the years in Essene doctrine, as well as for variety within the order during any given period. It is evident that the sect of the scrolls was not a small "splinter group," and that its sectarian literature was enormous. That such a major sect could have been unnoticed by Josephus and others is incredible.[50]

Other scholars have been hesitant to identify the sect of the scrolls with the Essenes. It is stated that there are real differences and that the scrolls should not be used as a yardstick to measure the accuracy or errors of Philo and Josephus. Moreover, the differences are incompatible with the assumptions that both groups can be called by the same name or that in Josephus the term *Essene* is sufficiently broad to cover these differences. For "accurate historical knowledge" it is safer to speak of the people of the scrolls and the Essenes as belonging to the same sect type.[51]

Whichever judgment may be deemed the more defensible, the following observation would seem to be justified by the evidence: The scrolls enable us to recognize that the Essenes of the first century and earlier, or the sects of the Essene type reflected in the scrolls and the classic sources, "root profoundly in older Judaism." They were not an exotic growth upon the life of Israel. The motivation for the separatist tendencies within this type of sectarian Judaism is now seen to be derived from the Torah, especially its priestly laws concerning ritual purity, and from Jewish "apocalypticism," a movement and a literature, to be described

[49] The following studies provide a compend of similarities as well as differences: Burrows, *D.S.S.*, pp. 279–294; M. Burrows, *More Light on the Dead See Scrolls* (1958), pp. 263ff. [hereafter, *More Light*]; W. H. Brownlee, "A Comparison of the Covenanters of the Dead Sea Scrolls with Pre-Christian Jewish Sects," *Biblical Archeologist* XIII (1950): 50–72; C. T. Fritsch, *The Qumran Community* (1956), pp. 104–110.

[50] F. M. Cross, Jr., *Ancient Library*, pp. 70ff. especially n. 33, p. 72; Schubert, *Dead Sea Community*, pp. 42ff.; K. G. Kuhn in *The Scrolls and the New Testament*, ed. K. Stendahl (1957), pp. 65f., 97, and n. 7, p. 265 [hereafter, Stendahl, *Scrolls*]. See Milik's reconstruction of various phases of Essenism, *Ten Years*, pp. 80–98.

[51] Burrows, *D.S.S.*, p. 294; idem., *More Light*, pp. 273f.

below, which had a decisive influence upon early Christianity. The apocalyptic overtones of sectarian Judaism of the Essene type, muffled by the Hellenizing apologetic of Josephus and Philo, are clearly sounded by the testimony of the scrolls. Thus we are provided a consistent theological background for understanding the distinctive beliefs and peculiar expressions of piety found within a major branch of sectarian Judaism. Many aspects of Essenism which before the discovery of the scrolls were considered paradoxical and perhaps the result of faulty reporting are now placed within an intelligible frame of reference.[52]

"A Fourth Philosophy"

The group described by Josephus as "a fourth philosophy" has been commonly identified as the Zealots, whom he accused of causing the Great Rebellion of the Jews in A.D. 66.[53] According to Josephus also, the origin of the "fourth philosophy," as distinguished from the philosophies of the Pharisees, Sadducees, and Essenes, goes back to Judas the Galilean.[54] Judas and his insurrectionists are reported as agreeing with the Pharisees in all respects except their "ineradicable passion for liberty." "The madness of this party," Josephus adds, drove them, "in desperation into revolt from Rome" during the governorship of the procurator Florus (A.D. 64–66).

It is misleading to speak of the Zealots as though a party by that name was organized throughout the Roman period. Perhaps it is more accurate to say that the same sentiments which had given rise to the revolt of the Jews against the Seleucids in the second century B.C. continued to live, and came to expression in the sporadic revolts against the Romans, finally leading to the Great Rebellion. Thus the Zealots in the seventh decade of the Christian Era represent the ascendancy of the same militant philosophy fostering the "home rule" spirit as that which inspired the zeal of Judas Maccabee and the fighting Hasideans, and of Judas the Galilean in the first decade. A governor's arbitrary abuse of his powers, or Rome's usurpation of the authority belonging to God, led some Pharisees and Essenes to abandon the passive resistance to aliens which was characteristic of their parties. It is probable that Josephus has obscured the connection between Jewish nationalism in the Maccabean and the Roman periods and that apologetic motives led him to glorify the former and to condemn the latter.[55]

THE RELIGION OF THE MASSES

A few statistics will show that the description which Josephus gives of the make-up of ancient Judaism for his Greek and Roman readers is far from com-

[52] F. M. Cross, Jr., *Ancient Library*, pp. 76ff., 92ff.; Schubert, *Dead Sea Community*, 80ff. Regarding the pacifist question, perhaps the Qumran folk believed only in one great "Holy War," that of the end. Essenes participating in the war A.D. 66–70 (Josephus) may have identified it as the "Holy War."

[53] *Antiq.*, XVIII. i. 1–10; cf. *The Mishnah*, Sanhedrin 9:6, p. 396.

[54] *War*, II. viii. 1.

[55] W. R. Farmer, *Maccabees, Zealots and Josephus* (1956), pp. 18–22; S. Johnson, *Jesus in His Homeland* (1957), pp. 94ff.

plete. It is estimated that in the time of Jesus there were 500,000 to 600,000 persons living in Palestine. According to Josephus, the total number of Pharisees, Sadducees, and Essenes came to more than 30,000. Thus the descriptions of various parties in Josephus do not cover 90 percent or more of the Jews in Palestine. Another fact should be kept in mind. There was an excess of 3,500,000 Jews living outside the Holy Land in New Testament times. Perhaps these Jews constituted as much as 7 percent of the population of the Roman Empire. It is claimed that there were more Jews residing in Alexandria than in Jerusalem, more in Syria than in all Palestine. What were the distinguishing characteristics of the religion of these "Hellenistic Jews," as they are called? [56]

An attempt will be made to answer this question in detail in Chapter 13. Many Jews living in Palestine at the time of Christian origins had been born and reared in cities of the Dispersion. Some scholars have been prone to exaggerate the differences between the beliefs and practices of the Jews of the Dispersion and those of Palestine, but Hellenistic Jews represent still another type within Judaism. Their native tongue was Greek; their "Bible," the Septuagint. Some of them doubtless formed themselves into separate synagogues, and these assemblies were frequented by Gentile inquirers.

Attention should be given the religion of the average native-born Jew living in Palestine, if for no other reason than that there were so many of them. What were the beliefs and practices of the common people, known in the Talmud as the *amme ha-ares* (peoples of the land)? Josephus wrote that the Pharisees exercised the greatest influence upon the masses. Since Josephus was a Pharisee, he may have done less than justice to the influence of other parties or sects, especially the Essenes. Although the latter were semimonastic, they had community centers in many villages and cities.

Jesus declared that the multitudes were "like sheep without a shepherd." [57] Many Jews were ignorant of the Torah and its traditional interpretations, and hence careless in their performance of the prescribed ceremonial and moral rules. Thus it may be concluded that the Pharisees, who held the respect of the *amme ha-ares,* did not associate with them nor actively seek to convert them. It is reported that the common people heard Jesus gladly. Some of his disciples were drawn from the "peoples of the land."

The masses did not represent the true Jewish piety of the first century; "a romantic aura of piety" has been associated with the common man. [58] Of course there were good men and women among the *amme ha-ares.* While they did not know or practice the minute details of the Law, they were sincere in their beliefs and religious practices. Nevertheless, we must suppose that the masses of men, then as now, thought of religion, if at all, prudentially. When urged to be "more religious," they would doubtless have asked how it would help them; how meet the economic and political distresses of their time; what promises it held for their

[56]Statistics based on J. Jeremias, *Jerusalem in the Time of Jesus,* trans. F. H. and C. H. Cave (1969), p. 205; Enslin, "New Testament Times, II. Palestine," in *Interpreter's Bible* (1951), vol. 7, p. 112 [hereafter, *IB*].

[57]Mark 6:34.

[58]Enslin, *Beginnings,* pp. 127f.

future? When strong men arose, such as Judas the Maccabee, Judas the Galilean, John the Baptist, Jesus of Nazareth, unnamed Zealot leaders, or Simon ben Kosibah, multitudes were ready to respond for weal or for woe. It is because of this fact that we must give special attention to the various types of hope held out to the masses in New Testament times. One cannot always distinguish the platforms and promises of modern political parties, since they appeal to the felt needs and wishes of the masses. Similarly it is not possible to distinguish the views which were clearly characteristic of any Jewish party, sect, or movement in New Testament times. We have noted the difference of opinion as to which party or sect produced several books of the Pseudepigrapha. It seems best therefore to examine the variety of hopes according to the writings which advance them, considering these writings chronologically.

ANCIENT JEWISH ESCHATOLOGIES

Eschatology is a term which the modern student of the New Testament should understand and use intelligently, not simply because the term is much in vogue in the scholarship of the twentieth century but because eschatology represents an important aspect of the religion of the Bible in its Old Testament, but more especially in its New Testament, expression. The term is derived from the Greek word *eschaton*, meaning end. By its use in Christian theology, eschatology came to be associated with death, the intermediate state, resurrection, the Last Judgment, Heaven, and Hell. But when the writers of the Bible speak of "the end," or "the end of the days," or of "the Age (or World) to Come," much more is implied than life after death.

The eschatology of the Bible is rooted in Israel's faith that history is the arena of God's activity, that His purposes are accomplished in and through the historical processes. Almost from the beginning, the Hebrews believed that their nation had been destined to serve the divine purpose in a special way. This was Israel's doctrine of election. The pre-exilic prophets assert this faith with special clarity and force. In the nation's early history pivotal events had occurred which were understood as God's mighty acts. Viewed in retrospect, these represented the successive stages in the working out of God's purposes for mankind.

A corollary of this perception of a directing providence was the prophets' clear recognition of the existence of evil in history. They were acutely aware of the terrible rebellions of God's chosen people, in the past and in their own generations. They witnessed the rise of rulers who defied God and usurped powers which belonged to Him alone. They saw that empires, established upon unrighteousness, collapsed, and they considered this the judgment of God upon the pride of men. When the prophets pondered man's capacity for evil, they were grim pessimists. But when they considered the power and mercy of God they were convinced that He continued to direct the course of history toward some ultimate purpose, which would not only reveal the glory of God but bring to fulfillment Israel's high calling.

Most of the prophets, from the eighth century B.C. on, looked forward to the consummation of "the Day of the Lord" and grounded the validity of their religious interpretations of history upon the realization of this hope. They were confident that the ultimate issues of history must be understood in the light of this divine purpose or goal. In the eighth century B.C. the popular idea was that "the Day of the Lord" would be a good time for Israel. The prophets argued that the coming day would be a time for the triumph of God and thus only of the righteous in Israel, if any such men could be found.

The beginning of what is commonly known as Israel's messianic hope may be reflected in the prophecies of Isaiah of Jerusalem and his contemporary, Micah. According to these prophets, the future deliverer of Israel will be an ideal king, like David.[59] The actual kings of Judah in succeeding generations seriously declined from this prototype, yet later prophets, Jeremiah and Ezekiel, kept alive the Davidic ideal.[60]

Some scholars have detected in Ezekiel's oracles the beginning of a separation of Israel's messianic hope from the Davidic dynasty. Whether or not this is the case, Ezekiel did seem to be more interested in the restoration of the temple than the monarchy. Possibly the prophet was responsible for giving impetus to an alternative type of messianism, involving a priest rather than a king. With the editing of the priestly tradition of the Law during the Babylonian exile, which provided for the consecration of the priest by anointing, the way was prepared for a transference of the title *messiah* to the ruling priest.[61]

After the restoration of the Jews from their Babylonian captivity, the hope of the good time coming revived. When a descendant of the Davidic house was restored to power in Jerusalem, patriotic prophets revived the older type of messianism.[62] In eschatological passages attributed to the latest of the prophets, however, the Davidic hope is often conspicuous by its absence. At the same time, the earlier prophets' faith that the coming day would bring a divine judgment upon evil was explicitly reaffirmed.

200–63 B.C.

Let us consider now various eschatologies which were being offered the Jews in New Testament times. Ecclesiasticus reflects the broadly humanitarian spirit of the Jewish sage, Jesus the son of Sirach. Yet one passage presents his vision of the great day coming, and reflects not only his nationalistic fervor but the persistence of several strands of the prophetic eschatology of the Old Testament.

> And the Lord will not delay,
>   neither will he be patient with them,

---

[59]Is. 7:10ff.; 9:1ff.; 11:1ff.; Mic. 5:2ff.

[60]Jer. 23:5f.; Ez. 34:23f.

[61]For a discussion of this exilic and postexilic eschatology, detached from any specifically Messianic elements, see R. H. Fuller, *The Foundations of New Testament Christology* (1965), pp. 26ff. [hereafter, *Foundations*].

[62]Hag. 2:23ff.; Zech. 3:8ff.; 4:7ff.; 6:9ff.

> till he crushes the loins of the unmerciful
> and repays vengeance on the nations;
> till he takes away the multitude of the insolent,
> and breaks the scepters of the unrighteous. . . .
>
> Hasten the day, and remember the appointed
> time,
> and let people recount thy mighty deeds.
> Let him who survives be consumed in the
> fiery wrath,
> and may those who harm thy people meet
> destruction.
> Crush the heads of the rulers of the enemy,
> who say, "There is no one but ourselves."
> Gather all the tribes of Jacob,
> and give them their inheritance, as at the
> beginning.
> Have mercy, O Lord, upon the people called
> by thy name,
> upon Israel, whom thou hast likened to a
> first-born son.
> Have pity on the city of thy sanctuary,
> Jerusalem, the place of thy rest.
> Fill Zion with the celebration of thy wondrous
> deeds,
> and thy temple with thy glory.
> Bear witness to those whom thou
> didst create in the beginning,
> and fulfil the prophecies spoken
> in thy name.
> Reward those who wait for thee,
> and let thy prophets be found
> trustworthy. . . .[63]

Other passages in Ecclesiasticus speak of the restoration of the house or kingdom of David, and allude to the coming of Elijah the prophet before the judgment.[64]

Owing to its contents and purpose, there is little eschatology in 1 Maccabees. In this writer's time Israel's great day might seem to some persons to have come. Yet at his death, Mattathias voiced the traditional hope of the restoration of the dynasty of David.[65]

The Book of Judith contains the following gruesome dirge.

> Woe to the nations that rise up
> against my people!

---

[63] Ecclus. 35:18; 36:8–16; 47:11.

[64] Ibid., 45:25; 48:10 (cf. Mal. 4:5f).

[65] 1 Macc. 2:57. Note that the expectation of "the prophet," ibid., 4:46 and 14:41, indicates that the present days are an interim until the coming of the Messianic Age.

> The Lord Almighty will take
> vengeance on them in the day
> of judgment;
> fire and worms he will give to their
> flesh;
> they shall weep in pain for ever.[66]

Tobit's song of thanksgiving echoed the more positive element in traditional eschatology: the peace, security, and joy of Jerusalem,[67] the ingathering of exiled Jews, and the conversion of the nations.[68] The poet of 1 Baruch also gloried in Jerusalem's good time to come. He exulted in the gathering of the dispersed Jews, in language reminiscent of 2 Isaiah.[69]

In these writings dating from the period 200 to 100 B.C., the "day" that is coming remains an event within history. But alongside these one must set books which describe "the coming age," or "the end of the days," in other ways. These writings are known as apocalypses, and the descriptions of the end which they contain, apocalyptic eschatology. The term *apocalypse* is derived from the Greek word *apocalypsis,* meaning revelation. Some readers of this book have been introduced to Jewish apocalyptic writings by a study of Old Testament literature dating from the postexilic period. The best way to learn what an apocalypse is like is to read some of these books: however, it may be helpful to list some of their distinguishing characteristics.

Pseudonymity: Since it was believed that the age of authentic prophecy had ended, Jewish seers in New Testament times deliberately took for pen names Enoch, Moses, Daniel, Ezra, and so on. It is doubtful that anyone purposed to deceive, or that the reader assumed that such books were really ancient.[70]

Secrecy: An apocalypse is commonly represented as something which had been, or ought to be, kept secret.[71] This air of mystery relates to the conception that the book contains a prevision by men in the long ago.

The division of history into periods: The vision of the end in an apocalypse is usually preceded by a historical survey. But it is strangely telescoped history, divided into eras of special length and possessing special characteristics.[72]

Determinism: All the events of history have been divinely predetermined. There are so many kings and empires before the coming of the end; so many and no more.[73] The periods of history rush on toward their appointed goal.

---

[66]Jth. 16:17.

[67]Tob. 13:9-12.

[68]Ibid. 14:5-7.

[69]Bar. 4:36f.

[70]H. H. Rowley, *The Relevance of Apocalyptic* (rev. ed., 1955?), pp. 35f. [hereafter, *Relevance*]. See also D. S. Russell, *The Method and Message of Jewish Apocalyptic* (1964), for a delineation of this and other characteristics of apocalyptic writings, pp. 104ff. [hereafter, *Jewish Apocalyptic*].

[71]Cf. Dan. 8:26; Asmp. M. 1:16f.; 1 En. 1:2, etc.

[72]Unfulfilled OT prophecies sometimes provided the mystical numbers for plotting these divisions. Dan. 9:1ff.; 1 En. 89:59ff.

[73]Dan. 7:2f.; Asmp. M. 12:4ff.

Belief in the nearness of the end: Intense expectation is present on almost every page of an apocalypse. The writer's pen decrees history's grand denouement. The last judgment will soon take place. The golden age is near.

The other-wordly, or cosmic, dimension: Unlike that of the earlier prophets of Israel, the apocalyptist's vision of the end is not an event in history. A new heaven and a new earth will be created. The dead will rise, and the living be transformed into angelic beings. The Age to Come is not the extension or reformation of existing conditions. The end breaks into history, obliterating the present evil age, and is itself the beginning of a new series of events belonging to another order of existence.

Pessimism: The apocalypses are pessimistic concerning man's nature and human remedies for the existing situation. Doom seems inevitable unless God intervenes. Yet, in one sense, the writers of apocalypses are stubbornly optimistic in the belief that God still rules in the kingdoms of men. For them, the darkest hour precedes the dawn; the "labor pains" bring forth the new Creation.[74]

Dualism: The presence and the strength of evil in the present age are due to the influence of supernatural demonic powers. Such a belief accounts in part for the pessimism of the typical apocalypse. Evil is a problem which requires for its solution more than human arms or intellect. God and his angels must intervene in the struggle, for the powers of evil have seemingly won the day.

Mythological symbolism: The visions of an apocalypse "are frequently unvisualizable."[75] It is easy to dismiss these bizarre word pictures as indications that the writers are pathological persons. Yet it must be recognized that they were endeavoring to describe the unexperienced, the unknown. Perhaps they were driven by their subject matter to employ fantastic images. Some of these visions are artificial, and may in fact represent the reworking of an image used by an earlier writer. We must allow for poetic license in these impressionistic word pictures, and chronological order ought not to be imposed upon them.

Let us consider now several writings which are commonly dated in the time of the Maccabean kings. The person who has not studied the Book of Daniel should read chapters 2, 6 through 9, and 12. The persecutions of Antiochus Epiphanes provide the setting in life for these apocalyptic visions. For the writer of Daniel, this crisis demanded a vindication of divine justice, if not of vengeance. The judgment foreshadows the triumph of "the saints of the most high."[76] While the hope of the Jewish nation's superiority is expressed, there is no good time coming for the Jews. The idea of the resurrection of the dead appears, and the hope for retribution in a world beyond history.[77]

The oldest sections of 1 Enoch envision the judgment as the coming of the holy and great One, bringing cosmic upheaval and terrible distress upon the earth.

---

[74]Rowley, *Relevance*, pp. 153ff.

[75]A. H. Wilder, *Eschatology and Ethics in the Teaching of Jesus* (rev. ed., 1950), p. 30 [hereafter, *Eschatology and Ethics*]; Moore, *Judaism*, vol. I, p. 343.

[76]Dan. 7:9–18. 1, 2 Macc. are important for an understanding of the setting of Daniel. 2 Macc. also offers the hope of resurrection as an incentive to heroism and martyrdom.

[77]Dan. 12:1ff.

A destruction of the wicked is depicted, of wicked angels as well as of men, and the coming age is described as one of spiritual well-being, peace, and justice.[78] In the final visions the traditional hope of an altogether terrestrial good time is given in a vision of the "new Jerusalem." [79] In what may also be early material, the figure of a messiah appears, "the white bull with large horns." This image does not describe a superhuman being. His righteousness is magnified, but only as that of a first among equals.[80]

Other writings which express the eschatology of the Hasmonean period are Jubilees, the Testaments of the Twelve Patriarchs, and, very probably, the Qumran Manual of Discipline. None of these books can be classed an apocalypse, but they contain apocalyptic passages. Jubilees makes no mention of an individual messiah descended from the house of David, unless he is referred to in the passage concerning "a prince" of Judah "over the sons of Jacob." At any rate, this author saw "princes and judges and chiefs" coming forth in the end time from Levi.[81] In the Testaments and the Manual the coming of several eschatological leaders is also predicted; among them a messiah arising from the house of Aaron.

Although the Testaments contain both Jewish and Christian materials, differing widely in their date of origin, and set forth ethical injunctions for the most part, prophecies from the Hasmonean times concerning the Age to Come are found in some of them. In the Testament of Levi we find a "little apocalypse." After the rule of corrupt priests, God will "raise up . . . a new priest, to whom all the words of God shall be revealed; and he shall execute a righteous judgment upon the earth for a multitude of days." [82] In the Testament of Judah, the crown of the priesthood is given to Levi, but the crown of civil rule to Judah "until the salvation of Israel (and of repentant Gentiles) shall come." [83] At "the end of the days" each tribe is blessed by angelic powers, but God himself blesses Levi. In the Testaments, "Beliar" [Belial] has become a personification of all evil, and at the end the "spirits of deceit" are cast into "the fire of gehenna." [84] The righteous arise to receive the reward for their deeds, in the bliss of a new Jerusalem, and glorify the Lord forever.[85]

According to the Manual of Discipline (1QS), the members of the sect "shall be ruled by the first laws with which the men of the community began to be disciplined until the coming of a prophet and the anointed ones of Aaron and Israel." [86] The messiah of Aaron is clearly a priestly messiah, while the messiah

---

[78]1 En. 80:3ff.; 99:4ff.; 19:1ff.; 1:3ff.; 25:3ff.

[79]Klausner, *Messianic Idea*, pp. 277, 283f.; 1 En. 90:17ff.

[80]1 En. 90:37f. Did the hope still persist in the early years of Maccabean rule that divine deliverance would be wrought by a righteous warrior?

[81]Bk. Jub. 31:13ff. Note also 23:25ff.

[82]Test. of Levi 18:2ff. It may be necessary now to date the XII P in the first or second century: Milik, *Ten Years*, pp. 34f.

[83]Test. of Judah 21–25; cf. Test. of Simeon 7:1–3, and Zech. 4:12–14.

[84]Test. of Levi 18:2; Judah 25:3; Reuben 2:1f.

[85]Test. of Dan 5:9–13.

[86]1QS ix, 10f. Cf. reference to a "Cave Four" fragment in F. F. Bruce, *Second Thoughts on the Dead Sea Scrolls* (1956), pp. 77f., in which the same three figures appear [hereafter, *Second Thoughts*].

of Israel may refer to a lay figure.[87] In the Qumran Manual there appear the divisions of time characteristic of the apocalyptic writings, and the conviction of predetermined seasons and of the final period or end, at which time Beliar is cast into "eternal fire." The righteous are promised eternal felicity, not merely as God's chosen people, but individually as "sons of light."[88]

ca. 63–1 B.C.

Of the documents commonly assigned to the first half-century of Roman rule in Palestine the following are of special interest: the Psalms of Solomon, the Similitudes of Enoch, the Qumran Habakkuk scroll (1QpHab), and the Cairo–Damascus document (CD). In these writings one sees an increased interest in the personality of a coming messiah. This may have been a repudiation of the Maccabean kings as messiahs. Chapter 17 of the Psalms of Solomon is evidently an indictment of the Hasmonean usurpers, as well as of Rome the oppressor:

> Behold O Lord, and raise up from them their king,
> > The son of David
> Against the time which thou, O God, chooseth for him
> To begin his reign over Israel thy servant,
> And gird him with strength to shatter unrighteous rulers,
> And to purge Jerusalem from Gentiles that trample her
> > Down to destruction. . . .[89]

This messiah's triumph inaugurates the new Age in which Jerusalem becomes the center of the world. Gentiles serve under the messiah's yoke; the Jewish exiles are gathered in; Palestine is redivided among the tribes. Yet there is hardly a trace of interest in material prosperity. The rule of righteousness is the theme of the poet. The only discipline that will be needed in the new Israel is the power of the spirit exercised by the Davidic king-messiah who will be "instructed by God." What a travesty upon this hope were the Herods whose military discipline was soon to be felt throughout the land. Elsewhere in the Psalms of Solomon there is reference to the resurrection of the righteous unto eternal life, and to the wicked who are doomed to perish.[90]

In the Similitudes of Enoch a personal messiah stands in the center of the Messianic Age. He is designated "the righteous one" or the "elect one." When he appears, mighty kings are to be destroyed or else handed over to the righteous.[91] Heaven and earth will be transformed for the dwelling of the elect.[92] In chapter 46 we have a reworking of the vision of Daniel 7. The coming of "the son of man" is described. He will "raise up mighty kings from their seats, and

---

[87]Cf. 1QSa ii, 11ff.; cf. 1QS vi, 5ff.; 1QSb v, 20; CD (A) vii, 20 (ix, 9).

[88]1QS i, 18; ii, 8, 17f.; iii, 13ff.

[89]Pss. of Sol. 17:21ff.

[90]Ibid., 3:16; 13:10; 15:15.

[91]En. 38:1ff. The Similitudes may be the work of a first- or second-century author. Note the Qumran fragments, Milik, *Ten Years*, pp. 33f.

[92]En. 45:4–6.

the strong from their thrones." He will "break the teeth of sinners . . . darkness will be their dwelling, and worms will be their bed." Is this "son of man" in Enoch a collective figure for Israel, as in Daniel, or a messiah? Scholars are divided on this question. In either case the manifestation of the son of man is associated with the glory of Israel, as well as with the enlightenment of Gentiles. In the Similitudes, the Messianic Age is described as a time when nature will be transformed and the dead will be raised. Whether this resurrection was considered a universal one is not explicitly indicated, but emphasis is placed upon the future of "the righteous and holy" who, in that day, will learn from a messiah "the secrets of wisdom."[93] Later chapters describe the severe troubles leading up to the end: the sending forth of "the angels of punishment" and the binding in chains of the wicked, and their imprisonment in the place of destruction.

In the Cairo–Damascus document there is but one messianic figure, the "Messiah of Aaron and Israel."[94] The argument that the sect represented by this document expected the resurrection and return of the "Teacher of Righteousness" as the Messiah falls short of being convincing. It is more probable that the Teacher became for his followers a prototype of the Messiah, or that he was considered to be one whose mission foreshadowed certain functions to be fulfilled by a messiah. Several references in the Damascus document and the Qumran Habakkuk commentary suggest that the sect believed that the invasion of the Kittim (Romans?) represented the tribulations at "the end of the days"; that the wealth and spoil of the last priests of Jerusalem would soon be delivered into their hands; and that the elect of Israel, "the sons of Zadok," would stand "in that day."[95] Here also is the thought of periods of fixed time decreed by God. The judgment is by fire of brimstone which will become a purging of all worshipers of idols, of all wicked from the earth.[96] There is also the idea that, by the elect, God will judge and chastise all the nations. But God's mercy will be shown "unto thousands to them that love him, and them that wait for him unto a thousand generations."[97]

A.D. 1–70

The two Jewish writings to be discussed in this section were probably written during Jesus' lifetime but before the earliest Gospels were compiled. This was the period of the rule of Herod's sons and of the first procurators. These were the years of mounting tension leading up to the Great Rebellion against Rome. At one time it was thought surprising that so few apocalyptic writings from this time had survived. The discovery of the apocalyptic literature of the Qumran

---

[93]En. 50–51.

[94]CD xiii, 1 (XV, 4); xiv, 19 (XVIII, 8); xix (B), 21–xx, 1 (IX, 29). See K. G. Kuhn, in Stendahl, *Scrolls,* pp. 58–60.

[95]CD iv, 4 (VI, 2); xiii, 20–23; 1QpHab ii, 6.

[96]CD ii, 6 (II, 4); xix (B), 9f. (IX, B, 10–13).

[97]CD xx (b), 22ff. (IX, B, 45ff.).

sect has filled this lacuna. We now know that early apocalyptic writings were still being copied and read and that new ones were being composed. Fragments of Jubilees, the Testaments of the Twelve Patriarchs, Daniel, and other known and unknown apocalypses have been found in the Dead Sea caves. It is evident that these writings constituted the literature of the Qumran sect up to the time of their abandonment around A.D. 64.

The writer of the Assumption of Moses, the first-century document in the Pseudepigrapha, employs the common stock of apocalyptic images and ideas, especially those of Daniel and 1 Enoch. Moses relates to Joshua the history of Israel down to the beginning of the reigns of Herod's sons.[98] At this point the history breaks off, for the writer believes that the end has come.

A Levite, Taxo, is urged to withdraw to a cave with his seven sons and die at the hands of the wicked rather than transgress the Torah. Yet God will avenge their deaths, for

> His kingdom shall appear throughout all creation,
> And then Satan shall be no more,
> And sorrow shall depart with him.
> Then shall be filled the hands of the angel who
>   stands on high [Michael]
> And he shall forthwith avenge them of their enemies.
> For the heavenly one will arise from his royal throne . . .
>   and the earth shall tremble, to its end shall it
>   be shaken . . .
> Then thou, O Israel, shalt be happy!
> And thou shalt mount upon the neck and wings of the eagle
> And (his days) shall be ended.
> And God will exalt thee, and cause thee to reach
>   to the heaven of the stars,
> To the place of their habitation. . . .[99]

Is this coming victory of God to be realized on earth? Or is it to be beyond history? This much is clear: it is God, not men, who will establish this kingdom. It has been suggested that since there is no thought of a general resurrection, the writer's vision closes with a glimpse of the eternal blessedness of the righteous in the heavenly world. Others hold that the figures of Israel's exaltation are conventional ones depicting the restoration of the Jewish nation to power and glory. Taxo's heroism is reminiscent of that of Mattathias. Did some "left-wing" Pharisee (or militant Essene or Zealot) grossly miscalculate the power of Rome? Was he convinced that heroic faith in God would enable the Jews to throw off the yoke of the Herods in the same way the yoke of the Seleucids had been removed? Did he call upon Taxo and his sons to take up the Maccabean banners? This victory day, whether on earth or in heaven, is a projection of the deep hatreds and nationalistic aspirations shared by many Jews of the period.

The same questions of interpretation are raised by the reader of the Qumran

[98]Asmp. M. 6:7–9; cf. *Antiq.,* XVII. x. 2.
[99]Asmp. M., 10:1–9 (T. W. Manson, *Servant-Messiah,* pp. 31f.).

scroll, the War of the Sons of Light Against the Sons of Darkness (1QM). This curious writing ostensibly contains instructions for the eschatological campaign against the army of "Belial and the men of his lot." It also prescribes the correct ceremonial procedures and equipment for the warring priests, so that they may avoid defilement in the forthcoming slaughter. The whole piece is shot through with apocalyptic sentiments, and the document ends with a sadistic war poem, followed by blessings and curses.[100] It is possible that the "mighty man . . . the man of glory" in the war chant of this scroll is to be identified with the sect's "Messiah of Israel," for by his side stands his superior, the high priest. The military scroll speaks with confidence that God "will send eternal help to the lot he has redeemed by the power of the angel . . . Michael," to exalt "the dominion of Israel over all flesh."[101]

After A.D. 70—Early Second Century

There have survived two apocalypses which most scholars believe to have been written after the fall of Jerusalem in A.D. 70: "the Ezra apocalypse" (2 Esdras or 4 Ezra), and "the apocalypse of Baruch" (2, or Syriac, Baruch). It is commonly agreed that one of the two writers has imitated the other, but no agreement has been reached as to their relationship. The differences in the writers' attitude to the Torah is a subject of great interest. The author of 2 Esdras succumbed to the deepest pessimism of the apocalyptists. The law had proved to be a standard almost impossible to attain. It is therefore Israel's condemnation. 2 Baruch exulted in the Law. Like Hillel and like the rabbis at Jamnia, the author saw obedience to the Torah as a practical program, Israel's greatest joy and hope.[102]

The eschatology of Esdras is not reducible to a single pattern of thought. The indebtedness of the writer to earlier apocalypses is everywhere present. The first vision declares the end to be near at hand. It is to be heralded by desolations in the earth and heavenly portents, and by the rule of an unexpected one (who is not identified).[103] A second vision presents premonitory signs: the opening of the book of judgment, the blast of the trumpet warning of the end.[104] A third vision portrays the new Jerusalem. The Messiah will be revealed to those who have not died. He will remain on earth for four hundred years, after which there will be a universal death and seven years of silence. Then comes the general resurrection and the great judgment, at which time men will be delivered to gehenna or to paradise.[105] The fourth vision concerns a woman who appears to be desolate and sorrowful; she is transformed into a woman of surpassing beauty. The figure represents the transformation of Jerusalem, which is in ruins, into the city that is to come.[106] Visions six and seven are original adaptations of imagery

[100]1QM xii, 10ff.
[101]Ibid., xvii, 5ff.
[102]R. H. Charles, *Religious Development between the Old and New Testaments* (1914), pp. 250f.
[103]2 Esd. 4:44ff.
[104]Ibid., 6:11ff.; cf. Rev. 5ff.
[105]2 Esd. 7:26ff.
[106]Ibid., 9:38ff.

drawn from Daniel. There is a symbolic sketch of history leading up to the prediction. The three-headed eagle may well be a transparent symbol of Rome. The destroying lion is declared to be the Davidic Messiah, who delivers the righteous.[107] Daniel's "son of man" image is also introduced as a personification of the Messiah. He consumes those who war against him "with the breath of his mouth." Here the Messiah appears to be a transcendent, a more than human, figure. The militant, nationalistic spirit of the earlier visions has quite evaporated.[108]

It has been said that 2 Baruch more closely than any other apocalypse sets forth messianic hopes resembling "those in the earliest parts of the Talmud and Midrash."[109] The end is preceded by twelve periods producing great terrors and torments. Little interest is shown by this writer in the person of a messiah. He is both a man of war and of peace. But the glories of the Messianic Age are vividly described. Nature will produce unimagined marvels, and great peace shall prevail. The heavenly Jerusalem will indeed descend to earth and endure "until the time is fulfilled." Then the Messiah returns to heaven (there is no mention of his death), and "all who have fallen asleep in hope of him shall rise again."[110] In this unending new world, the people Israel, inclusive of proselytes, will shine in brightness as the stars and have the face of angels. Yet this change in personal appearance will not prevent recognition. In this blissful state there will be neither toil nor sorrow.[111]

The writings and rabbinic traditions after A.D. 70 make clear the following fact: Although stunned and disillusioned by the tragic outcome of the war with Rome, Israel maintained its confidence in God and in the imminence of the Messianic Age. With the rebirth of hope there seems to have arisen a new zeal for the nation's destiny, a longing for the redemption of Israel, a scanning of the horizon for the appearance of a messiah.[112]

We have reached the end of New Testament times and, looking backwards, observe a fact of great importance for understanding the eschatology of Jesus and of the early Church. There had not emerged in ancient Judaism a uniform or consistent hope for the future. To speak of "the messianic hope" of the Jews is misleading, since no single solution for the ills of the present prevailed. There was no fixed utopian dream which brought satisfaction to all men. Hence unresolved tensions are evidenced between hope for the nation and its historical destiny, and hope for the achievement of individual blessedness in some other world, perhaps discontinuous with the present one.

This diversity of ideas is clearly evidenced in the uncertainty as to the manner of God's redemption of His people. Would He act directly, or through angelic or human agency; through a messiah, or through anointed ones? If through a

---

[107]Ibid., 11:1ff.
[108]Ibid., 13:1ff.
[109]Klausner, *Messianic Idea*, pp. 331ff.
[110]2 Bar. 25:1ff.; cf. 70:1ff.
[111]Ibid., 29:4f.; 73:1ff.; 48:50; 50:2ff.
[112]Klausner, *Messianic Idea*, pp. 394–403; Rowley, *Relevance*, pp. 105ff.

man, then what Israelite ideal or ideals of rulership would that man fulfill? Moreover, what would be achieved at "the end of the days"? National prosperity, or the universal triumph of righteousness? Would Israelites be vindicated and the heathen punished, or would idolatry and corruption be overcome everywhere? Would Gentiles turn to God and learn His truth and experience His mercies? And, finally, what would be the sequence of these last days? Would the age of the messiah be coterminous with the Age to Come? Or would the messiah's time be an extension of the present age, a kind of intermediate period of good times for the Jews, before the end?

Questions of this sort are given no definitive answers. Yet, through all of the diversity and perplexity of religious and political aspiration, there persisted this faith: God must act, He will deliver those who trust in Him, His purposes will be accomplished! The Christian movement arose out of this inchoate medley of hopes for a better day, those crosscurrents of pessimism and optimism, of nationalistic fervor and broader sympathies, of this-worldly hopes and other-worldly dreams. Eschatological images and symbols achieved a tremendous power to move the spirit of men. They became the vehicle for expressing the faith and hope of the earliest Christians. This potent imagery was reformulated in the creative intuitions of Jesus and of the earliest interpreters of his person and mission.

chapter five

A NARRATIVE OF
CHRISTIAN BEGINNINGS
Acts 1–12

a   b   c

(a) Obverse: Denarius depicting the profile of Tiberius laureate (A.D. 14–37); reverse: seated female figure (Livia as Peace/Justice). (The Chase Manhattan Bank Money Museum) (b) Obverse: Sestertius of Gaius (Caligula) A.D. 37–41. Obverse: head of Gaius laureate; reverse: the emperor's three sisters—Agrippina (security), Drusilla (peace) Julia (good fortune). (American Numismatic Society) (c) Bronze coin of Herod Agrippa I (A.D. 37–44). Obverse: Royal parasol with fringe; reverse: Three ears of barley. (The American Numismatic Society)

A view of the southeastern wall of old Jerusalem, adjacent to temple area, showing joining of Herodian construction (left) to a portion of the wall (right) probably rebuilt by Zerubbabel in late 6th century B.C. (Courtesy James Charlesworth, Duke University, who stands at the juncture)

Roman theatre at Caesarea, a seacoast city freed by Pompey 63 B.C. and given to Herod the Great by Augustus in whose honor the city was renamed, and later residence of Herod Agrippa I. (Israel Information Services)

Gaius Caesar (Caligula), A.D. 37–41. The emperor's brief popularity was followed by a severe illness which, historians claim, left him insane. Herod Agrippa I, a friend of the youthful Caligula, dissuaded the emperor from establishing his image in the Jerusalem temple. (Alinari)

Tiberius inscription from Caesarea bearing the name of Pontius Pilate. (Israel Department of Antiquities and Museums)

Iᴿ JESUS had been only a teacher in Israel—even for as brief a time as eighteen months—he might still be remembered. Some of his extraordinary sayings and parables might have been treasured by his disciples, as were the utterances of the ancient rabbis. Besides, the story of Jesus' martyrdom might have secured his fame. Such speculation, however, is profitless, for Christianity did not originate in this way. Jesus' disciples claimed that certain events had taken place shortly after his death which revealed the true meaning of Jesus' life for history. The God of Israel had performed a mighty act, mightier than all the deeds recorded in the scriptures, which set these former revelations in a totally new light. By the power of the living God Jesus had been raised from death. His identity as Messiah had been vindicated. But more than this. "The stone which the builders rejected" had indeed "become the chief cornerstone."[1] All power in heaven and on earth had been given to Jesus as the Christ. It was as though a veil had been lifted from the eyes of Jesus' disciples. They were witnessing the fulfillment of the scriptures. The long-awaited "Day" of Israel's redemption was at hand. The "Age to Come" had arrived and the purpose of God for His creation moved toward its glorious consummation.

The proclamation of Jesus' disciples seems as remarkable to men today as to the world of the first century, if not more so. Accordingly, it is not the curiosity of the historian alone which leads us to ask what were the beliefs of the earliest Christians, and how they came to hold them and to share them. Let the reader recall what has already been written about the literary sources of Christianity. The New Testament provides no direct testimony to the period immediately following Jesus' death. Yet there are four books containing indirect evidence of the highest value: the three earliest Gospels and the book of Acts. Paul's letters are all earlier, but the materials used by the compilers of these books are more primitive. In them the facts concerning the origin of Christianity are reported more extensively than in Paul's letters, although the latter give valuable supplements.

Because a number of matters have been discussed since the reading of Chapter 2, let us review here the plan of study. The first reading from the New Testament is its narrative of the earliest days of the Church, Acts 1–12. This account needs to be studied critically, supplemented, and sometimes modified, by information which can be gleaned from other sources (Chapters 5–7). Against this background will be traced the earliest stages in the formation of the gospel tradition (Chapter 8). Then the composition of the three Gospels Matthew, Mark, and Luke will be studied (Chapter 9). Part One will conclude with a sketch of the Ministry of Jesus (Chapters 10–12).

[1]Ps. 118:22; Acts 4:11.

94

ACTS 1–12: INITIAL IMPRESSIONS

Reading the New Testament is the most important part of any study concerning it. Just so, the first twelve chapters of Acts should be read now, before consideration of what others have said about Acts.

The book begins with a statement which links it with another writing of the New Testament. Acts 1:1–2 is, in fact, a secondary preface recalling the first four verses of the Gospel of Luke. It would seem, therefore, that Luke 1:1–4 stands as a general preface to Luke–Acts. The importance of this observation will be noted later, in this chapter and again in commenting on the origin of the third Gospel.[2] For the present let us consider two other literary features of Acts.

The narrative contains a number of general summaries. Some persons have detected in these statements the writer's organization of his book. For example, verses 6:7, 9:31, and 12:24 apparently mark the progressive development of the program proclaimed by the risen Christ in the introduction of Acts:

> You shall be my witnesses in Jerusalem (cf. 6:7) and in Judea and Samaria (cf. 9:31) and unto the end of the earth (cf. 12:24).[3]

Other summary statements are interspersed throughout Acts. In the first five chapters may be noted the following examples: 2:41–47; 4:32–37; 5:11–16, 42. At first glance they seem merely to link together stories of various types. Yet it is likely that in them the author's interpretation of his narrative is revealed. If most of the stories in Acts were drawn from oral tradition, as many believe, these general summaries were not found in the "sources." A folk tradition treasures particular stories. Folk stories become "history" when someone perceives in them a pattern of meaning, treats them as typical, and draws general conclusions from them.

A second feature of the Acts is the interlarding of its narrative with speeches delivered by principals of the story, Peter and Paul, or by lesser persons, such as Stephen and Gamaliel. The value of the speeches in Acts for the historian of the early Church will be considered below. Let it suffice here to observe that, whatever their source or sources, the speeches in their present form are compositions of the writer of Acts. If he followed a literary convention of his time, the author interpreted the narrative by means of such speeches.

The following outline draws attention to the general summaries and speeches in Acts.

An Outline of the Acts of the Apostles, 1–12

A. Introduction: Days of preparation for witness, 1:1–26:
    1. Secondary preface, 1:1–2 (see Luke 1:1–4)
    2. Jesus' contacts with, and promises to, the apostles after his passion, 1:3–5
    3. The ascending Lord prescribes a program for his witnesses, 1:6–11
    4. The brethren close the ranks of the twelve, 1:12–26

[2] See below, pp. 224ff.

[3] Acts 1:8. The fulfillment of the final prophecy is illustrated in the narrative from 9:32 onward, bringing the course of events to a point where the readers of Acts could continue it.

B. The witness of the Spirit-filled company, 2:1–47:
    5. The Lord gives the Spirit, 2:1–4
    6. Each hearing his own tongue, 2:5–13
    7. Peter's Pentecost speech, 2:14–40
    8. Summary: results of the proclamation—conversions and communal living, 2:41–47
C. Missions in Jerusalem: Successes and threats, 3:1–5:42:
    9. Peter heals a lame man, 3:1–11
  10. Peter's speech in the temple, 3:12–26
  11. The arrest and examination of Peter and John, 4:1–7
  12. Peter's speech before the council, 4:8–12
  13. The apostles are threatened and released, 4:13–22
  14. Prayers of gratitude bring a fresh outpouring of the Holy Spirit, 4:23–31
  15. Summary: the common practice of sharing, 4:32–37
  16. The deception of Ananias and Sapphira, 5:1–10
  17. Summary: signs and wonders, 5:11–16
  18. A second imprisonment; a courageous stand; Gamaliel's speech; the apostles' release, 5:17–41
  19. Summary: undaunted witnesses, 5:42
D. Missions of the Hellenists in Judea and Samaria, 6:1–8:40:
  20. Appointment of the Seven, 6:1–6
  21. Summary: numerous converts including a large group of priests, 6:7
  22. The arrest and arraignment of Stephen, 6:8–7:1
  23. Stephen's speech, 7:2–53
  24. The stoning of Stephen, 7:54–8:1a
  25. Summary: the scattering of the Hellenists; the persecuting activities of Saul, 8:1b–4
  26. Philip proclaims Christ to the Samaritans, 8:5–13
  27. Peter and John, representing Jerusalem, confirm the work of Philip, 8:14–25
  28. Philip and the Ethiopian eunuch, 8:26–40
E. First account of Saul's conversion, 9:1–31:
  29. The vision near Damascus, 9:1–9
  30. The ministry of Ananias, 9:10–19
  31. Paul preaches, escapes death in Damascus, 9:20–30
  32. Summary: the well-being of the Church in Judea, Galilee, and Samaria, 9:31
F. First missions to Gentiles, 9:32–11:30:
  33. Peter at Lydda and Joppa, 9:32–43
  34. Peter's speech at Caesarea; the conversion of the household of Cornelius, 10:1–48
  35. Peter explains his action in Jerusalem, 11:1–18
  36. Church at Antioch is founded, 11:19–20
  37. Summary: "the hand of the Lord was with them," 11:21
  38. Barnabas is sent from Jerusalem, 11:22–24
  39. Barnabas finds Saul, 11:25–26a

40. Summary: disciples are first called "Christians" at Antioch, 11:26b
41. Agabus prophesies famine; the relief visit to Jerusalem, 11:27–30
G. Persecution in Jerusalem under Herod, 12:1–25:
42. Martyrdom of James the brother of John; Peter's arrest and escape from prison, 12:1–19
43. The death of Herod, 12:20–23
44. Summary: marking the progress of Christianity, and of the narrative in Acts, 12:24–25

The writer of Acts was convinced that divine power accounted for the origin and rapid spread of the Christian Church. Its earliest representatives had experienced the inspiration of the Holy Spirit.[4] The Pentecost story makes it clear that this event is presented as an eschatological occurrence. The writer declares that the writers of Psalms 2 and 69, inspired by the Holy Spirit, spoke beforehand concerning incidents in the life of the early Church.[5] The Holy Spirit had spoken also through the prophets foretelling these "last days."[6] Jesus had given commandment to the apostles "through the Holy Spirit." Jesus had been "anointed with the Holy Spirit and with power" at the beginning of his Ministry; so also were the apostles.[7]

The location and length of the Cornelius story lay stress upon this theme: Through divine power and direction the mission of the Church was carried forward.[8] The hero of Acts is Saul (Paul), the champion of the Gentile mission of the Church. But behind the work of Paul lay the divine initiative. Visions were granted Peter and Cornelius, and when Peter first proclaimed to a Gentile household the good news concerning Christ, the Spirit was given as at Pentecost.[9]

The repetitious use of a term in the general summaries of Acts provides an explicit confirmation of this central conviction of its author. The proclamation, or increase, of "the Word" produced Christianity and furthered its rapid expansion.[10] In the Cornelius story it is made clear that this "Word" is "the good news" concerning Jesus the Christ.[11] This "Word" is "of God," for, as the author affirms, divine power had been revealed in Jesus' Ministry and manifested in the lives of men "chosen by God as witnesses."[12] Accordingly, we may conclude that for our author "the Word" is the Christian gospel, a message concerning God's action in Jesus the Christ. Moreover, men are enabled by God to receive the gospel since its effective power depends upon the inspiration of the Holy Spirit.[13]

---

[4]2:4; 4:8, 31; 6:3, 5; 7:55; 11:24. This possession is described as a gift of God (1:4; 5:32; 8:20; 11:17) or of the ascended Christ (2:33, 38).

[5]1:16ff.; 4:25ff.

[6]2:16ff., 30f.; 3:18; 7:52; 10:43.

[7]1:2; 10:38.

[8]10:1–11:18; 15:1–14. M. Dibelius, *Studies in the Acts of the Apostles*, trans. M. Ling (1956), pp. 109ff. [hereafter, *Studies*].

[9]10:44ff.; 11:15-17

[10]4:4; 6:4; 8:4; 10:36f.; 11:19.

[11]10:36.

[12]4:31; 6:7; 8:25; 11:1; 12:24.

[13]10:44.

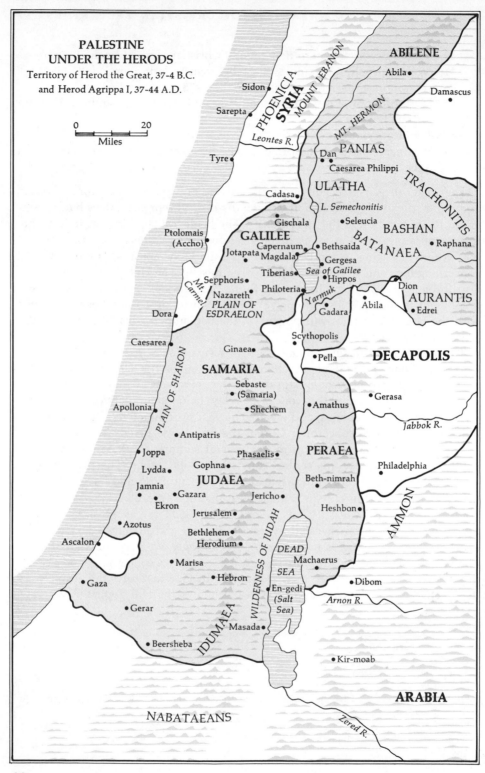

**PALESTINE
UNDER THE HERODS**
Territory of Herod the Great, 37-4 B.C.
and Herod Agrippa I, 37-44 A.D.

0   20
Miles

ABILENE

Abila

Damascus

Sidon

PHOENICIA

SYRIA

MOUNT LEBANON

Sarepta

Leontes R.

MT. HERMON

PANIAS

Tyre

Dan

Caesarea Philippi

Cadasa

ULATHA

L. Semechonitis

Gischala

Seleucia

TRACHONITIS

BASHAN

Ptolomais
(Accho)

GALILEE

Capernaum

Bethsaida

BATANAEA

Raphana

Jotapata

Magdala

Gergesa

Sepphoris

Tiberias

Sea of Galilee

Hippos

Mt. Carmel

Nazareth

Philoteria

Dion

Dora

PLAIN OF
ESDRAELON

Yarmuk

Gadara

Abila

AURANTIS

Edrei

Caesarea

PLAIN OF SHARON

Ginaea

Scythopolis

Pella

DECAPOLIS

SAMARIA

Sebaste
(Samaria)

Amathus

Gerasa

Apollonia

Shechem

Jabbok R.

Antipatris

Joppa

Phasaelis

PERAEA

Lydda

Gophna

Philadelphia

Jamnia

JUDAEA

Beth-nimrah

Ekron

Gazara

Jericho

Heshbon

AMMON

Jerusalem

Azotus

Bethlehem

WILDERNESS OF JUDAH

Ascalon

Herodium

DEAD

Machaerus

Marisa

SEA

Gaza

Hebron

En-gedi
(Salt
Sea)

Dibom

Arnon R.

Gerar

Masada

IDUMAEA

Kir-moab

Beersheba

ARABIA

NABATAEANS

Zered R.

98

Another important conviction of the writer is revealed in his general summaries and in the speeches of Acts. He reports that the first disciples of Jesus sought in every way to relate their beliefs and practices to contemporary Judaism and to the scriptures of the Jews. They continued to live as loyal Jews.[14] At the same time, they fearlessly condemned their leaders and people for rejecting the Christ, and pleaded with them to repent the crime of the cross.[15] Many students of Acts have concluded that the author was guided in his selection and treatment of traditional stories by his intention to show that Christians are true Jews. The only offense of the first Christians is that they responded in faith and obedience to the coming of the Messiah. Christians are, therefore, the true congregation of Israel, "the sons of the prophets and of the covenant."[16] Yet, for our writer, the earliest Christians were more than a sect within Judaism—whether or not they fully realized this. They were the community of the Messiah called to bear witness "to the end of the earth," and to bring to fulfillment God's purpose of salvation.[17]

It would be premature to state the aim of the writer of Acts, drawing upon these first impressions. The entire narrative must be taken into account, as well as the contents of the Gospel of Luke, which was almost certainly written by the same person for some of the same reasons. Yet it is already clear that whatever the particular occasion for the writing of Acts, its author was an enthusiastic exponent of Christianity. He was not an unbiased reporter, but a Christian who used Christian sources. He was assured that the rise and rapid advance of Christianity had been accompanied by spiritual phenomena attesting its divine origin. He was convinced that the community of believers in Jesus as the Christ formed the true, eschatological congregation of Israel. He selected episodes to illustrate and confirm these special convictions and interests. Moreover, the author seems to be writing for readers who are sympathetic to Christianity, or at least familiar with the hopes of Israel contained in their scriptures, whose authority is beyond doubt.

It becomes necessary to discuss the question of authorship. Our judgment of the value of any work depends to some extent upon our knowledge of its author and of his sources of information. It is natural also to ask whether the writer's personal interests and preconceptions have obscured important facts or intruded distortions into his narrative of Christian origins.

ANCIENT CHURCH TRADITION CONCERNING ACTS

There is evidence that Acts, if not considered holy scripture, was a Christian classic at the beginning of the second century.[18] But the earliest testimony of its origin dates from the last quarter of the same century. It is probable that Irenaeus

---

[14]2:46; 3:1; 10:14, 28; 11:2.
[15]E.g., 3:17ff.
[16]2:17, 21, 38f.; 3:25.
[17]1:8; 9:4–6, 13–15; 10:45–48; 11:17f.
[18]W. L. Knox, *The Acts of the Apostles* (1948), p. 2 and note [hereafter, *The Acts*].

spoke for the Church of the West when he wrote, around 180, that "Luke an attendant of Paul" wrote Acts.[19] More explicit evidence is provided in the Muratorian canon, a late second century canon published by L. A. Muratori in 1740, which lists the convictions of the Church at Rome around 180–200:

> . . . the Acts of all the Apostles were written in one volume. Luke compiled for the most excellent Theophilus what things were done in detail in his presence, as he plainly shows by omitting both the death of Peter and also the departure of Paul from the city when he left for Spain.[20]

An ancient introduction to the Gospel of Luke is known as the "anti-Marcionite prologue," for its defense of the full text of the Gospel against the abbreviated version edited by Marcion, the second-century heretic. This prologue may furnish the earliest references outside the New Testament to Paul's companion and physician, Luke:

> Luke is a Syrian of Antioch, a doctor by profession, who was a disciple of apostles, and later followed Paul until his martyrdom. He served the Lord without distraction, unmarried, childless, and fell asleep at the age of 84 in Boeotia, full of the Holy Spirit. . . .

> He, . . . impelled by the Holy Spirit, wrote this whole gospel in the region of Achaea . . . and afterwards the same Luke wrote the Acts of the Apostles. . . .[21]

It is often said that a presumption favoring the Lucan authorship of the Third Gospel and Acts is that Luke was not a prominent person in the apostolic age or later. Is it likely, one is asked, that anonymous writings should have been ascribed to a person who was neither an apostle nor a follower of "the twelve"? It might be answered that any evidence which the New Testament affords could have been observed by second-century Christians as well as by modern ones. The same data used to corroborate the tradition of Lucan authorship today might have given rise to this tradition.

Luke in the New Testament

Certain passages in Acts are marked by a shift from the third person to the first person plural. These "we" passages are (11:28?), 16:9–18, 20:5–15 (16–38?), 21:1–18, 27:1–28:16.[22] The natural conclusion is that they are extracts from a diary of one of Paul's companions. The question therefore arises: Who was with Paul during the times and places noted in the "we" passages? For the answer one can

---

[19] *Against Heresies*, III. 13.3; cf. III. 14.1ff.

[20] This phraseology excludes from the canon various apocryphal "Acts" of apostles. Earlier lines (2–8) comment upon Luke's authorship of the Third Gospel.

[21] Cited from R. G. Heard, *An Introduction to the New Testament* (1950), p. 74 [hereafter, *Intro.*]. See also *Journ. of Theo. Studies* n.s. VI (1955): 7ff. [hereafter, *JTS*]. Paul Feine and Johannes Behm express skepticism concerning these prologues (Feine-Behm-Kümmel, *Intro.*, pp. 103, 343).

[22] Consult commentaries on the problem of 11:28 and 20:16–38.

turn to several letters traditionally ascribed to Paul, but Colossians is of special interest.[23] Some of Paul's companions mentioned in Colossians are ruled out, for they are distinguished by name from the diarist in the "we" sections. Furthermore, if the diarist was a Gentile Christian, as has been commonly inferred from his interests, the field of choice is narrowed. The most likely candidate becomes "Luke the beloved physician."[24]

A comparison of the language and a style of the "we" sections and the rest of Acts has led most scholars to conclude that if Luke was the diarist he was also the compiler of the whole of Acts.[25] Furthermore, if Luke was the author of Acts he was also the author of the Third Gospel, for the prefaces of the two books link them as parts of a single work. The "trump card" sometimes used by defenders of the ancient Church tradition is that the medical language of Luke–Acts proves that the author was a physician. This argument has met with vigorous objections.[26] Yet the medical interest of the writer of Luke–Acts cannot be denied, and his choice of terms is, at the least, compatible with the tradition that he was a physician.[27]

This brief summary may lead the reader to conclude that the case for tradition is strongly supported by the internal evidence of the New Testament. But the principal grounds for objecting to the Lucan authorship of Acts have not been mentioned. These are, first, the suspicions that the sources underlying Acts, and their treatment by its compiler, militate strongly against acceptance of this tradition; and second, that the discrepancies between the narrative and Paul's letters and also the theology of Luke and of Paul are such that a companion of the Apostle could not have written Acts. The second objection is the more serious. It will be examined in more detail in Chapter 14. The question of the sources is considered below.

MODERN CRITICISM AND ACTS 1–12

Many modern scholars judge that the book of Acts imperfectly fulfills the title ascribed to it by tradition. It is not a record of the acts of all the apostles, but a fragmentary selection of those of Peter and a longer, but nonetheless sketchy, description of the acts of Paul. Much attention was given in the late nineteenth and early twentieth centuries to the historical limitations of Acts. The following were noted with respect to the early part of the narrative:

[23]Col. 4:7ff. See below, pp. 463ff. Cf. 2 Tim. 4:10f., which may contain a fragment of a genuine letter of Paul; see below, pp. 506ff.

[24]C. S. C. Williams, *The Acts of the Apostles* (1957), pp. 3f. [hereafter, *The Acts*]. J. Munck, who accepts with some diffidence the ancient tradition of Lukan authorship, disputes the usual assumption that the author was certainly a Gentile-Christian, *Acts, Anchor Bible,* vol. 31 (1967), pp. xxx ff. See also the Appendix (to vol. 31), W. F. Albright (pp. 264ff.), in which it is argued that Luke was a Jewish convert.

[25]Williams, *The Acts,* pp. 5f.

[26]W. K. Hobart, *The Medical Language of St. Luke* (1882); cf. H. J. Cadbury, *Style and Literary Method of St. Luke* (1920), and *JBL* XIV (1926): 190ff.

[27]Williams, *The Acts,* pp. 4f.

Omissions: As the story of Acts unfolds, chronological notes are few and far between and gaps in the sequence of events are easily detected. A few questions will suggest some important omissions. What happened to the majority of Jesus' Galilean disciples and to his work in Galilee?[28] For example, what happened to John? In Acts, John is a mute "extra" alongside Peter. Later traditions contain contradictory reports. Did he suffer early martyrdom, or live for many years at Ephesus?[29] How did James the brother of Jesus become a Christian? How did he attain pre-eminence in the Jerusalem church?[30] By what means and at what times did Christianity become established in Rome, in Alexandria?

Anachronisms: Some of the brief chronological notes which the author does introduce raise serious difficulties. In Acts 5:36 Gamaliel refers to two Jewish insurrections, one led by Theudas, the other by Judas the Galilean. According to Josephus, the author of Acts has reversed the order of these events.[31] Add this evidence to the alleged anachronisms relating to Paul's career, and considerable doubt is cast upon the historical value of Acts.

The author's credulity: Modern historians have often been offended by the miraculous in Acts, as well as by the mixture of credible stories with others which are prima facie "legendary." Did the writer possess sources of various sorts, and has he accepted them all at their face value?

Two types of opinion were advanced as a result of the investigation of such data as that given above. Either the author might have told more and reported it more objectively, but did not because of his special bias or tendency; or the fragmentary nature of the early chapters results from the limitations imposed upon the author by his own experiences and by the nature of the sources at his disposal. Nineteenth-century critics of Acts tended to favor the former alternative. The writer's partisan bias often prompted him deliberately to select certain incidents and to ignore others, as well as to distort the facts he did present.[32] By the turn of the century most New Testament scholars seemed to prefer the second explanation for the limitations of Acts as a history of the early Church. There was little disposition among them to deny that the author had a bias. But that he deliberately falsified history in the interests of some partisan tendency was dismissed as incapable of proof and as highly improbable.[33] Nevertheless this question of the effect of the author's purpose upon his writing continued to be raised.

[28]Note Acts 9:31; cf. Mark 14:28, 16:17.

[29]Acts 3:1, 4, 11; 4:13, etc. See below, pp. 552f.

[30]One could say that James is introduced almost surreptitiously in Acts 12:17.

[31]_War_, II. 8. 1; VII. 8. 1; _Antiq._, XVIII. 1. 1; XX, 5, 1f. On the reckoning of Josephus, Luke is guilty of a serious anachronism, attributing to Gamaliel, speaking before A.D. 36, a reference to an event occurring after A.D. 44.

[32]For a discussion of the "Tubingen criticism" and of its influence, see Foakes-Jackson and K. Lake, _Beginnings of Christianity_ (1942), vol. II, pp. 363–395, 408–443 [hereafter, _Beginnings_]; G. H. C. Macgregor, "Acts," _IB_, vol. 9, pp. 12ff.; A. M. Hunter, _Interpreting the New Testament, 1900–1950_ (1951), pp. 105ff. [hereafter, _Interpreting_].

[33]Macgregor, _IB_, vol. 9, p. 15.

THE QUESTION OF THE SOURCES AND THE DATE OF ACTS

Studies in the nineteenth and early twentieth centuries concerning the lost sources employed by "Luke" in his composition of Acts, as well as speculation concerning its date of publication, led to inconclusive results. Yet the search for the most probable answers to these questions cannot be neglected. An understanding of Luke's place in the development in early Christianity relates partially to one's choice of alternative solutions in these matters, and in the consequences one draws from them.[34]

As long as the Third Gospel and Acts were ascribed to the diarist, and the diarist was identified as "Luke the beloved physician," some of the persons and churches supplying him with information could be surmised. Paul knew the leaders of the Jerusalem church before and after his conversion. John Mark, the cousin of Barnabas, could have been of valuable assistance to Luke in writing about the earliest days of Christianity.[35] The diarist had direct access to the local traditions in Jerusalem, Caesarea, and, possibly, Syrian Antioch.[36]

"Source critics" have insisted that all presuppositions concerning the authorship of Acts should be put aside if the internal evidence is to be considered fairly. The narrative, they say, discloses "seams" in its fabric, indicating a piecing together of earlier documents. Variations in language, style, and points of view, which are clues to the identification of these sources, can be detected. By the turn of the present century many scholars had concluded that at least two major documents underlie the first half of Acts. One of these sources, "J," originated in Jerusalem: the other, identified by the symbol, "A," was assigned to Antioch. Some scholars point to evidence for a third, a Caesarean source, "C." The contents, relative age, and value of these hypothetical documents have been vigorously debated by scholars.[37] Solutions of vexing problems in Acts have been made to rest upon a number of these source theories.

A new factor was introduced into the discussion by the publication of C. C. Torrey's thesis that a single, Aramaic document underlies the first half of Acts.[38] Torrey sought to prove that the diarist of Acts translated the whole of chapters 1–15 from an Aramaic document composed by a Jerusalem Christian, perhaps as early as A.D. 49–50. He based his hypothesis upon certain passages in which an obscure Greek text becomes intelligible when translated into Aramaic. His

[34]H. Conzelmann in Keck and Martyn, *Luke–Acts*, pp. 298ff.; Feine-Behm-Kümmel, *Intro.*, pp. 123ff. Cf. Munck, *Acts, Anchor Bible*, vol. 31, pp. xxxvi ff.; H. J. Cadbury, *Acts, IDB*, vol. 1, pp. 34ff.

[35]Gal. 1–2; Col. 4:10, 14.

[36]Acts 21:15ff. (cf. 8:4ff.); if 11:28 may be accounted a "we" passage, the author of Acts was connected with Antioch (note "anti-Marcionite prologue," above; also Eusebius, *Historia Ecclesiastica* III. 4. 7 [hereafter, *H. E.*]).

[37]Adolf Harnack's analysis was widely influential: J, 1-5; A, 11:19–30; C (based on local and J traditions), 8:5–40. To these documents were added traditions originating from the three centers, and a Pauline source, 9:1–30. See Macgregor, *IB*, vol. 9, p. 18; Foakes-Jackson and Lake, *Beginnings*, vol. II, chap. 5.

[38]C. C. Torrey, *The Composition and Date of Acts* (1916).

case has fallen short of conviction, however, since other Aramaic scholars have judged that Torrey's most important examples are not supported by linguistic evidence. It is not denied that "Aramaisms" are to be found in the early chapters of Acts, but these are hardly sufficient to support the unity of Acts 1–15.[39]

The development of a new technique for literary analysis of the books of the Bible, "form criticism," will be discussed in Chapter 8 since the method has been most widely applied to the study of the Gospels. It should be noted here, however, that the form criticism of Acts has given rise to doubt that the author used written sources. The most that source criticism establishes is that there may be distinguished blocks of material which probably represent independent traditions. Whether written documents or oral traditions underlie Acts cannot be proved, but many scholars believe that evidence supports the latter conclusion. Separate the stories in Acts from their editorial framework and they bear the marks of an oral tradition which had become fixed in its forms through the application of this tradition to the various needs and interests of the earliest Christian communities. The question of the preliterary history of each narrative unit in Acts—or at least of each type of unit—needs to be studied before generalizations are made about the historical value of the whole.[40]

The speeches in Acts have attracted special interest in all discussions concerning the origin of its traditions. It is generally agreed that whatever the number and the nature of the book's sources, the more than twenty speeches in Acts are compositions of its author. In inserting these speeches into his narrative he was following an established literary convention. The following passage from Thucydides, written five centuries before Christ, has attracted the attention of many interpreters of Acts:

> As to the speeches that were made by different men . . . it has been difficult to recall with strict accuracy the words actually spoken, both for me as regards that which I myself heard, and for those who from various sources have brought me reports. Therefore the speeches are given in the language in which, as it seemed to me, the several speakers would express, on the subject under consideration, the sentiments most befitting the occasion, though at the same time I have adhered as closely as possible to the general sense of what was actually said.[41]

Was Thucydides justifying his free composition of speeches, or claiming that, wherever possible, he has subjected himself to the control of facts? The debate of scholars concerning the intention of this classic passage has brought into prominence important questions concerning the purpose of the speeches in Acts. Has the writer "adhered as closely as possible to the general sense of what was

---

[39] M. Black, *Aramaic Approach to the Gospels and Acts* (2d ed., 1954), pp. 8ff. [hereafter, *Aramaic Approach*]; W. L. Knox, *The Acts*, pp. 18ff.; Macgregor, *IB*, vol. 9, p. 18.; R. A. Martin, "Evidence of Aramaic Sources in Acts I–XV," *NTS* XI (1964): 38ff.

[40] Dibelius, *Studies*, 9ff., 126f.; W. L. Knox, *The Acts*, pp. 16ff.

[41] *Hist.*, I. 22. Cadbury's translation, *The Making of Luke–Acts* (1927), p. 185. The common practice of Greek and Latin historians was to use speeches to display their powers of imagination and rhetoric and to introduce editorial comment. Foakes-Jackson and Lake, *Beginnings*, vol. 5, pp. 402ff.; Dibelius, *Studies*, pp. 138ff.; Williams, *The Acts*, pp. 36f.

actually said," or have his theological concerns shaped the speeches to such an extent that the original situations are no longer depicted? This question cannot be ignored in the interpretation of any of the speeches in Acts.[42]

Acts closes with Paul awaiting trial in Rome. Roman Catholic and some Protestant scholars have held that at this point the narrative had caught up with events. It may be assumed, they say, that Acts was written between 60 and 70, probably in the early years of that decade. When the author wrote, he had reason to suspect that Paul's friends in the East would see his face no more,[43] but the Apostle's martyrdom had not occurred. The fact that the writer shows no familiarity with Paul's letters is thought to support this early dating of Acts. His failure to mention the fall of Jerusalem in A.D. 70 has also been noted.[44]

Most Protestant scholars believe that Acts was written at a later time because of its relation to the Third Gospel. Many date the Gospel of Luke around A.D. 80–85.[45] Therefore Acts, its sequel, is commonly dated within the period 85 to 90. The abrupt ending of Acts can be accounted for by the probable assumption that its readers could continue the story beyond that point. They doubtless knew of Paul's death, as did the author who reveals this fact in the farewell chapters, 20–21. It is likely that the purpose of Acts did not call for an account of Paul's martyrdom.

Scholarly interest in the book of Acts has clearly shifted in recent years. Attention no longer centers primarily upon Luke as a historian, or upon questions concerning the credibility of his sources or testimony. Rather, scholars have sought to appreciate and articulate the work of Luke the theologian. Important research by Martin Dibelius upon the literary style and special interests of the writer of Acts greatly stimulated this inquiry.[46] Modern studies on Luke–Acts, published in Germany for the most part, no longer picture Luke "as a somewhat shadowy figure who assembled stray pieces of more or less reliable information, but as a theologian of no mean stature who very consciously and deliberately planned and executed his work . . . Luke was not primarily a historian who wanted to give a record of the past for its own sake, but a theologian who, by way of historical writing, wanted to serve the church of his own day amid the questions and perils that beset her."[47]

[42]For a general discussion of the problem, see Feine-Behm-Kümmel, *Intro.*, pp. 117ff.; Cadbury, *Acts, IDB*, vol. 1, pp. 33ff.

[43]Acts 20:25, 38.

[44]Williams, *The Acts*, pp. 13ff; For a statement of the view that Acts was written during Paul's two-year imprisonment at Rome, as a positive testimony (not a legal defense) in Paul's behalf, see Munck, *Acts, Anchor Bible.* For a summary of the complex problems relating to the date of Acts, see Conzelmann in Keck and Martyn, *Luke–Acts*, pp. 298ff.

[45]See below, pp. 224f.

[46]The English translation of Dibelius' "studies," cited in note 8, was based on a 1951 German edition. Another noteworthy influence was the essay by P. Vielhauer on "The Paulinism of Acts," published in Germany in 1950 (Eng. trans. 1963), in which it was argued that Luke's theology only remotely resembled Paul's theology: Keck and Martyn, *Luke–Acts*, pp. 33ff.

[47]W. C. van Unnik, "Luke-Acts, A Storm Center in Contemporary Scholarship," in Keck and Martyn, *Luke–Acts*, pp. 23f.

A Working Hypothesis

Questions concerning the authorship of Acts, the nature and treatment of its sources, and the date of its writing, are all interrelated questions involving in one way or another the historical value of the book. It is doubtful that fully satisfactory answers to these questions can be reached. Yet with respect to the problem of authorship three main alternatives present themselves:

According to one, Luke is the writer of the Third Gospel and of the whole of Acts. For his second volume he drew upon his own diary and notes, and a variety of other sources.

According to a second alternative, Luke is the writer of the "we" sections, and possibly of several passages which provide their setting. A later editor compiled the whole of Acts 1–15 and the intervening parts of chapters 16–28.[48] The same unknown writer composed the Third Gospel. Although the latter part of this theory is resisted by a few persons, the affinities in language and style between the Gospel and Acts, and their common preface, seem to demand an assumption of common authorship.[49]

A third alternative also impugns the authenticity of the late second-century tradition on the ground of internal evidence, but holds that Luke–Acts was composed by an author who is otherwise unknown. The accounts of Paul in Acts, and its references to his preaching, are claimed to be at such variance with evidence concerning the Apostle's career and theology drawn from his own letters, that the hypothesis must be abandoned that all of Acts, including the "we" sections, was composed by Luke or some other missionary companion of Paul. The unknown author used (sparingly) the first person plural in portions of his narrative to call attention to eyewitness testimony, and perhaps to give the reader a feeling of direct participation. A close scrutiny of these "we" passages reveals, however, the untenability of the hypothesis that the author of Acts drew upon his own firsthand experience.

The present writer adopts the first alternative as the basis of a working hypothesis for further study of Acts 1–12. Luke wrote Acts after the Gospel, probably within the period 85 to 90.[50] These assumptions must be provisional since any decision depends upon a study of the Third Gospel, and especially of the differences between the Paul of the Acts and Paul revealed in his own letters. The adoption of this hypothesis rests upon the present writer's judgment that criticism of Luke–Acts has disclosed nothing which compels the conclusion that a companion of Paul could not have written these volumes.

To hold that Luke was the diarist as well as the writer of Luke–Acts means that the latter part of Acts contains much eyewitness testimony. But the same assumptions imply that Luke possessed a relative scarcity of information con-

---

[48]See Foakes-Jackson and Lake, *Beginnings*, vol. II, pp. 158f., 298ff.

[49]Williams, *The Acts*, pp. 6f.

[50]Note the improbable proposal that an early draft of the Third Gospel was sent to Theophilus as a "first treatise," after which Acts was written (ca. A.D. 66); then, on the basis of Mark's outline, Luke produced the Third Gospel as we have it, intending but never completing a revision of Acts. C. S. C. Williams, *Expository Times* LXIV (1953): 283ff. [hereafter, *Exp. T.*]; cf. H. G. Russell, *Harvard Theo., Rw.* XLVIII (1956): 167ff. [hereafter, *HTR*].

cerning the early churches. He spent but a few weeks in Judea. When Luke wrote of events long past, it may have been difficult, if not impossible, for him to fill in the gaps of his memory and notes. If Acts was written in Greece, as one early tradition implies, or at Rome, as was more generally believed, there were probably few persons, and fewer records, available to assist him. In view of considerations such as these, it will not be possible to accept, unconditionally, what Luke has written in the first part of Acts. Instead, the following critical principle will be applied in the next two chapters. Where the early narrative in Acts agrees with what is reported by Paul, or in other New Testament sources of the earliest period, we shall place a high estimate upon Acts. But where the narrative conflicts with these parallel traditions, we shall be less confident.

THE PURPOSE OF LUKE–ACTS

Full weight should now be given to the general preface, Luke 1:1–4. Herein Luke declares that his purpose is similar to the aim of earlier Christian authors. He also compiled "a narrative of the things which have been accomplished [that is, fulfilled] among us." [51] The conclusion follows that a confessional interest controls the content and purpose of Luke–Acts. In both volumes Luke proclaims the gospel.

The preface also shows Luke's recognition of an uncertainty on the part of his reader. He writes to Theophilus: "that you may know the truth concerning the things of which you have been informed [or "instructed"]." Nothing is known of this Theophilus. The word could have been a personification ("friend of God") rather than a person's name. Yet the deference shown "the most excellent Theophilus" is more understandable if an individual is being addressed. Does the author's respect for his reader suggest a Roman of equestrian status? The social position of Theophilus must remain an uncertainty. It is more important that we consider the relation of Theophilus to the Church. The deferential address suggests that he was not a Christian. This impression is strengthened when it is asked why Theophilus should need "to know the truth" about Christian origins. Apparently he had withstood the gospel, or, at least, full participation in the life and mission of the Church. Whatever the cause for uncertainty, whether lack of adequate instruction or inaccurate information, Luke wrote to overcome it.

It is unlikely that Luke's books were written for Theophilus alone. The dedication in the preface, and the division of the narrative into two parts, identify Luke–Acts as "literature" similar in kind to writings of the age intended for the public. Did Luke know that the problem of Theophilus was the problem of many persons? Perhaps, he thought, Theophilus might become a patron of the work, underwriting the expense of copying it. The preface does not reveal all we should like to know. For clues to Luke's purpose and to the problem of Theophilus one must turn to the contents of the books.[52]

[51]Luke 1:1. Note the words, "it seemed good to me also," v. 3.
[52]Cadbury, *Making of Luke–Acts*, pp. 194ff. Cogent objections to the hypothesis that the "secondary preface" (Acts 1:3–14, or a part of it) is an interpolation are set forth in Feine-Behm-Kümmel, *Intro.*, pp. 109ff.

Let us recall the concerns of the author of Acts described at the beginning of this chapter, revealed especially in summaries and speeches he composed.[53] The origin and growth of the Church is presented as evidence of a fresh incursion of divine power into history, bringing to fulfillment the hopes of the people of God. To belong to the Christian community is to become a member of the true Israel to whom the promises and the covenant belong. Now it is unlikely that persons with little knowledge of, or interest in, Judaism would have understood this approach to Christianity or this interpretation of its origin. At least Luke must have been assured that his readers were inclined toward belief in the God worshiped by the Jews and toward a reverence for the scriptures of Israel.

This evidence points to the conclusion that Luke–Acts was written for those Gentiles who were known to the Jews as "devout men" or "God-fearers." Numerous Gentiles had been attracted to the monotheistic faith and moral ideals of Judaism at this time. Although they had not become proselytes, they attended the synagogues, "gave alms liberally" to the Jews, and "prayed constantly" to the God of Israel.[54] According to Acts, these God-fearers had heard Christians proclaim the gospel in Jewish synagogues. Many had become converts; others had held back.[55] There were many aspects of Christianity intrinsically appealing to Gentiles.[56] But for the God-fearers among them there were reasons for resistance to the gospel. Did conversion to Christianity mean that a person could no longer worship the God revealed in Israel's scriptures? Had not the Jewish nation rejected as blasphemous the claims concerning Jesus? Was the gospel a corruption or a fulfillment of Israel's hope?

For Gentiles who had gratefully received from the synagogue the Septuagint it was a serious matter that the Christian gospel had been rejected by the Jewish nation and that, with the passage of time, the offense had not been overcome. Luke's selection, and treatment in Acts, of the "fulfilled-among-us" events makes it probable that Theophilus, and the circle of "devout men" he represented, belonged to this group. Luke would have his God-fearing readers "know the truth": the rejection of the gospel by Jews and its acceptance by Gentiles, far from giving cause for offense, was indeed the fulfillment of the scriptures. By the power of his Holy Spirit, the God of the Septuagint had spoken through the scriptures of these "last days," in which the Messiah had been revealed and vindicated, and his disciples inspired to bear faithful witness to his mission. Members of the ancient people of God who had resisted the gospel resisted the Holy Spirit and thereby forfeited their privileges and their inheritance.[57] To accept Jesus as the Messiah and "to continue in the apostles' teaching and fellowship" is truly to belong to Israel, truly to reverence the scriptures, and to inherit the promises made to God's covenant people. It is consistent with this understanding

[53]Feine-Behm-Kümmel, *Intro.*, pp. 117f.
[54]Acts 10:2; Luke 7:2–5.
[55]Acts 13:16, 26; 14:1ff.; 17:1, 4; 18:4, etc.
[56]E.g., D. W. Riddle and H. H. Hutson, *New Testament Life and Literature* (1946), pp. 102f.
[57]Acts 3:17–26; 7:51. A. C. Winn, "Elusive Mystery: The Purpose of Acts," *Interpretation* XIII, no. 2 (1959): 151ff.

of Luke's purpose that he "does not claim that the church has replaced Israel as the people of God, nor does he call Gentile believers Abraham's children . . . Luke wants to make it clear beyond doubt that in the course of events due respect has been paid to the priority of Israel . . . The main point would be that the continuity with [Israel's] history has in no way been broken, either by the emerging of Gentile Churches, or by the exclusion of disobedient Jews." [58]

It is probable that another dimension of the purpose of Luke is revealed in the early chapters of Acts. Luke reports that the earliest Christians were forced to defend themselves before the established order. Several arrests and trial scenes are reported.[59] Luke makes it clear, however, that the Jewish authorities who held their powers under Roman rule were unable to condemn the apostles as political offenders. When official action was taken against them, they were vindicated by heavenly visions, or they were released from prison by divine intervention.[60] The judicial death of Herod who "laid violent hands" upon some in the Church is reported, and the conversion of a notorious persecutor.[61] Luke seems sensitive to a political dimension of the religious problem facing men like Theophilus. He is intent upon resolving misgivings they may have, based on derogatory reports of subversive acts and teachings of Jesus and his followers.

There is some evidence from other New Testament books that the Christian church existed in an uneasy tension with Rome when Luke–Acts was written.[62] Judaism was an officially recognized religion, but the Christian communities composed of Jews and Gentiles could not take for granted that this toleration would be extended to them. Some scholars have held that the principal purpose of Luke–Acts is the defense of this privilege: since Judaism is recognized, so also is Christianity, for Christians are true Jews. But this is not probable.[63] The extent to which Luke's narrative has been consciously shaped as "a political apology" remains questionable. Yet from his reading of Luke–Acts, Theophilus learned that Christians are not only "the sons of the prophets and of the covenant" which God gave to the father of Israel, but also that Jesus and his apostles were law-abiding Jews, deserving therefore the toleration and legal support of responsible persons in the Empire.[64]

The above paragraphs suggest that a missionary motive prompted the author to write Acts as a sequel to his Gospel, and that a subsidiary apologetic interest affected his selection and treatment of materials.

[58]N. A. Dahl, "The Story of Abraham in Luke–Acts," in Keck and Martyn, Luke–Acts, pp. 151f. See Acts 2:39; 3:17ff.; 7:2ff.; 13:26; 26:6; also Luke 1:55, 72f.

[59]Altogether there are ten trials in Acts. Note 4:1–22; 5:17–42; 6:12–7:60. (The others are 16:19–24, 35–40; 17:6–9; 18:12–17; 22:30–23:10; 24:1–23; 25:1–12; 25:23–26:32.) Besides, in Acts there are numerous mob scenes and official investigations.

[60]7:55f.; 5:17ff.; 12:1–9; 16:25ff.

[61]12:21–23; 8:3; 9:1ff.

[62]See below, pp. 477ff.

[63]Williams, The Acts, p. 15.

[64]See H. Conzelmann's exposition of Luke's views concerning the relation of the Church with Judaism and the Roman Empire, and of Luke's theological foundations of his defense of the Church, The Theology of St. Luke, trans. G. Buswell (1960), pp. 137ff. [hereafter, St. Luke].

Two contrasting positions would deny the adequacy of this statement of the purpose of Luke–Acts. The first of these claims that it is possible to define more precisely the author's theological interests. It is not enough to "type" the first readers of Luke–Acts, or to speak of its author's intention as missionary or apologetic, or both. Such generalizations hide the real problems instead of solving them. The purpose of Luke–Acts is discovered by observing closely the author's redactional techniques, his editorial selection and revision of the traditions at hand, and by relating his work to similar or contrasting developments in early Christianity as these are reflected in contemporary documents. Several German scholars who have written from this point of view are agreed that a principal stimulus for Luke's theological writing was provided by the delay in Christ's (second) coming. The fact that the expectation of the imminent return of Christ had been proved wrong by the course of events, called into question the veracity of the *kerygma* of the earliest Christians.[65] By the way Luke edited and rearranged the traditional gospel materials about Jesus, and by composing a "history of the Church" as a sequel, Luke presents a reinterpretation of the Christian message, replacing the eschatology of Jesus and his first disciples by quite a different outlook. The same evidence is used to show that Luke's perspective is unlike Paul's. In Luke–Acts, Christ is proclaimed as the revelation and instrument of God's plan of redemption at the "center of the history of salvation" dividing the first epoch, that of Israel, from the third and last epoch, that of the Church. In addition, Luke is portrayed as the first representative of that "early Catholicism" which developed in the postapostolic age.

There are good and sufficient reasons for concluding that these definitions of Luke's theology are inadequate. Why should it be supposed that the abandonment of apocalyptic eschatology is a necessary prerequisite to interest in the Church as a missionary and institutional phenomenon? The Qumran scrolls demonstrate that an intensely eschatological community of the first century could have an active interest in discipline and order as well as sound doctrine. Moreover, it can be shown that the writer of Acts still stands within the framework of the primitive Christian eschatology and perspective concerning the history of Israel and the Church. Although differences between the theologies of Luke and Paul cannot be denied, eschatology is not the area of substantive dissimilarity.[66] There is also insufficient evidence to justify the use of the imprecise term "early Catholicism" as descriptive of Luke's view of the Church.[67]

A second recent position may be noted. It is that neither the purpose of Acts nor the theology of its author can be delineated systematically from a careful

---

[65]Conzelmann, *St. Luke;* Käsemann, *Essays.* Also P. Vielhauer in Keck and Martyn, *Luke–Acts,* pp. 45ff.; C. K. Barrett, *Luke the Historian in Recent Study* (1961), concludes that the impending threat of Gnosticism provided Luke an additional stimulus [hereafter, *Luke*].

[66]Feine-Behm-Kümmel, *Intro.,* pp. 98ff., 120ff.; W. C. van Unnik, "The 'Book of Acts' The Confirmation of the Gospel," *Novum Testamentum* IV (1960): 43ff. [hereafter, *Nov. Test.*]; J. Rohde, *Rediscovering the Teaching of the Evangelists,* trans. D. Barton (1968), pp. 175ff. [hereafter, *Teaching of the Evangelists*].

[67]U. Wilckens, "Interpreting Luke–Acts in a Period of Existentialist Theology," in Keck and Martyn, *Luke–Acts,* pp. 69ff.

study of his work. H. J. Cadbury is representative of those who have reached this conclusion. After many years of study, Cadbury opines that either the author of Luke–Acts was motivated by a variety of aims, or else he failed to make clear in his preface and elsewhere in the text a single, comprehensive purpose in writing.[68]

[68] *Acts, IDB,* vol. 1, par. 9f., pp. 37ff. W. G. Kümmel writes ". . . the large number of well-grounded proposals concerning the purpose of [Acts] make it questionable whether an unequivocal answer to this question is possible . . . as necessary as it is to the understanding of the theological meaning of the reports to attempt to discover the motives which control the composition of the individual narratives . . . so it is dangerous also here to attempt to know these motives too precisely. . . ." Feine-Behm-Kümmel, *Intro.,* pp. 115, 120.

BELIEFS OF THE
FIRST CHRISTIANS

Mosaic of the Triumphant Christ, whose resurrection is depicted here as raising the saints imprisoned to eternal life (1 Peter 3:19ff.?). From the Church of St. Luke, near Delphi. (Rev. Dr. Raymond V. Schoder, sj)

Dome of the Rock, a chief shrine of Islam, located on the site of Herod's temple and originally of Solomon's temple. (Israel Information Services)

An earlier picture of the temple area, sacred to Jews, Christians and Moslems, showing ruins from various periods of its long history. (Burton Holmes from Ewing Galloway)

"Head of Christ", an oil painting by the modern French artist, Georges Rouault, reminiscent of ancient images on catacomb walls. (Cleveland Museum of Art, Gift of Hanna Fund)

PUBLIC statements of a community's faith by its chief spokesmen are obviously primary source material for historical study. Ostensibly the early chapters of Acts present such testimony in speeches attributed to the Apostle Peter. A summary of four such speeches is given in Acts 2:14–40, 3:12–26, 4:8–12, and 10:34–43. Alongside these passages should be placed the first sermon of the Apostle Paul, recorded in Acts 13:16–41. What is the historical value of these traditions? It is not possible to give a simple, unequivocal answer to this question; however, these five speeches are of capital importance in researching the beliefs of the earliest Christians.

There is no reason to doubt that the author of Acts composed these passages, following a literary convention of historians in the Greco–Roman period.[1] It is not surprising that some of the speeches in Acts shed more light upon the writer's aims and beliefs, and the conditions existing in the churches of his own time, than upon the life situations underlying his reports. This is especially true with respect to the longer speeches, e.g., the address attributed to Paul on the Athenian Areopagus, Acts 17. The short missionary addresses of the apostles, however, are material of a special type. That the writer of Acts freely composed these is unlikely.[2] His personal background and experience differed from that of the earliest Christians in Jerusalem. It is probable that Luke had been won to Christianity through the missions of Paul. Although this can not be demonstrated, one may conclude that the Church traditions most familiar to the writer of Acts were expressed in terms refracted by Christian missions to Hellenists. Yet the five short speeches of Peter and Paul proclaim an interpretation of the person of Jesus and of his mission which is relatively undeveloped. They do not reflect the influence of that distinctive interpretation of the gospel known to us from Paul's letters.[3] Luke must have been confident that these missionary speeches summarized the traditional gospel of the early Church.[4]

[1] Dibelius, "The Speeches in Acts and Ancient Historiography," *Studies*, pp. 138ff.

[2] C. H. Dodd, *Apostolic Preaching and Its Developments* (1936), pp. 29ff. [hereafter, *Apostolic Preaching*]; Dibelius, *Studies*, pp. 165f.; W. D. Davies, *Invitation to the New Testament* (1966), pp. 50ff. [hereafter *Invitation*]. Ulrich Wilcken's thesis, that the speeches of the apostles in Acts "are not evidence of an early, still less earliest, primitive Christian theology, but [are summaries] of Lucan theology in the closing years of the first century," is set forth and examined critically in Rohde, *Teaching of the Evangelists*, pp. 202ff.

[3] P. Vielhauer, in his influential essay "On the 'Paulinism' of Acts" (Keck and Martyn, *Luke–Acts*, pp. 33ff.), concludes "that the Christological statements of Paul, in Acts 13:16–37 and 26:22f., are neither specifically Pauline nor Lucan but are the property of the earliest congregation." Conzelmann (*St. Luke*, p. 17) argues that theological motivation led Luke to distinguish the *kerygmas* of the primitive church and his times.

[4] Black, *Aramaic Approach*, pp. 36ff., 206f. W. L. Knox, *The Acts*, pp. 18ff. It is perhaps fruitless

The Aramaic coloring of passages in these speeches provides further evidence of their primitive character. The awkward expressions they contain are not typical of Luke's style and offer no support to theories of free composition. Perhaps one is justified in surmising that at such places Luke struggled with an Aramaic tradition. On the assumption that these obscure passages are "translation Greek," good sense is made of some of them by turning them back into the native speech of the Jewish–Christian apostles.[5]

A SUMMARY OF EARLY CHRISTIAN BELIEFS

Such considerations as the above encourage us to believe that these five speeches, critically examined, disclose some common, central convictions of the first Christians. These beliefs may be outlined as follows:

A momentous announcement: The goal of God's purpose in choosing Israel, anticipated by prophets and apocalyptic writers, has now been reached. God's final acts in history are now being revealed.

Peter, on Pentecost, interpreting the ecstatic behavior of the disciples, declares:

> . . . this is what was spoken by the prophet Joel: "And in the last days it shall be . . ." (2:16f.)

Or, again, in Solomon's porch:

> . . . what God foretold by the mouth of all the prophets . . . he thus fulfilled. (3:18; cf 10:43)

Likewise Paul announces:

> We bring you the good news that what God promised to the fathers, this he has fulfilled to us their children . . . (13:32f.)

Something momentous had happened. What was it? What gave these men their confidence that they were witnessing the coming of "the end of the days"? It was this: Israel's Messiah had been revealed. God had appointed as the Christ Jesus of Nazareth. This identification of the expected messiah is the central thesis of the five speeches in Acts. It is especially noteworthy that in each case the defense of this claim follows along much of the same lines.

The manifestation of the Christ: One, the heir to David's throne is Jesus, Peter declares:

---

to ask how this living tradition had been transmitted to Luke. Yet since these sermons led to baptism (2:38; 10:47) it is possible that the substance of the early preaching was kept alive in baptismal traditions. The liturgies and homilies associated with baptism and the Lord's Supper would have tended to preserve the traditions of the earliest Aramaic-speaking churches.

[5] W. L. Knox, *The Acts*, p. 20. See R. A. Martin, "Syntactical Evidence of Aramaic Sources in Acts 1-XV," *NTS* 11 (1964): 38ff.; cf. Cadbury, *Acts, IDB*, vol. 1, par. 8, pp. 34f., who insists upon the inconclusiveness of source identifications on the bases of style, because of the author's own stylistic variations.

> [David] being a prophet and knowing that God had sworn with an oath to him that he would set one of his descendants upon his throne, spoke of . . . the Christ . . . this Jesus. . . . (2:30–32)

Paul also stresses this aspect of fulfillment:

> Of this man's [David's] posterity God has brought to Israel a savior, Jesus, as he promised. (13:23)

Two, John's preaching of a baptism of repentance prepared for the coming of the Messiah. The relation of John the Baptist's mission as herald to that of Jesus as the Christ was very probably stressed by the earliest preachers. Note Acts 10:37 and 13:24f.[6]

Three, the mighty works of Jesus had signified his vocation. This point is made by Peter at Pentecost:

> Jesus of Nazareth, a man attested to you by God with mighty works and wonders and signs which God did through him in your midst, as you yourselves know . . . (2:22)

And again, in the house of Cornelius:

> . . . God anointed Jesus of Nazareth with the Holy Spirit and with power . . . he went about doing good and healing . . . for God was with him. (10:38)

Four, the climax of the historic mission of Jesus the Christ was his crucifixion. It had been a criminal action. Nevertheless, it was according to the will of God as the scriptures testify.

Notice how Peter's Pentecost sermon stresses this twofold significance of the cross of Jesus:

> . . . this Jesus, *delivered* up according to the definite plan and foreknowledge *of God*, you *crucified* and killed *by the hands of lawless men.* (2:23)

> Let all the house of Israel know assuredly that God has made him . . . Christ, this Jesus whom you crucified. (2:36)[7]

Five, the crowning vindication of Jesus' messiahship is his resurrection.

> God raised him from the dead and made him manifest unto witnesses . . . to us who were chosen by God. . . . (10:40f.)[8]

The event of the resurrection was presented by Peter and Paul as more than a personal victory for Jesus over death. The resurrection was proclaimed to be God's vindication of Jesus as the Messiah, as the event which provided the clue to the meaning of his historic Ministry which ended at the cross. Thus the resurrection of Jesus meant a continuation of his mission under conditions which could not be frustrated. This faith is expressed in the idea that God had highly

---

[6] F. V. Filson, *Jesus Christ the Risen Lord* (1956), p. 46 [hereafter, *Jesus Christ*].
[7] 3:13f.; 4:10; 5:30; 10:39; 13:27–29.
[8] 2:32; 3:15; 4:10; 5:30–32; 13:30f., 35.

exalted Jesus and given to him all power, in order that as Messiah he might fulfill God's purpose for man's redemption.

The manifestation of the Spirit in the community of believers in Jesus the Christ was itself proof that Jesus had been raised from the dead. His present power was felt as a new and unprecedented spiritual force. It is important for the reader to grasp this point. The recital of what God had accomplished through Jesus in *the recent past* led the apostles to interpret the crucial significance of the *present moment* for Israel. Moreover, faith in the resurrection of the Christ led the earliest Christians to forecast *the future consequence* of his manifestation in history. Then on the grounds of what had happened, of what was taking place and would soon occur, the preaching of the apostles concluded with an urgent appeal to their hearers. The following references support this summary of the apostles' perspective.

The consequences and the appeal: The presence of the Holy Spirit meant that the community of believers in Jesus the Messiah constituted the true people of God. These earliest Christians believed that they were that eschatological community to whom God, by the prophets, had promised forgiveness and final blessedness in the new age. In apocalyptic terms, believers in Jesus the Christ were "the saints" inheriting the promises of God (cf. Dan. 7:18, 21f.). Under the leadership of Jesus as "Lord," and through the instrumentality of the Holy Spirit, God was gathering together his elect people.

We have seen that in the prophetic and apocalyptic descriptions of the coming Day of the Lord the thought of judgment and of salvation appear side by side. So it is in these speeches in Acts. The response of the hearers to the message of Peter and of Paul was, in any case, a fateful one. The summons of the apostles was the *final* appeal of God to his covenant people:

> All the prophets who have spoken, from Samuel and those that came afterwards, also proclaimed these days. You are the sons of the prophets and of the covenant which God gave to your fathers. (3:24f.)

Yet for Peter and for Paul, as for the prophets, the call of God could have disastrous consequences:

> And it shall be that every soul that does not listen to that prophet ["the prophet like unto Moses"; for the Christians, a type of the Messiah] shall be destroyed from the people. (3:23)

It is not this threatening note which was stressed, however, so much as the note of confidence and joy. God had now provided ultimate deliverance through Israel's leader, savior, and lord. The hoped-for salvation of the people of God was now being accomplished, the good news of peace proclaimed. Accordingly, the apostles proclaimed God's forgiveness, the indwelling of the Spirit, and freedom from everything from which the Torah offered to free men but could not.

The speeches also imply that God's purpose for the salvation of men in and through Jesus the Christ, now being fulfilled, would be perfected or consummated in the future.

To the crowd in Solomon's porch, Peter declared that God would

> Send the Christ appointed for you, Jesus, whom heaven must receive until the time for establishing all that God spoke by the mouth of his holy prophets from of old. (3:20f.)

Only in this passage is the future coming of Jesus as the Christ forecast explicitly. But Peter's reference elsewhere to Jesus as "the one ordained by God to be judge of the living and the dead" clearly implies a future manifestation of his authority.[9]

Throughout these speeches the principal emphasis of the speakers was upon what had already happened. Unlike the writers of Jewish apocalypses, the early Christians did not believe that events to come would provide the decisive clue to the significance of the present. For them the Messiah had been revealed. The day of Judgment and of salvation had come; believers in Jesus the Messiah formed the eschatological people of God. Nevertheless, the experience of Christ's resurrection and the gift of the Spirit left the disciples with a sense of incompleteness which only intensified their hope. The reign of God, inaugurated by Jesus the Christ, moved toward its consummation. Thus the future would bring to their appointed end those realities which had already been given in Jesus the Christ, and partially realized through the gift of the Holy Spirit.

Also, since God had sent His Messiah and made him Lord of all, the time for decision had come. Men were called to turn to God in repentance and trust, to receive his offer of forgiveness, to be baptized as an outward sign of repentance and personal acceptance of Jesus as the Christ, and to share in the blessings of the new age which was promised.

The target of the missionary speeches in Acts was the conscience of the hearer. All five of them lead to the conclusion that Israel's rejection of Jesus the Christ, in the persons of their leaders, had been a terrible sin. But the forgiveness offered, more than the smitten conscience, probably moved Peter's hearers to repentance. The apostles proclaimed the cross to be an instrument of divine blessing, not of condemnation. Yet remorse and belief in God's willingness to forgive were not sufficient. To repent and believe meant that the hearer must confess that he was himself involved in these events in a radically personal way. There was indeed for him "no other name under heaven" by which he must be saved. Repentance and belief, therefore, expressed in the outward act of receiving baptism, meant a personal acknowledgment of sin, and a confession of Jesus as the Christ sent from God. It meant also a readiness to enter into the life of that community of faith, worship, and obedience which acceptance of Jesus as Messiah had brought into existence.[10]

---

[9] 10:42; cf. 1:6, 11; H. J. Cadbury, "Acts and Eschatology," in *Background of the New Testament and Its Eschatology*, ed. W. D. Davies and D. Daube (1956), p. 315 [hereafter, Davies and Daube, *Background*].

[10] Filson, *Jesus Christ*, p. 53. A. Schlatter: "The apostolic preaching culminated in the offer of baptism . . . its purpose was not merely the acceptance of an idea: it demanded a definite act." *The Church in the New Testament Period*, trans. P. Levertoff (1955), p. 9 [hereafter, *The Church*].

The outline above presents the common pattern of convictions set forth in the early speeches of Acts. It is true that such a formal synopsis can be misleading. There are some variations in the form and content of the speeches. Items were not always introduced by the speakers in this precise order; sometimes one or more of them may have been omitted altogether. Yet in every case *the story of Jesus was interpreted eschatologically.* The Christ who had come and who is to come is Jesus. Events of the recent past and present "fulfilled" the Old Testament scripture, that is, its history of salvation.

These speeches have been referred to as the "preaching" of the early apostles. Now that we have sketched their general content, it may be observed that the word *preaching,* as commonly understood today, is not altogether appropriate. The New Testament term, translated "preaching" in the English versions, is *kerygma.* The Greek noun *keryx* designated a herald or town crier. Hence the verb formed from the root meant "to announce" or to "proclaim," and the substantive form— *kerygma*—signified a public announcement or proclamation. It is a sound judgment, therefore, to say that, in the New Testament, *kerygma* refers primarily to the message proclaimed by the apostles, not to the act of preaching. *Kerygma* in the New Testament has for its object Jesus the Christ, or what God has done through Jesus the Christ. Much of what goes under the term today would not have been called "preaching" in the early Church.

The apostles used another term in referring to their "proclamation," the word *euangelion,* which meant "good news." It is this term which, through the Old English—God's story—is translated "gospel."

To "preach the gospel" did not mean to offer men advice or to tell others about one's experiences or to criticize individual or public morality, but to tell the story of a Jew called Jesus the Christ through whom the prophecies made to Israel were being fulfilled, in whose life, death, and resurrection God was acting conclusively for the salvation of men.

In this connection it is important to notice a third term used by the author of Acts: the word *martyria,* commonly translated "witness" or "testimony." For some modern readers the terms *to bear witness* or *to give one's testimony* connote the sharing of religious experiences. As in the case of "preaching," however, "witness" in Acts always has for its object certain events revealing God's action in and through Jesus the Messiah.[11] The apostles reported their personal experiences, it is true; yet by their testimony they drew attention not to themselves but to the mighty acts of God accomplished in Jesus the Christ.

A Traditional Gospel?

Our confidence in the speeches of Acts as providing a brief summary of the apostles' *kerygma* or "gospel," of their "witness" to Christ, is supported by reference to the letters of Paul. A summary of the earliest missionary "preaching" is not

---

[11] 2:32; 3:14f.; 5:30–32; 10:39. See W. C. van Unnik, "The Book of Acts: The Confirmation of the Gospel," *Nov. Test.* IV (1960): 54ff.

given in these writings since they are addressed to persons who were already believers. In interpreting and applying the gospel, Paul could assume a familiarity with its essential confessional statements. Moreover, since Paul wrote to communities that were predominantly Gentile, he did not merely repeat what the earliest Christians had proclaimed in their missions to the Jews. There is a passage in one of Paul's letters, however, written within twenty-five years after the crucifixion of Jesus, which is highly significant. In writing to the Corinthians, Paul reminds them of the terms in which he "preached the gospel" to them:

> I delivered to you as of first importance what I also received, that Christ died for our sins in accordance with the scriptures, that he was buried, that he was raised on the third day in accordance with the scriptures, and that he appeared to Cephas [Peter], then to the twelve . . . he appeared also to me. (1 Cor. 15:3–8)

Paul wished to emphasize the reality of Christ's resurrection as the basis of a Christian's hope in the resurrection of the body. Whatever his personal convictions in the matter, they were supported by a "gospel" which was, and had always been, constitutive of Christianity:

> Whether then it was I or they [the Jerusalem apostles] so we preach and so you believed. (1 Cor. 15:11)

Evidently Paul's proclamation and the proclamation of the first Christians were very much the same, and Peter, James, and the others in Jerusalem concurred in this judgment.[12]

There are other passages in Paul's letters where his interpretations are supported by an appeal to commonly accepted "tradition."[13] From these passages the following outline of a pre-Pauline *kerygma*, which the apostle himself proclaimed, may be reconstructed:

The hoped-for age, which the prophets foretold, has dawned:
The Christ has come who is Jesus,
  Descended from David;
  Who was crucified because of the sin of man but also in accordance with the scriptures;
  Who was designated Son of God (Messiah) in power by his resurrection from the dead;
  Who was exalted to the right hand of God that he might be Lord both of the dead and of the living.
Believers in Jesus the Christ are the saints upon whom the end of the ages has come,
  the Israel of God receiving the Spirit by hearing the gospel with faith;
  Who have been delivered from this present evil age,
  Who await the coming of the Lord Jesus from heaven as judge and as savior.[14]

This basic pattern of beliefs strikingly resembles the outline of the early speeches in Acts. As we shall observe at appropriate places, it may be said to

---

[12] Gal. 2:1–9.

[13] Dodd calls attention to several passages in 1 Cor. where Paul distinguishes the fundamental content of a traditional gospel and his own distinctive interpretations of it; *Apostolic Preaching*, pp. 9ff. R. Bultmann, *Theology of the New Testament*, trans. K. Grobel (1951), vol. I, p. 60 [hereafter, *Theology*].

[14] Rom. 1:1–4; Gal. 4:4; Rom. 8:34; Col. 3:1; Rom. 14:9; Gal. 6:16; 3:2; 1:4; 1 Thess. 1:10; 5:2, 9.

underlie the whole of the New Testament. The language and forms of expression vary widely from writer to writer. Nevertheless, a common core of convictions concerning Jesus is not only presupposed by all of the New Testament books, but determines everything that is said in them. This is not to claim that a uniform theology—a system of doctrine, or even a stereotyped verbal pattern of ideas—was achieved in the early Church. The Christian gospel won acceptance among men of many types with various backgrounds and experiences. The gospel was understood and proclaimed in a variety of ways. Nevertheless, within this diversity of exposition may be detected broad areas of agreement among the New Testament writers, manifesting the essential unity of the whole. The development of various aspects of the gospel does not seem to have resulted in any radical modification of the gospel itself. This "gospel" remains the basic frame of reference, and a common acceptance of it by the writers of the New Testament is the foundation of that unity within diversity which may be found in its books.[15]

CHRISTOLOGY IN THE EARLIEST CHURCH

In seeking to understand the beliefs of the earliest Christians we are now faced with an important question: Can anything be inferred from these speeches of Acts, and from other early sources, concerning the Christology of the primitive Church? *Christology* is a theological term referring to Christian beliefs concerning the person or nature of Jesus Christ. In what way or ways did the apostles elaborate their faith set forth in the *kerygma:* The Messiah who is to come is Jesus?

The reader of Acts has doubtless noticed that whenever the early Christians proclaimed the gospel they referred to passages from the Old Testament. There is every reason to believe that this feature of the narrative is authentic and that it affords a clue as to how Jesus' person and his role in history were interpreted by Christians in the earliest period. Some scholars have argued that the first Christians simply transferred to Jesus the Jewish doctrines of the coming Messiah. It does not take much thought to recognize that this principle of transference will not carry one very far. In New Testament times there was no such thing as a normative Jewish doctrine of *the* Messiah. It may be difficult in some places to decide to what extent the missionary speeches in Acts reflect the Christology of the earliest Church, or the Christology of Luke and the Church he knew at the end of the century, or intermediate developments. Yet it is evident that these forms of Christology are unlike any known types of Jewish messianism in the first century. Some of the scriptures employed in Acts had not received a messianic interpretation in pre-Christian Judaism. Passages of scripture were used by Christians to prove that Jesus is the Messiah, since he fulfilled them. The Christian

---

[15] Christian denominations and sects have sometimes resulted from a magnification of certain aspects of the NT teaching to the neglect of this underlying "proclamation" or "gospel." The latter provides the norm for evaluating any particular group's emphases, as well as the rallying point for a common recognition of the essential message of all Christian churches.

application of these scriptures to Jesus are, therefore, "testimonies," bearing witness to the earliest estimate of him.

What messianic titles were applied to Jesus in the primitive Church and how were they understood?[16]

Christ: In the *kerygma* of Acts, *Christ* is a title rather than a name.[17] Paul's letters support the relative primitiveness of this feature of the Christology of Acts. By the time the Apostle wrote, Christ had become a mere appellative (Jesus Christ or Christ Jesus). "The Christ" would have been a formula conveying little or no meaning to the Greek.

Joseph Klausner has written: "At first the only difference between Jews and Christians was that the former believed that the Messiah was still to come, and the latter that the Messiah had already come."[18] This judgment has been contested by those who believe that the earliest Christians expected Jesus' coming, not his return, as Messiah.[19] According to this position, the principal distinction between Jews and the first Christians was that the latter claimed they knew *who* the Messiah would be. God had declared Jesus, the Galilean prophet and teacher, the Christ who is to come. This position does not seem to reflect adequately the early Christian confessions. The belief that Jesus was the Messiah, and that he would soon be manifested as such to all the world, marked off the earliest Christians from the rest of Jewry, in spite of the common elements in their religion. This eschatological perspective of Jesus' Jewish disciples was a radical modification of any existing type of Jewish messianism, and defined the nature of their mission to, as well as their forthcoming struggle with, the synagogues of Israel.[20]

Son of David: We have seen that belief in a messiah of Davidic descent was a popular one in New Testament times, symbolic of the longing of the Jews for national independence and greatness. It is not true to say that no Jew would have accepted Jesus as Messiah unless it could be shown that he was descended from David, for this expectation was not everywhere shared. Just the same, the presence of such a claim in the early *kerygma* attests its importance.

Paul's statement in the introduction of his Letter to the Romans (1:3) shows that Jesus' Davidic descent was a cardinal point in the Jewish–Christian *kerygma.* Aside from appealing to a traditional belief, this reference has no relation to the argument in Romans. It is instructive to compare this pre-Pauline formula with Acts 12:33ff., as well as with the reference in Acts 2:24ff., to the enthronement

---

[16] In Chapter 11 it will be asked whether some of the early Christian confessions can be traced back to the consciousness of Jesus. There are methodological reasons for limiting our interest here to the question under discussion.

[17] Cadbury, in Foakes-Jackson and Lake, *Beginnings,* vol. 5, pp. 357f.

[18] Klausner, *Messianic Idea,* p. 526.

[19] Bultmann, *Theology,* vol. I, pp. 33f., 42ff.: The *kerygma* of the earliest Church "kept quite within the frame of Jewish expectation." M. Goguel, *The Birth of Christianity,* trans. H. C. Snape (1953), pp. 102f. [hereafter, *Birth*]; J. Weiss, *History of Primitive Christianity,* trans. and ed. F. C. Grant (1937; reprinted, *Earliest Christianity,* 1959), vol. I, pp. 118f. [hereafter, *Earliest Christianity*].

[20] Schlatter, *The Church,* p. 9; O. Cullmann, *Christ and Time,* trans. F. V. Filson (1950), pp. 81ff.; Fuller, *Foundations,* pp. 158ff., believes that the title *Messiah* (without the article) was an early Christian synonym of and substitute for Son of man, as the latter was applicable only to sayings of Jesus.

of David's descendant. It is thereby possible to see how early Christians offered a radical modification of a prominent strain of traditional Jewish messianism. The old prophecies concerning "the raising up" of a Davidic Messiah or "Son" were applied to the resurrection and exaltation of Jesus. The day of the enthronement of the Davidic king was understood to have taken place on Easter day. In the Old Testament and later Jewish texts this enthronment of David's son refers to the eschatological hope that Israel's national glory would be restored and that a Davidic king would rule over all the nations of the earth. In early Christian eschatology, it was proclaimed that Jesus' eternal rule as the Davidic Son was to be fully established by God in the future.[21]

The rare occurrence of "Son of David" in the gospel tradition as a term applicable to Jesus' historic Ministry, is therefore understandable. Indeed, the persistence in oral tradition of the sayings reported in Mark 12:35ff. provides an explicit early Christian rejection of the currently popular "Son of David" messianism.[22]

Son of man: Only in Acts does the title "Son of man" appear with reference to Jesus. Stephen, the dying martyr, declares that he sees Jesus as "the Son of man standing at the right hand of God" (7:56).[23] "Son of man" as a title for Jesus was more widely employed in the earliest Jewish–Christian communities as an interpretative image of Jesus' mission than the virtual omission of the term from Acts leads one to believe. In the most primitive strata of the gospel tradition, the exaltation of Jesus after his death was the exaltation of the Son of man, and the glorious, future coming of Christ was described as the coming "on the clouds" of the Son of man.[24]

We have seen that this Son of man imagery was derived from the apocalyptic tradition of Judaism, directly or indirectly from Daniel 7:13. It is a much disputed question whether or not Jesus had spoken of himself as the Son of man and, if he had, the relation of his use of the symbol to its application in Daniel.[25] In any case, those who preserved the traditions concerning Jesus, which were later to find their literary deposit in the Gospels, were surely convinced that Jesus had been, and was destined to be, this Son of man of Daniel's vision. The application, if not the meaning, of "Son of man" as a messianic title was extended during the oral transmission of this gospel tradition. This evidence can be satisfactorily explained only upon the assumption that Christians identified him with the

[21] 2 Sam. 7:12ff.; Pss. 2:7ff, 89; Is. 55:3ff.; Pss. Sol. 17, 18; Rev. 3:7; 5:5; 22:16; Acts 2:33f.; Luke 1:32. E. Schweizer has shown how OT and Jewish texts were reinterpreted in the primitive church: "The Concept of the Davidic 'Son of God' in Acts and its Old Testament background," in Keck and Martyn, *Luke–Acts*, pp. 186ff.; Fuller, *Foundations*, pp. 162f; Otto Betz, *What Do We Know about Jesus?* (1968), pp. 93ff. [hereafter *Jesus*].

[22] Mark 10:46f.; 11:9f. See below, p. 312.

[23] Yet when Stephen is being stoned, he cries out to Jesus as "lord."

[24] Bultmann, *Theology*, vol. 1, p. 49; Weiss, *Earliest Christianity*, vol. 1, pp. 126ff. H. E. Tödt, *The Son of Man in the Synoptic Tradition*, trans. D. M. Barton (1965), pp. 226ff. [hereafter, *Son of Man*]; Fuller, *Foundations*, pp. 143ff.

[25] See below, pp. 303ff.

apocalyptic "Son of man," the title that was current for a time in the early, predominantly Jewish–Christian communities.

The absence of any explicit Son of man Christology in New Testament books other than the Gospels might, at first sight, suggest that the early faith had little influence upon the subsequent Christology of the Church. Yet indirect allusions to Daniel in Paul's letters and also in Revelation indicate that it was an important source of testimonies to Christ. It may be argued that Paul interpreted the Son of man as a symbol of the community of the end time, in line with Qumran and Pharisaic eschatologies, as may be suggested by his declaration (I Cor. 6:2) that "the saints will judge the world." [26] Very probably Daniel 7, in combination with Ps. 110:1, was an especially significant context for interpreting Jesus as the Christ destined to come as God's final agent in judgment and in salvation. [27] Moreover, the Son of man Christology may underlie the descriptions of Jesus as "The Man" in the distinctive expositions of Christ's person and work found in Paul's Corinthian and Roman letters, and also in the Letter to the Hebrews.

A satisfactory explanation for the discontinuance of "Son of man" as a title for Jesus, and of its omission from the speeches in Acts summarizing the primitive *kerygma,* is not difficult to find. Outside of Aramaic-speaking communities, *bar nasha* (Son of man) would have been considered a strange and unintelligible term. The retention of an Aramaic title for Jesus would have provided an unnecessary obstacle to Gentiles. Moreover, a literal translation of the term into Greek produces a puzzling barbarism. It seems, therefore, that "Son of man" was retained only as a self-designation of Jesus in the gospel tradition. In expositions of the *kerygma* its place was taken by other "titles," which expressed in more adequate ways the convictions which "Son of man" had originally conveyed. At any rate, Luke retained the early usage in his Gospel and nearly abandoned it in Acts. [28]

Lord: In a number of places in Acts the term Lord (*kyrios*) is applied to God. In Peter's Pentecost speech, however, it is proclaimed that God had made the crucified Jesus "both Lord and Christ." Alongside this reference should be placed those passages in which appears the combination "Lord Jesus."

This evidence is insufficient to support the claim that "the Lord" was a messianic title in the early Christian communities. [29] It is highly improbable that any Aramaic-speaking Jew would have used the expression "the Lord" (*Mar*), either as referring to God or to a messiah. The practice of speaking of Jesus as "the Lord," absolutely, represents an innovation in the Hellenistic churches. There are a number of reasons, however, for believing that the basis of this Christological

---

[26] Betz, *Jesus,* p. 111.

[27] C. H. Dodd, *According to the Scriptures* (1952), pp. 67ff. [hereafter, *Scriptures*]; N. Perrin juxtaposes John 19:37 and Rev. 1:7 to show the influence also of Zech. 12:10ff., in reinterpreting Dan. 7:13: *Rediscovering the Teaching of Jesus* (1967), pp. 181ff. [hereafter, *Rediscovering*].

[28] Acts 1:9–11 should be noted where Christ's coming "with clouds" provides an indirect reference to Dan. 7:13. A Son of man Christology may underlie the reference to a "man appointed by God" who is to "judge the world," Acts 17:31.

[29] Bultmann, *Theology,* vol. I, pp. 51f., follows the classic argument of W. Bousset. The latter is fairly summarized for English readers by A. E. J. Rawlinson, *The New Testament Doctrine of the Christ* (1926), pp. 231ff.

title, so popular in the later Church, must be traced back to the original Aramaic-speaking Christian community. Of special importance is the currency in the early Church of the Aramaic term *maranatha* (our Lord, come!) as an ejaculatory prayer. That the Greek term *kyrios* should have come from the Aramaic *maran* is certainly more probable than that an originally Gentile description of Jesus should have been adopted by Aramaic-speaking Christian communities in time for Paul to refer to *maranatha* as a traditional form of prayer.[30]

The use of "our Lord" as a messianic title in the earliest Church is confirmed by the New Testament writers' frequent use of Psalm 110:1. It is directly cited in Mark (12:36) and in Hebrews (1:13), as well as in Acts (2:34f.), with reference to the exalted Christ.[31] The presence of this Old Testament testimony in writings which are independent of one another supports the view of the author of Acts: Psalm 110:1 was a fundamental text of the early *kerygma*. It provided a foundation for the later use of the title, Lord, as proclaiming both the present and future significance of Jesus as the Christ. As "Lord," Jesus was "at the right hand of God," until such time as his enemies were vanquished or reconciled.

Son of God: The author of Acts declared that, following his conversion, Paul "proclaimed Jesus in the synagogues of Damascus saying, 'he is the Son of God'" (9:20). It is quite evident that Luke believed Jesus to be the Son of God. He knew also that the term had become a Christian synonym for the Jewish "Messiah."[32] Nevertheless, in the summaries of the early Christian *kerygma*, "Son of God" as a title for Jesus is noticeably absent.

This evidence ought not to be interpreted as meaning that Jesus was not believed to be the Son of God in the earliest, Aramaic-speaking Christian communities. The introduction to Paul's Letter to the Romans (1:3) clearly implies the existence in the early period of this belief. Jesus had been declared "Son of God in power" because of his resurrection.[33] Moreover, the use of Psalm 2 as a testimony to Jesus in Acts 4:25f and 13:32f, which parallels Hebrews 1:5 and 5:5, strongly suggests that Luke knew it to be an early, traditional interpretation of Christ's person.[34]

It is sometimes stated that "Son of God" was a messianic title in pre-Christian Judaism and that by this means it entered into the primitive *kerygma*. Proof of this is lacking. The Old Testament writers used "son of God" as a term appropriate to angels, to Israel, to kings and other outstanding persons. Yet it was, at most, a term with messianic potential. There is no evidence for messianic application

---

[30] A. D. Nock, *Early Gentile Christianity and Its Hellenistic Background* (1964), p. 33; W. Foerster and G. Quell, "*Kyrios*," in *Theological Dictionary of the New Testament*, trans. and ed. G. W. Bromiley, vol. III (1965), pp. 1039ff. [hereafter, *Theological Dictionary*]; E. Schweizer, "Discipleship and Belief in Jesus as Lord from Jesus to the Hellenistic Church," *NTS* II (1955): 92f.; E. Schweizer, *Lordship and Discipleship* (1960), pp. 56ff. [hereafter, *Lordship*]; Fuller, *Foundations*, pp. 156ff.

[31] Also Heb. 1:3; 8:1; 10:12; 12:2; Mark 14:62; Acts 5:31; 7:55; Rom. 8:34; and 1 Peter 3:22.

[32] Acts 9:22; Luke 22:67, 70.

[33] Bultmann, *Theology*, vol. 1, p. 50. The precise origin and meaning of the pre-Pauline formula and of the testimony, Ps. 2:7, remains in debate. See Fuller, *Foundations*, pp. 165ff.

[34] For the recognition of Ps. 2 as messianic see also Rev. 12:5, 19:15.

of Psalm 2:7 in ancient Judaism until the writing of 4 Ezra; that is, after A.D. 70.[35] Nevertheless, the Jewish background of the term sheds some light upon the problem before us. The title "Son of God" at first may have signified simply a belief in Jesus' exaltation as king-Messiah, as the one ordained by God to rule his people, conveying much the same meaning as the title "our Lord." It is indeed very improbable that meanings which the title later gathered to itself in Gentile Christianity were any part of the beliefs of Jewish-Christians in the early period. For example, there is no evidence that such ideas as the pre-existence of Jesus, or of Jesus having been begotten by God or by the Spirit of God, were known in the early Jerusalem community.

The prophet like Moses: There is "no evidence at all in favor of the view that Jewish writers of the first century or even much later ever interpreted Deuteronomy 18:13ff. as being predictive of the Messiah, or of the coming of a specially great prophet like Moses." Lack of evidence at the time led the editors of *The Beginnings of Christianity* to declare that Acts 3:22–24 and 7:37 could not reflect the beliefs of Jewish–Christians in Jerusalem.[36] It is certain now, from eschatological passages in manuscripts found at Qumran, that this categorical statement needs serious qualification. We have seen that in the Manual of Discipline it is commanded that the community shall live according to its present way of life "until the coming of a prophet and the anointed ones of Aaron and Israel" (1QS ix. 11). In Qumran Cave Four, a group of Messianic scriptures was found beginning with Deut. 18:18. It is possible that "the teacher of righteousness" was related to this "prophet like Moses."[37]

The primary evidence that the earliest Jewish–Christian church interpreted Jesus' mission explicitly in terms of this Mosaic prophet is found in Acts 3:12ff. The close association of testimonies from Deuteronomy and Isaiah (52:13; 53:11) strongly suggests that Jesus was conceived as the one who, in his historic Ministry, had been manifested as the eschatological prophet-servant.[38]

That the author of Acts preserves this early Christological concept in speeches attributed to Peter (and Stephen, Acts 7:37) is supported by the presence of the Mosaic-prophet motif in early strata of the synoptic gospels. Within these traditions one also detects echoes of the Isaianic language pertaining to the servant.[39]

The relation of the revival of prophecy and messianic speculation is reflected in Mark 6:15 and 8:28, and parallels. In John's Gospel the juxtaposition of a particular eschatological prophet and the Messiah becomes clearly manifest in the question whether John the Baptist or Jesus could be identified with one or

---

[35] That "Son of God" may have earlier become a Jewish title for messiah in some quarters is possibly to be inferred from the Aramaism reflected in Mark 5:7: Filson, *Jesus Christ*, p. 148. Note also the "Messianic Florilegium" (4Q), Schubert, *Dead Sea Community*, pp. 119f.; Fuller, *Foundations*, p. 32.

[36] Foakes-Jackson and Lake, *Beginnings*, vol. 1, pp. 403–408; also Cadbury in *Beginnings*, vol. 5, pp. 371f. With respect to the absence in rabbinic literature of interest in Moses as a type of the Messiah, cf. D. Daube, *The New Testament and Rabbinic Judaism* (1956), pp. 11f.

[37] F. F. Bruce, *Second Thoughts*, p. 77; W. H. Brownlee, "Messianic Motifs of Qumran and the New Testament," *NTS* III (1956): 17.

[38] Fuller, *Foundations*, pp. 167ff.

[39] Ibid., pp. 169ff.

the other of these expected ones.[40] The background for such a tradition in Palestinian Judaism has now been recovered. Whereas in the Qumran eschatology, the new prophetic lawgiver was distinguished from other messianic figures, the early Christians averred that he had come in Jesus the Christ.

Servant: Twice in Peter's speech in Solomon's porch (3:3, 26) and twice in a prayer attributed to the disciples (4:27, 30), Jesus is designated "servant" of God. The term (*pais*) is not used in the later chapters of Acts. Does its appearance in portions preserving ancient traditions mean that "Servant" was a messianic *title* applied to Jesus in the earliest period? Many scholars have answered yes. It is true that the term used is ambiguous. *Pais* can be translated "child" (or "youth") equally well; yet it is very probable that the meaning "servant" is the only one possible in Acts.[41] As far as the evidence goes, *pais* does not seem to have been a messianic category of any importance in Hellenistic Christianity. It occurs only in liturgical passages. The application of the term to Jesus as a title must represent an early Jewish–Christian usage.[42]

If this conclusion is accepted, then it is important to ask what meaning the titled conveyed. The most plausible suggestion is that the servant passages of Isaiah provided the context for interpreting the person of Jesus as Messiah. The writer of Acts states that Philip's proclamation of Christ to the Ethiopian eunuch was grounded upon Isaiah 53 (8:26–30). The reader's confidence in Acts, as preserving at this place a genuine element in the Christology of the early Church, is strengthened by observing the author's application of the title "the righteous (One)" to Jesus. The servant Songs of Isaiah were recognized as sources for testimonies to Christ in the earliest preaching.[43]

The absence in Paul's letters of a Servant Christology based upon the Isaianic prophecies, as well as its presence in later writings, may seem to deny this early origin. It is true that Paul does not exploit these scriptures in offering his distinctive interpretations of the person of Christ.[44] The apostle's avoidance of "servant" as a messianic title may have been due to its use in the Jewish-Christian communities. Or, the servile and unscriptural associations of "servant" to non-Jews could have led Paul to drop it in correspondence with churches containing many Gentiles.[45] But a consideration more important than these is the fact that Paul was mainly interested in explicating the significance of Christ's present and future work; his servant role was fulfilled in Galilee and Judea (2 Cor. 4:5; 5:14ff.).

Summary

It is now possible to make a few observations. Speaking generally, Luke's record of the beliefs of the earliest communities concerning Jesus' person merits our

[40] John 1:20f.; 7:40f.

[41] Cadbury in Foakes-Jackson and Lake, *Beginnings*, vol. 5, pp. 365, 369; W. Zimmerli and J. Jeremias, *The Servant of God*, trans. H. Knight and others (1957), pp. 85ff.

[42] *The Servant of God*, pp. 83f.

[43] Ibid., pp. 85f. Cf. M. D. Hooker, *Jesus and the Servant* (1959), pp. 107ff. She denies that the evidence supports this judgment. See the judicious discussion of this issue in Fuller, *Foundations*, pp. 151ff.

[44] See below, pp. 457f.

[45] Hooker, *Jesus and the Servant*, p. 109; W. L. Knox, *The Acts*, p. 73; Schweizer, *Lordship*, pp. 50f.

confidence. He presents a group of Jewish–Christians reinterpreting scriptural categories in the light of a common understanding of their relation to recent events. Evidently some of these Christian testimonies had not heretofore been considered messianic prophecies by the Jews. Luke was surely familiar with the newly acquired meanings of these scriptural images and titles in Gentile congregations. He is sensitive to the fact that some of the earliest designations had fallen into disuse. Where the original traditions conveyed to his readers ideas alien to the thought of the earliest witnesses, Luke may have modified them. Yet even at such places it is unlikely that Luke conformed his sources to these later developments to any considerable extent. When Acts is read with an eye toward Paul's teachings concerning Christ, additional support is found for the primitive character of Luke's traditions.

Modern redaction criticism which focuses on Luke's own theological perspectives can obscure these important observations. There is a danger that once Luke's distinctive theology is found, embedded in the tradition, that the former is allowed to overshadow the latter. If it can be assumed that Luke was in possession of early tradition, which few would deny, one may believe that he did not regard this tradition merely as source material, but as, in some sense, "apostolic testimony" to Christ. Certainly he applied these earlier Christian testimonies to his own situation, to the mission of the Church in his time; yet, we may believe, with the intention of remaining faithful to the primitive *kerygma* preserved in the tradition.[46]

It was a matter of great importance to the future of Christianity that these early testimonies to Christ be preserved. By reason of their heritage and mentality, the first Jewish–Christians were monotheists. They were not given to metaphysical speculations. They were bound to think of Jesus as the Messiah with respect to his functions within history, to God's saving acts in the past, and to the hopes which Israel's prophets had envisioned. In setting forth the significance of Jesus they appealed therefore to scriptural images. Yet the earliest Christians manifestly recognized that the facts of their experience radically altered the traditional hopes of the Jews. The categories of Jewish eschatology were strained to the breaking point since, for the early Christians, only Jesus' Ministry and Resurrection explained them. It could now be seen that these scriptures had anticipated the *kerygma*; but before the events of the Ministry the *kerygma* was present only as unfulfilled promise.

Among persons whose convictions were grounded in the nonrecurring events of a particular man's life, no notions of a demigod would have arisen. Among such, the genuine humanity of Jesus of Nazareth would have served as a check upon tendencies toward myth-making. Nor indeed were conditions present in

---

[46] W. L. Knox, *The Acts*, p. 78; Macgregor, "Acts," *IB* vol. 9, p. 41; C. F. D. Moule, "The Christology of Acts," in Keck and Martyn, *Luke–Acts*, pp. 159ff. Cf. J. C. O'Neill, *The Theology of Acts in Its Historical Setting* (1961), pp. 118ff. While acknowledging the impress of Hellenistic missions upon the Christologies in Acts, R. H. Fuller (*Foundations*) detects pre-Lucan beliefs in the speeches of Acts; H. Flender, *St. Luke, Theologian of Redemptive History*, trans. R. H. and I. Fuller (1967), p. 2 [hereafter, *St. Luke*].

the earliest Christian churches for Christological formulations in any technical sense. It was only when persons of Greek mentality began to assign false meanings to the earlier confessions that the need was felt for formal doctrines concerning Jesus the Christ. Nevertheless, the witness of the first Christians provided the raw materials for all subsequent Christological confessions.[47]

MANIFESTATIONS OF THE HOLY SPIRIT

How were the early Christians' experiences of the Holy Spirit understood by them? This question calls attention to some unique features of the Acts narrative perplexing to the historian and seeming to lack logical consistency. Nevertheless, the question cannot be set aside if one is to understand "pneumatism" in the primitive church, as well as in later Christian theology.[48]

Did the First Christians Have the Experiences Reported in Acts?

Some historians of the early Church deny that such things as "speaking in tongues," miracles of healing, prophesying, and so on, were manifested at Jerusalem. These phenomena, it is said, first appeared in the Pauline churches where the membership, including Jews of the Dispersion, had been subjected to Oriental or Greek influences not felt in Jerusalem. Moreover, it is claimed that the writer of Acts was not himself familiar with such phenomena. They were no longer current in the Church of his period. He knew only that they had been in evidence as Paul had planted the gospel upon Gentile soil. Accordingly, he mistakenly supposed that such phenomena were everywhere exhibited. Christians in Jerusalem did not understand their experiences as the first Christians in Galatia or at Corinth understood theirs.[49]

First of all, let us notice that there is no sufficient reason for denying to the primitive Church a consciousness of the Holy Spirit's activity. Passages in the Gospels imply that the existence of the Church presupposes that the gift of the Spirit had been given to Jesus' disciples. Mark reports that John the Baptist had declared that "He who is mightier than I" will baptize men "with the Holy Spirit" (1:8). Since in Mark's narrative there is no indication that this event took place during Jesus' historic Ministry, Mark 1:8 reflects the traditional conviction that the Spirit was the postresurrection gift of Jesus the Christ to his disciples.[50] The account of the mission of Jesus' disciples reported in Matthew 10:1–23 is a passage of special interest since it reflects the views of a Palestinian, Jewish-

[47] For a further discussion of the crucial importance of the earliest confessions, see G. Dix, *Jew and Greek: A Study in the Primitive Church* (1953), pp. 27f. [hereafter, *Jew and Greek*].

[48] "Pneumatism" is a term derived from the NT word *pneuma* (spirit). It signifies interpretations of the actions of a spirit power or powers in relation to human existence.

[49] Goguel, *Birth*, pp. 95ff.

[50] Cf. Mark 13:11.

Christian community.[51] There is nothing in the incident itself to confirm Matthew's implication that the disciples were at that time endowed by the Spirit for their mission. Thus Matthew 10:19f. adds further support to the view set forth in early chapters of Acts: shortly after Jesus' death his first disciples had been enlightened and empowered by the Holy Spirit, and had proclaimed that the promise of Jesus was being fulfilled in them.[52]

There is no adequate ground for rejecting as unhistorical such external manifestations of the Spirit as are noted in Acts, even though one may suspect that Luke has not always understood the phenomenon he reports. To deny that "speaking in tongues," miracles of healing, prophecy, and other such "signs and wonders" could have accompanied the emergence of the Jewish–Christian church is to overlook the eschatological convictions expressed in the Jerusalem *kerygma*. External marks of religious fervor or inspiration such as these would not have been manifested among Jews who were convinced that the age of ecstatic prophecy had closed. Nevertheless, ancient Judaism expected that at "the end of the days" the Holy Spirit would again be revealed, not as a transient possession of warriors, kings, or prophets but as God's gift to his covenant people.[53] Peter's reference to the prophecy of Joel as having been fulfilled (Acts 2:15f.) is thus an appeal to an important strain of Jewish expectation, and emphasizes the faith of the early Christians that the era of the Spirit had indeed dawned with the enthronement of Jesus the Messiah.

"Signs and Wonders" in Acts

The descriptions in Acts of the pneumatic phenomena in the early Church include some puzzling and seemingly discrepant elements. This is true with respect to the occasions for the earliest Christians' reception of the Holy Spirit. In Acts 2:1-4 the disciples were all together when suddenly they were possessed by the Holy Spirit. In 4:21-23, when the company of the disciples "had prayed . . . they were all filled with the Holy Spirit." At a later time, the Spirit came upon Samaritan believers as a result of the prayers of Peter and John; yet we are also told that "the laying on of the apostles' hands" occasioned this gift of the Spirit (8:14-24; cf. 19:1-7). Paul himself is said to have received the Spirit in this way, through the hands of a disciple in Damascus named Ananias (9:17-19).

Another equivocal aspect of Luke's account of the earliest manifestations of the Holy Spirit concerns baptism. Peter's words at Pentecost imply that the gift of the Spirit was normally expected as an immediate consequence of baptism

[51] C. K. Barrett, *The Holy Spirit and the Gospel Tradition* (1947), pp. 127ff. For the origin of Matthew's Gospel in a Palestinian, Jewish-Christian community, see below, pp. 211ff.

[52] Heb. 2:3f.; 6:4f.; 1 Peter 1:12 provide independent evidence that pneumatic phenomena had been manifested in the early Church and ought not therefore to be thought the product of environmental factors restricted to the areas and period of Paul's early missions.

[53] "We cannot doubt that the Rabbinic Judaism of the first century would have regarded the Messianic Age or the Age to Come as the era of the Spirit," W. D. Davies, *Paul and Rabbinic Judaism* (1948), p. 216 [hereafter, *Paul*].

(2:38). Yet Acts reports that the Samaritans received the Spirit some while after they had been baptized in the name of the Lord Jesus (8:16f.). At other times, the manifestation of the Spirit precedes baptism (9:18; 10:47f.). The most we can say is that Luke testified that the rite of baptism and the reception of the Holy Spirit were identifying marks in early Christianity, the one completing the other. The relation between the rite and the gift is not clear in Acts.[54]

The external marks of the indwelling of the Spirit are also variously reported in Acts. In chapter 2 we are told that those who were filled with the Spirit "began to speak in other tongues." Luke understood this to mean that the apostles spoke the various native languages of the mixed population in Jerusalem. It would seem, however, that "speaking in tongues" on the day of Pentecost ought to be explained in the same way the phenomenon is explained elsewhere in the New Testament. The apostles probably were not given the power to speak foreign languages (would that the Spirit conferred this gift, you say). Rather, their speech must have become garbled as they attempted to express themselves under great emotional stress. We are told that bystanders thought them drunk. Yet to other "Jews and proselytes" these emotional utterances of Peter and his company stirred up recollections of God's mighty acts in history and stimulated a more sympathetic response. Very probably there was nothing miraculous about the audible sounds uttered by the apostles. The history of religions affords many parallels to the behavior of the crowds at Pentecost. For the student of such phenomena, the important considerations are the content of the spiritual insights which result from such overwrought emotional states and the ethical consequence after such moments of ecstasy subside.

Some persons have concluded that the writer's misunderstanding of the phenomenon "speaking in tongues" reveals his inability to distinguish between authentic early traditions, and later legendary accretions. To this extent one's confidence in Acts is shaken. In forming an opinion in this matter two things should not be overlooked. First of all, no further mention is made in Acts of the overcoming of language barriers under the inspiration of the Spirit, although the phenomenon "speaking in tongues" is reported again.[55] In the second place, there is reason to believe that Luke composed chapter 2 as a "curtain raiser," so to speak, for his story of Christian beginnings. He was interested primarily in the symbolism which this traditional story provided, rather than in supporting its interpretation of pneumatism. In Jewish haggadah there is a midrash which teaches that God revealed his Torah on Mount Sinai in the seventy languages of mankind.

[54] Have some later conceptions of the office of the Apostle been imposed upon the earliest traditions prior to Luke's record? Acts 19:1–7 suggests that the gift of the Spirit is obtained through official channels: Williams, *The Acts*, pp. 291ff. It is possible that Luke's source reflects a moment when baptism might have fallen apart into two sacraments, the one, immersion in water, signifying the cleansing of sin; the other, the laying on of hands, the gift of the Spirit: O. Cullmann, *Baptism in the New Testament* (1950), pp. 11ff.

[55] See 10:44–46; where reference is made to ecstatic praises of God, and 19:6, where speaking in tongues is associated with prophecy as in the thought of Paul; cf. 1 Cor. 13:1f.; 14:2f., etc. See K. Lake, "Glossolalia and Psychology," *The Earlier Epistles of St. Paul* (1919), pp. 241ff. [hereafter, *Earlier Epistles*].

Only Israel had hearkened and obeyed. Other rabbis told how Moses had ascended to heaven to receive the Torah. From thence he brought it unto Israel as God's gift. It is also significant that the traditional harvest festival, Pentecost, had come to be associated in ancient Judaism with the giving of the law. It is therefore possible that Luke, or more probably the writer of his source, had composed the Pentecost story as a Jewish–Christian midrash.[56] As in Jewish haggadah, interest turns away from the actual happening as understood by those who experienced it, and focuses upon some *meaning* of the story *for faith* in the present. The Pentecost story presaged for Luke the beginnings of Christianity's worldwide mission. It may be objected that the gift of the Holy Spirit is not elsewhere associated with Sinai. Yet it is peculiarly characteristic of Luke to use a traditional story as a frontispiece anticipating later developments in the narrative.[57]

Besides "speaking in tongues," Luke reports, the first believers in Jesus the Christ wrought miracles of healing. Such events were understood as "signs and wonders," either manifesting the Holy Spirit in the Messianic Age, or evidencing the power of the risen Christ. The healing of a lame man in the name of Jesus occasioned the first hostility of Jerusalem authorities to the disciples (3:1ff.). Such episodes attracted a large following, and the apostles' use of the name of Jesus in healing led outsiders to seek access to his power.[58]

Some students have discounted these miracle stories. Luke's writings reveal a personal fondness for miracles, especially for miracles of healing, which has contributed to his uncritical use of popular "wonder stories." Yet according to the earliest Gospels the disciples believed healing of the sick a part of their mission as well as of Jesus' Ministry. The Gospels also report that the power of "the name" of Jesus, in dealing with the demon-possessed, had led persons outside of the disciple band to employ it.[59] Moreover, like Peter in Acts, Paul testifies in his letters that miracles of healing were wrought among his converts. He also attributes them to the power of the risen Christ, or the Spirit.[60] It seems reasonable, therefore, to conclude that Luke is here reporting early traditions. That he should have magnified the miraculous elements in the narrative is of course more understandable than that he should have treated them skeptically. At the same time, it is noteworthy that very little notice is taken of this aspect of the Holy Spirit's work in the later letters of Paul and in the New Testament books after his time.[61] Such evidence represents the reduction of an emphasis which was prominent in the earliest days. Belief in miracles of healing was an inevitable accompaniment of the initial outbursts of Christian enthusiasm. Such miracles happened again where they were expected. That the disciples believed that Jesus could and did heal through them can scarcely be doubted.

[56] W. L. Knox, *The Acts*, pp. 80ff.

[57] Cf. Luke's relocation of Mark 6:1–6 in the Gospel (Luke 4:16–30). In Acts, Luke goes on to report how many of these peoples of the Dispersion did hear, and heed, the Apostles' witness to God's mighty acts, and did see for themselves evidences of the Spirit's power.

[58] Acts 3:11; 4:21; 5:12; 8:4–13.

[59] Mark 10:1; 9:38ff.; Matt. 7:22.

[60] Gal. 3:5; 1 Cor. 12:10; Rom. 15:19.

[61] W. L. Knox, *The Acts*, pp. 88ff.

The particular problems raised by these stories for the modern reader should not cause one to lose sight of their meaning for the first Christians.[62] Peter and the others were not "faith-healers" in the popular sense of this term, either in the first or twentieth centuries. Healing was always for them the result of faith and prayers, always a mighty work of God. The apostles did not use the healing powers given to them for selfish aims. They may have been less loath than Jesus to consider such power "proof" of the validity of their gospel; yet, in their ministry of healing they revealed that they had been close to Jesus. They knew from experience that if God did at times help them in extraordinary ways, if He prevented certain perils from overtaking them, possession of the Holy Spirit would not free them from all resistance and danger. On the contrary, the power of the Spirit manifested in such healings worked to stir up hostility against them.[63]

THE COMMUNITY CONSCIOUSNESS OF
THE ESCHATOLOGICAL CONGREGATION

The descriptions in Acts of pneumatic phenomena in the early Church may remain puzzling to the modern reader. Luke's major interest, however, should not be overlooked. He was more impressed with other signs of spirituality than "tongues as of fire," or sounds "like the rush of a mighty wind." The practitioner's techniques in miracles of healing are barely noticed. But he delights in reporting the amazing moral achievements of the first followers of Jesus: their boldness in declaring and defending their beliefs and actions, their self-effacing acts of mercy, their practical concern for the well-being of all who belonged to their group. The statements contained in Acts 2:42–47 should be recalled here.

It is highly improbable that Luke imposed this strong consciousness of community upon the primitive traditions, even though he may have idealized it. In ancient Judaism the hope of the manifestation of the Spirit in the Age to Come reflected a persistent social reference. By means of His Spirit, God would create in the last days a people—usually conceived as a reconstituted Israel—to inherit the blessings of the new age. Where such ideas were held, a corollary of faith in the coming of a messiah was belief in the emergence in history of the eschatological congregation.[64]

Pneumatism in early Christianity can best be understood in the light of these ancient Jewish conceptions. As the next chapter will illustrate, the beliefs and practices of the Essenes may have brought into sharp focus this communal aspect of Jewish eschatology. The followers of Jesus were, like these sectarians, and unlike the associations of the Pharisees and other parties within Judaism, conscious that they were already the eschatological congregation, the community of the last days. Nevertheless, the gift of the Holy Spirit is only anticipated in Essenism, while the early Christians believed that the eschatological events were taking place. With the coming of the Messiah, now risen from the dead, they

[62] See below, pp. 277ff.
[63] Schlatter, *The Church*, p. 18.
[64] Bultmann, *Theology*, vol. I, pp. 37f.

were being called out of Israel to become the people of God who would soon inherit His glorious kingdom.

It is not possible, therefore, to understand the communal spirit in primitive Christianity apart from an appreciation of the theological perspective of the *kerygma*. It cannot be accounted for by appealing to sociological conditions, such as the poverty of many within the group; nor to political developments, such as the hostility of the Jerusalem Sanhedrin. Nor do environmental factors, such as the influence of Essene communities, give sufficient explanations.

Luke reports that some early Christians "sold their possessions and goods and distributed them to all, as any had need" (2:45; 4:36f.). It would be wrong to assume that the earliest Christians developed a communistic society. There was no organized communal production among them and the common purse was made up of voluntary offerings.[65] The arguments for the value of a communistic economy can never be made to rest upon its alleged existence in primitive Christianity. But the obligation of the Church to provide for the material needs of all its members is exemplified in this early impulse toward the voluntary sharing of property.

Fortunately for the future of Christianity the Holy Spirit was originally received and interpreted by persons whose conceptions of the divine Spirit were patterned upon Jewish models. Christianity was first proclaimed as a way of life for the true Israel of God, renewed and inspired by the divine Spirit. Thus all who believed Jesus to be the Christ "were together and had all things in common" (2:44). The history of Christianity might have been quite different if the popular views concerning spirit-possession held by representatives of the Oriental mystery religions, or by Greek mantics, had predominated in the formative period of Christian origins.[66] The first disciples of Jesus understood what was happening to them in the light of the experiences and the teachings of the prophets of Israel, as these were currently interpreted. Unlike the devotees of the many Hellenistic religions, the first Christians did not cultivate the Spirit; that is to say, they did not seek to induce states of ecstasy leading to the suspension of consciousness or of rationality. When we consider Paul's missions, we shall learn that many religions of the Hellenistic age tended to relieve the individual of his responsibilities toward society. The spirituality of individuals in the church at Corinth, influenced by popular religious conceptions, tended to be void of social responsibility. But from its earliest days the Christian Church fostered and sustained a strong sense of community among its members.

Still more important for the future was the fact that the leaders of the early Church were men who had known Jesus personally.[67] In him whom they worshiped as the bearer of the divine Spirit, they had a concrete standard by which to judge the workings of the Holy Spirit, in themselves and in their community.

---

[65] The action of Ananias and Sapphira was morally reprehensible, not because they retained some of their property, but because of their deception in pretending to give every thing they owned, 5:1–11.

[66] See below, pp. 397, 404, and 485f.

[67] Schlatter, *The Church*, p. 17.

chapter seven

EARLY CHRISTIAN ORGANIZATION, MISSIONS, AND OPPOSITION

a   b   c

(a) Antioch stater of Augustus, 27 B.C.–A.D. 14 (30 pieces of silver). (The British Museum) (b) Coin minted in Alexandria. Obverse: Tiberius; reverse: the glorified image of Augustus. (The American Numismatic Society) (c) Bronze of Herod Agrippa (A.D. 37–44). In view of the second commandment, the "King Agrippa" inscription was accompanied by the emblem of a royal parasol. Once more, following procurator's rule, there was a Jewish monarch in Judea. (The American Numismatic Society)

137

The Damascus Gate (16th century A.D.) marks the site of a gate in the wall constructed by Herod Agrippa I (A.D. 41–44). Hadrian's Gate, recently excavated, is shown in the lower left. (George Rodger from Magnum)

Samaria regained its early prominence under Herod I who began an elaborate building program in 30 B.C. The king honored Augustus by renaming the city Sebaste and by constructing a large temple, the ruins of which are seen above. See Acts 8:5ff. (Rev. Dr. Raymond V. Schoder, sj)

Khirbet Qumran: In this picture one views from the tower the walls of a two-storied building housing the sect's scriptorium (left of center). Many scrolls found in the caves were doubtless written here. At the top of the photograph runs the long narrow Hall of the Congregation. (Courtesy of James Charlesworth, Duke University)

HOW were the earliest Christian churches organized? When asked this question the reader of Acts may despair of his source. He finds some evidence that authority was vested in the membership, referred to as "the assembly" or "the brethren." Yet the twelve "apostles" figure prominently as a group though not as individuals, with the exception of Peter. Indeed, from the beginning of the narrative "the twelve" refers apparently to a closed circle of leaders holding exceptional prestige and prerogatives. Then there are "the seven" drawn from a disaffected group in the Jerusalem church called "Hellenists." To these men special duties were delegated. Several references are made to "elders" in company with the apostles. The reader is at a loss to know what status they held. Besides all this, Acts testifies to the supremacy of Peter in the primitive Church. Yet when James, a brother of Jesus, is introduced, the reins of authority seem to have passed into his hands.

How is one to evaluate this evidence? After a student has reviewed the opinions of several scholars, he might suppose that the early chapters of Acts reflect not one but at least three different types of organization. Perhaps Luke's description is a composite of early traditions and later developments. Can critical scholarship recover the original order, if indeed such a thing existed?

THE ORDER OF THE COMMUNITY

In part, the diversity of opinion on the order of the earliest Christian churches can be attributed to the ecclesiastical bias of scholars. Christians have long been divided concerning the organization of the Church. Three types of order have come to predominate in Christendom: Congregational, Presbyterian, and Episcopal. Representatives of each type have sought to defend the superiority and authority of their own polity by appealing to Acts, as well as to other New Testament sources. There is also some reason to believe that the political views of particular scholars, relating to three roughly corresponding types of constitution—democracy, oligarchy, monarchy—introduce a further subjective factor into historical research. Nevertheless, neither theological nor political partisanship wholly accounts for the complexity of the question before us. The evidence in Acts is equivocal; and when it is viewed in conjunction with the testimony of Paul's letters and later Christian writings, the situation is little altered. The failure of New Testament scholars and church historians to reach any significant agreement as to how the early Christians organized themselves, or to demonstrate how

140

one type of church order evolved into another, argues for the complexity of the problem.[1]

Inevitably the early Christians were influenced by the organizational forms and procedures of Judaism in this period. It is, therefore, noteworthy that the order of the community of Essenes established near the Dead Sea bears striking resemblance to the description in Acts of the organization of the primitive Christian communities.[2] Individual members of the order founded at Qumran were responsible to its leading priests, yet each man's responsibilities were defined according to his relation to the entire membership, to "the many." Within the community at Qumran there was a council of twelve laymen and three priests.[3] The community of the Cairo–Damascus document also possessed an inner circle, six laymen and four priests called "judges."[4] The highest ranking official, according to both sources, was a presiding priest known as the "superintendent." Unquestionably, such superintendents and councils held great authority within the Essene communities. Yet it is improbable that any important administrative action was taken without the participation of the full assembly of the sect. In all things the Essenes "took council together."

The procedures of the Christian assemblies may be compared with these gatherings of "the many" in the Essene communities.[5] The position held by the twelve apostles in the early chapters of Acts was roughly that of the council of twelve in the Qumran community, in that they were honored as men of exemplary piety and best fitted to be the bearers of the community's traditions. The position of Peter, and later of James, resembled that of the superintendent who headed the Essene communities. Their relation to the brethren was that of a shepherd to his flock.[6] The interpretation of the eschatological role of "the twelve" in both apocalyptic groups is grounded upon some of the same Old Testament testimonies.[7]

There were of course some notable differences between the hierarchical organization and government of the Essene brotherhood and that of the Christian brethren at Jerusalem. Although Luke reports that "a great many priests" became members of the Jerusalem church (6:7), priests held no special status in the Christian community by virtue of their hereditary office. We hear of no probationary members in the early church comparable to the novitiates at Qumran,

[1]See below, pp. 487ff.

[2]B. Reicke, "The Constitution of the Primitive Church in the Light of Jewish Documents;" also S. E. Johnson, both in Stendahl, *Scrolls*, pp. 143–156, 129–142. Munck, *Acts, Anchor Bible*, C. S. Mann, in Appendix, pp. 276ff. J. A. Fitzmyer, "Jewish Christianity in Acts in Light of the Qumran Scrolls," in Keck and Martyn, *Luke–Acts*, pp. 233ff.

[3]1QS viii, 1. F. M. Cross, Jr., *Ancient Library*, pp. 230ff.

[4]CD x, 4–10.

[5]Acts 1:23; 4:32; 6:1ff. For a discussion of the "parallels" in the Corinthian and Jerusalem congregations, see Munck, *Acts, Anchor Bible*, pp. 278ff.; cf. Fitzmyer in Keck and Martyn, *Luke–Acts*, pp. 247ff.

[6]CD xiii, 7–19. The highest ranking priest in the Essene communities, the *mebaqqer* ("superintendent"), corresponds to the early Christian bishop, *episcopos*. Both officials are referred to as "shepherds." Cf. 1 Pet. 5:2f.

[7]Cf. 1QS viii, 5–8 with Rev. 21:14; Matt. 16:18; Gal. 2:9; Eph. 2:20; Luke 22:30.

although stern discipline is administered to offending members in both communities. No common work was assigned to the brethren in Jerusalem. These differences are sufficient to eliminate the idea that the earliest Christians modeled their order after that of some Essene community. Besides this, a number of features of the early Church in Acts resemble the constitution of nonsectarian Jewish synagogues, like, for example, the custom of laying on of hands and the appointment of "elders."[8]

Whatever one's judgment concerning the possibilities of Essene influence upon Christianity, the Dead Sea Scrolls provide documentary evidence that there existed in Palestine an apocalyptic community older than Christianity which was organized as a legislative assembly, at once democratic and unequal, with a council of twelve and a superintendent. There is no reason to suppose that Luke's description of the organization and government of the earliest churches is an artificial reconstruction embodying illogical and anachronistic elements. It is very plausible that the earliest Christians appropriated features of an Essene community organization, as well as a number of synagogue practices, in developing the order of their communities. In every case, however, we may be sure that these customary forms and procedures underwent radical modification under the influence of the Christian *kerygma*. This modification will be particularly evident when we consider the meaning of the cultic acts of the early Church, baptism and the community meal.

Let us consider now two questions: What were the activities of the original "apostles," especially Peter, in the earliest period? How can the rise to leadership in Jerusalem of James, the brother of Jesus, be explained? These two questions are important both for our survey of the history of the oral traditions concerning Jesus, and for understanding several crucial issues confronting Paul at the beginning of his Christian mission.

The Twelve and James the Lord's Brother

According to some scholars, the author of Acts assigns to the twelve apostles a position in the primitive Christian community which is founded upon late ecclesiastical tradition. One such view is that by the end of the first century it was commonly assumed that the eyewitnesses of Jesus' Ministry were the rightful bearers of tradition, that twelve disciples—and twelve only—had been chosen by Jesus, and that upon the authority of "the twelve" the whole existence of the Church depended. It is judged that this tradition, recorded in Acts and in other late New Testament writings, is entirely different from the picture given by Paul's early letters. Some writers have supposed that the origin of "the twelve" may be traced to an apocalyptic conceit concerning the role of Israel's twelve princes in the final judgment.[9] We are told that belief in the Church as the new Israel

---

[8]The *presbyteroi* ("elders") in the early Christian churches probably served the same functions as the elders of the synagogues. Cf. Acts 11:30 The establishment of the early Jewish–Christian synagogues is suggested by Acts 2:46, 4:31, 5:12, 21:46, and 6:9.

[9]Rev. 21:14; Eph. 2:20.

gave rise to legends concerning the Messiah's call, choice, and commissioning of "the twelve."[10]

Skepticism regarding this feature of the Acts narrative is not warranted. The Christian Church grew from a company of men who had known Jesus in his life and at his death, and who had borne witness to his resurrection. Jesus' Galilean disciples must have held a unique and unrivaled position in the earliest days, twelve of them forming an inner circle of leadership.[11] At the same time in the development of tradition, the influence of "the twelve" was probably exaggerated. It is surely significant that none of the original group, with the exception of Peter, were remembered as making any special contribution to the life of the church in Jerusalem.[12] Only their corporate witness to the *kerygma* seemed important.[13] That such prestige should attach to a person's function in relation to his community and its faith, without valuing that person's individuality, may seem very odd to us. Yet in the Qumran community there was an analogous situation.

Various explanations have been offered for the scattering of "the twelve" at an early date and for the eclipse of their influence as a group. Probably the principal reasons are (1) the change in membership of the primitive church, and (2) the critical situation in Jerusalem, which grew out of the persecution and dispersion of "the Hellenists" and which reached a climax in the violent actions of Herod Agrippa I.

Doubtless many of the Jews who came into the Christian community after Pentecost differed in their outlook from the Galileans. Priests and Pharisees were among the new converts (6:7, 15:5); these might be expected to adhere more closely to the Torah and the customary forms of piety than did the disciples who had known Jesus and first believed in him. The contempt which residents of Jerusalem and Judea had for Galileans might have contributed subtly to a lack of confidence in "the twelve" as the most capable leaders. Add to this, Luke's notice that the apostles were less interested in attending to administrative responsibilities than in proclaiming the gospel (6:2, 4), and one can easily see how functions originally belonging to "the twelve" passed into the hands of others. Even before the threat of Herod Agrippa I (12:1–3), some of the original twelve probably returned to Galilee. Few of these men possessed Peter's intelligence or force of character. When Paul came to Jerusalem approximately three years after Jesus' death, he saw besides Peter "none of the other apostles except James the Lord's brother" (Gal. 1:18f.).

According to Acts, Peter remained the undisputed head of the primitive church,

---

[10]Weiss, *Earliest Christianity*, vol. I, pp. 45ff. It is noteworthy that the lists in the NT of Jesus' disciples do not agree except in the number, twelve, and that the terms *disciple* and *apostle* are applied to others.

[11]K. Lake, "The Twelve and the Apostles," in Foakes-Jackson and Lake, *Beginnings*, vol. V, pp. 37–59; L. E. Elliott-Binns, *Galilean Christianity* (1956), pp. 54ff.; V. Taylor, "The Twelve and the Apostles," *The Gospel According to Mark* (1952), pp. 619–627 [hereafter, *Mark*].

[12]Or elsewhere for that matter, with the exception of John; see below, pp. 552ff. According to early chapters of Acts, John is only Peter's mute companion (3:1, 11; 4:3, 7, etc.). Herod's murder of James (12:1ff.) suggests that he was known to be a ringleader. For brief references to other disciples, Eusebius, *H.E.*, III. 5. 2; 7. 8; for their legendary acts, E. Goodspeed, *The Twelve* (1957).

[13]Schlatter, *The Church*, pp. 10f.

as chief spokesman for "the twelve"—at least until the time of his departure to Samaria (8:14ff.). It is sometimes said that the author of Acts does less than justice to the status of James in the earliest community. But Paul's statement in the Galatian letter, noted above, implies that James had not as yet become pre-eminent. The purpose of Paul's first visit to Jerusalem following his conversion to Christianity was, he tells us, "to visit Cephas [Peter]."[14]

Although there is some uncertainty as to the position of James in the very earliest days, it is nevertheless clear that before long he had supplanted Peter as head of the mother church. Both of our sources report this astonishing fact. When Paul speaks of his second visit to Jerusalem, fourteen (or perhaps eleven) years later, James is named first among the "pillars" of the Church (Gal. 2:9). When at last James is introduced in the Acts narrative, it is Peter himself who acknowledges him head of the Jerusalem community (Acts 12:17).

The transference of authority to James should probably not be understood either as a weakening of Peter's influence in the Jerusalem church or as the severing of his connection with it. The impression one gains from the early chapters in Acts is that Peter's missions beyond Jerusalem were supervised by the mother church even though they were carried forward on his own initiative. Peter was still accountable to the brethren (8:14, 25, 11:2f.). James' rise to leadership resulted from the fact that Peter exchanged his role as superintendent in the mother church for that of traveling missionary. At the same time, Peter retained an official connection with the community headed by James.[15] The implications of this are important for understanding Peter's later actions.

RITUAL IN THE EARLY CHURCH

Baptism

In Chapter 6 attention was drawn to the fact that in Acts the relation of baptism to the pneumatism of the early Church is confused. This is sometimes explained as the failure of Luke to harmonize sources containing conflicting traditions. Luke lacked sufficient information about Christian beginnings. Being familiar with the theology and mode of baptism in the churches of his time, he read these back into the earliest period. Such considerations have led some to conclude that baptism was not an original rite, or at least not everywhere practiced in the primitive Church.[16]

There is a more adequate explanation for lack of clarity in this matter. Luke emphasizes the fact that the divine plan is always thrusting outwards, and works a step ahead of the organized community. The spirit falls on Cornelius and his associates before their baptism (10:44), and Apollos is already burning with the

---

[14]The dominant position of Peter is further attested by the preservation of Jewish–Christian tradition, Matt. 16:17–19; Luke 22:31, etc. Bultmann, *Theology*, vol. 1, p. 59.

[15]O. Cullmann, *Peter*, trans. F. V. Filson (2d. ed., 1962), pp. 44ff.

[16]Weiss, *Earliest Christianity*, vol. I, pp. 50f.; II, p. 623; C. T. Craig, *The Beginning of Christianity* (1943), pp. 140f. [hereafter, *Beginning*]; *IB*, vol. 9, pp. 48f.

spirit (18:25) before he receives official instruction. "[Luke] is less interested in, and less profound in his treatment of, the sacraments than Paul. He sees the church not as an established hierarchical institution dispensing salvation but as a loosely-knit evangelistic and pastoral organism."[17]

Baptism was administered in all the earliest communities. Paul assumes that Christians had received baptism.[18] That from the beginning this was so is supported by early traditions recorded in the Synoptic Gospels. Baptism of disciples by Jesus was unknown; therefore the traditions which contrast the baptisms initiated by John and by the disciples of Christ were used to emphasize the significance of Christian baptism.[19]

The important question remains. How did Christian baptism originate and what was its meaning? For an answer one need not turn to the Jewish practice of baptizing Gentile proselytes, which may have existed in the first century. Neither are Essene lustrations a satisfactory model suggesting direct influence. Still further afield than these Jewish parallels, so-called, are the ritual washings of certain Hellenistic mystery religions.[20] Christian baptism was adopted from the practice of John the Baptist and his followers. One is assured that this orientation is properly historical by the preservation of the tradition that Jesus was himself baptized by John, and by the association in the *kerygma* of John's mission with that of Jesus the Messiah.[21] For John the rite of baptism was closely connected with his proclamation. It signified a cleansing from sin in anticipation of God's judgment. John felt that this judgment, so near at hand, was to be executed by the Messiah.[22] The early Christian belief that John had heralded the Messiah who had come is sufficient to account for the adoption of John's baptism as the rite of initiation into the Christian community.[23]

In relating early Christian baptism to John's baptism, justice must be done to their differences. The point has been stressed that the earliest Christians did not, like John, merely anticipate the new age. For them the eschatological events were already occurring. Thus baptism could hardly have had the same meaning to the earliest Christians that it had to John's disciples.[24] Besides this, a difference in their conceptions of sin and of guilt would have distinguished the rites of the

[17]Barrett, *Luke*, p. 75.

[18]1 Cor. 12:13; Rom. 6:3; cf. Acts 19:1-6.

[19]Mark 1:8 and pars.; Acts 1:5; 11:15f. The contrast is not between John's water-baptism and Christian Spirit-baptism, but between John's water-baptism and Christian water-and-Spirit-baptism. Williams, *The Acts*, p. 291. Christian anxiety that the two rites might be confused would have been early, not late. The tradition in the Fourth Gospel reflects an anxiety of another kind; see below, p. 585.

[20]Schlatter, *The Church*, pp. 31f. See below, pp. 343ff.

[21]Matt. 28:19 hardly represents the historical basis for Christian baptism although it provides an adequate theological explanation of its significance.

[22]See below, p. 272.

[23]H. Lietzmann, *The Beginnings of the Christian Church*, trans. B. L. Woolf (1937), p. 64 [hereafter, *Beginnings*].

[24]Bultmann's insistence that the early Christians knew Jesus only as the Messiah who was to come leads him to conclude that the meaning of the two baptisms "can hardly have been different." *Theology*, vol. I, p. 39.

two groups. John's baptism was for the remission of sins viewed from the perspective of the moral demands of the Torah and the prophets. Christian baptism was for those repenting the rejection of the Messiah whose mission brought to fulfillment God's former revelations. Finally, the bases for forgiveness were differently determined. John's baptism grounded forgiveness upon God's mercy toward the penitent, to be revealed in the coming judgment. Christian baptism grounded forgiveness upon the saving action of God already manifested in the cross and resurrection of the Messiah. Since these differences must have been felt from the beginning, it is very doubtful that there ever was a time when Christian baptism was not associated with the name of Jesus the Messiah and with the gift of his Spirit.[25] The Christian rite was a distinctive one by reason of its connection with the *kerygma*.

The Community Meals in the Earliest Period

Acts reports that the early Christians were accustomed to meet together for "the breaking of bread" (2:42, 46).[26] These words imply something more than the partaking of ordinary food.[27]

The Gospels report that on occasions when Jesus had eaten with his disciples commonplace actions had been given special religious significance. Moreover, accounts of the resurrection appearances of Jesus tell of the renewal of Jesus' fellowship with the disciples and of their recognition of him in "the breaking of bread."[28] The community meals of the earliest Christians were doubtless a deliberate continuation of this table fellowship with Jesus which the original disciples had enjoyed. The presence of the risen Messiah was keenly felt when the earliest Christians assembled in their homes for "the breaking of bread." Luke's reference to their gladness (2:46) implies further significance. Did the meal intensify the apocalyptic expectations of the primitive Christians? Perhaps the Messiah would appear in the midst of his people in "the breaking of bread," to establish his glorious kingdom! Viewed in this light the early Christian meal was a joyful anticipation of the messianic feast in the Age to Come.[29]

Was "the breaking of bread" also a commemoration of Jesus' Last Supper with "the twelve?"[30] On this scholars have sharply divided. Serious consideration need not be given to the opinion that the New Testament accounts of the Last Supper do not properly record an event of Jesus' passion. But many have believed that

[25]Acts 2:38; 10:48; 1 Cor. 1:13; 6:11; 12:13.

[26]Note also Acts 20:7, 11.

[27]In pious Jewish homes the principal meal was commonly begun with a prayer thanking God for daily food, after which bread was broken and its fragments distributed. But it is unlikely that Luke estimated the significance of "the breaking of bread" as merely providing further evidence that the early Jewish–Christians had followed traditional forms of piety and gained a reputation for their generosity.

[28]Mark 6:30ff. and pars.; Luke 24:28ff.; John 21:4ff.; Acts 10:40.

[29]Acts 2:46–3:8; cf. 5:12f., 26, 42.

[30]See below, pp. 313ff.

the tradition which Paul "received" (1 Cor. 11:23ff.), and the celebration of "the Lord's Supper" familiar to Paul and interpreted by him (1 Cor. 10:16–21), were unknown to the earliest Christians in Jerusalem. They knew nothing of a cultic act consisting of breaking bread and drinking wine in the faith that by this means believers in the Messiah could participate in his body and blood, becoming fellow-members of a body of which the Messiah was the head. Such sacramental notions, which are explicitly developed by Paul, were unknown to Jesus and to his Jewish disciples. This idea of a cult meal, growing out of the action of its founder, was derived from the mystery religions of the Greco–Roman world. The Christian sacrament of the Lord's Supper, or the Eucharist, was a product of Hellenistic Christianity.[31] According to these several theories of Hellenistic origin it would be an anachronism to understand the "breaking of bread" in Acts as having any cultic significance. The fellowship meals of Jesus with his disciples, which were continued for a while in the earliest churches, should not be thought of as "sacramental celebrations."[32]

Evidence will be presented in Chapter 12 for the view that the peculiar form and meaning of the Christian bread-and-cup ceremony originated from the Last Supper. By a comparison of three independent traditions—Paul, Mark, Luke—the significance which Jesus ascribed to this meal can be recovered. Whatever uncertainty may remain as to the actual words which were spoken, broken bread and the wine cup were used by Jesus to signify the meaning and the outcome of his death. By taking part in this meal Jesus' disciples, believing him to be the Messiah, were offered forgiveness and promised a share in the blessings of the Age to Come. One of these blessings would be the renewal of table fellowship with him.[33]

It is reasonable to assume that a fundamental unity belonged to the meal rites of early Christianity and that the several traditions of a later time developed out of this original complex of ideas. One principal type was connected with the symbolism of the broken bread and focused upon the Christians' consciousness of Jesus' living presence and hope of his imminent return. Another principal type derived its central meaning from the wine cup, which signified the participation of all believers in the saving benefits of the death of the Messiah. Yet it is doubtful that "the breaking of bread" in Acts refers to community meals which did not include the use of ceremonial wine. The early Christians may have used this phrase, as a familiar reference to their bread-and-cup ceremony, to prevent outsiders from profaning its significance. Against the background of pagan cultic

[31]A view given wide currency by the German scholar W. Bousset and given an original development by Bultmann. See *Theology*, vol. I, pp. 40f., 57f., 144ff.

[32]As in 1 Cor. 11:20–34; Jude 10–12. For early, noncanonical literature, H. Lietzmann, *Mass and Lord's Supper*, trans. D. H. G. Reeve (1953—), pp. 161–164, 188–212.

[33]The position of the writer is that the NT accounts of the Last Supper yield a common core of early tradition, although they reflect later liturgical developments. A comparison of this tradition with late Jewish meal customs and messianic expectations supports its Palestinian origin. Had these traditions been shaped by Hellenistic sacramental conceptions, the NT accounts would have been quite different. See further below, pp. 313ff.

ceremonies, the meaning of the wine cup easily could have been desecrated.[34]

The description of what happened at the community meals of the early Church rests, in part, upon arguments from silence. It is tempting to fill in the picture by appealing to the community meal practices of the Essenes. The brief notices in Acts invite this comparison. The Christian meals were, like those of the Essenes' community, complete meals and cultic in character. Moreover, if the Markan text of the Last Supper was preserved in the early Jewish–Christian communities, and influenced their own meal customs, the following point is noteworthy. In Mark 14:22–24 Jesus' blessings over the bread and wine occur together, presumably before the supper, as in the Essene cult meal. Paul declares that "after supper" Jesus took the cup. Perhaps by the time of Paul this liturgical formula had become established. The Essene and the older Christian procedures were not recalled. It was assumed that the common Jewish meal custom of blessing the wine after supper had been observed by Jesus and his earliest followers.[35]

In their meal customs another influence of Essenism upon early Christianity can probably be discerned. The same caution should be observed in this case, however, as in that of baptism. The Christian meal fellowships were integrally related to those which Jesus had held with his disciples and which, from the time of the Last Supper and the Easter meals, were conceived to mediate that salvation which God offered unto men in and through the Messiah's death and resurrection.

THE SCATTERING OF THE BRETHREN

The Acts narrative introduces the "Hellenists" and "Hebrews" so abruptly (6:2) that their identity has remained a matter for conjecture. Many persons hold that these fleeting references in Acts, viewed along with other evidence, shed light upon important developments in early Christianity. They help to explain why certain traditions concerning Jesus' Ministry have been preserved in the form we find them in the four Gospels. They also provide a background for understanding the fateful conflict which arose between the Jerusalem church and the Christian community at Antioch, and provide a stage for the emergence of the Apostle Paul as missionary to the Gentiles.

Who Were "The Hellenists" and "The Hebrews"?

Since the term *Hellenist* is not found in contemporary Christian or non-Christian writings, its usage in Acts is the essential clue to its meaning.[36] A few scholars have held that Luke employs this rare word as a synonym for the common term *Hellenes*, which he also uses. In both terms he makes reference to persons Greek

---

[34]J. Jeremias, *The Eucharistic Words of Jesus*, trans. A. Ehrhardt (1955), pp. 72ff. [hereafter, *Eucharistic Words*]; R. E. Brown, "The Unity and Diversity in New Testament Ecclesiology," *Nov. Test.* 6 (1963): 298ff.

[35]1QS vi, 1ff.; 1QSa ii, 14ff.; Kuhn in Stendahl, *Scrolls*, p. 73.

[36]Acts 6:2; 9:29. See commentaries for the textual problem concerning 11:20.

by race and upbringing.[37] Another view, proposed after the discovery of the Dead Sea Scrolls, is that the Hellenists were Jews converted to Christianity from the sectarian group which treasured these writings, or from some order similar to the one living at Qumran. This identification is a fascinating one, providing a possible bridge between Essenism and early Christianity. If it is tenable, an explanation would be given for some of the similarities we have been noting, and a link might be found connecting the primitive Church with writings such as John's Gospel or the Letter to the Hebrews.[38] This theory has not found many supporters however, and it must appeal to several highly speculative judgments; for example, that *Hellenist* was a term in the primitive Church no longer understood by Luke.

The usual view, which is likely to be correct, is that by the term *Hellenist* Luke wished to identify those Jewish–Christians "whose habitual use of the Greek language implied a certain detachment from the narrowly nationalistic outlook and the severe legalism of the typical Palestinian Jews." [39] The author's references suggest also that he had in mind Jews, and perhaps some proselytes, whose native connections were with the Dispersion rather than with Jerusalem. By his use of the term *the Hebrews* it is likely that Luke identifies only Aramaic-speaking Jews who were drawn into the early church from the *amme ha-ares* (peoples of the land). The group may have included converts from the Essenes and possibly Samaritans, although neither group is mentioned as such in Acts.[40]

One scholar, drawing attention to similarities between Samaritan views of Old Testament history and those held by Stephen according to Acts 7, advances the novel view that "the Hebrews" in Acts 6 identify Samaritan Christians exclusively.[41] If this theory is credible then one must conclude that Luke no longer understood references to "the Hebrews" in the early Church. Indeed the usual explanation given for the tensions within the Jerusalem congregation must be abandoned. According to this theory both the Hellenists (Hellenized Jewish–Christians) and the Hebrews (Samaritan–Christians) were minority groups within the Church which threatened its missions among the Jews of the city.

In the light of the historical background which has been surveyed, one can easily see why Palestinian Jews considered Hellenistic influences a threat to their

[37]Cadbury, in Foakes-Jackson and Lake, *Beginnings*, vol. V, pp. 59ff.; *IB*, vol. 9, p. 88.

[38]O. Cullmann, "The Significance of the Qumran Texts for Research into the Beginnings of Christianity," in Stendahl, *Scrolls*, pp. 25ff. See Fitzmyer's criticism in Keck and Martyn, *Luke–Acts*, p. 238. H. J. Schoeps and others argue that a connection between the Essenes and "the Hebrews" in Acts might have existed.

[39]C. H. Dodd, "History and Doctrine of the Apostolic Age," in *A Companion to the Bible*, ed. T. W. Manson, (1946) [hereafter, T. W. Manson, *Companion*]; Lietzmann, *Beginnings*, p. 70. It is possible that the term was coined by Palestinian Jews as a disparaging designation, i.e., Hellenists = paganizers. M. Simon, *St. Stephen and the Hellenists in the Primitive Church* (1958), pp. 12ff. [hereafter, *St. Stephen*]; J. Munck, *Paul and the Salvation of Mankind*, trans. F. Clarke (1959), pp. 218ff. [hereafter, *Paul*]; C. S. Mann (Munck, *Acts, Anchor Bible*, p. 302) suggests that "Hellenized-Jews" best translates Luke's *Hellenistai*.

[40]Fitzmyer in Keck and Martyn, *Luke–Acts*, pp. 238f.

[41]See the essay by W. F. Albright and C. S. Mann, "Stephen's Samaritan Background," in Munck, *Acts, Anchor Bible*, pp. 285ff., presenting Abram Spiro's hypothesis.

way of life and why, as a reaction, separate synagogues had been established in Jerusalem by Jews of the Dispersion (6:9). The Hellenists did not adhere to the forms of piety so dear to the Pharisees of Judea and the priests in Jerusalem. On the other side, the "Hellenists" might have felt that their interests and interpretation of the gospel were slighted by the majority in the Christian community. Possibly the specific grievance reported in Acts 6 was only a symptom of broad differences in belief and practice.

Stephen, the First Christian Martyr

The seven leaders appointed by "the disciples" to administer the "daily distribution" are not called "deacons" by Luke. It is anachronistic to consider their functions the same as those of men bearing this title at a later time. The author of Acts presents the seven as clearly subordinate to "the twelve." This judgment clearly predominated in the assembly of "the many." Yet the actions of Stephen and of Philip, two of the seven, indicate no reluctance on their part to act independently.

The unity of the primitive church was threatened. That a disruption did not occur may be due to two factors: (1) the deviant partisans were expelled from Jerusalem as a result of Stephen's preaching and martyrdom; and (2) there was a greater readiness on the part of Peter and John, than on the part of the majority among the Jewish–Christians of Jerusalem, to maintain fellowship with the scattered brethren and with the Christian communities established by them.

The historical value of the story of Stephen's martyrdom has been widely discussed (6:8–8:1). Some have argued that the Acts account is not consistent. Perhaps two traditional stories—one of a mob action, another of a formal trial—have been combined. Interest has centered chiefly upon the problem of Stephen's speech and its relation to the narrative setting in Acts.

Some scholars state that Stephen's speech is not a defense against "the false charges" brought against him.[42] Assuming, then, the irrelevance of the speech, several types of explanation for its content are given. Two of these may be noted to indicate the complexity of the problem. It has been argued that Luke's source contained the story of the martyr, but gave no account of Stephen's self-defense. Accordingly, Luke composed a speech for insertion here. If this is the explanation, then the crucial question becomes that of the author's purpose. Did Luke seek to reconstruct the lines of Stephen's defense? Or was he providing the reader with an example of the kind of preaching which led to Stephen's death? Or does the speech expound the unfolding purpose of Acts and not Stephen's ideas? Other scholars have thought that Luke's source contained a speech of Stephen, but that either this version was an edited one or Luke himself did the editing. In either case, theories of this type bring into prominence the question of the editor's motive.

Can the drift of Stephen's self-defense be recovered by a critical analysis of

[42]Dibelius, *Studies*, pp. 167ff.; Simon, *St. Stephen*, pp. 1f.; 39ff. Goguel, *Birth*, pp. 172ff.

Acts 7? Is it necessary to choose between the two types of explanation noted above? Most of the problems which have given rise to these proposals are taken into account if it is assumed that Stephen's speech is Luke's composition, but that he relied upon a story of the martyrdom which set forth the gist of Stephen's defense. There are no serious objections to the position that Acts 7 reports what Stephen might have spoken before his death, and, less vehemently perhaps in his sermons in Hellenistic synagogues.[43] At the time of his arraignment Stephen may have recognized the futility of offering a rebuttal of the charges brought against him. Thinking it was his last chance, he delivered an impassioned, partisan address. Whether or not he was able to complete it is uncertain.[44]

If the speech in Acts represents the true tendencies in Stephen's proclamation, we may say that he attacked the parochialism of the Palestinian Jews who had rejected Jesus the Messiah. He argued that the traditional accounts of God's revelations unto Israel afforded no justification for a slavish attachment to the soil of the Promised Land. Indeed, most of the important revelations and providential acts of God had taken place outside of Palestine—Mesopotamia, Egypt, Midian, and Sinai. Furthermore, the patriarchs had not been buried in the land of the Jews but in Shechem, inhabited in Stephen's time by the hated Samaritans (7:14-17). Woven into this theme is a second one, that the people of the old covenant had always been rebellious (7:9, 39-43, 51-53). The building of the temple itself by the degenerate Solomon, and the persistence of the nation's misguided pride in the temple, vividly illustrate the failure of Israel. The nation had not understood the true intentions of God's revelations in history which were now reaching fulfillment with "the coming of the Righteous One."

Stephen stood for a Christianity emancipated from that Jewish nationalism which was centered in the temple cult in Jerusalem. In part, Stephen's outlook was that of many Hellenistic Jews. But his disparagement of the temple was profoundly shocking to them, as well as to native-born Jewish converts in the Church.[45] Stephen's understanding of the teaching of Jesus apparently provided him with his new perspective upon Israel's institutions, the Law as well as the temple. It is unlikely that Stephen, any more than Jesus, wished to dispute the divine origin of either Law or temple (7:44f., 38, 53). His attack was directed to persons who, upon the authority of the Law, had crucified the Messiah, and who not only sought to disguise their apostasy by regular performance of the temple ceremonies, but used the temple to support their belief in an exclusive claim upon God. It would have been natural for persons so accused by Stephen to suppose that the authority of both the Law and the temple was under attack.[46]

[43]IB, vol. 9, p. 92; Craig, Beginning, pp. 147f.; W. L. Knox, St. Paul and the Church at Jerusalem (1925), pp. 39ff. [hereafter, Jerusalem]; Simon, St. Stephen, pp. 39ff.

[44]Apparently Luke considered the charges brought against Stephen to be unfounded; so also did the earliest Christians, else they would have repudiated Stephen. It is doubtful that either understood the full implications of Stephen's teachings.

[45]See below, p. 349.

[46]Cf. Simon, St. Stephen, pp. 48ff. Abram Spiro's hypothesis, that the speech of the "Samaritan Christian," Stephen, reflects his ingrained animus against Jerusalem Jews, offers a radically different explanation of Stephen's polemic and its offensiveness. See above, note 41.

We shall see that some of Jesus' actions and teachings appear to warrant Stephen's exposition of the Christian *kerygma*. This Hellenist brought into prominence a revolutionary aspect of the gospel which was concealed under the adherence of the apostles, and "the Hebrews" in the Church, to the Law and temple practices.[47] Moreover, in several respects Stephen anticipated Paul and, perhaps more directly, the teaching of the Letter to the Hebrews and the Gospel of John. At the same time, it is doubtful that Jesus or Paul, or any other early exponent of Christianity, went to such lengths as did Stephen. No one else claimed that, from the outset of their institution, the Law and the temple led to false developments, to a perversion of God's revelation in Israel's history.[48] Had Stephen lived he might have ranked with the greatest of the apostles.[49] Nevertheless, Saul of Tarsus was better fitted than he to interpret the mind of Christ concerning the purpose of the Torah. Besides this, the unknown apologist who wrote the Letter to the Hebrews was better fitted than Stephen to proclaim that Christ's person and sacrifice had replaced the need for the Jewish temple with its priesthood and sacrifices.[50]

Missions in Samaria and at Antioch

According to Acts "a great persecution arose against the church in Jerusalem" after Stephen's violent death. Those who were suspected of sharing his radical views fled the city into the regions of Judea, Samaria, and Phoenicia. Some migrated northward as far as Antioch. Others went to the island of Cyprus (8:1; 11–19). Luke's account of the gradual breakdown of the conservatism of the Jewish–Christians remaining in Jerusalem, and of the stages whereby Christianity penetrated to the Gentile world, is programmatic (1:8). Some of these missions may have been contemporaneous. There were certainly others which Luke does not report. The importance of the missions to Samaria and Antioch and of the consequent developments, which Luke stresses, can scarcely be doubted.

Students of the Old Testament will recall that the Samaritans were of mixed Gentile and Jewish blood, and that a separation of Samaria from the traditionally Jewish territories took place in the fifth century B.C. A Samaritan holy city and temple had been established at Gerizim. This temple was destroyed in 128 B.C. by the Maccabeans. Hatreds between the Jews of Judea and Galilee and the Samaritans had intensified through the years of Roman rule. Philip's proclamation of the Christian gospel in Samaria was therefore an epoch-making departure. Nevertheless, the church at Jerusalem maintained a connection with these churches founded upon the Samaritan soil. Peter and John, representatives of the twelve, were sent to observe the work of Philip.

The traditions reported in Acts 8 may contain some legendary material and be a composite of sources of unequal value; yet the substantial historicity of the

---

[47]Dodd, in T. W. Manson, *Companion*, p. 394.
[48]W. L. Knox, *Jerusalem*, pp. 50f., n. 10; pp. 54f., n. 24.
[49]*IB*, vol. 9, p. 92.
[50]Simon, *St. Stephen*, pp. 98ff.

developments reported may be maintained. Pro-Samaritan and anti-Samaritan traditions in the four Gospels not only confirm an early Christian mission among the Samaritans, but imply that some of the original apostles had labored in this region.[51] Several convictions of the apostles, growing out of their understanding of the gospel, led them to accept the Samaritan Christians, however much they may have been prone to share the antipathies of the Jerusalem Jews toward them. In the first place, the eschatological conception of the community of the Messiah implied that all confessors of Jesus the Christ composed one congregation. Moreover, the apocalyptic hopes of the earliest Christians, centering around Mount Zion as the dwelling place of those who awaited the return of the risen Lord, implied that Jerusalem was the earthly habitation of this congregation.[52] But most important was the original disciples' reliance upon the Spirit, upon its manifestations as a guarantee and a guide. Philip's preaching had been accompanied by typical pneumatic phenomena (8:6f). Confronted by this evidence, Peter and John gave little if any thought to the practical complications which developed when it became known in Jerusalem that Samaritans had received the apostles' "laying on of hands."[53]

An event of far-reaching consequence took place when some of the "scattered brethren" came to Antioch and "spoke to the Greeks" (6:20). Antioch was the seat of the imperial legate of the province of Syria and Cilicia and, as such, ranked as the capital of the East. According to Josephus, Antioch was the third city of the Empire, in importance exceeded only by Rome and Alexandria. The population was predominantly Gentile and hence the language and culture of the city were Greek. There was a large Jewish colony in Antioch. From its foundation the city's Christian community was composed of both Jews and Greeks.

The reader's first impression may be that Luke was very casual in noting the establishment of Christianity in this strategic city and the beginning of a Christian mission to Gentiles. But the concluding sentence reporting this event should be noted (11:26). For the first time the followers of Jesus were designated "Christians" (Christ-followers). Those who coined this nickname were outsiders.[54] For such persons, Christ would be considered a personal name, not a title. Yet, although the religious nature of the attachment of the followers of Christ to him was not understood by people in Antioch, they sensed that these men stood apart from the various Jewish parties and sects of the city. In Antioch the word *Christian* identified a new religion. Subsequently the Acts narrative makes it clear that Luke considered the Gentile mission of the Church a vigorous offspring of the community at Antioch.[55]

[51]Luke 9:51–56; 10:29–37; 17:11–19; John 4. Cf. Matt. 10:5.

[52]Lietzmann, *Beginnings*, p. 73.

[53]Cf. Acts 10:44–47; 11:12ff. In the light of this evidence the statement in 8:15–17 is suspect. Perhaps Luke wishes to show that Christians constituted a fellowship of the Spirit. Note 2:16f.

[54]Despite Bickerman (*HTR* 42 (1949): 109ff.), it is unlikely that followers of Jesus gave this name to themselves. The NT references to this term imply its use by outsiders only: Acts 26:28; 1 Peter 4:16.

[55]See below, pp. 354ff.

In other regions the "scattered brethren" spoke "to none except Jews" (11:19). There is much evidence to support this statement. Apart from expressed indications of the will of God concerning particular individuals and their own initiative—Cornelius or the Ethiopian eunuch—the Jewish-Christians limited their appeal to the synagogues of Palestine and the Dispersion.[56] This limitation of the outreach and vision of the Jewish-Christian missions before Paul accounts in large measure for the widespread opposition to Paul within the churches. It also helps to explain why so much of the gospel tradition, preserved in churches outside of Palestine as well as within it, bears the impress of Christian disputations with Jews.

Luke's report of the sending of Barnabas from Jerusalem to Antioch further supports this view that the development in Antioch was a new departure (11:22–24). The choice of Barnabas, rather than Peter or one of "the twelve," may have been caused by the latter's absence from Jerusalem. Whatever the reason, the selection of Barnabas was fortunate. Peter, whose actions in the Cornelius story indicate that he shared the narrow outlook of most of the Jewish-Christians, may not have received readily and joyfully the Gentile Christians at Antioch (11:23). The conservatism of Peter, however, should not be contrasted too sharply with the enlightenment of Barnabas. Peter was pliable to the Spirit's direction, and Barnabas later aligned himself with the reactionary Jewish-Christians at Antioch. Neither Peter nor Barnabas was destined to become the champion of Gentile Christianity. The greatest service which Barnabas rendered the early Church was his introduction of Saul [Paul] to "the Christians" at Antioch.[57]

EARLY CONFLICTS WITH JEWISH AUTHORITIES

Acts 12 reports that for a second time violent measures were taken to kill the Christian movement in Jerusalem. We have seen that the initial outbreak of violence had led to the scattering of some of the brethren. Here is reported the martyrdom of the first of "the twelve." Herod Agrippa I killed James, one of the sons of Zebedee, and arrested Peter. The latter's life was saved by an escape and flight from Jerusalem. Problems of chronology loom large in this portion of Luke's narrative.[58] Some of these will concern us later when we investigate Paul's contacts with the church in Jerusalem. The crisis described in Acts 12 centers our attention for the present upon a question deserving brief notice. What conclusions can be reached concerning the attitude of the Jewish authorities toward the earliest Christians?

A brief summary of the situation according to the earlier chapters in Acts may be helpful. The first conflict with Jewish authorities followed the healing of the lame man at the gate of the temple (3:1ff.). Luke reports that "the priests and the captain of the temple and the Sadducees" arrested Peter and John, held them overnight, and, at a hearing the next morning, forbade them "to speak or teach

[56]Philip's actions are no exception, IB, vol. 9, pp. 108, 113; Dix, Jew and Greek, pp. 30f.
[57]Acts 11:25f.
[58]IB, vol. 9, pp. 154f.

at all in the name of Jesus." Shortly afterward "the apostles" again were arrested and put "in the common prison" (5:17ff.). A miraculous escape took place during the night and at daybreak the same men resumed their teaching in the temple area. An arraignment before the Sanhedrin followed, and Peter's defiant attitude led many of the council members to clamor for his death. Gamaliel, a celebrated Pharisee, counseled that the followers of the crucified Messianic pretender be left in peace. In his opinion this movement, like so many others of the same type, would come to nothing. The apostles were beaten, charged again to desist from preaching, and released.

Some historians have seriously questioned the authenticity of these episodes. Perhaps they are legends drawn from different sources but reporting some of the same improbable incidents. Such clashes with the Jewish authorities are inconsistent with Luke's direct statements, which declare that the early Christians stood well in the estimation of the Jews of Jerusalem. The Sadducees might have regarded the rapidly growing Christian community as a threat to the peace. They may have investigated the situation, but it is unlikely that any official repressive measures were taken. The peace enjoyed by the Christians in Jerusalem was first broken by Stephen and his sympathizers. After their departure persecution ceased. Herod's martyrdom of James and the miraculous escape of Peter are overlaid with legend. It is, therefore, impossible to disentangle from this story anything which can be called historical, aside from the fact that James was an early martyr and Peter narrowly escaped death in Jerusalem. That James' death would have "pleased the Jews" is scarcely credible.[59]

This skepticism with regard to Acts is ordinarily rejected as going too far. There may be some doublets and anachronisms in the narrative, but Luke is undoubtedly correct in reporting that the first opposition came from the Sadducees rather than from the Pharisees. This group would have had cause to fear the possible political consequences of the movement. Yet so long as Jesus' followers did not cry for vengeance, or oppose the temple, there was no need for violent repressive action. Moreover, under the Roman procurators it would have been difficult to devise an effective method of persecution, even with the aid of the Pharisees. But the Pharisees had no reasons for such persecution and many reasons for cautious tolerance. Most of the early Christians were zealous for the Torah and Jewish traditions, and some of the Pharisees had become identified with the movement. The tolerant attitude of Gamaliel and its acceptance is entirely credible.[60]

We have seen that the preaching of Stephen created a new situation. Whereas Judaism could be tolerant of internal differences, of messianic pretenders, and of attacks upon national sins, there was one thing which had to be resisted with the utmost urgency: a denial of the divine origin and absolute validity of the Torah. As in the case of Jesus, so in the case of Stephen, any man deserved death whose teaching was understood as attacking the whole economy of Israel's religion.

[59]Goguel, *Birth*, pp. 454ff.

[60]*IB*, vol. 9, p. 81; J. Weiss, *Earliest Christianity*, vol. I, pp. 138f.; W. L. Knox, *Jerusalem*, pp. 1ff.; Schlatter, *The Church*, pp. 82ff.; Reicke, *New Testament Era*, pp. 188ff.

The cause for the murder of James by Herod Agrippa I, and of the reaction of the Jews in Jerusalem to this deed, is at first sight not clear. Herod's action should not be understood as condemnation of the entire Christian community, but only of some of its leaders. Did he recognize that popular Jewish opinion in Jerusalem was disturbed by the fact that the Hellenists, Samaritans and perhaps Essenes, and others from among the *amme ha-ares,* were being received into the local community, and that uncircumcised Gentiles were being admitted elsewhere? Herod's eagerness to be recognized as a zealous advocate of Judaism could have prompted him to "lay violent hands" upon those Christian leaders responsible for permitting such serious deviations. If this was the cause of Herod's action, many pious Jews of Jerusalem would have felt it was justified. The short duration of this persecution may have been due not only to Herod's death (A.D. 44), but also to the fact that leadership of the Christian community passed into the hands of that other James who, as we have noticed, adhered strictly to the Torah and traditions of Judaism.[61]

By way of summary we may say that with the exception of two brief periods of violence, the earliest Christians enjoyed some immunity from official interference. They were free to bear witness to the gospel in the temple area and in various synagogues of Jerusalem, and to meet together within the walls of the city. Immunity from persecution did not mean freedom from controversy with the Jews. Far from it. It was not easy for the early Christians—who felt themselves bound to expose the guilt of their people—to maintain a close relationship with the Jews in the hope of winning their acceptance of the gospel. A Jewish–Christian community with a mission to the Jews existed in Jerusalem at least until the Jewish war with Rome. The existence and influence of this mother church was destined to be short-lived. Nevertheless, its impress is stamped upon the surviving traditions about Jesus, and the career of Paul is inextricably related to the church in Jerusalem and to its leaders, who never understood him.

[61]Reicke, *New Testament Era,* pp. 198ff.; Goguel, *Birth,* pp. 465ff.

EARLY ORAL AND WRITTEN TRADITIONS CONCERNING JESUS

Three sculptured panels (c. 1930) in limewood on the reredos, Duke University chapel, depicting Jesus with the doctors in the temple, Jesus before Pilate, and the entombment. (Ted Sparks, Duke University)

Galilean shepherd and flock. The imagery of Christ as shepherd is most fully developed in John 10 (cf. Ezek. 34), but several similitudes and parables in the Synoptic tradition reflect Jesus' life in Galilee and his familiarity with shepherd/sheep relationships. E.g., Mark 6:34; Luke 15:3ff. (Israel Government Tourist Office)

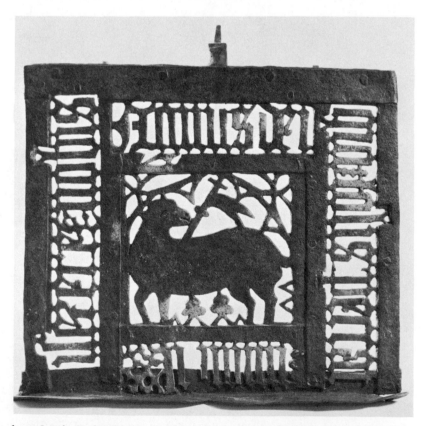

The Triumphant Lamb. Early Christians associated Jesus' death with the slaying of the Passover Lamb. 1 Cor. 4:7; 1 Pet. 1:18.; cf. Rev. 5:6. The vicarious benefits of this sacrifice are celebrated in John 1:29 as in later eucharist liturgy, inspiration for this iron altar panel of the fifteenth century. (Ernest Brummer Collection of Medieval and Renaissance Decorative Art, Duke University Museum.)

The Jordan River. The setting of several narratives in the Gospels. There is some doubt about the traditional site of John's baptism of Jesus, south of Jericho, but Jesus crossed the Jordan in this vicinity on his fateful journey to Jerusalem. (Israel Government Tourist Office)

THE early Christian Church expanded by boldly proclaiming Jesus the Messiah, ordering the common life of its membership, and withstanding various threats to unity and survival both from within and without.

The first followers of Jesus formed small communities of Aramaic-speaking Jews gathered around some of his original disciples and members of his family. These folk understood themselves to be of the Israel of the Age to Come. Their spiritual fervor, which found expression in ecstatic speaking and healings, tended to distinguish them outwardly from their fellows. Yet in many respects they appeared pious and loyal Jews; so they wished to remain. While they might have been regarded for some while as another sectarian movement within Judaism, within a brief span of ten to fifteen years the community had a phenomenal growth unparalleled by any other separate synagogue or Jewish community in Palestine. Greek-speaking Jews and proselytes, natives of other regions of the Roman empire living in Judea, as well as Samaritans, joined the movement. At Antioch in Syria, Greeks were numbered among "the Christians." At its growing edge, the primitive Church broke free of its provincial beginnings and became an inclusive fellowship. Yet the original community remained in Jerusalem, confronted with one crisis after another.

A view of the spread of Christianity could focus attention, as Luke does in Acts 13, upon the missions of the Apostle Paul. Instead, one may turn from Acts and consider the three earliest Gospels of the New Testament—Mark, Matthew, and Luke. In all probability, Paul proclaimed the Christian gospel in the regions reported in Acts 13–28, and composed his letters to the churches, before any Gospels were written. Nevertheless, the Gospels preserve traditions concerning Jesus' Ministry which, for the most part, had taken shape in the churches of Palestine and Syria during the first two decades of the Christian movement. It is quite possible that by the time Paul was brought to Antioch by Barnabas, and his great missions were begun, these essential traditions concerning Jesus' Ministry had become well established. Of course, the transmitters and editors of this early tradition selected from it, and interpreted and applied it, according to the needs and interests of the churches. But it is not probable that subsequent developments altered beyond recovery the earliest traditions.[1]

---

[1] The tradition was formulated "during the first twenty years of the Christian movement, and appears to have been largely accomplished by the time of Paul, who seems to regard the tradition as already fixed." A. M. Perry, "The Growth of the Gospels," *IB*, vol. 7, p. 73; Luke 1:2. Perry's statement has substantial validity, although the history of the synoptic tradition reveals persistence into the second century "of a living, free tradition of sayings of Jesus, out of which the Gospels have come," and which "did not come to an end with the writing of the Gospels." Perrin, *Rediscovering*, p. 34. See further, below, pp. 579ff.

The stories of Jesus which the earliest Gospels contain are those which the first Christians cherished and passed on to others. These are the traditions most useful in declaring, confirming, and defending the Christian *kerygma;* in instructing converts in the rites, discipline, and way of life of the Christian communities; and in inspiring believers to endure suffering and maintain hope. The Church's memory of Jesus is, at every point, intimately related to the life and thought of the earliest Christians, and the communities described in the Acts provide the historical matrix of the gospel tradition. Whatever else the Gospels of the New Testament may be, they are the literary deposit of the oral preaching, teaching, and worship of the primitive churches. Having just concluded a study of the exact period in which these formative influences were active, we deem it appropriate to consider the history of the gospel tradition. In this way one moves forward from the early Church to the origin of the three earliest Gospels. Then, through the eyes of these writers, one views the Ministry of Jesus and seeks to recover his teaching.

EARLIEST TRADITIONS

The Passion and Resurrection

The proclamation and defense of the *kerygma* called for repeated references to the Ministry of Jesus, especially to its closing days. It was essential to show that events in Jerusalem confirmed rather than denied the claim that the Messiah who is to come had been manifested. It was the manner of Jesus' death and his appearances to chosen witnesses which above all else confirmed for the Christians the gospel they professed: God had revealed the Messiah in his sufferings unto death, and in his resurrection.

There can be little doubt which part of this testimony most seriously offended both Jews and Greeks. Writing to the Corinthians, Paul acknowledges that "the word of the Cross" was a "stumbling-block to the Jews and folly to the Gentiles." [2] For the Apostle this "word" was the message of the resurrection of the crucified Jesus. Thus it is not difficult to see why the Jews took offense at the cross of this man. To affirm the resurrection of one who had been judged a blasphemer, and crucified, was, for the Jews, a scandal indeed.

As we have seen, the earliest Christians viewed Jesus' death as a treacherous murder. Yet connected with this idea was the belief that Jesus' rejection had not frustrated but, instead, accomplished the will of God.[3] At once the question was raised: How is one to validate these unheard of claims? Rational arguments would not suffice for the Jews. The only way to relate the crucifixion of Jesus to the divine purpose concerning God's Messiah was to appeal to his former revelation in law and prophecy. But alongside this proclamation of the necessity of the cross, its divine foreordination, there was also the deeper problem of the meaning of the cross, a question which, in any event, Jewish–Christians would have pressed

[2] 1 Cor. 1:23.
[3] Luke 24:25ff.; Acts 2:23–31; 3:18; 10:43; 13:27, 29, 32ff.; 1 Thess. 2:14f.; 1 Cor. 15:3f.

upon themselves. "Precisely because of Jesus' resurrection the question had to arise as to why Jesus had to go the way of suffering to the cross . . . If subsequently God was to manifest in the resurrection his divine power, why did God permit Jesus' rejection by the Jews?" [4] Thus for the purpose of "clarifying its own understanding of the momentous events out of which it emerged, and also for the purpose of making its gospel intelligible to the outside public," the earliest Church had to demonstrate that in the course of Jesus' Ministry specific scriptures had been fulfilled.[5]

The early Christians were also compelled to answer another question: Had Jesus been a criminal and blasphemer, as his enemies maintained, or a blameless person, as the disciples declared? The innocence of Jesus and the determination of responsibility for his death could have been established only by stating the circumstances of his arrest, trial, and crucifixion.[6] Many a person who took pride in Roman law would have wanted this information in some detail.

It is unlikely that the earliest witnesses felt a need for a connected narrative following the burial of Jesus. They thought it sufficient to report that particular persons had visited the tomb and found it empty and that Christ had appeared to individuals and to groups afterwards. It is probable that brief stories of appearances of Jesus to his disciples were offered as a confirmation of the summary statement in the early proclamations concerning the resurrection. The resurrection tradition in the Gospels bears the marks of the early oral and corporate witness of the Church.[7] The same motives which prompted the preservation of these stories led also to the early formulation of lists of specific persons who had seen the risen Christ after his death and burial. These too seem to have become an essential element of "the received tradition."[8] The longer, more detailed narratives in the Gospels of Christ's appearances, and the circumstantial stories of the finding of the empty tomb, bear the marks of more personal motives. Perhaps these stories were first offered as evidence of the resurrection in the worship of believers rather than in the Church's witness to outsiders. Some of them are associated with "the breaking of bread," which may point to their origin in the meal ceremonies of the earliest Christians.[9]

In the previous chapter the position was taken that "the breaking of bread" in the household assemblies of the primitive Christians was a deliberate renewal of the Last Supper memories of the disciples in the light of their Easter experiences

---

[4] W. Pannenberg, *Jesus—God and Man* (1968), p. 246 [hereafter, *Jesus*].

[5] Dodd, *Scriptures*, p. 14; Goguel, *Birth*, p. 103; R. Bultmann, *The History of the Synoptic Tradition*, trans. J. Marsh (1963), pp. 280ff. [hereafter, *History*]; Pannenberg, *Jesus*, pp. 246f.

[6] Weiss, *Earliest Christianity*, vol. I, p. 189; V. Taylor, *The Formation of the Gospel Tradition* (1935), pp. 44ff. [hereafter, *Formation*]. While Paul Winter (*Trial of Jesus*) too sharply separates religious and historical interests, he demonstrates that complex factors contributed to the growth of the passion traditions in the early Church.

[7] E.g., Matt. 28:8ff.; 28:16ff.; John 20:19–21. C. H. Dodd, "The Appearances of the Risen Christ," in *Studies in the Gospels*, ed. D. H. Nineham (1955), pp. 9ff. [hereafter, Nineham, *Studies*]; Taylor, *Formation*, pp. 59ff.

[8] 1 Cor. 15:1ff.; cf. Luke 24:33f.

[9] E.g., Luke 24:13–35; John 21:1–14. Dodd, note 7 above, pp. 13ff. Cf. Bultmann, *History*, pp. 284ff.; H. Anderson, *Jesus and Christian Origins* (1964), pp. 192ff. [hereafter, *Jesus*]; Pannenberg, *Jesus*, pp. 88ff.

and their advent hope. It is unlikely that the rehearsal of Jesus' words and actions which gave meaning to this early Christian ceremony merely called to mind the events on that night "when Jesus was betrayed." The historical setting of the Last Supper, within the story of the passion which it interpreted, would have been provided. The worship then as well as the preaching of the earliest Christians influenced the formation of the passion narrative and the selection and preservation of various stories supporting faith in the resurrection.

Stories Concerning Jesus and John the Baptist

Interest in the relation of the missions of Jesus and of John the Baptist tended to fix in the memory of Jesus' disciples incidents dating from the beginning of his Ministry. The early *kerygma* emphasized that Jesus' messiahship was heralded by the martyred prophet. Moreover, the similarities and differences between the baptismal rites of the disciples of John and the earliest followers of Jesus drew attention to the actions and the proclamations of the two men. Some of the gospel tradition concerning John was probably shaped by a rivalry which developed between Christians and the disciples of John. But the principal interest which led to the preservation of much important information about John and his relation to Jesus is doubtless reflected in the summaries in Acts of the early preaching: Jesus' messiahship was confirmed by the witness of the word of God spoken through the prophet John. The role of John was that of herald or forerunner of the Messiah.

God's Promised Salvation and Jesus' Mighty Works

We have seen that the earliest witnesses called attention to "the signs and wonders" which God wrought in the Ministry of Jesus the Messiah. In the description of Jewish eschatologies in Chapter 4 notice was taken of the belief that when the new age dawned the power of Satan or Belial would be overcome by the power of God. As in former days, so at "the end of the days," God would reveal his power and saving purpose unto Israel by mighty acts and by His outstretched arm. For the earliest Christians, Jesus' mighty works were essential tokens that these last days were at hand. Doubtless, many incidents drawn from Jesus' healing Ministry were recalled and reported again and again by the earliest preachers, and the form and content of these stories were influenced by the various scriptures associated with "the end of the days" in popular Jewish eschatology.

This perspective of the earliest witnesses makes improbable the view that the miracle stories were related merely to prove Jesus' supernatural power, or to support the authority of his teachings, or to illustrate his sympathetic and compassionate nature. The powers manifested in Jesus' Ministry were proclaimed to awaken faith in the eschatological fulfillment of God's saving power, revealed for the redemption of Israel.[10]

[10] T. W. Manson, *Jesus the Messiah* (1946), pp. 56ff.; A. Richardson, *The Miracle-Stories of the Gospels* (1941), pp. 16ff. [hereafter, *Miracle Stories*]. Note Acts 3:1–16; R. H. Fuller, *Interpreting the Miracles* (1963), pp. 46ff.

Early Interest in Decisive Moments in Jesus' Ministry

It is sometimes supposed that in the absence of any practical need for, or interest in, a connected story, the true course of events of Jesus' Ministry was forgotten in the decades following Easter. Consequently the element of chronology in the Gospels is the result of the editorial joining of originally unconnected stories. The earliest preachers usually did not tell the story of Jesus' Ministry from its beginning to its close, nor show how one incident followed upon another as cause and effect. If the detailed itinerary of Jesus' Ministry had been given prominence in the preaching of the first generation of Christians, the outlines and plans of the Four Gospels would be more uniform than they are. In none of them is the sequential pattern of events unbroken. Yet it is very unlikely that there ever was a time in the early Church when all interest was lacking in the succession of events.[11] The passion story itself raised questions concerning previous phases of Jesus' Ministry. What had Jesus done and said to provoke the hostility which confronted him when he came to Jerusalem? Was Jesus forced to visit the city, or did he go there of his own accord? Did his death come as a surprise? If he journeyed there voluntarily did he give his disciples any reason for doing so? In order to answer such questions as these, the earliest disciples would need to recall brief sequences of the Ministry.

THE APOSTLES' TEACHING

According to Acts, the earliest converts "devoted themselves to the apostles' teaching."[12] What was the nature of this teaching which accompanied and followed upon the apostles' proclamation? According to some scholars a clear distinction can be made between the *kerygma* and *didache* (teaching) of the early Church. Whereas the *kerygma* proclaimed the good news of God concerning Jesus the Messiah, and had for its object the interpretation of his coming, the *didache* set forth the nature of man's response to the gospel, and had for its object the interpretation of the moral demands of the new life of obedience to Jesus as Lord.[13] This distinction, if drawn too sharply, can hardly be maintained. The author of Acts associates the apostles' teaching with their *koinonia* (their "fellowship," or more probably, their "sharing" of all things), as also with the breaking of bread and the prayers. The early Christian teaching included instruction in the moral practices of the order, but the religious rites of the community must also have been subjects for teaching.

As a basis for the authority of their teaching, the apostles made repeated

---

[11] O. Piper, "The Origin of the Gospel Pattern," *JBL* LXXVIII, pt. II (1959): 115ff.; Taylor, *Formation*, pp. 38ff., 174f.; C. H. Dodd, "Framework of the Gospel Narrative," *New Testament Studies* (1953), pp. 1-11; R. H. Fuller, *The Mission and Achievement of Jesus* (1954), pp. 51ff. [hereafter, *Mission*]; H. Riesenfeld, "The Gospel Tradition and Its Beginnings," *Studia Evangelica:* Bd. 73, pp. 61ff.

[12] Acts 2:42.

[13] C. H. Dodd, *Gospel and Law* (1951), pp. 10ff.; Heard, *Intro.*, pp. 31f.

reference to sayings of Jesus. Moreover, in their disputations with fellow Jews, in their interpretations of scripture, and in their rejection of certain of the traditions of the elders, appeal was made to pronouncements of Jesus.

Jesus' Parables and Other Sayings

According to the earliest Gospels, Jesus' characteristic manner of teaching was by parable. Many of these parables were told and retold because of their immediate relevance to problems confronting the early Church. Our sources show that Jesus also used similitudes in his teaching. For example, in speaking of the manner in which gifts should be offered to the poor, Jesus said, "sound no trumpet before you as the hypocrites do in the synagogues and the streets that they may be praised by men."[14] Sometimes Jesus made a point by using a terse paradox, such as, "many that are first will be last and the last first."[15]

In order to clarify the appropriateness of the parables and other pictorial teachings of Jesus the apostles would often provide a brief narrative setting for them in his Ministry. The pronouncement of Jesus was the center of interest, however, and close attention was not given to questions of time or place, or to the names or numbers of persons involved. Nevertheless, many facts about Jesus were preserved as the setting for some authoritative saying of Jesus.[16]

Not all of the parables and shorter sayings of Jesus depended for their meaning upon a memory of their context in Jesus' Ministry. Doubtless many of Jesus' words were directly applicable to new situations. Moreover, in their eagerness to support their own points of view by appealing to Jesus, or to scripture, it is possible that some of the earliest teachers of the Church occasionally constructed a fitting word and ascribed it to Jesus. It is quite possible also that some early Christians, who had not themselves heard Jesus teach, unintentionally expanded the traditions concerning him.

In the course of the discussion above, a question of great importance has arisen: To what extent have the experiences of the early Church influenced the record of Jesus' actions and words? Was a truly historical impression of Jesus' Ministry preserved during the period between Easter and the earliest written records?

THE METHOD, VALUES, AND LIMITATIONS OF "FORM CRITICISM"

Students of the Gospels have long recognized that Jesus is known through the medium of a tradition which was transmitted by word of mouth for some time. In recent years, this period has been much investigated, and a critical method has been developed for studying the preliterary stages of the gospel tradition. This method originated in Germany and received the name *Formgeschichte* (form-

[14] Matt. 6:2.
[15] Mark 10:31; cf. Matt. 10:39; 23:12.
[16] Heard, *Intro.*, p. 31.

history). In English-speaking countries the method is commonly known as "form criticism." Two of the pioneer form critics were Martin Dibelius and Rudolf Bultmann.[17] It is not possible in any brief statement concerning form criticism to do justice to the contributions of these and other scholars who have developed and refined the method. A description of form criticism can give some assessment of its values as well as its limitations. The effects of form criticism upon the study of the Gospels have been far-reaching.

The following axioms disclose the method and purposes of form criticism.

(a) The stories and sayings of Jesus were first circulated in small independent units. This assumption rests upon the observation that many of the stories in the Gospels are linked by vague chronological or geographical connections which appear to be editorial. These secondary passages are easily detected in Mark because of the abrupt transitions in this Gospel; they are obscured by the more skillful editing of Matthew and Luke.[18] Yet some of the same incidents appear in different settings in the Gospels and bear out the view that the evangelists had stories before them "like a heap of unstrung pearls."

Most form critics agree that the account of Jesus' passion circulated as a connected story from the earliest days, for the reasons noted above. The narrative of passion week is thus a noteworthy exception to the first "rule" in form critical research. Indeed, the passion story was probably the nucleus about which accumulated, in snowball fashion, various fragments of tradition concerning Jesus, preserved without certain reference to the situations which had occasioned them.[19]

(b) These self-contained stories found in the Gospels can be classified according to their literary forms or types. This assumption rests upon the observed fact that the oral traditions and literary presentations of primitive cultures follow relatively fixed forms and definite styles. It is claimed that "no matter what folk's tradition be under scrutiny . . . similar units reappear—similar not so much in content as in structure, length and tendency. In other words, a given folk at a given time is likely to use a limited number of types of unit, into one or another of which by an instinctive mnemonic economy it pours the content of each particular tradition. These several types are the forms or categories from which form criticism gets its name."[20]

There has been wide agreement as to the identification of two common forms of narrative tradition in the Gospels, although the labels for them have been various.

The Pronouncement Story: Pronouncement stories contain a briefly narrated scene in which there is a unity of time and place. The scene serves as a frame for an

---

[17] *Form Criticism: A New Method of New Testament Research,* ed. F. C. Grant (1934) [hereafter, *Form Criticism*]; R. Bultmann, "A New Approach to the Synoptic Gospels," *Journ. of Rel.* V, no. 6 (1926): 337ff.; M. Dibelius, *From Tradition to Gospel,* trans. B. L. Woolf (1934); Bultmann, *History;* Taylor, *Formation.*

[18] Bultmann in F. C. Grant, *Form Criticism,* p. 26.

[19] The conclusion should not be hastily drawn that a tradition of the passion, once fixed, was handed on without changes. See Winter, *Trial of Jesus,* pp. 5f., and pp. 178f. below.

[20] K. Grobel, "Form Criticism," *IDB,* vol. 2, p. 320.

important saying of Jesus. The situation is depicted in the briefest possible way; for example, "one Sabbath he was going through the grain fields." Then follows a word or action which sets things in motion; for example, "his disciples began to pluck ears of grain." Some pronoucement of Jesus is reported; for example, "the Sabbath was made for man not man for the Sabbath." Usually the narrative ends with a brief note concerning the response of bystanders; for example, "the Pharisees went out and immediately took counsel . . . how to destroy him."

Several kinds of stories in the Gospels are presented in this form: the controversy stories;[21] brief conversations of Jesus with eager inquirers;[22] episodes ending in a word which sheds light upon Jesus' person.[23] In every case, the interest centers in a memorable saying of Jesus.

The Miracle Story: The typical miracle story of the Gospels is longer and more detailed than the pronouncement story. In order to portray both the seriousness of the suppliant's situation and wonder of Jesus' power, the circumstances are described; for example, the story of the raising of Jairus' daughter. The description of how the miracle occurred is concluded with a brief report of the results. Frequently the impressions upon bystanders are recorded as an additional means of confirming the miracle.[24]

Besides the pronouncement and the miracle story, the Gospels contain other units of narrative.

Legends: In their form, legends resemble the tales, or fragments of tales, concerning saints or holy men in Christian as well as in non-Christian traditions. In them a biographical interest is dominant. Typical of such stories are those concerning "the twelve," or other persons associated with Jesus; for example, Zacchaeus or Pilate's wife.[25] Some of the stories concerning Jesus directly are considered legendary in form; for example, Luke's story of Jesus at twelve years of age.[26]

"Myths": Some stories describe the words or the works of a divine being. The distinction between legend and myth is much disputed among form critics, but it is commonly agreed that, in their form, the stories of Jesus' temptation and transfiguration may be classified as myth.[27]

Parables and other forms reporting Jesus' teaching: The form of the parable has numerous parallels in Jewish tradition. Although the Hebrew word for parable describes numerous types of teaching, it commonly refers to a word picture drawn from some everyday human experience, intended to evoke a value judgment on the part of the hearer. The nonparabolic teaching of Jesus in the Gospels is more difficult to classify according to form. One form critic analyzes it into four

[21] E.g., Mark 2:1-12, 23-28; 3:1-6, etc.
[22] E.g., Mark 10:17-22; 12:28-34; Matt. 11:2-19, etc.
[23] E.g., Mark 6:1-6; 10:13-16; Luke 9:57-62; 11:27-28, etc.
[24] Mark 5:22-24, 35-43. Other examples, Mark 1:23-27, 40-45; 4:35-41; 5:25-34; Luke 7:11-17.
[25] Matt. 14:28-33; Luke 5:1-11; 19:1-10; Matt. 27:19. Dibelius, *Studies,* pp. 104ff.
[26] Luke 2:41-49.
[27] Matt. 4:1-11—Luke 4:1-13; Mark 9:2ff. and pars. Taylor's preference for "stories about Jesus" is understandable, but this is not a literary form.

groups:[28] One, the "wisdom" sayings of the proverbial type familiar to students of the Old Testament, of ancient Judaism, and of the teaching of Oriental sages generally;[29] two, prophetic and apocalyptic utterances which proclaimed the coming kingdom of God and called for repentance, promising salvation to those who are prepared and threatening the unrepentant;[30] three, sayings concerning the Torah and its traditional interpretations, similar in form to the familiar oracles of the prophets against external piety;[31] four, the first person singular sayings, the "I-type," conveying the teacher's sense of authority; for example, "behold, I send you forth . . ." "behold, I give unto you . . ."[32]

(c) The third assumption of form criticism is that the relative age and historical value of the gospel units of various types can be determined; that is, the preliterary history of the different forms or types. Once a gospel unit is identified and its stylistic characteristics noted, the necessary foundation has been laid for distinguishing the original story from its secondary amplifications. The age and value of a story is determined by its appearance, either as an original or "pure" form belonging to its type, or as a form bearing the marks of development.

It is admitted by all form critics that this stage of analysis is very difficult and "one to be pursued with great caution."[33] Yet, by observing how Matthew and Luke revise Mark, it is possible to deduce certain regularities in their editing process, and to assume that the same "laws" apply in the transmission of the precanonical tradition. A study of the manner in which the gospel tradition was handed down in the later Church, as evidenced in the "apocryphal gospels," also helps to identify the "laws" characteristic of the earliest development. Finally, the general principles which seem to govern the transmission of popular folk tales in a variety of cultures can be applied to early Christian tradition.

An example may show the significance of this critical procedure. In his study of the parable type, one scholar has stated that several "laws of transformation" can be observed in the tendency to embellish the details of a traditional parable, to transfer to the Christian community the meaning of parables originally addressed by Jesus to his opponents or to the crowd, to shift the emphasis of the parable from an eschatological to a hortatory interpretation, to interpret the parables allegorically, to form collections of parables which are alike, thus giving rise to a fusion of two or more of them, and to produce a change in the point of parables because of the change in setting, or by the addition of sayings which generalize their meaning. It is claimed that when such observations are taken into account it is then possible to recover the original meaning of the parables.[34]

(d) The fourth assumption of form criticism is one which openly or tacitly

---

[28]Bultmann, History, pp. 69ff.

[29]E.g., Matt. 6:34b; 12:34b; cf. Luke 14:7–11; Prov. 25:6f.

[30]Prophetic-type: Luke 10:23f.; 6:20f. Apocalyptic-type: Mark 13:24–27; Luke 17:26f.

[31]Mark 7:15; 10:11f.; Matt. 6:2–18.

[32]Matt. 10:16; Luke 10:19f.

[33]Bultmann in F. C. Grant, Form Criticism, pp. 28f.

[34]Jeremias, The Parables of Jesus, trans. S. H. Hooke (rev. ed., 1962), pp. 23ff. [hereafter, Parables].

guides the whole tedious undertaking of classifying literary units of the gospel tradition and of tracing the laws intrinsic to each type. It is the conviction that a "setting in life" for each unit may be found in the early Church, and that the witness of the earliest Christians determined both the form and, in many instances, the content of the stories in the Gospels.

In recent years, form criticism has been used as a method to recover the meaning for Jesus of his recorded deeds or words. Yet it was recognized by the early form critics that the step back to "the Jesus of history" involves the exercise of additional interests and methods, and can only be taken with the aid of other tools. They persisted in raising a more modest question which, they were convinced, was a prior one, and a question which could be answered with greater assurance: Why was this or that particular word or deed of Jesus *remembered,* and what led to its *modification,* by the earliest Christians?

So much for the methods of form criticism. A few words should be written about the positive contributions of this "school." For two reasons the values of form criticism have been overlooked or denied. In the first place, the earliest exponents of the method denied the historicity of the "editorial framework" of Mark's Gospel, and declared that the Gospels "do not enable us to know either the outer course of the life of Jesus or his inner development." [35] In the second place, extravagant claims were made concerning the utility of the method. For these reasons it was inevitable that form criticism should be condemned in certain quarters as an ephemeral thing, entirely negative and sometimes perverse. At the same time a truth was obscured which should have been obvious. Form criticism is a method which can be used by scholars of different theological persuasions. The element of a scholar's personal bias in any analysis cannot be disallowed. The application of the technique does not predetermine the results, nor does it lead inevitably to one set of conclusions. It is evident now that form criticism has not produced a "school" of theology.

Form criticism has demonstrated that each unit of the gospel tradition links Jesus' deeds and words with the faith and life of his followers. The witness of the early Church was not merely oriented toward the past history of a man who was dead, but to a present experience, and to a belief in the continuing importance of Jesus' work and words. Thus it was considered more important to obey Jesus than to retain in memory the precise words which he taught on any specific occasion. It was more important to appreciate the meaning of the Christian meal rite for the participant than to record precisely the proceedings of Jesus' Last Supper.

At no point did the preservers of the gospel tradition adopt the "detached view" of the historian or biographer who labors that the things of the past be remembered. Nor did early Christian curiosity dwell upon aspects of Jesus' personality which were of no importance to faith; for example, the color of his eyes and hair, the sound of his voice, or characteristic gestures when teaching. Form criticism reminds us that the earliest Christians never indulged "in scene painting for its

---

[35]Bultmann, "A New Approach . . . ," (see note 17 above), p. 359. See below, pp. 188ff.

own sake."[36] Neither did they base the validity of Jesus' teaching upon the verbal infallibility of their reports.[37]

Form critics have recognized that since each unit of the gospel tradition served some concrete religious interest, a definition of its setting in the life of the early Church defines the modern situation in which these stories are apt to be appreciated in their meaning and power. For example, Jesus' teaching on almsgiving is most germane when you give alms; the teaching on prayer, when you pray.[38]

Form critics have emphasized that the Gospels are a social possession. The traditions they contain are not the recollection of a few individuals, but represent the corporate testimony of a witnessing and worshiping community. Thus the possibility of fabrication by several persons of limited intelligence and comprehension is completely ruled out. But the point has more important implications. Personal reminiscences cherished by friends are often quite different from the corporate testimony which a group gives to its leader. In the latter instance the most valuable traditions are selected, culled, supported, and verified through constant repetition, and shaped into their most useful forms.[39]

Form criticism has demonstrated that the Gospels are valuable sources for knowledge of the earliest Christian churches. From a study of the various units in the Gospels, many interests and problems of the Palestinian communities, as well as the history of later developments, can be inferred. These results sometimes supplement and correct the data afforded by Acts and Paul's letters.[40]

These values are of considerable importance. At the same time, form criticism has serious limitations, which may now be indicated.

It is commonly believed that form critics have gone too far in ruling out all interest in the early Church in the course of events in Jesus' Ministry, or in the strategy of his actions.[41] It is not clear why the first generation of Christians should have been completely disinterested in an outline of Jesus' Ministry, whereas the second generation of believers felt a need for one. It is granted that the thinning of the ranks of eyewitnesses and the geographical expansion of the Church afforded an impulse for Gospel writing. Yet is it unlikely that the eyewitnesses left behind them only vivid recollections of particular happenings and isolated sayings, apart from any information concerning their setting. The broad outline of Jesus' Ministry must have become the common property of a large number of Christian teachers and communities.

Form critics have frequently overlooked the influence of "eyewitnesses and ministers of the word" (Luke 1:2). Some writers claim that the gospel was a

[36] R. H. Lightfoot, *The Gospel Message of St. Mark* (1950), p. 102 [hereafter, *Mark*]; P. Minear, "Form Criticism and Faith," *Religion in Life* 15, no. 1 (1945): 46ff. [hereafter *Rel. in Life*].

[37] Minear (see note 36 above), p. 48.

[38] Ibid., p. 47. "The Church not only remembered and reported facts. It lived them. If we have understood this, we are near to the secret of the Gospels." C. H. Dodd, *About the Gospels* (1950), p. 22.

[39] F. C. Grant, *Gospels*, pp. 1f.; Perry, *IB*, vol. 7, p. 71.

[40] K. Kundsin, "Primitive Christianity in the Light of Gospel Research," in F. C. Grant, *Form Criticism*, n.16, pp. 79ff.; Bultmann, *Theology*, vol. 1, pp. 33–62.

[41] See above, note 11.

product of unconscious "social processes." But it is positively misleading to suggest that the traditions concerning Jesus were left to the mercy of a group of anonymous, relatively illiterate people who were not aware that the events they had witnessed were epoch-making. Jesus' disciples placed a high premium upon veracity in reporting the essential elements in their tradition. Being Jewish, they were possessed of a conservative mentality. It is doubtful that their mental attitudes can be compared to those of naively credulous storytellers in many primitive societies.

This consideration has led two Scandinavian scholars to question the appropriateness of several important form critical assumptions and procedures. It is urged that the true setting-in-life of the tradition of Jesus' words and deeds is the activity of Jesus himself who, as a teacher, trained his circle of disciples to memorize and recite as "holy word" those things he wished them to learn and impart to others.[42] The picture of Jesus as rabbi, which these Scandinavian scholars have drawn, does not seem to correspond either to the situation in ancient Judaism or the early Church.[43]

It is, however, the merit of these studies that they stress the importance of Jesus' impact upon his disciples as a formative influence upon the gospel tradition. If the setting of the more important incidents or sayings had been seriously dislocated in the oral narrations of Christians, Jesus' own disciples were in a position to restore them to their proper setting.

It should never be forgotten that Jesus' first disciples exerted an influence upon the first generation of Christians far greater than their numbers.[44] Some of these apostles visited communities in which the gospel traditions were being shaped. They would not have permitted radical displacements of events; for example, of Peter's confession of Jesus as the Christ, which one form critic places after Easter.[45] Besides this, Jesus' sayings are cast in forms easy to remember. The tenacity of the Oriental memory should not be forgotten when modern examples of distorted storytelling, based upon mere memory, are given.

Form criticism holds the early Christians responsible for "creating" more of the stories and sayings of the Gospels than is likely. It is one thing to ask what motive the early Church might have had for reporting a particular deed or saying. It is another to ask what motive led to its invention. Yet some form critics seem to assume that the questions are the same. It is much more probable that the interests of the early Christians led them to select, interpret, and apply stories

[42] H. Riesenfeld, "The Gospel Tradition and Its Beginnings," *Studia Evangelica:* Bd. 73, pp. 43ff.; Gerhardsson, *Memory and Manuscript.*

[43] M. Smith, "A Comparison of Early Christian and Early Rabbinic Tradition," *JBL* 82 (1963): 169ff.; W. D. Davies, "Reflections on a Scandinavian Approach to 'The Gospel Tradition,'" *Nov. Test. Suppl.* 6 (1962): 3ff.; Anderson, *Jesus,* pp. 309ff.; Betz, *Jesus,* pp. 20ff.

[44] The tendency, beginning with M. Dibelius, to discount the role of the twelve in the shaping of the early Jesus-tradition has been countered by Jacob Jervell, who appeals to Paul's letters for support of his thesis that "from the beginning the early church possessed an apostolic tradition." *New Testament Abstracts* 8 (1963): 56f. [hereafter, *NT Abstracts*].

[45] Bultmann, *History,* pp. 257ff., 427. This is not to deny that theological motives have prompted some arrangements which do not permit a recovery of the original setting; see pp. 180ff; 188ff.

of Jesus, than that the same interests led them to create stories. If the latter had been the case one might expect to find in the Gospels echoes of Paul's ideas, or a closer identity of the teaching of the Gospels and Acts. Would we not expect to find Jesus and his disciples "speaking in tongues," or engaging in disputations concerning Gentiles and their membership in the community of Jesus and his disciples? [46] Again, if a large part of the tradition was created by communities *lacking historical perspective* and only giving expression to their own interests, how does one account for the presence in the Gospels of stories derogatory to revered leaders of the early Church? Or what of sayings in the same Gospels which seemingly compromise the conceptions of Christ's person which prevailed when the Gospels were written? [47]

In the application of the form critical method, it is commonly assumed that the gospel tradition chiefly affords information concerning the earliest Christians. The Gospels are valuable sources for the recovery of Christian beginnings, but their primary value lies in their witness to what Jesus said and did. The tendency on the part of form critics to rule out historical or biographical interests, as though these were no part of the evangelists' purpose, is a skeptical defeatism concerning the history of Jesus. One writer has described this defeatism as "a transient nightmare of gospel criticism." [48] Happily, in many quarters, scholars are wakening from this nightmare, and expressing a sober confidence that the "quest for the historical Jesus" in the Gospels is not a dead-end passage.[49]

A final weakness of form criticism is the inability of the method satisfactorily to classify all of the units of the gospel tradition. Some material in the Gospels does not yield the allegedly "pure" forms which must be restored if the study is to recover the original settings. There is material in the Gospels intractable to form critical analysis. This raises the question whether or not form can be the decisive factor in tracing to its origin the preliterary history of the tradition in all of its parts.

The conclusions of form critics often run beyond the limited literary evidence upon which they are made to rest. Questions concerning the substance of a story are confused with the history of its form. This confusion has been introduced into the study by using terms to classify stories which are more descriptive of the scholar's judgment concerning the stories' contents than their forms. To identify as "mythical" various stories whose forms are not identical is surely to express a historical judgment concerning their substance. This tendency to pass from judgments based on form to judgments based on substance is especially evident in the form critical analyses of the miracle stories. A critical mind should ask

[46] B. S. Easton, *The Gospel Before the Gospels* (1928), pp. 85ff.; T. W. Manson, "Present-day Research in the Life of Jesus," in Davies and Daube, *Background,* pp. 214f.

[47] E.g., Mark 8:32f.; 9:19, 34; 14:26ff.; T. W. Manson, *Jesus the Messiah,* p. 50. Perrin (*Rediscovering,* pp. 25ff.) dismisses these aforementioned "weaknesses" of form criticism on the assumption "that the early Church absolutely identified the risen Lord of her experience with the historical Jesus . . . and that the modern [Western] distinction is quite foreign to the early Church." The validity of this "absolute" assumption is, of course, the principal question at issue. See further pp. 235ff.

[48] D. M. Baillie, *God Was in Christ* (1948), pp. 54ff.

[49] See further, pp. 236ff.

whether or not any particular miracle happened, but the answer depends upon broader considerations than a literary analysis of the miracle-story type. To describe a story as a "pure" or a "mixed" type hardly provides a sufficient criterion for distinguishing the credible from the incredible.

THE BEGINNING OF WRITTEN ACCOUNTS

Luke's Gospel begins with the declaration that "many have undertaken to compile a narrative of the things which have been accomplished among us . . ." (1:1). We have no way of knowing the number of such writings in existence at the time (ca. A.D. 80–85?), nor when the traditions concerning Jesus were first committed to writing. Yet many scholars agree in identifying one of these "narratives" earlier than Luke's Gospel. Few doubt that he knew Mark's Gospel and used it as a source for his "orderly account." It is also probable that Luke had access to another source which was available to Matthew.

Source criticism of the Gospels in the modern period is a development of research upon "the synoptic problem." For more than a century scholars have been convinced that the measure of agreement among Matthew, Mark, and Luke can be explained only as the result of literary interdependence. These three Gospels have come to be known as the *Synoptic Gospels* because it has been judged that the three evangelists "view together" the Ministry of Jesus. The evidence upon which this assumption rests may be readily seen by placing the three Gospels in parallel columns, forming a synopsis or "harmony." Comparative study reveals striking differences as well as similarities among them. Thus "the synoptic problem" is: how can these similarities and differences be explained most satisfactorily?

During the course of the nineteenth century every conceivable relation between the Gospels was explored, some scholars working together, others independently. By the turn of the twentieth century a solution of the synoptic problem had been reached. It is known as "the two-document hypothesis." This theory declares (a) that Mark was the first of the Gospels to be written, and that Mark's narrative was used by the writers of Matthew and Luke as a source; (b) that Matthew and Luke also used a second document which may be described as a compendium of Jesus' teaching. This second document is commonly referred to by the symbol Q (*Quelle* is German for "source").

The primacy of Mark and the probability of Q explain the striking resemblances among the three synoptics and partially explain the similarities between Matthew and Luke which distinguish these Gospels from Mark. The evidence for these statements is here set forth:[50]

The priority of Mark: The following considerations provide a cumulative case supporting the priority of Mark:

(a) Common subject matter. The Greek text of Mark contains 661 verses. Of these, 601 are found in Matthew and in Luke. Matthew reproduces 90 percent

---

[50] A detailed statement of the case is presented in B. H. Streeter, *The Four Gospels* (1924), pp. 151ff.; F. C. Grant, *Gospels,* pp. 40ff.; Feine-Behm-Kümmel, *Intro.,* pp. 35ff., 42ff.; Perry, *IB,* vol. 7, pp. 61ff.

of the subject matter of Mark; Luke better than half of it. Only three of Mark's 88 paragraphs are missing from the other two.[51]

(b) Common outline. The sequence of Mark's narrative is supported either by Mark or by Luke. In the earlier portions of his Gospel, Luke adheres to Mark's order; in the latter portions of Matthew, agreement with Mark's outline is noteworthy. Where either departs from Mark, the other is usually found supporting him, and there is no case where Matthew and Luke agree together against Mark in a point of arrangement.[52] It is also noteworthy that the parallelism in the order of Matthew and Luke begins where Mark begins and ends where Mark ends.

(c) Common order extends to words and sentences. In spite of the fact that Matthew frequently abbreviates the source material derived from Mark, a characteristic to be discussed below, it has been estimated that Matthew employs 51 percent of the actual words of Mark.[53] Although Luke revises the rough style of Mark more extensively than does Matthew, it is significant that many of Mark's details, omitted by Matthew, are found in Luke. As a result, where it appears that Luke is dependent upon Mark, slightly over 50 percent of Mark's words are reproduced. The proportion of verbal agreement of Luke with Mark rises to 69 percent when words of Jesus are quoted.[54]

(d) Concurrence in the use of unusual words. The fact that rare words and rough constructions found in Mark reappear in Matthew and Luke calls for special attention. This linguistic data can be appreciated only when viewed in a Greek synopsis, but its importance cannot fail to be noticed by anyone. It is not likely that these rare words and harsh constructions were transmitted to three independent writers through an oral tradition which was subject to the transformations noted in the foregoing discussion of factors present in this period, nor is it likely that Mark "butchered" the grammatical constructions of Matthew and Luke.

(e) The meager amount of agreement between Matthew and Luke. Alongside the data listed above should be placed facts such as the following: Although Luke's agreement with Mark is over 50 percent, his agreement with Matthew in the same sections declines to 42 percent. Luke's agreement with Matthew against Mark is less than 6 percent.[55]

Such evidence as that discussed has led a majority to conclude that Matthew and Luke made use of Mark. It is sometimes declared that their copies of Mark must have been different from the text of modern editions upon which these

[51]Could these data point to Mark's use of Matt. or Luke? This is improbable since Mark's narrative is the more detailed. Is it credible that Mark omitted much that is in Matt. and Luke in order to "pad his stories," then introduced vivid but often inconsequential detail? Mark takes 194 words for the feeding of the five thousand; Matt. and Luke, 157.

[52]Streeter, Four Gospels, pp. 151, 161f.

[53]Oxford Studies in the Synoptic Problem (1911), pp. 85ff. [hereafter, Oxford Studies].

[54]Streeter, Four Gospels, p. 160; Perry, IB, vol. 7, pp. 62f.

[55]Statistical summaries may fail to remove the suspicion that more might be made of the alternative that Luke used Matt. or vice versa. For those weighing the first of these—the more probable of the two—let it be asked, is it credible that Luke carefully separated Jesus' sayings from their context in Matt. and relocated them, removing all trace of Matthean interpretations?; Cf. R. T. Simpson, "The Major Agreements of Matthew and Luke against Mark," NTS 12 (1966): 273ff.

comparisons are based. If the common source used by Matthew and Luke was our present Mark, then we may ask what explanation is provided, first, for their omission of whole sections of Mark's text, and second, for the minor agreements of Matthew and Luke against our present Mark. One answer to these questions is based on the assumption that an earlier edition of Mark ("Ur-Marcus," or Proto-Mark) was used by the late evangelists. This theory has failed to commend itself to most source critics. The omissions of Mark can be explained upon other assumptions, and the minor agreements may be attributable either to accidental concurrence due to the evangelists' improvements of Mark's diction, or to a reflection of similar theological views or influences. It is also probable that there occurred some accidental assimilation between the text of Matthew and Luke in the process of copying.[56]

The probability of Q: Remove the Markan passages from Matthew and Luke, and approximately two hundred verses remain which parallel one another closely. On the basis of the criteria listed above it has been argued that a second source was employed by the first and third evangelists. As noted above, this source has been designated by the symbol Q. The existence of Q cannot be other than hypothetical since it is not extant, and can be recovered only from Matthew and Luke.

The difficulties of reconstructing this lost writing can be appreciated when we consider the use of Mark. A reconstruction of Mark out of identical passages in Matthew and Luke would result in a Gospel three-fourths the length of its present text. Moreover, the order in which Matthew and Luke use their common, non-Markan material is very different, as may be seen in the outline on page 176. Even though it is probable that Luke has ordinarily preserved the original order of his sources, it can never be more than a probability that this was the case in his use of Q.

It is not surprising that there should be wide differences of opinion concerning the nature of Q.[57] Some scholars use the symbol merely to refer to that collection of stereotyped tradition used by Matthew and Luke in addition to Mark, and hold that part of this tradition may well have reached the synoptists through independent channels of oral traditions. There are others who are willing to dispense altogether with the hypothesis of a written source. This is surely going too far. Yet it is a natural reaction against the subjectivity of some who have claimed that Q was originally a "Gospel."

Perhaps Q should be used as a symbol designating only those verbal parallels

[56] Streeter, *Four Gospels,* pp. 168ff., 293ff. Cf. J. P. Brown, "An Early Revision of the Gospel of Mark," *JBL* LXXVIII, pt. III (1959): 215ff.; Feine-Behm-Kümmel, *Intro.,* pp. 49f. W. R. Farmer marshals the arguments of a minority who still question the fundamental thesis of Mark's priority (*The Synoptic Problem,* 1964), contending that Mark depends on Matt. and Luke, and Luke on Matt. He argues that in reaching the two-document solution of the synoptic problem unwarranted theological hypotheses have forced the evidence into "objective proofs." Yet Farmer and others who have seriously questioned the consensus of synoptic source criticism have failed to establish more satisfactory alternative solutions. Cf. Perrin, *Rediscovering,* pp. 34f.

[57] V. Taylor, "The Original Order of Q," in *New Testament Essays,* ed. A. J. B. Higgins (1959), pp. 246ff.; Feine-Behm-Kümmel, *Intro.,* pp. 50ff.; Tödt, "Q in Recent Research," in *Son of Man,* pp. 235ff.

in Matthew and Luke that were not derived from Mark. It is not mere fancy, however, which supposes that the content of Q may have extended beyond the limits of these parallels. Since Matthew and Luke omitted some things from Mark, is it not likely that they were also selective in their use of a second source? Some passages found only in the First or Third Gospel are embedded in a complex of the Q tradition, and resemble it in style and thought. It is reasonable to hold that such material originally belonged to the Q source. Moreover, it is easier to explain the absence of some of these sayings from one Gospel as omissions from Q than to suppose that their location in the other Gospel is merely editorial.[58]

It is sometimes supposed that Q was used in the composition of Mark. Passages in Mark which echo sayings in Q are the Beelzebub controversy (3:22–30), sayings of Jesus on the responsibilities of witnesses (4:21–25), teaching in connection with a mission of the twelve (6:7–11), sayings concerning discipleship (9:35–37, 41–50), and condemnation of the Pharisees (12:38–40). A theory of literary dependence is neither a necessary nor a probable explanation for these resemblances. At least some of the sayings of Jesus collected in Q must have circulated apart from this source, in the oral tradition of the Church.

The outline of Q which is given below is rigorously conservative. Several passages found in other reconstructions have been omitted where there is considerable debate.[59] Although minimal, this outline may enable the reader to visualize the content and arrangement of the document, as well as the different order of its sections in the two Gospels.

AN OUTLINE OF THE SAYINGS SOURCE

	Luke	*Matthew*
A. John the Baptist and Jesus:		
1. The proclamation of John	3:7b–9, 16b–17	3:7b–12
2. The temptations of Jesus	4:1b–12	4:1–10
3. Jesus' teaching	6:20–49	(cf. parallels 5–7; *10:24f; 12:33–35; 15:14*)
4. Response to Jesus' proclamation		
a. Centurion's faith	7:6b–9	8:8–10
b. Emissaries from John	7:19, 22f, 24b–28, 31–35	*11:3–11, 16–19*
B. Jesus and his disciples:		
5. Two applicants	9:57b–60	8:19–22

---

[58] Note Luke 9:60b–62 (cf. Matt. 8:19–22—Luke 9:57–62); F. C. Grant, *Gospels*, pp. 45f.

[59] F. C. Grant, *Gospels*, pp. 59f.; T. W. Manson, *The Sayings of Jesus* (1949), Table of Contents [hereafter, *Sayings*]. For a conjectural reconstruction of the text of Q, A. M. Hunter, *The Work and Words of Jesus* (1950), pp. 131ff. [hereafter, *Work and Words*]; A. Harnack, *Sayings of Jesus*, trans. J. R. Wilkinson (1908), pp. 253ff.

		Luke	Matthew
	6. Mission charge	10:2f, 5, 12	9:37f;
			10:11, 15–16a
	7. Woe to Chorazin, etc.	10:13–15	11:21–23
	8. Privileges of discipleship	10:21b–24	11:25–27; 13:16f
		11:9–13	7:7–11
C.	Jesus and his opponents:		
	9. The Beelzebub controversy	11:17–18a, 19f, 20–23	12:25–28, 30
	10. The return of the Evil Spirit	11:24–26	12:43–45
	11. The sign for this generation	11:29b–32	12:39f; 42, 41
	12. Concerning the light	11:34	7:22–23a
	13. Against the Pharisees	11:39, 42f, 49–51	23:25, 23, 6, 34–36
	14. Fearless confession	12:5–9	10:28b–33
D.	The future:		
	15. Cares and the coming kingdom	12:22b–31, 34	6:25–33, 21
	16. Watchfulness and faithfulness	12:39–40, 42–46	24:43–51a
	17. Parables of mustard seed and leaven	13:18f, 21	13:31b–33
	18. The table fellowship in the kingdom	13:28f	8:11f
	19. Lament over Jerusalem	13:34f	23:37–39
	20. Discipleship in the time of crisis	16:13, 16–18	6:24; 11:12f; 5:18, 32
	21. The day of the Son of man	17:24, 26f, 30, 37b	24:27, 37–39, 28

Upon the assumption that Q was a written source, various views concerning its origin have been advanced. Several scholars have conjectured that Q was originally a compendium of Jesus' teaching composed in Aramaic by Matthew the disciple of Jesus. This theory, and the fragment of second-century tradition upon which it rests, will be noted in the next chapter. Suffice it here to say that the hypothesis is unconvincing. Concerning the date and the place of origin of Q, one can only appeal in inferences from its content and from its use by Matthew and Luke. The fact that Q contains so little controversial matter—90 percent of it is positive teaching—has led many to conclude that it was composed as a manual of instruction for converts. Its teaching was probably intended for Gentile Christians. Antioch has been considered the most likely place for its origin. "Probably a date between A.D. 50 and 60 would command most general assent for the writing of Q."[60]

[60] Heard, *Intro.*, p. 52; T. W. Manson, *Sayings*, p. 20; Feine-Behm-Kümmel, *Intro.*, pp. 55ff., 85.

Other Types of Records

Having identified two of the sources used by Matthew and Luke in the composition of their Gospels is it now possible to locate others? What about Mark's Gospel? Is there evidence that the earliest evangelist relied on written as well as oral traditions? Affirmative answers may be given to these questions; yet anyone seeking to reconstruct the contents of documents earlier than Mark and Q must resort to speculation. At the same time it is highly probable that certain *types of writing* can be identified.

On the basis of observations concerning the collection of oral traditions, it can safely be surmised that the first "narratives" concerning Jesus were not literary productions. These came into existence as the by-product of the preaching and teaching of the Church. Various situations in the earliest communities determined the types of writing which would be needed. For example, brief fragments of the gospel tradition might have been written for reading by Jewish–Christian teachers as a supplement to the synagogue lessons. Perhaps before very long, such lessons were substituted for readings from the scriptures. Other fragments might have been compiled for traveling missionaries or other "ministers of the word." With the aid of such documents, teachers could illustrate the *kerygma,* instruct new converts in "the apostles' teaching," and inspire them to endure persecutions.

For the most part, these earliest writings would have circulated in the form of brief "tracts" or "fly-sheets." Yet, as time passed, longer and more complex writings might have been composed for the immediate use of particular congregations, or for the purpose of preserving their treasured traditions. Some scholars have supposed that such precanonical groupings lay before the evangelists as documents, and were inserted en bloc into the Gospels. We cannot be certain of this. Some of these traditions were perhaps grouped in the oral period and committed to writing for the first time by the evangelists themselves. A margin of uncertainty must be allowed in the matter. Yet it may be concluded that some complexes of gospel tradition had been written down before the Gospels were composed. Several of these may be listed below.

Passion narratives: As noted earlier, the passion narrative was very probably a noteworthy exception to the rule that the earliest stories concerning Jesus were self-contained and circulated separately. The constant repetition of the passion narrative in early Christian preaching and worship gave it a form and an outline. The content of the passion story was never so rigidly fixed as to preclude either abbreviations or additions in detail. The passion stories which became established at different centers would reflect these variations. At the same time, the interchange from one community to another of early church leaders served as a check upon fanciful developments. Details prized in one community would be introduced into the passion story of another. The story told in the most important churches, where tradition was associated with the testimony of one of "the twelve," would tend to replace local versions.[61]

[61] Taylor, *Formation,* pp. 170f.

After the recording of the passion narrative in the Gospel of Mark this version seems to have become normative for many Christian communities. Although the accounts of the passion in the Gospels of Matthew and Luke contain some additional material, they presuppose confidence in the Markan version. Numerous attempts have been made to trace the sources, or various strata of tradition, underlying Mark's "classic version" of the passion. While no agreement has been reached as to its precise content, it is commonly held that Mark's outline rests upon a narrative which had been earlier compiled out of Palestinian traditions for the needs of the Christian community in Rome. To this primary source, Mark added a group of stories connected with Peter as well as other stories, such as the anointing of Jesus, and his trial before the priests.[62]

Luke's Gospel probably provides further evidence for the existence of pre-canonical documents containing the story of Jesus' passion. In his final chapters, Luke has treated his Markan source with greater freedom than elsewhere. Verbal correspondence with Mark is about twice as great in Luke's account of Jesus' Ministry as it is in his account of the passion, and Luke introduces almost twice as many additions when he tells the story of the passion. Most significant of all is Luke's transposition of Mark's order of words and of incidents, four times as freely in his passion narrative as in following Mark's story of the Ministry. This evidence has led many to conclude that Luke had access to a passion narrative in addition to the one he found in Mark. It is possible that his "source" consisted in a cycle of oral tradition, but it is more probable that Luke had before him an alternate document.[63]

Allowing for uncertainty in respect to details one may conclude that, in the writing of Jesus' passion, Mark and Luke depended upon others who had earlier undertaken "to compile a narrative of the things which had been accomplished."

Testimony tracts: The Gospels frequently cite passages from the Old Testament as having been fulfilled by the events of Jesus' Ministry. It is probable that some of these texts were drawn by their writers from "testimony tracts." Some have been convinced that a Christian anthology of scriptural proof texts was composed in the primitive church. Yet sufficient evidence for this claim is lacking. The publication of testimony books was a later result, not the presupposition, of the work of the earliest preachers.[64] Yet some of the testimony tradition of the early Church was probably written down for propaganda purposes before the composition of the Gospels. Matthew affords evidence for the existence of one such collection.[65] It is not necessary to suppose that a need for such tracts was first

---

[62] Taylor, *Mark*, pp. 524, 653ff. Cf. W. L. Knox, *Sources of the Synoptic Gospels:* vol. I, *Mark* (1953), who judges Mark's passion story to be a conflation of two sources, one of which (following E. Meyer) is called "the Twelve Source," pp. 17ff., 115ff. [hereafter, *Sources*].

[63] A. M. Perry, *The Sources of Luke's Passion Narrative* (1920) [hereafter, *Luke's Passion Narrative*]; *IB*, vol. 7, p. 65; J. C. Hawkins, "St. Luke's Use of Mark's Gospel," in *Oxford Studies*, pp. 84ff. See V. Taylor's articles on recent defenders of a pre-Lukan passion narrative: "Theologians of Our Times," *Exp. T.* 74 (1962–63): 77ff., 262ff. Cf. J. M. Creed, *The Gospel According to St. Luke* (1950), pp. lxiii f. [hereafter, *St. Luke*]. See further, below, pp. 219ff.

[64] Dodd, *Scriptures*, p. 126.

[65] See below, pp. 203ff.

felt in bookish Gentile communities. Fragments of scrolls found in Qumran Cave 4 bear witness to the fact that Judean Essenes had composed miscellaneous collections of testimonies to support their eschatological views, as well as the verse-by-verse midrash pesher upon books of prophecy and the Psalms.[66]

Early genealogical lists: In confirmation of the claim that Jesus is the Messiah, the earliest preachers pointed to his Davidic ancestry. We have seen that very few of the Old Testament passages which described the Messiah as Son of David were preserved from the earliest traditions. Yet stress was placed upon the conviction that Jesus "was descended from David according to the flesh" (Rom. 1:3). Two lists tracing Jesus' descent through Joseph are found in the Gospels (Matt. 1:1–17; Luke 3:23–38). Differences between them suggest independent sources, and peculiar features in them suggest a documentary origin.

Traditions relating John the Baptist and Jesus: Interest expressed in early forms of the *kerygma* in the persons of Jesus and John the Baptist certainly gave rise to cycles of tradition concerning the two men. Stories of Jesus and John begin Mark's narrative as well as the Q source. Efforts have been made to break up this Q tradition into several shorter tracts. There are some reasons for concluding that the stories of Jesus and John may originally have been independent.[67]

Tracts reporting Jesus' mighty works: It is likely that the need for illustrating the early Christian proclamation that "Jesus went about doing good, because God was with him" led to collections of miracle stories. Single stories such as were reported orally might have satisfied the popular demand; yet there is some evidence that larger units had been compiled before the writing of the Gospels. Mark 4:35–5:43, which consists of four miracle stories, may be cited as an example. These stories illustrate various types of wonders wrought by Jesus, and probably a topical rather than a temporal sequence.[68]

Several other types of tracts listed below illustrate the thesis that collections of Jesus' teaching, as well as of deeds from the Ministry, had been written down before the composition of the Gospels.

Collections of conflict stories: The debate of Jesus with the synagogue continued unabated in the primitive Church. There is every reason to believe that the early Christians argued their points by appealing not to general principles, but to incidents from Jesus' ministry which preserved his typical sayings. As a result, stories reporting Jesus' sayings when opposed by the Pharisees tended to be grouped. The practical needs of the witnessing church for such collections overshadowed biographical interests and determined their forms. Two complexes of conflict stories in Mark invite attention (2:1–3:6, 11:27–12:37). In the arrangements and conclusions these sections contain prima-facie evidence that they are compilations earlier than Mark. Whether or not such "sources" were written or oral is uncertain. But it is probable that Mark knew these stories in the form of a tract and that he incorporated the tract into his narrative with a minimum of

[66]J. M. Allegro, "Fragments of a Qumran Scroll of Eschatological Midrashim," *JBL* LXXVII, pt. IV (1958): 350ff.; F. M. Cross, Jr., *Ancient Library,* pp. 218f., n. 39.

[67]W. L. Knox, *Sources,* vol. II, *St. Luke and St. Matthew* (1957), pp. 5f., 8.

[68]W. L. Knox, *Sources,* vol. I, pp. 39ff.; cf. Taylor, *Mark,* pp. 94f.

editing.[69] It is possible also that 7:1–23 represents a topical complex compiled earlier than Mark's Gospel, for Christian instruction or for use in disputations with the synagogue.[70]

Consider another block of tradition in the Gospels, commonly referred to as "the Beelzebub controversy" (Mark 3:22–27; Luke 11:17–18a, 19–20, and Matt. 12:25–28, 30). If this tradition was a pre-Markan tract, it was useful in answering the aspersions cast by members of the synagogue upon the early Christians' claim that Jesus' mighty works were evidence of his messiahship.[71]

Parable groupings: There are some indications that parable tracts had been compiled before the writing of the Gospels. Mark 4:1–34 provides an illustration. The interest and arrangement in this section is topical, and there are peculiarities in the text which are not characteristic of Mark. It is difficult to believe that oral tradition alone satisfactorily accounts for the transmission of this pre-Markan complex.[72]

It is possible that Luke's Gospel provides further evidence for the existence of parable tracts. The parable of the lost sheep, the lost coin, and the lost son (Luke 15) "form a sequence that may have been earlier than Luke's use of it."[73] The parable of the unjust judge, of the Pharisee and the publican, and of the pounds may have stood in another collection of three parables.

Tracts containing warnings and apocalyptic predictions: The first generation of Jewish-Christians experienced the mounting tensions leading up to the war of the Jews with Rome. Standing within, yet apart from, Judaism, they were faced with difficult decisions concerning involvement. Sayings of Jesus dealing with the fate of Jerusalem and the final issue of the coming tribulations greatly interested the early Christians. Sections of Mark and of Luke (Mark 13; Luke 21) are perhaps based upon tracts compiled by primitive Christians in Judea.

Literary analysis of Mark 13 has been complicated by the concern of scholars either to deny or to defend the authenticity of the entire discourse as one given by Jesus.[74] It is a popular theory that Mark 13:5–31 was a short apocalypse, composed by an unknown author in the sixties, which Mark took for a discourse of Jesus and placed in his Gospel. This "little apocalypse" theory was constructed upon questionable assumptions and its original statement can hardly be defended today. The precanonical history of Mark 13 is a complicated one. Yet the persisting efforts to recover the written source underlying it confirm the fact that the passage contains clues which lead to this conclusion.[75]

It is possible that Luke 21 is merely a revision of Mark 13, purposed to bring the latter's predictions into line with events accompanying the fall of Jerusalem

---

[69] Taylor, *Mark,* pp. 91f.; F. C. Grant, *Gospels,* p. 114.

[70] W. L. Knox, *Sources,* vol. I, pp. 52ff.

[71] T. W. Manson, *Sayings,* pp. 13, 84f.; W. L. Knox, *Sources,* vol. II, pp. 62ff.

[72] Jeremias, *Parables,* pp. 13f., 92ff.; Taylor, *Mark,* pp. 93f.

[73] S. McL. Gilmour, *Luke, IB,* vol. 8, pp. 14f.; W. L. Knox, *Sources,* vol. II, pp. 89ff.

[74] G. R. Beasley-Murray, *Jesus and the Future* (1954), Intro.

[75] T. W. Manson, *The Teaching of Jesus* (2d ed., 1935), pp. 260ff. [hereafter, *Teaching*]; Taylor, *Mark,* p. 498; W. G. Kümmel, *Promise and Fulfillment,* trans. D. Barton (1957), pp. 95ff. Cf. C. E. B. Cranfield, "St. Mark 13," *Scott. Journ. of Theo.* 6–7 (1953–54); Beasley-Murray, *Jesus and the Future,* Intro.

in A.D. 70. Yet it is probable that Luke's variations are due to his use of and preference for another version. Luke's interpolations suggest the existence of a second tract similar to the one upon which Mark 13 is based.[76]

We may conclude that the oral traditions concerning Jesus had begun to crystallize into written accounts before the writing of the earliest Gospels.[77] There is a large element of conjecture in reconstructing these earliest tracts, but there is enough evidence to show that the Gospels represent not the beginning—nor indeed the ending—but the climax of an effort to record Jesus' Ministry.

[76] T. W. Manson, *Sayings*, pp. 323ff.; W. L. Knox, *Sources*, vol. II, pp. 106ff.

[77] While not denying this as probable, many form critics presuppose only the so-called two sources, Mark and Q. Assuming that precanonical collections of tradition were grouped and edited, they reject the separation of "oral" and "written" sources. See Bultmann, *History*, pp. 321ff.; Feine-Behm-Kümmel, *Intro.*, p. 58.

chapter nine

THREE PORTRAITS OF JESUS

Matthew,
Mark,
and Luke

Portion of an early Christian sarcophagus (fourth century) symbolizing the Last Judgment. The Son of man separates the nations "one from another as a shepherd separates the sheep from the goats," Matt. 25:31ff. (The Metropolitan Museum of Art, Rogers Fund)

In the ancient Christian Church the vision of the "four living creatures" in the Book of Revelation (4:6ff; cf. Ezek. 1:1ff) provided emblems for the four Gospels. The lion may have been applied to Mark because this Gospel proclaims the royal dignity and power of Christ. Illustration from the Book of Cerne, an eighth century (?) collection of prayers. (University Library, Cambridge, England.)

The Emblem for Matthew's Gospel was a man, possibly because in this book Jesus' human ancestry is stressed. This and the other "living creatures" symbolizing the Evangelists are winged probably to signify their divine commissions as apostles. From the Book of Cerne. (University Library, Cambridge.)

Luke's Gospel was early symbolized by an ox because it was noted that his story of Jesus drew attention to sacrificial aspects of his ministry. From the Book of Cerne, so named because of its early possession by Cerne Abbey in Dorset. (University Library, Cambridge.)

P EOPLES' impressions of what Jesus was like are often the composite of traits drawn from all four Gospels of the New Testament. In this tendency is reflected a theologically sound instinct. None of the Gospels do full justice to the person of the Christ; in all of them the one Lord is proclaimed.[1] It is important, however, that the particular aims and distinguishing characteristics of each Gospel be recognized.

While the literary origins of the earliest Gospels are, first of all, to be understood as the product of an anonymous, oral tradition, it is erroneous to suppose that they are a haphazard mosaic of its surviving bits and pieces. One can believe that the Jesus-tradition might have become fragmented in this manner had it not been for the constructive, creative work of the four evangelists as well as some of their predecessors. Each Gospel possesses a unity and an individuality all its own, and each needs to be viewed apart as a full-length portrait of Jesus, and not merely as one of several sources, supplying mutually supplementary details when they are viewed together.[2]

Neither the names of authors nor dates were attached to the Gospels when they were written and first circulated. As long as the Gospels were not considered "scripture," questions of their origin and individuality were of no special significance. But by the later half of the second century questions had arisen concerning their authority, difference, and relative value. The following statement written around A.D. 180 and attributed to Irenaeus, Bishop of Gaul, reports the dominant tradition in the church at that time:

> Matthew published a written Gospel among the Hebrews in their own language, while Peter and Paul were preaching and founding the Church in Rome. After their decease, Mark, the disciple and interpreter of Peter—he also transmitted to us in writing those things which Peter had preached; and Luke, the attendant of Paul, recorded in a book the Gospel which Paul had declared. . . .[3]

The comparative study of the Synoptic Gospels in the modern period has cast shadows of doubt upon the truth of these traditions. One fact of great importance

[1]O. Cullmann, "Plurality of the Gospels as a Theological Problem," *The Early Church*, trans. S. Godmann (1956), pp. 39ff.

[2]For a lucid account of recent studies concerning the "theological motivations" of the Synoptic Evangelists, as revealed in their "collection, arrangement, editing, and modification of traditional material," etc., see N. Perrin, *What Is Redaction Criticism?* (1969). Extravagant claims however are made for the conclusions of these studies, and for the assumptions upon which they are based; cf. the greater reserve of Rohde, *Teaching of the Evangelists*, and Feine-Behm-Kümmel, *Intro.*, pp. 62ff., 75ff., 91ff.

[3]Eusebius, *H. E.*, V. 8, who cites a treatise of Irenaeus, *Against Heresies*, III. 1. i.

is the temporal priority of Mark, which has been established beyond reasonable doubt. The evidence set forth in the preceding chapter justifies a consideration of Mark before Matthew, notwithstanding the words of Irenaeus.

THE GOSPEL OF MARK

The Papias Tradition Concerning Mark

There is a Church tradition concerning Mark's origin which is earlier than Irenaeus. Around A.D. 140 Papias, Bishop of Phrygia, wrote a work entitled "Expositions of the Words of The Lord." From this work the following statement is cited:

> And the elder said this also: Mark, having become the interpreter of Peter, wrote accurately everything that he remembered, without however recording in order what was either said or done by Christ. For neither did he hear the Lord, nor did he follow him; but afterwards, as I said, [attended] Peter, who adapted his instructions to the needs [of his hearers] but had no design of giving a connected account of the Lord's oracles. So then Mark made no mistake, while he thus wrote down some things as he remembered them; for he made it his own care not to omit anything that he heard, or to set down any false statement therein.[4]

It is possible that this is the source of the tradition reported by Irenaeus, for Irenaeus knew the book by Papias. But reference of Irenaeus to the date of Mark may represent an independent tradition. The value of these second-century reports concerning Mark cannot be decided until one has closely examined the Gospel itself.

The Sources and Plan of Mark

There are, as we have seen, a number of internal indications that Mark's Gospel was composed of traditions of diverse origin. To what extent these were oral or written is difficult to say, but it is a safe assumption that some of Mark's materials had been grouped together previously. Accordingly, it is surely not correct to describe Mark as a transcript of Peter's reminiscences or a disciple's record of Peter's preaching and teaching. While it is true that Peter was present at many of the scenes reported in Mark, so that much of the narrative derives ultimately from him, Peter's testimony cannot account for the whole of the Gospel in its present form.[5]

Many attempts have been made to trace stages in the composition of Mark. The theory that Mark was written in Aramaic and later translated into Greek has failed to commend itself. The traditions underlying Mark had been transmitted in Greek for some while before the Gospel was written.[6] Another question still

---

[4] Eusebius, *H. E.*, III. 39.
[5] Heard, *Intro.*, p. 57.
[6] Perry, *IB*, vol. 7, pp. 67f.; F. V. Filson, *Origins of the Gospels* (1938), pp. 56ff. [hereafter, *Origins*].

in debate is whether or not the Greek Gospel of Mark appeared in several editions, some earlier and others later than the present Mark. It should be recalled that "Ur-Marcus theories" have been held to account for the omission in Matthew and Luke of several Markan passages, as well as for the minor agreements of the later evangelists against Mark.[7] Theories of an earlier edition of Mark have also been adopted to explain the alleged "doublets" in Mark, for example, 6:34–52 and 8:1–21; the disorder and lack of connection in the narrative, observed by Papias and many others since his time; and the presence in the canonical Mark of "Paulinisms," or of other secondary features suggesting revision. First-ranking scholars have disagreed as to whether or not some form of an "Ur-Marcus" hypothesis is necessary. Perhaps the majority would say no, on the ground that in its present form Mark is a unity in language, style, and thought. Moreover, there is not enough agreement between Matthew and Luke against Mark, where the two seem to be employing the Markan source, to support an "Ur-Marcus theory."[8] And, finally, evidence which has been used to defend the various theories of revision more probably indicates stages of development in the gospel tradition prior to its use by Mark, or else Mark's own editorial methods.[9]

Whatever the lingering uncertainties with respect to the oral and written "sources" underlying Mark, its original content and successive revisions, it is now commonly agreed that our present Gospel is the oldest surviving work of its type. The importance of two closely related questions is at once apparent: Did the author of the earliest Gospel possess a traditional account of the course of events in Jesus' Ministry, or is the plan of the Gospel largely one of his own devising? In either case we must also ask to what extent the purpose of the book has shaped and organized the traditions at hand. A variety of answers have been given to these questions. It will be helpful to consider a few of them for the light that they shed upon several puzzling features of this Gospel.

The "Markan hypothesis": This phrase defines a position widely held by critical scholars from the late eighteenth century to the twentieth. It was affirmed that Mark preserves the true, historical outline of Jesus' public Ministry. Most of the advocates of this hypothesis have believed that Mark not only reports the correct chronology of the Ministry but also traces the development of the disciples' ideas concerning Jesus, as well as Jesus' deepening consciousness of his mission as Messiah. It was assumed by exponents of the Markan hypothesis that Peter, and other representatives of the mother church in Jerusalem, furnished Mark with his information, facts which warranted the recognition of Mark as the basic history of Jesus' career.

In retrospect it is possible to see that the predominating views of scholars and theologians in the last century lent support to the Markan hypothesis. The

---

[7] See above, p. 175.

[8] Ur-Marcus theories have had a curious history. F. C. Burkitt sought to discredit them once for all (*Gospel History and Its Transmission, 1906* [hereafter, *Gospel History*]), but they continue to appear. See above, p. 175, note 56; H. A. Guy, *The Origin of the Gospel of Mark* (1955) [hereafter, *Origin*]. Taylor distinguishes Ur-Marcus, redaction, and compilation hypotheses, *Mark*, pp. 67ff.

[9] F. C. Grant, *IB*, vol. 7, p. 636; McNeile, *Intro.*, pp. 65ff.; Feine-Behm-Kümmel, *Intro.*, pp. 49f.

two-document solution of the synoptic problem had reversed the traditional view, at least as old as Augustine, that Mark was an abbreviation of Matthew. It was assumed therefore that since Mark is the earliest Gospel it is the most reliable. When studied alongside Matthew and Luke, and when compared with John, Mark seemed the least "theological." Since no earlier Gospel existed with which Mark could be compared, belief in the simplicity and objectivity of Mark's record was taken for granted. Most of the "lives of Christ" written in the nineteenth century were based upon the Markan hypothesis.[10]

In recent times this popular theory has suffered devastating attacks from several sources. Albert Schweitzer's review of the life of Christ in the research of the nineteenth century demonstrated the intrinsic weaknesses of this position. It was evident that the modern biographers of Jesus had been "obliged to read between the lines a whole host of things, and those often the most important, and then to foist them upon the text by means of psychological conjecture."[11] Many in our time continue to believe in the substantial historicity of Mark's outline of Jesus' Ministry, but it is clear that few care to defend the Markan hypothesis without serious qualifications.

The editorial framework hypothesis: Coincident with the development of form criticism as a tool of Gospel research there was proposed a view which represents a radical rejection of the Markan hypothesis. This position holds that Mark compiled his Gospel out of separate stories which had come to him from a variety of sources. The arrangement of the Gospel is the work of the evangelist, who superimposed upon his materials an editorial framework. For the most part there is little regard for chronological and topographical details in Mark, if indeed the evangelist was in a position to reproduce these. Instead the stories of Mark are grouped according to their subject matter, and the development of the "plot" of the Gospel is aided by the frequent use of connecting particles such as "immediately," "again," or the simple conjunctive, "and." Moreover, Mark has composed short, general summaries to punctuate his narrative, and these are readily distinguishable from the concrete stories they tie together.[12]

Many have concluded that there is no sufficient justification for this wholesale rejection of Mark's outline, as a scaffolding constructed by the evangelist.

The kerygmatic outline hypothesis: According to this view, the *kerygma* of the early Church had fixed in the oral tradition a summary of the Ministry of Jesus. Evidence for this is found in the skeleton outlines embedded in the speeches of Acts. When the outline of Mark is compared with the outline of these speeches,

---

[10] The Markan hypothesis was a useful weapon in striking down the Christ-myth theories of the late nineteenth century. "Liberal theology" also found an ally in the hypothesis. R. H. Lightfoot, *Mark*, pp. 5f.

[11] A. Schweitzer, *Quest of the Historical Jesus*, trans. W. Montgomery (1911), p. 330 [hereafter, *Quest*].

[12] A position linked with the name of Karl Ludwig Schmidt, whose untranslated German volume bears the title, *The Framework of the Story of Jesus;* Bultmann, *History*, pp. 338ff. Willi Marxsen's redaction criticism of the Second Gospel proceeds upon this assumption: *Mark the Evangelist*, trans. R. Harrisville (1969) [hereafter, *Mark*]. For a qualification of this thesis, see the works cited above, p. 164, note 11. For a rejoinder, see Nineham, *Studies*, pp. 223ff.

the conclusion is reached that Mark is an expansion of the primitive *kerygma* in narrative form.

This view is not a return of confidence in the Markan hypothesis. It is only claimed that the *kerygma* provided Mark with a broad outline of the course of events. But it is recognized that this outline was too meager to give a setting for all of the stories at hand. The conclusion is that Mark's plan is, in large measure, the work of the evangelist, but it is not an altogether arbitrary construction. Mark must have possessed a tradition of the course of events in Jesus' Ministry as well as many individual stories and larger complexes of tradition.[13]

This is an attractive hypothesis, but it is questionable that it can bear the weight which some of its defenders have claimed for it.

A theological understanding of history: All of the opinions which may be classified under this heading assume that Mark's Gospel is neither a biography nor an objective history of Jesus' Ministry. Instead, Mark may be described as a theological pamphlet. Traditional, historical materials have been brought together for a theological purpose. Among those who discern theological motifs in Mark there is a difference of opinion. Were these motifs embedded in the various traditions assembled by the evangelist, or do they represent his personal convictions? In either case, modern interest in the theology of Mark may be said to represent another reaction against the Markan hypothesis.

An early and influential example of the understanding of Mark as a theological work is the interpretation advanced by the German scholar Wilhelm Wrede.[14] Wrede drew attention to a datum of the synoptic tradition which is most distinctly set forth in Mark's Gospel, and may be termed "the messianic secret motif," the demons who seek to make Jesus' identity known are silenced.[15] Secrecy is enjoined after some of Jesus' mighty works have been wrought.[16] After Peter's confession the disciples are "charged to tell no one" that Jesus is the Christ.[17] Jesus withdraws from the crowds, embarking upon secret journeys and moving through Galilee incognito.[18] He gives private instruction to the disciples concerning the "mystery of the Kingdom of God" and other subjects.[19] Jesus is able to keep his messiahship secret as long as he is on earth. In fact, until the resurrection, Jesus remains unintelligible even to his disciples.[20] It is only then that the true recognition of who he is dawns upon them.

According to Wrede, these ideas do not belong to the authentic history of Jesus but are the imposition of a theological interpretation upon it. The real fact is that

---

[13]Dodd, *New Testament Studies*, pp. 9f.; A. M. Hunter, *The Message of the New Testament* (1944), pp. 31f. Cf. Feine-Behm-Kümmel, *Intro.*, pp. 62f.

[14]For a summary of Wrede's thesis, which is presented in an untranslated study (*The Messianic-secret in the Gospels*, 1901), see A. E. J. Rawlinson, *St. Mark* (1925), pp. 258ff. [hereafter, *Mark*]; Taylor, *Mark*, pp. 122ff.

[15]Mark 1:25, 34; 3:11f.

[16]1:55; 5:43.

[17]8:30; also 9:9.

[18]7:24; 9:30.

[19]4:10–12; 7:17–23; 9:28f., etc.

[20]9:32.

the idea that Jesus might be the Messiah had occurred to no one before the resurrection. Yet once the Easter faith was proclaimed, a tendency prevailed to interpret Jesus' nonmessianic ministry as the Ministry of the Christ. The absence of the proclamation of messiahship by Jesus and his disciples during his lifetime was thus accounted for in the early Church by "the dogma of intentional secrecy." Wrede did not believe that this dogma was invented by Mark. Rather he supposed that it was current in the church of Mark's day. The evangelist was responsible for fixing it in the synoptic tradition. Wrede's explanation of the origin of the messianic secrecy idea, and of the purpose served by this motif in Mark's Gospel, was vigorously contested in subsequent studies. Nevertheless, his perceptive analysis has continued to influence criticism.[21]

Upon the common assumption that Mark was guided by a particular theological interest or interests of his own, a variety of influences have been thought to explain the plan of his Gospel. Mark, it is said, is a liturgy. The use of Jesus-tradition in Christian worship determined the particular form of this Gospel. Some hold that its pattern and "plot" were influenced by Old Testament types and prophecies which, the evangelist believed, found fulfillment in Jesus' Ministry. In several studies, Mark's Gospel is described as a "sermon"—a proclamation of the *kerygma* of Jesus, crucified and risen, with an extended introduction containing traditional episodes from Jesus' Ministry, used as paradigms to inspire the faith and hope of Christians in Mark's own community and time.

It is probable that the various expositions of Mark's structure which are based upon the discovery of some all-encompassing theological motif or organizing principle are either overly subtle or systematic. It is only by indirection that Mark's theology is stated, and it is partially obscured by the mystery surrounding Mark's hero, as well as by the fact that traditional materials he has used reflect different origins and viewpoints. It is likely also that Mark's practical aims precluded a definitive articulation of a theology. These observations should not, however, inhibit a search for Mark's theological interests, some of which seem to be manifest in his Gospel.[22]

Because of the diversity of opinion concerning the source and development of the plan of Mark's Gospel, it is not surprising that a variety of outlines of its content have been proposed. The one given below assumes a theological orientation of the Gospel, and subordinates its incidental notes of time if not of place.

---

[21]J. M. Robinson, *The Problem of History in Mark* (1957), pp. 9ff. [hereafter, *Problem*]; Marxsen, *Mark*; Perrin, *What Is Redaction Criticism?*, pp. 12f.

[22]See comment in T. A. Burkill's *Mysterious Revelation* (1963), pp. 5f.; Bultmann, *History*, pp. 349f.; Feine-Behm-Kümmel, *Intro.*, p. 67. From time to time attempts have been made to see in Mark a reflection of Paul's theology, a view originating with G. Volkmar (1897) and popularized by A. F. Loisy and B. W. Bacon. See the latter's *The Gospel of Mark* (1925), pp. 221ff. The so-called "Paulinisms" in Mark appear to be commonplace teachings of the early Church; Paul's typical doctrines are not present in Mark. See Rawlinson, *Mark*, pp. xliii ff. Cf. Marxsen, i.e., Mark's appearance "checked a process of disintegration" which might have resulted from "the gnosticizing" of Paul's message, and thus was related to Paul in a different sense (*Mark*, pp. 213ff.).

An Outline of the Gospel According to Mark

A. Introduction: The beginning of the good news of Jesus Christ, the Son of God, 1:1–13: [23]
   1. The way is prepared, 1:1–8
   2. The beloved Son is anointed, 1:9–11
   3. The contest with evil begins, 1:12–13
B. The ministry of the hidden Messiah in Galilee and environs, 1:14–8:26:
   4. Summary: the proclamation of the kingdom of God, 1:14–15
   5. The call of four disciples, 1:16–20
   6. Summary: teaching with authority, 1:21–22
   7. Mighty works in and around Capernaum, 1:23–38
   8. Summary: visits to synagogues in Galilee, 1:39
   9. Controversies with the scribes, 1:40–3:6
  10. Summary: crowds by the sea; retirement to the hills with the twelve, 3:7–19a
  11. Charges brought against Jesus, 3:19b–35
  12. Parables concerning the mystery of the kingdom of God, 4:1–32
  13. Summary: private interpretation of the parables, 4:33–34
  14. Power over storms at sea, demons, death, and incurable disease, 4:35–5:43
  15. Enmity leads to wider journeyings and increased activity; missions of the twelve, 6:1–29
  16. The feeding of the five thousand and its sequel, 6:30–56
  17. The scribes raise the question of defilement, 7:1–23
  18. Summary: withdrawal to the region of Tyre and Sidon, 7:24–37
  19. The feeding of the four thousand, 8:1–10
  20. The Pharisees demand a sign and are refused, 8:11–13
  21. The mystery of the loaves; the leaven of the Pharisees, 8:14–21
  22. The gradual opening of blind eyes, 8:22–26
C. The Son of man journeys to Jerusalem to suffer and be glorified, 8:27–10:52:
  23. Peter confesses the Messiah; the first prophecy of the Son of man's death and resurrection, 8:27–33
  24. Sayings concerning the cost of discipleship and the coming of the kingdom "with power," 8:34-9:1
  25. A proleptic revelation of the hidden Messiah, 9:2–8
  26. Saying concerning the coming of Elijah, 9:9–13
  27. Exorcism of the deaf and dumb spirit, 9:14–29
  28. The second prediction of death and resurrection, 9:30–32
  29. Stories connected with the journey to Jerusalem 9:33–10:31
  30. Jesus walks ahead followed by fearful disciples; the third prediction of death-resurrection, 10:32–34
  31. Favors asked by James and John and the example of the Son of man, 10:35–45

---

[23] Mark's "introduction" may include vss. 14f. See the persuasive arguments of L. E. Keck, "The Introduction to Mark's Gospel," *NTS* 12 (1966): 352ff.

32. The blind beggar is given sight, 10:46–52

D. The hidden Messiah comes to Jerusalem, 11:1–13:37:

   33. Acted parables in Jerusalem: triumphal entry; cursing of fig tree; cleansing of the temple, 11:1–25 (26)

   34. Conflict stories in Jerusalem, 11:27–12:40

   35. Scene opposite the temple treasury, 12:41–44

   36. The apocalyptic discourse, 13:1–37

E. The passion and resurrection of the Messiah, 14:1–16:8:

   37. The plot against Jesus, 14:1–2

   38. The anointing at Bethany, 14:3–9

   39. Summary: the treachery of Judas, 14:10–11

   40. The Passover meal, 14:12–31

   41. Gethsemane, 14:32–42

   42. Betrayal and arrest; the flight of the disciples, 14:43–52

   43. The priest's hearing and condemnation of Jesus, 14:53–65

   44. Peter's denial, 14:66–72

   45. Trial before Pilate, 15:1–15

   46. The crucifixion, 15:16–36

   47. God's Son is revealed in dying, 15:37–39

   48. Summary: the attendant women, 15:40–41

   49. The burial, 15:42–47

   50. The visit of the women to the empty tomb, 16:1–8

The Gospel of Mark may be divided into two parts of almost equal length. Its first division describes the ministry in and around Galilee (A–B); its final division describes the one-week ministry in Jerusalem and its environs (D–E). These two divisions are joined by a brief, telescoped version of the journey to Jerusalem (C).[24] Almost coincident with these major geographical divisions are two centers of interest. In the first division, the emphasis is upon the conflict of the hidden Messiah who is opposed by demons and by the religious and civil authorities of Galilee. The motif of struggle in this phase of the Ministry is heightened by the tension which develops between Jesus and the crowds. The masses are filled with astonishment but are not able to understand the meaning of his proclamation, parables, or mighty works. This lack of understanding is shared in large measure by "the twelve." In the final division, the gathering gloom deepens, and, following a treacherous plot, an arrest under cover of darkness, hasty trials, and physical violence, Jesus is led forth to die in loneliness.

Beneath this story of tragedy runs a mysterious undercurrent of promise and hope. Indeed, the reader of Mark's passion narrative has been given in advance the clue which turns this tragedy into triumph. Predictions of the imminent suffering and death of the Son of man, in which his disciples are to participate,

---

[24] R. H. Lightfoot, *Mark*, p. 12. Cf. Marxsen's view (*Mark*, pp. 54ff.) that Galilee remains the important theological locale, even in Mark's passion narrative. In Mark's community the imminent return of Christ was expected in Galilee. For a trenchant criticism of Marxsen's thesis, see Rohde, *Teaching of the Evangelists*, pp. 113ff.

are joined with forecasts of the manifestations of a glory that is to come. The first prophecy of doom is linked with the transfiguration of the not-yet-glorified Son of man. The second and third predictions of Jesus' death end with the promise of resurrection.[25] In these passages there is a decided shift in the center of interest. The astonishment and awe excited in the first division of the Gospel by the mighty works of Jesus are now connected with his teaching concerning the cross as the road to victory. Only after tribulation comes the final glory. This theme is given impressive development in the only discourse of any length in Mark, chapter 13. In the passion narrative which follows, prophecies of future victory accompany the sentences of death.[26] At the conclusion of Mark, the burial of Jesus is followed by the discovery of the empty tomb.

The Origin of Mark

Let us now recall the second-century traditions concerning the writing of Mark. Perhaps most scholars would agree that the name *Mark* designates the author, or at least the compiler, of the Second Gospel. Mark was neither an apostle nor a person otherwise sufficiently prominent in the Church to have a purely anonymous writing attributed to him. But who was this Mark? The answer to this question in the second century possibly rested upon an inference drawn from I Peter 5:13. Mark had assisted Peter in "Babylon," that is, in Rome.[27] I Peter attests the currency of the belief—in the early years of the second century at the latest—that Peter and Mark were in Rome together. The tradition of Papias and Irenaeus may also presuppose a belief that Rome was the place of Peter's martyrdom. This martyrdom tradition finds support in a writing dating from the last decade of the first century, I Clement.[28] Since there is a tendency in ancient church tradition to bring together references to all persons of the same name, it is uncertain whether the author of the Second Gospel should be identified with the "John whose surname was Mark" who appears in Acts and in letters of Paul.[29]

Recent views concerning the "developed" character of Mark's sources, and the origin of the form of this Gospel, have tended to loosen its direct connection with Peter, and hence with the Mark who was his assistant. The words of Papias may be accounted for by the suggestion that the writer of the canonical Gospel used Mark's notes, and that what "the elder" had said about these was later applied to the Second Gospel.[30] Alternatively "the elder" may have referred to another document (possibly Q), and it was wrongly supposed by Papias that Mark was intended, since his Gospel contains much that seems to come from Peter.[31] Unfortunately, the contents of the Second Gospel provide little, if any, evidence for identifying its author.

[25] See outline above, C. 23–25; 28; 30.
[26] Mark 14:9, 25, 28, 62.
[27] Rev. 14:8; 16:19; 17:5, etc., 2 Bar. IX:1; Siby. Or. V. 143.
[28] Cullmann, *Peter*, pp. 89ff. See below, pp. 477f.
[29] Acts 12:12, 15; 13:5, 13; Col. 4:10ff.; Philemon 24 (2 Tim. 4:11).
[30] Guy, *Origin*, Summary.
[31] Heard, *Intro.*, pp. 54ff.; Cf. Enslin, *Beginnings*, pp. 384f.

What may be inferred from Mark concerning its date and place of origin? The apocalyptic discourse supplies the only indication of a date. A description of "the desolating sacrilege" and the destruction of the temple implies that these events have not yet taken place but are imminent, or that these events have just begun to happen.[32] This evidence is not fully conclusive, and some would prefer a date for Mark in the early 70s. There is nothing in Mark which clearly indicates its place of origin. It seems to have been written for Gentile readers and for persons unfamiliar with Aramaic and Jewish customs in Palestine.[33] The author has employed several Latin words, transliterating them into Greek.[34] While none of this evidence points conclusively to Rome, it is compatible with the tradition. Some favor a Palestinian provenience—Antioch in Syria; or more probably Galilee, appealing to the evangelist's evident interest in this region.[35] Others have conjectured that Alexandria was the place of its writing.

In spite of these uncertainties, it is safe to say that there are elements in the tradition concerning the origin of Mark which can be defended with confidence. The present writer believes that Mark originated in Rome during the years A.D. 64 to 69. It is easier to explain the inclusion in the New Testament of a Gospel not written by an apostle—a writing superseded by others incorporating its contents—if one assumes a special connection with Rome. The earliest tradition favors Rome and, as we shall see, there is much in the Gospel itself which presupposes conditions in Rome in the 60s.

The Purpose of Mark

As stated above, Mark's Gospel was written for Gentile readers. It should now be observed that it was addressed primarily to Christians. Several types of evidence support this view. Mark introduced his characters as persons known to his readers. If his purpose had been to win converts, we would expect an identification of persons, for example, of individuals healed by Jesus (to witness if I lie). A knowledge of the content of Jesus' teachings seems to be presupposed (such as are reported in the Q tradition). The superscription of the Gospel contains the double name "Jesus Christ," and the technical word "Gospel," implying that Mark wrote for readers who already shared the faith. There is evidence that Mark was concerned to acknowledge the urgency of the mission of the Church to outsiders. But Mark himself contributes to this task, not by writing a Gospel for the unconverted, but by furnishing the Church with a version of its traditional good news, to confirm faith and at the same time to expose the seriousness of unbelief, especially the unbelief of the Jews.[36]

[32] Mark 13:14–20.
[33] 5:41; 7:3f., 11, 34; 15:22.
[34] 5:9; 12:15, 42; 15:16, 39.
[35] Marxsen, *Mark*, pp. 54ff.
[36] Weiss, *Earliest Christianity*, pp. 689ff. The distinctions, intended for insiders or outsiders, can be too sharply drawn. See, e.g., C. F. D. Moule, "The Intention of the Evangelists," *The Phenomenon of the New Testament* (1967), pp. 104ff.

The "Annals" of the Roman historian Tacitus provide an important source of knowledge of the situation facing Christians in Rome in the 60s of the first century. It was rumored that the great fire which broke out there in the winter A.D. 64–65 had been started by Nero to make way for the enlargement of his palace complex and gardens. "Therefore," writes Tacitus,

> to dispel the report Nero made a scapegoat of others, and inflicted the most exquisite tortures upon a class hated for their abominations, whom the populace called Christians. The Christus from whom the name had its origin had been executed during the reign of Tiberius by the procurator Pontius Pilate. The mischievous superstition was thus checked for the moment, but was reviving again, not only in Judea, the original seat of the evil, but even in the capital, where all that is anywhere hideous or loathsome finds its center and flourishes. Accordingly some were first put on trial; they pleaded guilty, and upon the information gathered from them a large number were convicted, not so much on the charge of arson as because of their hatred of humanity. Wanton cruelty marked their execution. Covered with skins of wild beasts they were torn in pieces by dogs, and thus perished; many were crucified, or burned alive, and even set on fire to serve as an illumination by night, after daylight had expired. Nero had offered his own gardens for the spectacle, and exhibited races, mingling with the crowd in the garb of a charioteer, or himself driving. Hence, even for criminals who deserved extreme and exemplary punishment, there arose a feeling of compassion; for it was not, it seemed, for the common weal, but to glut the cruelty of one man, that they were being destroyed.[37]

There are aspects of Mark's Gospel which imply that it was written for a martyr church. As we have noticed, the theme of conflict is prominent in Mark. Jesus' Ministry begins with the proclamation that the kingdom of God is at hand. This apocalyptic idea carried with it the belief in the intensification of the struggle with evil as the present Age gives place to the new one. In his Ministry, Jesus had experienced the birth pangs of this Age to Come. As the foe of Satan he had contended with "wild beasts" and with the demonic in men.[38] The scribes of the Pharisees sought to "test" or tempt him;[39] also the disciples. Their thought that Jesus as Messiah could avoid suffering was declared to be the onslaught of Satan.[40]

Mark's story of the strong Son of God is told with a sensitivity to the conflicts which faced the embattled Church of his day. Almost from the beginning of the Gospel, Jesus' disciples are victims of the same antagonisms which Jesus suffered.[41] The shadow of the cross falls across their path.[42] They are not to find their security with Jesus, but they too are sent out to proclaim the coming kingdom and to war against the demons.[43] Has Mark selected for inclusion in his Gospel

---

[37] E. T. Merrill's trans. Cited in Rawlinson, *Mark,* pp. xvi f.
[38] Mark 1:13, 24.
[39] 8:11; 10:2; 12:15.
[40] 8:33. See Robinson, *Problem,* pp. 26ff.
[41] 2:18, 24.
[42] 2:20.
[43] 3:14; 4:14–17; 6:7–13, etc.

the stories of Jesus' power over the storms, and over the legion of demons possessing the untamed man, with a view to the fears which beset the Christians at Rome?[44]

From the conclusion of the first division to the end of Mark's Gospel, the vocation of the suffering Son of man and the vocation of his disciples are given a close and impressive correlation. In this central section is found a nucleus of discipleship sayings grouped with the predictions of Jesus' passion. The cost of discipleship is stressed: renunciation, the bearing of one's cross, the losing of one's life for the sake of Jesus *and the gospel*.[45] "Quite realistically Mark brings his hearer face to face with Jesus in such wise that the hearer's own history and situation in the church of around A.D. 66–70 correlates with the history of Jesus . . . Mark sets down beside the history of Jesus the church of his own day, living still in the anguish of the tensions of the present age in which the conflict between the Spirit and Satan is continued."[46]

Mark 13 has special bearing upon the situation confronting Christians in Mark's time, and upon his purpose in writing. It offers a challenge to those who are *hated* by all for the name of Christ (note the statements of Tacitus).[47] Jesus had predicted the sufferings his followers must endure, but when these begin, his disciples are to know that "the end is not yet" although imminent, and to be assured that "he who endures to the end will be saved."[48] In and through their sufferings, Christians are called to bear witness to the nations. For this task they are promised the support and guidance of the Holy Spirit.[49] At the end of the apocalyptic discourse stand the words: "And what I say to you I say to all, watch."

Again at Gethsemane Jesus' disciples are reminded of their weakness and of the need for constant watchfulness.[50] Why, we may ask, is Peter's denial given so much attention in Mark's passion narrative?[51] Did the author know that some of his readers had denied their Lord during the height of Nero's trials and persecutions, and had wept when they remembered?

It has been suggested that some words of another New Testament writer aptly describe the purpose of Mark:

> . . . let us run with perseverance the race that is set before us, looking to Jesus the pioneer and perfector of our faith, who for the joy that was set before him endured the cross, despising the shame, and is seated at the right hand of the throne of God. Consider him who endured from sinners such hostility against himself, so that you may not grow weary or faint-hearted. In your struggle against sin you [unlike others?] have not yet resisted to the point of shedding your blood.[52]

[44] 4:38, 40; 5:4; 6:48–50.

[45] 8:34–38; 9:33–50; 10:23–31, 35–45.

[46] Anderson, *Jesus*, pp. 244f. For an alternative situation—Galilean instead of Roman Christians—see Marxsen's *Mark*, pp. 161ff.

[47] 13:13.

[48] 13:7, 20, 27.

[49] 13:9.

[50] 14:38.

[51] 14:27–31, 54, 66–72.

[52] Heb. 12:1–4.

This statement emphasizes the practical note in Mark, but it is hardly a sufficient summary of the purpose of the Gospel. For Mark, Jesus certainly is more than the example for his martyr disciples. Jesus' life was given as "a ransom for many," and his death is understood as the shedding of "the blood of the covenant."[53] It has long been recognized that these ideas were in one way or another determinative of the Gospel's teaching.[54] But recent studies have demonstrated that, throughout his Gospel, Mark has oriented the traditions concerning Jesus toward his passion. For example, Mark's portrayal of John the Baptist makes him not only the forerunner of the Messiah but also of his passion.[55] Mark proclaims that Jesus can be understood only from the perspective of his cross, and "in the discipleship of suffering in which the paradox of God's action through Jesus is continued in the life of Christians (8:27ff)."[56] Jesus' disciples are to have a share in the consummation of God's kingdom that is to come, not because they take up their crosses and follow Jesus unto the end (which the original disciples could not do), but because, in obedience to the Father's will, the Son of God had suffered and died for them.

Modern expositors of Mark have seen the necessity of showing how their reading of Mark's theology coheres with Mark's understanding of the messianic secrecy motif which runs throughout his Gospel. It is probable that Mark attempted to maintain "a schema of the time of Jesus' earthly obscurity, followed by the time of his glory and heavenly Lordship over the church." At the same time, Mark narrates that the secret of Jesus' messiahship did not remain completely hidden during the course of the Ministry. It is unlikely that at such places one discovers evidence in Mark's tradition intractable to his theory. Rather, Mark thereby disclosed his belief "that the earthly activity of Jesus is already the locus of Revelation, the matrix of the 'time of salvation,' that the risen Christ who is proclaimed is identical with the Jesus who is the originator of the Gospel."[57] Mark was not concerned with such historical distinctions as are drawn by modern scholars, between "the Jesus of history and the Christ of faith," or indeed with clearly distinguishing the Ministry and post-Easter periods. For him, God's revelation in Jesus Christ, to which the Church bears witness, remains a mystery until it is comprehended by faith at the foot of the cross; the authority of the Messiah–Son of God remains an enigma and a scandal until the disciples learn to understand that the path to resurrection and glory, for Jesus and for his followers, leads through suffering and death.

Perhaps there were persons in the Church of Mark's day proclaiming the

[53]Mark 10:45; 14:24.

[54]Rawlinson, *Mark*, pp. xvii, lii; Taylor, *Mark*, pp. 124f.; *IB*, vol. 7, p. 633.

[55]Note the thematic synchronism in 1:14. The catchword "to be handed over" points to Jesus being handed over to his enemies, 9:31, 10:33, etc. (Marxsen). Also 6:14ff.; 8:28; 9:11ff.

[56]H-D. Knigge, "The Meaning of Mark," *Interpretation* 22 (1968): 79.; Keck, note 23 above, p. 362ff.

[57]Anderson, *Jesus*, p. 245. Burkhill, *Mysterious Revelation*, writes of Mark's tendency to distinguish the periods of Jesus' humiliation and glorification and of his counter tendency "to light up the darkest depths of the humiliation" with "the spiritual glory of the Messiah to be revealed fully at his awaited Parousia." For other explanations, after Wrede, of Mark's understanding of this half-concealed, half-revealed Messianic secret, see H-D. Knigge, note 56 above, pp. 53ff.

authority of Christ apart from his cross and rejecting the necessity of their own witness through suffering. Perhaps they were appealing to traditions from Jesus' Ministry which had become separated from their setting in the life of the obedient Son of God who had suffered unto death. If these conjectures are correct, then Mark's achievement was to orient the traditions once again toward the passion-resurrection of Jesus, thus restoring them to the only setting in which they could be understood "as the Gospel of God."

In order to delineate the purpose of Mark it is possible to divide in this way practical and theological aims. But they were not separated in the evangelist's mind. Mark was concerned to teach that the theological meaning of the cross can best be understood by one who has humbly prepared himself for a renunciation of self, for a life of service and, if need be, of suffering and martyrdom.[58] If this was true, then a martyred church possessed, and still possesses, the most satisfactory key to an understanding of "the mystery" proclaimed in Mark, and can best appreciate the intensity of its hope of glory.

The Ending of Mark

The oldest texts of Mark's Gospel conclude with the words "for they [the women] were afraid."[59] Some believe that Mark intended to conclude his Gospel with the report that the women ran away from the tomb, filled with astonishment or awe. This ending is held to be in accord with the abrupt and ungrammatical style of the evangelist. Besides this, Mark may have considered that Jesus' historic Ministry ended with the discovery of the empty tomb. The postresurrection appearances of Jesus were manifestations of the heavenly session of the Son of God.[60]

Expositions of Mark's theology have increasingly sought to demonstrate the congruence and suitability of 16:1–8 as an ending for this Gospel. If it was Mark's purpose "to encourage and exhalt a church in the throes of persecution to the gallantry of Christian faith, one could not imagine any more fitting conclusion than this, in which, with the brevity that yet says everything needful, the resurrection of Jesus Christ is held up as the pledge of God's breaking into history to end his people's night of sorrow."[61]

For many scholars it is not credible that Mark's Gospel should have ended with 16:8. Linguists have questioned the propriety of ending a book with a conjunction. There are anticipations of a postresurrection narrative provided in Mark 14:28 and 16:7. Would the evangelist have put down his pen before recording that these promises were fulfilled? It has been conjectured that Mark's Gospel ended with a Galilean episode, such as is told in John 21.

---

[58] Weiss, *Early Christianity,* pp. 693f.

[59] The passages printed after Mark 16:8 in the RSV should be read. Criteria of vocabulary, style, and content, and the mss. evidence support the conclusion that these endings are no part of the Second Gospel. Later scribes supplied them.

[60] R. H. Lightfoot, *Mark,* pp. 80ff.; Enslin, *Beginnings,* pp. 387f.

[61] Anderson, *Jesus,* p. 222; Feine-Behm-Kümmel, *Intro.,* pp. 71f.; Marxsen, *Mark,* pp. 80ff.

On the assumption that our present Mark is incomplete, two explanations have been offered. One of these is that the evangelist was interrupted before he finished. Perhaps a revision of the Gospel was contemplated but never accomplished. An alternative view is that Mark's conclusion was indeed written but that the Gospel was mutilated, either by some accident or through deliberate suppression. Accidental mutilation seems more probable. The worn ending of a papyrus scroll could easily be torn. Perhaps some surviving copy of Mark, if not the original, was partially destroyed in rioting against the Christians in Rome.

THE GOSPEL OF MATTHEW

In the early centuries of the Church, Mark's Gospel suffered through comparison with the Gospel of Matthew. The First Gospel was believed to be the writing of an apostle; the Second Gospel was not. Matthew was seen to contain nearly everything found in Mark, and much more. In the modern period, the "quest of the historical Jesus" tended to reverse this judgment. In the eyes of many scholars, Matthew's value as an historical source was diminished when compared with Mark. More recently, a common acknowledgment of theological tendencies in both Gospels has awakened interest in the discovery of Matthew's special value. Although one may point to a fluctuation of interest in this Gospel among scholars, it is doubtful that this has been true among the rank and file of Christians. Indeed, some of the major reasons for the early advocacy of Matthew were never lost sight of and still account for its popularity.

The Papias Tradition Concerning Matthew

As noted at the beginning of this chapter, the judgment of the Church at the close of the second century was that Matthew had been composed "among the Hebrews in their own language," during the ministries of Peter and Paul at Rome. Words of Clement of Alexandria, Tertullian, and Origen reveal the dissemination of this tradition which Eusebius attributes to Irenaeus. Later writers, notably Jerome, confirm its persistence. Again, a quotation from the lost book of Papias furnishes a likely clue to the source of this tradition. Following his reference to the comment of Papias concerning Mark, Eusebius writes:

> But concerning Matthew the following statement is made: "So then Matthew composed the oracles [sayings?] in the Hebrew language, and each one interpreted [translated?] them as he could." [62]

These traditions concerning the literary activity of Matthew raise many questions. The modern student is presented with a baffling number of alternatives. Yet this much may be said. Gospel criticism has seriously discredited the tradition

[62] H. E., III. 39. 16. In an earlier section Eusebius writes, "Matthew, having first preached to the Hebrews, when he was about to go to others, compensated for the loss of his presence . . . by delivering to them in writing his Gospel in their native language" (III.24).

of an apostolic authorship of the First Gospel. The burden of proof is clearly upon those who would defend it. Two objections are especially weighty: the First Gospel is preserved as a Greek writing, which manifests a dependence upon at least two Greek sources, Mark and Q; and the reliance of the first evangelist upon Mark and the nature of his revisions of Mark make it extremely doubtful that he should be identified with the apostle Matthew.[63] Independent judgments can be postponed until the sources of Matthew's Gospel and the plan and general characteristics of this work have been studied.

The Sources and Plan of Matthew

The criteria upon which Matthew's use of Mark may be established have been set forth in the preceding chapter. In the following table the order of Matthew 3–13 and Mark 1–4 is shown. Notice that Mark has provided the first evangelist with the framework of his Gospel, but also that Matthew has treated his source with "a mixture of deference and of freedom."[64]

MATTHEW'S USE OF MARK

	Matthew	*Mark*
1. John the Baptist	3:1–6 (7–10)	1:1–6
	11 (–12)	7–8
2. Baptism of Jesus	13 (14–15)	9–11
	16–17	
3. The Temptation	(4:1–11)	12–13
4. First preaching in Galilee	4:12 (13–16) 17	14–15
5. Call of the first disciples	18–22	16–20
6. Jesus in the synagogue at Capernaum	cf. *7:28–29*†	21–28
7. Healing of Peter's mother-in-law	cf. *8:14–15*	29–21
8. Sick healed at evening	*16 (–17)*	32–34
9. Jesus departs from Capernaum	. . . . . .	35–38
10. Preaching journey in Galilee	4:23–25*	39
11. The Sermon on the Mount	5:1–7:29	
12. Healing of a leper	8:1–4	40–45

†This summary statement is substituted for Mark 1:21. It seems to be a conflation of Mark 1:39, 3:10, 7, 8. Cf. Matt. 5:1–Mark 3:13.

*In spite of dislocation of Markan sections, note that Mark's order is retained.

[63] The persistence into the modern period of the opinion that Matthew, in its present or earlier form, was composed earlier than Mark and used by him as a source, should not be overlooked (e.g., B. C. Butler; A. Schlatter; P. Parker; W. R. Farmer). The various arguments in support of the priority of a basic Matthean source fall short of conviction. C. F. D. Moule, *The Birth of the New Testament* (1962), Appendix, G. M. Styler; Perrin, *Rediscovering*, pp. 34f.

[64] J. Moffatt, *Introduction to the Literature of the New Testament* (1918), p. 246 [hereafter, *Intro.*]; Bultmann, *History*, pp. 350ff.; Feine-Behm-Kümmel, *Intro.*, pp. 47f., 75.

	Matthew	*Mark*
13. Healing centurion's servant	(5–13)	cf. *1:23–28*
14. (Note nos. 7 and 8 above)	. . . . . .	
15. Jesus crosses the lake and calms	18 (19–21)	cf. *4:35†*
the storm	23–27	cf. *4:26–41*
16. Gadarene demoniac	28–34	cf. *5:1–20*
17. Healing of a paralytic	9:1–8	*2:1–12*
18. Call of Levi (Matthew)	9–13	*13–17*
19. Question about fasting	14–17	*18–22*
20. Healing of Jairus' daughter	18–26	cf. *5:21–43*
21. Two blind men healed	27–31	cf. *10:46–52*, only
		one man
22. Dumb demoniac healed	(32–33) 34	cf. *3:22*
23. The Mission Discourse	9:35 (10:5–6)	cf. *6:6, 34, 7*
	(8,16b)	*3:13–19*
	. . . . . .	*6:8–11*
	. . . . . .	*13:9–13*
	. . . . . .	*4:22*
	. . . . . .	*8:38, 34–35*
	–11:1	*9:37, 41*
24. John and Jesus	(11:2–19	. . . . . .
25. Woes on cities of Galilee	20–24	. . . . . .
26. Jesus' thanksgiving to the Father	25–30)	. . . . . .
27. Two conflict stories	12:1–4 (5–7) 8–14	*2:23–3:6*
28. Jesus heals the multitude	15–16 (17–21)	*3:7–12*
29. Jesus calls the Twelve	cf. *10:1–4*	*13–19a*
30. Accusations against Jesus	12:22–24	*3:19b–22*
31. A house divided	25–35 (36–37)	*23–30*
32. Against seeking signs	38–42	(cf. *8:11–12*)
33. Return of the evil spirit	43–45	. . . . . .
34. Jesus' true relatives	46–50	*3:31–35*
35. Parables of the Kingdom	13	*4*

From Matthew 14 onward, the first evangelist never drops the Markan thread. The fabric of his narrative is "embroidered" with Old Testament references—especially in the passion story—but Matthew does not seem to possess an alternative narrative sequence.[65] None of the extra incidents are connected, and when the question of their historical value is raised, one cannot rank them alongside the stories taken from Mark.[66]

Matthew has shown greater freedom in altering the order of his second major source than the order of Mark, but it is likely that he has shown the same respect for the wording of Q passages.

Brief attention may now be given to the question of the sources underlying

[65] Moffatt, *Intro.*, p. 247.

[66] Matt. 14:28–33; 17:24–27; 27:3–10, 19, 24f., 51–53, 62–66. See Streeter, *Four Gospels*, pp. 502f.

"special Matthew." The term applies to the approximately four hundred verses peculiar to the First Gospel, passages which are commonly identified by the symbol M.[67] Chapters 1 and 2 were probably composed by the first evangelist from local oral traditions. Yet, as earlier observed, the genealogy of Jesus which stands at the beginning may have been composed by another. Some verses in Matthew's account of the Ministry and passion are additions to Mark's stories.[68] Other M material is the testimony tradition. Eleven passages from the Old Testament are cited, "this was to fulfill what was spoken by the prophet. . . ."[69] Some or all of these testimonies may have come from a tract or from tracts used in the community which the first evangelist represents. Possibly a few units of the tradition found only in Matthew were derived from Q.[70]

In addition to these passages and a few editorial summaries, there still remains a large body of material peculiar to Matthew. This is concentrated in chapters 5–7, 13, 17, 18, 20, 23, and 24. Do these passages form a third major source of the First Gospel, which some have identified as the M document? The strongest support for this hypothesis is found in Matthew 5–7, as a study of the table on page 205 will show. The "special Matthew" in chapters 13–24 may have been drawn from the same source. But some of this material could have come from several smaller tracts or from oral tradition. The peculiar ways in which Matthew revised his "originals" make it difficult to reconstruct them. Because of the Jewish–Christian "atmosphere" of M, and the anti-Gentile bias of its teaching, many believe that it originated in the Jerusalem church.[71]

The reader is now in a position to see why the Gospel of Matthew is often referred to as "a revised and enlarged edition of Mark." Indeed we may use this description to summarize some of the editorial methods employed by the first evangelist.

We have already noted that Matthew revised Mark and Q by a partial re-arrangement of the order of his sources. A second characteristic of his revision is a compression of Mark's narratives. Thus, for example, the stories of the storm at sea, the Gadarene demoniac(s), Jairus' daughter and the woman with the hemorrhage, told in Mark in 821 words, are reduced to 357 in Matthew.[72] Doubt-less the first evangelist wished to make room for non-Markan material at his disposal and concluded that some of Mark's vivid detail was unedifying, or dispensable for other reasons. A third type of revision is an improvement of Mark's diction. He removed redundancies,[73] eliminated ambiguous statements,[74] and modified inelegant or irregular forms of speech.[75]

[67] Summarized by S. Johnson, *IB*, vol. 7, pp. 238.; Streeter, *Four Gospels*, p. 198.

[68] See table above, Sec. 2, Matt. 3:14f.; Sec. 27, Matt. 12:5–7; Sec. 31, Matt. 12:36f.

[69] Matt. 1:22f.; 2:15, 17f., 23; 4:14–16; 8:17; 12:17–21; 13:14f., 35; 21:4f., 27:9f. Cf. 25:56.

[70] Symbol: QMt, e.g., 10:24f. (cf. Luke 6:40 and Matt. 10:26–33 with Luke 12:2–90; also Matt. 22:11–14 (cf. Matt. 22:1–14 with Luke 14:16–24). Cf. Feine-Behm-Kümmel, *Intro.*, pp. 77f.

[71] Streeter, *Four Gospels*, pp. 231f., 254ff.; T. W. Manson, *Sayings*, pp. 21ff.; G. D. Kilpatrick, *The Origin of the Gospel According to St. Matthew* (1946), pp. 3ff. [hereafter, *Origin*].

[72] See table above, Secs. 15, 16, and 20.

[73] Cf. 8:16 and 26b with Mark 1:32 and 4:39.

[74] 13:58; cf. Mark 6:5f.

[75] Cf. of Greek texts needed here, but note Matt. 4:1 and Mark 1:12f.

Other revisions seem to have been prompted by doctrinal motives. Thus by means of editorial omissions or alterations there is a safeguarding of Jesus' power and goodness against detraction.[76] The same motives apparently led Matthew to revise Mark's references to Jesus' disciples and to offer a defense of "the twelve." [77] Other revisions of the substance of Mark's statements probably reflect doctrinal motives. Matthew increased the number of persons benefited by Jesus' mighty works.[78] He also conformed events more closely to Old Testament prophecies and made more explicit the apocalyptic utterances of Jesus in Mark.[79]

Matthew's enlargements of Mark may be summarized. First of all, Matthew added narratives at the beginning and end of his Gospel: the nativity stories, the extra incidents in the passion narrative, and the account of Christ's postresurrection appearances to chosen witnesses. Secondly, Matthew enlarged Mark by inserting at appropriate points the testimony tradition noted earlier, introducing these Old Testament passages with his characteristic formula. Finally, Matthew enlarged Mark's outline by dovetailing into it five or possibly six discourses. On four occasions, Matthew started with a section of Mark as a nucleus and expanded it by non-Markan supplements into a discourse or "sermon": Matthew 9:35–11:1 (Mark 6:7f); Matthew 13 (Mark 4); Matthew 18:1–19:2 (Mark 9:33f.); and Matthew 24:1–26:2 (Mark 13). Matthew's enlargement of the second of these passages from Mark is shown below:

The Composition of Matthew 13

1. 13: 1–9 . . . . Mark (4:1–9)
2. 10–13* . . . . Mark (4:10–12)*
(4:21–25)
3. 14–15 . . . . Special Matt.
4. 16–17 . . . . Q (Luke 10:23–24)
5. 18–23 . . . . Mark (4:13–20)
—* . . . . Mark (4:26–29)*
6. 24–30 . . . . Special Matt.
7. 31–32 . . . . Mark (4:30–32)
8. 33 . . . . Q (Luke 13:20–21)
9. 34–35 . . . . Mark (4:33–34)
10. 36–43 . . . . Special Matt.
11. 44–46 . . . . Special Matt.
12. 47–50 . . . . Special Matt.
13. 51–52 . . . . Special Matt.
14. (8:18, 23–27)* . . . . Mark (4:35–41)*

*Note Matthew's displacement of the order of Mark.

[76] 3:13–15; Cf. Mark 1:9; 12:9–14; cf. Mark 3:1–6 (note the omission of 5a); 13:55; cf. Mark 6:3.
[77] 20:20; cf. Mark 10:35, 12–59; cf. Mark 3:34. Occasionally reference to the disciples' ignorance or bewilderment is omitted (Mark 9:6; 10:32), or toned down (16:5–23; cf. Mark 8:14–33).
[78] Two demoniacs in 8:28–34; two blind men, 9:27–31; five thousand men *besides women and children* are fed, 14:21.
[79] E.g., 21:2, 4f., 7; 26:15; 27:3–10. Note Zech. 11:12f. Cf. Matt. 16:28 with Mark 9:1; Matt. 24:3 with Mark 13:4.

In this case three parables recorded in Mark 4 are expanded in Matthew 13 by means of the addition of discourses and parabolic tradition drawn from Q and "special Matthew."

The first in order of Matthew's discourses, chapters 5–7, is a unique composition. It is a collection of Jesus' teaching drawn from several sources and built into an outline provided by a sermon found in the Q source. The composition of this discourse is shown below:

THE COMPOSITION OF MATTHEW 5–7

1. 5:3–12—The Sermon in Q (Luke 6:20–23)
2. 13–16 . . . . Q (Luke 14:34–35; 11:33)
3. 17–37—Special Matt. (25–26—Q cf. Luke 12:57–59)
4. 38–48—The Sermon in Q (Luke 6:29–30; 27–28; 32–36)
5. 6:1–18—Special Matt.
   (9–13) . . . . (cf. Luke 11:2–4)
   (14–15) Mark (cf. Mark 11:25–26)
6. 19–34 . . . . Q
   (Matt. 19–21—Luke 12:33–34)
   (22–23—   11:34–36)
   (24—   16:13   )
   (25–34—   12:22–31)
7. 7:1–5—The Sermon in Q (Luke 6:37–38, 41–42)
   6—Special Matt.
8. 7–11 . . . . Q (Luke 11:9–13)
9. 12—The Sermon in Q (Luke 6:31)
10. 13–14 . . . . Q (Luke 13:23–24)
11. 15–27—The Sermon in Q
    (Luke 6:43–46)
    (13:26–27)
    (6:47–49)

In constructing these discourses, Matthew followed two literary conventions. One is known as the conflation of sources. At the outset it is evident that both Mark and Q contained versions of John's preaching. Matthew was therefore faced with two alternatives. Either he could choose one source and ignore the other, or he could combine features of both, "conflating" his sources. Ordinarily Matthew chose the second of these alternatives. An examination of sections 2–4 and 7–9 in the table on Matthew 13 above and sections 3 and 5 in the table on Matthew 5–7 will provide ample evidence for Matthew's practice of conflation. The second literary convention employed by Matthew is the practice known as "agglomeration." It consists in the joining of sayings, variously placed in the sources, to form large blocks of tradition developing a single subject or cognate themes.[80] In the Matthew 5–7 table we see this principle illustrated.

The above discussion of Matthew's revisions and expansions has been limited primarily to a delineation of his literary traits and miscellaneous motives explain-

---

[80] B. W. Bacon, *Studies in Matthew* (1930), p. 17 [hereafter, *Matthew*].

ing these. Several scholars have claimed that a careful study of Matthew's editorial practices discloses his overriding and independent theological interests. One writer claims that three major purposes have informed Matthew's redaction of his sources. He has "historicized" units of Mark's narrative by introducing temporal and geographical detail; and he has ordered the entire tradition at his disposal into three epochs: (a) the time of the fathers and the prophets, a time of preparation for (b) the time of Jesus, followed by (c) the time of the Church. Matthew has also "ethicized" the tradition of Jesus' Ministry and thereby manifested his own understanding of the proclamation of the Kingdom and its moral demands, which differs from that of other New Testament writers. Finally, Matthew's editing reveals indirectly his conception of the Church as an institution.[81] The purpose of Matthew will be discussed below.

It will be helpful now to view the structure of the entire Gospel. In the outline which follows, Matthew's insertion into the framework of Mark of major blocks of Jesus' teaching, to form five "discourses," is clearly shown.[82]

An Outline of the Gospel According to Matthew

A. Beginning of narrative: Birth and early ministry of Jesus the Messiah 1:1–4:25:
  1. Genealogy, the names and places associated with the origin of Jesus the Messiah, 1:1–2:23
  2. Ministry of John, 3:1–12
  3. Jesus' preparation and early ministry in Galilee, 3:13–4:25
B. The first discourse: The higher righteousness of the kingdom of heaven 5:1–7:29:
  4. Introduction, 5:1–2
  5. The blessings of the disciples, 5:3–12
  6. Their relation to the world, 5:13–16
  7. New law fulfills the old, 5:17–20
  8. New law contrasted with the old, 5:21–48
  9. New piety contrasted with the old, 6:1–18
  10. Other teachings, 6:19–7:12
  11. Warnings, 7:13–23
  12. Concluding parable, 7:24–27
  13. Summary, 7:28–29
C. Narrative continues: Jesus' mighty works 8:1–9:33:
  14. Descent from mountain and three healings, 8:1–17
  15. Interlude: teachings concerning discipleship, 8:18–22
  16. Three manifestations of Jesus' power, 8:23–9:8
  17. The independence of Jesus' disciples, 9:9–17
  18. Three miracles, 9:18–34

---

[81] Georg Strecker, "The Concept of History in Matthew," *Journal of the American Academy of Religion* (1967): 219ff. [hereafter, *Journ. AAR*].

[82] It may be objected that Chapter 23 adds a sixth "discourse," and that the identification of five owes its origin only to Bacon's improbable hypothesis that Matthew drew a conscious parallelism with "the five books of Moses." See Feine-Behm-Kümmel, *Intro.*, p. 75.

D. The second discourse: The mission and the marks of special disciples 9:35–11:1:
19. Introduction, 9:35–10:4
20. The first mission, 10:5–15
21. Warnings and counsel, 10:16–39
22. Rewards for those who aid disciples, 10:40-42
23. Summary, 11:1

E. Narrative continues: Jesus' rejection anticipated 11:2–12:50:
24. John the Baptist and the Coming One, 11:2–19
25. Mixed reception to Jesus' revelation, 11:20–30
26. Controversies, 12:1–50

F. The third discourse: Parables of the kingdom 13:1–58:
27. Introduction, 13:1–3a
28. Parables on receiving the word, 13:3b–23
29. Three parables concerning the future judgment, 13:24–43
30. Three other parables, 13:44–50
31. The scribe instructed in the kingdom, 13:51–52
32. A concluding example, 13:53–58

G. Narrative continues: The building of the Church 14:1–17:27:
33. Herod fears that Jesus is John, whom he had beheaded, 14:1–12
34. The five thousand are fed and Peter is taught to have faith, 14:13–36
35. The question of ritual cleanliness, 15:1–20
36. Jesus ministers to the Gentiles, 15:21–39
37. The demand for a sign rejected and disciples are warned against Pharisees and Sadducees, 16:1–12
38. Peter's confession and blessing, 16:13–20
39. Jesus speaks of suffering and of glory, 16:21–28
40. The transfiguration reveals the "beloved Son," 17:1–8
41. Disciples are told that John is the Elijah who has come, 17:9–13
42. Jesus heals as an example to disciples of need for faith, 17:14–21
43. Second prediction of suffering and glory, 17:22–23
44. Jesus gives disciples example in exercise of freedom, 17:24–27

H. The fourth discourse: Church problems 18:1–19:2:
45. The greatness of the child, and the value of "little ones," 18:1–14
46. When a "little one" sins, 18:15–35
47. Summary, 19:1–2

I. Narrative continues: Jesus goes to Judea 19:3–23:39:
48. Rigorous demands of discipleship, 19:3–20:28
49. Two blind men are healed, 20:29–34
50. Triumphal entry and cleansing of temple, 21:1–22
51. Controversies and parables of conflict, 21:23–22:46
52. Denunciation of "the scribes of the Pharisees"; the seven woes; the lament over Jerusalem, 23:1–39

J. The fifth discourse: The end of the Age 24:1–26:2:
53. Signs of the approach of the end, 24:1–36
54. On preparedness, 24:37–25:13

55. Three parables on readiness for judgment, 25:14–46

56. Summary, 26:1–2

K. Narrative continues: Jesus goes to his death 26:3–27:66:

57. The conspiracy; the anointing; the betrayal, 26:3–16

58. The Last Supper and Gethsemane, 26:17–46

59. Arrest and arraignment before the high priest, 26:47–68

60. Peter's denial, 26:69–75

61. Trial before Pilate, 27:1–26

62. The crucifixion of Jesus, 27:27–56

63. The burial, 27:57–66

L. The narrative ends: The resurrection 28:1–20:

64. The women at the tomb; Jesus' appearance to them, 28:1–10

65. The false witness of the guards, 28:11–15

66. Appearance to the eleven; their commission, 28:16–20

Several students of the First Gospel who have closely studied its distinctive subject matter and structure have attributed its distinction to one or more environmental factors. It has been urged that such a carefully constructed Gospel cannot be satisfactorily explained as merely the product of the evangelist's editing of sources. This Gospel was written to meet the needs of a particular Christian community. It is therefore probable that its traditions were shaped by that community's interests and activities.

One suggestion is that the traditions in Matthew had been used in the worship of a Jewish–Christian church. Its sources—Mark, Q, and M—had received sermonic exposition, possibly for as long as twenty years before the writing of Matthew. During this time gospel traditions were selected and grouped as "lections" to be read in public worship. Finally, the Gospel of Matthew was composed as "a kind of revised gospel book produced for the worship of the Church," conveniently incorporating in one volume the earlier lectionary material. Thus it is claimed that a liturgical milieu explains a number of features of the First Gospel, for example, the compression of its narrative (unessential details do not hold the attention of worshipers); the evangelist's use of regular formulae to end discourses as well as to introduce Old Testament passages; the presence in Matthew of direct speech and of question-and-answer discourse. The form of "the Beatitudes," "the Lord's Prayer," and certain other passages points to the origin of Matthew's tradition in liturgy.[83] From the beginning to the present day, Matthew has been used by the Church for its services of public worship.[84] Was the Gospel composed with these liturgical needs in mind? All answers must be speculative, since there is scant and equivocal evidence to support them. The extent to which readings from the scriptures had become fixed lections in the Jewish synagogues of the first century is uncertain. But even if such were used, it is questionable that Jewish–Christians would have adopted this practice. Some differences were deliberately cultivated.[85]

---

[83] Kilpatrick, Origin.

[84] S. Johnson, IB, vol. 7, pp. 231f.

[85] W. D. Davies in Davies and Daube, Background, pp. 124ff.

An alternative suggestion for the particular milieu of Matthew's Gospel is more probable and has much to commend it. This is the view that the Gospel was issued as a handbook by a "school," or brotherhood, of Jewish–Christian scribes. The systematic arrangement of the Gospel, the adaptation of its teaching to specific problems arising from a community's life, the concern for the position and the duties of leading disciples, point to its origin in a group devoted to study and instruction. The crowning achievement of the scholarship of "the school of St. Matthew" was its "ingenious interpretation of scripture which closely approaches . . . the *midrash pesher* of the Qumran Sect. . . ."[86]

This conception of the First Gospel as a manual of instruction for the Church is one which has persisted for some while among interpreters of Matthew. But various views have been held as to the purpose of such a manual. Was it composed for prebaptismal, for postbaptismal, or, more broadly, for ethical instruction? According to Acts, the *didache* of the early Jewish–Christian church prescribed a somewhat comprehensive pattern for the corporate life of the believers. We can now observe that the Christian way set forth in Matthew is also comprehensive. Is the First Gospel the literary deposit of the *didache* of some Jewish–Christian community? Probably so, but further delineation of the character of Matthew will be deferred until its origin has been discussed.

Authorship, Date, and Place of Origin of Matthew

In the light of the above observations, what may now be concluded about the second-century tradition concerning Matthew? Does the statement of Papias perserved in Eusebius refer to the First Gospel? In all probability, yes. Matthew was certainly in existence when Papias wrote. The conclusion therefore follows that Papias was misinformed, with respect both to the apostolic authorship of the First Gospel, and to its composition in Aramaic. The internal evidence of the Gospel discredits the comment of Papias. At the same time, there may be a kernel of truth in this tradition. Two alternatives have been proposed. A few hold that, in its reference to "the oracles," the Papias tradition refers to Old Testament prophecies about the Christ. It is not improbable that the apostle Matthew might have made a collection of these. The phrase, "each one interpreted them as he could," would suggest that these collected oracles were variously applied to the deeds and words of Jesus which seemed to fulfill them.[87] Or it could mean that "each one *translated* them [Matthew's testimonies] as he could" into Greek. This hypothesis in its various forms has encountered serious objections. A second, and also improbable, explanation for the basis of the Papias tradition is that it has reference to Q. Three of the statements reported by Papias have been thought applicable to this lost document: Q contained "the sayings" of Jesus, was originally composed in Aramaic, and probably existed in several translations. Moreover,

[86]K. Stendahl, *The School of St. Matthew* (1954), pp. 20ff. [hereafter, *School*]. See above, p. 52, note 45.

[87]Burkitt, *Gospel History*, pp. 126f. Stendahl's theory of a "school of St. Matthew" (noted above) derives these quotations, with greater probability, from the activity of Jewish–Christian scribes within the Church of the evangelist. Cf. Feine-Behm-Kümmel, *Intro.*, pp. 78f.

an Aramaic original of Q would imply that its author was a Palestinian Christian.[88]

Both of these views are no more than guesses advanced to explain the Papias tradition. Both erect one hypothesis upon others and depend upon the dubious assumption that a writing by an apostle would have been lost or superseded. Their value lies in this: they call attention to the fact that the name of the author of a source or source material might easily be transferred to a Gospel which incorporated it, especially when this Gospel came into competition with others claiming some apostle's backing. The substitution of the name of "Matthew" (Matt. 9:9) for the "Levi" of Mark 2:14 may have had some influence in establishing the tradition reported by Papias, but it is unlikely to be its sole basis.

The breakdown of the ancient Church tradition ascribing the First Gospel to Matthew means that its anonymous author can be identified only through his work. The Gospel implies that "St. Matthew" was not an apostle, writing his own recollections, but a Jewish–Christian whose native tongue was Greek and who had derived his knowledge of Jesus from oral and written traditions current in his own community.

The determination of the date of Matthew must take into account its use by Ignatius around A.D. 110 and its probable quotation in *The Teaching of the Twelve Apostles* and in *The Shepherd of Hermas*, both written before A.D. 150. But the content of Matthew provides the most significant evidence for fixing the time of its composition. The insertion of the following words into the parable of the marriage feast suggests that Jerusalem had fallen: ". . . the king was angry; and he sent his troops, and destroyed those murderers, and burned their city" (Matt. 22:7). The addition of the word "desolate" in Matthew 23:38 and Matthew's alteration of Mark 13:14 (Matt. 24:15) also suggest a date after A.D. 70. The phrase "to this day" (27:8) and the legendary character of this and other additions to Mark's passion narrative indicate a considerable lapse of time since the death of Jesus.

Assuming that Mark was written at Rome during the period A.D. 65 to 70, some time must be allowed for its dissemination, and for the establishment of Mark's authority in the East, to account for its influence upon Matthew. We are thus able to reduce the margin of probability to A.D. 75 to 110. A more precise dating than this depends largely upon the student's estimate of the appropriate temporal setting for the apocalyptic utterances in the First Gospel and for the Church situation which it presupposes. The present writer sees no convincing reason for dating the Gospel later than A.D. 80 to 85. Indeed, several factors support its composition during this period. There are suggestions in the Gospel that the hope of some persons in the near advent of the Son of man and of the end of the Age is waning, and that the evangelist is concerned to revive this hope. But it is not likely that a second generation of Christians is implied, as in the Apocalypse of John, especially in view of the retention of such sayings as Matthew 10:23, 16:28 and 26:64. The most natural reading of Matthew 24:9f. is that the "tribulation" is closely associated with the fall of Jerusalem, and that this passage was written not long after that event.

[88] T. W. Manson, *Sayings*, pp. 16ff.

The evidence of the Qumran scrolls calls into question the assumption that the existence of a church order, and of a writer's interest in discipline, necessarily imply that a Christian document is postapostolic in date and derives from a Gentile community. The conclusion reached with respect to Luke–Acts applies as well to Matthew. There is no need to suppose a late date for this Gospel because of its writer's concern for the Church and its disciplined life.[89]

Scholars are nearly unanimous in agreeing that the First Gospel was written in Syria or northern Palestine and that its early acceptance was due to its advocacy by the church at Antioch. Some evidence points to Antioch as the place of its writing, but other evidence is against this.[90] Of course, it is more important that one should know the character of the particular Christian community producing the Gospel than that its location should be identified. It is fortunate that one is able to speak with some confidence about the former, if not about the latter.

The Purpose of Matthew

In this section, evidence will be given for the view that Matthew wrote a manual of instruction to be used by teachers in the Church, in order to confirm faith that Jesus is the Messiah who fulfills Old Testament prophecies and Jewish apocalyptic hopes; that the community of believers in Jesus as Messiah is the New Israel, the people of the new covenant unto whom the promises of God are given; and that the words of Jesus the Messiah constitute the Law of God for the Church until the end of the Age.

First, more than the other evangelists, Matthew seeks to provide proofs that Jesus is the true Messiah of the Jews. From the beginning of his writing he is concerned to show that the facts of the gospel tradition correspond to law and prophecy. A genealogy showing Jesus' descent from Abraham and David introduces Matthew's Gospel. Isaiah, Micah, and Jeremiah foretold his birth and the signs attending it. Matthew retains the four passages in Mark identifying Jesus as Messiah and introduces this idea into his sources seven times.[91] Jesus in Matthew applies the title "the Christ" to himself. The title "Son of David" is related to Jesus twice in Mark, but Matthew ascribes it to him six other times.[92] Matthew's alterations of Mark 15:26 and 32 are probably motivated by the desire explicitly to claim for Jesus the title "king of the Jews."[93]

Matthew's use of Old Testament testimonies should be recalled here as an important illustration of this purpose. The manner in which these testimonies

---

[89]See above, p. 110; Davies, *Invitation*, pp. 209f. Supporters of a later date, ca. A.D. 100 or shortly thereafter, are Bacon, Grant, Enslin, Johnson, and Bornkamm.

[90]Streeter, *Four Gospels*, pp. 500ff.; cf. Bacon, *Matthew*, pp. 17ff; F. C. Grant, *Gospels*, pp. 140f.; Kilpatrick, *Origin*, pp. 124ff.

[91]Matt. 11:2; 16:20; 24:5; 26:68; 27:17, 22.

[92]1:1; 9:27; 12:23; 15:22; 21:9, 15. J. M. Gibbs, "Purpose and Pattern in Matthew's Use of the Title 'Son of David,'" *NTS* 10 (1964): 446ff.

[93]Cf. Matt. 27:37, 42. See G. Bornkamm, "End-Expectation and Church in Matthew," in G. Bornkamm, G. Barth, and H. J. Held, *Tradition and Interpretation in Matthew*, trans. P. Scott (1963), pp. 33ff. [hereafter, Bornkamm-Barth-Held, *Matthew*].

are introduced, cited, and interpreted is characteristic of the first evangelist, and probably of the "school" he represented. Such testimonies are not limited to "special Matthew" and thus cannot be said to characterize the views of his source only. The recognition of the similarity of type in the exposition of testimonies in Matthew and at Qumran—the midrash pesher—has provided a significant clue to the peculiarly mixed texts of the Old Testament appearing in the First Gospel. Among the Qumran scribes, the eschatological beliefs of the sect exerted a creative influence upon the scriptures. The same tendency is seen in Matthew's use of the Old Testament. The eschatological beliefs of the Church gave its scribes a new understanding of the prophecies which was unknown to those who spoke them and to later Judaism. The occurrence of events fulfilling these scriptures gave authority to the scribes to alter the prophecies to correspond to their fulfill-ment.[94] This principle of correspondence could also work in reverse. Prophecies were employed in Matthew's community to correct and to supplement the gospel tradition.

Matthew would also have his reader understand that Jesus is the Messiah *who is to come.* The advent of Jesus as the glorified Son of man, especially in his role as judge, is a central teaching of the First Gospel. Thirty times this apocalyptic title is used by Jesus in Matthew, and special emphasis is placed upon his role as ruler and as judge.[95] As Son of man Jesus will come (10:23) in the glory of his Father (16:27) or in his own glory (25:31) with his angels (13:41; 24:31). He will sit on the throne of his glory and judge the nations, rendering to every man according to his deeds (16:27; 19:28; 25:31). But the emphasis in Matthew upon Jesus' heavenly session does not imply that Jesus is separated from the company of his disciples until his glorious advent at the end of the Age. On the contrary, two aspects of the present relation of Jesus the Messiah to his disciples are stressed in the First Gospel: the presence of Jesus is known in the disciple community because he has willed to identify himself with his followers, and Jesus continues to be the Teacher of "his Church."

Evidence for the first of these statements is provided in the following passages. In Matthew 1:23, the keynote of the story of the birth of Jesus is sounded. The coming of the Messiah fulfills the prophecy of Isaiah "they shall call his name Emmanuel—God with us." In Matthew 18:20, in the middle of the Gospel, Jesus speaks of the Church and its prerogatives, declaring, "where two or three are gathered in my name, there am I in the midst of them." The last words of the Gospel re-echo this assurance of the presence of the risen Christ: "Lo, I am with you always, to the close of the age." Thus Matthew declares that in the person of Jesus the Christ, God is with men so long as the world lasts.[96] In this teaching, Matthew approximates the mystical conception of the apostle Paul that the Church is "the body of Christ." [97]

---

[94] Stendahl, *School,* pp. 196ff.; F. C. Grant, *Gospels,* pp. 147ff.

[95] Used in Mark 14 times; in Luke, 25.

[96] Dodd, *New Testament Studies,* pp. 60ff.

[97] Anderson, *Jesus,* pp. 225f. Cf. Strecker, note 81 above, p. 230, who argues that Matthew's theology "corresponds neither to the older Jesus-tradition nor to Pauline or Johannine theology."

Second, the belief that believers in Jesus the Messiah form the New Israel is clearly implied in passages in Matthew which emphasize that the Jews are no longer the people of God.[98] The woes of the nation are viewed as retribution for the crucifixion of the Messiah. The Jews had solemnly accepted responsibility for their action.[99] The tradition in the First Gospel was evidently assembled in some community which knew firsthand the bitterness of the controversies between the synagogue and Church. Answers which were given to the slanders of the Jews are recorded, and it is likely that words of Jesus condemning the Pharisees were brought together to serve as an indictment of unbelieving Jews. Matthew is the Gospel which equates Pharisee and "hypocrite."[100]

Matthew did not conceive of the New Israel as merely a purified remnant within Judaism, confessing the Messiah. The self-consciousness of the Church as separate from Judaism is manifested in the ruling concerning the temple tax.[101] Neither is it probable that Matthew considered the true people of God to be the Gentile Christians only. The "nation" to whom the Kingdom of God is given is the Church composed of Jews and Gentiles who confess the faith, first confessed by Peter: Jesus is the Christ. It is to this "Church" that power is given to interpret the Law of the old Israel; but it is also this Church which is given a universal mission.[102]

The absence from the other Synoptic Gospels of the word *Church* and its appearance twice in Matthew have led some scholars to refer to Matthew as "the ecclesiastical gospel."[103] The appropriateness of this term is especially evident in the fourth discourse.[104] In its treatment of an offending brother, the Church acts as an organized society with a rule of discipline. In the narrative which follows, a distinction seems to be drawn between ordinary disciples and those who would be "perfect."[105]

The Church of the First Gospel was conscious of the mixed character of its membership. Not only did this community contain members who would subject themselves to no law, but false prophets had arisen to lead men astray, and the love of many had grown cold.[106] According to the Matthean tradition, the rule of excommunication is not an absolute one. The penitent brothers must be forgiven.[107] The separation between "the good seed" and "the weeds," "the

[98] 13:10. Cf. Bornkamm, who observes rightly that one never reads in Matthew that Christians are the new or true Israel, the elect, the Church of the New Covenant, etc. He draws the dubious inference from this that the congregation which Matthew represented "had not separated from Judaism . . . the struggle with Israel is still a struggle within its own walls," *Matthew*, p. 39. Note the use of the terms *their scribes, their synagogue,* and *your synagogues,* 7:29; 9:35; 23:34. Rohde, *Teaching of the Evangelists,* pp. 79f.

[99] 27:25.

[100] 27:62–66; (1:3, 5f. ?). Note 23:1–36.

[101] 17:24–27. Cf. Bornkamm-Barth-Held, *Matthew,* pp. 196.

[102] 16:18f. and 18:17; 24:14 and 28:16–20.

[103] F. C. Grant, *Gospels,* pp. 134ff.

[104] See outline above, Sec. H, Matt. 18:1–19:2.

[105] 19:3–12, 16:22. Strecker, note 81 above, pp. 228ff.

[106] 5:19; 7:15f.; 24:11f.

[107] 18:21–35.

righteous" and "the evil," must await the final judgment.[108] Some interpreters of Matthew have concluded that the evangelist identified this mixed community, the visible Church, with the kingdom of heaven. It is unlikely that he did so absolutely. Matthew identified the kingdom of the "Son of man" with "the Church," for, like the Church, this kingdom contained "evildoers" and those who gave offense. Such persons would be purged in the last judgment.[109] But those who inherit the kingdom of heaven are only "the righteous."[110] For all practical purposes the teaching of Matthew is that those who enter the kingdom also enter the Church, at whose congregational meetings the risen Christ is present. The scribes and teachers of this community have the power "to bind and to loose," and their decisions are ratified in heaven.[111]

Third, closely related to the conception in Matthew of the Church as the New Israel is the idea that the teaching of the Messiah provides a new understanding of the Law or Torah of God. It can be objected that the use of the phrase *new Law* is a misleading if not incorrect indicator of Matthew's position. Matthew's understanding of the Law does not differ in principle from Jewish scribal tradition: rather, the question for Matthew and his Church is the right interpretation of the Law which has abiding validity.[112] Evidently the need had arisen in the Church of the First Gospel to insist that Christians were bound by law, that the life of righteousness was to be identified with observance of law. Yet this law is not identical with the old Law of Judaism. Nor is the "higher righteousness" understood by Matthew as a new legalism. Jesus' words were not intended "to destroy the Law;" yet they fill it with the meaning God had intended, a meaning which the teachers in Israel had failed to comprehend.[113]

The concept of Matthew as the Gospel of "the new Law" probably derives in part from Bacon's ingenuous theory that the topical arrangement therein of Jesus' sayings in five formal discourses stands as a conscious imitation of the five books of Moses. The internal evidence does not seem to support Bacon's hypothesis, but it cannot be denied that Jesus is portrayed as the new Moses by Matthew.[114] Like Moses, Jesus barely escaped death as an infant. Out of Egypt God called His Son, who was also tempted in the wilderness—as Moses and the children of Israel had been tempted. Like Moses, too, Jesus proclaimed the law of God from the mountain, and the new covenant like the old is sealed in sacrificial blood. Parallels such as these can lead into flights of fancy, but, beyond doubt, Matthew presents Jesus as the authoritative teacher of Israel whose words rightly interpret

[108] 13:24–30, 36–43, 47–50; 25:31–33.

[109] 13:41.

[110] 13:43; 25:34ff.

[111] Johnson, *IB*, vol. 7, p. 234.

[112] G. Barth, "Matthew's Understanding of the Law," in Bornkamm-Barth-Held, *Matthew*, pp. 153ff.; also Bornkamm, ibid., pp. 24ff.

[113] 5:17–20. Note Barth's attempt to identify the illusive antinomians who are opposed by Matthew's community; ibid., pp. 159ff.

[114] See above, pp. 204ff. Kilpatrick, *Origin*, pp. 107f. Cf. Bornkamm-Barth-Held, *Matthew*, pp. 35, 153ff.; Anderson, *Jesus*, pp. 222f., n. 65, pp. 340f.

the old covenant Law, and whose authority supersedes that of other teachers in Israel, past and present.

The "discourses of Matthew" present the law under which the Church is to live until the close of the Age. In them the motives of reward and penalty are prominent as an encouragement to Christians to do the will of God.[115] But the motive of imitating Christ and the perfection of God is fundamental.[116]

A careful analysis of the First Gospel leads to the question of its consistency. Some claim that its writer was pro-Jewish and that his understanding of Jesus' teaching is Judaistic. Others have recognized a decided Gentile bias; still others have seen that this bias is coupled with an anti-Jewish animus.[117] Recent studies have rightly emphasized the importance of the Gospel's concluding missionary charge (28:16ff.) as the key to understanding the theological presuppositions of Matthew. From this perspective one may conclude that Matthew's church "teaches a completely unqualified universalism" so that it is no longer possible to speak of *the evangelist's* "Jewish Christianity." The so-called "separatist passages," and those containing a legalistic understanding of Jesus' teaching, reflect views present in Matthew's source(s). Their preservation illustrates the evangelist's fidelity to the tradition he reports, but the contexts in which he places it manifest, on the one hand, that the alternatives—Jewish or Gentile Christianity—have been transcended, and, on the other hand, the grounds upon which Matthew's church proclaimed its universalistic faith.[118]

THE GOSPEL OF LUKE

The late-second-century tradition that Luke was the author of the Third Gospel has been reported above.[119] Possibly earlier, indirect support may be found in the dialogues of Justin Martyr. Justin speaks of the Gospels as "the memoirs of the apostles" and, at one place, refers to these as compositions "by apostles *and those who followed them.*"[120] The last clause may refer to Mark and Luke as followers, respectively, of Peter and Paul. Other evidence perhaps may be found in the "Anti-Marcionite Prologues." The conclusion of the prologue to the Third Gospel, which is cited in Chapter 5, apparently echoes the tradition reported by Irenaeus, but the biographical details in its first paragraph may represent an earlier tradition.[121]

[115] 5:19, 22–26, 29f.; 6:3f., 18; 7:1f., 19, 21–27, etc.

[116] 10:25 and 5:44–48.

[117] K. Clark, "The Gentile Bias in Matthew," *JBL* LXVI (1947): 165ff.; Feine-Behm-Kümmel, *Intro.,* p. 82; D. R. A. Hore, *The Theme of Jewish Persecution of Christians in the Gospel According to Matthew* (1968).

[118] The opposite positions advanced by Bornkamm-Barth-Held are attacked by W. Trilling and G. Strecker. See Rohde, *Teaching of the Evangelists,* pp. 74ff., 111f.

[119] See above, pp. 99f.

[120] *Dial.,* 103. 19.

[121] Heard, *Intro.,* p. 74. See also T. W. Manson, *Bulletin of the John Rylands Library* vol. 28, pp. 384ff. [hereafter, *BJRL*]. Note the skepticism of others concerning the value of these "prologues," Feine-Behm-Kümmel, *Intro.,* pp. 102f., 343.

If there had been no information more substantial then inferences to be drawn from the New Testament, it is unlikely that a Gospel would have been ascribed to Luke, who was neither an apostle nor a follower of one of "the twelve." In this book's introduction to Acts, it was acknowledged that the authorship of Luke–Acts must finally be decided upon the internal evidence. We turn, then, to consider the contents of the Third Gospel.

The Sources and Plan of Luke

Although the Third Gospel, like the First, represents a gathering together and an expansion of traditional source material, its creative writer cannot be described adequately as an editor. Luke's Gospel is an original work, reflecting its writer's special interests. It is true that Mark was Luke's principal source; yet the Third Gospel is more than a new edition of Mark. Luke has used Mark more sparingly than the author of the First Gospel and he has taken greater liberties with his source. Matthew employs over 90 percent of Mark; Luke slightly over 60 percent.

Luke preserves the order of Mark with remarkable fidelity. Of the 109 paragraphs before Luke 19, only three occupy a different position from parallels in Mark.[122] Up to the passion narrative, passages in Mark appear in the following sections: 4:31–44; 5:12–6:19; 8:4–9:50; 18:15–43. Luke's omissions from Mark, however, are noteworthy, especially the section Mark 6:45–8:26, commonly known as "Luke's great omission." It is not necessary or probable to account for these omissions by an appeal to some form of an Ur-Marcus theory. Several of them may be explained as Luke's avoidance of duplications.[123] Partial parallels to Mark in other sources are sometimes preferred.[124] Some of Mark's stories were thought misleading or unedifying to Gentile readers.[125] For the rest, we can assume that Luke needed room for non-Markan traditions which he favored. Luke's revisions of Mark's language are more drastic than Matthew's, but probably some of the same motives prompted him to make them. Like Matthew, Luke abbreviated some of Mark's stories. Even Mark's meager teaching tradition is somewhat abridged in Luke.[126] He removed redundancies, sometimes rewrote awkward passages, and replaced Mark's rough expressions with more elegant ones. Moreover, doctrinal motives may have determined several of Luke's revisions. Reverence is shown for the person of Jesus, and consideration for his disciples.[127]

Luke's practices of revision may be summarized as follows. He has exercised

---

[122] Luke 3:19; 6:12–16; 8:19–21. This statistic is based on *Gospel Parallels: A Synopsis of the First Three Gospels* (1949). The second of these passages introduces, and the third concludes, a section in Luke made up of non-Markan materials.

[123] Luke 11:14–22; cf. Matt. 9:32–34 (Q); Luke omits Mark 3:22–27; cf. Matt. 12:22–30.

[124] Note Luke's selection of the teaching concerning divorce (16:18; cf. Matt. 5:32 [Q]), and his omission of Mark 10:1–12.

[125] E.g., Mark 7:24–30; 11:12–14, 20–25.

[126] Luke 8:4–18; cf. Mark 4:1–29; 9:10–17. Cf. Mark 6:30–44.

[127] Luke 5:12; cf. Mark 1:40; 5:29f. Cf. Mark 1:15f. Note Luke's omission of Mark 14:50: "they all forsook him and fled," as well as his expansion of Mark 14:37: Jesus "found them sleeping *for sorrow*," Luke 22:45.

the greatest freedom in revising the situations contained in the introductions and conclusions to Mark's stories (although he seldom makes the temporal connections more precise). He is less free in revising the narratives themselves, although there are some significant alterations in detail. The words of Jesus are quoted most exactly.[128] The composition of Luke's passion narrative will be discussed later.

The hypothesis that Luke employed Q as a source has a high degree of probability, as we have seen. Most of the Q tradition is either located in one short section, 6:20–8:3 (known as Luke's "lesser interpolation"); or in another, much longer section, 9:51–18:14 (known as Luke's "greater interpolation"). Probably Luke held the order of Q, as well as that of Mark, in greater respect than did Matthew. We have observed that the first evangelist freely transposed, combined, and conflated his sources. Luke's practices are to select passages from one source and follow it to the exclusion of another, and to incorporate blocks from his sources. Reconstructions of the order of Q have ordinarily been based upon Luke. Some scholars would hazard the generalization that Luke's versions of Q passages are closer to their original wording than Matthew's. Others note the conservative tendency in Matthew's revisions of Jesus' discourses in Mark and apply a rule of thumb in reconstructing Q: follow Luke's order but Matthew's wording. But each passage needs to be studied separately.[129]

A considerable body of material remains after the subtraction of Mark and of Q. The following table identifies the passages prior to the passion story which are peculiar to the Third Gospel:

"Special Luke"

1. The birth and infancy of John and Jesus, 1 and 2
2. John's preaching to special groups, 3:10–14
3. The rejection at Nazareth, 4:16–30 cf. Mark 6:1–6
4. The miraculous catch of fish, 5:1–11 cf. Mark 1:16–20
5. Woes (from the Sermon on the Plain), (6:24–26)*
6. The widow's son at Nain, 7:11–17
7. The woman with the ointment, 7:26–50 cf. Mark 14:3–9
8. The ministering women, 8:1–3
9. The Samaritan villages reject Jesus, 9:51–56

*Passages in parentheses may not belong to L; some may have been drawn from Q. (L is the symbol used for "special Luke" here and on pages 219–220.)

[128] A noteworthy exception is 5:32, which may represent the language of the Church (cf. Mark 2:17 and Matt. 9:13). Bultmann, *History,* pp. 358ff., presents a detailed analysis of Luke's editorial revisions of Mark's narrative units and concludes that, in his literary use of Mark's arrangement, Luke "is more conservative than Matthew . . . because he is interested in an historically continuous and connective presentation. . . ." and, unlike Matthew, does not "make his account subservient to some systematic interest." pp. 362, 366. Cf., however, more recent studies which contend that Luke's use of Mark, and other sources, was directed by discernable theological interests. See above, p. 110, and further, below, p. 227.

[129] Creed, *St. Luke,* pp. lxv f.; Cadbury in *Making of Luke–Acts,* pp. 101ff. The problem of determining "the original Q" is a complicated one. Note "the Lord's Prayer" (Matt. 6:9–13—Luke 11:2–4).

10. The nature of discipleship, (9:61–62)
11. The return of the seventy, 10:17–20 cf. Mark 16:17–18
12. The parable of the good Samaritan, 10:29–37
13. Mary and Martha, 10:38–42
14. The friend at midnight, 11:5–8
15. The blessedness of Jesus' mother, 11:27–28
16. The parable of the rich fool, 12:13–21
17. Watchfulness and faithfulness, (12:35–46) cf. Matt. 24:43–51
18. The servant's wages, (12:47–48)
19. Repentance or destruction, 13:1–9
20. The woman with the spirit of infirmity, 13:10–17
21. The departure from Galilee, 13:31–33
22. The man with dropsy, 14:1–6
23. Teaching on humility, 14:7–14
24. Parables on building a tower and on going to war, 14:28–33
25. Parable of the lost coin, 15:8–10
26. Parable of the prodigal son, 15:11–32
27. The unjust steward, 16:1–12
28. The rich man and Lazarus, 16:19–31
29. The servant's duties, 17:7–10
30. Healing of ten lepers, 17:11–19 cf. Mark 1:40–45
31. The kingdom of God and the day of the Son of man, (17:20–37) cf. Matt 24:26–28, 37–41; 10:39
32. Parable of the unjust judge, 18:1–8
33. Parable of Pharisee and publican, 18:9–14
34. Zacchaeus, 19:1–10
35. Jesus weeps over Jerusalem, 19:41–44

It is almost universally believed that chapters 1 and 2 should be considered apart from the rest of "special Luke." The unity of the birth narratives and peculiarities of style and language distinguish these chapters from the remainder of the special material of the Third Gospel. Luke 1–2 may depend upon a pre-canonical written source or may be a composition by the evangelist based upon traditions from several "sources." In either case a Judean, or at least a Palestinian, origin for the tradition is probable.[130]

The heterogeneous character of the remainder of "special Luke" makes it intractable to topical arrangement. Both narrative and discourse are included. Some of the narratives peculiar to Luke may have been used by him in place of their partial parallels in Mark.[131] Some narratives amplify or illustrate Mark's outline.[132] Yet other stories have no connection with the Markan tradition. In their intrinsic value, these narratives contrast sharply with Matthew's haggadic

[130]Cf., Feine-Behm-Kümmel, Intro., pp. 95f. See further, below, p. 225.

[131]See table above, Secs. 3, 4, 7, and 11.

[132]E.g., in Mark, Jesus is accused of consorting with "tax collectors and sinners," but aside from the call of Levi (2:13–17) no evidence is given of this. See table, Secs. 7 and 34.

additions to Mark.[133] A special kind of discourse tradition is found in several parables in "special Luke" which depict types of character.[134] Three of these parables closely resemble those recorded in Mark and Matthew, but even these are unique in that they draw an analogy between some aspect of God's action and the acts of *unrighteous* men.[135]

Questions concerning the nature of "special Luke" and its influence upon the third evangelist become especially perplexing toward the end of the Gospel. It is a striking fact already noted that Luke's passion narrative differs considerably more from Mark than do the earlier portions of his Gospel. For the purpose of this study, the narrative is divided into two parts: Luke 22:1–13, in which the parallelism with Mark 14:1–16 is close; and Luke 22:14 through 23:56, in which the narrative is roughly parallel to Mark but the measure of agreement is less. The following table presents the problem graphically.

The Passion Narrative in Luke and Mark

	Luke's Passion Narrative	L	Mark
(i)	1. 22:1–2 the conspiracy		14:1–2
	2. .... the anointing at Bethany		3–9 (cf. Luke 7:36–50)
	3. 3–6 betrayal by Judas		10–11
	4. 7–13 preparation for the Passover		12–16
(ii)	5. 14 Jesus gathers with the apostles	(L)	17 "the twelve"
	6. 15–16 renewal of Passover in the kingdom prophesied	L	(25)
	7. 17–18 the cup saying	L	23–24
	8. 19 the bread saying		22
	9. 21–23 the traitor	21, 23 (L)	18–21
	10. 24–27 greatness in the kingdom	27 (L)	10:42–44 (45)
	11. 28–30 judgment of the tribes of Israel	(L)	(Matt 19:28)
	12. 31–34 Peter's denial prophesied	L	(14:29–31)
	13. 35–38 two-sword saying	L	. . . . . .
	14. 39 the way to Gethsemane		14:26
	15. .... stricken shepherd and scattered sheep		27–28
	16. 40 arrival at Gethsemane		32
	17. 41–42 "thy will be done"		35–36
	18. 43–44 the distress of soul	(L)	(33–34)
	19. 45–46 sleeping disciples		37–38

[133]E.g., see table, Secs. 6, 9, and 13.
[134]See table, Secs. 12, 16, and 28.
[135]See table, Secs. 14, 27, and 32.

Luke's Passion Narrative	L	*Mark*
20. . . . . Jesus prays a second and a third time		39–42
21. 47–53 Jesus taken captive		43–52
22. 51 Jesus forbids resistance; heals slave's ear	L	. . . . . .
23. 52–53 Jesus speaks to his captors		14:48–49
24. . . . . disciples flee; young man looses his linen cloth		50–51
25. 54–55 Jesus taken to high priests; Peter in courtyard		53–54
26. 56–62 Peter's denial		66–72
27. 63–65 Jesus is mocked	(L)	(65)
28. 66 before the Sanhedrin arraignment in the morning		(15:1a)
29. . . . . (trial at night)		14:55–65 (cf. Luke 22:67–71)
30. 67–71 trial when "day came"	(L)	(14:55–65)
31. 23:1 Jesus delivered to Pilate	(L)	(15:1b)
32. . . . . death of Judas		(cf. Acts 1:18–19)
33. 2 accusations of treason	L	. . . . . .
34. 3 Pilate's question	(L)	(15:2)
35. 4–5 Pilate asserts Jesus' innocence	L	. . . . . .
36. 6–12 Jesus before Herod	L	. . . . . .
37. 13–16 Pilate declares Jesus not guilty of death	L	. . . . . .
38. (17)–22a release Barabbas, crucify Jesus		6–14
39. 22b no crime deserving death		. . . . . .
40. 24–25 Pilate's sentence		15
41. . . . . king mocked by soldiers		16–20
42. 26 Simon bears the cross		21
43. 27–31 "daughters of Jerusalem"	L	. . . . . .
44. 32 note concerning two criminals		27 "robbers"
45. 33 Jesus is crucified		22–24
46. 34a "Father, forgive them"	L	. . . . . .
47. 34–35 lots for the garments		24–25
48. 36–38 "king of the Jews"		36, 30, 26
49. 39–43 "with me in paradise"	L	. . . . . .
50. 44 "darkness over the whole land" temple's curtain torn		33 38
51. . . . . the cry of desolation		34–36 cf. v. 36 Luke 23:36
52. 46b "Father, into Thy hands"	L	(37)

Luke's Passion Narrative	L	Mark
53. 47 centurion's remark	L	(29)
54. 48 distressed multitudes	L	. . . . . .
55. 49 women from Galilee		40–41 cf. Luke 8:3
56. 50–56 burial of Jesus		42–47

Notice that Mark continues to alternate with "special Luke" in the account of the passion. But observe (from the italicized passages) that the order of Mark's narrative has been transposed to an unparalleled extent.[136]

Luke's passion narrative is variously explained. One opinion is that "special Luke" contained a passion narrative, or a more inclusive source, which provided the conclusion of the Third Gospel, into which has been interpolated some contributions of Mark.[137] The alternative opinion is that Mark provided Luke the foundation for his passion story as for the preceding apocalyptic discourse.[138] It will be noted below that a decision in this matter affects one's view concerning the origin of Luke's Gospel and, to some extent, its historical value.[139]

Whatever the form or forms in which these traditions reached the third evangelist, the hypothesis has merit that "special Luke" originated in Palestine.[140] Passages from this source show Jesus' interest in "the poor" and there is a tendency to equate poverty and piety.[141] This may point to the church in Jerusalem. Yet an immediate derivation of "special Luke" from the earliest church may be excluded by the sympathy shown in the source toward the Samaritans.[142] The tradition also shows interest in Jesus' contacts with women,[143] and a fondness for the miraculous.[144] "The conjecture that much of this material took shape in the church at Caesarea is at least attractive."[145] Caesarea was a Greek-speaking city, in tradition the scene of Peter's first Gentile convert. It was the home of

---

[136] Mark's narrative is also rewritten and conflated with other material, a feature hardly to be found elsewhere in Luke. Some of Luke's "improvements" were probably introduced to provide smooth transitions to episodes which are inserted, e.g., Secs. 48f., while others stand as corrections of Mark, e.g., Secs. 7f.; 28–30.

[137] Perry, *Luke's Passion Narrative*; Streeter, *Four Gospels*, pp. 202f.; V. Taylor, *Behind the Third Gospel* (1926); P. Winter, "The Treatment of His Sources by the Third Evangelist in Luke XXI–XXIV," *Studia Theologica* 8 (1955): 138ff.; P. Winter, "On Luke and Lucan Sources," *Zeitschrift für die neutestamentliche Wissenschaft und die Kunde der älteren Kirche* 47 (1956): 217ff. [hereafter, *ZNW*].

[138] Moffatt, *Intro.*, pp. 274ff.; Creed, *St. Luke*, pp. lxiii f.; S. McL. Gilmour, "A Critical Examination of Proto-Luke," *JBL* (June 1948): 151ff.; *IB*, vol. 8, pp. 16ff.; McNeile, *Intro.*, pp. 61f; Feine-Behm-Kümmel, *Intro.*, pp. 94f.

[139] See further, below, pp. 223f.

[140] F. C. Grant, *Gospels*, pp. 62f.; Creed, *St. Luke*, p. lxvi. Cf. Cadbury in *Making of Luke-Acts*, pp. 66ff.

[141] Table, pp. 217f., Secs. 2, 5, 16, and 28.

[142] Table, pp. 217f., Sec. 9, 12, and 30.

[143] Table, pp. 217f., Sec. 6–8, 13, 15, 20.

[144] Table, pp. 217f., Secs. 4, 6, 20, 22, 30; *IB*, vol. 8, p. 14.

[145] Creed, *St. Luke*, p. lxx; Streeter, *Four Gospels*, p. 219.

Philip, the evangelist to Samaria, as well as of his daughters. Such a background suits the internal character of "special Luke." The date for the assembly of this material is a question related to the composition of the Third Gospel.

An Outline of the Gospel According to Luke

A. Preface to Theophilus: 1:1–4
B. Birth and childhood of John and of Jesus: 1:5–2:52:
   1. Annunciations to Zechariah and to Mary, 1:5–56
   2. John and Jesus are born, 1:57–2:20
   3. Jesus' infancy; the boy of twelve, 2:21–52
C. Preparation for the Ministry: 3:1–4:13:
   4. John the Baptist, 3:1–20
   5. Jesus' baptism, ancestry, temptations, 3:21–4:13
D. The Galilean ministry: 4:14–9:50:
   6. The fame of the teacher, 4:14–15
   7. Rejection at Nazareth, 4:16–30
   8. Healings in and around Capernaum, 4:31–44
   9. Call of the first disciples, 5:1–11
   10. Controversies with Pharisees, 5:12–6:11
   11. Call of "the twelve," 6:12–16
   12. The Sermon on the Plain, 6:17–49
   13. Deliverance from death, 7:1–17
   14. Jesus and the Baptist, 7:18–35
   15. A woman of the city, and other women who accompanied Jesus 7:36–8:3
   16. Jesus teaches by parables; performs mighty works (traveling with the disciples), 8:4–56
   17. The mission of "the twelve" and the departure from Galilee, 9:1–11
   18. Feeding the five thousand, 9:12–17
   19. Peter's confession: Jesus' first prediction of his sufferings and those of the disciples, 9:18–27
   20. The transfiguration, 9:28–36
   21. Failings of the disciples, 9:37–50
E. The journey to Jerusalem: 9:51–19:27:
   22. Hostile Samaritans; half-hearted disciples, 9:51–62
   23. The mission of the seventy, 10:1–24
   24. Jesus answers questions, 10:25–42
   25. Teaching on prayer, 11:1–13
   26. Demon exorcism, 11:14–26
   27. Hearing the Word; seeking signs; shedding light, 11:27–36
   28. Discourse against Pharisees and lawyers, 11:37–54
   29. Warning the disciples, 12:1–13:9
   30. Healing and teaching in the synagogue on the Sabbath, 13:10–21
   31. Reversal of fortune, 13:22–35
   32. Healing and teaching around a dining table, 14:1–24

33. The cost of discipleship, 14:25–35
34. Three parables on God's love for the lost, 15:1–32
35. Teaching on the use and abuse of riches, 16:1–31
36. Teaching on causing sin, on forgiveness and duty, 17:1–10
37. The grateful Samaritan, 17:11–19
38. Teaching concerning the kingdom of God and the Son of man, 17:20–37
39. Two parables on prayer, 18:1–14
40. Teaching on entering the kingdom, 18:15–34
41. A blind beggar receives his sight, 18:35–43
42. Jesus in Jericho, 19:1–27

F. The days in Jerusalem: 19:28–24:53:
43. The triumphal entry; the cleansing of the temple, 19:28–46
44. Controversies with the Jewish authorities, 19:47–21:4
45. Warning and predictions concerning things to take place, 21:5–38
46. Preparation for the Passover meal with the disciples, 22:1–13
47. Institution of The Lord's Supper, 22:14–23
48. A farewell discourse, 22:24–38
49. Jesus goes to the Mount of Olives and is betrayed and arrested there, 22:39–53
50. Jesus is denied by Peter; reviled by his guards, 22:54–65
51. Hearing before the council at dawn, 22:66–71
52. Jesus before Pilate, 23:1–5
53. Jesus examined by Herod, 23:6–16 (17)
54. Jesus delivered to the Jews by Pilate, 23:18–25
55. The journey to the cross, 23:26–32
56. Miracles at the site of the crucifixion and in Jerusalem, 23:33–45
57. Witness of the dying Christ and of the centurion, 23:46–49
58. The burial of Jesus, 23:50–56
59. The empty tomb is discovered, 24:1–11 (12)
60. The risen Christ on the road to Emmaus, 24:13–35
61. Christ's appearance and reminder to the disciples in Jerusalem, 24:36–49
62. The farewell, 24:50–53

According to some scholars, an analysis of the structure of the Third Gospel sheds further light upon its origin. The fabric of the finished work reveals certain "seams" which make possible the recovery of various materials used, and the manner of their editing, and also reveals stages in the process whereby they were joined. It is claimed that if one subtracts the Markan material from Luke there is left a gospel-like document composed of alternating sections of the Q and L traditions. There remains an account of the Galilean ministry[146] and almost the entire journey to Jerusalem.[147] Moreover, the non-Markan passages in the concluding division of the Gospel read like an independent passion and resurrection

[146] See the Outline of the Gospel, Secs. 11–15.
[147] Secs. 22–39 and 42.

narrative.[148] It is claimed also that Luke's account of the preparation for the Ministry of Jesus, as well as the beginnings of his work in Galilee, are almost wholly independent of Mark.[149] The conclusion is that this material represents the "first draft" of the Third Gospel, which is called by proponents of the theory, "proto-Luke." Subsequent to the publication of Mark, slightly over half of Mark was inserted into "proto-Luke," which remained the framework of the Gospel, and the nativity stories were prefixed to the whole. Thus our present Gospel of Luke came into existence.[150]

The importance of the proto-Luke hypothesis lies in its defense of the Third Gospel as an independent, documentary witness to Jesus' Ministry, parts of which were written down at least as early as Mark and confirm much of the latter's outline and substance. It is also said that this hypothesis provides some internal evidence compatible with the traditional view of the origin of the Third Gospel. Proto-Luke might have been written by a companion of Paul as early as A.D. 60, in Caesarea or in Rome.

Although the proto-Luke hypothesis has these attractive features, it has not commended itself to the majority. We have already noted that many are convinced that Mark is the framework for the whole of Luke's Gospel. Several of the passages which are crucial to a proto-Luke theory probably represent the evangelist's editing and expansion of Mark from oral traditions, rather than parts of an independent writing. If a few of these more doubtful passages are conceded, "the gospel-like document" called proto-Luke dissolves into an amorphous collection of traditional materials.[151]

The Origin of Luke

There is nothing in the Third Gospel that is decisive with respect to authorship, aside from the evidence that the native language of the evangelist was Greek. The internal evidence is consistent with the tradition that Luke was a Gentile Christian.

There is some evidence in the Gospel which provides a clue to its date. A comparison of Luke 19:41–44 and 21:20–24, with their Markan parallels, suggests that Luke looked back upon the siege and destruction of Jerusalem.[152]

Two critical assumptions make the margin of uncertainty concerning the date of Luke very narrow indeed: the dependence of Luke upon Mark, and the writing of Acts before or during the last decade of the first century. The Third Gospel was probably completed within the period A.D. 80 to 85. The absence of any

---

[148] Secs. 43, 45, and 47–62.

[149] Secs. 4–7 and 9.

[150] Streeter, *Four Gospels*, pp. 199ff.; V. Taylor, *The First Draft of the Third Gospel* (1927); F. C. Grant, *Gospels*, pp. 127ff.

[151] S. McL. Gilmour, note 138 above, pp. 151ff.; Feine-Behm-Kümmel, *Intro.*, pp. 92ff.

[152] This is likely even though it be argued that Luke's description echoes the LXX accounts of previous Jerusalem disasters rather than the A.D. 70 seige.

evidence of Luke's use of Matthew, and vice versa, points to a date for Luke closely approximating that of the First Gospel.

The presence in Luke of the Q and L traditions and the author's claim that he had been in touch with "eyewitnesses and ministers of the word," suggest that materials for the Gospel were gathered in Syria and in Palestine—whether by himself or others one cannot say; however, this internal evidence tallies well with the tradition that Luke had been with Paul in Antioch and in Syria. Scant data exist for locating the place where the Third Gospel was composed. Various inferences have been drawn from passages in Luke–Acts to defend or to discredit the second-century tradition that the author wrote in Achaia (Greece), but none of these arguments is conclusive.

For an interpretation of Luke, an identification of the writer's purpose or interests does not depend upon certain information concerning either its date or place of origin.

The Purpose of Luke

The following notes on the Third Gospel presuppose the fundamental unity of Luke–Acts; also a recollection of the discussion of the purpose of this two-volume work in Chapter 5 (it may be helpful to read again this discussion).[153] It is of course possible that Luke had a different intention in composing his Gospel than in writing Acts, but this is not probable in view of his general preface. A study of the Gospel supports the conclusions that the two works were conceived with complementary purposes, if not with a single, wholly consistent, aim.

Some of Luke's interests, discerned in the early chapters of Acts, are also manifested in the Gospel. The beginning and conclusion of the Gospel, and the tradition called "special Luke," merit particular attention. Although Luke employed various "sources," it is likely that he consciously made them serve his intention in writing to Theophilus.

Birth and childhood of John and Jesus, 1:1–2:52: For his Gentile readers, Luke supplied the setting of the Messiah's birth within a circle of pious Jews. He has recorded one of the most valuable accounts of the life, worship, and national hopes of Palestinian Jews in the first century B.C. And yet, it is Luke's nativity story which places the birth of the Jewish Messiah upon a map of world history. By calling attention to the emperors who reigned when Jesus was born and when John inaugurated his mission, Luke emphasized the importance of these events to citizens of the Empire.[154] The aged Simeon who has ardently hoped for "the consolation of Israel" is inspired by the Spirit to declare that the child Jesus will become "a light for revelation to the Gentiles . . ."[155]

"The role of the Spirit in the Nativity stories recalls the role of the Spirit in the history of the church in Acts . . . As the Spirit is the initial force behind Luke's

---

[153] See above, pp. 107ff.
[154] Luke 2:1ff.; 3:1ff.
[155] 2:25ff.

insistence upon universalism in Acts, so it is the Spirit-filled Simeon who makes the major forecast of this universalism in the nativity story."[156]

In several important ways Luke's nativity narrative gives prescience of a dominant theme running through his account of Christian beginnings. Christianity is a world religion: its "savior" is the Messiah of the Jews, but also of all mankind. Thus Luke anticipates the ending of his second book to Theophilus, in which he has Paul proclaim to the Jews, after attempting "to convince them about Jesus both from the Law of Moses and the prophets": "Let it be known to you then that this salvation of God has been sent to the Gentiles; they will listen."[157]

Preparation for the Ministry, 3:1–4:13: Luke alone among the evangelists extended the Baptist's citation from Isaiah 40 to include the prophecy: "And all flesh shall see the salvation of God."[158] Also only Luke records that the multitudes flocked to John and were exhorted by him. Does Luke suggest in this way a distinction between the true people of God, receiving John's baptism or, at least, raising unanswered questions as to the implications of his presence, and the leaders of Israel who reject John's proclamation?[159] The location of the genealogy of Jesus is probably intended to show that Jesus was Son of God by descent, as he had been by divine choice, and by the anointment of the Spirit at his baptism. Yet, unlike Matthew, Luke carried Jesus' ancestry beyond Abraham the father of the Jews, to Adam the father of mankind.[160]

Luke's tradition prior to the Galilean ministry of Jesus gives prominence, as was noted above, to the work of the Holy Spirit; all persons participating in the miracle of the Messiah's birth were "filled with the Holy Spirit." Luke read in Mark that John the Baptist had predicted that Jesus would baptize with the Holy Spirit. The coming of the Spirit, therefore, authenticated John and his proclamation. After Jesus had received baptism with water, "the Holy Spirit descended upon him in bodily form as a dove . . ."[161] "Full of the Holy Spirit," Jesus returned from the Jordan and "was led by the Spirit for forty days in the wilderness."[162] The guidance of the Holy Spirit in the Ministry of Jesus, as well as in the witness of his followers, is a pervasive theme in Luke–Acts. While praying, both Jesus and his disciples receive the direction of the divine Spirit.[163]

The Galilean ministry, 4:14–9:50: Luke omitted Mark's summary of the proclamation of Jesus at the beginning of his Ministry, and substituted for it an illustration of his preaching at Nazareth.[164] The position and treatment of this section indicate clearly some of the interests of the third evangelist. Under the inspiration

---

[156]H. H. Oliver, "The Lucan Birth Stories and the Purpose of Luke–Acts," NTS 10 (1963): 224f. Notice should be taken of the juxtaposition of *Spirit* and *power* in Luke's birth narratives. See especially 1:35; also 1:17, 67, 80; 2:25ff.; 4:14 (cf. Mark 1:14; Matt. 4:12).

[157]Acts 28:23, 28.

[158]Luke 3:4ff.; cf. Mark 1:2f.; Matt. 3:3.

[159]3:7, 10, 15. Cf. Matt. 3:7 (Q).

[160]3:23–38.

[161]3:22.

[162]4:1, 14.

[163]4:19; 10:21 (cf. Matt. 11:25); 9:29; 21:36; 22:40ff.; 24:49.

[164]4:15–30.

of the Spirit, Jesus declares the dawning of the age of promise. But Jesus reminds his hearers in the synagogue that God had benefited non-Jews through his servants the prophets. The murderous attack upon Jesus by the Galileans is predictive of his cross. But his rejection by Jews results in the liberation of his message to the Gentile world.

In Luke's introduction of the Ministry of Jesus he emphasizes, more emphatically than Mark, that the time of salvation is a present reality. He does not substitute for Mark's hope of an imminent coming of the kingdom, a wholly different conception of fulfillment. But Luke's principal focus is upon the significance of the Ministry of Jesus as the decisive time of salvation—time which incorporates also the Church's mission (Luke–Acts)—rather than upon the temporal newness of the Parousia of Christ.[165]

Non-Markan passages in Chapter 7 deserve notice. The dialogue between Jesus and the centurion is almost identical in Matthew and Luke, suggesting that the story was derived from the Q source. But in the narrative framework of Luke's version, his special interest is manifested. He identified the centurion as a "God-fearer" whose contact with "the Lord" was through Jewish elders and friends.[166] This centurion, like the centurion Cornelius in Acts, probably represented men like Theophilus who had been brought to receive the salvation of God through the Jews and their scriptures. The gospel was meant for all men. It was received by those who had only God's mercy to fall back upon; for example, a bereaved widow and mother, and another woman who is a social and religious outcast.[167] These are but two of the many women to whom, Luke tells us, Jesus had brought good news of the kingdom of God.

The journey to Jerusalem, 9:51–19:27: Luke's long special section begins with a report of Jesus' presence in Samaria and with a tradition which associated his Ministry with this people long held in contempt by their Jewish neighbors.[168] Surely the third evangelist appreciated the significance of these contacts, as would Theophilus. Did they not show how Jesus broke down barriers of prejudice and national feeling? In this fact was the possibility and promise of a world mission which the apostles were destined to carry forward. Only Luke reports the mission charge of Jesus to "the seventy."[169] Recall that in the Torah seventy is the number of all the nations of the earth. Although this is not a Gentile mission, it is likely that Luke's readers would take it to be a mission among the Samaritans, and predictive of the wider mission which was to come. Luke included two units which reveal Jesus commending Samaritans who put Jews to shame by their behavior.

---

[165] Conzelmann (*St. Luke*, pp. 95ff.) holds that Luke deliberately recast his sources, thus renouncing the early Christian expectation of the imminent Parousia. In its place, Luke presented the time of Jesus and the extended time of the Church as successive stages in God's plan of salvation. Moreover, Luke is the first NT writer to appeal "to the phenomenon of the Spirit as a solution of the problem of the delay of the Parousia." Cf. Feine-Behm-Kümmel, *Intro.*, pp. 100ff.; Rohde, *Teaching of the Evangelists*, pp. 176f.

[166] 7:1–10; cf. Matt. 8:5–13.

[167] 7:11–17, 36–50.

[168] 9:51ff.

[169] 10:1–20.

A Samaritan exemplifies the good-neighbor spirit, and only the Samaritan among the ten lepers who are healed returns to express gratitude to his benefactor.[170]

"The lighted lamp" saying of Jesus is found in Matthew and in Luke but its application is instructive with respect to the different purposes of these Gospels. In Matthew the light is to give illumination to those who are already in the house; in Luke the light guides those who are outside it.[171]

Other interests of Luke have been discovered in his greatly expanded version of Jesus' journey to Jerusalem. Jesus' preparation of his disciples for their future mission, as witnesses to his word and work, is prominent here. Special attention also falls upon the word of forgiveness toward the penitent, which especially distinguishes the Gospel of Jesus. Indeed, chapters 15–19 have been called "the gospel of the outcast." In this section there is "a great concentration of teaching, chiefly in the form of parables, the purpose of which is to demonstrate God's care for those whom men despise and condemn," [172] and, one should add, to teach his rebuke of man's self-righteous pride. Luke gave more space than the other evangelists to the traditions revealing Jesus' love for the outcasts and sinners. The story of Jesus and Zacchaeus summarizes an important aspect of the Third Gospel: "For the Son of man came to seek and to save the lost." [173] In reading this section of Luke's Gospel, Theophilus could not fail to see Jesus portrayed as a friend of humanity.

The very fact that Luke epitomizes Jesus' Ministry as a "journey" may have some complementary relation to his depiction of the witnessing disciples as "those of the way." [174] Luke envisions God's purpose of salvation reaching its fulfillment *in this whole progression of events*, defined more broadly than the passion-resurrection of the Jewish Messiah. The conclusion of Jesus' Ministry is unfolded by Luke as the death, resurrection, and ascension of the Christ; but also included is his gift of the Spirit to chosen witnesses, who are with him in "the way," and his final manifestation as universal Savior and Judge.

Days in Jerusalem: the Crucifixion and Resurrection narratives, 19:28–24:53: Before turning to Luke's passion story, notice should be taken of his version of Mark's "little apocalypse." [175] Luke's account roughly parallels Mark 13, but his rearrangements suggest that although he also believed the end would come suddenly, Luke wished to show that God had filled, with eschatological significance, the time beforehand. It is hardly correct to conclude, as some have claimed, that Luke had completely given up the imminent expectation of the Christ of glory, and has substituted the phenomenon of the Holy Spirit as a solution of the problem of delay. But it does seem to be true that for Luke the early realization of the Church's advent hope did not hold, as it did for Mark, an urgency of concern.

---

[170] 10:29–37; 17:11–19.

[171] 11:33; cf. Matt. 5:15.

[172] T. W. Manson, *Sayings*, p. 282.

[173] 19:1–10.

[174] W. C. Robinson, Jr., "The Theological Context of Luke's Travel Narrative (9:51ff.)," *JBL* 79 (1960): 20ff.

[175] 21:5–36.

The importance of the time of Jesus and of his Church is emphasized more strongly in the Third Gospel.[176]

In Luke's account of the trials and execution of Jesus his innocence is stressed. It is plausible that Luke sensed that his readers might not understand the disturbance in the temple, and abbreviated the story of the cleansing.[177] Yet for Luke, Jesus' daily presence and teaching in the temple held great significance. "It is in the temple that the final manifestation of who Jesus is, is now given in view of his imminent passion."[178] Passages from "special Luke" relating to Jesus' trial explicitly state that the charges brought against him were unfounded. Jesus had committed no violent or treasonable act. Especially noteworthy are the repeated statements of Pilate and the centurion's protest: "Certainly this man was innocent."[179] Luke noted that the pious Jewish councilman, Joseph, had not consented to the crime of the cross.[180]

It is often declared that Luke emphasizes the guilt of the Jews while exonerating the Romans. Yet, with the possible exception of 23:13, the rulers and not the people oppose Jesus and clamor for his death.[181] Even though apologetic interests are found in the passion story they do not dominate the scene of Jesus' death. Luke portrayed the intensity of Jesus' sufferings, and the anguished emotions of those who watched him die.[182] One of the robbers was converted by the sight of Jesus.[183] Surely Luke witnessed, in and through his moving narrative, to the faith expressed by Paul: although the cross is "folly" to Gentiles, "it is the power and wisdom of God to those who are called, both Jews and Greeks."[184] In his story of Jesus' sufferings, Luke appealed to the conscience and the will of his reader.

As in the other three gospels, so in Luke the Easter story begins with the discovery of the empty tomb. But Luke has reworked the traditional materials at hand to emphasize that the fulfillment of the promises of God to Israel are "accomplished" in Jerusalem. Luke's ubiquitous interest in the fulfillment of scripture in Jesus' Ministry is prominent in his special Easter story, the Road to Emmaus.[185] "And beginning with Moses and all the prophets [the risen Jesus, present with his disciples yet hidden from them,] interpreted to them in all the scriptures the things concerning himself." It is clear that "Jesus occupies for Luke the center of the line of 'sacred history,' going back to Israel and forward to the

[176]See above, note 165.

[177]19:45.

[178]Conzelmann, *St. Luke*, p. 78. Cf. Luke 2:25–38. K. Baltzer, "The Meaning of the Temple in the Lukan Writings," *HTR* 58 (1965): 263ff.

[179]23:47 (cf. Mark 15:39). See also 23:4, 13–16, 20b, 22.

[180]23:50f.

[181]See summary of evidence and the argument that Luke absolves the people, but not their rulers, advanced by G. Rau, *NT Abstracts* 10 (1966): 546. Cf. Conzelmann, "Luke's Treatment of the Question of Guilt," *St. Luke*, pp. 90ff.

[182]22:63f.; 23:11, 27, 36, 39, 48.

[183]23:40–43.

[184]1 Cor. 1:23f.

[185]Luke 24:13ff.

epoch of the Church. The things concerning Jesus of Nazareth, which took place in Jerusalem in those days, are the culmination of God's history with Israel." [186] Thus Jerusalem, which in Jewish prophecy was the locus of the eschatological salvation for all nations, became the origin point of the apostle's mission to the Gentiles.

The last words of Jesus reported in the Third Gospel anticipate Pentecost and the second part of the work written to Theophilus. Yet the words reach backward as well as forward: a Christian mission "to all the nations" was the declared purpose of God, foreshadowed in the scriptures of the Jews, and now brought to fulfillment in the Ministry of Jesus and in the witness of his disciples to Christ "the Lord."

The most common title for Jesus in the Gospel for the Gentiles is "the Lord." [187] It is a usage which is peculiar to the Third Gospel among the synoptists and raises the question of the possible influence of Paul and Hellenistic Christianity. We have seen that the Church of the second century believed that the Gospel by Luke was the gospel according to Paul. As in Acts so in Luke's Gospel, the distinctive features of Paul's theology are conspicuous by their absence. Yet, beyond question, Luke shared the vision of the great apologist for the Gentile mission. Although in Luke's Gospel the word *church* does not appear, the idea of a universal community is traced to its foundation, which is the "catholic" spirit of Jesus. The breadth of his human interest led inevitably to the founding of a community in which there would be "neither Jew nor Greek, bond nor free, male nor female." [188] Luke's second volume revealed how this intention became a reality.

[186] Anderson, *Jesus*, p. 229.
[187] Creed, *St. Luke*, p. lxxv.
[188] Gal. 3:28.

chapter ten

THE MINISTRY OF JESUS

Prolegomena

The western shore of the Sea of Galilee at Tiberias, a city built by Herod Antipas c. A.D. 25 as the capital of his tetrachy, and named in honor of Tiberius Caesar (A.D. 14–37). The lone boat in the picture heads north to Capernaum. Cf. John 6:23. (Israel Government Tourist Office)

Fisherman casting his net into the Sea of Galilee. While much fishing was done from small boats in Jesus' time some fish were gathered in by nets thrown into the sea. See Matt. 13:47ff. (Israel Government Tourist Office)

Via Dolorosa (Way of the Cross): a narrow street in the Old City of Jerusalem connecting the site of Pilate's Judgment Hall and the present Church of the Holy Sepulchre. The traditional route taken by Jesus on his way to Calvary. (The Matson Photo Service, Alhambra, California)

What can be known about Jesus of Nazareth? What did he teach and what did he do? What was the setting and duration of his life? Can one know the strategy of his Ministry? Is it possible to learn from the Gospels what were Jesus' thoughts concerning himself, his fate, and the future of his work?

Today's answers to the above questions are often equivocal and tentative. Frequently one finds that scholars give less space to their answers than to defending their lack of confidence in such matters. Most historians, as well as theologians, among the ranks of Christian scholars believe that a substantial knowledge of the man Jesus is crucially important for the continuing proclamation and mission of the Church. Yet there is little consensus among them as to how much of this knowledge of Jesus is obtainable and important. There is some agreement as to the methods one may legitimately use, but the conclusions that are reached thereby often differ widely.

The preceding chapters may partially explain how and why this situation developed. Many studies of the Gospels in the last half century have been based upon the assumption that the information contained in the Gospels is that memory of Jesus which early Christians cherished and passed on to others; that the units of the Jesus-tradition which survived were those most useful in advancing and supporting the Christian *kerygma* and community. The application of form criticism to the study of the Gospels has gone far to validate this assumption. This is widely recognized, even by those who have serious reservations concerning some of the conclusions of individual form critics. The Gospels of the New Testament are a literary deposit of the preaching, teaching, and worship of the first generation of Christians, and it has been shown that those interests have left their imprint upon the precanonical "sources," either oral or written or both.

But the Gospels are more than this. Further progress toward understanding them has been made on the assumption that the evangelists selected and organized the Jesus-tradition at hand according to their own theological interests. We have seen that a commonplace axiom of form criticism is that the chronological and topographical outlines of Jesus' Ministry in the Gospels are, to a large extent if not altogether, the editorial accomplishment of their writers. This axiom has been the basis of several important treatises, which were noted in the last chapter, on the theologies of the Gospel authors. From a study of the structure of Mark and of the other Gospels, and the editorial techniques employed in them, clues have been derived for a recovery of the distinctive theologies of the evangelists or, at least, their theological tendencies.

These developments in synoptic criticism have unquestionably intensified the problematical nature of Jesus-research. "Must we not recognize that Jesus is not only screened from us by the beliefs of early Christians, which have colored the oral tradition and written sources about Jesus, upon which the Gospel writers drew, but also by the minds of the Gospel writers themselves? Do not Matthew, Mark and Luke, as interpreters, cast their own mantles around Jesus so that he himself is hidden more and more from our eyes?"[1]

The force of these questions and of the acknowledgments they imply are not to be denied. It is now commonly conceded that the investigation of Jesus' history is a far more complex task than earlier historians seem to have recognized. While a more adequate understanding of the origin and nature of the Gospels has not led scholars to despair of these books as sources for knowledge of Jesus, it is apparent that the outcome of nineteenth-century research upon the Gospels, and the theological issues which were sharpened by this research, have had a sobering if not inhibiting effect upon recent scholarly attempts to describe Jesus.

THE QUEST OF THE HISTORICAL JESUS, OLD AND NEW

At the turn of the present century, Albert Schweitzer published a devastating criticism of the major "lives of Jesus" written by German and French scholars between 1778 and 1901 and based ostensibly on data which the Gospels provide. The English title of Schweitzer's book gave a popular name to this prodigious literary effort: "the quest of the historical Jesus." Schweitzer demonstrated that the confusing variety of biographies which he reviewed may be accounted for by the rationalistic or romantic biases of their authors, and by the psychological conjecture which they had foisted upon the data of the Gospels to make plausible their own descriptions of Jesus' personality.

It was left to other critics to point out that the failure of the nineteenth-century "quest" to discover "the real Jesus" was caused by a more basic error, an error which Schweitzer had failed to recognize and which also vitiated his own effort. These biographers, as well as their sharp critic, had based their work on the presupposition that the overbearing influence of Christological dogma was the *only* serious obstacle to recovering the real Jesus. It was assumed that even from the days of the early Church, Jesus had been more or less misunderstood, so that the writers of the Gospels themselves, wittingly or unwittingly, had obscured the essence of what Jesus taught as well as the real meaning of his actions. But now, at long last, scientific historiography has enabled competent scholars to gain access to the true facts. Schweitzer's principal complaint was that those who had searched for the real Jesus in modern times had not been sufficiently objective. This fault Schweitzer himself sought to overcome.[2]

During the early decades of this century, when form criticism was leading the way to a more adequate understanding of the preliterary history of the Gospel tradition, and exposing the arbitrary use of faulty source theories by the "objective" biographers of Jesus, two leading European theologians, Karl Barth and

[1] Davies, *Invitation*, p. 132.
[2] Anderson, *Jesus*, pp. 18f.

Rudolf Bultmann, were questioning seriously the legitimacy of this century-long quest. "Historicism" was the pejorative term used to condemn the methodology of these biographers of Jesus, a methodology which many philosophers of history and historians were repudiating. But more serious to these theologians was the conviction that the quest itself was invalid according to the Christian proclamation and faith.

The impact of the objections raised by Bultmann upon subsequent developments was especially strong because the Marburg theologian had pioneered in applying the methods of form criticism to the New Testament, and was in the process of publishing the successive editions of his *History of the Synoptic Tradition.* As early as 1929 Bultmann wrote:

> It is not permitted to go beyond the proclamation, using it as a source in order to reconstruct the historic Jesus with his messianic consciousness, his inwardness or his heroic character. This would be precisely the "Christ according to the flesh" [2 Cor. 5:16] who belongs to the past. It is not the historic Christ who is the Lord, but Jesus Christ as he is encountered in the proclamation.[3]

In Bultmann's later defense of his position, in answer to some of his students who sought to modify it, he reiterated that the Christ of the *kerygma,* and not the person of the historical Jesus, is the object of a Christian's faith. The man whom the *kerygma* addresses is neither able, as has been commonly supposed, "to free the picture of the historical Jesus from the dogmatic overlay which had concealed it in the primitive Christian message, nor may he inquire behind the kerygma for a legitimation offered by historical research." In his various responses to persons seeking to appraise or reappraise his position, Bultmann persisted in denying both the theological necessity and the historical possibility of knowing Jesus as he really was, how he lived, and what he taught before his crucifixion.[4]

Following Bultmann's major contributions, the course of Jesus-research flowed into two main channels. On the one hand, the writings of some New Testament scholars in this country and abroad revealed that the unfulfilled expectations and methodological errors of their predecessors had not established the futility of "the quest of the historical Jesus." As one writer has observed, "the resilience of the historical approach" is a phenomenon to be taken into account in a survey of recent trends.[5] On the other hand, one may distinguish a group of scholars by the more direct influence of Bultmann's theology and form critical judgments upon their work. They began what has been called, "a new quest of the historical Jesus." This descriptive phrase, useful at the outset in identifying the special viewpoint

[3] These lines are from an essay by R. Bultmann, quoted in S. Neill, *Interpretation of the New Testament* (1964), p. 271; the complete essay may be found in *Glauben und Verstehen,* vol. 1 (2d ed., 1954), p. 208.

[4] R. Bultmann, "The Primitive Christian Kerygma and the Historical Jesus," in *The Historical Jesus and the Kerygmatic Christ,* ed. C. E. Braaten and R. A. Harrisville (1964), pp. 15ff. [hereafter, *Historical Jesus*]. For a concise statement of Bultmann's position, emphasizing the influence of Heidegger and Kierkegaard, see J. B. Cobb, Jr., "The Post-Bultmannian Trend," *Journal of Bible and Religion* XXX (1962): 3f. [hereafter, *JBR*]; for the influence of M. Kähler, cf. Perrin, *Rediscovering,* pp. 219ff.

[5] Anderson, *Jesus,* pp. 56ff.

and contributions of several major scholars, who are named below, begs the question: How "new" is the new quest? "Post-Bultmannian" is a preferable identification since this term does not focus directly on this question which may detract from other more material issues. "Post-Bultmannian" identifies the program of those scholars who acknowledge the seriousness of the issues which Bultmann raised, yet who seek to modify his position through the application of some basic insights and skills which Bultmann taught.[6]

One important conviction may be said to unite the great majority of scholars engaged today in Jesus-research, however they may be distinguished as groups or as individuals. Unlike Bultmann, they affirm the necessity and possibility of postulating a continuity and substantial agreement between "Jesus as he was" and the Christ to whom witness was borne in the Christian *kerygma* of New Testament times. They have seen that Bultmann's insistence on the theological irrelevance of knowing "Jesus as he was" threatens to reduce the Incarnation to a symbol of timeless truth, and encourages a revival of Christ-myth theories. They agree that there is no stability in a position which affirms Jesus' historicity as well as his full humanity, as Bultmann does, but denies the interest of faith in the "features and traits" of Jesus' personal life, and in the actual teachings and happenings of his Ministry. But to insist on the relevance of Jesus as he was leads at once to the problem: How can this knowledge be established? There is indeed "no logical connection between theological necessity and historical possibility."[7] If one must acknowledge the misguided attempts and failures of earlier generations, how is one to avert them, and achieve a greater measure of success?

More Modest Claims, and a More Rigorous Methodology

Brief notice should be taken of the encouragement which has come to Bultmannian scholars from an understanding of history, and of the person or self, derived from several modern philosophers, especially Wilhelm Dilthey, Martin Heidegger, and R. G. Collingwood. Some of Bultmann's keenest students, identified in the section above only as a group, have sought to modify their teacher's "existentialist theology" by a reapplication to the Jesus-tradition of some of the basic insights which Bultmann had received from these philosophers. Each of the following German scholars has written one or more programmatic essays on the recovery of important aspects of Jesus' history in the *kerygma* of the Gospels: Ernst Käsemann, Günther Bornkamm, Hans Conzelmann, Gerhard Ebeling, and Ernst Fuchs.[8] One of these men, Bornkamm, has set forth the results of his post-

[6]Special features of the post-Bultmannian program are described below.

[7]Van A. Harvey, "The Historical Jesus, the Kerygma, and Christian Faith," *Rel. in Life* 33 (1964): 433.

[8]E. Käsemann, *New Testament Questions of Today*, trans. W. J. Montague (1969), pp. 23ff. [hereafter, *New Testament Questions*]; G. Bornkamm, *Jesus of Nazareth*, trans. I. and F. McLuskey, 1960), pp. 9–26 [hereafter, *Jesus*]; H. Conzelmann, "Method of Life-of-Jesus Research," in Braaten and Harrisville, *Historical Jesus*, pp. 54ff.; G. Ebeling, *The Nature of Faith*, trans. R. G. Smith (1961), pp. 58ff.; E. Fuchs, *Studies of the Historical Jesus*, trans. A. Scobie (1964), pp. 11ff.

Bultmannian studies in a systematic sketch of Jesus' Ministry. Bornkamm's book, bearing the title in English translation of *Jesus of Nazareth,* has won the respect it deserves as a worthy sequel to Bultmann's *Jesus and the Word.*

James M. Robinson, an American scholar, wrote an important monograph setting forth the rationale for the post-Bultmannian program.[9] According to Robinson, "the nineteenth century saw the reality of 'historical facts' as consisting largely in names, places, dates, occurrences, sequences, causes, effects—things which fall far short of being the actuality of history, if one understands by history the distinctively human, creative, unique, purposeful, which distinguishes man from nature." The new, "existentialist" view of history seeks the purposes and meanings lying behind the facts. "The dimension in which man actually exists, his 'world,' the stance or outlook from which he acts, his understanding of his existence behind what he does, the way he meets the basic problems and the answer his life implies to the human dilemma . . . such matters as these have become central in an attempt to understand history." Moreover, in seeking to know a man of the past, the new historian also focuses upon "the significance he had as the environment of those who knew him, the continuing history his life produces, the possibility of existence which his life presents to me as an alternative. . . ." [10] Thus the study of history, of what life meant to a man in the past, questions the meaning of one's personal life or selfhood in the present.

The Bultmannians apply this "new" understanding of history to Jesus. Through his sayings concerning the kingdom of God, his words concerning the Jewish Torah, and especially his parables, the modern historian, writes Robinson, gains "sufficient insight into Jesus' intention to encounter his historical action, and enough insight into his understanding of existence presupposed in his intention to encounter his selfhood." [11]

Whereas the old quest for a knowledge of Jesus' personality was foredoomed to failure, because of false expectations respecting the Gospel sources, it is claimed that the post-Bultmannian program is a promising one. The Gospels are recognized as "kerygmatic history," but as such they are said to contain source materials especially suited to the new type of inquiry. "For the kerygmatic interest of the primitive Church," Robinson claims, "would leave unaltered precisely those sayings and scenes in which Jesus made his intention and understanding of existence most apparent to them." [12] In its Christological utterances the *kerygma* explicitly set forth Jesus' own selfhood, and called upon the hearer to discover, in Jesus' understanding of existence, one's own true selfhood. Thus, according to Robinson, the new historiography has opened up "a second avenue of access" to the historical Jesus. The serious student of the Gospels may now encounter Jesus as he was, and therefore he is able to approximate the experience of the original disciples, "who had both their Easter faith and their factual memory of Jesus." [13]

[9] *A New Quest of the Historical Jesus* (1959) [hereafter, *New Quest*].
[10] Ibid., pp. 28f.
[11] Ibid., p. 70.
[12] Ibid., p. 69.
[13] Ibid., pp. 85f.

Whether in fact this particular angle of vision opens the way to a knowledge of Jesus as he was, as well as to the meaning of discipleship, has been a subject of much debate. It is a worthy aim for the historian to seek to know how Jesus understood himself and how he wished to be understood by his disciples, a purpose of scholarship which should never be foreclosed. But anyone who thus interprets Jesus in modern categories must submit to rigorous tests his results, however appropriate to Jesus these categories of interpretation may seem.[14] "The peril of modernizing Jesus" besets the twentieth-century existentialist as it did the nineteenth-century rationalist or romanticist.

It is not permissible today to minimize the difficulties of Jesus-research. The dangers of subjectivity—the inevitable influence of ideological presuppositions— are especially perceptible here, if not in one's own work, then in that of others.[15] Add to this fact the observations made above concerning the nature of the sources at the historian's disposal: one can only find the history of Jesus within the fragmentary, "kerygmatized" material preserving the witness of the apostles and others within the early churches and edited by the evangelists with their particular viewpoints. The conclusion follows that "only by methodologically pure and critical work can the received traditions be made useful for a historical description of Jesus."[16]

This section concludes with a report of methodological procedures used by many contemporary scholars as they have attempted to advance from an analysis of the Gospel tradition to a description of Jesus as he was. These procedures employ these criteria: the criterion of dissimilarity; the criterion of multiple or cross-sectional attestation; and the criterion of coherence.[17]

The first two criteria have been considered especially useful in identifying "authentic sayings" of Jesus. The criterion of dissimilarity refers to teaching which for various reasons cannot be derived from ancient Judaism or attributed to the early Church. But special attention may be called to certain actions of Jesus which appear offensive, or at least startling, to foe and friend alike. An example of a saying of Jesus meeting this criterion is his use of "abba" ("father" or "my father") in addressing God. Jesus' baptism by John, signifying repentance of sins, is an example of an action of Jesus satisfying this criterion.

It is noteworthy that whatever may be discovered through the application of the criterion of dissimilarity, one possesses "only a critically assured minimum."[18] Explicit claims concerning Jesus' person would seem to be eliminated from his teaching by this criterion, since it is at least extremely probable that any such self-affirmation would, in Christian circles, have been applied to the risen Lord.

[14]V. A. Harvey and S. M. Ogden, "How New Is the 'New Quest of the Historical Jesus'?" in Braaten and Harrisville, *Historical Jesus*, pp. 197ff.; Anderson, *Jesus*, pp. 149ff. R. E. Brown, "After Bultmann, What?" *Catholic Biblical Quarterly* XXVI (1964): 5ff. Cf. J. M. Robinson, "The Recent Debate on the New Quest," *JBR* XXX (1962): 168ff.; Perrin, *Rediscovering*, pp. 232f.

[15]Anderson, *Jesus*, pp. 97ff.; N. A. Dahl, "The Problem of the Historical Jesus" [hereafter, "Historical Jesus"] in Braaten and Harrisville, *Kerygma and History*, pp. 150ff.

[16]Dahl, "Historical Jesus," p. 151.

[17]Perrin, *Rediscovering*, pp. 39ff.; H. K. McArthur, "Survey of Recent Gospel Research," *Interpretation* 18 (1964): 39ff.; Anderson, *Jesus*, pp. 99f.

[18]Dahl, "Historical Jesus," p. 156.

Furthermore, only Jesus' highly original teaching can be identified in this way. It is however improbable that Jesus teaching was in all respects radically different from the Judaism of his day. The application of this criterion represents the extreme opposite of the position taken by other scholars who insist that one should begin with the whole or maximum of material and, when in doubt, favor the witness of tradition.

The criterion of multiple or cross-sectional attestation identifies sayings of Jesus which either in their form or content, or both, are found in more than one of the sources underlying the Synoptic Gospels. An example of the application of this method, and of the materials so identified, may be found in C. H. Dodd's *History and the Gospel* and in T. W. Manson's *The Teaching of Jesus.* By exercising this criterion, scholars have discovered Jesus' proclamation concerning the coming of the kingdom of God, and the Son of man; his attitude toward the Torah, and especially, toward persons treated by others as society's outcasts—"the tax collectors and sinners" of the Gospels. Some scholars claim that this criterion rarely attests specific sayings of Jesus.[19] But by its application one may discover some things more important than isolated sayings, namely, authentic features and traits of Jesus, and thus be led to an understanding of his intention.[20]

The criterion of coherence examines and accepts as authentic Jesus-tradition which coheres with sayings or actions identified by other criteria, especially by the criterion of dissimilarity. Some persons would apply this criterion only to material found in the earliest sources or strata of the gospel tradition,[21] but the possibility cannot be excluded that authentic sayings were preserved in secondary literary sources. Of course this criterion must be used with caution. Sayings which have "the ring of authenticity," or actions which are "characteristic of Jesus" appear differently to different men.

The persisting quest of historians to learn what Jesus was really like has been compared with "the work of the archaeologist who attempts to restore an old monument of which only the foundation and a few scattered stones remain."[22] As a scientist he will make one or more sketches in an attempt to picture the monument as it stood. No one will deny the usefulness of these archaeological drawings. At the same time the scholar will be expected to call attention to points in his sketch "where exact knowledge ends and his tutored imagination has taken over." When he has discovered the precise spot where a few of the stones originally lay, he will value this precious evidence far more than the total monument he has reconstructed by his inferential methods.

In a similar fashion, sketches of the historical Jesus will continue to be drawn in the absence of sufficient information to reconstruct his life after the order of a modern biography. Some of the sketches drawn by scientifically competent scholars have great value and, like the hypothetical reconstructions of great archaeologists, become the impulse for further research and advance knowledge.

[19] Perrin, *Rediscovering,* p. 46.
[20] Anderson, *Jesus,* p. 100.
[21] Perrin, *Rediscovering,* p. 43.
[22] Dahl, "Historical Jesus," p. 155.

Over an extended period, however, "an expansion of our exact knowledge of primitive Christianity and of Judaism in Jesus' time" may mean more for modern man's rediscovery of Jesus than many imaginative sketches portraying him as he probably was.

Non-Christian Sources and Their Value

Although the student of the history of Jesus is dependent upon books of the New Testament, especially the three earliest Gospels, there is just enough information about Jesus in Jewish and pagan writings to anchor him in history. It is important that this evidence be reviewed. In an earlier critical period a few scholars argued that the Christ of the Gospels was a myth, or a symbol fortuitously associated with the life of a man who had never lived. More recently, radical form critical views have threatened to uproot the Christian Gospel from the solid earth of Jesus' unique historical existence.

The earliest Jewish testimony to Jesus is found in the *Antiquities* of Josephus. The following passage in Book XX is commonly considered genuine:

> Ananias called the Sanhedrin together, brought before it James, the brother of Jesus who was called the Christ, and certain others . . . and he caused them to be stoned.[23]

Another passage is found in Book XVIII. It describes Jesus as a teacher and a miracle worker, reports that "Pilate condemned him to be crucified," and that he was raised from the dead in fulfillment of prophecy. This passage is almost universally considered to be a Christian insertion, but whether in whole or in part is a matter of conjecture.[24]

It is impossible to believe that Josephus knew nothing about Christian origins. The explanation of his almost complete silence must be found in the historian's apologetic motives. Writing as a Pharisee and for the Romans, Josephus studiously avoided commenting upon messianic movements within Judaism. This explanation does not rest solely upon an argument from silence, for in telling of John the Baptist and his tragic fate, Josephus conceals from his readers the messianic import of John's proclamation and baptism.[25]

The references to Jesus and to his followers in the Talmud are designed to contradict the claims of the Christian gospel, and are therefore of little independent value. Two plausible reasons have been given for the scarcity of references to Jesus and to Christianity in the Talmud. In the first place, events of the period are seldom noted; for example, no reference is made to the Maccabean Revolution! In the second place, the origin of the Christian sect in the disturbed

---

[23] XX. ix. 1.

[24] XVIII. iii. 3. For examples of efforts to reconstruct an original reference to Jesus in Bk. XVIII, see M. Goguel, *The Life of Jesus*, trans. O. Wyon (1933), pp. 75ff. [hereafter, *Jesus*]; Klausner, *Jesus*, pp. 55ff; R. Dunkerley, *Beyond the Gospels* (1957), pp. 34ff. Against such attempts to recover an original statement it has been argued that Origen, who cites three times the Josephus passage referring to James, makes no allusion to this ostensibly earlier, fuller statement.

[25] See below, p. 271.

period leading up to the great rebellion in A.D. 66 to 70 must have seemed to many rabbis an ephemeral thing. Thus by the time of "the sages of the Talmud," when Christianity was an established religion, the original events were no longer remembered, and the popular stories concerning Jesus "were turned into subjects of ridicule." The Jewish scholar Joseph Klausner summarizes the statements of the Tannaim about Jesus which are found in the Talmud. The founder of Christianity was remembered as a rabbi whose name was Jesus of Nazareth, who practiced sorcery and beguiled Israel, who mocked the words of the wise, who expounded scripture in the same manner as the Pharisees, who had five disciples, who said that he was not come to take away from the Law or to add to it, who was hanged as a false teacher and beguiler on the eve of the Passover which happened on the Sabbath, and whose disciples healed the sick in his name.[26]

The earliest Latin passage in which Christ is mentioned is found in the correspondence of Pliny the Younger, a governor of Bithynia, with the Emperor Trajan, noted in the first chapter of this book. In a letter usually dated in A.D. 112, Pliny reports that his investigation had convinced him that the Christians were a crudely superstitious folk. On certain days they assembled before dawn and "sang hymns to Christ as to a God."[27] About the same time, Pliny's friend, Tacitus, recorded in his Annals the persecution of Christians under Nero. This passage, noted in connection with the study of Mark, reports that "Christ was put to death in the reign of Tiberius by the procurator Pontius Pilate."[28]

References in Roman literature to Christ and early Christianity are rare. This is not surprising. As late as the second century the whole movement was considered a "mischievous superstition," according to Tacitus. In Roman literary circles Christianity was just another contemptible Oriental cult. Why did it matter if its own account of its origin was real or fictitious?[29] Although the comments of Latin authors are of very little value to this study of the history of Jesus, it is interesting that Roman society became aware of Christ as "an object of worship and the historical founder of a religious community." The same twofold witness is given to Jesus throughout the New Testament.[30]

New Testament Sources Other than the Synoptic Gospels

Paul's letters provide the earliest literary evidence that Jesus lived. From them can be gleaned the following items: Jesus was a man born of a woman who belonged to the race of Abraham and to the family of David. He lived under the Jewish Law. His meek and gentle manner was noteworthy.[31] He died upon

---

[26]Klausner, Jesus, p. 19. See also Davies, *Invitation*, pp. 66f.

[27]X. 96.

[28]See above, p. 196. The passage in Suetonius cited in Chapter 2 (Life of Claudius 25.4) should also be noted. If "Chrestos" is a corruption of Christos, then Suetonius supposed that Christ had been in Rome ca A.D. 49, so little was the historian interested in Christianity's account of its origin.

[29]Cf. Herodotus, who fails to mention Zoroaster in writing of the Persian religion; and Dio Cassius, who says nothing of Simon ben Kosibah in commenting upon the Jewish revolt in Hadrian's time.

[30]C. H. Dodd, "Life and Teachings of Jesus," in T. W. Manson, *Companion*, p. 367.

[31]Gal. 4:4; 3:16; Rom. 1:3; 9:5; 15:8; 2 Cor. 10:1.

a cross. The Jews brought about his death, just as they had killed the prophets before him.[32] At a last meal with his disciples on the night of his betrayal, Jesus had distributed bread and wine as his body and blood.[33] Paul mentions the burial of Jesus, and he lists certain individuals and groups to whom Jesus appeared, beginning three days after his death.[34] Paul refers to the fact that Jesus had brothers among whom was James. He notes that "apostles" were associated with Jesus and names two of them, Peter and John.[35]

Besides these allusions to facts of Jesus' history, Paul witnesses to some of Jesus' teaching and to the importance which was placed upon it in the early Church. Two explicit references to "commandments of the Lord" are found in I Corinthians.[36] These commandments are reported in slightly different wording in the Synoptic Gospels.[37] Other passages in Paul's letters may allude to teachings of Jesus embodied in the Synoptic Gospels. For example Romans 12:14, 13:7, and 14:13–14 probably reflect the influence of Jesus' words.[38] Paul could assume that his readers would be familiar with Jesus' teaching, and that the authority of his words would be self-evident to Christian converts.

Among New Testament books written by others, the Letter to the Hebrews deserves special attention. Like the third evangelist, the author of Hebrews claims that his witness to Christ was attested "by those who heard him."[39] It is in the interest of the writer's theology to show that Christ's sacrifice was effective because he had been a real man.[40] He had learned perfect obedience to God through temptations and sufferings unto death which are the common lot of men.[41] Apparently, a story of Jesus' life and death which presented him as a man who was radically obedient to the will of God provided the essential basis for this writer's Christology.[42]

Brief comment should be made here on the value of the Fourth Gospel as a source for the history of Jesus, although the matter will be treated fully in a later chapter.[43] The fourth evangelist selected the literary form of a "gospel" to expound his theology. Thus there is at least a superficial similarity between John and the Synoptic Gospels. Moreover, the exposition of the person and work of the Christ in the Fourth Gospel is based upon traditional units of the Ministry, some of which are partially parallel to those recorded in the Synoptic Gospels. There

[32]Gal. 3:1; 1 Cor. 1:23; 1 Thess. 2:15.
[33]1 Cor. 11:23ff.
[34]1 Cor. 15:4ff.
[35]Gal. 1:19; 2:9.
[36]7:10f.; 9:14.
[37]Concerning divorce, Mark 10:11f. and pars.; concerning the laborer and his wages, Matt. 9:10b and Luke 10:7b. Goguel, *Jesus*, pp. 121ff; Dodd, *Gospel and Law*, pp. 46ff.
[38]Cf. Matt. 5:43ff. and Luke 6:27f.; Mark 12:17 and pars.; Matt. 7:1f. (Luke 6:37); Mark 7:14ff.
[39]Heb. 2:3.
[40]Heb. 2:10ff.
[41]Heb. 4:15; 5:7ff.; 9:27f.
[42]Heb. 12:1f., 13:12f. presuppose that a knowledge of his life was widespread. Cf. 1 Peter 2:21f.; 1 Tim. 6:13f. Goguel, *Jesus*, p. 128.
[43]See below, pp. 571ff.

are, however, striking differences in the form and content of John from those of the other three Gospels. The fourth evangelist's reflections upon the meaning of particular episodes from the Ministry have become so fused with the traditional stories themselves that in many instances their earlier forms can scarcely be recovered. It can also be shown that the traditional teaching of Jesus has been refracted in the Gospel of John. Three influences have been united in the evangelist's mind: the sayings of Jesus as he received them; the interpretations of Jesus which were known to the evangelist through Church tradition; and the influence which was exerted upon his mind by acquaintance with the Hellenistic–Jewish thought of his age. The fusion of these elements makes it difficult, in any particular discourse in John, to distinguish between an early understanding of Jesus' teaching—in some instances perhaps his actual words—and what is read into it in the light of the evangelist's experience and special purposes. It cannot be said that efforts to recover the sources underlying the Fourth Gospel have been successful. Suffice it to say, John's Gospel cannot be used for the history of Jesus in the same way as the Synoptic Gospels. Harmonies of the four Gospels do violence both to the synoptists and to John. The special values of the Fourth Gospel can best be appreciated when it is studied as an independent work in its own setting. When this has been done, the two types of gospel portraiture can be viewed intelligently as complementary sources for understanding Jesus Christ.[44]

Agrapha and the Apocryphal Gospels

The canonical Gospels were composed of oral traditions and of written sources of various types. With their "publication" the reservoir of gospel tradition was not completely exhausted, as the writer of the appendix to the Fourth Gospel, with pardonable exaggeration, maintained.[45] Some of this tradition was preserved in ancient Christian writings which are still being discovered.

The term agrapha (unwritten things) is used—though not always with the same meaning—to identify a portion of this noncanonical tradition. Agrapha may be defined as units of tradition (mostly sayings of Jesus) not found in the standard text of the canonical Gospels.[46] Several sources of the agrapha may be noted. The letters of Paul contain some which have been cited. Another example of an agraphon in the New Testament is the word of Jesus reported in Acts 20:35, "it is more blessed to give than to receive." Ancient manuscripts of the New Testament provide a second source of agrapha. After Luke 6:5 in the sixth-century manuscript Codex Bezae, the following incident is recorded:

> On the same day, seeing someone working on the Sabbath, he [Jesus] said to him, "Man, if indeed you know what you are doing, you are blessed; but if you do not know, you are cursed and a transgressor of the Law."

[44]Perrin, Rediscovering, pp. 48f.
[45]John 21:25.
[46]Coined to identify uncanonical sayings of Jesus which cannot be traced to their source, the term is ordinarily employed in this more inclusive sense.

In most cases agrapha of this type are easily identifiable as scribal additions. But the authenticity of a few, such as the one just cited, has been maintained.[47]

A third source of agrapha are the writings of the Church Fathers. Probably Bishop Papias was the first of the fathers to collect the sayings of Jesus not recorded in the Gospels. The result was five volumes entitled *Expositions of the Words of the Lord.* Unfortunately, Papias was not a very intelligent man, as Eusebius observed, and citations of agrapha from the collection of Papias suggest that the work was of little value. Agrapha in the works of Justin Martyr, Clement of Alexandria, Origen, and a few others deserve more serious consideration. Take this passage from Origen, for example:

> I have read somewhere that the Saviour said . . . "He that is near me, is near the fire; he that is far from me, is far from the kingdom."[48]

Still another source of agrapha are the Egyptian papyri which have been found during the past century. Especially noteworthy are the Oxyrhynchus Papyri in which one agraphon ordinarily follows another without context, introduced by the formula "Jesus says." An example reminiscent of Matthew 18:20 may be given:

> Jesus says: Wheresoever there are two, they are not without God, and where there is one alone, I say, I am with Him. Lift up the stone, and there shalt thou find me; cleave the wood, and I am there.[49]

Did most of these agrapha originally stand in some gospel, or are they isolated sayings taken from the oral tradition which persisted alongside of written gospels? Since the discovery of several "gospels" in the Coptic language in the vicinity of Nag-Hammadi (Egypt) in 1945 or 1946, support is given the former alternative.[50] At least one may say that isolated sayings found their way into gospel manuscripts, from which they were cited by the Fathers of the Church.

The existence of extracanonical gospels is attested in Christian literature of the second and third centuries. With the eventual canonization of Matthew, Mark, Luke, and John, most of these rival gospels were destroyed, or became the property of special groups who found them congenial to their doctrines. Some of these extracanonical gospels have been discovered in ancient manuscripts of various dates and states of preservation. It is difficult to classify these "remains" chronologically, and to identify the documents of which they were originally a part. In

[47] J. Jeremias, *Unknown Sayings of Jesus* (1957), pp. 49ff. [hereafter, *Unknown Sayings*]; Dunkerley, *Beyond the Gospels*, pp. 121ff.

[48] Jeremias, *Unknown Sayings*, p. 54. The same saying is found in the Coptic *Gospel of Thomas*, trans. A. Guillaumont, Puech, Quispel et al. (1959), Log. 82, p. 45. Note Jesus' use of fire as an eschatological symbol, Mark 9:49; Luke 12:49. See the *Apocryphal New Testament*, trans. M. R. James, (1924), pp. 33ff.

[49] Oxyr. pap. 1, 4. In the Matthean word, Jesus promises his presence to those who pray in his name; in this agraphon, to those who labor. See E. Hennecke and W. Schneemelcher, *New Testament Apocrypha* (1963), vol. 1, pp. 97ff.

[50] J. Doresse, *The Secret Books of the Egyptian Gnostics*, trans. P. Mairet (1960), pp. 116ff. [hereafter, *Secret Books*]; W. C. van Unnik, *Newly Discovered Gnostic Writings*, trans. H. H. Hoskins (1960), pp. 7ff.

writings of the Church Fathers some of the same works may be referred to by different titles.[51]

Two types of apocryphal gospel material may be distinguished. The first contains a pious "embroidery" upon some aspect of canonical tradition, or upon traditions approximately parallel to those in the Gospels. The Protoevangelium of James provides an excellent example of this type. It contains legends relating to Mary, Joseph, Jesus' birth and childhood. The passion and resurrection narrative in an extant fragment of a Gospel of Peter also belongs to this type. These traditions are pure invention for the most part, but some early reminiscenses may be preserved. Tendentious gospels are a second type of apocryphal material. These contain traditions which were collected in sectarian groups to support the community's special interests. Examples of such writings are the Gospel of the Egyptians and the Gospel of Basilides. Among the Chenoboskion manuscripts are well-preserved specimens of apocryphal gospel traditions of the second type; for example, the Gospel of Truth, and the Gospels of Thomas and of Philip.

Until very recent times it was commonly held that in the apocryphal gospels the history of Jesus has been "irretrievably smothered beneath legend and fantasy."[52] Here and there in the midst of "worthless rubbish" discoveries of a "priceless jewel" have been claimed. The continuing discoveries of papyrus fragments stood as reminders that questions concerning the value of extracanonical traditions should be held in suspended judgment. The remarkable Nag–Hammadi discoveries have led some to opine that the historian is now in possession of some agrapha which may be as authentic as sayings of Jesus in the Synoptic Gospels. Among these newly recovered Coptic documents, the Gospel of Thomas holds special interest for Jesus-research. It contains no narrative but only sayings of Jesus, similiar in form to the Oxyrhynchus Papyri, and parables which, in their content but not in their setting, resemble Matthew's Gospel. The yet unsettled question is the relationship between Thomas and the Synoptic tradition, but evidence seems to favor their independence.[53] It is indeed possible that the recovery of lost stories and sayings of Jesus may "supplement our knowledge here and there in important and valuable ways."[54] But it is unlikely that these new discoveries will substantially revise that history of Jesus which can be learned from the Gospels of the New Testament.

Problems of Chronology

A natural but unwarranted assumption is that the evangelists shared the interests of historians in questions such as the following: When was Jesus born? What was the duration of his Ministry? And when did he die? Answers to these

---

[51]James, *Apocryphal New Testament*; Dunkerley, *Beyond the Gospels*, pp. 102ff.

[52]Hunter, *Work and Words*, p. 16.

[53]H. Montefiore, "A Comparison of the Parables of the Gospel according to Thomas and of the Synoptic Gospels," *NTS* 7 (1960–61): 220ff.; O. Cullmann, "The Gospel of Thomas and the Problem of the Age of the Tradition Contained Therein," *Interpretation* 16 (1962): 418ff.; H. Koester, "Gnomai Diaphoroi," *HTR* LVIII (1965): 290ff. Cf. H. K. McArthur, "The Dependence of the Gospel of Thomas on the Synoptics," *Exp. T.* 71 (1960): 286ff.; R. M. Grant, "Two Gnostic Gospels," *JBL* 79 (1960): 1 ff.

[54]Jeremias, *Unknown Sayings*, p. 32; Dunkerley, *Beyond the Gospels*, pp. 15f., 163f.

questions can be derived only from information introduced into Gospels for reasons other than chronology. Such evidence as exists provides an insecure basis for positive conclusions. Reconstruction of the chronology of Jesus' history is bound to contain speculative elements. Principal evidence from the Gospels will be listed below, along with the available data from sources external to them. Then the two principal types of "solutions" will be described.

When was Jesus born? According to Matthew and Luke, Jesus was born "in the days of Herod." Matthew's narrative implies that Herod died shortly after Jesus' birth. Now we have noted that King Herod ruled from 30 to 4 B.C.[55] However one estimates the value of the nativity stories of the gospels, it is difficult to believe that theological motives established the relation of Jesus' birth to the last years of Herod's reign.

According to Luke 2:1, Jesus was born in the time of a census commanded by Caesar Augustus and carried out in Palestine by Quirinius, governor of Syria. Two difficulties may be noticed. According to Josephus, Quirinius enrolled the peoples of his domain in the year A.D. 6, which action caused an insurrection among the Jews.[56] Moreover, it seems that it was Sentius Saturninus, not Quirinius, who was governor of Syria during the last years of King Herod. The mention of the census in Luke's birth narrative presents evidence therefore which complicates rather than clarifies the question before us.[57]

The duration of Jesus' Ministry: The association of the careers of John the Baptist and of Jesus in the New Testament makes pertinent any reference to the beginnings or the end of John's mission. Luke's formal introduction in 3:1ff. is evidence of primary importance. Yet only one item in it affords any precise dating: "In the fifteenth year of the reign of Tiberius Caesar . . . the word of God came to John . . ." Tiberius became emperor on August 19, A.D. 14. Luke therefore dates the beginning of John's mission in the year A.D. 28–29. Luke probably based his calculation on a synchronization of the Syrian and Roman calendars and intended the year 27–28[58]

According to Mark 1:14, Jesus' ministry in Galilee began after the arrest of John by Herod (Antipas). Efforts to establish the date of John's arrest have not been successful, nor have the accounts in the Gospels and in Josephus of John's martyrdom yielded any secure evidence for determining the subsequent withdrawal of Jesus from Herod's domain and the termination of his work in Galilee.

In Luke 3:23 it is stated that Jesus was "about thirty years of age" when he "began his ministry." It is hazardous to make precise this approximate estimate. It is sometimes claimed that the passage in John, 2:13–21, which describes a visit

[55] To speak of Jesus' birth as occurring four years "before Christ" is patently absurd. This "error" is traceable to the calculations of Denis the Little, who in the 525th year of the Era of Diocletian was charged by Pope John I to fix the movable date of Easter. In the course of the monk's calculations, Denis dated Jesus' birth December 25, 754. On the authority of Pope John, 754–5 became A.D. (Anno Domini) 1. Since the older calendar dated Herod's death in 750, the new calendar dated it 4 B.C.

[56] *Antiq.*, XVII. xiii. 5. Cf. Acts 5:37.

[57] G. B. Caird, "Chronology of the N. T.," *IDB*, vol. 1, p. 600. See below, pp. 321ff.

[58] Goguel, *Jesus*, p. 224. Cf. Caird, note 57 above, p. 601.

of Jesus to Jerusalem at the Passover shortly after the Ministry began, contains a valuable chronological notice.[59] After Jesus had cleansed the temple, the Jews demanded some "sign" of his authority. Jesus replied, "Destroy this temple, and in three days I will raise it up." Supposing Jesus to have been speaking of Herod's temple, his antagonists exclaimed, "It has taken forty-six years to build this temple, and will you raise it up in three days?" Since Herod's temple was not completed until the days of Albinus (A.D. 62–63), most authorities take the protest of the Jews to mean that for forty-six years the temple had been under construction. According to Josephus, Herod began his temple in the eighteenth year of his reign. Assuming the factual character of this dialogue in John, and that the Passover in the year A.D. 27 or 28 is indicated, this clue seems promising. Yet the setting of the incident in the Fourth Gospel involves a broader problem. John dates Jesus' cleansing of the temple at the outset of his Ministry; Mark, followed by Matthew and Luke, locate it before the Passover of Jesus' crucifixion. Does the date A.D. 27–28 mark the beginning or the end of Jesus' Ministry?

Various references in the Gospels note seasonal changes during the course of the Ministry. According to Mark 2:23–28, it is the harvest season (April to June). Mark 6:39 indicates that the feeding of the five thousand took place in the vicinity of the Sea of Galilee when the grass was green (January to March). Three Passovers, as well as other Jewish feasts, are noted in the Gospel of John.[60] Whether any of these references provide authentic chronological notes is a much debated question.

When did Jesus die? References in the Gospels to the officials presiding over Jesus' trials locate the crucifixion within the years 27–33. Pilate was procurator from A.D. 26 to 36. According to Matthew 26:3, Caiaphas was high priest when Jesus was condemned. At one place Josephus infers that Caiaphas was deposed in A.D.36, but later remarks imply an earlier deposition.[61] A date for the crucifixion later than A.D. 33 would be excluded if this be so. The chronology of Paul's life also renders a later time improbable.[62]

According to all four Gospels, Jesus' crucifixion took place on Friday. Mark suggests that the fateful day was fifteen Nisan, since the last supper, a passover meal, had been held after sunset on Thursday. In the Fourth Gospel, Jesus' crucifixion occurred on the fourteenth day of Nisan, coinciding with the slaying of the Passover lambs. Can a choice be made between these traditions?

Since the Jewish calendar is based on a lunar-solar system of reckoning, chronologists have sought to cull from ancient astronomical records the time of the full moon in the month of Nisan from A.D. 26–36. The conclusions of some scholars have been utilized. According to one, the crucifixion occurred on fifteen Nisan A.D. 30, or on fourteen Nisan A.D. 33.[63] According to another, A.D. 27 is the

[59] Goguel, *Jesus*, pp. 227f.
[60] John 2:13, 6:4, and 12:1.
[61] *Antiq.*, XVIII. ii. 2.
[62] See below, p. 384f.
[63] Achelis of Koenigsberg, 1902. See Riecke, *New Testament Era*, pp. 176ff., who dates Jesus' death 14 Nisan, A.D. 33, employing historical data only.

only year in which Christ might have died on fifteen Nisan; A.D. 30 and 33 are the only two years when the crucifixion could have occurred on fourteen Nisan.[64] The large element of uncertainty in all such "scientific" calculations seriously limits their value.[65]

Reconstructions of the chronology of Jesus' Ministry have ordinarily been based on one of two alternatives. The choice lies between a Ministry of from one to two, or from two to three years' duration, depending on whether the primary value is given to the course of events in Mark or in John. On the one hand, defenders of the Johannine chronology have tended to follow its notations concerning Jewish feasts and have harmonized with this pattern references in the Synoptic Gospels. The most popular dates for the longer Ministry are A.D. 26–29 or 27–30. On the other hand, defenders of the primary value of Mark's outline have usually rejected the idea that John's Gospel is constructed upon a chronological scheme. They have contended that nothing in the Gospels suggests that the Ministry of Jesus lasted more than one or two years.[66] Some exponents of this view have been willing to accept John's account of a longer ministry in Jerusalem than the synoptic outline implies.[67] Alternative dates for the shorter Ministry are 26–28, 27–29, or 28–30 depending chiefly upon how one determines "the fifteenth year of the reign of Tiberius Caesar" (Luke 3:1) and the relation of the beginning of Jesus' Ministry to the work of John the Baptist.

It is commonly held that the birth of Jesus occurred in the year 7–6 B.C. The most significant aspect of the continuing debate on chronological problems concerns the date of Jesus' death. Neither the day of the week nor the year matters so much as the day of the month. Whether or not Jesus' Last Supper was a Passover meal is considered by some persons to provide a principal clue to Jesus' interpretation of his death.[68]

AN OUTLINE OF JESUS' MINISTRY

The materials for writing a biography of Jesus do not exist. This admission need not lead, however, to the negative conclusion that "the outline of the Gospels does not enable us to know either the outer course of the life of Jesus or his inner development."[69] It is probable that the plot of Mark's Gospel preserves a substantially trustworthy (though incomplete) account of the course of events

[64] J. K. Fotheringham, *JTS* XXXV (1934): 146ff.

[65] Goguel, *Jesus*, p. 227; Jeremias, *Eucharistic Words*, pp. 10ff.

[66] C. H. Turner, "Chronology," in J. Hastings, *Dictionary of the Bible*, vol. 1 pp. 403ff.; Hunter, *Work and Words*, pp. 18f. G. Ogg, *Chronology of the Public Ministry of Jesus* (1940), argues for a 2–3 year Ministry, A.D. 29–30 to 33. Cf. Caird, note 57 above, p. 603, A.D. 28–30.

[67] T. W. Manson, *BJRL* XXXIII (1951): 271ff.; C. H. Dodd in T. W. Manson, *Companion*, pp. 371f.; cf. Goguel, *Jesus*, pp. 271ff.

[68] Caird, note 57 above, p. 603. On the question of the Last Supper's relation to Passover, see below, pp. 313f.

[69] Bultmann, *Existence and Faith*, p. 52. Cf. the statement of G. Bertram, German form critic, cited in Goguel, *Jesus*, p. 59.

in Jesus' life and of the chief phases of his Ministry. Beginning with Mark, we may reconstruct a broad outline of Jesus' activity which is intelligible in itself and which has a solid claim to represent what actually happened.[70] A large number of the incidents in the Synoptic Gospels are historical. Of course there is no way of proving the accuracy of these versions. But to rest the argument for their historicity upon the possession of a complete and detailed chronology is impossible and unnecessary. Few students of the lives of men in antiquity will demand such exactness. Moreover, many of Jesus' teachings may be learned through a critical study of the synoptic tradition. The so-called Q passages of Matthew and Luke, and much of the discourse tradition exclusive to the First and Third Gospels merit our confidence as reflecting the substance of Jesus' ideas. Historical methods are often incapable of sharply separating the precepts and parables of Jesus from the application of such teaching by his disciples. Yet a patient study of the Gospels will show that such teaching as can be recovered is consistent with his action.

In the remainder of this section the outline of Jesus' Ministry will be sketched. Our reading of Mark disclosed that the first part of Jesus' Ministry was centered in Galilee, the latter part in Judea. This division of the principal scenes of Jesus' activity reappears in Matthew and Luke, despite the differences in editorial aims and methods. That these areas were the principal foci of Jesus' Ministry finds further support in the summary statements of the apostle's *kerygma* in the early chapters of Acts. Between the Galilean and Judean periods of the Ministry in Mark, as well as in Matthew, Jesus traveled in regions to the north and northwest of Galilee. Luke's omission of many of Mark's episodes relating to this period obscures this area of the Ministry in the Third Gospel. Yet it is unlikely that Luke offers a variant historical tradition. He has introduced stories which do not fit into the Markan framework, but he provides no clear itinerary of his own. The reader of Luke 9–18 learns that Jesus made a somewhat leisurely progress through the central districts of Palestine toward Jerusalem.[71]

Because the chronological connections are loosest in Mark 7–9, it is reasonable to suppose, as Luke seems to have done, that more time should be allowed for a ministry in Perea and Judea and, perhaps, in Jerusalem itself.

On the basis of these general observations, and upon evidence set forth in the section on chronology, the main stages of Jesus' Ministry and their approximate duration may now be conjectured:

A.D. 27 Fall–Winter   The appearance and proclamation of John the Baptist; Jesus' baptism and temptation in the wilderness.[72]

A.D. 28 Early Spring   After John's arrest Jesus begins his Ministry in Galilee in the towns surrounding the Sea of Galilee; he preaches in

[70]Recent "redaction criticism" of the Gospels has tended to reinforce the skepticism of form critics concerning the historical value of Mark's plot. See, e.g., G. Strecker, "The Passion and Resurrection Predictions in Mark's Gospel," *Interpretation* XXII (1968): 421ff.

[71]Luke's "great interpolation" (9:51–18:14) preserves traditions of Jesus' contact with the people of Samaria, which have left traces in John. While, in the Fourth Gospel, Jesus' Ministry alternates between the two districts, John 7:1f. marks a transition. After this there is no return to Galilee.

[72]John reports that Jesus worked for a short while alongside the Baptist in Judea, 3:22f.; 4:1. See Goguel, *Jesus*, p. 242; V. Taylor, *The Life and Ministry of Jesus* (1955), pp. 64ff. [hereafter, *Life*].

the synagogues and heals; he also carries on his work in the open and by the lakeside; a popular following is gained but the hostility of the scribes of the Pharisees is provoked; an inner circle of disciples is drawn to Jesus.

Early Summer | A mission of the disciples; a popular demonstration by the Sea of Galilee; the feeding of a multitude.

Summer | The suspicions of Herod Antipas are aroused; Jesus leaves Galilee and with his disciples wanders to the north; in the vicinity of Caesarea Philippi, Peter confesses that Jesus is the Christ.

Fall–Winter | Jesus goes to "the region of Judea and beyond the Jordan." [73]

A.D. 29 Spring | Jesus makes his triumphal entry into Jerusalem and within the week is arrested, tried, and crucified.

There are elements of speculation in the above sketch. Yet in the main it is supported by the traditions, sufficiently well at any rate to provide a narrative framework for interpreting the history of Jesus.

Before this interpretation is attempted, we should give attention to some of the prominent themes which underlie Jesus' Ministry and which give coherence to the story as a whole. This is the most hazardous step in the whole undertaking of historical reconstruction. Because there have been varying conceptions of the central themes intrinsic to the story of Jesus, many different "lives" have been written. There is an inevitable element of subjectivity in this aspect of Gospel criticism. Yet a recognition of this fact should not discourage us in the search for clues sufficiently comprehensive to provide an intelligible framework for the Ministry. If such clues are not derived from the Gospels themselves, they will be introduced into the story by the reader, wittingly or unwittingly. By failing to take the texts before us with sufficient seriousness, we tend to alter or supplement them to suit our own taste. We should not decide beforehand that clues for interpreting the history of Jesus are not a part of the history itself. All the relevant passages in the Gospels—understood in the light of their first-century Palestinian setting, insofar as this is possible—provide the historical norms of interpretation.

THE PROCLAMATION OF THE KINGDOM OF GOD

There is an impressive agreement among students of the Gospels that Jesus' teaching concerning the kingdom of God is basic to an understanding of his Ministry. According to the earliest Gospels, as will be seen below, the coming

[73] The better part of a year may be implied by Mark's narrative, 6:39–14:1ff. John 7:32ff. reports Jesus' presence in Jerusalem during the feasts of tabernacles and dedication (Sept.–Oct. and Dec.). Did Jesus retire from Jerusalem and labor in "the region of Judea and beyond the Jordan" (Mark 10:1) until the final Passover? Several units of the synoptic tradition, contrary to Mark's plot, imply that Jesus had been in Jerusalem before his passion, e.g., Luke 13:34; Matt. 23:37; Mark 11:1–10. See note 45 above.

of the kingdom of God was proclaimed by Jesus throughout his Ministry. "His teaching, his healings and exorcisms, the task of the Twelve, his whole campaign and even his death, all serve to make good this proclamation and the faith that inspires it."[74]

References in the Synoptic Gospels to Jesus' teaching concerning the kingdom may be grouped under four headings: statements explicitly proclaiming the coming of the kingdom of God; statements implying its coming; sayings of Jesus concerning the sorts of persons who are to receive or enter the kingdom; and the parables of the kingdom.

Proclaiming the Kingdom

Mark:

1. . . . Jesus came into Galilee, preaching the gospel of God, and saying, "The time is fulfilled, and the kingdom of God is at hand; repent, and believe in the gospel." Mark 1:14–15 (Matt. 4:17)

2. And he said to them [the disciples], "Truly, I say to you, there are some standing here who will not taste death before they see the kingdom of God come with power." Mark 9:1 (Matt. 16:28–Luke 9:27)

3. "Truly, I say to you [the disciples], I shall not drink again of the fruit of the vine until that day when I drink it new in the kingdom of God." Mark 14:25 (Matt. 26:29; cf. Luke 22:16, 18)

Q:

4. "I tell you, among those born of women none is greater than John [the Baptist]; yet he who is least in the kingdom of God is greater than he." Matt. 11:11–Luke 7:28

5. "Whenever you [the disciples] enter a town and they receive you, eat what is set before you; heal the sick in it and say to them 'the kingdom of God has come near to you' [Matt: is at hand]. . . ." Matt. 10:7–Luke 10:8, 9 (11)

6. "Thy kingdom come, thy will be done. . . ." Matt. 6:10–Luke 11:2

7. ". . . if it is by the Spirit [Luke: finger] of God that I cast out demons, then the kingdom of God has come upon you." Matt. 12:28–Luke 11:20 (cf. Mark 3:22–27)

8. "I tell you, many will come from east and west and sit at table in the kingdom of God, while the sons of the kingdom [Luke: "workers of iniquity"] will be thrown into outer darkness; there men will weep and gnash their teeth." Matt. 8:11–12–Luke 13:28–29

9. "From the days of John the Baptist until now the kingdom of God has suffered violence, and men of violence take it by force. The law and the prophets were until John." Matt. 11:12–Luke 16:16[75]

---

[74] A. Wilder, *New Testament Faith for Today* (1955), p. 74: C. T. Craig, "The Proclamation of the Kingdom," *IB*, vol. 7, pp. 145ff.; Perrin, *Rediscovering*, p. 54.

[75] For this emended text, see Kümmel, *Promise and Fulfillment*, pp. 12f. Cf. N. Perrin, *Kingdom of God in the Teaching of Jesus* (1963), pp. 171ff. [hereafter, *Kingdom*]. The following passages are probably editorial additions: Luke 4:43 (cf. Mark 1:38); Luke 9:11 (cf. Mark 6:34); Luke 9:60 (cf. Matt. 8:22); Luke 21:31 (cf. Mark 13:29); and Matt. 24:14 (cf. Mark 13:10, 13b).

"Special Luke":

10. Being asked by the Pharisees when the kingdom of God was coming, he answered them, "The kingdom of God is not coming with signs to be observed; nor will they say, 'Lo, here it is!' or 'There!' for behold, the kingdom of God is in the midst of you." Luke 17:20

Proclaiming (by Implication) the Kingdom

Mark:

11. And Jesus said to them [the people who asked why his disciples, unlike John's, did not fast] "Can the wedding guest fast while the bridegroom is with them? As long as they have the bridegroom with them they cannot fast. The days will come, when the bridegroom is taken away from them, and then they will fast in that day." Mark 2:19–20[76]

Q:

12. And Jesus answered them [the disciples of John], "Go and tell John what you hear and see [the signs and proclamation of the kingdom of God?]: the blind receive their sight and the lame walk, lepers are cleansed and the deaf hear, and the dead are raised up, and the poor have good news preached to them. And blessed is he who takes no offense at me." Matt. 11:4-6-Luke 7:22–23 (cf. saying No. 7)

13. "Blessed are the eyes which see what you see [the signs of the kingdom?]. For I tell you that many prophets and kings desired to see what you see, and did not see it, and to hear what you hear [the proclamation of the kingdom?], and did not hear it." Luke 10:23–24-Matt. 13:16–17

14. "The queen of the South will arise at the judgment with the men of this generation and condemn them; for she came from the ends of the earth to hear the wisdom of Solomon, and behold, something greater [neuter adj., the kingdom of God?] than Solomon is here. The men of Nineveh will arise at the judgment with this generation and condemn it, for they repented at the preaching of Jonah, and behold, something [sic] greater than Jonah is here." Luke 11:31–32; Matt. 12:41–42[77]

"Special Luke":

15. He [Jesus] opened the book [of Isaiah], and found the place where it was written, "The Spirit of the Lord is upon me, because he has anointed me to preach good news [of the kingdom?] to the poor . . . to proclaim the acceptable year of the Lord." Luke 4:17–19 (in place of Mark 1:15)

Receiving and Entering the Kingdom of God

Mark:

16. And he said to them [the twelve], "To you has been given the secret of the kingdom of God [Matt.; Luke: given to know the secrets of], but for those outside everything is in parables." Mark 4:11

---

[76]See also Mark 2:21–22.

[77]For other passages referring to a "day" of judgment associated with the appearing of the Son of man, see below, pp. 261f.

17. ". . . if your eye causes you to sin, pluck it out; it is better to enter the kingdom of God with one eye than with two eyes to be thrown into hell. . . ." Mark 9:47

18. . . . and he said to them [the disciples], "Let the children come to me, do not hinder them; for to such belongs the kingdom of God. Truly, I say to you, whoever does not recieve the kingdom of God like a child shall not enter it." Mark 10:14–15

19. . . . and Jesus looked around and said to his disciples, "How hard it will be [Luke: it is] for those who have riches to enter the kingdom of God! . . . It is easier for a camel to go through the eye of a needle than for a rich man to enter the kingdom of God." Mark 10:23, 25

20. And when Jesus saw that he [the scribe] answered wisely, he said to him, "You are not far from the kingdom of God." Mark 12:34

Q:

21. "Blessed are you poor [Matt.: poor in spirit], for yours is the kingdom of God [Matt.: heaven]." Matt 5:3–Luke 6:20

22. ". . . seek first his kingdom, and these things [clothing, food, drink] shall be yours as well." Matt. 6:33–Luke 12:31[78]

"Special Matthew":

23. "Blessed are those who are persecuted for righteousness' sake, for theirs is the kingdom of heaven." Matt. 5:10

24. "Whoever then relaxes one of the least of these commandments and teaches men so, shall be called least in the kingdom of heaven; but he who does them and teaches them shall be called great in the kingdom of heaven. For I tell you, unless your righteouness exceeds that of the scribes and Pharisees, you will never enter the kingdom of heaven." Matt. 5:19–20

25. And he said to them [the disciples], ". . . every scribe who has been trained for the kingdom of heaven is like a householder who brings out of his treasure what is new and what is old." Matt. 13:52

26. "I will give you [Peter and the other disciples] the keys of the kingdom of heaven, and whatever you bind on earth shall be bound in heaven, and whatever you loose on earth shall be loosed in heaven." Matt. 16:19 (cf. Matt. 18:18)

27. "Whoever humbles himself like this child, he is the greatest in the kingdom of heaven." Matt. 18:4

28. ". . . and there are eunuchs who have made themselves eunuchs for the sake of the kingdom of heaven." Matt. 19:12b

29. Jesus said to them [the Pharisees?], "Truly I say to you, the tax-collectors and the harlots go into the kingdom of heaven before you!" (The tax-collectors and harlots "believed John" [the Baptist]). Matt. 21:31b

30. ". . . I tell you [Pharisees?], the kingdom of God will be taken away from you and given to a nation producing the fruits of it." Matt. 21:43

31. "Then the king will say to those at his right hand, 'Come, O blessed of my Father, inherit the kingdom prepared for you from the foundation of the world. . . .'" Matt. 25:34

[78] Matt. 7:21 is not listed here as belonging to the Q source. Cf. Luke 6:46.

"Special Luke":

32. Jesus said to him [a candidate for discipleship], "No one who puts his hand to the plow and looks back is fit for the kingdom of God." Luke 9:62

33. "Fear not, little flock, for it is your Father's good pleasure to give you the kingdom." Luke 12:32

34. "You are those who have continued with me in my trials; as my Father appointed a kingdom for me, so do I appoint for you that you may eat and drink at my table in my kingdom, and sit on thrones judging the twelve tribes of Israel." Luke 22:28–30[79]

Parables of the Kingdom

Mark:

35. And he said, "The kingdom of God is as if a man should scatter seed upon the ground. . . ." Mark 4:26–29

36. And he said, "With what can we compare the kingdom of God, or what parable shall we use for it? It is like a grain of mustard seed. . . ." Mark 4:30–32 (cf. No. 37 below)[80]

Q:

37. "It [the kingdom of God] is like a grain of mustard seed . . ." Matt. 13:31–32-Luke 13:18–19

38. "It [the kingdom of God] is like leaven. . . ." Matt. 13:33-Luke 13:20–21

39. One of those who sat at table with him [Jesus] . . . said . . . "Blessed is he who shall eat bread in the kingdom of God!" But he said to him, "A man once made a great banquet and invited many. . . ." Luke 14:15–24 (cf. Matt. 22:2–14)[81]

"Special Matthew":

40. ". . . the kingdom of heaven may be compared to a man who sowed good seed in his field; but . . . his enemy came and sowed weeds. . . ." Matt. 13:24–30 (note also 13:36–43)[82]

41. "The kingdom of heaven is like treasure hidden in a field. . . ." Matt. 13:44–46

42. "Again, the kingdom of heaven is like a net which was thrown into the sea. . . ." Matt. 13:47–50

43. ". . . the kingdom of heaven may be compared to a king who wished to settle accounts with his servants. . . ." Matt. 18:23–25

44. "For the kingdom of heaven is like a householder who went out early in the morning to hire laborers. . . ." Matt. 20:1–16

45. "Then the kingdom of heaven shall be compared to ten maidens who took their lamps and went to meet the bridegroom. . . ." Matt. 25:1–13

[79] Luke 18:29b appears to be an editorial addition. Cf. Mark 10:29.

[80] Mark's parable of the fig tree (13:28f.) may originally have been a parable of the kingdom. Cf. Luke 21:31. Mark's parable of the vineyard may also be compared with the banquet parable, no. 39.

[81] The Q parable of the cloud and the south wind may be a parable of the kingdom, Matt. 16:2f. and Luke 12:54ff.

[82] Matt. 13:19 is clearly an editorial gloss. Cf. Mark 4:15.

Several conclusions widely held today are now given:

One, upon Jesus' lips, the phrase *kingdom of God* did not denote a territory or social order under the rule of God. At least this was not its primary reference. The Aramaic term which underlies the Greek of the Gospels means kingship rather than a kingdom or a domain. The term expressed the faith of Israel that God is king. Many would paraphrase the kingdom of God to read "the reign of God," for it connotes the sovereignty of His will in history.[83] Yet even the terms *reign* or *rule* are not adequate, if one thinks of them as abstract concepts. "The kingdom of God is the power of God expressed in deeds; it is what God does wherein it becomes evident that he is king . . . it is quite concretely the activity of God as king." [84]

Two, there is no difference in meaning between the kingdom of God and the kingdom of heaven, the latter phrase being that which Matthew prefers. "Heaven" was a pious periphrasis for the unspeakable Name.

Three, in proclaiming the coming of the kingdom, Jesus was not announcing a slowly evolving movement within history, or an event which men could bring or "build" by adhering to the principles of Jesus' ethic. Whereas the parables of growth have been interpreted in this way, most scholars reject this reading of them on the basis of nonparabolic teaching concerning the kingdom.[85] Jesus believed that God manifested His rule in history in His own time and way.

Four, when Jesus spoke of the kingdom of God as "coming" he spoke of an eschatological hope. It is true that in ancient Judaism the phrase *kingdom of God* could refer to a present reality perceived by faith: God rules His world; He always has and He always will. It was possible to speak of this everlasting kingdom as an established reality whenever and wherever God's people acknowledge His supremacy and obey His will. But it is unlikely that any of the passages above can be properly understood in this way. In proclaiming the "coming" of the kingdom of God, Jesus testified to his generation that God would usher in that new Age to which the prophets and writers of apocalypse had looked forward. This day of judgment and of salvation was "at hand."

Beyond these areas of agreement, interpretations diverge as to the meaning of Jesus' teaching. In the main, three viewpoints may be distinguished: Jesus taught that the coming of the kingdom was an imminent, altogether future event; Jesus taught that the kingdom of God had come in the course of his Ministry; or Jesus taught that the future kingdom of God was already in some sense being manifested in his Ministry. The first two viewpoints have the advantage of simplicity and logical consistency. The third may be suspect as representing a middle-of-the-road position. Expositions of this, as of paradoxical statements generally, can fall short of being convincing by reason of their vagueness. Yet the third viewpoint has this obvious advantage: It takes into account all of the above sayings concerning the kingdom which merit our confidence as reporting Jesus'

[83]Note saying no. 6, above, p. 252.

[84]Perrin, *Rediscovering*, p. 55.

[85]Sayings nos. 22–30 and 39–44. See the article *"Basileus"* by K. L. Schmidt, K. G. Kuhn, G. von Rad, and H. Kleinknecht in *Theological Dictionary*, ed. Bromiley, vol. I (1964), pp. 564ff.

teaching. For this reason it is a more widely accepted interpretation than either the first or the second.

The third viewpoint will be presented in the next chapter as reflecting the perspective of Jesus throughout his Ministry. Representative statements of the first and the second alternative positions will now be given.

The view that Jesus was determined by a belief in the imminent coming of the kingdom of God, after the manner of Jewish apocalyptic expectations, has been forcefully maintained by Albert Schweitzer.[86]

According to Schweitzer, Jesus was obsessed by an apocalyptic vision. He was convinced that the birth pangs of the new Age were being experienced in his time. The final judgment of God would soon fall upon Satan and other invisible demonic powers. The day determined by God for the establishment of His kingdom was at hand. The Son of man would appear on the clouds as the agent of divine judgment and of salvation. The dead would be raised, and the deeds of men, both good and evil, would receive their reward. The condemned would be cast into a fiery pit, and the righteous would enter upon a life of unending bliss, living as angels and enjoying forever the presence of God.

After Jesus' contact with the Baptist, he expected these last things. At his baptism, Jesus became convinced that he was the Messiah-designate. Yet he did not make this belief a part of his public preaching. Indeed, since he identified himself with the apocalyptic Son of man who would come in clouds of glory, he made no personal claims in the brief period of his public teaching.[87] He offered his disciples no private instruction. His sole purpose was to set in motion the apocalyptic program of events. When Jesus sent out "the twelve" on a mission in Galilee he expected the End to take place before they had completed their tour (Matt. 10:22–23). He did not expect to see them again in "this present Age." When this expectation was not realized, Jesus revised his forecast, as well as the conception of his personal role in relation to the End.[88] His death was to be the apocalyptic "tribulation" precipitating last things. The predestined kingdom of God was to be taken by violence. Jesus and his disciples became the penitent stormtroopers "engaged in forcing on and compelling the coming of the king-

---

[86] Schweitzer, *Quest,* pp. 348ff.; idem., *Mystery of the Kingdom of God,* trans. W. Lowrie (1950). Whatever one's view of its details, Schweitzer's thesis that "consistent eschatology" provides the essential clue to Jesus' mission makes him the foremost representative of the futurist position. Schweitzer challenges his critics to render a more probable explanation of some of the most crucial texts in the Gospels. Schweitzer's foremost "disciple" is M. Werner, *The Formation of Christian Dogma,* trans. S. G. F. Brandon (rev. ed., 1957). See Perrin, *Kingdom,* pp. 37ff.; also G. Lundström, *The Kingdom of God in the Teaching of Jesus,* trans. J. Bulman (1963), pp. 77ff. [hereafter, *Kingdom*].

[87] In this way Schweitzer explains the Messianic secret motif. "The eschatological solution . . . at one stroke raises the Markan account as it stands, with all its disconnectedness and inconsistencies, into genuine history." *Quest,* p. 335.

[88] "The fact which alone makes possible an understanding [of Jesus] is lacking in Mark (sic, cf. note 87) . . . without Matt. 10–11, which is historical as a whole and down to the smallest detail, everything remains enigmatic . . .," Schweitzer, *Quest,* pp. 358, 361. The decisive influence of Schweitzer's reading of Matt. 10 upon the development of his theory is stressed by Perrin, *Kingdom,* pp. 32f.

dom."[89] Thus Jesus' journey to Jerusalem was "the funeral march to victory." The Messiah of the coming kingdom

> lays hold of the wheel of the world to set it moving on that last revolution which is to bring all ordinary history to a close. It refuses to turn and he throws himself upon it. Then it does turn and crushes him. Instead of bringing in the eschatological conditions, he has destroyed them. The wheel rolls on, and the mangled body of the one immeasurably great Man, who was strong enough to think of himself as the spiritual ruler of mankind and to bend history to his purpose, is hanging on it still. That is his victory and that is his reign.[90]

According to Schweitzer, Jesus' eschatology and his ethical teaching form a consistent whole, His radical demands comprise the ethic of the interval, *Interim-ethik*, a heroic world-denying ideal appropriate to the last days. In his famous metaphor, Schweitzer affirmed that "the late-Jewish Messianic world view is the crater from which bursts forth the flame of the eternal religion of love."[91]

Let us consider now the position which represents the opposite pole of the theory just examined. Some scholars hold that, far from patterning his life upon the rigidly deterministic scheme of Jewish apocalypse, Jesus through his teaching reveals his radical break with this scheme. His announcement of the coming of the kingdom was indeed based upon current apocalyptic expectations. Yet, in employing the language and symbols of apocalypticism, Jesus gave them a quite original interpretation. It is not wise to assume, as does Schweitzer, that the content of the idea of the kingdom of God, as Jesus meant it, may be filled in from the speculation of apocalyptic writings. Neither in his action nor in his words does Jesus imply an early end of the world. Both are, in fact, inconsistent with such a belief. Jesus' proclamation "that the kingdom of God had already come dislocates the whole eschatological scheme . . . the eschaton has moved from the future to the present . . . from the sphere of expectation into that of realized experience."[92] At the same time, Jesus' thought remains "eschatological" in its orientation. The coming of the kingdom in his Ministry is, as in prophecy and apocalyptic, the ultimate, decisive act of God in history.

This position which opposes all futurist interpretations of Jesus' perspective goes by the name of "realized eschatology." Its foremost representative in the English-speaking world is C. H. Dodd.[93] According to Dodd, Jesus came into Galilee proclaiming that the kingdom of God had come. Explicitly and by im-

---

[89] Schweitzer, *Quest*, p. 355. See saying no. 9 above, p. 252.

[90] Ibid., p. 369.

[91] A. Schweitzer, *Out of My Life and Thought* (1933), p. 69. Schweitzer concluded that Jesus' actions and words are better than his apocalyptic "dogma." The latter belongs to an outmoded world view which Jesus himself destroyed by "forcing" the eschatological program into actual history. It is natural that moderns should place a high premium upon Schweitzer's reading of the Gospels since he exemplified in his own life so many of the traits of the Man they portray. Yet Schweitzer's sketch must be examined with the same critical seriousness with which Schweitzer examines the "lives" written by others. See further, pp. 279, 290f.

[92] C. H. Dodd, *Parables of the Kingdom* (1936), p. 50 [hereafter, *Parables*].

[93] Dodd in T. W. Manson, *Companion*, pp. 373ff. A critical review of the evidence is set forth in Dodd, *Parables*. See also Hunter, *Work and Words*, pp. 68ff., 101ff.

plication, Jesus announced that the eschatological Day is a present fact.[94] This view is given support and illustration in Jesus' parables, which depict in vivid and variable imagery "the arrival of a zero hour in human experience." The kingdom of God confronts men with a crisis and demands of them decisive action. Moreover, Jesus' miracles are tokens that "the powers of the kingdom of God were abroad."

Jesus' proclamation carried with it the implication that the Messiah had come. He chose the mysterious title "Son of man" to disclose to those who could hear it the "mystery of the kingdom of God." He used this symbol to reveal the truth that "in his own life of service and conflict, in suffering and in death, God was at work bringing in His kingdom and that beyond suffering and death lay eternal glory in which He should reign as the Lord of a redeemed humanity." [95]

Dodd does not overlook the predictive element in the Gospel tradition. He holds, however, that predictions of Jesus belong to different planes of thought which have been confused. While some of Jesus' words refer to forthcoming historical events, others refer to "events of a wholly supernatural order." Predictions concerning the fall of Jerusalem, his death, and the tribulations of his disciples belong to the former group. But sayings concerning the coming of the kingdom subsequent to Jesus' Ministry speak of realities transcending history. It is probable that Jesus used the traditional apocalyptic language concerning "last things" to speak of ultimate truth, of the glories of a world beyond this. Yet "his future tenses are only an accommodation of language." "The kingdom of God in its full reality is not something which will happen after other things have happened. It is that to which men awake when this order of time and space no longer limits their vision."

There are passages in the Gospels which seem to foretell a period of waiting between Christ's resurrection and return. According to Dodd, it is not probable that these passages truly represent the teaching of Jesus. In this case it is not the intent of Jesus' words which have been misunderstood. Rather, his words have been reapplied to a new situation. A setting in the life of the Church has replaced the original setting in Jesus' Ministry. An example of this is given in the so-called "eschatological parables" of Matthew. When these are studied in the light of Jesus' teaching, applying the principles of form criticism, the conclusion is reached that they are parables originally intended "to enforce his appeal to men to recognize that the kingdom was present." When the historic crisis with which Jesus confronted men had passed, these parables were adopted by the Church to enforce its appeal to men to prepare for the second and final crisis which the Church (through its misunderstanding of Jesus' teaching) believed to be approaching.[96]

[94] Dodd considers the above sayings in the following order: 7, 1 (the phrase "at hand" is rendered "has come"), 12, 13, 11, and 9.

[95] Dodd in T. W. Manson, *Companion*, p. 374.

[96] Some of Dodd's "disciples" have gone further, claiming that the apocalyptic sayings in the Gospels are the result of early misinterpretations and editorial distortions, e.g., Heard, *Intro.*, pp. 246ff. So also other scholars, F. C. Grant, *The Gospel of the Kingdom* (1940), and H. B. Sharman, *Son of Man and Kingdom of God* (1943).

Dodd believes that the eternal significance of history was revealed in the Ministry of Jesus, once and for all time. It is not necessary, nor indeed likely, that Jesus expected an imminent end of the world. Much of Jesus' teaching "implies that human life will go on, under much the same outward conditions, with the same temptations and moral problems, and the same need for forgiveness and grace, as well as of daily bread." [97] Accordingly, Jesus' commandments do not constitute an *Interim-ethik* but a moral ideal for men who have "received the kingdom of God" and who are henceforth living in the new age in which God's judgment and grace stand revealed.

The reader of Dodd's exposition of Jesus' teaching cannot but be impressed by the brilliance of this scholar whose writings form such a significant contribution to an appreciation of the New Testament. Dodd has dealt conscientiously and critically with all of the relevant passages of the Gospels. Yet it does not seem that this exposition of Jesus' perspective is fully adequate. The particular texts which stand in the way of accepting the thesis that Jesus uniformly taught a "realized eschatology" will be examined in the next chapter.

The attempts to order Jesus' teaching along the lines of either a "consistent" or a "realized" eschatology have failed to convince most scholars. Rather it is concluded that Jesus' thought centered around two foci, neither of which can be ignored or explained away. One focus of Jesus' teaching is "the eschatological crisis precipitated within the ministry . . . the other focus is the eschatological consummation which, within the framework of the ministry, remains a future event." [98] The message of Jesus can be understood only if it is recognized that he proclaimed both the coming of the kingdom in the future and its present reality. In some sense the coming kingdom was already making its presence felt; in another sense, it had not yet fully come. Such teaching cannot be regarded simply as a particular form of Jewish apocalyptic. At the same time, it cannot be completely detached from the historical context of apocalyptic thought.

The student will doubtless ask whether such apparently paradoxical teaching may be shown to form integral parts of a consistent whole. In the final analysis the question becomes: Can this perspective yield a sketch of Jesus' history which is more intrinsically probable than those which are offered by Schweitzer and Dodd? Before such a sketch is attempted it is important to have before us yet another group of sayings in the Gospels. In the above discussion it has been noted that closely related to the explication of Jesus' teaching concerning the coming of the kingdom has been the interest of scholars in sayings in the Gospels concerning the Son of man.

[97] T. W. Manson, *Companion*, p. 376. Dodd examines the relation of eschatology and ethics in the teaching of Jesus in *Gospel and Law*, pp. 53ff.
[98] C. K. Barrett, "New Testament Eschatology," *Scott. Journ. of Theo.* 6 (1953): 231; Lundström, *Kingdom*, pp. 232ff.; Perrin, *Kingdom*, pp. 159ff. Cf. Perrin, *Rediscovering*, in which a sustained effort is made to interpret the words present and future as signifying experiential rather than temporal realities. See also Bornkamm, *Jesus*, pp. 90ff.

THE SON OF MAN IN THE SYNOPTIC GOSPELS

The presence of the phrase *Son of man* in the Gospels holds a particular fascination for students of the history of Jesus. According to the earliest evangelists, "Son of man" became Jesus' favorite self-characterization. The phrase is employed in no other context except when Jesus himself speaks. Passages referring to the Son of man may be grouped under three classifications: the future coming of the Son of man; the present prerogatives or fortunes of the Son of man; and the imminent sufferings, death, and resurrection of the Son of man. The following table sets forth this threefold tradition, according to the sources in which it is found.

The Future Coming of the Son of Man
   Mark:
1. ". . . whoever is ashamed of me and of my words in this adulterous and sinful generation, of him will the Son of man also be ashamed, when he comes in the glory of his Father with the holy angels." Mark 8:38 (Luke 9:26; cf. Matt. 16:27)
2. "And then they will see the Son of man coming in clouds with great power and glory. And then he will send out the angels, and gather his elect from the four winds, from the ends of the earth to the ends of heaven." Mark 13:26 (Matt. 24:30–31–Luke 21:27)
3. ". . . and you [members of the Sanhedrin] will see the Son of man sitting at the right hand of Power, and coming with the clouds of heaven." Mark 14:62 (Matt. 26:64; cf. Luke 22:69)

    Q:
4. "And I tell you, everyone who acknowledges me before men, the Son of man [Matt: "I"] also will acknowledge before the angels of God; but he who denies me before men will be denied before the angels of God." Matt. 10:32–33–Luke 12:8–9
5. "But know this, that if the householder had known at what hour the thief was coming, he would have been awake and would not have left his house to be broken into. You also must be ready; for the Son of man is coming at an hour you do not expect." Matt. 24:43–44–Luke 12:39–40
6. And he said to his disciples, "The days are coming when you will desire to see one of the days of the Son of man, and you will not see it. And they will say to you, 'Lo, there!' or 'Lo, here!' Do not go, do not follow them. For as the lightning flashes and lights up the sky from one side to the other, so will the Son of man be in his day . . . as it was in the days of Noah, so will it be in the days of the Son of Man . . . likewise as it was in the days of Lot . . . so will it be on the day when the Son of man is revealed." Luke 17:22–30; (cf. Matt. 24:26f, 37–41)

   "Special Matthew":
7. "When they persecute you [the disciples] in one town, flee to the next; for

truly, I say to you, you will not have gone through all the towns of Israel, before the Son of man comes." Matt. 10:23

8. "The Son of man will send his angels, and they will gather out of his kingdom all causes of sin and all evildoers, and throw them into the furnace of fire . . . then the righteous will shine like the sun in the kingdom of their Father. . . ." Matt. 13:41–43

9. Jesus said to them [the disciples], "Truly, I say to you, in the new world, when the Son of man shall sit on his glorious throne, you who have followed me will also sit on twelve thrones, judging the twelve tribes of Israel." Matt. 19:28 (cf. Luke 22:28, 30)

10. ". . . then will appear the sign of the Son of man in heaven, and then all the tribes of the earth shall mourn. . . ." Matt. 24:30a[99]

11. "When the Son of man comes in his glory, and all the angels with him, then he will sit on his glorious throne. Before him will be gathered all the nations. . . ." Matt. 25:31ff.

"Special Luke":

12. ". . . when the Son of man comes, will he find faith on earth?" Luke 18:8

13. ". . . watch at all times, praying that you may have strength to escape all these things, and to stand before the Son of man." Luke 21:36[100]

The Present Prerogatives or Fortunes of the Son of Man

Mark:

14. ". . . the Son of man has authority on earth to forgive sins. . . ." Mark 2:10 (Matt. 9:6–Luke 5:24)

15. And he said to them [the Pharisees], "The Sabbath was made for man, not man for the Sabbath; so the Son of man is lord even of the Sabbath." Mark 2:27–28 (Matt. 12:8–Luke 6:5, both omitting v. 27)

Q:

16. "For John came neither eating nor drinking, and they say, 'He has a demon'; the Son of man came eating and drinking, and they say, 'Behold, a glutton and a drunkard, a friend of tax collectors and sinners. . . .'" Matt. 11:18–19–Luke 7:33–34

17. . . . a man [Matt: a scribe] said to him, "I will follow you wherever you go." And Jesus said to him, "Foxes have holes, and birds of the air have nests; but the Son of man has nowhere to lay his head." Matt. 8:19–20–Luke 9:57–58

18. "This generation is an evil generation; it seeks a sign, but no sign shall be given to it except the sign of Jonah. For as Jonah became a sign to the men of Nineveh, so will the Son of man be to this generation." Luke 11:29–30 (cf. variant Matt. 12:39–40)[101]

---

[99] Possibly an editorial addition (cf. Mark 13:24ff.), similar to Matt. 16:28 (cf. Mark 9:1).

[100] Luke 22:69 is probably an editorial modification of Mark 14:62.

[101] The recovery of this saying, to say nothing of its meaning, is notoriously difficult. To which of the three types of saying does it belong? Luke 6:22 is probably no part of Q. Cf. Tödt, *Son of Man*, pp. 123f. Matt. 13:37 is usually considered secondary, ibid., pp. 93, 135.

"Special Luke":

19. And Jesus said to him [one of those who murmured against him] "Today salvation has come to this house, since he [Zaccheus, a tax collector] is also a son of Abraham. For the Son of man came to seek and to save that which was lost." Luke 19:9–10

The Imminent Sufferings, Death, and Resurrection of the Son of Man

Mark:

20. And he [Jesus] began to teach them that the Son of man must suffer many things, and be rejected by the elders and the chief priests and scribes, and be killed, and after three days rise again [Matt, Luke: "on the third day be raised"]. Mark 8:31 (Matt. 16:21–Luke 9:22)

21. And as they were coming down the mountain [of transfiguration], he charged them [Peter, James, and John] to tell no one what they had seen, until the Son of man should have risen [Matt.: "is raised"] from the dead. Mark 9:9 (Matt. 17:9)

22. . . . he was teaching his disciples, saying to them, "The Son of man will be delivered into the hands of men, and they will kill him . . . after three days he will rise [Matt.: "he will be raised on the third day"]." Mark 9:31 (Matt. 17:22–23; Luke 9:44 omits the prediction of the resurrection)

23. "Behold, we are going up to Jerusalem; and the Son of man will be delivered to the chief priests and the scribes, and they will condemn him to death, and deliver him to the Gentiles; and they will mock him, and spit upon him, and scourge him, and kill him; and after three days he will rise." Mark 10:33–34 (note variants, Matt. 20:18–19–Luke 18:31–33)

24. ". . . the Son of man also came not to be served but to serve, and to give his life as a ransom for many." Mark 10:45 (Matt. 20:28; cf. Luke 22:27)

25. "For the Son of man goes, as it is written of him, but woe to that man by whom the Son of man is betrayed!" Mark 14:21 (Matt. 26:24–Luke 22:22)

26. ". . . the hour has come; the Son of man is betrayed into the hands of sinners." Mark 14:41 (Matt. 26:45; cf. Luke 22:48 below)

"Special Luke":

27. . . . Jesus said to him, "Judas, would you betray the Son of man with a kiss?" Luke 22:48[102]

Several observations are now noted concerning the above passages.

1) The primary reference of the phrase in the Gospels is apocalyptic. It recalls directly or indirectly a vision in the book of Daniel, chapter 7. Whether this Danielic symbolism is more immediately derived from later apocalyptic writings, especially the Similitudes of Enoch, is a question that is still in debate.[103]

Some scholars have attempted to deny the apocalyptic connotation of the phrase Son of man in the Gospels. Its primary reference, it is said, is to the prophecy

---

[102] This passage may have belonged to Luke's special passion narrative (see above, pp. 219ff.), though it could be an editorial gloss (cf. Mark 14:45f.). Luke 17:25 and 24:7 appear to be editorial.

[103] See below, pp. 304ff.

of Ezekiel.[104] If Jesus did apply the phrase to himself, it was a mere periphrasis for "I." The Aramaic term normally meant *any* man, but in a particular sense it could mean *this* man. A rejection of the apocalyptic reference of Son of man in the Gospels is not convincing. While Ezekiel's usage may afford a context for understanding some (though not all) of the sayings in the second group above, it fails to do so for those belonging to the first and third groups. The association of the Son of man with the coming "Day" suggests that the phrase is related to Jesus' proclamation of the coming kingdom, whether by Jesus himself or the early Church, and that both phrases are derived from Jewish apocalyptic eschatology.

2) A corollary of the above observation is that the phrase primarily denotes sovereignty. In Christian devotion, Son of man often signifies Christ's humanity, while Son of God declares his divinity. Yet it is not lowliness or mortality that is emphasized in the Son of man symbolism in the Synoptic Gospels. In them, as in Daniel, the phrase signifies the destiny of someone who is given authority to judge and to rule the nations. At the same time the Son of man in Daniel 7, as in the Gospels, symbolizes the destiny of man who comes out of suffering unto victory.

3) If the apocalyptic connotation of Son of man in the Gospels is warranted, it is probably used therein as a title for a messiah who is the bearer of divine judgment and salvation in the last days. A German scholar, Hans Lietzmann, argued that the Aramaic *bar nasha* could not have been a title. Few if any agree with this conclusion today.[105] Unquestionably *bar nasha* was the ordinary colloquial word for "man." But in a special context it could mean "The Man," as for example, "the righteous" could mean "The Righteous One." It is possible that some of the traditional Son of man sayings in the Gospels report teachings of Jesus which intended no direct reference to the Danielic image. Yet such instances are the exception and not the rule.

Beyond these basic points of agreement the judgments of scholars have proliferated to an astonishing degree.

4) Many scholars are convinced that, sooner or later, Jesus identified himself in some way with the Son of man. Even among these, however, there is a wide difference of opinion as to whether this identity was conceived to be a present fact or a future prospect, or both. Did Jesus speak of himself as being the Son of man during his Ministry and/or did he think of himself as the one destined to become this Son of man in the future?

Beginning with the assumption of identity, and seeking an answer to the questions formulated above, we are offered the same principal alternatives in interpreting the Son of man passages in the Gospels as those concerning the kingdom. The ordering of the evidence in one case has seemed to prejudice the pattern of interpretation in the other. For example, since for Schweitzer the kingdom of God comes in the immediate future, Jesus also proclaimed, as an

---

[104] J. Y. Campbell, "Son of Man," in *Theological Word Book*, ed. Alan Richardson (1950); P. Parker, "The Meaning of Son of Man," *JBL* 60 (1941): 231f. Note C. C. McCown, "Jesus, Son of Man: A Survey of Recent Discussion," *Journ. of Rel.* 28 (1948): 1ff.; and Higgins, *New Testament Essays*, pp. 123ff. F. H. Borsch, *The Son of Man in Myth and History* (1967), pp. 21ff., 34ff. [hereafter, *Son of Man*].

[105] Higgins, *New Testament Essays*, p. 125.

altogether future event, the coming of the Son of man. Jesus did not believe that he was the Son of man; he only believed that he was destined to become such.[106] For Dodd, since the kingdom came with Jesus, the Son of man had also come. Quite consistently Dodd affirms that "there is no coming of the Son of man after his coming in Galilee and Jerusalem." Reference to the future "Day" of the Son of man stands for "timeless fact . . . that which cannot be experienced in history is symbolized by the picture of a coming event, and its timeless quality is expressed as pure simultaneity in time—as the lightning flashes."[107]

The present writer believes that the attempts to bring the Son of man tradition within the frame of a "consistent" or a "realized" eschatology have been no more successful than in the case of the teaching concerning the kingdom. Rather the portrayal of Jesus as the Son of man in the Synoptic Gospels contains the same polarity of *now* and *not yet*. The kingdom has not yet come; nevertheless Jesus' proclamation, parables, and mighty works declare that God's rule is already making itself manifest. Even so, Jesus is not yet the *glorified* Son of man; nevertheless, he acts on earth as already possessing the authority of one who is destined to bring to fulfillment Daniel's vision. The mystery of the kingdom which Jesus proclaimed is the presence in history of a reality which will be manifested in the future "in power." Similarly, the secret of the Ministry is not that Jesus was the Messiah. Rather, it was the *nature* of his Messianic mission, his relation to the coming kingdom, that remained a secret. There were none who would believe, before the cross and resurrection, that the Son of man must suffer and die in order to reign.

5) Another range of questions and conclusions appears if one accepts as a basic assumption the view that, during the course of his Ministry, Jesus *did not proclaim himself* the Son of man, even the one destined to become the Son of man. Several important studies of the Son of man sayings listed above have reached the conclusion, to which Bultmann was led by his form critical studies, that only those which refer to "the future coming of the Son of man" are authentic sayings of Jesus. In these passages Jesus speaks of someone other than himself, and reference is therein made to the exaltation, not resurrection, of the Son of man.[108]

Working beyond this point, other scholars have been particularly impressed by the evidence that seldom if ever in the Synoptic Gospels is Jesus' teaching concerning the kingdom of God brought into relationship with the Son of man sayings attributed to him. The conclusion is that the two conceptions arose from different sources and premises, a conclusion supported by the evidence that the two conceptions are not clearly linked in the Judaism of Jesus' time.[109] It has

---

[106] Schweitzer, *Quest*, pp. 363ff.

[107] So Dodd interprets sayings such as no. 6, above; *Parables*, p. 108; Hunter, *Work and Words*, pp. 106ff.

[108] Bultmann, *History* p. 152; Bornkamm, *Jesus*, pp. 161f.; Tödt, *Son of Man*, pp. 55ff., 114ff., 141ff.; Fuller, *Foundations*, pp. 119ff.

[109] Matt. 13:37ff. and 16:28 are usually considered editorial. Philipp Vielhauer advanced the view that since the Kingdom of God was a principal part of Jesus' proclamation, none of the Son of man sayings belong to the authentic teaching of Jesus. H. M. Teeple, "The Origin of The Son of Man Christology," *JBL* LXXXIV (1965): 213ff. Cf. Tödt, *Son of Man*, pp. 27ff.

been urged also that Jesus' proclamation of the kingdom reflects such an intensity of belief in the immediacy and finality of God's action in the present that there is no room between Jesus and the coming kingdom for the coming of a second eschatological figure.[110]

6) A very different approach to the derivation of the Son of man sayings is taken by Eduard Schweizer, who argues that only the sayings about the present prerogatives and powers of the Son of man (group two, above) have the strongest claim to be authentic teaching of Jesus.[111] In these passages the Son of man is one "who lives a lowly life on earth rejected, humiliated, handed over to his opponents, but eventually exalted by God and to be the chief witness in the last judgment." [112] This picture, according to Schweizer, was probably derived by Jesus from the Jewish conception of the humiliation and exaltation of righteous men.[113] Thus the Son of man may have been for Jesus a concept independent of that of the kingdom, as it is represented in the earliest strata of the synoptic tradition. According to Schweizer none of the sayings in groups one and three, listed above, are indisputably authentic since they are post-Easter in their present forms.

In view of this variety of opinions, the Son of man tradition cannot be used with the same degree of confidence as the kingdom of God sayings, as providing a basic, underlying theme in the Synoptic Gospels giving coherence to the fragmentary data of Jesus' history. Nevertheless, at significant points, anyone's reading of the Son of man tradition plays an important, if not determinative, role in his reconstruction of the Ministry of Jesus.

[110]Käsemann, *Essays*, pp. 43f. R. H. Fuller, *New Testament in Current Study* (1962), pp. 391f.; Perrin, *Rediscovering*, pp. 164ff.

[111]E. Schweizer, "The Son of Man," *JBL* LXXIX (1960): 119ff.; idem., "The Son of Man Again," *NTS* X (1962–63): 256ff. See also, J. A. T. Robinson, *Jesus and His Coming* (1957). Cf. Borsch, *Son of Man*, pp. 36ff.

[112]Schweizer, "Son of Man," note 111 above, pp. 121f.

[113]See M. Black, "The Son of Man in Recent Research," *BJRL* XLV (1962–63): 305ff.

chapter eleven

THE MINISTRY OF JESUS IN GALILEE

Mount of Temptation rising sharply from the Jordan Valley. Traditional site of Jesus' temptation (Matt. 4; Luke 4), so identified because of "the very high mountain" from which Jesus is said to have viewed "all the kingdoms . . ." (symbolized by Herod's Jericho?). (Ewing Galloway)

The sounding of the shofar—Jewish ritual and signaling instrument (meaning a "wild ibex" but usually translated "ram's horn"). Associated in synagogue services with God's provision of the ram in Gen. 22, a scripture read during the New Year's services. (Israel Government Tourist Office)

The Road from Jerusalem to Jericho descends nearly 4,000 feet through the desolate wilderness of Judea, the setting of Jesus' parable of the Good Samaritan, Luke 10. (Ewing Galloway)

The ancient mosaic of Jesus' miracle of the loaves and fish (Mark 6:3ff and pars.) is today housed in a Benedictine monastery on the shore of the Sea of Galilee. (Israel Government Tourist Office)

I N THE early Church it was proclaimed that Jesus' Ministry had begun with the mission of John the Baptist. Historians must adopt this point of departure, for, in the preaching and baptism of John, Jesus received his first impulse to public action. No man exerted a greater influence over Jesus. For him, as for the apostles, John was the greatest of all the prophets. His career marked the boundary between the old age and the new.[1]

BEFORE THE MINISTRY

The facts relating to John's birth and early life are shrouded in legend. Luke 1–2 can hardly be used directly for historical reconstruction.[2] Yet from this tradition one learns that John's parents were of priestly descent, and that he had lived in the wilderness of Judea before "the day of his manifestation to Israel."[3] While in this desolate region, John received his call. Since the discoveries at Qumran, some scholars have concluded that prior to his public life John was in contact with the sect of the scrolls. Perhaps John lived for a while at Khirbet Qumran; he may have been orphaned (Luke 1:17) or sent there by his parents.[4] Josephus reports that Essenes "adopted other men's children" and "molded them in accordance with their own principles."[5] Others, supposing that John's childhood was spent with his parents, suggest that John became a novitiate at the Qumran monastery in his early twenties. Perhaps when he went to Jerusalem to be ordained to the priesthood, the conduct of the priests provoked John to indignation and he fled to the wilderness. All speculation aside, it is noteworthy that the presence in the wilderness of both John and the dissident priests at Qumran was inspired by the summons from the prophecy of Isaiah: "In the wilderness prepare the way of the Lord. . . ."[6] Both John and the Qumran priests believed that the last days were at hand, both demanded from their fellow

[1] Matt. 11:7ff.; Luke 7:24ff.; 16:16 (Q); Acts 1:21; 10:36f.

[2] See further, below, pp. 321ff.

[3] Luke 1:80; 3:2; Matt. 3:1. How John maintained life in the wilderness is something of a mystery. It was recalled that his diet had been limited to "locust and wild honey." Doubtless John's sympathizers believed that he had been sustained by divine providence, as had Elijah, his prototype; John's enemies attributed his survival to black magic, Matt. 11:18; Luke 7:33 (Q).

[4] W. H. Brownlee in Stendahl, *Scrolls,* p. 35. See Burrows, *More Light,* pp. 56ff.

[5] *War,* II. ii.1. K. Schubert lists evidence supporting the opinion that John's father held views similar to the Qumran sect: *Dead Sea Community,* pp. 126f.

[6] Isaiah 40:3 (Mark 1:3 and pars.; 1QS viii. 13–16). It should be noted that others besides Essenes lived in the desert for religious convictions. See Josephus' description of such an ascetic named Banus, *Life,* 2:11.

Israelites a thoroughgoing repentance, and both practiced a ceremonial immersion in water.[7] The proximity to Qumran of John's preaching also has been urged as a basis for his acquaintance with Essene beliefs and practices. Probably John knew of the Essenes; yet it is only a possibility that he had ever been a probationer in one of their settlements.

John's Proclamation and Appeal

The following passages in the Synoptic Gospels describe the person and proclamation of John the Baptist: from the earliest Gospel (most of which is used by Matthew and Luke)—Mark 1:2-8; from Q—Matthew 3:7-12, Luke 3:7-9 and 15-17; and from "Special Luke"—Luke 3:10-14.

Josephus also provides a description of John's mission:

> John, called the Baptist, . . . was a pious man who bade the Jews who practiced virtue and exercised righteousness toward each other and piety toward God, to come together for baptism. For thus, it seemed to him, would baptismal ablution be acceptable, if it were used not to beg off from sins committed, but for the purification of the body when the soul had previously been cleansed by righteous conduct. . . .[8]

According to Christian sources, John heralded the imminent day of judgment. He forecast that God's retributive punishment would soon fall upon apostate Israel. The "wrath to come" was impending: the ax lay at the root of the unfruitful trees, corrupt men would flee the terrors of the coming judgment like vipers slithering before the burning stubble of the harvest field, the harvester held the winnowing fork in his hand to clear the threshing floor.[9] Besides, the synoptists report that the prophet claimed to be the unworthy forerunner of one mightier than himself who would destroy the wicked with his fiery breath or spirit.

John appealed to the multitudes who came to hear him at the fords of the Jordan, urging them to repent while there was yet time. He required that their repentance be accompanied by a baptism in the river, and followed by moral actions appropriate to the new life to which God called them. He allowed none of his hearers to take comfort in the fact that he had Abraham for his father.

The account of Josephus differs widely from this description of John, but few would consider the *Antiquities* a more objective record.[10] In accord with his tendency to relate Jewish teachings to Greek philosophy, Josephus transformed the fiery eschatological prophet into a preacher of virtue not unlike the Stoics, and John's baptism became a ritual washing like the neo-Pythagorean lustrations which signified a corresponding inward and outward purity. It is not surprising that Josephus obscured the messianic character of John's following.

[7] Cf. John 1:6-8, 15, 19ff.; 3:22ff. See below, pp. 590, 593.
[8] *Antiq.*, XVIII. v. 2.
[9] For this apocalyptic image of the Judgment, cf. 4 Ezra 4:30ff.
[10] See above, p. 241. Cf. M. S. Enslin, "Once Again: John the Baptist," *Rel. in Life* XXVII (1958): 557ff.

Much interest has centered around John's rite of baptism. Two problems can be distinguished: the question of John's originality, and the relation of John's proclamation to his form of baptism.

One need not look beyond Judaism for near parallels to John's baptism. It has been widely held that John's rite was modeled upon the practice of baptizing Gentile proselytes, although it cannot be proved that this custom antedates John.[11] Those who assume the currency of proselyte baptism emphasize that this water bath afforded John a suitable model for an initiation ceremony. Unlike other Jewish washings it was a once-for-all event. Perhaps John deliberately applied to "the children of Abraham" a rite devised by them to benefit pagans, thus declaring his conviction that the whole Jewish nation had gone astray and needed to be reconstituted as the people of God.[12]

In recent times there has been revised an early theory which relates John's baptism to Essene ritual washing. John's references to the eschatological baptism by fire or the spirit, or both, parallel the expectations of the Qumran sect. Yet, unlike the Essene "purifying waters," and despite the implications of the comment of Josephus, John's baptism was a nonrecurring act. Baptism in the river Jordan was not the first in a series of ablutions similar to the Essene bath of initiation, or else there would have been no basis for its comparison with Christian baptism.[13] Moreover, there is not the slightest evidence that John's candidates passed through a period of probation, or were examined by a council, or that through baptism they were admitted into a community of discipline. John's public ministry was entirely independent of the priests at Qumran.[14]

It is a sound conclusion that the form of John's baptism was determined by the nature of his proclamation. Whatever partial parallels existed in Jewish lustral practices, John drew upon apocalyptic imagery which frequently represented the inexorable divine judgment as a stream of fire, sometimes issuing from the throne of God or as the fiery breath of a messiah.[15] John's baptism may have been performed in the streams of the Jordan because running water was necessary to the symbolism of submersion in this river of fire. Repentant individuals were to enact in advance their acceptance of the eschatological judgment of God. Apparently it was John's conviction that by a humble submission before God in the present, one could be assured of divine forgiveness in the future judgment. The originality of John's baptism consists in the fact that it dramatized the substance of his eschatological proclamation.[16]

[11] Craig, *Beginning*, p. 69; T. W. Manson, *Servant-Messiah*, pp. 43ff. See *NTS* 1 (1954): 150ff.; 2(1956): 193ff.

[12] As evidence that such a radical position can be attributed to John, cf. 1QM 1, ii; 1QH vi. 7f.; CD 2:14–3:20, Brownlee, in Stendahl, *Scrolls*, p. 37. The Qumran folk considered themselves the true Israel; outsiders belonged to the realm of Belial.

[13] Cf. 1QS vi.14ff., ii. 19,iii.6; *War*, II. viii. 5 and 7. This is disputed by some scholars, e.g., Albright (Munck, *Acts*, Anchor Bible, pp. 281ff.).

[14] Schubert, *Dead Sea Community*, pp. 80ff. H. H. Rowley, "Baptism of John and the Qumran Sect," in Higgins, *New Testament Essays*, pp. 218ff. John had disciples who learned from him certain disciplines of the spiritual life, but he does not seem to have gathered disciples or organized a sect. On the contrary, he directed his hearers to the coming One "mightier than I."

[15] Dan. 7:10f.; 4 Ezra 13:10f.; 2 Thess. 2:8; Rev. 8:5ff.

[16] C. H. Kraeling, *John the Baptist* (1951), pp. 117ff. [hereafter, *Baptist*]. See now, 1QpHab iii. 28ff.

John's Baptism of Jesus

When Jesus came from Galilee to hear the fiery prophet, he presented himself for baptism. Mark's notice (1:9) is clearly historical, for the early Church cannot have been responsible for originating the tradition that Jesus submitted to John's "baptism of repentance for the forgiveness of sins." Only Matthew provides an explanation (which must have arisen in the Jewish–Christian community of the First Gospel) to guard against misunderstanding: Jesus' repentance was a positive act, the fulfillment of "all righteousness." [17]

Since the Gospels were written from the standpoint of faith and not primarily as biographies, it is probably fruitless to speculate upon the question of the meaning to Jesus of his baptism. Yet the question will arise: Were the early Christians responsible for bringing together Psalm 2:7 and Isaiah 42:1, thus representing Jesus' baptism as his anointment to be the servant-Messiah, or did Jesus at some later time (in his training of the disciples) so interpret his calling? Mark 1:10f. implies an intensely private experience, but Matthew 3:17 and Luke 3:22 describe a public revelation. [18]

John's Martyrdom and His Significance

Before taking leave of John and following Jesus into the wilderness, we should give brief attention to the prophet's fate, and also to the judgments of Jesus and his followers concerning John. The imprisonment and death of John are reported in Mark 6:17–29. These events were recorded also in the passage from Josephus cited earlier:

> . . . when everybody turned to John—for they were profoundly stirred by what he said—Herod feared . . . an uprising (for the people seemed likely to do everything he might counsel) he thought . . . it better to get John out of the way in advance, before an insurrection might develop, than . . . be sorry not to have acted once an insurrection had begun. So because of Herod's suspicion, John was sent as a prisoner to Machaerus . . . and there put to death. But the Jews believed that the destruction which overtook the army came as a punishment to Herod, God wishing to do him harm. [19]

Herod's arrest of John is credible. Not only would the ruler's suspicions have been aroused by John's popular following, but the prophet's moral exhortations might have given rise to criticism of Herod and to popular scorn. Christian sources clearly support John's influence over the masses. Yet the Markan account of John's arrest and martyrdom, like Luke's account of his birth, is probably legendary. [20]

---

[17] Luke puts the baptism in a subordinate clause, probably viewing the fact as relatively unimportant beside the experience of Jesus at the time. Second-century Christians offered more elaborate explanations (see James, *Apocryphal New Testament*, pp. 6ff.). Although Jesus was at no time reluctant to humble himself before God, Matt. 3:14f. is probably secondary since it implies John's recognition of Jesus. Note 21, below.

[18] See further, pp. 308f.

[19] *Antiq.*, XVIII. v. 2. For an account of the defeat of Herod's armies, *Antiq.*, XVIII. v.

[20] See Rawlinson, *Mark*, pp. 80ff.

The account which Josephus gives of John's martyrdom, of the defeat of Herod's armies, and of the popular reaction may be substantially factual.

The Q tradition reports that John sent from his prison a delegation to Jesus asking, "Are you he who is to come or shall we look for another?"[21] If John had previously identified Jesus as "the Mightier One," then his question could imply disillusionment, or at least uncertainty as to the correctness of his earlier expectation. But John's question may reveal no more than the beginning of his active interest in the work done by his Nazarene convert.

Although John's prison walls cannot be penetrated to learn his final attitude towards Jesus, the Synoptic Gospels provide several glimpses of the significance which the Church attributed to John. Is it possible that one or more of the following passages reflect also Jesus' estimate of John's mission? Notice should be taken of Mark 9:11–13 (Matt. 17:10–13); Matthew 11:7–12; Luke 7:24–28, 16:16 (Q); Matthew 11:14f. (M). According to the Q passage, Jesus recognized John to be a true prophet. In this context his words, "and more than a prophet" suggest further the belief that John had been the one destined to herald the Age to Come. If these words go back to Jesus, then support is given to the view that he also identified John as the Elijah of traditional expectation, the messenger sent to prepare the way for the coming of the Lord. In Matthew 11:12, and its variant Luke 16:16, we may possess authentic reminiscence of Jesus upon John's death. John had suffered that violence to which men are exposed who stand at the threshold of the coming Age and who are obedient to the call of God.[22]

Jesus' Temptation in the Wilderness

In the Synoptic Gospels the baptism and temptation of Jesus are presented as two phases of one critical experience in the life of Jesus. The Spirit possessing him at the moment of his baptism "drove him" to seek the seclusion of the wilderness. The historical sequel to Jesus' baptism is reported in Mark 1:12f., and a narrative of this temptation was contained in the Q source.[23] Some scholars, with an eye to Mark's simple declaration that Jesus was "tempted by Satan," consider the Q account an impressive commentary, in parable form, on the entire course of Jesus' Ministry. The very fact that Jesus was tempted inspired some Christian teacher to reflect upon the courses of action Jesus might have taken but had rejected at various stages of his career.[24] If we read it as a Jewish–Christian midrash, its lesson was that the old children of God had proven faithless; Jesus, by his great trust in God, had qualified as the representative head of the new

[21] Matt. 11:2ff.; Luke 7:18ff. J. A. T. Robinson conjectures that John thought "the One who should come" was Elijah, "Elijah, John, and Jesus . . ." NTS 4 (1958): 263ff.

[22] Kraeling, Baptist, pp. 137ff. Goguel's judgment that Jesus broke with John has little support (Jesus, pp. 271ff.). Cf. Robinson's view that Jesus accepted, then later rejected, John's Elijah redivivus teaching, note 21 above.

[23] Matt. 4:1ff.; Luke 4:1ff. Did Matthew's order of the last two temptations stand in the Q source? Daube, New Testament and Rabbinic Judaism, pp. 406ff.

[24] Bultmann, History, pp. 253ff.; W. E. Bundy, Jesus and the First Three Gospels (1955), pp. 62ff. [hereafter, Jesus].

Israel, the true Son of God. Unquestionably the narrative has symbolic features which reflect the story of Israel's wilderness experience. Yet it is as improbable that anyone in the early Church would have had the imagination to create this narrative, as it is that the idea of Jesus' temptation originated in the Church. The Q account possibly preserves the substance of an internal conflict which Jesus faced before his active ministry began. Jesus might have told his disciples this story as it stands in Matthew's version. We cannot of course be sure of this.

John's preaching aroused the hopes of many in the advent of a messiah. It is natural to expect that Jesus considered the course of his life's work in terms of such popular expectations. In the story of Jesus' baptism the term *messiah* does not appear, yet as Jesus identified himself with his people, and joined with them in their ardent longing for the salvation of God, he may have felt himself called to a life work which, for its characterization and measurement, demanded certain aspects of current messianic hope. It is against the background of this complex of Jewish messianic expectation that one may search for significant clues to Jesus' thinking and the moral courage of his decisions in the wilderness.[25]

Jesus' first temptation, the challenge to transform stones into bread, may be explained in one of two ways. That which gave the suggestion power may have been the seeming contradiction in Jesus' own experience "between the love of God which called him to his task and the acute privation, the hunger and weakness, into which he had been brought."[26] Had not God given signs to the leaders whom he had called to serve his people?[27] It is probable, however, that Jesus was first tempted to fulfill the hope of his people that, in the age of the Messiah, there would be a miraculous abundance of food. Had not Moses given bread in the wilderness when Israel hungered?[28]

In the face of this temptation, either to seek a sign of his divine calling or to satisfy the will of the people and to provide the Messiah's "day of plenty," Jesus found guidance in recalling the ancient truth: "Man shall not live by bread alone." Out of Egypt God had called his son, yet Israel had suffered hunger, a condition which should have led God's people to trust in his power to fulfill his promises.

The form of the second question is linked to the first by the repetition of the conditional word *if.* If God had called a man to serve the nation, then surely the nation would be provided a sign of his authority. Yet this time the suggestion is not that Jesus rely upon miraculous power to deliver himself or his people from an existing danger, such as hunger. It is proposed that Jesus court disaster. Moreover, the force of the temptation is supported by scripture: It is impossible to put too much trust in God. To Jesus such reasoning was not only specious but patently evil. To put God to the test is not to trust him. In doing so, Israel had proved to be a rebellious "son" while in the wilderness; Jesus would not so tempt God.

[25] Hunter, *Work and Words*, pp. 38ff.; T. Ferris, *The Story of Jesus* (1953), pp. 21ff.; F. Dostoevsky, *Brothers Karamazov*, 5.

[26] W. Manson, *The Gospel of Luke* (1930), p. 37.

[27] Ex. 4:1ff.

[28] Ex. 16. Cf. John 6:30f.

In the third temptation, Jesus is confronted with "all the kingdoms of the world" and their glory. We have noted the persistence into Jesus' day of the idea that a messiah would hold temporal power. There were many in Jesus' day who were able to justify their use of evil means in order to bring to pass the Jewish dream of independence. "The home-rule party" seemed determined to follow a demonic policy, using deceit, murder, and terrorism, to liberate God's people from their unhallowed enemies. The Sadducees were doing much the same thing—coming to terms with evil. True, they were pursuing an opposite course, one of compromise and appeasement. Yet doubtless they could have sanctified their means by appealing to the fact that the maintenance of the status quo allowed the Jews a modicum of self-rule and freedom to practice their religion. Did Jesus, obsessed with the thought that he had been called to proclaim to Israel the coming of the kingdom of God, consider various programs which in his time were being urged in the name of piety and patriotism? Did he see in these programs of violence or compromise a capitulation to the kingdom of evil? Again a word from the narrative of Israel's wilderness sojourn comes to Jesus as a divine admonition: "You shall worship the Lord your God, and Him alone shall you serve." God's kingdom must come in God's own way. Jesus would not further his Ministry in ways which are not themselves righteous. He would not grasp for power, however much it is thought the Messiah was meant to possess it and exercise it.

THE GALILEAN MINISTRY

"Now after John was arrested, Jesus came into Galilee, preaching the gospel of God and saying, 'The time is fulfilled, and the kingdom of God is at hand;[29] repent, and believe in the gospel.'" (Mark 1:14f.) Like John the Baptist, Jesus was moved to action by his conviction that the eschatological Day was fast approaching. Like John also, Jesus called upon his hearers to repent. But the emphasis of Jesus lay not upon the threatening "wrath to come." Instead he spoke of the imminent coming of the reign of God as good news and, in the actions of his Ministry, *he became more than a herald:* "Jesus not only issued a call to repentance but with full authority he granted to men the salvation expected in the future."[30] We may note also that Jesus was no ascetic. There is no trace in the earliest strata of the gospel tradition of Jesus' baptism of disciples. Hence he did not linger in the wilderness or stand by the side of running streams attracting people to himself. Rather, he moved from place to place, speaking in the synagogues or in the open countryside.

The earliest Gospel makes it clear that two kinds of activity were typical of Jesus' itinerant ministry in Galilee—teaching and healing. We have seen Mark's particular interest in Jesus' power over demons, but he does not neglect to report that Jesus' teaching astonished the people. "He taught as one who had authority, and not as the scribes" (Mark 1:21f.).

[29] Dodd's rendering "the kingdom of God has come" is to be rejected. See Fuller, *Mission*, pp. 20ff.; cf. Perrin, *Kingdom*, pp. 64ff., who argues that the lexicographical evidence remains *sub judice*.
[30] Pannenberg, *Jesus*, p. 217; Betz, *Jesus*, p. 34ff.

The Call of the First Disciples

Shortly after the Ministry began, Jesus called disciples. Mark reports that two pairs of brothers, fishermen by trade, were invited to follow Jesus and to help him in his work.[31] The call of another disciple, a tax collector named Levi, is singled out by Mark.[32] Such stories may reveal ways in which Jesus gathered other disciples. Yet, strange as it may seem, the gospel traditions do not enable us to know positively even their names.[33] Some scholars have identified stages in the relations of Jesus with his disciples. First there was the call of an indeterminate number of disciples, followed by the appointment of "the twelve," then the commissioning of "apostles." Some suppose that Jesus' formal choice of twelve men was "an acted parable" proclaiming his intention "to create a new Israel."[34] It is probable that the synoptists recognized that the elders representing the twelve tribes of Israel provided a type of Jesus' selection of twelve men. It is possible that at the end of his Ministry Jesus treated these disciples as the nucleus of the true Israel. That Jesus consciously restricted his disciples to twelve is not consonant with his call to others to "follow" him. Jesus sought to extend his popular following, yet never without fair warning that his disciples must be ready at all times to make costly sacrifices.[35]

The Mighty Works of Jesus

Two closely related questions will be considered in this section. Is it possible to know Jesus' attitude toward his mighty works? Can the actual situations from the Ministry be reconstructed from the miracle stories of the Gospels? In attempting to answer both questions earlier observation should be recalled. The *kerygma* of the earliest Church, supported by the claim that God had wrought "signs and wonders" through Jesus the Christ, ensured the preservation of miracle stories from the Ministry. It would not be correct to describe all, or even most, of these stories as "wonder tales," created from apologetic motives unrelated to the Christian proclamation and moral teachings. Nevertheless, their forms in the Gospels do reflect stages of development, the special interests of the synoptists, as well as the earlier influences exerted during the course of their oral transmission.[36] We have seen that the Q story of Jesus' temptation reports his decision not to use marvelous power either to help himself, or for self-exhibition as a means of attracting attention or compelling belief. It should be noticed now that throughout the Ministry Jesus did not extricate himself from dangers, nor was

---

[31] Mark 1:16ff. (Matt. 4:18ff.). The variant, Luke 5:1ff., may be a postresurrection story, cf. John 21:4ff. The alacrity of the disciples' response suggests that there were earlier contacts (note John 1:40ff.). But cf. T. W. Manson, *Servant-Messiah*, pp. 68f.

[32] Mark 2:14 (Matt. 9:9).

[33] Cf. Mark 3:16ff.; Matt. 10:2ff.; Luke 6:14ff. (Acts 1:3); John 1:45ff., 14:22. See above, pp. 142ff.

[34] Hunter, *Work and Words*, pp. 60f.; Bornkamm, *Jesus*, pp. 144ff.

[35] Matt. 8:19ff.; Luke 9:57ff.; Matt. 10:34ff.; Luke 12:51ff.; 14:26f.; Mark 10:21 and pars. Very probably the number of Jesus' disciples fluctuated from time to time.

[36] See above, p. 163. Richardson, *Miracle Stories*, pp. 20ff.; Fuller, *Interpreting the Miracles*, pp. 24ff., 46ff.; Betz, *Jesus*, pp. 63ff.

**PALESTINE
IN THE TIME OF JESUS
and the Early Church**

Tetrarchy of Herod Antipas

Under Roman Procurator

Tetrarchy of Lysanias

Tetrarchy of Philip

0   20
Miles

ABILENE

Abila

Damascus

Sidon

Sarepta

Leontes R.

MOUNT LEBANON

P H O E N I C I A (**Roman province**)

S Y R I A

MT. HERMON

Tyre

Jordan R.

PANIAS

Dan • Caesarea Philippi

ITURAEA

TRACHONITIS

Cadasa

ULATHA

L. Semechonitis

Gischala

Seleucia

BATANAEA

GALILEE

Capernaum

Raphana

Ptolomais
(Accho)

Magdala • Bethsaida

GAULANTIS

Jotapata

Cana •

*Horns of
Hattin* △

Sea of Galilee

Gamala

Sepphoris •

Tiberias

Dion

Mt.
Carmel

Nazareth •

*Mt.
Tabor* △

Yarmuk R.

AURANTIS

Dora •

Nain

Gadara

Edrei

*PLAIN OF
ESDRAELON*

Capitolias

Caesarea •

Scythopolis •

Bethabara

DECAPOLIS
(**semi-independent
under Romans**)

Ginaea •

Pella

PLAIN OF SHARON

SAMARIA

Samaria
(Sebaste) • △*Mt. Ebal*

Gerasa

Apollonia •

Shechem • • Sychar

Amathus

River Jordan

Jabbok R.

Antipatris •

Joppa • Arimathaea •

Phasaelis •

PERAEA

Lydda •

Gophna •

Archelais •
• Ehraim

Beth-nimrah

Philadelphia

Bethel •

Jamnia •

Gazara •

Jericho •

Mt. of Olives

Ekron • Emmaus • △

Julias

Heshbon

Azotus •

Jerusalem •
Bethlehem •

Bethany
•

AMMON

Ascalon •

Herodium •

Callirhoe •

JUDAEA

Marisa •

*DEAD
SEA*

Machaerus •
Dibon •

Gaza •

Hebron •

WILDERNESS OF JUDAH

En-gedi
(*Salt
Sea*)

Arnon R.

Gerar •

Juttah •

Carmel •

Areopolis •

Raphia •

Masada •

A R A B I A

Beersheba •

IDUMAEA

Kir-moab •

N A B A T A E A N S

Zered R.

he willing to comply with the demands of men that he produce signs in support of his authority. He refused to give such signs and spoke of men's desire for them as morally reprehensible.[37]

The fact remains, however, that Jesus did perform mighty works. His antagonists were unable to deny this. They could only impugn the source of his powers and his motives for exercising them. Mark 3:19b–27 is particularly instructive in this regard. But the importance of this passage lies chiefly in its revelation of Jesus' reason for alleviating the suffering of a particular group of persons, the demon-possessed. It was God's will that "the strong man—Satan—be bound by a stronger power." Jesus' victory in the wilderness was to be extended into the Galilean ministry. It is instructive to contrast here the defensive attitude of the Qumran community in its battle against evil spirits.[38] Matthew and Luke incorporated into this Markan passage a detached saying which they found in the Q source:

> ". . . if it is by the finger [Matt.: Spirit] of God that I cast out demons, then the kingdom of God has come upon you." Luke 11:20 (cf. Matt. 12:28)

This saying provides a further insight into Jesus' attitude. In his mighty works the powers of the Age to Come were being manifested. It could therefore be said that the eschatological kingdom had come.[39] Noteworthy also is Jesus' condemnation of Chorazin and Bethsaida, Galilean cities where, according to Matthew, "most of his mighty works had been done":

> "Woe to you . . . for if the mighty works done in you had been done in Tyre and Sidon, they would have repented long ago . . . it shall be more tolerable on the day of judgment for Tyre and Sidon than for you."[40]

Since "the time is fulfilled," Jesus' acts stand in a particular relation to the eschatological judgment. The mighty works of Jesus should lead to repentance and to belief in the good news. In the absence of this response, the final judgment of the Galilean villagers was being sealed.

At first sight it may seem that the above evidence is contradictory. On the one hand, Jesus refuses to give signs. On the other hand, he regards his mighty works as signs validating his proclamation and testifying to its fulfillment. But the apparent contradiction disappears when it is noted that Jesus believed that the merely curious, the seekers after signs, would never be able to understand the true significance of his acts. "Those who had eyes to see," had "been given the secret of the kingdom of God." Sooner or later those persons would recognize that Jesus' acts were signs.[41] That Jesus was acutely sensitive to subjective attitudes

---

[37] Mark 8:12 and pars. The saying "no sign shall be given . . ." is doubly attested, see Matt. 12:38ff.; Luke 11:29ff.

[38] Betz, *Jesus*, p. 60.

[39] Kümmel, *Promise and Fulfillment*, pp. 105ff.; Perrin, *Rediscovering*, pp. 63ff. Cf. Fuller, *Mission*, pp. 25ff. Jesus' reply to John's question from prison implies the same: the OT prophecies of the last days are being fulfilled in Jesus' marvelous acts (Matt. 12:2ff.; Luke 7:18ff.).

[40] Matt. 11:20ff.; Luke 10:13ff. (Q).

[41] Mark 4:10ff. and pars.; Matt. 13:16f.; Luke 10:23f. (Q); Mark 8:17ff. (Matt. 16:8ff.).

of persons toward him or, better, to the actions of God as King exercising his power through him, is supported by the numerous references to situations when faith or unbelief conditioned his willingness, though not his power, to perform mighty works.[42]

Brief attention is now given to the question of the credibility of the miracle stories of the Gospels. The matter is exceedingly complex, for historical study can neither avoid this question nor answer it. Moreover, a simple *yes* or *no* to the query "Did Jesus perform miracles?" is difficult, if not impossible, for many persons. One's total world view is involved, as well as one's estimate of Jesus.[43]

A discussion of Jesus' miracles raises a whole series of fundamental questions: What is meant by the term *miracle*? An act allegedly occurring in the natural world which is flatly contradictory to nature, or merely an occurrence inexplicable on the basis of what is presently known about nature? Or does the term *miracle* imply belief in an act initiated by a Power beyond nature? But, then, how does one define *nature*? Is nature a closed system of known and predictable laws? Or does the term merely signify what may be known at any given time about the probable action or interaction of physical or psychological phenomena? Moreover, the question "Did *Jesus* perform miracles?" requires a comprehensive summing up of all the evidence concerning him. Suppose, for example, a person's judgment is that Jesus was only a man. Such a person might accept as credible some of the healing miracles (although explaining them differently). He would probably reject the so-called "nature miracles." But suppose the reader believed that in Jesus the spirit of the living God was uniquely embodied. Then belief in the "grand miracle," the incarnation, removes for him the principal reason for taking offense at the lesser miracles. The point is that we cannot hope that "the assured results" of historical research, or a battery of theological arguments, can solve for anyone the problem of miracles. There is an indispensable element of personal bias in any answer to the question before us, however well one may be equipped as historian or philosopher.[44]

Recognition of the limits of historical criticism should not discount the religious value of raising the question of credibility. Indeed, there are three factors which encourage the exercise of critical faculties, and which provide more or less "objective criteria" for a decision concerning the credibility of any particular miracle story.

First of these factors is the sufficiency of the evidence. Most persons would agree that some miracle stories in the gospel tradition are better attested than others. Is it not reasonable to believe that a substantially factual account has been given of the feeding of the multitude by Jesus, since it occurs in all four Gospels, and to value somewhat less highly the story of Jesus changing water into wine, which occurs only in the Fourth Gospel? It is possible that Christian motives have

---

[42] Mark 2:5 and pars.; 5:34f. and pars.; 6:1f. (Matt. 13:53ff.). For a valuable discussion of the meaning for Jesus of faith, in relation to his exorcisms and healings, see Perrin, *Rediscovering*, pp. 132ff.

[43] Hunter, *Work and Words*, pp. 58f.; Richardson, *Miracle Stories*, pp. 123ff.

[44] Richardson, *Miracle Stories*, pp. 128ff.

so affected the development of some of the miracle stories that it is pointless to ask what "actually happened."

Second, the miracles of the Gospels were reported by persons who did not consider "secondary causes." Many things attributed to the direct activity of God or of Satan in New Testament times are otherwise explained today. The reader of the Gospels is therefore justified in "rationalizing" some of the miracles, provided that his "explanations" do not caricature the evidence or make the early Christians appear as fools or knaves.[45] This point will be discussed below.

Third of the factors is the total witness of the Gospels concerning the nature of God's action in Jesus the Christ, which provides a context for considering any particular story. The question here is not whether Jesus might have done this or that wonder, but whether he would have done it in view of his teaching reported elsewhere. This criterion of coherence must be employed with great caution. How indeed can a person say that any particular act of Jesus is "out of character" without presumptuously assuming that he has fully comprehended Jesus? Nevertheless, the suspicion that some of the miracles are incongruous with Jesus, when his words and work are considered together, warrants a search for explanations other than those which appear on the surface.[46]

An illustration of the second factor will be given. The accounts of Jesus' exorcism of demons are apt to be particularly offensive to the modern reader. Belief in demon-possession was almost universal in the first century, and many mental and physical maladies were diagnosed in this way. Doubtless Jesus' power over persons so affected was great and his exorcisms created a strong impression upon the masses. Yet few scientists today would hesitate to describe such beliefs as superstition; that is, as the tendency of men in antiquity to ascribe to supernatural agency phenomena which were not understood. Perhaps some would argue that in our present state of knowledge the possibility of demon-possession should not be rejected. But most moderns believe that the evidence is insufficient and that the symptoms of those who believed themselves to be "demon-possessed" are to be otherwise explained.

Did Jesus believe in demon-possession? It is sometimes conjectured that he accommodated himself to the beliefs of his contemporaries in order to establish a basis for curing them. Demon-possession was a dreadful factor in their minds which could not be overcome if he attacked it as an illusion. It seems more plausible, however, that Jesus really shared the limitations of his age. Unless we suppose that throughout his Ministry he was omniscient—a position which qualifies his true humanity—it is no more difficult to believe that Jesus held some views which modern science has discredited, than it is to admit that he held mistaken views concerning the authorship of Old Testament books.[47]

---

[45] Some, but by no means all, rationalizations are intended to explain away the miraculous. A "scientific explanation" need not deny God's activity in any particular happening. A believer may gladly receive more adequate knowledge of the mysteries of God's action.

[46] H. E. W. Turner, *Jesus, Master and Lord* (1954), pp. 181ff.

[47] It is nonetheless true that the mentally ill are sometimes the victims of forces that seem to lie altogether outside their control.

Advances in psychosomatic medicine make it possible for modern readers to explain many of the miracles of the Gospels differently. Certain maladies once believed to be incurable and the result of physical causes are now recognized to be functional disorders resulting from psychological maladjustment. For example, certain types of skin disease may have been wrongly diagnosed as leprosy. Certain types of blindness and paralysis may have been due to psychological not to physiological causes. It is not intended to imply that Jesus was simply a psychologist many centuries ahead of his time, but rather, that "what is now known about nature" has a direct bearing on the healing stories of the Gospels. Some of the so-called "modern parallels" demonstrate that much that Jesus did was not "against nature." At the same time, the evidence of the dramatic progress of a science yet in its infancy enforces the wisdom of refusing to accept only those miracles of Jesus which today's scientists can accomplish. The Christian is not alone in his unwillingness to dogmatize concerning what was possible for Jesus, but Christians especially will not wish to press their conclusions upon others.[48]

In summary, the miracles of Jesus should neither be dismissed nor too highly valued. They were part of Jesus' Ministry, but only a part. For Jesus' disciples—then as now—they were signs, pointing to a significance in Jesus which went beyond them. But for those who sought "signs and wonders" as ends in themselves, Jesus' miracles did not bring satisfaction. Apparently Jesus did not intend that they should open the eyes of men who were otherwise blinded, or serve as "objective proof" relieving his disciples of the subjective uncertainty of their faith.

Jesus and the Torah

The powers of the coming kingdom were already attacking directly the sources of evil and bringing health and joy unto men. For Jesus, this meant that the time was fulfilled for a willing acceptance of the demands as well as the gifts of God. With utmost urgency he laid upon the conscience of his hearers the necessity of immediate, unreserved obedience to the will of God. Jesus' eschatological summons to repentance and proclamation of the good news provide the proper context for understanding his teaching.

Jewish eschatology was inseparably related to the Torah. God would deliver and finally vindicate His people upon the condition that His covenant law be honored and obeyed. In proclaiming the demands of the will of God whose kingdom is near, it would be expected that Jesus would relate his teaching to the Torah of Israel. It is clear from the Synoptic Gospels that he did so.

Jesus was received by his contemporaries as a rabbi. He taught in the synagogues of Galilee and gathered around him a band of "disciples." With these pupils, and with the scribes, Jesus debated questions of the law. Like the rabbis, Jesus taught in parables and coined many proverbial sayings. Modern Jewish

[48] Is it needless to say that no one becomes a Christian by believing, and no one ceases to be a Christian by not believing, all of the miracles recorded in the Gospels?

scholars have gleaned numerous tannaitic parallels to the teachings of Jesus. In his appearance and manner of speaking Jesus appeared to many to be a rabbi.[49]

More important than the evidence above is the fact that like the scribes Jesus accepted without question the authority of the scriptures. Perhaps some of the sayings of Jesus which appeal to scripture texts originated in the controversies between the early Church and the synagogue. But recognition of Jesus' reverence for the authority of the scriptures does not depend upon a few, isolated citations. It is broadly attested by the pervasive, one might almost say unconscious, use which Jesus made of the language of scripture.[50]

Some scholars have held that Jesus did not accept the authority of the whole Torah, that he distinguished between its ethical and its ceremonial commandments.[51] For Jesus the former were basic and permanent, the latter were peripheral and transitory. It is doubtful that this generalization can be maintained. After curing a leper Jesus sent him to the temple to offer for his cleansing "what Moses commanded."[52] Moreover, Jesus recognized the sacrificial cultus which the Torah prescribed.[53]

Jesus' attitude toward the oral law, "the traditions of the elders" (Mark 7:5), is at first sight perplexing. Yet it can be affirmed confidently that Jesus did not in principle reject all scribal interpretations. He probably wore the garment prescribed by the Pharisees for the righteous. His synagogue attendance is again noteworthy, for this assembly was sanctioned and regulated by the oral law only. Some of the traditional practices of the pious, which were not explicitly scriptural, he commented upon without disapproval. In discourses with Pharisees he accepted as valid some of their principles of interpretation.[54]

Despite this evidence, the zealous and most influential champions of the Torah, the Pharisees, found Jesus' action and teachings scandalous and grew to distrust his piety. It was evident to them that he was not a typical rabbi. It took no specialist to see this, for the masses detected that he was not like the scribes.[55] How then are we to define this difference? Two sayings of Jesus reported by Mark which—by implication—proclaim the presence of the kingdom of God are especially noteworthy here. Jesus' similitude of the rejoicing wedding guests (Mark 2:18-20) carried his conviction that the time had come for a release from the

[49] Mark 9:5; 10:51; 11:21; 14:45; 1:21, 39, etc. "It is incredible that they [the early Christians] would transform into a rabbi him whom they looked upon as messiah," R. Bultmann, *Jesus and the Word*, trans. L. P. Smith and E. H. Lantero (1934), pp. 58ff. [hereafter, *Jesus*].

[50] Heard, *Intro.*, pp. 115f.; H. Branscomb, *Jesus and the Law of Moses* (1930), pp. 119ff. [hereafter, *Jesus*].

[51] See above, p. 253, saying 11. Perrin, *Rediscovering*, pp. 78ff.

[52] Mark 1:40ff. and pars.

[53] Mark 11:15ff. The saying, Matt. 5:23f., is not antagonistic to the cultus. It answers the question, how is one to offer sacrifice? Cf. *The Mishnah*, Yoma 8:9, p. 172. "Special Matt." emphasizes Jesus' loyalty to the temple, Matt. 17:27; 23:17, 19.

[54] Branscomb, *Jesus*, pp. 125ff. Some of this evidence has been used by Paul Winter (*Trial of Jesus*) to argue that Jesus was a Pharisee, and that Jesus' disputes with the Pharisees in the Gospels originated in the Christian Church, not in the history of Jesus. For a successful refutation of this skeptical portion of Winter's thesis, see Betz, *Jesus*, pp. 76ff.

[55] Mark 1:22 and pars.

normal requirements of the Torah and tradition; the similitude of the patched cloth (Mark 2:21f.), that Jesus' teaching was bursting their bounds. A reading of several of the "conflict stories" of the Gospels is instructive when guided by the question: When Jesus was accused of deviating from the Torah and its traditional interpretations, what did he reply?

The Sabbath: Mark 2:23–28 and 3:1–6, and pars., and Luke 13:10–17 and 14:1–6 reveal that Jesus and his disciples were accused of profaning the Sabbath. In the first story, Jesus met the Pharisees' objections to his disciples' action by tacitly acknowledging that they had "worked," by noting that a precedent had been set when David and his men had eaten food for priests unlawfully, and by declaring that "the Sabbath was made for man." It is likely that the David incident (I Sam. 21:1ff.) had been the subject of discussion among the Tannaim.[56] In the rabbinic traditions extant, it is judged that the lives of David and his men had been in jeopardy. Jesus' disciples were not in such dire need. And yet he defended them. Their casual needs were more important than Sabbath rules.[57] In the other stories which report Jesus' action on the Sabbath, the same attitude is disclosed.[58] None of the persons healed by Jesus had been in any immediate danger. It was enough for Jesus that God never proscribes acts of mercy. If it is permissible to pull an ox out of the ditch on the Sabbath, then surely God wills on this day that humans who are suffering be given immediate relief.

Contact with "sinners": The following passages which report Jesus' contacts with "sinners" reveal a second characteristic of Jesus' attitude toward the Torah and its traditions: from the earliest Gospel—Mark 2:14–17; from Q—Matthew 11:16–19, Luke 8:31–35, and Matthew 18:10–14; Luke 15:3–7; from "Special Matthew"—21:31, and from "Special Luke"—Luke 7:36ff. 15:8ff., 18:10ff. and 19:2ff.[59]

The Hebrew phrase _'amme ha-ares_ (peoples of the land) originally identified the country folk or, as we might say, the masses. We have seen, however, that the rabbis used it to designate peoples who were deficient in their knowledge of the Torah and its traditions and who were careless in performing the religious observances of "the righteous."[60] The rabbis' _'amme ha-ares_ and the "sinners" of the Gospels refer to the same people. From these _'amme ha-ares_ the Pharisees separated themselves for fear of ceremonial defilement and temptations to impiety. They classed such "sinners" with violators of the grave precepts of the Torah, robbers and adulterers, and with "tax collectors," that notorious group of apostates, the hated symbols of Jewish subjection to foreign rule.[61]

The Synoptic Gospels show that Jesus befriended "sinners." Rabbinic sources

[56] Branscomb, _Jesus,_ p. 145.

[57] The Halakah—"the Sabbath is given for you, and not you for the Sabbath" (Mekilta Ex. 31:13)—is no true parallel to Mark 2:27, for the Jewish saying clearly implies, given _to keep._

[58] Mark 3:1ff. and pars.; Luke 13:10ff.; 14:1ff.

[59] C. H. Dodd notes the importance of the convergence of this evidence, _History and the Gospel_ (1938), p. 94. Note also the story reproduced in some mss. of John (7:53ff.) and in other mss. of the Third Gospel (after Luke 21:38).

[60] See above, pp. 77f.

[61] Note rabbinic references in Branscomb, _Jesus,_ pp. 131ff.

record that there were many *'amme ha-ares* in Galilee. From this folk Jesus had selected his own disciples. He lived with "sinners." He ate in their homes. But this free association was highly offensive to the Pharisees. Jesus and his disciples flouted the program of social ostracism necessitated by the ideal of a holy people. Jesus defended these attacks by saying: "Those who are well have no need of a physician, but those who are sick; I came not to call the righteous, but sinners." "The Son of man [or I] came to seek and to save that which was lost."[62] These "lost sheep of the house of Israel" were his special care. God willed and rejoiced in their salvation. The danger therefore of eating untithed food in the homes of sinners, or of otherwise incurring ceremonial defilement through association with them, meant nothing to Jesus.

Ritual defilement: Mark 7:1–8 preserves a story in which Jesus' disciples are criticized for eating with unwashed hands, thereby incurring ritual defilement. Mark explains this "tradition of the elders" for his Gentile readers. The whole incident has been considered by some scholars as an anachronism. The prescription that all pious Jews, as well as priests, eat their food in a ceremonial state of purity is first attested in second-century rabbinic traditions. Yet this story need not be discounted, although Mark's "all the Jews" should not be pressed. Some of the Pharisees, as well as the Essenes, of Jesus' day may have advocated and practiced such ritual cleansing. In any event, it is clear that Jesus would have had no sympathy for the scribes' criticism of his disciples. He did not enjoin them to observe the laws of priestly purification.

Divorce: The Torah provides that a husband might present his wife a certificate of divorce if he found "some unseemly thing [indecency, RSV] in her" (Deut. 24:1). In Jesus' day neither rabbinic sanction nor wife's consent were necessary in divorce proceedings, but the question had arisen how Deuteronomy 24:1 should be interpreted. The tannaitic "pair" Shammai and Hillel differed as to what constituted "unseemliness." The former rabbi maintained that infidelity was intended; the latter held that burning a husband's dinner was an unseemly thing.[63] According to Mark and the Q tradition, Jesus became involved in this debate. He taught that divorce was contrary to the will of God whatever the cause.[64] In taking this position, Jesus rejected the final authority of an explicit provision of the written Torah. In doing so, however, Jesus appealed to the Torah. He found in its story of creation the divine sanction for his teaching that marriage ought to be an indissoluble union. Jesus did not consider that he was repudiating the Torah, but interpreting its basic intention.[65]

Vows: Again, in Mark 7:9–13, Jesus spoke of the comparative worth of two

---

[62] Mark 2:17 and pars.; Luke 19:9.

[63] *Mishnah*, Gittin 9:10, p. 321.

[64] Mark 10:2ff. and pars.; Matt. 5:32 and Luke 16:18 (Q). The exceptive clause in Matt. 5:32 and 19:9 represents the judgment not of Jesus but of the Jewish–Christian community of the First Gospel. Mark and Luke, as well as Paul (1 Cor. 7:11), agree against Matt. (possibly also "Special Matt.," Matt. 19:10).

[65] In seeking to apply this and other moral absolutes of the Gospels, it should be remembered that "Jesus was not legislating for life's failures, but proclaiming the perfect will of God in the light of the dawning of His reign," Craig, *Beginning*, p. 95. See further, below, pp. 293ff.

statutes of the Torah. In this case, however, one law is not reinterpreted in the light of the other. A situation is described in which two grave precepts of the Torah are opposed, the law concerning the performance of vows (Deut. 23:21ff.) and the law requiring children to honor their parents (Ex. 20:12; Deut. 5:16). This paragraph in Mark may be all that remains of a "pronouncement story." At any rate, its setting in Mark appears to be topical. Uncertainty must therefore remain concerning the situation of the Ministry which provoked Jesus' sharp criticism of the scribes.[66] It was a vicious "human tradition" to teach that God held inviolate vows which interfere with such plain duties as the respect and care owed one's parents.

Attached to this story is a compend of Jesus' teaching concerning defilement, Mark 7:14–23. It is probable that the arresting words reported in verse 15 were spoken by Jesus, and that the discussion and interpretation which follow had been formulated in the Gentile church, as a reaction to this provocative saying and to its interpretation by conservative Jewish–Christians. Some have concluded that Mark 7:15 sums up Jesus' attitude toward the legalism of the scribes of the Pharisees:

> ". . . there is nothing outside a man which by going into him can defile him; but the things which come out of a man are what defile him."[67]

Could Jesus have meant to nullify all of the commandments concerning food laws and purification? Some persons think so, but others argue that Jesus' sole interest was to teach that the inner springs of attitude and action must be cleansed before anyone is righteous in God's sight. Internal cleanliness is therefore more important than external conformity to the laws of cleansing; but Jesus had no intention of repudiating the latter *in toto*. In support of this interpretation are the words of Jesus which scorn certain scribes who cleanse "the outside of the cup and the plate," but inside were "full of extortion and rapacity."[68]

It is easier to understand the controversy in the Jerusalem church between the Hellenists and Paul on the one hand and the Christian Pharisees or Hebrews on the other if we assume that from the first this saying of Jesus was capable of both interpretations. Several aspects of the evidence thus far reviewed could be urged in support of either position. But we must look beyond the conflict stories of the Gospels to understand Jesus' attitude toward the Torah. Of special importance are the sayings which are funded in the Sermon on the Mount, Matthew 5–7.

The antitheses of Matthew 5:21–48: Two serious misunderstandings can result if these antitheses are considered out of relation to other teachings in the Gospels—an exaggerated disparagement of Pharisaism and a misconception of the novelty of Jesus' teaching. By no means all the scribes of the Pharisees were guilty of superficiality and hypocrisy, nor possessed of the spirit of revenge and hatred

[66] For the critical problems relating to Mark 7, see Taylor, *Mark*, pp. 334ff.; Branscomb, *Jesus*, pp. 156ff.

[67] See also the Q passage, Matt. 12:35; Luke 6:45.

[68] Matt. 23:25; Luke 11:39 (Q). Craig, *Beginning*, pp. 98f. Cf. Perrin, *Rediscovering*, pp. 149f.

toward their enemies. Furthermore there are some rabbinic parallels for the "I say unto you" passages of Jesus. It is possible to conclude that Jesus' rejection of the sayings of "the men of old" was not a repudiation of the whole of Judaism, but only of a certain development in it represented by those scribes who had most actively opposed him. Such reasoning does not obscure the fact, however, that Matthew 5:21–48 does not epitomize the teaching of any individual or group within ancient Judaism. Indeed it is unthinkable that any scribe would have set over against the demands of the Torah the righteousness which God requires, for such an attitude would imply the supersession of the authority of the law.[69]

The first thing to observe about the content of these statements is that Jesus teaches that persons who submit merely to the formal requirements of God's commandments have, in fact, disobeyed him. Jesus does not say that true obedience cannot exist when the formal demands of the law have been met. But for Jesus true obedience must include more than this. True obedience "exists only when a man inwardly assents to what is required of him . . . when the whole man *is* what he does, when he is not *doing something obediently,* but *is* essentially obedient."[70] Notice some of the examples Jesus gives. Any man who shuns adultery but keeps lust in his heart has not understood the requirement of God's commandment, which is complete purity. He who merely refrains from perjury has by no means fulfilled the divine will, which is absolute truthfulness.[71]

It would be a fallacy to conclude that the rabbis taught only an ethic of conformity to the letter of the law. Many sayings show their conviction that God demands an obedience which goes beyond external conformity to His commandments.[72] Nevertheless, it was inevitable that the scribes concerned themselves primarily and practically with the *what* of action, even though they recognized the fundamental importance of the *how*. In opposition to this scribal tendency, Jesus took a position which threatened the whole structure of law. He separated obedience from the formal, legal authority of Torah and tradition. To the scribes, this position implied something more than a reformation of the law.

There is a story in the Gospels, slightly different in its two versions, which may provide the essential clue to Jesus' attitude revealed in the conflict stories and in the above statements. The reader should refer to Mark 12:28ff. (Matt. 22:34ff.) and to Luke 10:25ff. ("Special Luke"). Rabbinic tradition discloses that the scribe of this story raised a stock question to which the rabbis had given various answers. For example, a Gentile on the verge of becoming a proselyte challenged Hillel to teach him the whole law while he stood on one foot. Hillel replied: "What is hateful to thee do not to anyone else; this is the whole law and the rest is commentary; go and study."[73] According to Luke, Jesus' answer

[69] H. Windisch, *The Sermon on the Mount*, trans. S. McL. Gilmour (1951), pp. 144ff. [hereafter, *Sermon*].

[70] A definition of true or "radical" obedience given by Bultmann (*Jesus*, p. 77) and representing, in this writer's opinion, the position of Jesus.

[71] Matt. 5:27ff.

[72] See Branscomb, *Jesus*, pp. 231ff.

[73] Shabb. 31a., cited from T. W. Manson, *Teaching*, pp. 297f. Cf. Tobit 4:15. Sifre Lev 19:18 reports that R. Akiba had said: "'Thou shalt love thy neighbor as thyself—this is the greatest general principle of the Law.'"

to the scribe was: "Do this, and you will live." The answers of Hillel and of Jesus are by no means the same. Hillel subsumes the teaching of the Torah under a single general rule. From this principle all of the other laws can be deduced. But Hillel's opinion did not lessen the importance of any of the commandments, or release him or anyone else from obeying them all.

The same may be said concerning the men of Qumran. Philo summarizes the piety of the Essenes as love toward God and one's neighbor. But since Qumran found the will of God in the commandments "in the last resort the attempt to pass beyond concrete demands to the heart of God itself failed. The synthesis of the will of God into a simple basic law crumbled constantly, constantly disintegrated into a multitude of individual commandments."[74] For Jesus, the two love commandments are assigned a priority which is neither logical nor relative, but absolute. They are themselves sufficient without any supplement whatever as a complete guide to anyone who wishes to live.[75]

Jesus read in the Torah, in Deuteronomy 6:4, the divine summons that man bow his will in complete obedience to God. Now that the kingdom of God was at hand, this and this alone mattered. Yet for Jesus a man who wills what God wills must love his neighbor as he does himself. This commandment Jesus also read in the Torah, Leviticus 19:18. For Jesus this was not just another commandment to be ranked next in order after "the first and the greatest." Jesus realized that the attitude which persons take to a neighbor—to every man with whom they come in contact—is an attitude determined by the attitude taken toward God. Those who would enter the kingdom of God must be wholly submissive to His will, renouncing their selfish wills, setting aside their own claims, and they must stand before their neighbors prepared to sacrifice for them as for God.[76]

It has often been noted that these love commandments are as little legal as possible. A man may be compelled on the Sabbath to abstain from all sorts of activities designated "work." But he cannot be compelled to love God completely, nor his neighbor as himself. There are no enforceable rules which can specify and measure degrees of obedience to such commandments. It would seem therefore that Jesus did renounce the formal authority of the Torah as a compend of rules, equally valid, equally binding. Yet because he drew the love commandments from the Torah, he could say, "I have come to fulfill the law."

In this connection the meaning of the following passage must be studied:

> "Think not that I have come to abolish the law and the prophets; I have come not to abolish them but to fulfil them. For truly, I say to you, till heaven and earth pass away, not an iota, nor a dot, will pass from the law until all is accomplished. Whoever then relaxes one of the least of these commandments and teaches men so, shall be called least in the kingdom of heaven; but he who does them and teaches them shall be called great in the kingdom of heaven. For I tell you unless your

---

[74]Betz, *Jesus*, pp. 44f. (Philo, vol. IX, *Every Good Man Is Free*, 83f.)

[75]T. W. Manson, *Teaching*, p. 305. Matt. 22:40, another variant of Mark 12:31b, seems to affirm logical not absolute priority, but Matthew may not have so understood it.

[76]Bultmann, *Jesus*, pp. 114ff.

righteousness exceed that of the scribes and Pharisees, you will never enter the Kingdom of Heaven" (Matt. 5:17–20).[77]

In their substance these words may indeed go back to Jesus, although we may suspect that the preserver of "Special Matthew" had not understood them.[78] For Jesus the law was a God-given guide, at least for this present age, but only if all of its parts were subordinated to the love commandments. When in any concrete situation the weightier matters of the laws were involved, then, as we have seen, Jesus did not hesitate to brush aside the iotas and dots of the Torah as well as the minutiae of scribal tradition. The righteous man accepts the claim of God by obeying his commandments. But these never proscribe love. Legal righteousness comes to naught when it is secured at the expense of a single neighbor who is in need of love.

It is not sufficient to say, however, that Jesus radicalized the law, subordinating all its parts to the love commandment. In contrasting his own understanding of the will of God with the Mosaic Law and its traditional interpretation, Jesus acted in accordance with his proclamation of the coming of the kingdom of God. His mission was to reveal the new law of God, which, according to some persons and groups in ancient Judaism, was to be given to the community of Israel at the end of the days.[79]

Teaching by Parable

Jesus' teaching is revealed in his parables as well as in the conflict stories and controversial sayings of the Gospels. We cannot distinguish sharply between these materials as though they are different in type. If we use the term *parable* in its original and broadest sense, it may be said that Jesus seldom if ever taught except in parable. His poetic and imaginative mind conceived ideas in realistic images. His maxims and short pronouncements as well as his "parables" are pictorial and dramatic.[80] But the parables in narrative form, considered as a whole and apart from the similitudes and proverbial sayings of Jesus, provide material of special value for a recovery of Jesus' teaching.

The modern student is aware of two pitfalls in the study of Jesus' parables. First, far from being evidence of Jesus' originality in the manner and method of his teaching, the parables reveal the essential likeness of Jesus to the scribes and rabbis of his day.[81] Ancient Jewish traditions provide many formal parallels to

[77] It is not possible that the first evangelist believed that Jesus had bound his disciples to the details of the Torah, for the antitheses make clear the meaning of the statement which precedes them. For Matthew's community it is the higher righteousness which Jesus taught, not the scribal tradition, which is binding in the Church.

[78] The evidence converges to support the opinion that the M tradition originated in a reactionary group (the Christian Pharisees in Jerusalem?). Cf. note 61 above. See above, p. 203.

[79] Qumran provides evidence of this belief in the expectation of a new, eschatological Torah. Perrin, *Kingdom*, pp. 76ff., 204. Cf. W. D. Davies, *Torah in the Messianic and/or Age to Come*, *JBL* Mon. Ser. V. vii (1952); Käsemann, "The Problem of the Historical Jesus," *Essays*, pp. 36f.

[80] Mark 2:17, 19ff.; Matt. 5:39ff. (Luke 6:29f.); Matt. 6:2f., etc.

[81] H. J. Cadbury, *What Manner of Man* (1947), pp. 34f.

the parables of the Gospels. It can be shown also that much of the imagery employed by Jesus in his parables resembles the biblical imagery used in some of the Qumran scrolls.[82] Furthermore, it must be recognized that the parables may reveal indirectly the teaching of Jesus. Form critical studies have shown that some of the parables were transformed by their oral transmission, by their re-application to situations facing the early Church.[83] Yet it may be said that recent studies have not diminished the grounds for confidence that the parables, taken as a whole, bear "the stamp of a highly individual mind." They are works of art whose author can rarely be in doubt.[84] In vivid and various images the parables of Jesus exhibit some of the essential elements in his teaching.

Several recurrent themes are prominent in the parables. Especially noteworthy is the motif of growth and the harvest.[85] The motif of the absent master is hardly less prominent.[86] Indeed, several parables utilizing either or both of these themes focus upon the idea of great expectations, and emphasize the necessity of waiting patiently or alertly for their fulfillment. It is easy to say that the interest of the early churches in the consummation of the kingdom of God and in the return of the absent Lord explains the presence in the Gospels of such parables. Yet apart from some modifications in their application, these parables surely originated in the mind of Jesus and reveal his principal concerns.[87]

Another recurrent theme of the parables is the pathetic proclivities of men to make excuses when it is time for decisive action, or, as a variation on this theme, man's tragic unpreparedness for the days of opportunity and his refusal to recognize, when caught unawares, that his was the fault in having put other interests first.[88] Again, it is easy to show that parables such as these served practical ends in the early Church. But the presence of so many of them attests their origin in the teaching of Jesus. Apparently he was sensitive to the tendency in all men to excuse themselves and to evade their responsibility under God.

Like the stories of Jesus' mighty works, many parables of the Gospels reveal Jesus' conviction that the eschatological hope of Israel would soon be fulfilled, that the kingdom of God was at hand. Jesus' parables which have reference to the kingdom of God have been listed.[89] In some instances the preface is secondary which reads, "the kingdom of God is like. . . ." Nevertheless, the study of these parables, apart from their editorial setting, often supports the view that the reality of the kingdom is their implied premise. The farmer waits with assurance for the harvest which is ripening, in spite of small beginnings and of the mysterious hiddenness of nature's powers;[90] servants await the master's return with mixed

---

[82] Betz, *Jesus,* pp. 48ff.

[83] See above, pp. 168, 181.

[84] Dodd, *Parables,* p.11.

[85] Mark 4:26ff.; 4:1ff. and pars.; Matt. 13:24ff.; Mark 4:30ff. and pars.; Luke 12:13ff.; Matt. 20:1ff.; 21:28ff.; Mark 12:1ff. and pars.; Mark 13:28ff.

[86] Luke 19:12ff.; Mark 12:1; 13:34; Matt. 24:45 and Luke 12:42 (Q); Matt. 25:14f.

[87] Cadbury, *What Manner of Man,* pp. 39ff.

[88] Matt. 22:1ff.; Luke 14:15ff. (Q); Matt. 8:21f.; Luke 9:59ff. (Q); Matt. 24:43ff.; Luke 12:35ff. (Q); Matt. 25:1ff.

[89] See above, p. 255.

[90] Note 85, above.

feelings of hope and fear—he is coming soon but will they be prepared?[91] The leaves of the fig tree are signs that the summer's end is close;[92] a cloud arises in the west, a shower is imminent, or a south wind rises warning that scorching heat approaches;[93] a treasure is found, but one must act at once to seize the opportunity;[94] a man is on the way to trial, he must be quick to clear himself;[95] a great banquet is prepared, invitations are being sent out, if the righteous who are bidden are refusing, then "sinners" must be seated at the board.[96] The people to whom Jesus spoke were in the position of the various characters of these parables. A crisis had arisen. The parables reveal Jesus' belief that the kingdom of God is at hand, for weal or for woe.[97]

A large number of parables reveal that Jesus kept in the forefront of his teaching God's mercy to "sinners."[98] The coming of the kingdom was "good news to the poor." Most of these parables of the Gospels were preserved as weapons against the synagogue or, perhaps, "Pharisees" in the Church. But it is probable also that they originated in controversy. We have seen that the scribes rejected Jesus because he gathered "sinners" around him and assured them of God's forgiveness, apart from obedience to the Torah. The parables reveal that Jesus sought to teach his critics that it is the "sinner" who can best realize the extent of God's goodness;[99] that the "righteous" have no reason for their indignation that the "good news" is being proclaimed to the poor;[100] that it is God's nature to seek the lost and to rejoice greatly when they are found, as when they return.[101]

But there are other parables which are intended to stir Jesus' hearers to repentance. In view of the attitudes of many, the imminence of the kingdom is the imminence of catastrophe. The parables of the faithful and wise servant, of the talents (or pounds), and of the doorkeeper were probably addressed to the ranking scribes of Israel.[102] To them much had been entrusted, and now the judgment of God is soon to be revealed. The parable of the mote and the beam was probably directed to the Pharisees, as well as the similitude about blind leaders of the blind who fall into the ditch with those whom they guide.[103] The parable of the fig tree appears to warn of the fate of Israel as a whole, whereas the parable of the wise and foolish builders is a warning of Jesus to his own disciples.[104] Apparently Jesus used the parable to warn various groups that the

[91] Note 86, above.
[92] Mark 13:28f.
[93] Matt. 16:2f.; Luke 12:54f. (Q).
[94] Matt. 13:44ff.
[95] Luke 12:58f.; Matt. 5:24f. (Q).
[96] Matt. 22:1ff.; Luke 14:15ff. (Q).
[97] Dodd's defense of a "realized eschatology" of the parables falls short of conviction. See Fuller, *Mission*, pp. 44ff.; Kümmel, *Promise and Fulfillment*, pp. 127ff.; Jeremias, *Parables*, pp. 115ff., 230.
[98] Luke 7:36ff.; 15:1ff.; Matt. 21:28ff. Jeremias, *Parables*, pp. 124ff.; Perrin, *Rediscovering*, pp. 90ff.
[99] Luke 7:47.
[100] Matt. 21:28ff.; Matt. 22:8f.; Luke 14:21 (Q); Mark 12:9.
[101] Luke 15:7, 10, 32.
[102] Matt. 24:45ff.; Luke 12:42ff. (Q); Matt. 25:14ff.; (Luke 19:12ff.); Mark 13:33ff. Jeremias, *Parables*, pp. 53ff.
[103] Matt. 7:3ff.; Luke 6:41f. (Q); Matt. 15:12ff.; Luke 6:39.
[104] Luke 13:6ff.; Matt. 7:24ff., and Luke 6:47ff. (Q).

kingdom comes as judgment upon those who spurn the will and the word of God.

What is man to do in view of the coming crisis? Jesus gave his answer in many parables. Men are to become again like little children, that is to say they are to be little before God, to be trusting, and to find their security in his love.[105] The parables of the servants' wages and of the laborers in the vineyard emphasize Jesus' belief that man's obedience to all of the commandments does not put God in his debt, that all the rewards of God are, in the final analysis, the outcome not of human merit but of divine grace.[106] Accordingly, those who await the coming of the kingdom cannot pride themselves in their righteousness nor take security in it, but must be humble before God. Humility is certainly a predominant theme in Jesus' teaching, in his action, and in his attitude to God. In the age that is coming, God *is King.*

This repentance and self-abasement before God must be followed by recognition of the cost of "entering" or "receiving" the kingdom. The way of the penitent is not easy. The door is a narrow one that leads to life.[107] In vivid imagery Jesus warns his hearers not to act without counting the cost. The expense of a tower must be estimated by its builder; a king must muster his troops before a compaign, or else there may be embarrassing shortages.[108] The plowman must set his eye on a mark ahead, lest, looking back, he should run a crooked furrow.[109]

What, according to Jesus, are the characteristic marks of those who await in penitence and faith the coming of the kingdom and who have made, or are ready to make, the necessary sacrifices? The twin parables of the hidden treasure and of the pearl speak of the unprecedented joy of those who have found the one thing of supreme value.[110] But above all else, Jesus expected men to learn the spirit of forgiveness and forbearance toward one another, and to love both friend and foe. In the parables of the unmerciful servant and the prodigal son, Jesus teaches that the requirement of forgiveness is grounded in the limitless willingness of God to forgive, to show mercy to the undeserving.[111] In the parable of the good Samaritan, Jesus depicted neighbor-love in action.[112] Besides the extended metaphors of Jesus' parables, concrete examples of neighbor-love are given in brief picture-words: "If anyone strike you on the right cheek, turn to him the other also. . . . If anyone forces you to go one mile, go with him two miles. Give to him who begs from you. . . . Sell your possession and give alms. . . ."[113] Such precepts are not reducible to statute laws, to a code morality. Rather they remain a continuous stimulus to the imagination, prodding the hearers of Jesus to consider what such forbearance and love require of them in concrete situations.[114]

[105] Mark 10:15 and pars.; Jeremias, *Parables,* pp. 190f.
[106] Luke 17:7ff.; Matt. 20:1ff.
[107] Matt. 7:13f.; Luke 13:23f.
[108] Luke 14:28ff.
[109] Luke 9:61f.
[110] Matt. 13:44ff.; Perrin, *Rediscovering,* pp. 87ff.
[111] Matt. 18:23ff.; Luke 15:11ff. See also Matt. 6:12, 14f., and Luke 11:4 (Q).
[112] Luke 10:25ff.
[113] Matt. 5:39ff.; Luke 6:29f.; Mark 10:21 and pars.
[114] Dodd, *Gospel and Law,* pp. 73ff.

Let us conclude this section by asking why Jesus taught in parables. There is a passage in the earliest Gospel, Mark 4:10–12, which appears to answer this question. It is said that Jesus used parables in order to obscure his teaching from the masses. Further on, it is reported that Jesus found it necessary to disclose the meaning of his parables to his disciples in private. In parallel passages, Matthew and Luke do not explicitly declare that it was Jesus' intention to conceal his message, yet they acknowledge that his parabolic teaching resulted in obscurity.[115] There is reason to feel that Mark 4:10ff. and its parallels do not represent the aim of Jesus. The fact that the Gospels relate so many of these parables without interpreting them, and that persons other than Jesus' disciples are said to have understood their meaning, provides a qualification of this theory of concealment.

Two principal explanations for the presence of this saying in the Gospels have been given. Some have held that the saying is not authentic but represents the view of some Gentile Christian community in which the interpretation of the parables had become obscure, a view influenced, perhaps, by Pauline teaching concerning the hardening and rejection of Israel (cf. Rom. 9–11). Others, following Wrede, view the passage as evidence of "the dogma of intentional secrecy."[116] A third explanation rests upon the conviction that Mark 4:11f. is a primitive, Palestinian tradition.[117] Perhaps an early Palestinian Christian mistakenly concluded that Jesus, like the Essene scribes, intended his teaching for the brotherhood only. Other scholars assume that the Gospels give an unauthentic version of a genuine saying of Jesus, and seek to reconstruct its original form. It has been suggested that Jesus used the Aramaic word *mathla* ("riddle," or "dark saying"), which has been translated "parable," and the Aramaic particle *de*, which can mean "who" as well as "so that." Thus Jesus said that whereas the twelve possessed "the secret of the kingdom of God," for "those outside" everything remained obscure, who indeed saw and heard but did not perceive.[118] Perhaps Jesus' comment was influenced by his recognition that the results of his proclamation and that of the prophet Isaiah were similar. In this case the context of the prophet's ironic words may shed light upon the meaning of Jesus' words. While the original form of this saying can only be guessed, few can believe that Jesus used parables to mystify the masses. His picture-words were intended to reveal, not to conceal, the truth.

Intention and Motivation

It is not possible to do justice to the problems which have arisen when students of Jesus' parables and precepts turn from a discussion of their setting in the

---

[115] Matt. 13:13; Luke 8:10.

[116] Bundy, *Jesus*, pp. 223f.

[117] Jeremias, *Parables*, pp. 13ff. Cf. Dodd, *Parables*, pp. 13ff.

[118] T. W. Manson, *Teaching*, pp. 76ff. Jeremias acknowledges this possibility but prefers the translation: "in order that they (as it is written) may 'see . . . , unless they turn and God will forgive them.'" Perhaps the saying referred to Jesus' preaching in general and not only to the parables (Jeremias, *Parables*, pp. 17f.).

Ministry to questions of interpretation and modern relevance.[119] What meaning has the teaching of Jesus within the framework of his proclamation of the coming kingdom? To what motive or motives did Jesus appeal by way of enforcing his radical demand that the will of God be obeyed?

Opinions vary widely as to Jesus' intentions. Did he expect literal fulfillment of his commandments? Roman Catholicism has held that the Gospels contain proper imperatives upon whose fulfillment salvation depends. Yet the practical tendency has been to view Jesus' counsels of perfection as binding only upon members of monastic orders. Speaking generally, it may be said that Protestants conclude that the moral demands of Jesus are not practical and are, in some instances, impossible of fulfillment. On rare occasions there have been persons, like Tolstoi, who have sought to follow literally his words. Yet "it has been widely held by orthodox Protestants that the absolute standards of Jesus are calculated to drive man to a sense of failure and despair and so to prepare them for the message of salvation in the cross alone."[120]

In the nineteenth century a view became prevalent which dominates the thought of many today. Jesus was not laying down rules, it is said, either for the Church or the world. Rather he was describing fundamental attitudes or dispositions. Far from wishing to put a heavier burden of law upon his disciples, Jesus sought to reveal the inadequacy of a legalistic understanding of God's will. He taught men what they should *be* rather than what they should *do*. By these interpreters, Jesus' picture-words are considered extreme and exaggerated illustrations, driving home to the consciences of his hearers certain fundamental moral principles.

Probably Jesus did not mean that his parables and precepts should be understood as new laws. But there is every reason to believe that he wished to be taken seriously. It is not possible to say that Jesus was concerned with what a man is and not with his actions. The saying about the tree and its fruits precludes a theoretical separation between being and doing, between character and conduct.[121] Jesus did not allow his hearers to be satisfied with general feelings of benevolence. Jesus' teaching was embarrassingly specific and concrete.

Albert Schweitzer has insisted that any sound interpretation of Jesus' intentions must do justice to the intrinsic connection between his eschatological proclamation and his moral demands. This is an important point, but it can be understood without recognizing that Jesus' teaching is an *interim-ethik*. Where in the Gospels does Jesus demand heroic sacrifices of his disciples because of the shortness of time? Where is it suggested that it is the period of crisis that gives Jesus' teaching its validity? The place of the eschatological sanction in Jesus' teaching is discussed below.

C. H. Dodd has suggested that each of Jesus' precepts and parables indicates, in a dramatic picture of some actual situation, the *quality* and *direction* of a person's action, action which conforms to the standard revealed in God's actions in history. Take, for example, the command to turn the other cheek. Pictured here is the

---

[119] See A. Wilder's "The Sermon on the Mount," *IB* vol. 7, pp. 160ff.; Windisch, *Sermon*, pp. 44ff.
[120] Windisch, *Sermon*, p. 161.
[121] Matt. 7:15ff.; Luke 6:43ff. (Q); Matt. 5:16.

man of great patience whose love and respect for other persons however objectionable enables him to hold in check his pride and natural desire to retaliate. Here is one who imitates the patience and love of God, his forbearance under affronts, a respect for men which does not coerce their freedom. It is impossible for anyone to say that such precepts are kept, or that they can be kept in their full scope. Nevertheless, Jesus gives the categorical command that man's attitudes and actions ought to have this quality and direction. In making the effort—if it is honestly made—men obey God's will. Their very efforts have in them the quality, and move in the direction, which God demands. Yet it can never be said of Jesus' precepts what a certain man said of the ten commandments, "All these I have kept from my youth." Even though Jesus' precepts are obeyed, they are not fulfilled, for they open up possibilities of effort and action which are not attained. According to this interpretation, the precepts of Jesus cannot be transferred directly from written page to action. They become, through reflection and through effort, increasingly a part of any individual's total outlook upon life, the bias of his mind and will. Thus they find expression in actions appropriate to the changing moral situations which confront him.[122]

When we turn to ask what was the motivation to which Jesus appealed, it is clear that Jesus' hope of the coming kingdom moved him to speak of future rewards and penalties.[123] Since Jesus believed that the time of God's decisive action in history was at hand, he held before men the inevitable consequences of their own choices. Yet such future retributions are not represented as arbitrary or external inducements. Alongside teaching of this type there appear words of Jesus which, at first sight, seem contradictory. The parables of the servant's wages and of the laborers in the vineyard distinctly oppose all human calculation of rewards from God, expressly deny that man can have any sort of claim before God.[124] Moreover, Jesus commands love of enemies for no other reason than that God is "kind to the ungrateful and selfish."[125]

> Jesus, with the instinct of a consummate teacher, speaking as he is to simple people, casts his vision of moral consequences into concrete pictures of compensation, "hire," reward and punishment . . . the mind of Jesus senses the terrible and glorious issues of human choice . . . this is not a consciously artistic or deliberate move; it is the natural action of the imagination. Nevertheless, when we wish to grasp the essential appeal made by Jesus for repentance and obedience and righteousness . . . these vistas of reward and penalty are definitely subordinate to the call upon men to act worthily of those who are sons of the Father in heaven, and in ways consonant with his glory.[126]

---

[122] Dodd, *Gospel and Law*, pp. 73f. See also, Pannenberg, *Jesus*, pp. 232f. and 236ff.; Perrin, *Rediscovering*, pp. 146ff.

[123] Matt. 5:3ff.; Luke 6:20ff.; Matt. 5:21ff., 7:1f., etc.

[124] See note 106, p. 292.

[125] Matt. 5:44ff; Luke 6:27ff., esp. v. 35 (Q). Bultmann, *Jesus*, pp. 78ff.

[126] Wilder, *Eschatology and Ethics*, pp. 138, 141. See also Perrin, *Kingdom*, pp. 194ff., 201f., who finds in Matt. 6:12 "the key to the understanding of the relationship between eschatology and ethics in the teaching of Jesus."

In the final analysis, we conclude that the ethical demands of Jesus were grounded in his understanding of the character of God.

Response in Galilee to Jesus' Teaching and Healing

Two incidents are located in the Gospels, near the close of Jesus' Galilean ministry, that appear to represent strategic turning points in the narrative: the mission of Jesus' disciples and Jesus' feeding of the multitude.[127]

It is probable that the principal reason for the disciples' mission was Jesus' eagerness to announce the imminence of the kingdom of God to as many people as possible while time remained. The power of God would be with the disciples to heal, and they were to call men to repentance and faith.[128] Embedded in the account of this mission is the ominous notice that Herod, receiving reports of the activities of Jesus and the disciples, spoke of having beheaded John the Baptist.[129] This traditional story is not untouched by early Christian apologetic. As it reads, it may do less than justice to the actual hostility toward Jesus of Herod Antipas and his partisans. The combined oposition of Herod and the Pharisees probably precipitated Jesus' decision to send forth the disciples.[130]

Jesus' action in feeding the multitude apparently resulted in a crisis in his relations with the Galileans. The question will naturally arise, what is the meaning of this story? It is puerile to suggest that during an afternoon picnic by the lakeside Jesus taught a lesson in sharing. Yet a literal multiplication of loaves and fish is difficult to reconcile with Jesus' refusal in the wilderness to turn stones into bread, and with his unwillingness in Galilee to give signs of his authority. It is probable that this meal was celebrated with a large company of Galilean followers in anticipation of the feast which Jesus believed would soon be enjoyed in the kingdom of God. Jesus frequently used the banquet image in parables and sayings, recalling prophetic and apocalyptic symbolism.[131] In another way, in deed as well as in word, Jesus expressed his conviction that the Age to Come was near.

Whatever uncertainty remains as to the circumstances and original significance of this story, the immediate results of the feeding of the multitude are evident. Jesus promptly sends the disciples away by boat, persuades the crowds to go home, and seeks the seclusion of the hills. Why were such actions necessary? John's Gospel records a plausible explanation. The masses wished to make Jesus their king! After this, Jesus abandoned his work in Galilee.[132]

[127] Mark 6:6ff. and pars.; Mark 6:30ff. and pars. See also John 6:1ff.

[128] For comment upon Schweitzer's reading of Matt. 13:23, see p. 257, note 88.

[129] Mark 6:14ff. and pars.

[130] Mark 3:6 and pars. Since the sequence of conflict stories in Mark forms a topical complex, the reader should be warned against assuming too precipitous a break in the relations of Jesus and the Pharisees. Cf. Luke 13:31ff. (L). See Goguel, *Jesus*, pp. 343ff.

[131] Luke 14:15ff.; Matt. 22:1ff. (Q); Matt. 25:1ff.; Luke 6:21 (Matt. 5:6). Cf. Is. 25:6ff.; Moore, *Judaism*, vol. II, pp. 363ff. Daube, *New Testament and Rabbinic Judaism*, pp. 36ff. On the question of the miracle, see Taylor, *Mark*, pp. 121f.

[132] Mark 6:45ff. (Matt. 14:22ff.); John 6:15. Was Jesus at this time confronted by "a Maccabean host with no Judas Maccabeus, a leaderless mob a danger to themselves and everyone else"? T. W. Manson, *Servant-Messiah*, pp. 70f.

One might suppose that Jesus' popularity among the *'amme ha-ares* in Galilee would have warranted the continuation of the Ministry there. Yet in the parable of the sower, Mark 4:1ff., there is revealed Jesus' awareness that his message was not deep-rooted in the minds and wills of the masses. People came to be healed and to marvel at Jesus' teachings. But they had not repented nor believed his proclamation of the coming of the kingdom nor surrendered themselves to the will of God.[133]

Why did Jesus abandon work in Galilee? Various answers have been given: the failure of the disciples' mission; the attempt of the multitude to draft Jesus as a leader according to popular expectations; Jesus' inner constraint to discover what his disciples thought of the Ministry, or to know the extent of their loyalty; his desire to escape arrest by Herod and a fate like that of the Baptist; his desire to concentrate upon the training of the Twelve. Perhaps the explanation lies in a combination of circumstances. But one can only theorize, for the evidence is implicit at best.

[133]Jesus' rejection at Nazareth may have afforded him forewarning of the offense which would be taken by other Galilean communities sooner or later, e.g., Bethsaida and Chorazin. Mark 6:1ff. (Matt. 13:53ff.) Luke, employing an independent source, makes the incident at Nazareth a prelude to the Ministry, 4:16ff. It is doubtful that Jesus ever anticipated mass conversions, or that the synoptic traditions support those biographers who depict a "Galilean springtime."

chapter twelve

THE MINISTRY OF JESUS
BEYOND GALILEE AND IN JUDEA

a   b   c

(a) A Tyrian shekel, silver coin traditionally used for payments by Jews to the temple treasury. "The thirty pieces of silver" given to Judas were either coins like this or Roman imperial silver, Matt. 26:14f.; 27:3ff; cf. Matt. 22:15ff. (The Chase Manhattan Bank Money Museum)   (b) Lepton of Pontius Pilate (A.D. 26–36) The fifth procurator's coins differed radically from those of his predecessors. He adopted pagan cultic objects as symbols, such as the augur's wand impressed on the copper coin above. (The Chase Manhattan Bank Money Museum)   (c) Small bronze coin of Herod Agrippa I (A.D. 37–44), possibly "the widow's mite" (Mark 12:41ff), unless the two coins of the gospel story were leptons struck by Pilate or Gratus. (The Chase Manhattan Bank Money Museum)

Aerial View of Mt. Tabor, showing also the Valley of Jezreel, approximately six miles southeast of Nazareth, traditionally identified as the Mount of Transfiguration (Mark 9:2ff. and pars.). Numerous churches and monasteries have been erected on its summit. (Georg Gerster from Rapho-Guillumette)

Garden of Gethsemane (Mark 14:32; Matt. 26:36) on the Mount of Olives where, according to the Gospels, Jesus agonized in prayer before his arrest, trials and crucifixion. This view is westward toward Jerusalem, across the Kidron Valley. The Golden Gate is in the background. (Ewing Galloway)

A view of Bethlehem, six miles south-southwest of Jerusalem. The birthplace of Jesus. Only the terrain is reminiscent of New Testament times, since no remains earlier than the fourth century have been found. (TWA photograph)

THE itinerary of Jesus after his retirement from Galilee is variously reported in the Gospels. Mark narrates that he led his disciples "into the region of Tyre and Sidon." Assuming that there was a brief excursion into this territory beyond Galilee, it is not surprising that a few stories of encounters of Jesus with non-Jews have survived. But there is no evidence that he sought to extend his Ministry among these Gentiles.[1] In the vicinity of Caesarea Philippi, Peter confessed his faith that Jesus was the Messiah whom he had been expecting.[2]

A MOMENTOUS CONFESSION AND ANNOUNCEMENT

The historicity of the incident at Caesarea Philippi has been denied by some scholars. It seems improbable, they say, that the disciples' confession, "Jesus is the Messiah," occurred during the Ministry. Moreover, it is argued that Jesus did not at this time foresee his death and resurrection. The passion predictions, so-called, reported in Mark 8:31 and 10:32f., are prophecies after these events. The post-Easter faith was projected backward into Jesus' Ministry, by Mark or by Christian witnesses before him.[3]

It can hardly be questioned that these sayings in the Gospels concerning Jesus' death and resurrection reflect the happenings themselves. Yet this critical judgment is not sufficient reason to conclude that Jesus' Ministry was originally nonmessianic. The Gospels provide strong support for the position "that Jesus actually awakened Messianic expectations by his coming and by his Ministry, and that he encountered the faith which believed him to be the promised Saviour. The faith which is expressed by the two disciples at Emmaus: 'But we hoped that he was the one to redeem Israel.' (Luke 24:21) seems to express quite accurately the conviction of the followers of Jesus before his death. This, too, is the only explanation of the attitude of the Jewish authorities and of Pilate's verdict."[4] The

---

[1] Mark 7:24ff. Luke abandons Mark's account of journeys to the north. See the judicious comments of S. Johnson concerning Jesus' contacts with Gentiles, *Jesus in His Homeland*, pp. 78ff., and J. Jeremias, *Jesus' Promise to the Nations* (1958) [hereafter, *Jesus' Promise*].

[2] Mark 8:27ff. and pars.

[3] See above, pp. 190f., Bundy, *Jesus*, pp. 291ff.; Bultmann, *History*, pp. 257ff.; idem., *Theology*; vol. I, pp. 26ff. Cf. G. Strecker, "The Passion and Resurrection Predictions in Mark's Gospel," *Interpretation* XX (1968): 421ff., who affirms that a pre-Marcan traditional unit is found in Mark 8:27–29, 31, 32–33 but, for insufficient reasons, concludes that its provenience cannot have been the historical life of Jesus (p. 437).

[4] Bornkamm, *Jesus*, pp. 169ff.; Betz, *Jesus*, pp. 85ff.; C. K. Barrett, *Jesus and the Gospel Tradition* (1967), pp. 23f. [hereafter, *Jesus*].

302

question of Jesus' awareness of impending sufferings and death is discussed in the next section.

On the assumption that Mark's account of Peter's confession of Jesus' Messiahship contains an historical kernel, how is one to explain the report of Jesus' response?

Although the term *messiah* had no fixed meanings, as our review of the evidence has shown, popular Jewish messianism was closely associated with the political independence and the national sovereignty of the Jews. If Jesus had made public a claim to be a messiah, or if he had encouraged others to make the claims for him, false hopes would certainly have been aroused that he was launching a political, perhaps a military, campaign. This was far from Jesus' intention, as the narratives of the Temptation and the Galilean ministry reveal. Yet it was inevitable that within the circle of Jesus' serious hearers the question should have arisen: What is the relation of the herald of the kingdom to its coming? It is not surprising that during the course of his Ministry Jesus reminded some persons of John the Baptist, or that others identified him with traditional eschatological figures such as Elijah or "the prophet." Mark has probably exaggerated the extent to which the recognition of Jesus as a messiah was kept secret, yet it is not probable that the secrecy motif is altogether a post-Easter interpretation.[5] Mark does report that when Jesus approached Jerusalem a blind beggar, Bartimaeus, hailed him as "Son of David," and that Galilean pilgrims welcomed him to the city with shouts of victory for "the kingdom of our father David that is coming."[6] The result was that within a few days Jesus was executed as a messiah, or, from the viewpoint of the Romans, a revolutionist. One may with reason suspect that messianic speculation centered around Jesus during the Galilean ministry and that he sought to quiet a premature, misguided popular movement. When Peter confessed his belief, "You are the Messiah," Jesus recognized that the term *as Peter understood it* should not be applied to him.[7]

From the moment of Peter's confession, Jesus turns to explain to "the twelve" his understanding of his destiny and of theirs. He demands of the disciples a loyalty to himself, not only an acceptance of his proclamation. The mission and fate of the "Son of man" becomes the principal subject of this teaching.[8]

The Meaning of Son of Man on Jesus' Lips

Since twelve of Mark's fourteen Son of man passages follow Peter's confession, some scholars have held that Jesus did not use *bar nasha* as a title until after this event, or, if so, "Son of man" was only a colloquial way of speaking of man prior to Peter's confession. One influential scholar has expressed the view that Jesus did not apply the term to his person alone and in a special sense until the final

[5] Mark's theory of the parables (see above p. 293), and his treatment of the discomfited demons, possibly reflect a theological extension of a genuinely historical element in the tradition.

[6] Mark 10:46ff.; 11:1ff. and pars.

[7] Mark 8:31 and pars. C. H. Dodd in T. W. Manson, *Companion,* pp. 382f.

[8] See the above table, pp. 261ff.

crisis of the Ministry. Before this, when speaking of the Son of man, Jesus had intended "the saints of the Most High," directly recalling the vision and interpreted symbolism of Daniel 7. "The Son of man" stood for that company of penitent sufferers whom Jesus called out of Israel. These men, together with Jesus, formed corporately the Son of man, destined to share the blessings of the Age to Come in which God alone would be king.[9]

These positions must be made to rest upon several dubious assumptions. If Jesus first used Son of man at the time of Peter's confession, Mark 2:10 and 28 must be explained. It is easy to say that these passages are "Christian comments," which, of course, they are in their present forms, but why should their substance be denied to Jesus? It has been suggested that Jesus used *bar nasha* on these occasions as periphrasis for "I" or, again, that the weight of the belief that Jesus had on occasions spoken of the Son of man, ostensibly referring to himself, had resulted in the extension of the term in the Jesus-tradition of the early Church. Thus some traditional "I" sayings were converted into Son of man sayings.[10] The view that up to the very end Jesus used Son of man only as a corporate image—the community of the Messiah—is almost a pure assumption. No texts of the Gospels afford direct support for such usage.[11]

Unless the contention can be sustained that Jesus did not at all speak of the Son of man, there is a simpler and more probable interpretation. It is this: Early in his Ministry Jesus identified himself with the coming Son of man, not only in speaking with his disciples, but in his public proclamation. There is no reason why Jesus should not have used *bar nasha* as a self-designation, unless this would have been tantamount to saying, "I am Israel's Messiah." But on the basis of the evidence available, it cannot be said that this Danielic symbol had become a popular messianic title.[12] Jesus' use of the term would have been vague and not a little puzzling from the first. The public would have been able to read into Jesus' use of Son of man only that which they had already learned from his teaching and his actions.[13] Moreover, and this is a more important consideration, by adopting an eschatological symbolism which was only loosely related to traditional messianic expectations, Jesus was able to provide the subject of his teaching

[9]T. W. Manson, "Realized Eschatology and the Messianic Secret," in Nineham, *Studies* pp. 215ff.; also V. Taylor, *IB*, vol. 7, pp. 118f.

[10]That Jesus could have used *bar nasha* in Mark 2:10, 28 merely to refer to man *qua* man is not credible. See M. Hooker, *The Son of Man in Mark* (1967), pp. 81ff. [hereafter, *Mark*]; I. H. Marshall, "The Synoptic Son of Man Sayings in Recent Discussion," *NTS* 12 (1966): 342f.

[11]Indeed some passages expressly exclude it—Matt. 11:19; Luke 7:34 (Q), in which the Son of man is contrasted to John the Baptist (Schweizer, *Lordship*, pp. 44f.). Cf. Taylor, *Mark*, pp. 383f.; C. J. Cadoux, *The Historic Mission of Jesus* (1941), pp. 90ff.

[12]In 1 Enoch 37–71, the Danielic Son of man is probably identified with the Davidic Messiah (see above, p. 263), but since Jesus' teaching nowhere reflects the influences of this apocalypse it is unlikely that he assumed its influence on the masses. This is not undisputed. The basic question involves the date of these Enoch passages, and the suspicion that they contain late, Christian interpolations. See Higgins, *New Testament Essays*, pp. 125f.

[13]"The title 'Son of man' offers no answer but merely poses a question, like that provoked by Jesus' Ministry: 'What can this mean?' (Mark 1:27), 'Who is this man?' (Mark 4:41)." Betz, *Jesus*, p. 112.

such content and significance as he desired. At the same time, in relating his Ministry to the coming of the Son of man, Jesus could proclaim that in his own words and deeds God's purpose, set forth in Daniel's triumphant vision, would be fulfilled in history and beyond it.[14]

Many objections can be raised to this view that Son of man was originally a self-characterization of Jesus, and that by this Danielic image he taught the meaning of his mission and destiny. Attention has been given in Chapter 10 to the complexity of this problem, and to the numerous alternative explanations of the origin of the Son of man Christology in the Gospels.[15] All of the theories, alternative to the one offered here, pose some serious problems. Compelling arguments can be marshalled in suppport of the position that early, Aramaic-speaking Christians confessed that Jesus the Messiah and risen Lord of the Church was the Son of man who is to come. Two factors argue against the view that the original application of the title Son of man was given to Jesus at a relatively late period, in Hellenistic–Christian churches. First, this Christology is imbedded in the Q tradition; and second, the manner in which the suffering, death, and vindication of Jesus as Son of man is presented in Mark's Gospel lends support to the primitiveness of this interpretation.[16] Some scholars have held that early, anonymous Christian "prophets," in the name of Christ, put the term into the mouth of the historical Jesus.[17] It is difficult to believe this. Would these early Christian witnesses have refrained, almost without exception, from using this title in other contexts? The reader is reminded again of the fact that Son of man is a phrase confined almost exclusively to Jesus' speech in the Gospels. This fact puts a strong burden of proof upon any who would deny that the term in some sense goes back to Jesus. Applying the criterion of dissimilarity, it is unreasonable to conclude that such sayings as one finds in Luke 12:8, and its parallels in the Gospels, originated in some early Christian community.[18] It is not credible that the Church should have created sayings which seem to make a distinction between Jesus and the Son of man.[19]

The view that Jesus never spoke of himself as Son of man, but only proclaimed the coming of another, whom he so designated, also contains serious difficulties. When it is recalled that Jesus believed John the Baptist to have ushered in the new age, and that his own word and action inaugurated the kingdom of God, one may well ask what place there would have been in Jesus' teaching for the coming of some other eschatological figure. Apart from these few Son of man texts, there is no evidence that Jesus expected one greater than or equal to himself who would be manifested in the coming kingdom of God.

[14] While it may seem incredible that Jesus would have consciously chosen a self-designation which was vague and mysterious, Jesus knew the extent to which the Twelve shared the popular eschatologies and might well have wished to avoid clearly messianic titles. See Knox, *Sources*, vol. II, pp. 143ff.; I. H. Marshall, note 10 above, pp. 350f.

[15] See above, pp. 263ff.

[16] See above, p. 265.

[17] Käsemann, *Essays*, pp. 110f.; Perrin, *Rediscovering*, pp. 185f.

[18] Bultmann, *History*, pp. 151f.; Bornkamm, *Jesus*, p. 176.

[19] R. Otto, *The Kingdom of God and the Son of Man* (1938), p. 163. Cf. Perrin, *Rediscovering*, pp. 188f.

It seems a justifiable conclusion, then, that Jesus identified himself with the *coming* Son of man. But are we not able to say more than this? What of those texts in which Jesus seems to speak of his present fortunes and authority as those belonging to the Son of man, and of other texts which foretell his sufferings and resurrection as the mission and fate of the Son of man? We have noted that some scholars declare that only those sayings which prophesy the heavenly glorification of the Son of man in the future are authentic, that Jesus thought of himself as Son of man designate, so to speak. As noted above, it is the present writer's conviction that some if not all of those sayings are authentic which report that Jesus understood his present authority and fortunes as deriving from the fact that he was called to be and become the Son of man. Eduard Schweizer and others have defended satisfactorily sayings in the Gospels which depict the Ministry of Jesus as already that of the Son of man.[20]

When one turns from an examination of these texts separately, support for deriving from Jesus the teaching they contain is found in Jesus' proclamation of the kingdom of God. One can apply here the criterion of coherence or consistency. For Jesus, the kingdom had not come in its fullness, yet in his Ministry—his proclamation, his mighty works, his supersession of the formal authority of the Law as it applied to the present age, his teaching by parable—Jesus declared that the coming rule of God was already being manifested in history. Likewise, Jesus' claim to authority, while grounded in his election and faithful witness to God's kingdom as Son of man, is not fully realized; nevertheless, because he is fulfilling the role of Son of man he will be vindicated and exalted as such by God, and stand as the chief witness in the last judgment.

Some scholars have resisted strenuously the view that the same polarity of "now and not yet" existed in Jesus' thinking concerning the revelation of the Son of man that is found in his teaching concerning the coming of the kingdom of God. It is true that there are no primary texts in the Gospels which link directly the kingdom and the Son of man. Yet these allegedly disparate sayings are juxtaposed in the same strata of the Gospel tradition, and what is said about the Son of man corresponds closely with what is said about the kingdom.[21]

Another form of the argument opposing the view that Jesus thought of his Ministry as that of the Son of man, is that the prophecies in the Gospels of the future coming are never brought into direct relation with the prophecies of Jesus' passion and resurrection as Son of man. The common practice of separating the Son of man tradition into three types of sayings, as was done in Chapter 10, should be recalled. It is true that sayings in group one refer to the exaltation or glorification of the Son of man, while sayings in group three refer only to his resurrection. This observation has led some to conclude that there is a discrepancy in the gospel tradition, and since exaltation appears to be the more primitive concept than the resurrection of Jesus, the authenticity of the group one sayings, as deriving from Jesus tradition, is confirmed.

[20]E. Schweizer, "The Son of Man," *JBL* LXXIX (1960): 119ff.; idem., "The Son of Man Again," *NTS* 10 (1962): 256ff.; I. H. Marshall, note 10 above, pp. 339ff.
[21]Barrett, *Jesus*, pp. 32f.

There is, however, no a priori reason why Jesus should not have spoken of the vindication of the Son of man alternatively as resurrection and as exaltation. While some texts of the Gospels relate these alternative modes of speech very closely indeed, the relationship is not sufficiently coherent and unified to support their origin in the witness of post-Easter community. The detachment and reserve in Jesus' speech concerning the future role of the Son of man, the lack of explicit teaching relating his present work and God's future vindication, are more adequately explained as resulting from Jesus' own readiness to accept his present mission and fate as Son of man, and to give this the principal focus in his teaching: Suffering and death he must endure before the Son of man appears as a witness in the last judgment, when God's kingdom, that cannot be destroyed, will be established.

Several Son of man sayings may appear to contradict this almost exclusive focus of Jesus upon accomplishing his present mission. One may point especially to passages found in the "little apocalypse" of Mark 13 and its parallels. It must be recalled, however, that a great many scholars hold that this discourse is a composite document originating in the early Church.[22] Many if not all of these sayings might be genuine utterances of Jesus. But the total effect of the discourse creates an impression inconsistent with Jesus' teaching elsewhere. Mark's own purposes, as well as the theological and practical interests of the early Church, have decisively affected the form and content of Mark 13.

Most of the sayings of Jesus referring to the future coming of the Son of man emphasize the unpredictability of this event.[23] Even in Mark 13 there is a passage which stresses this fact. The following words provide a strange ending to a discourse ostensibly providing a "blueprint" of the End:

> Truly I say to you, this generation will not pass away before all these things take place . . . But of that day or that hour no one knows, not even the angels in heaven, nor the Son, but only the Father. Take heed, watch; for you do not know when the time will come.[24]

Apparently Jesus' certainty of God's imminent vindication of his word and work was joined with a disinterestedness in calculating its calendar date.[25]

FOREBODINGS OF DEATH; INTIMATIONS OF ITS MEANING

When did Jesus first realize that his Ministry would result in humiliation, suffering, and death? The question admits no certain answer. The forebodings

---

[22] See above, p. 181.

[23] See sayings 5, 6, 12, and 13 above, pp. 261f.

[24] Mark 13:30ff. See also Mark 9:1; 14:62 and pars.; and Matt. 10:23 (M).

[25] The analogy of the perspective of the OT prophets is frequently and fittingly noted. The belief that God would *certainly* fulfill his purpose led to the conclusion that he would do so *speedily*. Like the prophets and writers of apocalypse, Jesus foreshortens the future; yet, unlike the latter, he does not indulge in fanciful, detailed speculation concerning the final events. See Bultmann, *Theology*, vol. 1, p. 5; T. W. Manson, *Teaching*, pp. 269ff.

of death which are repeatedly attributed to Jesus in the Gospels have been dismissed by some as later Christian interpretations. It is said that Jesus did not go up to Jerusalem to die, but to continue the Ministry there. We say again that the predictions in the Gospels of the specific circumstances of Jesus' rejection in Jerusalem doubtlessly reflect the Church's knowledge of events which led up to the Cross. But this admission by no means renders unauthentic all of the forecasts of suffering and death. Jesus taught that the coming of the kingdom brought the most intense conflict with evil. Those who do the will of God must be prepared for the utmost renunciation of self, even unto death. After John's martyrdom, it was obvious that heralds of the End faced the same dangers as prophets of the past. Toward the close of Jesus' ministry in Galilee he was surely sensitive to the gathering storm of opposition.[26] Mark 8:32 (Matt. 16:22) shows that for Peter, "Messiah" and suffering were intolerable contradictions. But Jesus' sharp rebuke of Peter revealed his conviction that the necessity of suffering is grounded in the will of God and not merely in the schemes and plots of his enemies. When his disciple suggested otherwise, Jesus experienced once again the onslaught of the devil.

It is at this place that one can see the appropriateness of the term *Son of man* as the subject of Jesus' prophecies concerning his suffering and death. It is precisely in this context in the Gospels that the third usage of the Danielic image is found: "The Son of man must suffer many things and be rejected . . ." As one writer has reminded us, "The Son of man [in Daniel] is not simply one who appears at the end of time to act as judge: rather it is because he is Son of man *now*—i.e., elect, obedient, faithful, *and therefore suffering* that he will be vindicated as Son of man in the future . . ."[27]

The sayings of Jesus found in Mark 8:34–9:1, which speak also of the sufferings of the disciples, appear to be a topical collection. Yet it is not enough to conclude that in inserting them after the story of Peter's confession and Jesus' first prophecy of his passion, Mark shows editorial insight. It is to such a setting that they naturally belong.[28] The story in Mark 10:35ff. supports the view that Jesus led his disciples toward Jerusalem knowing full well the serious crisis that awaited them. Like Peter, the sons of Zebedee anticipated the glories to be shared by the community of the Messiah in the coming kingdom. Jesus assured them that the future was indeed in the Father's hands, and certain. But, for the present, they must drink the cup which he·was destined to drink and be baptized with his baptism.[29]

Do the Gospels reveal that Jesus had given thought to the meaning of his death? If so, did he share this with the disciples? Many scholars have answered these questions in the affirmative, believing that Jesus found a central clue to the

[26]Dodd, *Parables*, pp. 57ff.; Bornkamm, *Jesus*, pp. 154f.
[27]Hooker, *Mark*, p. 190 (italics mine); Barrett, *Jesus*, pp. 35ff.
[28]Taylor, *Mark*, p. 380; Barrett, *Jesus*, pp. 49ff.
[29]Jesus use of "the cup" (Mark 10:38f., 14:36 and pars.) corresponds to the predominant OT usage, symbolizing divinely appointed suffering. For baptism as a reference to death, cf. Luke 12:50 (Q?). The common assumption that Jesus knew from the beginning that *a cross* would be his destiny (e.g., Hunter, *Work and Words*, pp. 92ff.) rests upon too great confidence in Mark's "evidence."

meaning of his death in Isaiah 53 or in some of the Psalms which speak of the righteous sufferer, or in both. In these scriptures one reads of the sufferings of the righteous which are patiently borne in obedience to the will of God, and in them the faith is expressed that sufferings have a vicarious value, that they are God's means of redeeming men from evil. It is not possible to prove that Jesus found in "the Servant Songs of Isaiah" a key to the meaning of his death. Some have argued that the earliest strata of the Gospel tradition provide no support for this assumption. Yet it can be shown that Jesus' teaching, especially his teaching concerning the sufferings of the Son of man, reflects at numerous points the influence of the latter half of the Book of Isaiah. Jesus does not speak of himself as "the Servant." This title is nowhere the subject of his pronouncements concerning his mission or fortunes. Yet it is probable that Isaiah's Servant supplies the principal scriptural basis for the predicate: "The Son of man goes as it is written of him. . . ."[30]

The story called "The Transfiguration" presents special problems for the historian. Some are content to treat it as a legend. A few have supposed that it originated as a postresurrection story and that at a later time it was read back into the Ministry.[31] Most readers of Mark, following Matthew and Luke, understand this story as the account of a vision which Jesus' disciples experienced resulting from Peter's confession, Jesus' surprising reaction to it, and his forecast of the sufferings of the Son of man.[32] While few persons would claim to know what actually happened on this mountain, it is probable that at this time Peter, James, and John became convinced that Jesus was indeed their hope, even though the mystery of a suffering messiah was to remain for them a stumbling block. They knew that they must wait upon his words and follow him. Still it was with fear and trembling that they did so.[33]

THE MINISTRY IN JUDEA AND BEYOND THE JORDAN

Passing through Galilee, escaping (so far as it was possible) the public eye, Jesus came into the region of Judea.[34] We have seen that many writers consider that Mark telescoped Jesus' Ministry leading up to his final visit to Jerusalem.

[30]See T. W. Manson, *Jesus the Messiah*, pp. 154ff., Zimmerli and Jeremias, *The Servant of God*, pp. 98ff., O. Cullmann, *The Christology of the New Testament* (1959), pp. 81, 175, 183f. Representative studies maintaining that Jesus was not influenced by the suffering servant image of Is. 53 are C. T. Craig, "The Identification of Jesus with the Suffering Servant," *Journ. of Rel.* XXIV (1944): 240ff.; Bultmann, *Jesus*, pp. 213f.; Tödt, *Son of Man*, pp. 152ff. For notice of extensive literature on the subject, and diverse appraisals, see the author's, "The Servant Motif in the Synoptic Gospels," *Interpretation* XII (1958): 28ff; Hooker, *Jesus and the Servant*, p. 23; Fuller, *Foundations*, pp. 115ff.

[31]Mark 9:2ff. and pars. See Taylor, *Mark*, pp. 386ff. Cf. Bundy, *Jesus*, pp. 304ff. C. H. Dodd has shown that form critical analysis of the transfiguration gives no support whatever to the theory that the story is an antedated postressurection tradition (Nineham, *Studies*, p. 25).

[32]A. Schweitzer's reversal of the order—transfiguration, Peter's confession—is a psychological conjecture, the very thing he deprecates in other scholars.

[33]Mark 10:32. T. W. Manson suggests that the story of Peter's vision has been influenced by the messianic passage, Deut. 18:15 (*Servant-Messiah*, p. 75).

[34]Mark 9:30; 10:1.

We cannot be sure, however, that Mark possessed any record at all of Jesus' movements during this time. None of the narratives strung together by Mark's incidental notes of Jesus' forward progress is strictly relevant to the circumstances of the journey.[35] Luke mentions a frustrated attempt to enter "a village of the Samaritans." This incident probably has no chronological significance. Jesus may have journeyed into the region of Samaria. Limited contacts with members of this hated group resulted in mutual appreciation, but the evidence hardly deduces a ministry in Samaria.[36] There seems no reason to doubt that in leaving Galilee behind, Jesus deliberately "set his face" to go to Jerusalem.[37]

According to the Fourth Gospel, Jesus arrived at the Holy City during the eight-day harvest feast of Tabernacles (September–October). Opposition to his Ministry soon arose from the chief priests and Pharisees. But in spite of this Jesus remained in Jerusalem or its environs until the feast of Dedication two months later. Once again, we are told, Jesus crossed the Jordan and, seeking greater privacy, took his disciples to a village less than twenty miles northwest of Jericho, Ephraim.[38] Some scholars have accepted these chronological notices in John as authentic and used them to expand Mark's reference to a ministry in Judea. One has suggested that a written source underlies John 7–10.[39] There is a close correspondence between issues debated by the Tannaim and the controversial dialogues between Jesus and "the Jews" in this section of the Fourth Gospel.[40] Moreover, certain passages in the Synoptic Gospels have been thought to hint that Jesus' final Passover visit to Jerusalem was not his first but a return visit. Apparently he was well known in the city.[41] Possibly Mark's story of the cleansing of the temple, and associated incidents, were wrongly placed. Some features of these episodes are more easily understood if they are situated, not at Passover time, but some six months earlier at the feast of Tabernacles. Such reading of the evidence is, however, too precarious to be fully convincing.[42]

LAST DAYS IN JERUSALEM

The passion narratives of the Gospels are, as has been observed, full of detail and, in each, the sequence of events is closely connected. The first impression is that historical reminiscences were retained here to a greater extent than was

[35] Mark 10:17, 32, 46; 11:1. Taylor, *IB*, vol. 7, p. 132.

[36] Luke 9:51ff. See also Luke 10:30ff.; 13:22; 17:11ff.; and John 4:4ff. Cf. Matt. 10:5f.; 15:24. Johnson, *Jesus in His Homeland*, pp. 82ff.; Jeremias, *Jesus' Promise*, pp. 19ff., 42f.

[37] Luke 9:51; 13:31ff. For discussions of the question, why did Jesus go to Jerusalem, see Taylor, *IB*, vol. 7, p. 131; T. W. Manson, *Servant-Messiah*, pp. 75ff. Goguel seeks by source criticism to distinguish the development of various traditions (*Jesus*, pp. 392ff.).

[38] John 7:2ff.; 10:22, 40; 11:54.

[39] Goguel, *Jesus*, pp. 244ff.

[40] W. F. Howard, *IB*, vol. 8, pp. 583ff.

[41] E.g., Matt. 23:37ff.; Luke 13:34ff. (Q); Mark 10:1b, 46f.; 11:3; 12:12; 14:2, 13f., 49.

[42] Goguel, *Jesus*, pp. 420ff.; Craig, *Beginning*, p. 123; Manson, *BJRL*. XXXIII (1951): 271ff. Cf. Taylor, *Mark*, pp. 461f.

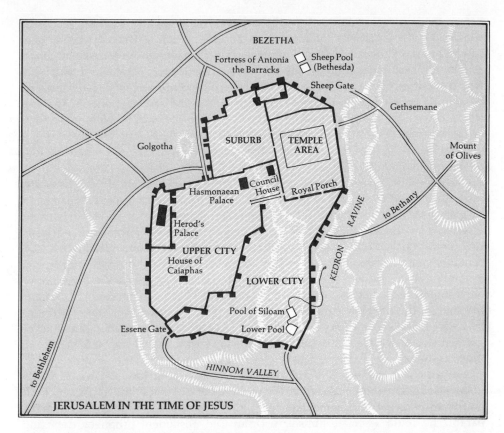

JERUSALEM IN THE TIME OF JESUS

the case in earlier portions of Jesus' story. And this is doubtless true. It must be remembered, however, that the passion of Jesus was "preached" from the earliest days of the Church, and that apologetic and missionary motives surely influenced the narratives: the earliest witnesses were convinced that Jesus' death was by no means "accidental"; God's purpose was fulfilled in and through it, although those men who brought Jesus to his cross were fully responsible for their actions.[43]

The high incidence of references to the fulfillment of "scripture" in the passion narratives inevitably raises questions which cannot be answered positively: To what extent was "proof from prophecy" added later as a result of Christian interpretation? Were scriptural passages "creative" of some of the detail in the story? Although scholars differ with respect to the historicity of its details, "nothing would be more wrong to deny that there is any historical truth in the story . . . simply because the church's faith was specially concerned with this piece of tradition, and has filled it in with the aid of passages from the Old Testament."[44]

All of the Gospels agree that Jesus' last visit to Jerusalem occurred a few days

[43]See above, pp. 118, 161f.
[44]Bornkamm, *Jesus*, pp. 157f.

before the Passover.[45] At this time the city was teeming with pilgrims. They had come from every place to commemorate the redemption of Israel from bondage by the grace and power of God. From the time of his arrival in Jerusalem, Jesus' actions are best understood as acted parables. Like the Old Testament prophets, who sometimes dramatized their oracles concerning coming events, Jesus declared by actions more eloquent than words the meaning and outcome of his Ministry. It is probable too that, like the prophets' "signs," Jesus' actions were more than vivid illustrations. The relation of Jesus' deeds to realities to come were as yet unseen, but Jesus acted in the faith that what he was doing was instrumental to their fulfillment.[46]

Consider, first, the story of the triumphal entry into Jerusalem.[47] One may ask the probable meaning of this demonstration for the crowd who participated in it, and then what meaning the incident might have had for Jesus. It is often asserted that the disciples and other Galilean pilgrims who accompanied Jesus to Jerusalem hailed him as Messiah. It must be noticed, however, that Mark 11:9 contains citations from a Hallel Psalm which was regularly sung by pilgrims at a number of Jewish festivals. Even the unusual cry, "Blessed be the kingdom of our father David that is coming," does not hail Jesus as a messiah.[48] Perhaps the sight of the city alone, and the joy of their festival journey, led the multitudes to voice their intense eschatological hopes. At the same time, the spreading of garments and leafy branches before Jesus shows that special homage was being given to him.[49]

Against the background of this tense situation the action of Jesus is to be understood. Jesus could not control the outbreak of popular enthusiasm. He could not avoid personal involvement in this nationalist demonstration. But by acted parable he could associate himself with an Old Testament prophecy depicting a messiah without pomp, a king of peace. As at the time of Peter's confession, Jesus was unable to deny the homage paid him, but the disciples and the crowd could be shown the only kind of leadership he offered them. In retrospect this day of his "visitation" would be understood.

There is irony in this situation. Unknown to themselves, the crowds shout for the restoration of David's kingdom, confessing that in Jesus, as he goes to his death, the kingdom of God is coming. There was on Jesus' part no deliberate messianic claim. This may explain why neither the priests nor the Romans took any notice of the incident. But the truth was soon to dawn upon those who had eyes to see—the truth concerning the messianic secret and the mystery of the kingdom of God.[50]

[45] Mark 11:9f. and pars.; John 12:12ff.
[46] H. Wheeler Robinson, "Essay on Prophetic Symbolism," in *Old Testament Essays*, ed. D. C. Simpson (1927), pp. 10ff. Cf. Is. 20; Jer. 27–28; Acts 21:10ff.
[47] Mark 11:1ff. and pars.; John 12:12ff.
[48] "The Son of David," Matt. 21:9, is doubtless an editorial gloss. Cf. 21:12. Schweitzer's view that Jesus was hailed as the Elijah who is to come deserves serious consideration.
[49] Kümmel, *Promise and Fulfillment*, pp. 115f. Note 2 Kings 9:13; 1 Macc. 13:51 (John 12:13).
[50] Kümmel, pp. 117f; Taylor, *Mark*, p. 452. This entry of Jesus "would be inconceivable without his powerful claim that the kingdom of God is dawning in his word, and that the final decision will turn upon himself." Bornkamm, *Jesus*, p. 158. Note the fourth evangelist's comment, John 12:16.

The second acted parable of Jesus is the cleansing of the temple.[51] Again it is not altogether clear what happened on this occasion. How was Jesus able to drive from the large Court of the Gentiles the money-changers and sellers of sacrifices, and to prevent the area from being used as a thoroughfare? Jesus' action cannot have been intended as a reform measure only. Shortly afterwards he left the temple and the city, and traffic was resumed. But Jesus' action could have been understood as a messianic sign, and it probably was so intended. In Old Testament prophecies and in ancient Jewish traditions, the Messianic Age is associated with the renewal of the temple and with the expectation that in that day Gentiles will worship at Mount Zion.[52] The people generally may not have understood this messianic significance of the disturbance in the temple. Mark reports that it was Jesus' teaching there which astonished the multitudes.[53] But, for the chief priests, such popular demonstrations were the stuff from which messianic movements began. They might have been totally blind to the purposes of Jesus, but his action in the temple had challenged their authority and offered a serious threat to the peace. A tense situation was developing which required that they be cautious.

Some of the conflict stories which follow this incident in the temple may have been situated earlier in the Ministry of Jesus.[54] Nevertheless, it is likely that the stories concerning the challenge of Jesus' authority and his views on the traditional resurrection hope belong to the passion week.[55] Jesus' reaction to the question put to him by representatives of the Jerusalem Sanhedrin was similar to his response to persons who on other occasions had demanded his credentials. He gave a veiled reply, yet he did not avoid the crucial issue. How can anyone tell whether a man's authority is from God or not, unless he is concerned above all else to do His will? Apparently, Jesus considered that the Sadducees were incompetent to adjudicate such a question since they recognized no incongruity between the concessions operating in the Court of the Gentiles and God's purposes for His temple. Later on, the Sadducees put to Jesus their stock question designed to reduce to absurdity the belief of the Pharisees in a general resurrection. In his reply, Jesus dismissed as profitless all idle curiosity concerning the manner of the resurrection and turned to the ground for belief in it as a fact. In the Torah, which the Sadducees considered to be the sole authority, God is revealed as "the God of the living." Jesus taught that the faithful of all ages enjoy unbroken communion with Him.

The Last Supper of Jesus is the third of his acted parables in Jerusalem.[56] The interpretation of this event is, as we have observed earlier, partly determined by

[51] Mark 11:15ff. and pars. (Cf. John 2:13ff.)

[52] Mark 11:17 (Is. 56:7); Ezek. 43:6ff., 44:5ff., etc. Jeremias, *Jesus' Promise*, pp. 57ff. Jesus' action may have been inspired by Mal. 3:1ff., as many believe, but there is no purging of the priests. Perhaps Zech. 14:21b is the prophecy fulfilled.

[53] Mark 11:18. Cf. Luke 19:47f.; John 7:14f. Instead of acting to rid Jerusalem of Gentiles, Jesus provided for their worship at the temple.

[54] E.g., Mark 12:28ff. Cf. Luke 10:25ff. Taylor, *Mark*, pp. 101, 468.

[55] Mark 11:27ff.; 12:18ff. and pars.

[56] Mark 14:12ff. and pars.

the answer given to the question: Was the Last Supper a Passover meal? The following table presents the sequence of events associated with this important Jewish feast, and approximate times according to modern reckoning:

Nisan 14: The day of preparation.

Noon   Use of leaven and leavened foods prohibited.

1:30 P.M.   Slaughter of the daily evening sacrifice.

2:30 P.M.   The offering of this sacrifice. From this time until sunset everyone fasted. The Passover lambs were slain.

Nisan 15: The day of Passover, or the first day of Unleavened Bread.

Around 6:30 P.M.   Sunset, the end of Nisen 14: The beginning of Nisan 15; the Passover was celebrated.

Mark, followed by Matthew and Luke, report that Jesus' Last Supper was a proper Passover eaten in the early hours of Nisan 15. The Gospel of John, however, presents contradictory statements. It is reported that when Jesus was tried before Pilate, the Passover had not been eaten by the priests.[57] In view of these discrepant versions the reader must decide between the following alternatives: Either all that happened from the Last Supper to the burial of Jesus took place on the day of Passover, 15 Nisan, which in the year Jesus died fell on a Thursday/Friday; or these final events occurred on the day of Preparation which in that year was Thursday/Friday, Nisan 14.[58]

Some readers may ask: Is this question of time a vital consideration? Might not Jesus have eaten the Passover with his disciples twenty-four hours beforehand, knowing that he would be dead when the feast was celebrated? The problem is not disposed of so simply, for the essential question remains: Does the account of the Last Supper in the oldest traditions display the characteristic features of a Passover meal? Opposite sides have been taken on this question. Some have said that arguments favoring a Passover meal are that it was celebrated in Jerusalem in the evening; that Jesus and his men formed a group of typical size; that they reclined while eating; that the traditional Passover bread and red wine were given ceremonial interpretation; that the poor were remembered, songs of thanksgiving sung, and afterwards a journey was taken within the limits of the city.[59] But there are serious objections. Would Jesus' disciples and the mob have carried arms on the evening of Passover? During that night would the Sanhedrin have met, tried, and condemned Jesus? Assuming that an extraordinary Council meeting was held, would the high priest have violated the law by tearing his robe in protests of blasphemy? Would Jesus have been executed on the day of Passover? Would he have been taken down from the cross, prepared for burial, and entombed during the feast?[60]

[57] John 18:28. See also 19:14, 31, 42.

[58] All harmonizing efforts have failed. See Jeremias, *Eucharistic Words*, pp. 5ff. A third possibility may be noted: that the arrest, trial, and crucifixion might have taken longer than a single night and morning (Black in Higgins, *New Testament Essays*, pp. 19ff.).

[59] Jeremias, *Eucharistic Words*, pp. 14ff.

[60] Jeremias seeks to meet the objections (ibid., pp. 37ff.), but some of the rabbinical evidence is late, and some of the analogies of doubtful validity.

Various efforts have been made to explain the solemnities of the Last Supper upon other than a Passover setting. Some say it was a *kiddush* (consecration); that is, a meal-time, ritual sanctification of holy days, notably of the Sabbath. Others have compared Jesus' Last Supper with his disciples to a Jewish *haburah* (fellowship) meal. But arguments in support of either of these alternatives are tenuous to say the least.[61] We have seen that some of the features peculiar to Jesus' last meal in the Markan version, and unexplainable by Passover customs, are possibly taken from Essene cult-meal practices such as are described in the texts from Qumran.[62] Since it cannot be said that the historical questions have been satisfactorily answered, it is probably best not to make the interpretation of Jesus' actions and words at the Last Supper dependent upon a Passover setting.

It cannot be denied that the supper traditions are fragmentary and lack consistency. Which of these accounts is the most apt to be authentic: the "tradition" Paul had "received" (reported in the earliest literary source, I Cor. 11:23ff.), the Markan version (Mark 14:17ff.; Matt. 26:20ff.), or the tradition drawn from "Special Luke" (Luke 22:15ff.)?[63] The present writer believes that Mark's Gospel reports the oldest form of Jesus' words:

> Distributing bread to his disciples, Jesus said: "Take; this is my body." And when the cup was given to them, he said: "This is my blood [of the covenant] which is poured out for many.[64] Truly, I say to you, I shall not drink again of the fruit of the vine until that day when I drink it new in the kingdom of God."

Our interpretation of these words should be dependent upon the following facts. In his parables Jesus had spoken of the coming kingdom as a banquet or feast. He had employed this image in feeding the multitude, and possibly at other fellowship meals with his disciples. Jesus had spoken of giving his life as a ransom for "many." He had also spoken of his forthcoming suffering as his "cup." And now, Jesus distributed bread as representing himself on the eve of his death; he handed around the wine cup promising the disciples a share in the eschatological kingdom made possible by his death. No longer does Jesus expect them to die with him. But they were to have a share in the benefits of his death, in the consequences of his death. By eating and drinking, the disciples were given the privilege of experiencing in advance the "messianic banquet." To Jesus, they were the Israel of the Age to Come. They were being allowed to experience in the present those benefits soon to be realized when the kingdom of God came "in power."

This is a remarkable thing that Jesus does for his disciples. Before the night was over, one of these men was to deny him. All were to forsake him. Since

---

[61] Ibid., pp. 21ff.

[62] See above, p. 148.

[63] For the evidence favoring the longer text of Luke and its independence, Jeremias, *Eucharistic Words,* pp. 87ff.

[64] The possibility must be seriously considered that Paul preserves the oldest form—"this cup is the new covenant in my blood," since it is difficult to believe that a Jew would have commanded the drinking of blood, and since the Markan phrase "my blood of the covenant" is not possible in Aramaic. Kümmel, *Promise and Fulfillment,* pp. 120f.; Jeremias, *Eucharistic Words,* pp. 133f.

Jesus knew this, it can be said that his action at the Last Supper was his most impressive declaration that the gifts of God are given to undeserving men. Jesus came, as he said, "not to invite the righteous, but sinners."[65]

Gethsemane; the Betrayal; Peter's Denial

When Jesus left "the upper room" with "the twelve," he went toward the Mount of Olives, a usual trysting place at nightfall. In a garden called Gethsemane Jesus lingered. Separating himself from the disciples, he fell upon his knees in agony of spirit: "Abba (Father), all things are possible to Thee; remove this cup from me; nevertheless, not my will, but thine be done."[66] It is not surprising that this scene should be reported with slight variations in the Gospels, for the disciples were at some distance removed, and dozing. Yet it is beyond question that on this night Jesus knew that his ordeal was imminent, that he recoiled from it, that he experienced a terrible anguish. It is equally certain that Jesus' serenity at the time of his arrest was not a stoical courage. Through communion with God as "Father," he had found the spiritual resources enabling him to accept violence and death.[67]

At this point a question may be raised which could have been dealt with at numerous points in the Ministry. Whence arose the belief of early Christians—most explicitly set forth in the First and Fourth Gospels—that Jesus was (and is) "the Son of God"? Several answers have been given to this important historical question. That the title arose *ab extra* in Hellenistic Christianity, under the influence of the common notion that the great saviors of mankind were divine men or "sons of God," is now commonly denied. We have earlier pointed to the strong reasons for believing that the term *Son of God* was applied to Jesus by the earliest, Aramaic-speaking Church.[68] We face now a new possibility: that by his attitude to God, by the relation in which he stood to God (most evident in moments of prayer), Jesus revealed himself to his disciples. The impression of the quality of his inner life, a life of complete obedience to the will of God as "Father," an impression strengthened and transfigured for the eyes of faith in the resurrection, led Jesus' disciples to confess him "the Son of God."[69]

In the earliest strata of the synoptic tradition Jesus rarely speaks of himself as "the Son," if indeed this absolute was possible in Aramaic. It is probable that these passages are best explained as confessional statements of the early Church.[70]

---

[65] Dodd in T. W. Manson, *Companion,* pp. 386f.

[66] Mark 14:26, 32ff. and pars. Cf. John 12:27ff. and 18:11, which appear to be echoes of a precanonical Gethsemane tradition.

[67] Luke 22:42 and John 12:28f. lay stress upon this fact implicit in the Markan narrative (Goguel, *Jesus,* pp. 492ff.) Cf. Barrett, *Jesus,* pp. 46ff., who conjectures that Jesus' cry in Gethsemane and his "cry of desolation" from the cross lead one to conclude that Jesus hoped for God's intervention in establishing his kingdom, that he was disappointed, yet remained determined to be loyal.

[68] See above, pp. 127f.

[69] T. W. Manson, *Teaching,* pp. 89ff.; Fuller, *Mission,* pp. 80ff.; Schweitzer, *Quest,* p. 43.

[70] Mark 12:6 and pars.; 13:32 (Matt. 24:36); Matt. 11:27 and Luke 10:22 (Q). Cf. Mark 1:1; 1:11 and pars.; Matt. 4:3 and Luke 4:3 (Q); Luke 4:41 (cf. Mark 1:34, 3:11); Matt. 16:16 (cf. Mark 8:29; Luke 9:20); Mark 9:7 and pars.; Matt. 26:63 (cf. Mark 14:61; Luke 22:67); Mark 15:39 (Matt. 27:54; cf. Luke 23:47).

He who had been "designated Son of God in power . . . by his resurrection" could, with propriety, be confessed "the Son" during his Ministry. Since Jesus' baptism was his first public act of self-humiliation, from that time he had actually become a true Son, fulfilling the vocation of Israel. It is unlikely that the early confessors were any more able than we are to know what had been "the religious experiences" of Jesus. But this the disciples of Jesus had known: he had fulfilled a scriptural ideal of the obedient Son. Although he had not claimed the title "the Son of God," he had acknowledged God and spoken to God as a child to his earthly father. The disciples could not forget that Jesus had not only used the regular term of Jewish piety—*abhi* (my father)—but that at critical points in the Ministry the language of his prayer was, as we might say, the language of familiarity—*abba* (father).[71]

In the garden of Gethsemane Jesus was arrested. The temple police, accompanied perhaps by deputies, were led to the spot by Judas Iscariot, "one of the twelve."[72] In this way the authorities were able to avoid an open arrest of Jesus, a thing they had feared would result in a riot. Did Judas sell to the authorities his inside knowledge of Jesus' nocturnal meeting place? Albert Schweitzer has suggested that for a price Judas revealed the messianic secret, reporting to the priests Peter's confession and the incident of Jesus' anointment in Bethany as the Messiah. Conjectures as to the possible motives for Judas' act, which can only be described as a betrayal, began in the first century and persist in the present.[73] Such curiosity is understandable, but since it is not possible to provide historical confirmation for any of these "explanations," there is little profit in raising the question of motive. Jesus himself could only say: "Woe to that man . . . It would have been better for that man if he had not been born."[74]

The story of Peter's denial is woven into the synoptic story of Jesus' trial.[75] Yet it is appropriate to consider it here. The Gospels variously report that Jesus had predicted Peter's denial.[76] Why should this be considered a prophecy after the event? Peter's brashness and self-confidence are broadly attested in the Gospels, and reports of Jesus' rebuke of his disciples' foolishness refer to his foreknowledge of their behavior based on his understanding of their natures. The story of the denial is told with such vivid detail that some have suspected a legendary origin, or else the whole is attributed to a storyteller's art.[77] But is it credible that anything like this could have arisen in early Christian traditions? It is a sad fact that not even Peter, the man Jesus likened to a rock, remained loyal in the crisis. Jesus faced abuse and death without any human supports.

---

[71] J. Jeremias, *The Prayers of Jesus* (1967), pp. 11ff. It may be more important for the student to consider "what attitude Jesus took to his work and what kind of authority he exercised over his disciples, than to ask what title he accepted or rejected," since none of the traditional titles had clear denotations. S. Johnson, *Jesus in His Homeland*, pp. 136ff.

[72] Mark 14:43ff. and pars. Cf. John 18:2ff.

[73] Mark 14:3ff. (Matt. 26:6ff.). Cf. Luke 7:36ff.; John 12:1ff. Schweitzer, *Quest*, p. 394.

[74] Mark 14:21 (Matt. 26:24).

[75] Mark 14:66ff. and pars. Cf. John 18:17, 25ff.

[76] Mark 14:26ff. (Matt. 26:30ff.). Cf. Luke 22:31ff.

[77] Mark 9:33ff. (Luke 9:46f.); Luke 9:54f.; Mark 10:35ff. (Matt. 20:20ff.); Mark 14:37f. (Matt. 26:41).

Condemnation by the Chief Priests and by Pilate

The accounts of the trials of Jesus in the Gospels are not without difficulties, both historical and legal. The table below offers a reconstruction of the principal course of events, but it is not possible to harmonize the various details in the Synoptic Gospels.[78] Many scholars have observed that in the development of the trial tradition there is a progressively heightened tendency in the Gospels to shift the responsibility for the crucifixion of Jesus from the Roman government to the Jewish people.[79] The legal problem arises out of the fact that the examination of Jesus in the high priest's house conforms to none of the judicial proceedings set forth in the rabbinical tractate, *Sanhedrin*. Moreover, in the time of Jesus the Sanhedrin exercised authority as a legislative and administrative organ as well as a judicial body.[80] Probably the hearing before the high priest should not be termed a trial but "grand jury proceedings," with or without the consent of the Pharisees, to determine the charges which should be preferred in the court of the procurator.[81]

The following table presents a possible reconstruction of "the judicial process":

1. Examinations by the Jews
   a. After his arrest, Jesus is informally examined in the high priest's house.[82] His captors mock him.[83]
   b. At dawn the Sanhedrin is convened.[84] Evidence is sought that Jesus had spoken of destroying the temple (presumably considered a messianic act) but without success.[85] Finally, the high priest, Caiaphas, asks the direct question, "Are you the Christ . . . ?" The force of Jesus' qualified affirmative seems to have been: Messiah is your word; it is as the Son of man that I shall be manifested to you, and to all.[86] The nature of Jesus' reply caused the high priest to cry "Blasphemy!"
2. Trial before Pilate
   a. Jesus' accusers state that he is guilty of treasonable words and deeds, that he claims to be "a king."[87] Pilate marvels that Jesus makes no effort to defend himself, but judges the prisoner to be politically harmless.[88]

---

[78] Mark 14:43ff. and pars. Cf. John 18:12ff.

[79] Winter one-sidedly redresses the balance (*Trial of Jesus*). Cf. the judicious comment of Barrett, *Jesus*, pp. 53ff. *The Trial of Jesus*, ed. E. Bammel (1970).

[80] *Mishnah*, pp. 386ff. See Winter, *Trial of Jesus*, p. 27.

[81] Taylor, *Mark*, pp. 644ff.; Bundy, *Jesus*, pp. 514ff.; Betz, *Jesus*, p. 87.

[82] Luke 22:54; John 18:12ff.

[83] Luke 22:63ff.

[84] Luke 22:66. Mark mistakenly concludes that a trial was held during the night, a brief consultation in the morning, 15:1. Black in Higgins, *New Testament Essays*, pp. 22f.

[85] Mark 14:55ff. and pars. That Jesus said something like this is supported by Mark 15:29. His refusal to reply to the accusation left its meaning uncertain. See Betz, *Jesus*, pp. 89ff., who holds that the temple saying is to be understood against the background of 2 Sam. 7 and its current Jewish eschatological interpretation. Cf. John 2:19.

[86] Note the variants in Mark 14:61f. and pars.

[87] Luke 23:2 is "correct as regards this point" (Bornkamm, *Jesus*, p. 164). Cf. John. 19:12ff.

[88] Note Luke's exaggeration of the truth for apologetic reasons, see above, p. 229. Luke's story of the trial before Herod, while not lacking realism, can scarcely be crowded into the morning. Goguel,

b. Pilate offers to release Jesus as a concession to the people, in accord with a local custom of granting amnesty to a prisoner, believing that Jesus is still a people's favorite. To Pilate's surprise (and the reader's), the release of an insurrectionist named Barabbas is demanded.[89] In the face of the priests' clamor and a popular demonstration, Pilate follows expediency rather than justice. He releases Barabbas and condemns Jesus to be crucified. Jesus is brutally mocked by the soldiers in their barracks-room.

The Crucifixion and Burial of Jesus

From the days of the Punic wars, the Romans had used crucifixion as capital punishment for slaves. This was an extreme form of torture which could last for a day or longer. Mark writes that Jesus was crucified between two thieves, that he refused opiates of any kind and died within six hours. By a harmonization of the Gospel traditions, the Church speaks of "the seven last words from the Cross." Only one of these stands in the Markan passion narrative, the loud "cry of desolation" based upon Psalm 22:1. Either it was known from actual hearers that Jesus had shouted thus, or else in the absence of testimony it was assumed that this psalm, which so strangly prefigured events of the passion, was fulfilled up to the last moment.[90] In either case, a word from scripture on the lips of a righteous man at death is no cry of despair.

It would have been a violation of Jewish law to have left Jesus' lifeless body hanging on the cross overnight.[91] Its removal was all the more urgent since death had occurred within a few hours of the Sabbath. Joseph of Arimathea risked public scorn in order to be loyal to the traditions of piety. After securing Pilate's permission, Joseph hastily laid the dead stranger's body in a tomb, and rolled a stone against its door. "The curtain seemed to have fallen on unrelieved tragedy."[92]

The Resurrection of Jesus

Since the life of Jesus like that of any man ends with death, some New Testament scholars consider that the closing pages of the Gospels form the first part of the narrative of the early Church. Historical method may justify concluding the story of the Ministry of Jesus with his burial, but the fabric of the Gospel tradition is thereby torn at its end. The stories of the empty tomb and the postresurrection appearances of Jesus belong to the narratives of his passion. They are the conclusion to the good news of the Ministry, not its sequel.

No part of the gospel has excited greater interest and controversy than the testimony to the resurrection. Luke's report of the Athenians' response to Paul's

---

Jesus, p. 515, n. 1; Cf. Streeter's defense in *Oxford Studies,* pp. 229ff.; Black in Higgins, *New Testament Essays,* pp. 23f.

[89]Goguel, *Jesus,* pp. 516ff.; Rawlinson, *Mark,* pp. 227f. Winter is wholly skeptical of the Barabbas incident (*Trial of Jesus,* pp. 91ff.).

[90]Mark 15:34 (Matt. 27:46). Cf. Mark 15:24 (Ps. 22:18); 15:29 (Ps. 22:7).

[91]Deut. 21:22f.

[92]Hunter, *Work and Words,* p. 121.

preaching reflects the reaction of men to the Church's proclamation in all ages: "When they heard of the resurrection of the dead, some mocked; but others said, we will hear . . . again about this."[93]

The formation of the earliest Christian traditions concerning the resurrection of Jesus was discussed in Chapter 8. Lists of persons who had seen the risen Christ were reported by the earliest preachers, such as the one recorded in 1 Corinthians 15. To support these bare statements concerning the numerous witnesses, stories were told of Jesus' postresurrection appearances to his disciples, the resolution of their incredulity by his assurances to them, and the commands of the risen Christ. Several of the resurrection stories in the Gospels are the literary deposit of this earliest testimony. They bear the marks of "a tradition shaped and rubbed down to essentials in the process of oral transmission," for example, Matthew 28:8–10, 16–20, and John 20:19–21.[94]

Modern Christian scholars have assumed that these stories are the primary evidence for belief in the resurrection. It is noted that *none of the canonical Gospels describes Jesus emerging from the tomb.* The mere fact, it is said, that the tomb of Jesus (or of someone else?) was found empty is capable of many explanations and proves little if anything.[95] Moreover, one can trace in the traditions a tendency "to write up" the experiences of the women at the tomb. It is certainly true that *the disciples did not believe in Jesus' resurrection simply because they could not find his body. They were convinced because the living Christ appeared to them.*[96] Nevertheless, it is probable that the earliest testimony to the resurrection presupposes the fact of the empty tomb.[97]

The careful reader will note the discrepancies in the stories of the women at the tomb. Mark says they found the stone rolled back, and that upon entering the tomb they met a young man there. Matthew reports that they saw an angel descend and roll away the stone. Luke says that they saw two men. In John's Gospel, Mary Magdalene discovered that the stone had been taken away. She reported to Peter and another disciple who found the tomb empty, except for the grave cloths. Subsequently Mary herself looked into the tomb and saw two angels in white. The message to the women and their reactions are also variously reported. Did they, or did they not, find the disciples? And, if they did, what message did they deliver? Did any of these women see the Lord? Is it possible to recover an original account on the basis of which one can explain the origin of the other stories, or must independent witnesses be weighed one against another?

A critical consensus has not been reached on these questions. All would agree

---

[93] Acts 17:2.

[94] Luke 24:13–35, 36–49, and John 21:1–14 may also rest upon earlier traditions of the same type. In their present form, however, they are circumstantial narratives reflecting the storyteller's art rather than a corporate tradition: Dodd in Nineham, *Studies,* pp. 9ff. See the careful analysis of the variant traditions and attempted reconstruction, Anderson, *Jesus,* pp. 185ff.

[95] Note Matt. 28:11ff.

[96] Craig, *Beginning,* pp. 135f.

[97] Matt. 28:8, 16; Luke 24:21ff.; John 20:19. It is sometimes stated that Paul knew nothing of the empty tomb tradition. His words: Christ "died . . . was buried . . . rose again" seem to take it for granted; otherwise what point is there in the middle term? Cf. Anderson, *Jesus,* pp. 192ff.

that the events of Easter morning cannot be woven into a single narrative. But for some scholars the very nature of these discrepancies "proves" the fact of the empty tomb. For others the same data point to late and possibly legendary origins. In either case the traditions arose as particular expressions of faith in Jesus' resurrection and not as providing primary evidence proving its historicity.

Historians should begin their examination of the resurrection evidence with the experiences of the disciples. Unquestionably, the crux of the matter is here. Paul's "received tradition" stated that the risen Jesus had "appeared to Cephas [Peter], *then* to the Twelve." [98] Yet if one proceeds from this point, he soon encounters other puzzling discrepancies. What happened to Peter's story? Mark implies a first meeting with all of the disciples in Galilee, and Matthew reports the same. Luke and John report that it was in Jerusalem or in Judea that Jesus first appeared to the disciple band, although in "the appendix" of the Fourth Gospel a meeting in Galilee is reported. The question of the locale of the post-resurrection appearances is for some a matter of great importance, requiring a choice between Galilee or Jerusalem; for others, the question is of minor significance.

It may be a source of disappointment to some readers that the narratives in the New Testament do not provide cogent proofs for the resurrection. But, when we think of it, this is not surprising. Suppose for the sake of argument that evidence for the empty tomb could be undeniably established; this would not prove that Jesus was still alive, still less that, as the consequence of his death, Jesus had been invested by God with "all authority in heaven and on earth." [99] Or suppose that the manner or mode of Jesus' appearing could be "explained," that one's curiosity could be satisfied concerning the so-called "subjective" or "objective" factors, or both, which *caused* faith in the resurrection; it would not thereby be established that in this event a new age began in the history of the world, that God, by turning the defeat of his Anointed into triumph, gave to Jesus "the name which is above every name, that at the name of Jesus every knee should bow . . . every tongue confess that Jesus Christ is Lord, to the glory of God the Father." [100] Whatever the manner of his appearances, the risen Christ was only seen *for what he is* through the eyes of faith.[101]

THE NATIVITY TRADITIONS IN MATTHEW AND LUKE

At first sight it may seem strange to direct attention to the infancy narratives of Jesus in the First and Third Gospels at the close of his public Ministry. Is

[98] 1 Cor. 15:5.

[99] Matt. 28:18.

[100] Phil. 2:9ff.

[101] Luke 24:13ff. suggests that the first believers became sensible of the risen Christ as the scriptures were related to Jesus' Ministry, and in the breaking of bread. Through Word and Sacrament the eyes of faith behold him still. For lively discussions concerning the nature and relevance of *faith* in the resurrection of Jesus Christ, see Anderson, *Jesus*, pp. 205ff; G. W. H. Lampe and D. M. MacKinnon, *The Resurrection* (1966); W. Marxsen et al., *The Significance of the Message of the Resurrection for Faith in Jesus Christ*, ed. C. F. D. Moule (1968).

this not the very thing one has sought to avoid, to do violence to the perspective of the Gospels? Paradoxically, this is not the case. It was only after the Ministry of Jesus had issued in belief in his resurrection that there was any interest in the circumstances of his origin. The central events in the New Testament's witness to Jesus are his death and resurrection. His birth is viewed in the light of the interpretation of these events, and not vice versa.

Outside the opening chapters of Matthew and Luke, there are no references in the New Testament to Jesus' birth of the Virgin Mary.[102] Efforts have been made to discredit these passages by regarding them as scribal interpolations. But it cannot be said that the textual and literary evidence impugns their genuineness. The absence of all mention of the occasion of Jesus' birth in the Gospels of Mark and of John, in Paul's letters, and other writings earlier than Matthew and Luke, is not prima-facie evidence opposing these traditions. The most that these data prove is that in several important churches either nothing was known of unusual circumstances surrounding Jesus' birth, or, if the stories were current, they were not felt to contain any matter essential to the kerygma of the Church.[103]

In Chapter 9 consideration was given to the interests which might have led the first and third evangelists to adapt as well as to report the traditions of Jesus' nativity.[104] At this point let us admit the likelihood that the stories in the Gospels are traditional, and not altogether the creations of the evangelists, and raise the question: What is the historical evidence for the miracle?

It must be admitted that the nativity stories manifest irreconcilable differences in detail. There has been a freedom of development in this tradition which has no parallel in the Gospels. Both Matthew and Luke agree that Joseph was not the natural father of Jesus, but in almost all of the particulars they differ. Both report that Jesus was born in Bethlehem and reared in Nazareth, but there is no agreement as to cause of the movements of Jesus' parents. Neither evangelist directly describes the event of Jesus' birth. The language of their narratives is poetical, and influenced by Old Testament narratives and prophecies.[105]

The nature of this evidence leads some to affirm that the birth narratives are an insecure basis for the belief that Jesus was born of a virgin.[106] But others take the opposite position. It is said that the discrepancies in the stories are those most likely to have occurred before the facts of the case became the object of scrutiny some thirty years or so afterwards. Moreover, the central claims are doubly attested since two independent stories agree in reporting them.[107] Doctrinal considerations inevitably affect any individual's evaluation of this scanty evidence.

What then can we say? Can one surmise that the nativity stories rest upon

[102] Matt. 1:18–25; Luke 1:34f.

[103] J. K. S. Reid, "Virgin (Birth)," in Richardson, Theological Wordbook, pp. 275f.

[104] See above.

[105] Biblical rather than pagan influences are reflected, W. L. Knox, Some Hellenistic Elements in Primitive Christianity (1944), pp. 22ff.

[106] See, e.g., P. Gardner-Smith, The Christ of the Gospels (1938), pp. 61ff.; C. J. Cadoux, The Life of Jesus (1948), pp. 27ff.; Bundy, Jesus, pp. 36ff.

[107] Reid, note 103 above, p. 276; J. G. Machen, The Virgin Birth of Christ (1932), pp. 191ff.

a factual occurrence? Or are they legendary products of early Christian efforts to find Jesus' personal history in the Old Testament and ancient Jewish haggadah? Alternatively, can we explain their origin as a reflex expression, in narrative form, of the total impression made by Jesus upon some of his followers? Some persons may consider that these questions pose clear-cut options, but perhaps one should reckon with a combination of several, complex factors. There are kernels of fact in most legends. Figurative speech and song are the most adequate means of expressing the real meaning of certain events concerning which very little of a factual nature can be recovered. It is not surprising that among many who confessed Jesus to be "the Son of God" there would have been little disposition to doubt that Jesus came from God in a way that was wholly unique. If, as seems likely, the nativity stories of the Gospels had their original setting in the worship of early Palestinian churches, many different influences might have converged to give them their distinctive traditional forms.[108]

For many readers a discreet veil of reverent agnosticism must ever surround historical questions concerning Jesus' birth. But the value of the nativity stories of the Gospels is not thereby depreciated. Be they fact or fiction or a combination of both, the faith they express is a faith which the whole of the New Testament proclaims: Jesus came from God; it is not possible to "explain" him as merely the product of Israelite piety. In his historical existence he was a new creation, accomplished by the power of God in and through Israel's history "when the time had fully come."[109]

[108] P. Minear, "The Interpreter and the Nativity Stories," *Theology Today* 7 (1950): 358ff.; R. H. Fuller, "The Virgin Birth: Historical Fact or Kerygmatic Truth?" *Biblical Research* I (1956): 1ff.

[109] Gal 4:4. See F. V. Filson, *A New Testament History*, (1964), pp. 86f.

part **2**

EARLY EXPANSION OF
CHRISTIANITY AND
THE CAREER OF PAUL

chapter thirteen

THE ENVIRONMENT
OF GENTILE CHRISTIANITY

Statue of Dionysus, from the East pediment of the Parthenon. Originally a vegetation deity, this god was known to Romans by his Greek title, Bacchus, and honored chiefly as the god of the vine. The object of worship in a mystery religion, Dionysus assured his initiates participation in his divine nature. (Rev. Dr. Raymond V. Schoder, SJ)

This painting from Herculaneum depicts priests of the Egyptian goddess Isis, an underworld deity of procreation and rebirth, performing rites in her honor. In New Testament times, Isis personified several Semitic, Greek and Roman deities. (Alinari)

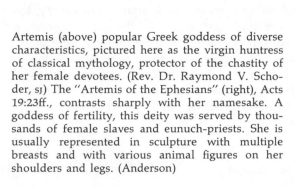

Artemis (above) popular Greek goddess of diverse characteristics, pictured here as the virgin huntress of classical mythology, protector of the chastity of her female devotees. (Rev. Dr. Raymond V. Schoder, sj) The "Artemis of the Ephesians" (right), Acts 19:23ff., contrasts sharply with her namesake. A goddess of fertility, this deity was served by thousands of female slaves and eunuch-priests. She is usually represented in sculpture with multiple breasts and with various animal figures on her shoulders and legs. (Anderson)

329

O NE Christian missionary towers above all others in the first generation because of his strategic role in transplanting the gospel of the early Palestinian Church to the great cities of the Roman Empire. He is Saul of Tarsus, better known as Paul, "bond-slave of Jesus Christ," the "Apostle to the Gentiles." The life and thought of this premier apostle now concern us. But before we consider his great achievement we must view that larger area of the world into which we are drawn when we return to the reading of Acts, and follow this with a study of the letters of Paul. The gospel was successfully transplanted in the Roman world because, we may say, the soil was prepared and the atmosphere conditioned for its rapid growth.

The most lasting effect of the conquest of Alexander was the dissemination of the Greek language and culture, and the consequent dissolution of many of the city-states and small kingdoms of Europe and western Asia. A common culture for all men was vigorously fostered in the numerous cities built by Alexander and his successors. This culture was the legacy of the golden age of Greece; yet in the process of its extension it was enriched by many Oriental contributions.[1]

The resistance to Hellenization by the Maccabees in Judea was symptomatic of a broader Oriental reaction to all Greek influences in western Asia and Egypt.[2] Yet in spite of this reaction, the mighty tide was not turned. The influence of Hellas continued to permeate the life of mankind. With the triumph of Rome, political stability made possible the flowering of a culture commonly called "Hellenistic."

The Roman genius for organization brought about the conditions for extending the Greek notion of the unity of all men. Yet with the unification of the world by Roman power, large masses of men were deprived of opportunities for participation in local government. Patriotism no longer furnished men an organizing principle for their thought and energies. Instead, they began the search for a meaningful existence in personal rather than in public affairs. The family, the trades, the professions became more important, and social life found expression in small associations of persons who shared common occupations or aspirations. Thus, as has been frequently observed, the dominant spirit of the Hellenistic Age had two components: cosmopolitanism and individualism. At first sight these components may appear contradictory. Yet the arts and sciences, the philosophies and religions of the Hellenistic Age afford evidence that they were complementary and broadly characteristic of the spirit of the times.[3]

[1] Pfeiffer, *New Testament Times*, p. 99.
[2] Ibid., p. 97.
[3] Ibid., pp. 98ff.; Riddle and Hutson, *New Testament Life and Literature*, pp. 5f., 14f.

330

Of principal interest to readers of the New Testament are the religions and philosophies of the Hellenistic Age which flourished in the regions beyond Palestine where Christian missions were begun. In this chapter the following topics will be discussed briefly: the national cults and the "mysteries" of Greece; the religion of imperial Rome; the popular appeal of the Oriental mystery religions; the widespread belief in astrology and magic; the religious interpretations of life offered by two popular "schools" of Greek philosophy; and the religions of a more speculative and mystical type attested in "the Hermetica" and in "pre-Gnostic" writings. The chapter will conclude with a brief discussion of the Jews of the Dispersion.

CULTS AND MYSTERY RELIGIONS

The Greek City-States

When the Greeks conquered the East they practiced on foreign soil some of the cults of their native city-states. With establishment of the Hellenistic cities, efforts were made to promote the worship of Zeus, Hermes, Apollo, Artemis and other nationally known deities of the Greek pantheon. Homer remained a first reading book in the schools.[4] The results, however, were meager, for the foundation of the Hellenistic kingdoms marks the twilight of the gods of Olympus. Their fate was sealed with the break-up of the Greek city-states.[5] The failure of the Olympian gods to conquer the East also resulted from the fact that the Greeks honored the gods of the vanquished countries. The foreign gods were given the names of Greek deities upon the assumption that they were the same, but the change in their names was not a change in their natures. For example, the Artemis worshiped at Ephesus was not the chaste Greek goddess but a sensuous mother diety of the mountains.[6] Early in the second century B.C. an attempt was made in Greece to revive the worship of the Homeric deities. New epiphanies and new oracles were claimed, especially of Apollo at Delphi; some new festivals were added to the traditional calendar. But the pomp and circumstance of public worship failed to disguise the loss of a living faith. When honors were accorded the Greek gods in Asia and Africa, they were mere formalities.[7]

Following the death of Alexander, a sense of insecurity was felt everywhere. The belief arose that Chance (Tyche) ruled the destinies of men. In some places, where the forms of national religion were without meaning, the Greeks personified Tyche and erected temples and statues in her honor. Tyche became the patron

[4] M. P. Nilsson, *Greek Piety* (1948). For a brief description of the cults of the Greek city-states, see S. V. McCasland, *IB*, vol. 7, pp. 88ff.

[5] The agnosticism of the fifth-century philosophers had been a strong corrosive influence, Pfeiffer, *New Testament Times*, pp. 128ff.; Nilsson, *Greek Piety*, pp. 70ff.

[6] Acts 19:23ff. At Lystra, Barnabas and Paul were worshiped as Zeus and Hermes, but to the townspeople they were not epiphanies of the Olympian gods but of local deities bearing their names, Acts 14:11ff.

[7] W. W. Tarn and G. T. Griffith, *Hellenistic Civilization* (3d ed., 1952), pp. 337f.; Pfeiffer, *New Testament Times*, p. 130.

goddess of a number of Hellenistic cities, for example, Antioch in Syria. Criticism and unbelief "had wrenched the tiller from the hands of the gods, and men were driven hither and thither at sea without a rudder, at the mercy of the waves." Tyche was the last stage in the secularizing of classical Hellenic religion.[8]

Nevertheless, one form of ancient Greek religion survived the wave of skepticism and unbelief—the "mysteries." Indeed, the spirit of the times was congenial to their revival. A *mysterion* was a sacred rite in which individuals participated by their own free choice. By means of it, initiates, called *mystai*, were brought into close relation to the deity honored. They were given a new nature, delivered from the cycle of reincarnation, and assured happiness after death. The "experience" of the *mystai* resulted either from an act done to them or by them, or from watching a sacred drama. Among the Greek mystery religions which flourished in the Hellenistic Age were the Eleusinian, the Dionysiac, and the Orphic.

The Eleusinian mysteries centered around Demeter, goddess of the field; Kore (Persephone), her daughter, the spirit of vegetation; and Hades (Pluto), god of the dead. It was believed that Hades carried Kore to the underworld for eight months of the year. The initiates of this mystery apparently believed that just as nature is reborn in the spring, so by participation in the secret rites of Eleusis, men were reborn and secured a blissful immortality.[9] Dionysus was originally a Thracian fertility god who became known as the god of wine (Bacchus). His early worshipers roamed the countryside in states of sacred intoxication, tearing living animals to pieces and eating their raw flesh. Through these wild revelries the spirit of the god, incarnate in the potency of nature's life-forces, was possessed and immortality gained. Such savage practices were no longer encouraged by the devotees of the Dionysian mysteries in New Testament times. Instead, it was taught that the meaning of the Dionysian myths had been revealed to the ancients by Orpheus. The fate of Dionysus, child of Zeus, was that he was destroyed by the Titans who, in turn, were destroyed by Zeus. Out of the ashes of the Titans man was created, who possesses both a divine and a destructively titanic nature. The soul, the divine element in man which derives from Dionysus, can be set free from its union with an inherently natural wildness only as it is liberated from the body. Orphism depicted the pleasures of the initiated and the horrible punishments of the wicked in the after life. Orphism stressed the sins and guilt of men and showed the way, through strict diets and ritual purifications, to an eternal salvation.[10]

Religion in Imperial Rome

The religion of early Rome was in many respects parallel to the polytheistic cults of the Greek city-states. Jupiter, the great god of the sky and weather, was

---

[8]Nilsson, *Greek Piety*, pp. 85f.

[9]See inscription honoring priests of Eleusinian mysteries, F. C. Grant, *Hellenistic Religion* (1953), pp. 15f. The cult spread from Eleusis to Athens and from thence to the world. Initiation was open to all classes.

[10]F. W. Beare, *IDB*, vol. 2, pp. 492f. See the Orphic texts, F. C. Grant, *Hellenistic Religion*, pp. 105ff.

worshiped with Mars, who doubled as the god of war and agriculture, and also Quirinius, a minor war god. Juno, the fertility goddess of the moon, was another local deity. Because of its central location, Rome was influenced by gods of surrounding states at an early date. From Latin neighbors came Diana, Hercules, Castor, and Pollux; from Greece, Demeter, Dionysus, Kore, Apollo, and others. With the exception of Apollo, the Greek deities were given Roman or Etruscan names.

One feature of Roman religion which distinguished it from that of ancient Greece was its priesthood. Although no priestly caste existed, the clergy were organized into a hierarchy of *collegia,* or boards. One priest, the *pontifex maximus* or chief pontiff, outranked all of his colleagues. The principal function of the priest was to see that the numerous sacrifices and other traditional rites were scrupulously performed. All right-thinking Romans believed that such observances were necessary to maintain *pax deorum* (peace with the gods).[11]

No more than the cults of the Greek city-states was the religion of early Rome able to maintain itself as a living faith after the extension of the Roman power into the Mediterranean world. The cults of the Capitoline gods lived on in the form of local patriotism, to be revived only as a means of its support. But it became evident after the Punic wars that the new world needed a religion as all-embracing as the empire itself. In place of the old state religion, imperial Rome attempted to establish the cult of its emperors. The idea of deifying men, either living or dead, was not native to Italy. It was taken over from the Greeks, who considered that a people's gratitude to heroes providing days of peace and social well-being was sufficient cause for paying them divine honors. Alexander and his successors had foreshadowed the emperor cult, but the first of the emperors, Augustus (27 B.C.–A.D. 14), established the practice when he declared the apotheosis of Julius Caesar (*Divus Iulius*) and dedicated a temple in his honor.[12]

During the reign of Caesar Augustus a deliberate effort was made to revive the old state cult and its *collegia* of priests. Although this "return to religion" had important political consequences, it did not succeed in breathing new life into the old dry bones. Instead, the Romans of the new "republic" venerated their living "savior." Augustus refused to permit Romans to worship him directly. Nevertheless, his "genius" was venerated, and the poets sang the praises of the reigning god and the dawn of the Golden Age. In the eastern provinces, temples were built in honor of Augustus and Roma and sacrifices offered to them. Herod the Great rebuilt Samaria, naming it Sebaste, the Greek equivalent of "Augustus," and erected a temple in the emperor's honor. The worship of the dead emperor, and of the "genius" of the living emperor as divine, had an important bearing upon the organization and solidarity of the Empire. The emperor cult gave to the heterogeneous Roman army a feeling of pride in the unity and greatness of the empire. Associated with the cult of the military standards, representing the

---

[11] H. J. Rose, *Religion in Greece and Rome* (1959), pp. 197ff.

[12] Antiochus IV called himself a god (see above, p. 37). He was represented on coins as the Olympian Zeus (see p. 31).

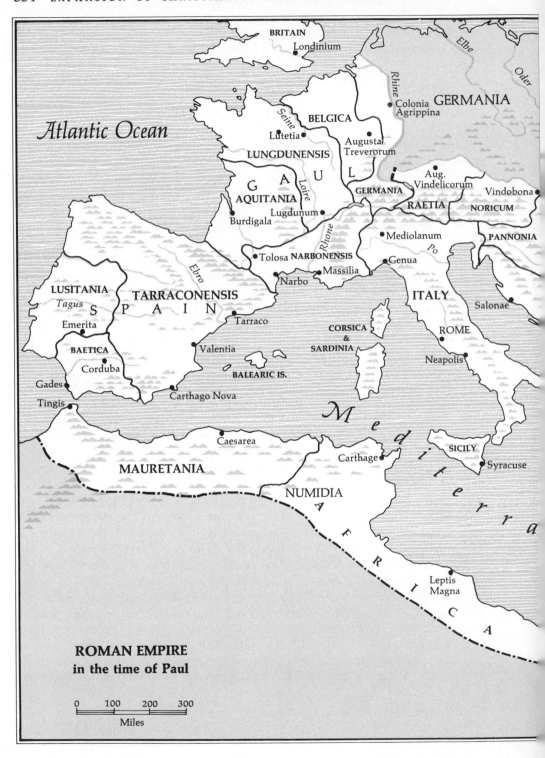

**ROMAN EMPIRE
in the time of Paul**

0   100   200   300

Miles

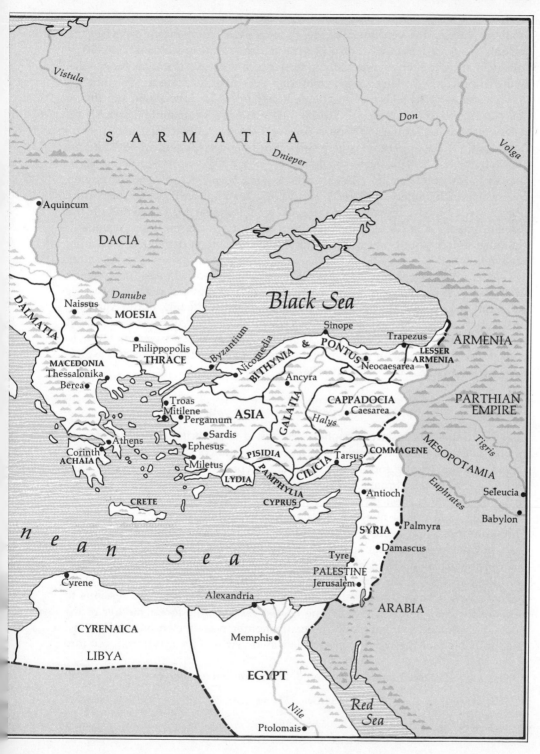

SARMATIA

Vistula

Don

Volga

Dnieper

Aquincum

DACIA

Danube

Black Sea

Naissus

MOESIA

ARMENIA

Philippopolis

THRACE

Byzantium

Sinope

Trapezus

LESSER
ARMENIA

Nicomedia

BITHYNIA &

PONTUS

Neocaesarea

MACEDONIA

Thessalonika

Bérea

Ancyra

PARTHIAN
EMPIRE

Troas

Mitilene

Pergamum

ASIA

GALATIA

CAPPADOCIA

Caesarea

Halys

MESOPOTAMIA

Sardis

Tigris

Athens

Ephesus

PISIDIA

Tarsus

COMMAGENE

Seleucia

Corinth

ACHAIA

Miletus

LYDIA

PAMPHYLIA

CILICIA

Euphrates

Babylon

CYPRUS

Antioch

CRETE

SYRIA

Palmyra

n e a n   S e a

Tyre

Damascus

PALESTINE

Jerusalem

Cyrene

Alexandria

ARABIA

CYRENAICA

LIBYA

Memphis

EGYPT

Nile

Red
Sea

Ptolomais

soldierly virtues, the veneration of the emperor was an important aspect of the legion's *disciplina Romana*.[13] It also became an important touchstone of political loyalty of subject peoples, especially in the eastern provinces. Among the peoples of the empire only the Jews were exempt from the cult of the state and its emperor. Anyone refusing to take part in simple ceremonies acknowledging the divine source of the benefits of the *pax Romana* was suspected of revolutionary activity. It was inevitable that tension should develop between Christianity and imperial Rome as the Church became largely Gentile in membership and was recognized as a religious society distinct from Judaism. To the representatives of the state, the Christian proclamation, "Jesus Christ is Lord," easily might be considered a treasonable statement. To Christian ears, the assumption by emperors of the titles "Son of God," "Savior," and "Lord" would appear blasphemous. Of the Roman emperors in New Testament times, Domitian was the most zealous in claiming divinity, but Gaius Caligula and Nero also sought divine honors during their reigns.[14]

Like all religions constructed by politicians, the emperor cult had fundamental weaknesses. It lacked all genuine religious content. It afforded no satisfactory substitute for a personal religion or philosophy.[15] Before the time of the Augustan Restoration, mystery religions from Anatolia, Syria, and Egypt had been brought to Rome. The policies of Augustus and those of his successors were not able to curb the popular appeal of these foreign cults that satisfied the needs and aspirations of the masses for a personal religion.

The Popular Appeal of Oriental Mystery Religions

Belief in divinely inspired prophetesses, called *sibyls*, originated in Greece, as did the idea that the state should collect, preserve, and consult these oracles upon whose fulfillment the fortunes of the state depended. Sibylline Books were introduced into Italy through Greek colonizers and provided the means of access to Rome for the earliest mysteries. Following a famine in the fifth century B.C., a Sibylline oracle was obeyed and a temple was built in Rome to Demeter, Dionysus, and Kore. In 205 B.C., after the long years of war with Hannibal, Rome was showered with volcanic stones on several occasions. Hannibal was no longer a serious menace, but Romans grew panicky and the Sibylline oracles were again consulted. It was learned that the enemy would not be defeated unless a Phrygian goddess was brought to Rome. Accordingly, a deputation went to Pessinus to procure the holy stone of Cybele, the *Mater Deum Magna* (great mother of the gods). Subsequently, a temple to the earth-mother was erected on the Palatine. It is probable that the worship of Cybele's lover, Attis, was also introduced into Rome at this time.

The Cybele-Attis mysteries centered in an annual spring festival. The cult

[13] Nilsson, *Greek Piety*, pp. 277f. C. D. Morrison, *The Powers That Be* (1960) pp. 83ff., 131ff. [hereafter, *Powers*].

[14] See below, pp. 477ff., 522, 556.

[15] It was even deficient as a social force; see Nilsson, *Greek Piety*, p. 178.

legend told of the love of Cybele for Attis. When the youth became unfaithful, the goddess drove him mad. He emasculated himself under a pine tree and died. The belief in the resurrection of Attis to become god of the underworld is implicit in the ritual. Like the Greek Eleusinian mystery, this Anatolian cult was related to the annual death and resurrection of vegetation. In Phrygia the spring festival was accompanied by wild orgies. Some of the male worshipers imitated Attis and sacrificed their virility to the gods, doubtless seeking to stimulate Cybele for her unending task of reproduction. The eunuchs who survived became priests of Cybele and wore women's clothing. Among Greeks and Romans they were known as "Galli."[16]

Having obeyed the divine command to receive the Great Mother, the Romans "took measures to keep her respectable and Roman."[17] There was a repugnance for the eunuch priests and their dress, and Roman youths were not allowed to become Galli. But the annual festivals continued and during the reign of Claudius (A.D. 41–54) they were made more elaborate and given official sanction. In Rome, Attis was a more popular god than Cybele because he promised his devotees life after death and deliverance from subjection to sensual appetites. Besides the public rites, the cult of Cybele–Attis probably had a number of mystic sacraments. A blood-bath of initiation, called the *taurobolium*, is known from a number of inscriptions. In this ceremony the devotee descended into a pit covered with a grate. Onto the grate was led a bull or a ram, adorned with garlands of flowers. The beast was mortally stabbed by the priest and the devotee drenched with its blood. From the pit the initiate emerged convinced that his sins had been washed away and that he was reborn forever. He was venerated by the crowds as one who had acquired something of the nature and power of deity.[18]

Egypt's contribution to the Greco–Roman mysteries was the cult of the god Osiris; his consort, Isis; and their son, Horus (or Anubis?). Accounts of the Osiris myth make it clear that the Egyptians worshiped a dying and rising god who offered men the hope of a happy immortality. Under the dynasty of Ptolemies, the mysteries of Osiris assumed a less markedly national character, and spread throughout the Greek world and thence to Italy. The Greeks at Alexandria called their god Sarapis (Osiris–Hapi: Gr. *Osorapis*) and gave him the attributes of Zeus, Hades, and other Greek deities. They hoped to unite in common worship the two races inhabiting the Ptolemaic kingdom.

When the worship of Sarapis–Isis first reached beyond Alexandria, it was confined to private associations, but later the cult was officially established in such prominent Greek cities as Athens, Thessalonica, and Delos. It is thought that the mystery became established at Rome during the time of Sulla (80 B.C.).

[16]See Lucian's description of the spring festival in F. C. Grant, *Hellenistic Religion*, pp. 116ff.; F. V. M. Cumont, *The Oriental Religions in Roman Paganism* (1911), pp. 46ff. [hereafter, *Oriental Religions*]; Pfeiffer, *New Testament Times*, pp. 149ff.

[17]Rose, *Religion in Greece and Rome*, pp. 273f.

[18]The *taurobolium* was also used for the consecration of priests. See the description of the rite, Barrett, *Background*, pp. 96f. The fullest account of the Osiris myth is given in Plutarch's *Iside et Osiride*, secs. 12–20, summarized in Pfeiffer, *New Testament Times*, pp. 141ff.

There it continued to win followers in spite of the repeated attempts on the part of the government to suppress it. Chapels to the Egyptian gods were torn down four times in the decade 58–48 B.C. but the cult was not to be denied. At last the mad emperor, Caligula, put up a temple to Isis in the Campus Martius (ca. A.D. 38). From this time the Egyptian mystery enjoyed the favor of the emperors.

The action of Caligula calls attention to the fact that Isis was often worshiped apart from the other Egyptian deities. While Sarapis was never invoked without Isis, she was often invoked alone. Indeed, of all the pagan deities of the Greco-Roman world, Isis was probably the greatest. She became identified with every goddess; yet the Lady of the Myriad Names was more than a composite deity. She had little in common with Diana the virgin huntress, as cold as her own moon; still less with Aphrodite, or with Athena, a man's goddess. Isis was a friend of women and the greatest of them all; she was a wife and mother who had suffered and who understood. It was no small part of the success of the Sarapis–Isis cult that for the first time in the pagan world one-half of the race had a friend in the court of heaven.[19]

There were many features which added to the popularity of this Egyptian mystery. The twice-daily sacrifices, the penitential practices, the continual round of duties performed by the black-stoled priests in the service of Isis impressed upon observers the reality of ever-present deities, ready and willing to enter into commerce with persons in need. Public ceremonies were regularly scheduled and at such times the image of Isis was displayed. The November festival was the passion and resurrection of Osiris. In the spring the festival of the launching of the symbolic ship of the goddess was held, at which time a gorgeous procession made its way from the temple to the seashore.[20]

We can know what the cult of Isis meant to individuals because of the second-century romance by Apuleius, *Metamorphoses* (which is known, since Augustine, as *The Golden Ass*). It is the story of a young nobleman named Lucius who is led by his adventures into careless dabbling in magic. As a result he is changed into the shape of an ass. After he has undergone many fantastic adventures, Isis appears to him in a dream, reveals her many divine names and powers, and speaks of her festival on the morrow. Lucius is told to approach the procession and take a rose from the priest's hand and eat it. Thus he will be rid of his animal nature. Isis claims his devotion and promises

> ". . . Your life will be happy, nay glorious under my protection . . . And if by acts of diligent obedience, faithful devotion, and steadfast self-discipline you deserve well of my godhead, you shall know that I and I alone have the power to prolong your life beyond the bounds appointed by your fate."[21]

Lucius obeys the command of Isis, and later becomes initiated into her mysteries. He is not permitted to divulge the cultic secrets but his hints are revealing:

[19]"Isis was a phenomenon which had not appeared in the Mediterranean world in historical times, but having once appeared has never since quitted it; she was the woman's goddess," Tarn and Griffith, *Hellenistic Civilization*, p. 359.

[20]Apuleius, *Metamorphoses*, XI. 8ff.

[21]Ibid. Quoted from A. D. Nock, *Conversion* (1933), p. 139. For excerpts from the *Metamorphoses*, describing the initiations of Lucius, see F. C. Grant, *Hellenistic Religion*, pp. 136ff.

I visited the bounds of death; I tread Proserpina's threshold; I passed through all the elements and returned. It was midnight, but I saw the sun radiant with bright light. I came into the very presence of the gods below and the gods above and I adored them face to face. . . .[22]

On the morning following these nocturnal revelations, Lucius was exhibited to a congregation of people in the dress of a sun god. Later on, Lucius passed through two other initiations and became a minor priest of Isis at Rome.

Brief notice should be taken of the cult of Mithra, a religion which spread with amazing rapidity throughout the Roman army and became, during the third century, a strong competitor of Christianity. One cannot appreciate the power attained by the mysteries of Mithra unless one learns of their ancient origin among the Aryans and of their development as a cultural export of Persia after Alexander's conquest. We must content ourselves here with a description of the mysteries of Mithra in the Roman Empire.[23]

According to the cult legend, the god Mithra had been born from a rock. After various exploits he caught and tamed a huge bull created by the Persian high god, Ahura–Mazda. Later Mithra slew this bull and from it there sprang the plants and animals useful to mankind. In early representations, Mithra is associated with the sun god, feasting with him and riding in his chariot. Indeed, by the time Mithra reached Rome in the first century B.C. he had become a solar deity. In later inscriptions he is invoked as *deus Sol invictus Mithras* (the unconquerable sun-god Mithra).[24] His birthday was celebrated when the sun, passing the winter solstice, began its movements toward its summer position, a date fixed at December 25.[25] Among his worshipers Mithra was exalted as a righteous and holy god, a lover of truth and a hater of deceit, the guardian of contracts and the inviolability of oaths.

The shrine of the Mithra cult, of which there are many ancient remains, consisted of a pillared vestibule which led to an underground grotto. In this dark cave there stood stone benches alongside walls and two altars in the center. On the back wall facing the entrance was a bas-relief of Mithra the bull-slayer. It is probable that these chapels were not used for public worship but for the initiation of men into the sacred mysteries. Only men were allowed to be devotees of Mithra. These passed through seven ascending stages of initiation, probably corresponding to the popular belief that the soul passed through seven planetary spheres on its way to the abode of the blest. The object of the initiatory rites was the progressive attainment of moral purity.[26] The initiate was promised eternal life in the general resurrection at the end of history, and an escape from the great conflagration which would finally consume all demonic powers and evil-doers.

[22] Nock, *Conversion*, p. 145. See A. J. Festugiere, *Personal Religion among the Greeks* (1954), pp. 68ff.
[23] See Cumont, *Oriental Religions*, pp. 142ff.; Pfeiffer, *New Testament Times*, pp. 161ff.
[24] Along with Cybele, Attis, and other gods; see F. C. Grant, *Hellenistic Religion*, p. 147.
[25] See "Origin of Christmas," Cullmann, *The Early Church*, pp. 21ff.
[26] The emperor Julian wrote of "the commandments" which Mithra taught his followers, but no record of the moral code of Mithraism has been preserved. It probably contained the soldierly virtues.

THE WIDESPREAD BELIEF IN ASTROLOGY AND MAGIC

We have already noted that when the small "worlds" of the Greek and Roman city-states were shattered by the political changes of the Hellenistic Age, the fear arose that human life was a plaything of blind Tyche or Fortuna (Lat. fortune). Many men turned to astrology in the hope of understanding the universe, and of finding security in it. Astrology is based on belief that the stars influence life on the earth and determine the fate of every man. The popular astrology of New Testament times was the adaptation by Greek science of ancient Babylonian observations and calculations concerning the movements of the heavenly bodies.

The logical implication of astrology is atheism, since belief that the cosmos is a giant, clocklike mechanism eliminates the possibility of interference by the gods. This conclusion was drawn by a few persons, notably by the avid student of astrology Emperor Tiberius, who reigned during Jesus' Ministry. In subsequent sections we shall see that Stoic philosophers and such religious mystics as the writers of the Hermetica had their own ways of coming to terms with astrological fatalism. But, for the masses, the belief in blind, merciless fate drove men into the arms of the priests of the mystery cults. The stars and other planetary "powers" were gods or demons (*daimones*) who could be appeased by sacrifices and prayers, or mastered by magical means. Some of the mystery religions readily embraced the beliefs of astrology and offered freedom from the tyranny of the *stoicheia* (elemental spirits of the universe). Thus Mithra, a solar deity, guided the souls of men through the planetary spheres; Attis was called "the shepherd of the bright stars"; and men like Lucius became convinced that Isis was the mistress over fate, able to prolong life beyond its appointed bounds.

Superstition and magic are weeds which grow in the same soil as religion. It is evident from our sources that many persons in the Roman Empire sought by magical means to overcome the demons and the fatalism of astrology. Magic was made a substitute for religion, as well as its adjunct. In Rome's golden age, Augustus sought to curb the traffic in sorcery and magical materials, as had the Athenians in the classical period of Greece, but with less success. The popular demand for love potions, conjurations, "the evil eye," amulets, statuettes of gods, and so on netted fabulous profits for businessmen. Prevalent also was belief in oracles, and in dreams and omens.[27]

THE POPULAR "SCHOOLS" OF HELLENISTIC PHILOSOPHY

Two philosophies arose at the beginning of the Hellenistic Age and were dominant in the period of Christian origins, Epicureanism and Stoicism. Both of these schools appealed to the educated who had lost faith in the traditional gods

---

[27] For a selection of magical papyri, see F. C. Grant, *Ancient Roman Religion* (1957), pp. 238ff.; Nilsson, *Greek Piety*, pp. 161ff.; R. Bultmann, *Primitive Christianity*, trans. R. H. Fuller (1956), pp. 146ff.; Morrison, *Powers*, pp. 75ff.

and were seeking some rational understanding of the nature of man and the world as an alternative to skepticism.

While Alexander's generals were fighting over political control of the world, a philosopher named Epicurus (342–270 B.C.) taught at Athens. His understanding of the physical world was based upon the theories of Democritus. Nothing exists except atoms moving downward in empty space. The human being is thus a chance compound of atoms which at death dissipate "like smoke." It is somewhat surprising that Epicurus believed in the existence of the gods. Yet he held that men could contemplate their blissful existence with a religious emotion devoid of fear and selfishness, for the gods have neither the power nor the interest to hurt or help human beings. They dwell in the empty spaces between the stream of atoms, far removed from the world. They know no trouble and give none to anyone else. In his ethical teaching, Epicurus affirmed that pleasure is the fulfillment of life. The good man has the capacity to enjoy pleasure and is untroubled by pain or fear.

The philosopher's mission was to deliver men from their dread of life and of death. Since Epicurus believed that the popular forms of religion encouraged fear of the gods and of what comes after death, he became the foe of the traditional cults. The great poem of Lucretius, *De Rerum Natura*, composed early in the first century B.C., provides the fullest exposition of the teachings of Epicurus and also reveals the ecstasy of a man delivered from dread of life's mysteries.[28] Yet the influence of Epicurus was not extensive. Stoicism offered a more satisfactory solution to the theoretical and practical problems of men in the Greco-Roman world. It therefore became "the noblest and most influential religion for intellectuals." Through its street preachers, Stoicism also became a popular religious philosophy.[29]

The founder of Stoicism was Zeno (336–263 B.C.), a contemporary in Athens of Epicurus. He taught in the "painted porch" (*stoa*) from which his philosophy derived its name. Two of Zeno's pupils, Cleanthes and Chrysippus, elaborated his system. A brilliant representative of Stoicism in the second century B.C. was Posidonius, the teacher of Cicero. During this century the religious mysticism latent in Stoic philosophy was developed under the influence of the contemporary revival of Platonism. Also the traditional polytheistic myths were allegorized to accommodate them to Stoic doctrines. After Posidonius, the ethics of Stoicism were emphasized by Seneca and Epictetus and the Stoic emperor Marcus Aurelius.[30]

The Stoics taught that ultimate reality is a rational *pneuma* (breath, or spirit). The universe is perpetually passing to and from alternative states: God in his proper being, the *Logos* (Pure Reason) or the Divine Fire; and the world in its

[28] Cited in Barrett, *Background*, pp. 72ff. See Pfeiffer, *New Testament Times*, p. 119.

[29] Pfeiffer, p. 140ff.; Bultmann, *Primitive Christianity*, pp. 135ff.; E. Bevan, *Later Greek Religion* (1950), pp. 1ff., 79f., 102ff.

[30] Seneca (A.D. 4–65); Epictetus (60–110); Marcus Aurelius (121–180). The writings of Zeno's earliest pupils have perished save for a few fragments quoted by other writers (see Barrett, *Background*, pp. 61ff.).

plurality of *spermatikoi Logoi* (seminal rational forms), into which the one Logos is distributed as sparks of the Divine Fire. "The whole of reality," wrote Chrysippus, "forms a unity because a breath permeates it throughout, and by it the universe is held together and stays together and forms an organic unity."[31]

As a consequence of this world view, the Stoic believed that everything that happens to men is in accordance with necessity, or "the providence which pervades the universe." This belief brought to the Stoic no terrors; he held in religious awe the universal law of Nature:

> Lead me, O Zeus, and thou, O fate,
> To the goal which you have ordained for me.
> I will follow without shrinking. Were I a miscreant,
> And would not follow, I should have to nonetheless.[32]

Since man in his essence is a spark of the divine, to live according to reason is "to live according to Nature" and to find true happiness. To attain this virtue requires constant self-examination and self-restraint. The "wise man" seeks to be wholly dependent upon Nature and completely independent of externals, as Epictetus wrote:

> I am free, I am a friend of God to render him willing obedience. Of all else, I may set store by nothing—neither by my own body, nor possession, nor office, nor good report, nor, in a word, anything else.[33]

The Stoic ideal was *apatheia* (freedom from all emotion). Reason must be the autocrat over the passions. An unfortunate person should be helped, the evil should be punished, without empathy.

It is easy to see that this ideal of self-sufficiency could lead to an individualistic and negative ethic. Happiness could be conceived as the withdrawal into oneself, the achievement of an inner serenity unaffected by the course of events in society. But Stoicism did not ordinarily lead to social indifference. It was believed that man is destined by nature for society and given duties to fulfill. Indeed, all beings endowed with reason constitute a single society in which reason is law.[34] Stoicism provided a theoretical basis for self-sufficiency and for universal brotherhood, thus fulfilling two essential aspirations of the uprooted individuals of the Hellenistic Age.

While the pantheistic world view of Stoicism differed widely from the polytheism of the popular cults, the Stoics did not war against the latter. Stoic doctrine was compatible with belief in the multiplicity of gods. The supreme god, the Divine Fire (habitually referred to by the traditional name, Zeus) was one; yet other reasonable beings besides men existed. The Stoics followed the Platonists in designating such beings greater than men "demons." These inhabited the ether

---

[31] Quoted in Bultmann, *Primitive Christianity*, p. 135.

[32] Ibid., p. 139, attributed to Cleanthes.

[33] *Discourses* IV. 3.9ff. See excerpts from the *Discourses* in Barrett, *Background*, pp. 66ff.

[34] ". . . the *Logos* which commands us what to do and what not to do is common. If this is so, then there is likewise a law in common. If this is so, we are fellow-citizens, and if so we are members of the same community . . . a single state." Marcus Aurelius, *Meditations*, IV. 4.

and were invisible. Stoics did not accept the popular mythologies in the literal sense but, according to Posidonius, even the obscenities in these myths could be explained as figurative expressions of truths taught plainly in Stoicism. Since the Stoics believed that man was by nature akin to God, the ceremonies of cultic religion had no significance. Prayer was the communion of the mind with God; whoever imitates God—that is, who lives according to Nature—has adequately worshiped him.[35] Nevertheless, the Stoics offered a rational defense of the value for society of the traditional religions, and many of them found expression for their religious aspirations in the popular cults. On the question of the survival of the soul, the Stoics were not fully agreed. Some denied personal immortality; others held that some souls survived the periodic world conflagrations wherein men and demons were reabsorbed into the Divine Fire. According to Stoic theory, Zeus alone was imperishable.

At the time of Christian origins, the Stoic platform extended from the classroom into the market place. Stoic preachers, like the early Christian missionaries, visited the teeming cities of the empire taking their message to all classes of men. The "soapbox" speeches of the Stoics gave rise to a new type of literature called the *diatribe* (conversation-discourse).[36]

MYSTICAL RELIGIONS OF THE GRECO-ROMAN WORLD

In its broadest sense, *mysticism* defines a tendency in all religions. But as ordinarily used by historians, mysticism describes the religion of persons who believe that they have experienced a direct knowledge of and communion with the divine. In this *unio mystica* the spirit of man is joined with the divine spirit and is set free from the limitations of mortality. Such an experience may be brief or prolonged, but in any case it transcends all ordinary conditions of human consciousness. The sensations of the mystic may result from the contemplation of some natural phenomena, but ordinarily they are thought to arise from supernatural revelation or illumination. The mystical type of religion discussed in this section is sometimes classed among the "mysteries," but it may be distinguished from the latter by its lack of dependence upon cultic rites. The only kind of initiation which these mystics recognized was the purely spiritual initiation into the truth about God, the cosmos, and man's nature revealed to the elect. From man's side, this truth could be gained only through the discipline of meditation.

There were intellectuals of the empire who found no lasting satisfaction in the popular philosophies and eventually turned to mystical or else to occult beliefs. The god of the Stoic, "being immanent in everything, satisfied to some extent

[35] Ibid., IX. 40. According to theory the Stoic god is hardly personal, yet in practice the Stoic often felt towards the encompassing Logos as towards a Person, a Father to be obeyed, to whom gratitude and praise could be offered. See Bevan, *Later Greek Religion*, pp. 14, 35, 106ff.

[36] Pfeiffer cites an excellent example in Horace, *Satires*, II. 3. Imitations of the diatribe, which echo Stoic themes, are found in the Hellenistic-Jewish writings, Wisd. of Sol. and 4 Macc.: Pfeiffer, *New Testament Times*, p. 143.

the mystical seeking of unity with the All . . . but the mystic demanded not only unity with God but also that he should be exalted. . . ." [37] God must be more than Reason or Spirit immanent in the world; he must be their transcendent Cause. It was under the pressure of this need that in the second century B.C. men were attracted to the mystical (or Pythagorean) element in Plato's philosophy. Plato's mysticism was fused with Stoicism, as in the teaching of the Stoic Posidonius, or else Platonism was maintained as a system tinged with Stoic ideas.[38] In New Testament times the mystical longings of many persons burst the bounds of rational thought and found personal satisfaction not in speculation but in an experience of divine illumination.

This is evidenced by the popularity of "the Hermetica," an extensive body of writings which has survived from the second and third centuries A.D. Some tractates belonging to this literature are dated in the first century. Thus it is possible that Hermetic teaching was known in New Testament times. The Hermetica are monuments to the cross-fertilization of Greek and Oriental thought which was characteristic of the Near East in Hellenistic and Roman periods. The Hermetic tractates are in the form of dialogues containing the communications of the god Hermes "Trismegistus" (thrice-greatest) to his sons, Tat and Asklepius.[39] The writers of the Hermetica probably did not form a "school," and their books were not the sacred canon of a "church." At the same time, small associations of mystics may have cultivated this Hermetic lore.

The doctrines of the Hermetica cannot be reduced to a consistent pattern of thought. Nevertheless, a Platonic–Stoic world view and a common religious spirit are manifest in them all. The Hermetists believed in one God, maker and father of the universe, and that knowledge of God provided the only way of man's salvation. God demands from men no cultic ceremonies. "The service of God is one thing alone, to refrain from evil." [40] This ethical demand concentrated upon personal purification and detachment from material things. The mind was set upon God and his eternity.[41] To possess this knowledge was to be a complete man and to partake of immortality:

> "O earth-born men," cries the prophet in the first Hermetic tractate, "why have you given yourselves over to death, when you have the right to partake of immortality? Repent, you who have made error your fellow-traveler and ignorance your consort. Depart from that light which is darkness! Leave corruption and partake of immortality!" [42]

[37] Nilsson, *Greek Piety*, pp. 126f.

[38] The amalgam of Platonic and Stoic ideas produced an *organon* for many writers of the Greco-Roman world who attempted a rational justification for religion. Bevan, *Later Greek Religion*, pp. xxvi f. See Festugiere, *Personal Religion among the Greeks*, pp. 123ff., for a description of this world view so congenial to the mystics' temperament.

[39] The Hermetists while writing in Greek claimed to be translating ancient books of the Egyptians. Hermes is the Greek equivalent of the Egyptian god, Thoth, the inventor of writing, the first master of wisdom. The epithet "thrice-greatest" is an Egyptian formula often applied to the gods.

[40] *Corpus Hermeticum*, X. 15 [hereafter, *C.H.*].

[41] C. H. Dodd, *The Interpretation of the Fourth Gospel* (1953), pp. 13f. [hereafter, *Fourth Gospel*].

[42] *C.H.*, I. 28.

According to the Hermetica, knowledge of the invisible and visible world, and of man's nature and destiny, has saving power. But this knowledge is not considered the product of rational observation or speculation. The writers believed that they were transmitting revelation and that the practical object of all knowledge is a vision of God. God wills to be known, and to know him is life eternal.

In the thirteenth tractate, the Hermetists' doctrine of regeneration is set forth. While waiting upon God, Hermes directs the process by which Tat passes through the experience of rebirth. Tat is required to discipline his mind and will, to renounce "the irrational torments of matter" inherent in his material body, so that the essential man in him can be liberated. And then follows a period of silence when Hermes and Tat wait upon "the powers of God" to possess Tat's nature and to expel the "torments." After the declaration by Hermes that Tat has been "deified by generation," Tat cries:

> "Father . . . I perceive things now not with bodily eyesight, but with the mystical faculty which the Powers have given me! I am in heaven, and on earth, in water and in air; I am in animals, in plants; I am a babe in the womb, and one that is not yet conceived, and one that has been born; I am present everywhere."

Tat is assured that he has "become a god and a child of One." After singing the hymn of rebirth, Hermes warns Tat not to divulge the mystery, and declares: "Now you know with your mind both yourself and our Father."[43]

THE RISE OF GNOSTICISM

The terms *gnostic* and *gnosticism* are used by modern writers in a bewildering variety of ways. Etymologically, the terms derive from *gnosis*, the Greek word for "knowledge." Through long usage among historians, "Gnostic" became a label for a large and somewhat amorphous group of speculative theological systems of the second century A.D. described by Justin Martyr and Irenaeus, and later by Hippolytus and others, in their refutations of heresies. Some scholars insist that the use of the terms should be limited to these Christian heresiologies.[44] But there are others who bring forward evidence to support the hypothesis that Gnosticism developed as a movement or way of thinking independent of Christianity, paralleling and probably antedating the latter's origin. This proto-Gnosticism, so-called, found expression in a great variety of writings ranging from serious philosophical discourse to wild speculative teachings based on astrological and magical lore. Yet within a rich profusion of forms one is able to trace a cluster

---

[43] Dodd, *Fourth Gospel*, pp. 44ff. Tractate 13 is one of the later Hermetic writings, and the possibility of Christian influence cannot be denied. Nevertheless, the substance of its teaching can be documented from other tractates which reveal no Christian influence.

[44] R. P. Casey, "Gnosis, Gnosticism and the New Testament," in Davies and Daube, *Background*, pp. 42ff.; J. Munck, "The New Testament and Gnosticism," in W. Klassen and G. F. Snyder, eds., *Current Issues in New Testament Interpretation* (1962), pp. 224ff. [hereafter, *Current Issues*].

of motifs, which has affinities with second-century, classical Gnosticism, and the term *gnostic* may be appropriately used in a broader sense.[45]

The origin of Gnostic motifs is a subject of vigorous debate. But it is widely held that a Gnostic movement absorbed features from Judaism before its interaction with Christianity. Conversely, the writings of several Jewish apologists and sectarian groups reflect Gnosticising tendencies. Perhaps it is a sound assumption to explain the rise of Gnosticism as a syncretistic phenomenon, like so many popular religions and philosophies of the Hellenistic Age, a fusion of Greek and Oriental thought.

After contact with Christianity, Gnosticism gathered momentum, and there arose "that rank growth of Christian, or semi-Christian and quasi-Christian systems" which are derided, and in some measure described, by the second-century Christian apologists.[46] It is a plausible but controversial theory that in the early period of Christianity's development Gnostic teachings were tolerated and that a mutual interpenetration of thought ensued; but that during the postapostolic age resistance and rejection set in. In this book the earliest manifestation of Gnostic ways of thought—pagan, Jewish, Christian—will be termed *pre-Gnostic* to distinguish these ideas or motifs from the Gnostic systems of theology attributed to teachers within, or on the fringe of, the Christian Church in the second century and later.[47]

Reconstructions of pre-Gnosticism inevitably contain speculative features. Sources earlier than Christian writings are meager in the extreme, and the problem of methodology is an acute one. Some scholars believe it is possible to work backward from late sources, some of which date from the fifth or sixth centuries A.D. They have been provided a wealth of new and earlier material in the Nag-Hammadi discoveries, which preserve approximately a thousand pages of original Gnostic writing containing ideas similar to those attacked by Irenaeus and others, and numerous variations thereof.[48] By abstracting from the known sources of developed Gnostic systems some common and interrelated themes, these scholars have attempted to recover modes of thought important to several New Testament writers, or at least to various persons and groups with whom New Testament writers interacted.

The constructive method described above is not inhibited by chronology and "has the advantage of presenting what early Gnostics may well have thought."[49] Nevertheless such synthetic abstractions should not be mistaken for the recovery of pre-Christian "sources." The problem for the interpreter is "to avoid reading back into first-century terminology the associations and connotations which that terminology does have in the second century," and at the same time to recognize,

[45]Bultmann, *Primitive Christianity*, pp. 162ff.; H. Jonas, *Gnostic Religion* (1958); R. M. Grant, "Gnosticism," *IDB*, vol. 2, p. 404.

[46]Dodd, *Fourth Gospel*, p. 101; Van Unnik, *Newly Discovered Gnostic Writings*, pp. 28ff.

[47]For the distinction commonly drawn between the terms *pre-Gnostic* and *proto-Gnostic*, see R. McL. Wilson, *Gnosis and the New Testament* (1968), pp. 16ff. [hereafter, *Gnosis*].

[48]Van Unnik, *Newly Discovered Gnostic Writings*, pp. 7ff.

[49]R. M. Grant, *IDB*, vol. 2, p. 404.

already in the first century "the emergence in embryonic form of incipient Gnostic systems which only come to full development later."[50] Because of the dangers of this method other scholars "refuse to admit that later developments can explain what earlier writers had in mind."[51]

The following tentative description attempts to set forth some of the motifs present in pre-Gnosticism. It must not be supposed that this basic pattern was everywhere explicit, or indeed found in any one document in this simple form. The principal characteristic of the pre-Gnostic world view is its radical dualism between the visible and invisible worlds. Ultimate reality—God, the Good, the Unknown Father—is supramundane and absolutely alien to anything human. Indeed, knowledge of this invisible reality cannot be attained by the mind of man unaided; it derives from supernatural revelation. Even so, knowledge thus given can only be expressed in negative terms. Over against God are other orders of being, a spin-off of the divine nature, represented perhaps as the creation of lower powers, who are termed demons, elemental spirits, and the like. At any rate, the imperfect world of man is dominated by these lesser powers; man's home is the innermost dungeon of the domain governed by these world rulers. Around and above man's world is a system of spheres or aeons—the *pleroma* (fullness)—which is the abode of the invisible spirits.

By his birth man belongs to the lowest order of beings. Yet the innate feeling in man, or in some men, that man is a prisoner in this world and under a fateful, destructive tyranny, indicates a primordial relation to the invisible world. In man's body, or in the bodies of elect men, a divine spark which is immortal is lodged. The liberation of this spark or spirit is possible through *gnosis*, that "knowledge" of the divine mysteries reserved for the initiated. The goal of Gnostic teaching is therefore the release of the inner life in man that he may participate in the life of the invisible, eternal world—the realm to which he belongs, from which he has fallen—and thus realize his true destiny. *Knowledge is power.* This is the faith of the Gnostic teacher. "He who knows what he is and whence he is can find his way home. He who knows the nature of the governing world and its governing powers can overcome these powers."[52]

One of the most controversial aspects of research concerning ideas intrinsically pre-Gnostic is the postulation of a redeemer myth. In numerous classical Gnostic systems it was taught that a redeemer descended to earth to impart knowledge about the unknown God and the divine spark in man. Having brought to men redemption by this *gnosis*, he ascended to the realms above. The question is: Did this myth of the Gnostic redeemer originate in Eastern antiquity and, in the course of time, influence Jewish, Christian, and pagan thinkers of the first and second centuries; or was the Gnostic redeemer myth a culmination of a long process of development which derived its principal content from Adamic speculation in Judaism or from Christian messianism or both? In several ancient myths there

[50]R. McL. Wilson, *Gnosis*, p. 23.
[51]R. M. Grant, *IDB*, vol. 2, p. 404.
[52]Dodd, *Fourth Gospel*, p. 113; Van Unnik, *Newly Discovered Gnostic Writings*, pp. 21f.

appear ideas of a Heavenly or Primal Man imprisoned in the material world and who, upon his release and ascension, left behind something of his nature to be recovered. But it is a broad leap of the imagination to assume that such pre-Christian ideas conveyed the full implications of the alleged Gnostic redeemer myth which, according to some, influenced the Christology of the writers of some New Testament books, e.g., Ephesians and the Fourth Gospel.[53]

The objectives of pre-Gnostic teachers were not unlike those of the Hermetists and the priests of the mysteries. They sought to provide the initiate a means of escape from bondage to matter, fate, and the demons, and to enable him to attain immortality. Yet pre-Gnosticism like Hermetism may be distinguished from the mysteries by the absence of public ceremonies and the cultus. Although the Hermetica are sometimes called "gnostic writings," there are reasons for distinguishing the two. In pre-Gnosticism, *gnosis* is less the knowledge of God than it is knowledge of the structure of the invisible, humanly incomprehensible, overworld. This knowledge is ordinarily conveyed in the form of myths. Myths are sparingly used in the Hermetic tractates, but the pre-Gnostic and Gnostic writings contain varied and complex mythologies. The self-centeredness of the Gnostic is another distinguishing feature. Knowledge of the invisible world is sought that men may possess self-understanding. The Hermetic writings make it clear that to "know God," to attain the vision of God, alone satisfies the needs of men. Such mystical piety is seldom found in the pre-Gnostic texts.[54]

It should be noted that the practical effects of *gnosis* upon human conduct produced two opposites: The enlightened could express their liberation of the spirit from the tomb of the body by adopting ascetic practices—dieting, sexual continence, and so on. Or the Gnostic doctrine of a radical freedom of the spirit of man from matter could lend encouragement to moral license.

JUDAISM OF THE DISPERSION

At the time of the birth of Jesus "it was not easy to find a place [in the whole world] where they [the Jews] had not penetrated, and which was not dominated by them."[55] The Jews of the Dispersion actively participated in the commercial and social life of the cities and villages of the Greco–Roman world, and sometimes enjoyed full citizenship rights. At the same time, they zealously maintained their national identity and religion and, where possible, some type of civic organization of their own. In Alexandria, for example, where the Jews were settled in unusually large numbers, theirs was a semi-autonomous community. In more sparsely settled

[53] See below, pp. 502f. and 586ff.

[54] Dodd, *Fourth Gospel*, pp. 101f.; R. M. Grant, *Gnosticism and Early Christianity* (1959), pp. 8f.; Nilsson, *Greek Piety*, p. 131. It should be noted, however, that Hermetic tracts were found at Nag–Hammadi; Van Unnik, *Newly Discovered Gnostic Writings*, p. 17; Doresse, *Secret Books*, pp. 241ff., 275ff.

[55] Strabo, quoted by Josephus, *War*, VII. iii. 3; also Philo, *Against Flaccus*, 7. (Strabo was a Roman geographer during the reign of Augustus.) For a history of Jewish settlements in foreign lands, see Pfeiffer, *New Testament Times*, pp. 166ff., 189.

areas, the synagogues served as centers of Jewish religious and political life.[56]

Like a magnetic pole, the temple in Jerusalem held the Jews of the Dispersion together. Thousands visited Jerusalem annually for the feast of the Passover, and every Jew of twenty years or older acknowledged his duty to support the temple with the yearly half-shekel tax. But more important for the preservation and propagation of Judaism abroad was the allegiance given to the commandments of the Torah. The Diaspora Jew was often ignorant of the burgeoning oral or unwritten Law formulated by the scribes of Palestine. Greek-speaking Jews could study the Septuagint, but language as well as geography rendered the teaching of the Mishnah (Hebrew) and the Gemarah (Aramaic) inaccessible to many. To the best of their ability Hellenistic Jews adhered to the precepts of the Law of Moses but generally speaking the standards of piety among Palestinian Jews were higher. At the same time there is some evidence that, under the influence of the text of the Septuagint, a tendency existed toward separation of Torah from the vital context of the covenant, and its "petrifaction" into "legalistic formulae."[57]

The sarcastic comments of such Roman writers as Horace and Juvenal indicate that the Jews impressed their Gentile neighbors by their observance of circumcision, Sabbath rest, and the avoidance of swine meat. Obedience to the ceremonial prescriptions of the Torah, together with monotheism, imageless worship, and ethical conduct were indeed the essential characteristics of Hellenistic Judaism.[58] This distinctive way of life made the Jews the object of both admiration and scorn among the Gentiles. By their belief that they were the chosen people of the one living and true God, by their ridicule of all forms of Gentile worship and idolatry, the Jews provoked some pagans to keen resentment. Yet, as we have observed, there was much in Judaism which attracted high-minded Gentiles. The synagogues of the Dispersion were sensitive to this opportunity and actively sought converts. "Propaganda and the mission to the Gentiles appear in the Septuagint as a specific task incumbent on Jewish piety." It should be recalled that the translation of the Hebrew scriptures into Greek helped bridge the "universes of discourse" separating East and West, and made effective missionary propaganda possible. As a result, proselytes and "God-fearers" were a conspicious element in the synagogues of the Dispersion.[59]

It remains for us to recognize the important consequence of this mingling of Jews and Greeks in the Greco–Roman world. It has been said that Gentiles "were attracted to Judaism first as a philosophy and later as one of the Oriental mystery cults offering eternal life."[60] Judaism is called a "philosophy" by several Roman writers, a misconception fostered by Jewish apologists. Josephus, as we have seen, identified the major Jewish parties and sects as the "four philosophies." Philo

---

[56] Where possible, separate lawcourts may have been maintained, e.g., Sardis (ca. 50 B.C.), Josephus, *Antiq.*, XIV. x. 17.

[57] H. J. Schoeps, *Paul: The Theology of the Apostle in the Light of Jewish Religious History*, trans. H. Knight (1961), pp. 29f. [hereafter, *Paul*]. It is however a common mistake, acknowledged by Schoeps, to draw sharp distinctions between Hellenistic and Palestinian Jews. See Davies, *Paul*, pp. 6f.

[58] Pfeiffer, *New Testament Times*, p. 184; Schoeps, *Paul*, p. 28.

[59] Josephus, *War*, VII. iii. 3; *Against Apion*, 2. 39. See above, pp. 50f., 108.

[60] Pfeiffer, *New Testament Times*, pp. 192ff.

of Alexandria taught that the religion of Moses was the highest philosophy. He attempted to demonstrate the correspondence between the Old Testament and the Stoicized Platonism of his time through an allegorization of the scriptures. In this he may be likened to Posidonius, who sought to show that Stoic doctrines could be found in the myths and cults of the popular religions. The books entitled the Wisdom of Solomon, the Letter of Aristeas, and 4 Maccabees are other Hellenistic–Jewish writings tinged with Platonic and Stoic doctrines. The author of 4 Maccabees adopts the form of a Stoic diatribe, and defines "wisdom" as did the Stoics "the knowledge of things human and divine, and their causes."[61] Thus effective expression is given of "the cultural pretension of Hellenistic Judaism": Wisdom–Torah is represented as the source of moral and spiritual education of humanity.[62]

The traffic was by no means one way. Evidence of the direct influence of Hellenistic Judaism upon pagan philosophers and religious writers is not plentiful. Nevertheless, the fascination of the Westerner for things Oriental, the afore-mentioned apologetic writings of the Jews, the dissemination of the Hebrew scriptures in Greek, were not without their effects beyond the limits of the synagogues. Some of the tractates of the Hermetica and pre-Gnostic texts reflect ways in which the Old Testament and ancient Jewish teachings contributed to the amalgam of Greek and Oriental thought. It may be argued that Jewish ideas were little understood by these Gnosticizing writers. But to some extent Greek and Jewish thinkers employed common speech and discourse. This fact holds obvious implications for the Gentile mission of the Christian Church.

It is easy to see how some Gentiles could have mistaken Judaism for an Oriental mystery religion. Proselyte baptism might have suggested the lustrations and baths of initiation into the mysteries. Jewish fasts and other penitential acts could have been related to the deprivation of the flesh advocated by the popular cults.

Judaism could better satisfy the religious aspirations of men in the Hellenistic Age than could the mystery religions. Judaism taught the unity of God and of the world, and satisfied the longings of individuals for a purification from the passions of the flesh and for eternal happiness. At the same time, the ceremonial and dietary laws, and the practice of circumcision, gave Judaism a national character which remained a deterrent to its missionary enterprise.[63]

[61] 1:16, Cf. *Cicero, De Officiis* 1.43; *Seneca, Epistle* 89. Lietzmann, *Beginnings,* pp. 92ff.; Bultmann, *Primitive Christianity,* pp. 94ff.
[62] Schoeps, *Paul,* pp. 30f.
[63] Pfeiffer, *New Testament Times,* pp. 193f.

chapter fourteen

THE ACTS NARRATIVE
OF PAUL'S MISSIONS

Roman pillars at Caesarea, coastal city c. 25 miles south of Mt. Carmel. Given to Herod the Great by Augustus; the official seat of the Roman procurators and residence of Herod Agrippa I. See Acts 8:40; 10:1ff; 18:22; 21:8. (Israel Government Tourist Office)

351

Antioch, on the Orontes, is the city where followers of Jesus were first called "Christians" (Acts 11:26). View of the gorge behind site of the buried, ancient city of Syria, capitol of the Seleucid Empire; one of the three greatest cities of the Greco-Roman world and an important center for the earliest Christian missions. (Rev. Dr. Raymond V. Schoder, SJ)

Ephesus: Ruins of Roman theatre and half-mile road to the harbor (now silted up). In this theatre occurred the riot, instigated by Demetrius in protest against Paul's preaching, Acts 19:23ff. Second century tradition associates John the apostle also with Ephesus. (Ewing Galloway)

The Appian Way, "queen of the long [Roman] roads" (Strabo), over which Paul travelled some 130 miles to his imprisonment at Rome (Acts 28:13f). (ENIT)

THE BOOK OF ACTS and the letters of Paul present the background and the foreground of a sketch of the Apostle's ministry. Acts traces the public events; the letters reveal the inner man, his thought and his essential teachings.[1] Accordingly, many efforts have been made to dovetail into the Acts' narrative the letters of Paul and an exposition of their contents. Aside from the fact that the chronology of Paul's letters is uncertain, it is possible that such synchronizations are more confusing than clarifying. The dramatic progress of the Acts' narrative and its impact upon the reader are greatly diminished by the interpolation of Paul's letters. If Acts is read in bits and snatches, as the background for a study of Paul's letters, the distinctive literary and theological features of the book are apt to be lost. The inevitable tendency is to interpret the language of Acts in the light of Paul's theology.[2]

A more disastrous consequence may result for the serious reader, who is alert to critical problems as they arise. The synchronization of Acts and Paul's letters becomes a task of such complexity and interest that too little thought may be given to the special contribution of each letter. Parts of Paul's letters may be dissected as containing clues to the solution of historical problems presented in Acts at the expense of appreciating the theological significance of each letter from the Apostle.

In this chapter it will be assumed that Acts 13–28 should be read as a unit. Only when it is important to acknowledge discrepancies or concurrences between events reported in Acts and by Paul will reference be made to the letters. Likewise, in the chapters on Paul's letters which follow in this book, Acts will not be referred to directly, unless items in its narrative clarify one's understanding of the Apostle's writings.

THE COMPOSITION OF ACTS 13–28

The "second half" of Luke's narrative of Christian beginnings is frequently known as the Acts of Paul. It is an appropriate title, for chapter 13 marks a decided shift in the author's interest from Peter and the Twelve to Paul. Nevertheless, the division of the book of Acts on this account is not without unfortunate results.

---

[1] A common judgment. The statement cannot stand, however, without qualifications. The most serious of these have been made by J. Knox, *Chapters in a Life of Paul* (1950), pp. 13ff. [hereafter, *Chapters*].

[2] The partitioning of Acts into halves, 1–12; 13–28, may be condemned for the same reason, for disrupting the unity of Acts, but internal considerations provide some justification for this division.

The introductory verses of chapter 13 make it quite clear that the story Luke tells is still *the story of what the risen Lord accomplished, through his chosen witnesses and by means of the Holy Spirit.*[3] Christians at Antioch were "worshiping the Lord" when they were directed by the Holy Spirit to proclaim the gospel, just as were the earliest Christians in Jerusalem. "In Jerusalem and in all Judea and Samaria" the apostles had borne their witness; now other disciples received power to proclaim the gospel "to the ends of the earth." The world mission of the Church has its origin in the divine will and prospers under the Holy Spirit's direction.[4]

Although the essential unity of Acts should not be overlooked, chapter 13 introduces a new series of events. We are told of the first extensive missionary journey undertaken by Paul, a mission which resulted in the opening of "a door of faith to the Gentiles."[5] It is also the first church-sponsored mission. Barnabas and Paul were not "free-lancing" missionaries, like Philip and the other "scattered brethren," but representatives of the congregation at Antioch. A single church stood behind the work of Barnabas and Paul, and sent them forth with fasting, prayer, and the laying on of hands.[6]

The author of Acts presents the story of Paul's missions in the form of a travel narrative. In addition to describing the chief centers of missionary activity, Luke notes the ports of embarkation (13:4, 13, and so on), landing points (13:5, 13, and so on), and other places to show the direction of the itinerary (14:24 and so on). One influential scholar has argued that this form of the narrative was determined by Luke's "travel diary." He relied on oral or written traditions in reporting the "first missionary journey"; yet he cast the whole into the form of his itinerary source, inserting numerous anecdotes and speeches. This compositional pattern was followed in the remainder of the Acts narrative, although the pattern is broken with Paul's arrest in Jerusalem. An alternative theory is that Luke composed the itinerary narrative using a firsthand account of one of Paul's companions which he edited and, by inserting "we," emphasized the eyewitness character of his source. The occasional disappearance of "we" may be due simply to Luke's desire at such places to exalt Paul.[7]

The Witness of Paul from Antioch to Rome
(An Outline of the Acts of the Apostles 13–28)

A. Mission of Barnabas and Paul to Cyprus and Galatia (the "first missionary journey"), 13:1–14:28:
  1. Commissioning of Barnabas and Paul at Antioch, 13:1–4
  2. Mission on the Isle of Cyprus, 13:5–12

---

[3] Acts 1:8.

[4] Acts 13:2,4.

[5] Acts 14:27.

[6] Acts 13:3; 14:26. The "laying on of hands" can hardly be considered the elevation of Barnabas and Paul to the rank of apostles; cf. Gal. 1:1.

[7] See Dibelius, *Studies,* pp. 5f.; W. L. Knox, *The Acts,* pp. 57f. Cf. E. Haenchen, " 'We' in Acts and the Itinerary," *Journ. for Theology and the Church,* ed. R. W. Funk, vol. 1, pp. 65ff.

3. Mission to Galatia begins, 13:13–14a
4. Paul's speech in the synagogue at Antioch of Pisidia, 13:14b–41
5. Results of this Sabbath meeting and the next, 13:42–48
6. Summary: departure from Antioch, 13:49–52
7. Summary: mission at Iconium, 14:1–7
8. Lystra: mistaken for gods, and stoned, 14:8–20a
9. Summary: preaching in Derbe, and the return journey, 14:20b–28

B. Controversy concerning the terms of salvation for Gentiles, 15:1–35:
10. Judean Christians at Antioch demand circumcision of Gentile converts, 15:1
11. Delegation to Jerusalem, 15:2–5
12. Jerusalem Conference convened, 15:6
13. Peter's speech, 15:7–11
14. Summary: the report of Barnabas and Paul, 15:12
15. James' speech, 15:13–21
16. The decree is dispatched, 15:22–31
17. Summary: instruction at Antioch, 15:32–35

C. Mission of Paul to Macedonia and Achaia (the "second missionary journey"), 15:36–18:17:
18. The altercation concerning John Mark, 15:36–40
19. Summary: Paul revisits Galatia; at Lystra he is joined by Timothy, 15:41–16:5
20. Paul is guided to Macedonia via Troas, 16:6–10 (Note travel diary, 16:9–18)
21. At Philippi: Lydia is converted, a slave girl healed, Paul and Silas beaten and jailed; the deliverance and public apology, 16:11–40
22. At Thessalonica and Beroea: summary of the mission, 17:1–15
23. Paul waits at Athens for Silas and Timothy, 17:16–21
24. The Areopagus speech of Paul, 17:22–34
25. At Corinth: Paul lives, works with Aquila and Priscilla; preaches in the home of a God-fearer adjacent to synagogue, 18:1–17

D. Mission of Paul to Asia (the "third missionary journey"), 18:18–19:41:
26. Brief visits to Ephesus, Jerusalem, Antioch, 18:18–22
27. Summary: Paul revisits Galatian and Phrygian disciples, 18:23
28. Apollos at Ephesus, 18:24–28
29. Paul's preaching at Ephesus results in a new "Pentecost," 19:1–7
30. Summary: the two-year Ephesian ministry, 19:8–12
31. Paul and the Jewish exorcists, 19:13–16
32. Summary: public book burnings, 19:17–20
33. The Roman journey projected, 19:21–22
34. The riot in Ephesus, 19:23–41

E. Paul visits the regions of Macedonia and Achaia; en route to Jerusalem, 20:1–21:14 (travel diary resumed, 20:5–15 [16–38?]):
35. Summary: Paul's mission of encouragement becomes an escapade, 20:1–6
36. Paul in Troas, 20:7–12

37. Summary: Paul plots his course in the light of Pentecost, 20:13–16
38. Paul's farewell speech to the Ephesian elders, 20:17–35
39. Summary: the voyage to Palestine, 20:36–21:7
40. Paul among the prophets at Caesarea, 21:8–14

F. Paul in Jerusalem, 21:15–26:32 (travel diary, 21:1–18):
  41. Upon arrival, Paul receives advice from James and the elders, 21:17–25
  42. Paul is dragged from the temple, 21:26–29
  43. Paul is mobbed; arrest by the tribune, 21:30–36
  44. Paul's self-defense: speech before the temple, 21:37–22:21
  45. A Roman citizen pleads his rights, 22:22–29
  46. Paul before the Council; another speech in self-defense, 22:30–23:10
  47. Divine assurance, 23:11
  48. A plot is disclosed; Paul sent to Caesarea with a letter to Felix the procurator, 23:12–35
  49. Paul accused before Felix; his speech of defense, 24:1–21
  50. Paul's trial delayed; Felix converses with the Apostle; Festus succeeds Felix, 24:22–27
  51. Paul accused before Festus; Paul appeals to Caesar, 25:1–12
  52. Paul's case laid before Agrippa; Paul's last defense before a court in Palestine, 25:13–26:32

G. Paul's voyage to Rome, 27:1–28:16:
  53. Experiences at sea logged by diarist

H. Paul at Rome, 28:17–31:
  54. Paul appeals to the local Jewish leaders, 28:17–22
  55. Paul's exposition of the gospel results in schism; Paul's statement concerning the hardening of the Jews, 28:23–28 (29)
  56. Summary: the two-year ministry at Rome, 28:30–31

THE ACTS STORY OF PAUL'S CONVERSION AND EARLY EXPERIENCES

"And Saul was consenting to his [Stephen's] death." Thus Luke introduces the man of Tarsus.[8] We are also told that Saul (Paul) zealously took part in the persecution which Stephen's martyrdom touched off in Jerusalem. "Entering house after house," Paul dragged both men and women "to prison." So bent was he upon extending the persecution of Christians beyond Jerusalem that he gained letters from the high priest and journeyed to Damascus.

What actually took place on the Damascus road is a mystery which becomes no less one by appealing to so-called parallels in the phenomenology of religious mysticism or to psychologists' data concerning visions and auditions. Luke's story in Acts 9:3–9, recounted in 22:6–11 and again in 26:12–18, brings us as near as possible to the actual event. Some light may be shed upon its significance, however, by reconsidering what had been some of Paul's experiences before it.

[8] Acts 8:1. At this point the following passages should be reread: Acts 8:1–3; 9:1–30; 11:19–30; 12:25.

The Apostle's declaration in Galatians 1:22, that he was "not known by sight to the churches of Christ in Judea," does not mean that the statement in Acts 8:3 is erroneous. Victims of Paul's persecutions would not have known him personally, and there were doubtless Christians from villages near Jerusalem who had only heard of this notorious Pharisee. Moreover, other statements lend support to Luke's account of Paul's early residence in Jerusalem, his zealous study of the Law. and his vigorous advocacy of its authority.[9]

Why was it that Paul was such an ardent persecutor of the Christians? In his letter the Apostle writes of those things in Christianity which make pious Jews indignant. There is such conviction in his words that we may be sure that he is remembering his old feelings. Since the Pharisees believed that the Law of Moses was God's greatest gift to man, a revelation of His nature and of His commandments, obedience to the Law was the essential condition of man's salvation. The Christians proclaimed God's mercy toward the undeserving, and told of a messiah who had befriended and brought God's salvation to "publicans and sinners." These untaught fishermen and common folk of Galilee were claiming that they were the new Israel to whom God was giving all the blessings promised to the fathers by the prophets. For Paul this so-called "good news from God" was an insult to the God of Mt. Sinai, a subversion of His holy laws, blasphemy. Finally, we may note that the idea of a crucified messiah was, to the Judaism Paul knew, a grotesque distortion of Israel's hope. Did not the Law expressly declare, "Cursed be everyone who hangs on a tree"? With whatever reasons Paul may have supported his persecutions, it is obvious that he did so from the highest religious motives.[10]

Paul's conversion was therefore a complete reversal of his former convictions. All at once he knew that he was wrong. He had been compounding the guilt of those of his party who had killed the Messiah. If Jesus had died for these Galileans, then to persecute them was to crucify the Messiah afresh. If forgiveness was being offered a man like himself, then the witness of the Christians was indeed "good news." It follows that such a gospel must be taken directly and deliberately to all men, "to the Jew first, but also to the Greek." As we shall see, Paul's conversion and his commission as an apostle to the nations are two parts of the same experience. As in his former days, this man's conviction led to action. Luke makes it quite clear that the only explanation for this about-face in Paul's life was a vision of Jesus Christ in his risen glory. And the Apostle himself insists upon this source of his enlightenment. He had not reasoned himself from error to truth.[11]

The conversion of Paul the Pharisee has been considered evidence supporting the early Christians' faith that Jesus was designated "Son of God in power . . . by his resurrection from the dead."[12] None of the Pharisees had joined Jesus'

---

[9]J. Knox's rejection of Jerusalem as the scene of Paul's education for the rabbinate, and of his activity as a persecutor of Christians, is hypercritical (*Chapters*, pp. 34ff). See M. Dibelius and W. G. Kümmel, *Paul*, trans. F. Clarke (1953), pp. 46f.

[10]Ibid., 50ff.; Weiss, *Earliest Christianity*, vol. 1, pp. 191f.

[11]Gal. 1:1, 11f.; 1 Cor. 9:1; 15:8.

[12]Rom. 1:4.

disciple band during his Ministry. In fact, among Jewish leaders, the Pharisees shared responsibility for his death. Even with the resurrection, the established order remained in power: Christ was victor over death, but not over Pharisaism. But the plot was not finished. It is the conversion of Paul, and in his achievements as the greatest of Christian missionaries, that the tragic conflict between the power of Jesus and that of the Pharisees reaches a crucial turning point. Jesus Christ "made me his own," wrote the Apostle, and again, "I have been crucified with Christ; it is no longer I who live, but Christ who lives in me . . ."[13] Was ever a victory more complete than that, after death, Jesus should have taken one of the most zealous representatives of a group that had sought his death and made of this man the greatest of all witnesses to the faith that "Christ crucified" is indeed the "power of God and the wisdom of God"?[14]

In the story of Paul are given the essential elements that distinguish all conversions, according to early Christianity: the conviction that Jesus is still alive; that he is man's only Savior—God's power for salvation; that Jesus as Savior and Lord calls men to witness to this faith in word and deed.

Some of Paul's testimony concerning his early days as a Christian casts a shadow of suspicion upon the complete accuracy of the story of Acts 9:10–30. For one thing, Paul declared that he became "an apostle not from men nor through man, but through Jesus Christ and God the Father, who raised him [that is, Jesus] from the dead . . ."[15] His statements seem to contradict the important role played by Ananias in Acts. Some have surmised that the currency of just such a story led Paul to make his emphatic denials in Galatians.[16] An alternative interpretation of our sources is more satisfactory. In Galatians, Paul sought to defend his independence of the Jerusalem apostles. Accordingly, one would expect him to "telescope" some of the details of his personal life and elaborate upon others.

It is important to recognize, however we explain these differences between Acts and Paul's letters, that the Apostle was convinced that he had received his call at the feet of the risen Christ and not from the hands of men.[17] No individual or hierarchy of men appointed Paul to his apostleship. In considering the significance to Paul's career of Ananias and of Barnabas, this fundamental fact must not be overlooked.[18]

Luke reports that for several days after receiving Christian baptism Paul stayed in Damascus. According to Galatians 1:17, Paul "went away into Arabia," a detail omitted in the three versions in Acts. Yet the stories are not contradictory. Paul tells the Galatians that he returned to Damascus after being in Arabia for a time, clearly implying an earlier stay in the city. Moreover, it is consistent with the man revealed in his letters that Paul should wish Christians in Damascus to know

[13]Phil. 3:12; Gal. 2:20.

[14]C. H. Dodd, *The Meaning of Paul for Today* (1920), pp. 13ff. H. G. Wood, "The Conversion of St. Paul," *NTS* 1 (1955): 276ff.; Munck, *Paul*, pp. 11ff.

[15]Gal. 1:1, 12, 15ff.

[16]Craig, *Beginning*, p. 164.

[17]Cor. 15:1ff.

[18]Weiss, *Earliest Christianity*, vol. 1, pp. 196f.

at once that he was a changed man, that he should begin at once to preach.[19]

It is sometimes thought that Paul's Arabian visit provided a time of retirement. Like some monk he prepared himself for his missionary journeys by living the hermit's life in the desert.[20] This is fanciful, for we are told by Paul that the churches in Judea heard that "he who once persecuted us is now preaching the faith he once tried to destroy."[21] Soon after his conversion Paul began evangelistic work. The plots of the Jews to kill him also suggest that he did not become a recluse, that his early advocacy of Christianity was a matter of public knowledge, provoking the fury of his former confederates.

Paul's own reference to his escape from Damascus contains a detail which is not present in the Acts account, but is reconcilable with it.[22] The synagogue authorities might have plotted with Nabatean soldiers, under an official of King Aretas, to lay an ambush for Paul should he attempt to escape. Years later, Paul calls attention to the fact that he had been lowered from the Damascus wall in a fish-basket. This incident was a source of humiliation to him. He had approached Damascus a proud Jew bearing letters from the high priest of Jerusalem; he left Damascus a fugitive from killers both within and without its walls. What a change had taken place! But the real change was in the heart of the man and not in the circumstances of the road.

"Out of the frying pan into the fire" might be said of Paul as he fled from Damascus to Jerusalem. Is it any wonder that "the disciples were afraid of him"? "But Barnabas took him, and brought him to the apostles."[23] Had it not been for Barnabas would Paul have seen Peter or James the Lord's brother? Would Paul have been able to remain with them for fifteen days, gathering eyewitness reports of Jesus' deeds and words?[24]

It was unlikely that Paul remained quiet in Jerusalem. He boldly proclaimed the gospel in the Greek-speaking Jewish synagogues of the city. Paul's preaching provoked a storm of protest. He was forced to flee Jerusalem, or be killed. Once again Paul needed friends. And there were "brethren" to help. From Caesarea he sailed to Tarsus.[25] What sort of welcome could be expected back home?

MISSION TO CYPRUS AND GALATIA

The choice of Cyprus as the launching point of the mission from Antioch may have derived from the wish of Barnabas to return to his homeland. But Luke's interest does not dwell upon the advantage which previous contacts might have

---

[19]E. Haenchen, "The Book of Acts as Source Material for the History of Early Christianity," in Keck and Martyn, *Luke–Acts*, pp. 268f.

[20]H. C. Kee and F. W. Young, *Understanding the New Testament* (1957), pp. 213f.

[21]Gal. 1:23.

[22]2 Cor. 11:32f.

[23]Acts 9:27.

[24]Paul reports that he visited Jerusalem "to get information from" Peter (Gal. 1:18): G. D. Kilpatrick in Higgins, *New Testament Essays*, pp. 144ff. Cf. Haenchen in Keck and Martyn, *Luke–Acts*, p. 269.

[25]Acts 9:28–30.

afforded. One episode is singled out for attention. The very first Roman official whom Paul encountered was favorably disposed towards hearing "the word of God."[26] In spite of the opposition of "a Jewish false prophet," the proconsul of Cyprus, Sergius Paulus, believed. Similar reactions to Paul's preaching are reported over and over again. The Apostle's troubles did not originate from the custodians of the Roman peace, or from the Gentile population, but from the Jews. Whatever the particular problem in the minds of Luke's first readers, the Acts account of Paul's "first missionary journey" brings this issue into the foreground. Luke wished to show why the missions of Jewish-Christians turned into missions to Gentiles. This change was not the result of failure on the part of the Apostle—of Paul no less than Peter and John—to work conscientiously for the conversion of the Jews. Paul and his companions regularly went first to the synagogue, not merely out of convenience, but because they were convinced that "it was necessary" that the word of God should be spoken first to the Jews.[27] The people of God must not have any grounds for complaint, or for excusing themselves.[28] Because of the violent opposition of "unbelieving Jews" to those who offered them divine forgiveness, Paul and his party turned to the Gentiles.[29]

It is doubtful that Acts 13:16–41 represents a free composition. We have seen that the resemblance of this speech to those of Peter and of Stephen has led many scholars to consider it a summary of the original gospel of the Church. At the same time, the Pisidian Antioch sermon is peculiarly appropriate to the occasion, and contains a few distinctive Pauline features. Luke had more than oral and written versions of typical early sermons to guide him. He had heard Paul preach to Jews and Greeks in the synagogues of the Dispersion.[30]

Among modern Protestants, the ranking of the great apostles of the Church is no more than a matter of personal preference. Yet when Luke wrote Acts, division of opinion on this question still threatened the unity of the Church and its gospel. In his selection of certain episodes and in the way he tells them, it would seem that Luke wishes to emphasize the equal stature of Peter and Paul. Note Acts 2:43 and 14:3, and then compare Paul's healing of the lame man at Lystra, and the similar mighty work wrought by Peter.[31] A part of Luke's purpose was to make sure that Paul's reputation would be second to none.

There is no warrant for the supposition, however, that Luke biased his story in favor of Paul, nor that the parallels with Peter which are drawn are inventions of the author of Acts, although they may have been adapted to serve his theological interests. To Luke such coincidences were due to divine providence; where the Holy Spirit was at work in men, howsoever different in personality, characteristic signs were observed.

The reaction of persons at Iconium and Lystra to the first Christian missionaries

---

[26] Acts 13:7.

[27] Acts 13:46; cf. Rom. 1:16; 9:1–5; 10:1.

[28] Acts 13:40, 46, 51; cf. Rom. 10:18–21.

[29] Acts 18:5ff.; 19:8f., etc.

[30] W. L. Knox, The Acts, pp. 94ff.

[31] Cf. Acts 14:8–11 and 3:1ff.

are consistent with the reputation of the peoples of this region. The Phrygians were highly emotional folk, easily excited to mob action and to mass movements. When Paul and his associates left the city of Antioch for the outlying districts, they showed great courage. They were almost lynched in Iconium, and at Lystra a very different but equally dangerous enthusiasm was manifested. According to an old legend, Zeus and Hermes had once visited the earth in disguise. None of the Phrygians had given them hospitality, with the exception of an old man and his wife. As a result the entire population was destroyed, but the two peasants were transformed into great trees when they died. The people of Lystra must have thought that history was being repeated, that Barnabas and Paul were the gods incognito. The ancient mistake would not be made over again.[32]

In appealing to the people of Lystra to abandon their idolatrous beliefs and practices, Paul argued from nature to nature's God. To the Jew, God's goodness was revealed in His patience in withholding His judgments upon evil men in history. But among pagans, who did not consider that history was ordered by a divine providence, the power and mysteries of nature awakened religious awe. Paul argued that the beneficent aspects of nature disclosed the claims of a Creator upon His creation.[33]

Note the contrast between the attitudes of the volatile crowds in verses 18 and 19.[34] From offering sacrifices to throwing stones certainly shows a radical change of heart on the part of the crowd. But the most remarkable feature of this story is the courage of Paul. Nearly dead from the pummeling, he spent the night in the city and, after a brief visit to Derbe, came back to Lystra to "strengthen the souls of the disciples." This act of courage probably had a more long-lasting effect upon the peoples in this region than Paul's sermons beginning with arguments from nature. At any rate, Paul proclaimed the gospel in word and in deed.

In 14:23 we have an interesting comment upon Paul's organization of new churches. The statement is tantalizingly brief. Yet it tells us that the Apostle was not content to win individuals as converts to the faith. He organized communities of believers.

We have seen that the forms of government in the earliest churches have been much debated. Acts 6:1–6 provides an example of a congregation choosing its officers. In two of Paul's letters he recognized the presence of certain senior members, perhaps formerly the elders of Jewish synagogues of the Dispersion, and declared that they deserve special prerogatives.[35] In Acts 14:23 we are told that elders were *appointed* in every church established during the "first missionary journey." In some of the outlying districts, where converts from paganism were

---

[32] Ovid, *Metamorphoses*, 8. 626ff. The indentification of Barnabas with Zeus may indicate his more impressive physical appearance. The apocryphal "Acts of Paul" contains the story of Thecla, an Iconium convert. This legendary account may possibly preserve a description of Paul's personal appearance: "a man of small stature, with his eyebrows meeting and a rather large nose, somewhat bald-headed, bandy-legged, strongly built, of gracious presence; for sometimes he looked like a man and sometimes he had the face of an angel." (Cited from *IB*, vol. 9, p. 185).

[33] Cf. Rom. 1:19f.

[34] With the account in Acts 14, cf. Paul's reference to being stoned, 2 Cor. 11:25.

[35] 1 Cor. 16:16; 1 Thess. 5:12f.

in the majority, elders were doubtless appointed by Paul and his associates, rather than chosen by congregational election. The search for a clearly normative pattern of church polity in the Acts and Paul's letters has not led to any unanimity of opinion.

It is, perhaps, more profitable to examine the accounts of Paul's missions for the light they shed upon the missionary enterprise of the early Church. More important than uniformity in organizational procedures is the vision of the task and its basic strategy. In Acts 13 and 14 we read of church-sponsored missionaries, moved by the Holy Spirit in a high moment of worship, going forth with the full support of their people. Wherever possible, the gospel is proclaimed by them against the background of the story of salvation revealed in the Old Testament. At other times advantage is taken of some local custom, belief, or situation, and a "natural" point of departure is adopted for the proclamation of the gospel. New converts are offered salvation but not security.[36] Guidance is given new disciples in organizing themselves, but such steps are taken in the atmosphere of worship, turning the confidence of young churches away from human founders to the Lord. From first to last, Luke represents the Christian mission as the work of "a living God."[37]

THE JERUSALEM CONFERENCE

Acts 15 presents to the historian of early Christianity some serious problems. Paul's account in Galatians of the discussions among the apostles concerning "the Gentile Question" does not coincide at every point with Luke's narrative leading up to the "Jerusalem Conference." It is perhaps too much to expect complete consistency in two sources written from different standpoints. Some scholars, however, have urged that such questions as Luke's authorship of Acts, the reliability of its sources, and even the integrity of Paul are at stake in these discussions. Thus the efforts to "harmonize" Acts 9–15 and Galatians 1–2 have attracted considerable attention.[38]

In studying Acts or Galatians it is important to keep the following in mind. There is no doubt about the final outcome of the debate in the early Church concerning the terms of admission for Gentiles. Nor is there any serious differ-

---

[36] Acts 14:22.

[37] Acts 14:23.

[38] Acts 9–15 report three visits of Paul to Jerusalem following his conversion: (a) the acquaintance visit, 9:26ff., (b) the famine-relief visit, 11:27ff., (c) the conference visit, 15:1ff. Galatians reports two visits only: (d) 1:18, (e) 2:1ff. Most scholars equate Acts 9:26ff. and Gal. 1:18. Therefore (a) = (d). See however, P. Parker, "Once More, Acts and Galatians," *JBL* LXXXVI (1967): 175ff. Accepting the majority opinion, (a) = (d), three explanations are possible: (b) = (e), or (c) = (e), or (e) = (b) + (c). A fourth alternative has been suggested, that (e) is not to be equated with either (b) or (c). For a detailed discussion, see Foakes-Jackson and Lake, *Beginnings,* vol. V, p. 195; J. C. Hurd, Jr., *The Origin of 1 Corinthians* (1965), pp. 15ff. [hereafter *1 Corinthians*]; C. B. Caird, "Chronology of the N. T.", *IDB,* vol. 1, pp. 605f.; G. Ogg, *The Chronology of the Life of Paul* (1968), pp. 72ff. [hereafter, *Chronology*].

ence of opinion concerning the significance of this historic decision for the future of Christianity. The only uncertainty lies in the precise sequence of events leading up to that decision.

What was this so-called "Gentile Question"? Acts 15:1–2 declare that some of the Jewish–Christians of Jerusalem insisted that Gentile converts to Christianity should be circumcised. These men (commonly designated "the Judaizers") held that until God's commandment is fulfilled, no assurance of salvation ought to be given to any male received into the Church.[39] Christian baptism was not a substitute for circumcision, any more than was Jewish baptism of Gentile proselytes in the synagogues. Circumcision was the sign of membership in the covenant community and the condition of God's covenanted mercies.

The fact that some of the first Christians championed this position is significant. But it was not a view held by only a handful of Jewish–Christians in Jerusalem. Paul's letters, especially the Letter to the Galatians, reveal that there were advocates of circumcision in Christian churches of the Dispersion.[40]

There was another aspect of the Gentile Question. The Judaizers of Jerusalem and elsewhere also insisted upon the continuing authority of the food laws of the books of Moses. They probably did not teach that Gentile converts were bound to observe all of these dietary regulations in order to be saved. But Paul was surely right in concluding that so long as distinctions were drawn between "clean" foods and "unclean" foods, Gentiles were being compelled "to live like Jews."[41] Unless all such food laws were abolished, the Christian communities would become hopelessly segregated, and the vision of a community in which Jew and Greek would be brothers in Christ would be an empty dream. Also, by refusing to eat with Gentiles, Jewish–Christians were guilty of insincerity; they were denying by their actions their pretensions to equality and unity in the Church.[42]

Without Paul's version of the great debate in Galatians 1 and 2, the reader of Acts 15 might fail to see that there is any connection at all between the stated purpose of the Jerusalem Conference and the final "decree."[43] Some scholars have supposed that Luke (or his source) has confused two or more situations and at least two different conferences.[44] Yet it is clear from Galatians that the two issues of circumcision and the observance of Jewish food laws were closely related. Both involved the fundamental question: Upon what does salvation rest in the Christian gospel? Is salvation ultimately the reward for a righteousness achieved by men in obedience to Law? Or does full assurance of salvation depend upon the glad response of faith to the proclamation of God's saving action in Christ?

Paul saw much more clearly than did anyone else this fundamental issue. If the position of the Judaizers had been adopted, believers in Jesus as the Christ would have been confined to a sect *within* Judaism. The practical effect of their

---

[39] Gen. 17:9ff.
[40] Gal. 5:2; 6:12f.; Phil. 3:2f.
[41] Gal. 2:14.
[42] Gal. 2:11ff.
[43] Acts 15:19f., 28f.
[44] E.g., *Weiss, Earliest Christianity,* vol. 1, pp. 258ff. See further, below, note 78, p. 402.

demands would have been to force Gentiles to become Jews before becoming Christians. The new mission to the Gentiles, begun by the Antioch congregation and spreading so rapidly, would have been set back. But more important than the practical handicap imposed upon subsequent missions to the Gentiles was the threat to the gospel itself. Paul was convinced that if Judaism's conception of a works-righteousness was accommodated to the Christian message of salvation, the cross of Christ would no longer effect its saving power. If salvation was to be won by obedience to the Law "then Christ died to no purpose."[45]

According to Acts 15 and Galatians, Peter, Paul, and even James reached the conclusion that circumcision ought not to be imposed upon Gentiles. Luke reports that in the discussions Peter laid emphasis upon the event which had opened his eyes, the conversion of Cornelius. The Spirit of God had made no distinction between the circumcised and the uncircumcised. Have Christians any right to do so?[46] Paul and Barnabas commended their missions among Gentiles by appealing to the "signs and wonders" wrought by the Spirit of God. All resistance broke down when James took the position that no other burden should be laid upon Gentile converts than certain "necessary things."[47] Whatever the significance of these "necessary things," it is apparent that circumcision was not among them.

It may surprise the reader that Paul assented to the proposal of James: Gentile converts were to avoid partaking of food previously offered in sacrifice to idols, and the eating of meat not killed in the Jewish ("kosher") way.[48]

Unless Galatians was written before the Jerusalem Conference (as some have supposed) it is strange that Paul makes no mention of this decree of Acts 15:20 in Galatians.[49] Stranger still, he does not refer to it when he is compelled to deal with the question of eating food offered to idols at Corinth.[50] Two explanations are suggested. Either Paul recognized the practical necessity of being conciliatory at the Jerusalem Conference and therefore agreed to the decree, or else Luke (or his source) erred in connecting the decree with this conference. In the former case, one must face the probability that Paul soon recognized that compromise was not possible in this matter. Some support for the view that the decree represented a later action of the Jerusalem church is given in Acts itself. On Paul's last visit to Jerusalem he was told by James of the decree. In reading Acts 21:5 one might easily suppose that Paul had not previously known of the decree or had any part in framing it. In any event, following the Jerusalem Conference Paul carried forward his Gentile mission convinced that no restrictions of any consequence had been placed upon him.

Acts and Paul's letters may be related in a number of ways, but the conclusion of the discussions in Jerusalem on the Gentile Question is beyond doubt. Luke's

[45] Gal. 2:21.

[46] It was probably argued that since Peter had baptized Cornelius *only* after God had provided evidence of his acceptance, this was a special case and did not waive the necessity of circumcision as a general rule.

[47] Acts 15:19, 28.

[48] Some mss. omit "fornication," others add "the golden rule" stated in a negative way. Were moral rules added to the text of a decree originally prescribing ceremonial regulations?

[49] Gal. 2:6–10, 14.

[50] 1 Cor. 8.

view was that traditional doctrines and practices were bound to give way to the witness of the Holy Spirit. The answer to the question which Paul asked the Galatians, exposing the untenable position of all efforts to impose legalistic interpretations upon the Christian gospel, was the crux of the matter: "Let me ask you only this: did you receive the Spirit by works of the Law, or by hearing with faith?"[51]

MISSION TO MACEDONIA AND ACHAIA

When Paul set sail from Troas for Macedonia he carried the gospel of Jesus Christ from one continent to another.[52] Of course the map of Paul's world was not the same as that of today's. The Romans referred to the Mediterranean as Mare Nostrum (our sea), and the crossing of the Aegean was from one province of the Roman Empire to another. Nevertheless, the modern reader can realize the dramatic significance of Paul's penetrations westward into regions destined to become a part of modern Europe.

Paul and Barnabas parted company at the outset of the "second missionary journey." Paul argued that John Mark should be left behind this time.[53] How could such a relatively small matter lead to "sharp contention" between friends of long standing? It is noteworthy that in his Galatian letter Paul wrote that Barnabas as well as Peter had been rebuked for shrinking from table fellowship with Gentiles. Perhaps the dispute over Mark ruffled feelings which were already severely strained.[54]

On this mission Paul journeyed overland to the Galatian cities. Silas (Roman name, Silvanus) was his companion, and another helper, Timothy, joined them at Lystra. In order to avoid needless antagonisms Paul circumcised Timothy "because of the Jews."[55] It was no sacrifice of principle to circumcise a half-Jew, and it was expedient to do so since Timothy would be visiting Jewish synagogues with Paul.

The brief notices of Paul's northward and northwesterly trip toward Troas have led to a variety of speculations.[56] Luke was interested only in stressing that the mission to Macedonia represented an urgent, divine call. Some plans had to be given up in order to follow the leadership of the Holy Spirit.[57]

A woman was Paul's first convert on the soil of Europe. Lydia was one of the highminded women of the Gentile society who had been attracted to Judaism, possibly because of its noble ideals of marriage and the home. In Philippi the

---

[51] Gal. 3:2.

[52] Acts 16:11.

[53] Acts 15:36ff. Recall 13:5, 13.

[54] Whatever the situation, Paul continued to associate Barnabas with him in his mission; cf. 1 Cor. 9:6. Mark seems to have redeemed himself in Paul's sight, 2 Tim. 4:11.

[55] Acts 16:3. Cf. Keck and Martyn, Luke-Acts, pp. 203f.; also p. 271.

[56] Acts 16:6f. See below, pp. 418f.

[57] It has been conjectured that Luke joined Paul's party at Troas, and that the author of Acts is none other than "the man from Macedonia."

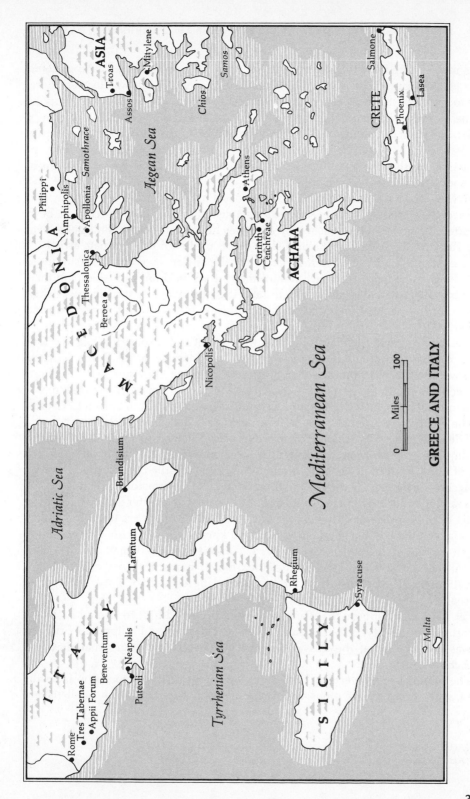

ASIA

Troas
Mitylene
Assos

Chios
Samos

Aegean Sea

CRETE
Salmone
Lasea
Phoenix

Philippi
Amphipolis
Samothrace
Apollonia

M
A
C
E
D
O
N
I
A

Thessalonica
Beroea

Athens

Corinth
Cenchreae

ACHAIA

Nicopolis

Mediterranean Sea

Adriatic Sea

Brundisium

Tarentum

Rhegium

Syracuse

Malta

S I C I L Y

I
T
A
L
Y

Rome
Tres Tabernae
Appii Forum
Beneventum
Neapolis
Puteoli

Tyrrhenian Sea

0   100
|————————|
Miles

GREECE AND ITALY

Jews met outside the city gate, by the river where the ceremonial washings could take place. It cannot be said for certain whether a synagogue was located there. But to this accustomed place of worship came Paul on the Sabbath and "spoke to the women who had come together." It is clear from Luke's identification of Lydia, and from the nature of her gracious invitation to the Christian missionaries, that she was a wealthy merchant. While it is true that Christianity held an attraction for the depressed classes of Roman society, persons from the top of the social scale also became converts.

In view of Paul's cordial relations with the Philippians one might wish that more details relating to the Apostle's establishment of this church had been reported.[58] But the author wishes only to show how Paul's stay at Philippi ended. The story of the healing of the mad slave girl is told with consummate artistry.[59] Insane persons had a curious fascination for the ancient world. It was supposed that the gods had deprived such folk of their sanity in order to make them their spokesmen. The reader cannot fail to note that the restoration of this wretched girl to mental health brought anger instead of joy to those who were interested in her.

The mob's attack upon Paul and Silas was violent and disorderly. The missionaries may have thought it pointless to protest brutal treatment. As Roman citizens they were supposedly immune from beatings and unjust imprisonments. But legal proceedings might result in long delays and restrictions upon their freedom of movement. Only when the situation became desperate did Paul appeal to Caesar.

The author's comment upon the bearing of Paul and Silas in the inner prison is indeed moving. No wonder "the prisoners were listening to them."[60] Freakish earthquakes were common enough in this region, we are told, and when we put out of mind modern penal establishments and consider the typical wooden-beam dungeons of the period, there is nothing incredible in the story that follows. At any rate, it is not this miraculous aspect of the story that interests Luke, but the effect of the courage and the responsible action of his prisoners upon the Philippian jailer. Filled with a shuddering fear, and knowing that his life was no longer worth anything, the jailer was ready to commit suicide. Whatever the jailer meant by his "Save me!" the apostles took him at his word. They offered him a salvation not from punishment for a supposed dereliction of duty, but for life eternal.

Let no reader suppose that Paul's wounded pride led him to demand a police escort out of the city.[61] For the sake of the gospel, and the Philippian Christians it was important that the missionaries be vindicated of charges that they had breached Roman law.

The winning of converts in Thessalonica brought further opposition from the Jews, who stirred up the mobs against the apostles, depicting them as aliens and

[58] See below, pp. 451ff.
[59] Acts 16:16ff.
[60] Acts 16:25ff.
[61] Acts 16:37.

insurrectionists.[62] In the uproar that followed, the city authorities intervened and the apostles were urged to move on to another place.[63]

At Beroea, the apostles were more favorably received. Luke notes, with a probable appeal to Theophilus, that confirmation of the gospel is to be sought by "examining the scriptures." Some Jews at Beroea gave an intelligent response to this argument from the Old Testament. They recognized that the gospel provided a key to the unity of the Bible and its message: the crucified Christ fulfills the Old Testament drama of salvation; and the cross itself is to be understood in the light of God's mighty acts in that history which led up to it.[64] Ironically, at Beroea Paul was subjected to persecutions like those he had given others: Jews from Thessalonica came to persecute the Christians, following the same course which Paul had determined to follow as a zealous Pharisee in his journey to Damascus. In the face of his antagonists, Paul must have seen his former self. The critical situation which developed at Beroea led to a temporary separation of Paul, Silas, and Timothy. Paul, we are told, was carried to Athens.[65]

Our imagination is quickened by the thought of Paul in the Athenian *agora* (marketplace) with its architectural gems and its monuments to the heroes and the gods. Just so, Luke's imagination must have been stirred. The Areopagus speech provides primary evidence of important aspects of Luke's theology. Neither in its style nor in its content does this sermon correspond to the gospel Paul proclaims in his letters. Is it possible that Paul would have claimed common ground between himself and the popular beliefs of his listeners? For example, where in his letters does Paul hold to the Stoic thesis that men are by nature akin to God?[66]

It is too much to claim that Paul's mission to Athens is derived from an eyewitness account, and that this speech is a verbatim report. Yet the difficulties in the way of accepting the substantial historicity of Luke's narrative at this point have been exaggerated.[67]

Luke mentions three types of response to Paul's preaching at Athens. In the first place, we are told that "some mocked."[68] The Epicurean and Stoic philosophers would probably be among this number. They contemptuously dismissed his ideas as a throwing together of scraps of learning picked up hither and yon.[69] When Paul proclaimed "Jesus and the resurrection," some supposed that he spoke

[62] Acts 17:4f.

[63] It is probable that the notice of "three weeks" suggests too brief a period for the mission in Thessalonica. See below, p. 88.

[64] Acts 17:11.

[65] Acts 17:14f.

[66] See "Paul on the Areopagus," Dibelius, *Studies*, pp. 26ff.

[67] B. Gärtner, *The Areopagus Speech and Natural Revelation* (1955); Macgregor, *IB*, vol. 9, 231f. Comparisons of Acts 17 and Rom. 1–2 must not obscure the importance of this section for a determination of Luke's distinctive understanding of the relation between the gospel and the world; cf. Flender, *St. Luke*, pp. 66ff.

[68] Acts 17:32.

[69] Acts 17:18.

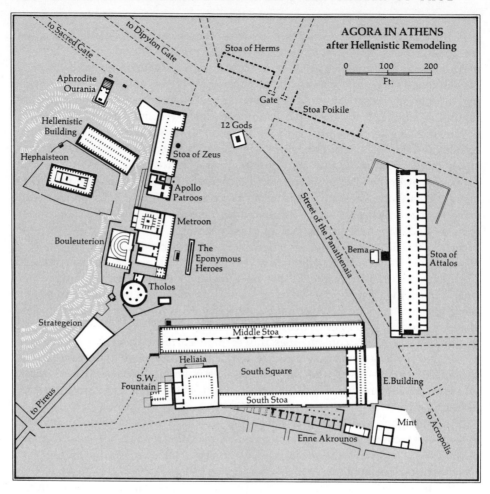

of "*foreign* divinities."[70] Finally, we notice that "some men joined him [Paul] and believed": an aristocrat named Dionysius, a woman named Damaris, and "others with them."[71]

Since there is no reference to a Christian church at Athens in New Testament times, it would seem that whatever the results of Paul's visit there, they were ephemeral. The intellectual atmosphere in Athens was not congenial to a religious philosophy of life commitment. A premium was placed upon the novelty of ideas, upon talk not action.

While waiting at Corinth for the arrival of Silas and Timothy from Macedonia, "Paul was occupied with preaching."[72] Luke's portrayal corresponds with the impression one gains from reading Paul's letters. Tireless, and unwilling to wait for

---

[70]*Anastasis* (Greek, resurrection) may have been mistaken for the name of a goddess.

[71]Acts 17:34. Cf., however, 1 Cor. 16:15. Paul's only indirect reference to his failure in Athens may be 1 Cor. 2:3 (Haenchen in Keck and Martyn, *Luke–Acts*, pp. 274f.).

[72]Acts 18:5.

one situation to become stabilized before starting other ventures, Paul never missed opportunities to proclaim the good news of Jesus Christ. Perhaps, as Paul wrote to the Corinthians later, he was spurred on to activity by his belief that "the appointed time has grown very short," that the "form of this world is passing away."[73] But it is more likely that the essential sanction for Paul's perseverance was the fact that he was constantly under the control of Christ's love for all men.[74]

A sidelight upon Paul's personality is afforded in the reference to his move from the synagogue to the house of Titius Justus next door. Perhaps Luke wished to show that although Paul reacted in a conventional way to the Jews who "opposed and reviled him," he did not abandon his kinsmen by race. The Jews and the God-fearers who frequented the synagogues had to be given every opportunity to hear and heed the gospel. It must have been galling to the Jews that "Crispus, the ruler of the synagogue, believed in the Lord." Continuing to preach within the shadow of the synagogue, Paul must have faced daily the scowling countenances of his enemies. Luke reports that the Lord was revealed to Paul in order that his fears of bodily harm might be allayed.[75]

The "trial" of Paul before Gallio in Corinth has some amusing aspects. Gallio saw through the tissue of trumped-up charges. He was not going to be imposed upon, nor was he willing to begin his rule in the region with a religious squabble. The incident is entirely credible: the roughing-up of Sosthenes by onlookers who are encouraged by Gallio's snub; Gallio's indifference to—perhaps amusement over—the commotion which followed. Gallio's judgment was not to be swayed by mob scenes.[76]

As usual, Luke brought his narrative of Paul's activities in one city to a close with a public hearing and a general disturbance. But this time the reason for Paul's departure is not given. Did Paul leave Corinth on his own initiative to visit Jerusalem at the Passover season?

PAUL IN THE ROMAN PROVINCE OF ASIA:
THE EPHESIAN MINISTRY.

With his conversion to Christianity Paul did not abandon completely the religion of his early years. Luke correctly reported that although Paul championed the freedom of the Gentiles concerning the requirements of the Law, he still honored many of them. No longer did his salvation, nor that of any man, depend on obedience to its letter, but the Law contained divinely sanctioned religious customs as well as moral commandments. "At Cenchreae," Paul "cut his hair, for he had a vow."[77]

[73] 1 Cor. 7:29, 31.
[74] 1 Cor. 9:16ff.; 2 Cor. 5:14f.
[75] Acts 18:6ff.
[76] For the importance of this notice in fixing the Pauline chronology, see below, pp. 384f.
[77] Acts 18:18b. This correspondence between Paul's and Luke's view of the Torah and its ceremonial features has been sharply denied by some scholars. See discussions of the issue in Keck and Martyn, Luke–Acts, pp. 37ff. (Veilhauer) and 194ff. (Bornkamm).

With Acts 18:22 the story of Paul's "third missionary journey" begins. One wishes that Luke had reported beforehand the nature of Paul's receptions at Jerusalem and at Antioch. Were relations with the leaders of these churches further strained at this time? Luke seems impatient to get Paul back to the mission field, to tell of his experiences at Ephesus, the principal city of the Roman province of Asia. But before he does this, he introduces Apollos, a brilliant Alexandrian who knew something about Christianity, but whose experiences had been limited. "He knew only the baptism of John," we are told.[78] This expression is cryptic. Perhaps Apollos knew a tradition which declared that John and Jesus were heralds of the coming kingdom of God, preachers of repentance. Like them, Apollos preached with eloquence and power concerning the coming judgment, and the heroic ethic required of those who were to share in the new age. But one thing Apollos lacked. He did not know that the Christ had come, that the new age had dawned, and that persons who were baptized "in the name of Jesus," as Christ and as Lord, were experiencing the very thing that had been promised—the power of the Holy Spirit. After Apollos had been instructed by Priscilla and Aquila—Corinthian converts of Paul left by him at Ephesus—Apollos came to know Jesus, not only as a historical personage, but as a living presence.

Paul labored in Ephesus for from two to three years, preaching daily in "the hall of Tyrannus." As we have noted earlier, Luke seems especially interested that Paul's ministry was marked with the same evidence of divine favor as had marked Peter's ministry in Jerusalem. Special notice is taken of the fact that "a number of those who practiced magic arts brought their books together and burned them in the sight of all."[79] According to several Latin and Greek authors, Ephesus was known the world over for its magic books, the "Ephesian Letters." It was thought that they would ensure safe journeys, success in love and business, and so forth. The public "book burning" in Ephesus doubtless created quite a stir.

Almost every sentence of Luke's story of the Ephesian riot can be supported by inscriptions or by references in ancient authors. Luke writes interestingly and with detailed accuracy.[80] The reputation of Ephesus as the guardian of the popular pagan goddess, Artemis, was jeopardized by the successes of the Christian mission. A temple of fabulous size and grandeur housing the image of Artemis attracted visitors to Ephesus from far and wide. Small silver images of Artemis were sold to devotees and tourists visiting the temple. Their makers were the first to complain when Paul's attack on idolatry began to make headway. Once again we have a vivid example of the power of patriotism and religion, when the two are associated, to rouse the masses of men to action. But the real fear of Demetrius and his salesmen was not the loss of the prestige of Artemis and of their city, but the more immediate loss of personal income.

The "town clerk" is, at first sight, an impressive figure. His speech is an appeal

---

[78] Acts 18:24f.

[79] Acts 19:19; cf. 5:12ff.

[80] Although it is surprising that such scant information is given about Paul's relatively long ministry at Ephesus: Williams, *The Acts*, pp. 222ff.; Cadbury, *The Book of Acts in History*, pp. 41ff.

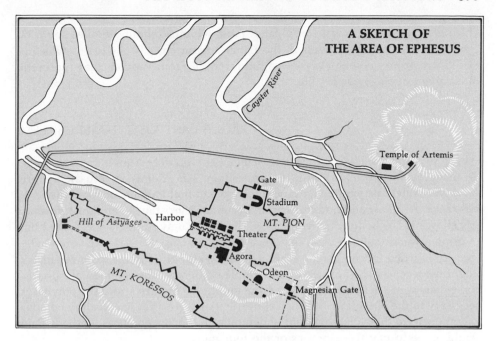

A SKETCH OF
THE AREA OF EPHESUS

to reason, civic order, and justice. Yet it is evident that his motives were mixed. His principal fear was not that injustice might be done to Paul and his travel companions, but that the Romans might intervene in local affairs if there should be a disturbance of the peace.

Luke's account of Paul's movements after leaving Ephesus makes it clear that his plans for visiting Jerusalem had top priority. Eventually he "must also see Rome"; but first, Palestine.

The brief excursion into Macedonia and Achaia may have been due to Paul's pastoral concern for his young churches, but since their representatives joined his party, the organization of this delegation may have been the purpose of this quick trip. For some while Paul had been collecting a fund for the destitute in Jerusalem.[81] Gentile churches would thus acknowledge their debt to "the mother church"; by this act the reluctant Jewish-Christians in Jerusalem might be moved to recognize the Gentile converts as true "sons of Abraham."

Two events marked Paul's stay of three months in Greece, probably at Corinth. Only one of these is mentioned by Luke—the plot against Paul. Did some persons plan to murder Paul on the high seas? Was the money Paul carried a motive? We are not told.[82] A more significant omission is Luke's failure to notice that while at Corinth Paul wrote his Letter to the Romans.[83]

At any rate, the plot prevented Paul from realizing his hope of arriving in Jerusalem at the Passover. He determined to make it for the day of Pentecost,

[81] 1 Cor. 16:1ff.; 2 Cor. 9:1ff.; Rom. 15:25ff.
[82] Acts 20:3.
[83] See below, p. 427.

which was celebrated seven weeks later. From Miletus (about 30 miles south of Ephesus) he sent for the elders of the Ephesian church.[84] Paul's words with his friends are, from one point of view, a sad farewell. From another, they represent an eloquent apology for his life.

PAUL'S LAST VISIT TO JERUSALEM

In spite of his fears in coming to Jerusalem, Paul did not resign himself to them. He made every effort to disarm the opposition. His friends in Jerusalem were faced with a delicate situation. Rumors had spread that Paul encouraged the Jews to forsake their Law and traditions upon becoming Christians. Paul must in some way show his "orthodoxy" if he hoped to dispel the ugly rumors concerning him. Four men, we are told, were in the process of observing the Nazarite vow.[85] The time approached for the purchase of the animals and other items to be sacrificed. Doubtless fees were also to be paid the temple barbers for the ceremonial haircuts. Some men were not able to give up gainful employment or to afford the purchases necessary to the Nazarite vow. Thus opportunities were afforded wealthy persons to demonstrate their piety without undergoing the inconveniences. Perhaps Paul would agree to pay the expenses of the four men.

Paul must have followed the suggestion of James and the elders with considerable reluctance.[86] Such an action could be interpreted as hypocrisy. It is probable that Paul knew that a compromise was necessary, which could be agreed upon without sacrificing his principles, even though his action might be interpreted wrongly. In this case the outcome of Paul's action was disastrous. Asian Jews were responsible for bringing a slanderous charge against Paul.

Whether Paul's antagonists really believed that he had carried into the temple his Gentile companion from Ephesus, Trophimus, or whether the whole thing was trumped-up, we cannot say. It was, of course, a very serious charge, involving a death penalty, and the reaction of the pious Jewish pilgrims, massed in Jerusalem for the festival, was instantaneous.[87] Maltreatment by outraged mobs was nothing new to Paul; however, the anger of the incensed Jews in Jerusalem was a murderous anger. If the Roman tribune (commanding about 1,000 soldiers) had not intervened, Paul would certainly have been lynched.

The tribune suspected that Paul was a notorious criminal, the Egyptian revolutionary who some time earlier had marched on Jerusalem with a large force.[88] Paul's Greek speech led the tribune to realize his mistake, and Paul was able to gain his consent to address the mob.

[84] Acts 20:18ff.

[85] Num. 6:1ff. Note Josephus, *Antiq.*, XIX. vi. 1.

[86] The varied reactions of historians to this episode underscore the difficulty and delicacy of Paul's dilemma; see Macgregor, *IB*, vol. 9, pp. 283f. Cf. Munck's account based on textual emendation, *Paul*, pp. 238ff.; Bornkamm in Keck and Martyn, *Luke–Acts*, pp. 204f.

[87] Josephus, *War*, V. ii, 1f.

[88] Ibid, II. xiii. 3f.

A touch of personal admiration is revealed in the author's comment: "Paul, standing on the steps, motioned with his hand to the people; and when *there was a great hush*, he spoke to them in the Hebrew language. . . ."[89] Tradition has it that Paul was not an impressive man in his physique and appearance. [90]

It is hard to believe that Paul could have spoken formally and at such length to this restive mob. Has Luke introduced proof of Paul's innocence by means of a conventional literary device, the speech? Paul's words are altogether appropriate to the occasion, and even mobs have been known to become quiet when someone yells, "Let the scoundrel have a chance to speak!" Paul stressed his strict loyalty to the Law by identifying himself with the people to whom he spoke. He once stood where they were standing, persecuting men like himself with a zeal no less than their own. It was true that a change had taken place, but Paul argued that he had not abandoned his old faith. He had rather found its fulfillment. The Christ of promise had revealed himself to Paul as being none other than Jesus of Nazareth, risen from the dead. Paul stressed the fact that a man of Damascus, "a devout man according to the Law, well spoken of by the Jews" had instructed him, confirming the continuity between God's revelation unto "the Fathers" and God's revelation in the Christ. To what conclusion was Paul's defense tending? The question is not answered in Acts for, with the mention of the word "Gentiles," the smoldering fury of the crowd was fanned into flame.

Claudius Lysias had little if any idea what Paul hoped to achieve by speaking. But it had by now become clear to Lysias that his prisoner had certainly roused the rabble. He was determined to get to the bottom of this grievance. He would torture the truth out of him. It was now imperative that Paul identify himself more fully. He spoke to Lysias of his Roman citizenship. We have already noted that Paul did not always use his "citizenship papers" as insurance against all physical harm and indignity. But few men survived the lashing of the scourge. It was one thing to die for Christ, if no honorable option presented itself; it was something else to throw one's life away.

Historians have raised serious questions about the events described in the concluding chapters of Acts. After Paul's declaration of Roman citizenship, one would think a Roman official either would release him or would assume responsibility for any judicial proceedings. Furthermore, Paul's "defense" is a diversion from the main issue, and the Apostle's identification with Pharisaism an incredible thing—inconsistent with his own statements. Again, who can believe that Paul's claim to share the Pharisees' belief in the resurrection would have won them over to his side?[91] The "trial" before the Jewish Sanhedrin is quite possible, however, upon the supposition that this body had formally lodged a complaint against Paul. Lysias would them be compelled to permit an airing of the charge. Paul's attitude in the court, and the tactical defense that he adopted, are also quite credible. The vivid details of the narrative contribute to the reader's sense of confidence in its historical value.

[89] Acts 21:40.
[90] See note 32 above. Cf. 2 Cor. 10:10.
[91] Macgregor, *IB*, vol. 9, pp. 294ff.; Weiss, *Earliest Christianity*, vol. 1, pp. 374f., n. 108.

The view is taken above that Paul acted with prudence in Jerusalem. Some aspects of the story of the "trial" might seem to deny this claim. He did not bother to begin his defense in the usual formal manner of address; he railed out against the court official, "the high priest Ananias."[92] Perhaps he added insult to injury by excusing himself, saying, "I did not know, brethren, that *he* [that a man with his reputation] was the high priest."

There is a kind of reckless abandon in Paul's bearing before the Sanhedrin, sharply contrasted with the regal dignity of Jesus before the same body and before Pilate. "When he [Jesus] was reviled, he reviled not in return; when he suffered, he did not threaten; but he trusted to him who judges justly."[93] It is not surprising that few if any men, even the great Apostle, measure up to Jesus' example. But again let it be said: Paul could not believe that his work was done. Jesus went to Jerusalem to die. Paul was determined to "see Rome."

Perhaps it is from this point of view that one must interpret Paul's words, "Brethren, I am a Pharisee, a son of Pharisees; with respect to the hope of the resurrection of the dead I am on trial."[94] It was a tactic designed to divide the court and to divert the body from the main question before it. As a Christian, Paul could argue that he was a Pharisee. The second part of Paul's claim raises a more serious question. He was not on trial concerning the hope of the resurrection. Perhaps Paul decided to throw "an apple of discord" among his judges, to remind them of the enmity existing between themselves, drawing attention away from their common enmity toward him.[95] Some have supposed that such an expedient, if adopted, would hardly have led to the violent dissension which followed. Yet Luke surely knew that this doctrinal dispute between the Pharisees and the Sadducees was an explosive one. It is possible that, like Stephen, Paul saw the futility of answering the specific charge brought against him, and that he took the opportunity to call attention to the centrality of the resurrection hope in the Christian gospel.

Sometime during the night following, Luke reports, Paul had another of his mystical visions. The Apostle became convinced that "the Lord stood by him," that he would indeed be given opportunity to "bear witness also at Rome."[96] But there is a threatening sequel in the story. Paul's enemies sought by devious means to circumvent "justice." Forty men, in a solemn confederation, planned to kill Paul, but a relative heard of the ambush and tipped him off.

Claudius Lysias recognized his duty and did it. A letter was dispatched to the governor Felix, and asylum provided for Paul at the seat of the Roman government in Palestine, Caesarea. According to the records, Antonius Felix was procurator in Judea from A.D. 52 to 59.

The three hearings of Paul's case recorded in Acts 24–25 are intensely interesting to some readers, repetitious and wearisome to others. It may be well for

[92] Acts 23:3.
[93] 1 Peter 2:22.
[94] Acts 23:6ff.
[95] Williams, *The Acts*, p. 248. Cf. Josephus, *Life*, 139ff.
[96] Acts 23:11.

all to recognize the probable reasons Luke has given so much space to them. For one thing, Paul's apologies stressed the relationship between the Old Testament and the Christian gospel. He argued, on the one hand, that the hopes of Judaism found fulfillment in Christ and, on the other hand, that Paul as a Christian Jew, far from forsaking the scriptures, had faithfully honored them. Even in his preaching to the Gentiles he had sought to fulfill the divine mission of the people Israel. Luke also may have been prompted to give so much space to Paul's hearings before governors and other officials since he knew that Theophilus (and readers of his station) would have a particular interest in the attitudes which officialdom had taken toward Paul as a guide to their own policies. And, finally, Luke surely wished to show that Paul did get to "see Rome" as the final outcome of a long chain of unforeseen and unpredictable circumstances.

In recognition of these theological and political interests of the author of Acts, some historians have suggested that his sources have been "written up." Perhaps the speeches are "doublets," since they contain similar features. The delay of Felix is puzzling, and the reasons given for it are unconvincing. But there are sound arguments in support of the veracity of Luke's account.[97] The circumstantial detail of the narrative gives credence to the whole. There is every reason to suppose that Felix found himself in a difficult corner. How could he gain from Paul's enemies the true facts of the case? The whole incident had begun in a mob scene; its instigators were unknown. Since they were "Asian Jews" they had probably returned to their homes. The only crime of which Paul was accused which was punishable by death was the charge that he had desecrated the temple. But it would be almost impossible to establish his guilt. If Paul had been "a nobody" Felix could have settled the tiresome affair as he pleased. But Paul was a Roman citizen, and Felix was a "freedman" (according to Tacitus).[98] Hence it was necessary for Felix to proceed with caution. Some degree of freedom was doubtless allowed Paul.

The arrival of the new governor, the procurator Festus, provided another opportunity for Paul's enemies to convict him.[99] We are reminded of the overtures of the Jews to Gallio. A special favor was requested of Festus by the group from Jerusalem: let Paul be returned to the scene of his "crime" for trial. Were the forty men still holding themselves to their vow? Festus, however, was no fool. Let the accusers come to Caesarea, he replied. When he returned, a hearing was set, and Paul was again given an opportunity to defend himself. This time Paul came directly to the point. In the months of waiting he had not been preparing legal briefs, but the issues had become crystal clear. "Neither against the Law of the Jews, nor against the temple . . . have I offended at all," Paul declared.[100] He was confident that no proofs of his enemies' charges on these scores would be forthcoming. Since the only matter worthy of investigation was the charge of sedition, there was no warrant for transporting Paul to Jerusalem, and Paul

[97] Weiss, *Earliest Christianity*, vol. 1, pp. 375f.; F. F. Bruce, "St. Paul in Rome," *BJRL* 46 (1964): 336ff.
[98] *Annals*, XII. 54; *Histories*, V. 9
[99] Acts 24:27; 25:1ff.
[100] Acts 25:8.

certainly did not desire it. But perhaps Festus was guided by considerations other than logic. Since Felix had been recalled for his inability to govern the Jews, Festus may have been inclined to accede to the Sanhedrin's request. What chance did Paul have in Jerusalem of seeing "justice" done? The situation was indeed desperate. He was therefore forced to seize upon his last defense. He appealed directly to Caesar. A step had now been taken from which there was no turning back.

Luke reported that Jesus, and after him, Peter, stood trial before one of the Herods. Now Paul was to have his turn. This time the Herod was the last of the dynasty, Agrippa II. Although he ruled Galilee and the territories to the northeast, he was also entrusted with the temple and with the appointments of the high priest. Herod was therefore associated with Festus in the rule of the Jews. Perhaps he came to Caesarea to pay a courtesy call on the new governor. Festus had an interesting case to call to Herod's attention. Opportunity was thus given for a fitting state occasion. Perhaps a Herodian could help Festus prepare his report to Caesar.

The scene that is portrayed is impressive: the king and the governor in their colorful robes; the notorious Bernice dressed for the occasion; the retinue of the court.[101] Before such pomp stood Paul, in chains, pleading for himself. This address is the most formally organized of the speeches of Paul in Acts. Has Luke given special attention to recreating this scene? One suspects that the plan of the defense was devised in the mind of Paul. Perhaps he was giving thought now to his appearance in Caesar's court. It was an impassioned apology for his life, and for his Lord.

The climax was nearly reached when Festus interrupted Paul. The ravings of a mad man, he cried! But Paul turned to Agrippa, recognizing his familiarity with the scriptures and with the traditions concerning Jesus and the early Church. Perhaps this background would give Agrippa a better basis for understanding. But, no, the king had had enough. Was Paul's eloquent plea beginning to disturb him? Like Pilate, he dismissed the truth with a sneer. But Paul was unquestionably innocent of the charge of sedition. In this all were agreed.

THE VOYAGE TO ROME

Luke's story of Paul's ship foundering in a storm, pounded to pieces upon the shoals, its passengers in the water narrowly escaping with their lives, has fascinating elements of surprise. It is no wonder that readers of Paul's voyage to Rome become absorbed in the nautical or heroic aspects of the story. But the narrative's theological significance ought not to be overlooked. Luke would not have gone to such lengths merely to tell an exciting episode.

By this time, the reader of Acts may have noticed that its ending closely parallels the conclusion of Luke's Gospel. Some have referred to Acts 21:1 as the beginning of "a passion narrative." Like his Lord, Paul went to Jerusalem to be rejected

[101]For gossip concerning Bernice, see references in F. F. Bruce, *Commentary on the Book of Acts* (1956), p. 434.

by the Jews, to suffer indignities at their hands, to be tried by the high priest, to be given a hearing before the Roman procurator and the regnant Herod. The storm and shipwreck appear as the nadir of Paul's fortunes. Yet the hope of reaching Rome was realized after all. The concluding chapters of Acts correspond in some ways to the crucifixion and resurrection of Jesus Christ. Yet for all the writer's admiration for Paul, the conclusion of Acts is surely not intended to glorify Paul as a man of superior wisdom, self-control, and courage, or as one whose superhuman qualities made him master of the situation. The reader is meant to realize that, from first to last, "the acts of the apostles" were wrought by God, in the fulfillment of his saving purpose for mankind in and through Christ and his Church.

Only when such considerations as the above are taken into account is there value in tracing the sea journey of Paul in some detail. Even then the commentator is bound to acknowledge that his own notes can hardly "improve" the narrative. Luke's abilities as a storyteller and historian are demonstrated impressively in the concluding section of Acts.

When, at long last, Paul arrived in Rome it was "to the Jew first" that he proclaimed the good news of Jesus Christ. One might suppose that after a quarter-century Paul would have abandoned all hope of laboring profitably among the Jews and turned his full attention to the Gentiles. But three days after arriving in Rome, he "called together the local leaders of the Jews."[102] The motive for his persistence is clear: "It is because of the hope of Israel that I am bound with this chain." Israel's hoped-for Messiah had come. This was the theme of Paul's preaching until the end.

No unfavorable report concerning Paul had come to the Jews in Rome, yet it is obvious that they were "primed" for him. They desired to hear Paul, but they made it plain that they knew that "this sect" (Christianity) was spoken against everywhere. Unable to go to the synagogue, Paul encouraged the Jews to come to his lodgings. There "from morning to evening" he attempted to "convince them about Jesus, both from the law of Moses and from the prophets." Once again there was a mixed reception. The passage which Paul cited from Isaiah was a popular "testimony" in the early Church to account for the resistance of the Jews to the preaching of the Messiah.[103]

It was beyond the scope of the writer's purpose to deal with the fate of Paul after "the two years" he resided in Rome.[104] To Paul these months were a time of opportunity. While waiting to appear before Caesar or for his prosecutors to bring their charge to Rome, he kept right on doing what he had always done. Within the limits imposed upon him, he earned his keep, preached, and taught.

The story of Paul's missions from Jerusalem to Rome ends on a note of victory. In the language of the writer of Acts, "quite openly and unhindered" is one word: *akolutos*. It expressed the faith of Luke, as well as of Paul: nothing could stop the advance of the Christian mission in the world.

[102] Acts 27:17.
[103] Cf. Matt. 13:14f.; John 12:40. Also Mark 4:12 (Luke 8:10).
[104] See Macgregor, *IB,* vol. 9, pp. 349ff.

chapter fifteen

PAUL'S LETTERS
TO THESSALONICA
AND TO CORINTH

a   b   c

(a) Coin of Claudius (A.D. 41–52), probably minted at Rome. Head of the emperor on the obverse; the draped female figures on the reverse may combine Nemesis, Pax and Victoria signifying that the emperor's victories bring lasting peace. (The American Numismatic Society) (b) Rome's peace with Parthia was reached in A.D. 63. The doors of the temple of Janus were solemnly closed. This sestertius, probably minted in A.D. 65, bears the head of Nero, laureate, bearded, on the obverse; the temple of Janus, showing a closed door (left side) on the reverse. (The American Numismatic Society) (c) Undated aureus bearing portrait of Nero wearing laurel wreath on the obverse; Salus seated, holding patera in right hand, on the reverse. (The Chase Manhattan Bank Money Museum)

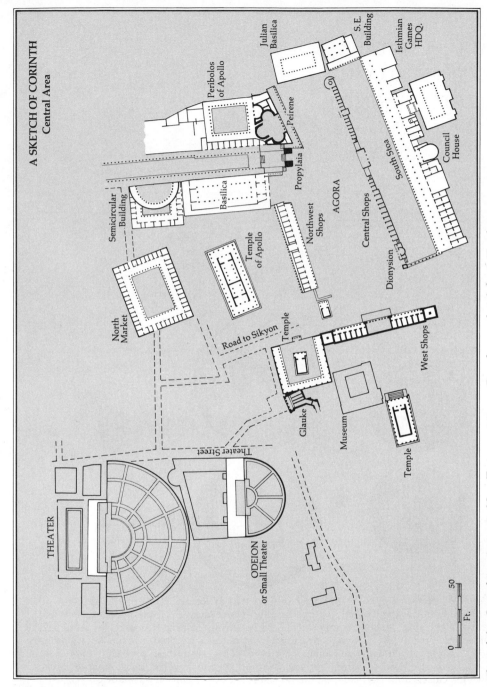

A SKETCH OF CORINTH
Central Area

THEATER

ODEION
or Small Theater

Theater Street

North Market

Semicircular Building

Basilica

Road to Sikyon

Temple

Glauke

Museum

Temple of Apollo

Northwest Shops

West Shops

AGORA

Peribolos of Apollo

Julian Basilica

Peirene

Propylaia

Central Shops

South Stoa

Dionysion

S. E. Building

Isthmian Games HDQ.

Council House

0   50
Ft.

Plan of the Corinthian Agora in New Testament times. Based on a sketch by J. Travlos. Report of Corinth excavations. (By permission, the American School of Classical Studies at Athens.)

382

View of the Corinthian Agora from the East. The South Stoa (far left) housed the Council hall, headquarters for Isthmian games, etc; the central terrace, running parallel to this Stoa, contained the Bema and shops. Paul stood on the pavement (center of picture) before Gallio, who gave his accusers a hearing from the Bema. (Courtesy of American School of Classical Studies at Athens.)

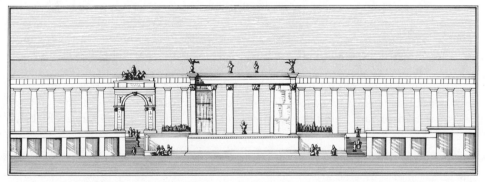

Sketch of a portion of the Central Terrace, Corinthian agora, with a reconstruction of the Bema. Based on a drawing by J. Travlos. (By permission, the American School of Classical Studies at Athens.)

T HE Apostle Paul appears in the titles of thirteen letters of the New Testament.[1] It is unlikely that he wrote three of these—1 and 2 Timothy, and Titus. Colossians and Ephesians are denied Paul by many scholars. Eight or possibly nine letters provide the primary sources for our knowledge of Paul and of his churches.

The chronology of the writings of Paul which have survived is still uncertain after prolonged debate. But the following order, allowing for a narrow margin of error in the dates, is probably correct and will be followed in this study.

1. 1 Thessalonians	(from Corinth)	A.D. 50
2. 2 Thessalonians		A.D. 50, a few months later
3. 1 Corinthians	(from Ephesus)	A.D. 55 or 56
4. 2 Corinthians	(from Macedonia)	A.D. 56
5. Galatians	(from Ephesus or Corinth)	A.D. 56[2]
6. Romans	(from Corinth)	A.D. 56 or early 57
7, 8. Colossians and Philemon	(from Rome)	ca. A.D. 61
9. Philippians	(from Rome)	ca. A.D. 62[3]

A fixed point is provided by an inscription found at Delphi which dates the proconsulate of Gallio from July 1, 51 to June 30, 52. Within that period fall the events reported in Acts 18:12–18. Other dates in Paul's career are determined by reckoning forward and backward from the Apostle's arrival at Corinth in A.D. 50, utilizing notes of time and place in the letters and in Acts.[4] Paul's conversion occurred within the period A.D. 33–35 and his martyrdom during Nero's persecution of Christians, A.D. 64–65. It therefore follows that all of Paul's letters were written toward the close of his career and within a comparatively brief

[1]In the KJV a fourteenth letter is assigned to Paul, the Epistle to the Hebrews. Modern scholars have rejected this surmise (cf. RSV), to which exception was taken in the ancient Church; see below, pp. 527ff.

[2]Some scholars believe that Galatians was dispatched from Syria in A.D. 49. See below, pp. 419f.

[3]It is possible that Philippians was written from Ephesus during an imprisonment of Paul (A.D. 53–56). See below, pp. 453ff.

[4]A. Deissmann, *St. Paul*, trans. L. R. M. Strachan (1912), pp. 235ff.; Feine-Behm-Kümmel, *Intro.*, pp. 179ff. See also, C. B. Caird, "Chronology of the N.T.," *IDB*, vol. 1, pp. 603ff.; Ogg, *Chronology*. cf. Knox, *Chapters*, pp. 81ff.; the evidence for "the usual chronology of Paul's letters" is reviewed skeptically by J. C. Hurd, Jr. (*1 Corinthians*, pp. 12ff.).

384

period. This observation inhibits the search for a progressive sophistication of Paul's theology, or for evidence that he gradually abandoned early Jewish-Christian for more universal Hellenistic thought-forms. If there was a development in Paul's thought during his active missionary career, it was the reflex of changing situations confronting him, and not the maturity which comes with transition from youth to age.

The arrangement of Paul's letters has sometimes been decided by the common themes to be found in two or more of them. It should not be forgotten, however, that the exigencies of the moment directed Paul in his correspondence as in his missionary journeys. Similar situations might have arisen at different times in different places. Paul's letters are an *ad hoc* disposition of special problems as these were brought to his attention. In every case his letters served as substitutes for, or preparatory steps toward, direct pastoral action. Because of the nonliterary nature of Paul's letters, the term *epistle,* which is commonly applied to them, can be misleading.[5]

The letters of Paul bear formal resemblance to the common types written during the period. Yet they are "like rare and attractive wild plants growing in the conventional and well-kept garden of contemporary Greek writers."[6] The Apostle's passionate concern led him to subordinate the well-turned phrase and the orderly application of his metaphors to forthrightness in speech. Apparently he visualized his readers and their reactions as he dictated his letters, and his words were charged with feeling.

It is this quality of passionate concern which draws the modern reader of Paul's letters into a vigorous dialogue. Behind the specific local conditions which confronted Paul and led him to write lie ever-present human concerns.

THE LETTERS TO THE THESSALONIANS

The Authenticity of the Letters and Their Relationship

Students of Paul declare that 1 Thessalonians is conspicuously characteristic of him in language and personal qualities. But two major difficulties are said to stand in the way of accepting Paul's authorship of 2 Thessalonians. First in importance is the matter of similarity and difference in language and style. Portions of 2 Thessalonians resemble so closely 1 Thessalonians that some interpreters suspect that Paul's ideas have been paraphrased by another person. Why, it is asked, should Paul have written almost identical letters to the same church within a short interval of time? Besides this verbal similarity, one must reckon with a difference in the tone of the letters reflected in their styles. The mood of 1 Thessalonians is warm, affectionate, personal; that of 2 Thessalonians, cool, formal, official, and, some would add, "grim and vengeful."[7]

[5]Deissmann, *St. Paul,* pp. 8ff.

[6]Lietzmann, *Beginnings,* p. 114. Note samples of letter writing preserved in papyrus fragments, Barrett, *Background,* pp. 27ff.

[7]F. W. Beare, *St. Paul and His Letters* (1962), p. 42; McNeile, *Intro.,* pp. 128f.; J. E. Frame, *Epistles of Paul to the Thessalonians* (1924) [hereafter, *Epistles*].

A second major objection relates to the alleged difference in the eschatology of the two letters. The writer of 1 Thessalonians expects an imminent coming of the Lord Jesus without signs.[8] In 2 Thessalonians it is declared that certain signs will precede the coming of Christ, and that an indeterminate time may elapse before the End comes.[9] By itself this objection to a single authorship is not serious. The notion that the End is near and that premonitory signs are to be expected are not mutually exclusive ideas in Jewish or Christian apocalypses. Nevertheless, some have concluded that since the language and style suggest that 2 Thessalonians is a pseudonymous writing, the different emphases in the eschatology of the two letters is also evidence of different authorship.[10]

A few scholars have been convinced by these considerations. But no criteria have been established for determining the psychological impossibility of Paul's authorship of 2 Thessalonians, and no consensus has been reached concerning the purpose of an alleged imitator of 1 Thessalonians.[11] Yet there are those who resist the traditional view in other ways, recognizing the force of these difficulties. Perhaps, it is said, Paul delegated Silvanus or Timothy to write one or the other of the letters.[12] Some have been persuaded by the theory advanced by Adolf Harnack and accepted, with some diffidence, by Kirsopp Lake.[13] Perhaps two letters were written by Paul in quick succession. 1 Thessalonians was addressed to Gentile Christians; 2 Thessalonians to a smaller group of Jewish–Christians who were in the church, to preclude misunderstanding of certain points in the longer letter. This view is attractive, but is it credible that Paul acknowledged a division of this sort in one of his churches, if indeed such a thing existed?[14]

A third explanation deserves serious consideration. This is the view that 2 Thessalonians is the earlier of the two letters. There are several cogent points in favor of reversing the canonical order which may be due simply to the respective length of the letters. In 1 Thessalonians the sufferings of the church are treated as belonging to the past, whereas in 2 Thessalonians they are at their height. Moreover, in the shorter letter Paul speaks of recently receiving reports of disorders in the community. The allusive references to disorders in the longer letter seem to presuppose Paul's earlier acknowledgment of them.[15] It is also claimed that the eschatological passages are more easily understood if the shorter letter preceded the longer one. After reading 2 Thessalonians, persons in the church might naturally have asked: If there is to be a delay in the coming of Christ, what hope have those who die in the meantime?[16]

[8]1 Thess. 5:1ff.

[9]2 Thess. 2:1ff.

[10]Feine-Behm-Kümmel, *Intro.*, pp. 187ff.

[11]M. S. Enslin (*Beginnings*, p. 244) suggests that early in the second century a Paulinist became convinced that Paul's adventist teaching was misunderstood. Cf. Beare, *St. Paul*, p. 44.

[12]F. C. Burkitt, *Christian Beginnings* (1924), pp. 128ff.

[13]Lake, *Earlier Epistles*, pp. 83ff.

[14]Note 1 Thess. 5:27.

[15]Cf. 2 Thess. 3:11 and 1 Thess. 4:10–12; 5:14.

[16]T. W. Manson, *Companion*, pp. 101f.; L. O. Bristol, "Paul's Thessalonian Correspondence," *Exp. T.* LV (1944): 223. If this suggestion be followed, 2 Thess. might have been written from Athens late in A.D. 49, 1 Thess. from Corinth early in A.D. 50. Cf. Feine-Behm-Kümmel, *Intro.*, p. 186.

While certainty is not possible, most scholars affirm Paul's authorship of both letters and hold that the difficulties have been exaggerated. The reader is encouraged to adopt this position as a working hypothesis. Furthermore, the situation and purpose of both letters is credible on the assumption that they were written in the canonical order.[17]

Interpretation of the Letters

Let us turn now to consideration of the letters themselves.

AN OUTLINE OF THE FIRST LETTER OF PAUL TO THE THESSALONIANS

A. Introduction, 1:1–3:13:
    1. The superscription, 1:1
    2. The thanksgiving, 1:2–2:16: for the faith, love, and hope of the Thessalonians (2-10); in recollection of his labor among them, and their welcome (2:1–16)
    3. Paul's longing to visit the church intensified by Timothy's return, 2:17–3:10
    4. Paul's prayer for the fulfillment of his hopes, and for the Thessalonians that they may be perfected in holiness, 3:11–13
B. A plea for more consecration, 4:1–12:
    5. Concerning sexual purity, 4:1–8
    6. Concerning brotherly love, 4:9–12
C. The coming of Christ, 4:13–5:11:
    7. Words of comfort concerning those who die beforehand, 4:13–18
    8. Words of encouragement for "the sons of light," 5:1–11
D. Exhortations to follow in the Christian way, 5:12–22:
    9. Respect and loving esteem for leaders, 5:12–13a
    10. Peace among brethren, 5:13b
    11. Patient consideration for the loafers, the faint-hearted, and the weak, 5:14
    12. Nonretaliation; good will to all, 5:15
    13. Joy; prayerfulness; thanksgiving in all circumstances, 5:16–18
    14. Spiritual gifts to be sought; all forms of evil to be avoided, 5:19–22
E. The conclusion, 5:23–28:
    15. Prayer; an assurance, 5:23–24
    16. Final requests, 5:25–27
    17. Benediction, 5:28

The reader gains a vivid impression that in the first part of this letter (A), Paul's relief is mingled with anxiety. He is grateful and relieved that the Thessalonian Christians have stood firm under very trying circumstances, but he is anxious lest impugners of his character and motives destroy his work and the confidence

[17]See the judicious comments in McNeile, *Intro.*, pp. 128ff.

which the church has placed in him. From the moment he left, Paul wished to return to Thessalonica. Timothy's report (and perhaps a letter from the church) had increased his longing.

Luke provides an account of Paul's departure from Thessalonica.[18] He reports that Jews in the city had stirred up the crowd against the missionaries, and a Christian named Jason and some others in the church had been brought before the city authorities, rightly identified by Luke as politarchs.[19] In the absence of the missionaries there was a judgment against them, probably condemnation by default. In his letter, Paul acknowledged that still others had sought to thwart the Christian mission in Macedonia. He wrote: "you suffered the same things from *your own countrymen* as you did from the Jews."[20] Would the new converts stand firm? Timothy was sent from Athens to encourage the church.[21]

When Timothy rejoined Paul at Corinth, Paul learned that the enemies of the church had been attacking the Apostle's behavior during the Thessalonian mission and making capital of his failure to return.[22] Suspicion had been aroused in the minds of some of Paul's converts. That Paul should have given so much space in his letter to a defense of his conduct and motives clearly implies that he felt the dire nature of the situation, but also was confident that his affectionate and reassuring words would overcome it.[23]

Timothy brought word of the courage and fidelity of the Christians at Thessalonica and Paul was greatly comforted (3). But there were still outstanding problems. Paul had been unable to give the Thessalonian Christians adequate instruction because of the abrupt termination of his mission. In his absence, serious misunderstandings had arisen.[24] The Thessalonians were ignorant of the gospel's teaching concerning the resurrection of the dead (7). Moreover, the hope concerning the coming "day of the Lord" had not been understood (8).

Paul gave new instruction concerning the resurrection of the dead.[25] He asserted that there was a qualitative difference between pagan and Christian grief and declared that the resurrection of Christians was assured in the resurrection of Christ. He did not develop this teaching, however, because the immediate problem at Thessalonica concerned the relation of the dead to the coming Day of the Lord. On the authority of a traditional saying of Jesus, Paul declared that those who are alive at the time of his coming would have no advantage over those who die beforehand. The dead would arise to participate in the eschatological victory of the Messiah and his community. Paul's apocalyptic imagery appears to us as

[18]Acts 17:5ff. The Thessalonian ministry was probably longer than three weeks. Cf. 1 Thess. 2:7ff.; 2 Thess. 3:7ff.; Phil. 4:15.

[19]See Cadbury, *Acts in History*, p. 41, and n. 21, p. 54.

[20]1 Thess. 2:14ff.

[21]1 Thess. 3:1ff. Not reported by Luke, but note Acts 17:14f.

[22]1 Thess. 3:6; Acts 18:5.

[23]The absence of apologetic statements in 2 Thess. indicates that the letter achieved its desired effects. Frame, *Epistles*, pp. 9f.

[24]1 Thess. 3:10; 4:13ff.

[25]It is unlikely that Paul had given earlier instruction on this aspect of the *kerygma*. Was it thought by some at Thessalonica that believers would not be subject to death?

fleeting and impressionistic. He offered his readers no full exposition of his eschatology.[26]

The Greek mind resisted the idea of a resurrection of the body although the belief was common that the souls of men were subject to reincarnations, being essentially immortal. Moreover, the Greeks thought of history as an ever-recurring circle, not as a forward-moving line of time directed towards a day of judgment and a general resurrection.[27] Doubtless Paul's eschatological proclamation baffled his Gentile hearers. But there is no evidence that on this account Paul resorted to speculative reasoning or to an allegorizing of Jewish apocalyptic symbols in describing the Christian hope. His contagious assurance that death brings no separation of the believer from his Lord, and that an eternal fellowship with Christ is promised must have brought comfort to mourners where knowledge failed. We have seen that in the Hellenistic Age confidence was placed in the illumination of the mysteries of life and death through revelation when rational thought was unable to penetrate the darkness.

The moral delinquencies of the Thessalonian Christians probably were related to their failure to grasp the full significance of the Christian hope (8). The Greek view of the human personality was dualistic. Where religion permeated philosophy, the belief was sustained that the spirit or mind of man was by nature divine or, if properly enlightened, destined to share the life of eternity. But the "flesh" of man had no decisive influence upon his "spirit"; his bodily impulses and actions were merely instinctive or morally indifferent. Only the disposition of man's mind or spirit affected his eternal destiny.

Paul inherited from Judaism a belief in the profound unity of man's nature as wholly related to God. Moreover, as a Christian apostle, Paul envisaged a new stature of manhood in Jesus Christ. He experienced the indwelling of the Holy Spirit and proclaimed the hope of the resurrection of the body. Accordingly, the Apostle's ideal was the life of total consecration, "umblamable in holiness" before God. Christians were called to be "saints," that is to say, persons who acknowledged that they were chosen by God and thus consecrated unto Him.[28] Paul employs the eschatological sanction to enforce this ideal. The Day of the Lord is near but it will come without warning, and the immoral will be punished.[29]

Paul taught that the Christian ideal of consecration had practical and comprehensive implications (5–6). Sexual purity meant abstinence from relations outside of marriage. The married were to have such respect for their mates and other persons that lust and adultery were forbidden.[30] Paul commended the Thessalonians for their "love of the brethren." Nevertheless, he reminded the "loafers" in the church that they lacked love unless they aspired to live quietly, minded

[26] A fuller statement is given in 1 Cor. 15; see below, pp. 404f.

[27] Cullmann, *Christ and Time*, pp. 51ff.

[28] 1 Thess. 2:11f.; 3:12f.; 4:3, 7f.; 5:23f.

[29] 1 Thess. 1:10; 2:16; 4:6ff.; 5:9.

[30] 1 Thess. 4:3ff. Does Paul's reference to "the weak" include those who have not attained this standard of sexual morality (5:14)?

their own affairs, worked with their hands, and were dependent upon nobody.[31] To the rest Paul wrote that love is always patient, even with loafers.[32]

Apparently the proclamation of the imminence of the Day of the Lord had led some Christians at Thessalonica to become overly excited. Their hope had reached such a feverish state as to be morally enervating. They had abandoned their work and become wards of the community. Paul reminded his converts that a proper understanding of the Advent hope would not lead to a fanatical other-worldliness, but to a tranquillity of mind, to such industry as would leave no time for meddling in others' affairs, and to an honorable independence which would command the respect of outsiders.

The patterns of ethical instruction in 1 Thessalonians are found in several non-Pauline letters of the New Testament and in other early Christian literature. This teaching is parallel in its forms to ethical instruction in Hellenistic writings generally. It is therefore probable that the Thessalonian letters contain typical expositions of "the Christian Way" in the Hellenistic churches.[33]

An Outline of the Second Letter of Paul to the Thessalonians

A. Introduction, 1:1–4:
   1. The superscription, 1:1–2
   2. The thanksgiving, expressing pride in the Thessalonians' steadfastness and faith, 1:3–4
B. The revelation of the Lord Jesus, 1:5–12:
   3. Rest for the saints from sufferings; the disobedient to be judged, 1:5–10
   4. Prayer: support for the believers; the glorification of Christ, 1:11–12
C. The revelation of the man of lawlessness, 2:1–12:
   5. The Day of the Lord has not come, 2:1–2
   6. After "the rebellion" comes the lawless one, 2:3–12
D. Words of comfort and encouragement, 2:13–17:
   7. Saints are called to obtain glory, 2:13–15
   8. Prayer for the elect, 2:16–17
E. Final appeals, 3:1–15:
   9. Request for prayer, 3:1–2
   10. Expressions of confidence in the Lord, and in the Thessalonians, 3:3–5
   11. Injunctions concerning the loafers, 3:6–15
F. The conclusion, 3:16–18:
   12. Benediction, 3:16
   13. Inscribed saluation, 3:17
   14. Second benediction, 3:18

A comparison of this outline with 1 Thessalonians will reveal the close resem-

---

[31] 1 Thess. 4:9ff.
[32] 1 Thess. 5:14.
[33] See above, pp. 164f. Dodd, *Gospel and Law*, pp. 12ff.; D. G. Bradley, "The Typos as a Form in the Pauline Paraenesis," *JBL* LXXII (1953): 238ff.

blance between the two letters. We may therefore proceed to the distinctive part of 2 Thessalonians (C), for it is here that we find the probable occasion for its writing.

Within a few weeks after dispatching his first letter, Paul learned that the problems at Thessalonica were more serious than he had supposed. This church was not only ignorant of the Christian hope concerning the dead and the dying, and needing encouragement in view of the coming Day of the Lord (D); there was a fundamental misunderstanding of this aspect of the Christian *kerygma*. Paul could not wait to visit the church, for some persons were misrepresenting his views and thereby causing great excitement. Moreover, the enemies of the church had stepped up their persecutions, and loafers in the church were creating a serious problem. A short letter was therefore written to recall his teaching while in their midst and to beg the Thessalonians to adhere to "the traditions" which had been passed on to them orally or by letter.[34]

As we shall see, it was not a total misrepresentation to declare, as some were doing, that Paul proclaimed a "realized eschatology."[35] Yet it is certain that at the time of the Thessalonian correspondence Paul shared the perspective of the early Church: the hope of Israel had not been completely fulfilled; salvation through Christ was a present reality and also a future hope.

It is futile to seek a full exposition of Paul's eschatology in 2 Thessalonians since he asked his readers to recall his teachings. His immediate purpose was to quiet the fanatical excitement in the church, not to detail a blueprint of the close of the age. As a result, certain of Paul's statements in this section defy understanding. The "rebellion" referred to the commonplace apocalyptic belief that religious apostasy precedes the coming of the Day of the Lord.[36] But what is the meaning of Paul's reference to "the mystery of lawlessness already at work"? And who is this "man of lawlessness," claiming divinity and enthroning himself in the temple? A further problem relates to the identification of the force or person "restraining" this lawlessness.[37]

Some have held that "the man of lawlessness" refers to an emperor or agent of Rome, and that by the mystery of lawlessness Paul meant the power regnant in the imperial administration. But it is consistent with other statements by Paul that Rome should be considered the restrainer not the cause of lawlessness.[38] Accordingly, others interpret Paul as referring to Judaism as "the mystery," and some leader—perhaps a wicked high priest—as "the man of lawlessness." Another suggestion can be traced, like the above alternatives, to ancient Christian sources. Paul, it is claimed, was the restrainer of the mystery of lawlessness, and that which restrained (or delayed) the revelation of the man of lawlessness was

[34]2 Thess. 2:15. That another letter on similar subjects would be needed so shortly after the first is sufficient cause for the sharpness and coolness of the Apostle's words.

[35]2 Thess. 2:2.

[36]2 Thess. 2:5f., 14. Cf. 2 Ezra 5:1ff.; Jub. 23:14ff.; Matt. 24:10ff.

[37]Both neuter (v. 6) and masculine (v. 7b) forms are used.

[38]Cf. Rom. 13:1ff.; see below, pp. 444f.

the Christian gospel, which must be proclaimed to the Gentiles before the End comes.[39]

It is probable that Paul had in mind definite historical situations and persons, but we cannot be certain of this. The Apostle's vision included more than the observable events of history. His thought is mystical and soars to cosmic dimensions. The revelation of the man of lawlessness, with "pretended signs and wonders," is described as "the activity of Satan." With the coming of the Day of the Lord the lawless one is to be slain as the result of a cosmic conflict. Paul's imagery contains some of the characteristic stage properties of Jewish and Christian apocalypses.[40]

While the two Thessalonian letters are not the greatest of Paul's writings, they are certainly distinctive and of undoubted value. They reveal in marvelous ways the personal and pastoral qualities of Paul, and also the strength and weakness of a small Christian community, but a few weeks old, struggling to understand the gospel of Jesus Christ and to maintain itself against overwhelming odds.

THE CORINTHIAN CORRESPONDENCE

Preliminary Questions

The narrative of Acts enables us to identify the period of the Apostle's contacts with the Corinthian Christians; Paul's letters shed remarkable light upon his relations with them.

Paul's mission to Corinth began in the winter of A.D. 49–50 and ended in the summer of 52.[41] After this, the Apostle returned to Judea and Syria. We are left to guess how long it was before the "third missionary journey" began, but it is probable that the visitation of the churches in the regions of Galatia and Phrygia was started in the early spring, A.D. 53.[42] The eventual destination of this trip was Ephesus, and Paul labored there for the better part of three years, A.D. 53–56.[43] Upon leaving Ephesus, he visited the churches in Macedonia and Achaia. Luke implies that this time Paul stayed at Corinth for three months before going through Macedonia en route to Jerusalem. His last visit to the Corinthians probably occurred late in A.D. 56.[44]

For the story of Paul's relations with the church at Corinth during the last two or three years of this period we turn to 1 and 2 Corinthians. But before these

[39]Cf. Mark 13:10; Acts 1:6ff.; 3:19f.; Rev. 6:1ff. Note the parallel in the Jewish notion that the Messiah's coming is delayed for the conversion of Israel; Elijah must first come. See Munck, *Paul,* pp. 36ff.

[40]Do Paul's words reflect the Antichrist myth of the Johannine circle? See pp. 563, 567. Perhaps it is an error to trace pre-Gnostic ideas in the Thessalonian letters; see R. M. Grant, *Gnosticism and Early Christianity,* p. 155f.

[41]Acts 18: see above, pp. 370f.

[42]Acts 18:18, 22f.

[43]Acts 19:1ff.

[44]Acts 21:1ff. Paul left Ephesus before Easter (Acts 20:5; 1 Cor. 16:8). Did the riot precipitate an earlier departure than planned? For a discussion of Paul's trials at Ephesus, see below, pp. 454f.

letters are studied, several questions relating to their integrity need to be investigated.

1 Corinthians was not Paul's first letter to the church at Corinth. In it he refers to another written earlier, and to a misunderstanding which it had caused.[45] The full text of this "previous letter" is lost, but numerous scholars have held that a fragment of it is embedded in the canonical writing 2 Corinthians. The six verses which follow 2 Corinthians 6:13 interrupt the train of thought, while 2 Corinthians 7:2ff. may be joined smoothly to 6:13. Moreover, it is thought by some that the teaching of this erratic "block" answers to Paul's description of his previous letter, and is of such nature as to necessitate clarification. Should it be concluded that the passage is a secondary insertion, its identity as a fragment of the "previous letter" is an attractive hypothesis. It must be recognized that the brevity of the "fragment" makes its preliterary history problematical in the extreme. But if for other reasons the integrity of 2 Corinthians is suspect, the plausibility of one or other of the fragment hypotheses increases.[46]

This reference in 1 Corinthians 5:9 to a previous letter is an important building block in the construction of one scholar's elaborate theory concerning Paul's early relations to the Corinthians.[47] Using 1 Corinthians as a source, he hypothesizes the content of Paul's original preaching at Corinth, Paul's previous letter, and the church's responses to it. Then, against this background, 1 Corinthians is interpreted as a careful statement which, on the one hand, avoids the enthusiasm typical of the Apostle's first preaching (which had misled some converts) and, on the other hand, modifies the too-restrictive positions which Paul's "previous letter" had commended. This ingenuous thesis has failed to commend itself, but a review of its construction sheds light upon several of the more difficult texts of 1 Corinthians.[48]

The unity of 1 Corinthians is usually assumed. A few scholars have divided the document into two or more letters, and still others have attempted to "restore" an original text by rearrangements. These efforts have attracted little interest, for they do not seem to provide any information about the development of Paul's dialogue with the Corinthians which is not afforded upon the assumption that 1 Corinthians is a single letter.[49].

The case is quite different with respect to 2 Corinthians. It is commonly held that 2 Corinthians 1–9 is actually Paul's fourth letter, to which has been attached, by another, a portion of a third letter from the Apostle. Near the beginning of

[45]1 Cor. 5:9.

[46]R. H. Strachan, 2 Corinthians (1953), pp. xv, 3ff.; Lake, Earlier Epistles, pp. 120ff., conjectures that other parts of the previous letter may be embedded in 1 Cor. Cf. Filson, IB, vol. 10, pp. 269f., who rejects the "previous letter" hypothesis. For arguments supporting a non-Pauline origin of this fragment, see J. Gnilka, "2 Cor. 6:14–7:1 in the Light of the Qumran Texts and the Testament of the Twelve Patriarchs," in Paul and Qumran, ed. J. Murphy-O'Connor (1968), pp. 48ff.

[47]Hurd, 1 Corinthians.

[48]C. K. Barrett, The First Epistle to the Corinthians (1968), pp. 6ff. [hereafter, First Epistle].

[49]Craig, IB, vol. 10, p. 6; J. Moffatt, The First Epistle of Paul to the Corinthians (1938), pp. xxiv ff. [hereafter, I Corinthians]. The authenticity of I Cor. is beyond question. See I Clem. 47:1; Justin Martyr, Dial. with Trypho, 33.

2 Corinthians one finds references to a severe and threatening letter from Paul which had grieved members of the church and caused Paul some emotional and regretful moments. 1 Corinthians could not possibly be this letter. But, in the view of many, 2 Corinthians 10–13 preserve it, or a part of it. In 2 Corinthians 1–9 Paul writes of his joy and great relief from a crushing anxiety. His "severe letter," or "sorrowful letter" as it is sometimes designated, and the presence of Titus at Corinth, had brought about a major change in the situation. Looking back upon the past crisis, Paul was exhilarated by the thought of the reconciling ministry of an apostle of Jesus Christ. In this frame of mind he was magnanimous to his opponents. In chapters 8–9 he seems to be closing this "thankful letter."[50] Many have concluded that it is psychologically impossible that after writing 1–9 Paul could have penned the angry and sarcastic remonstrance and self-defense which follow in 10–13. Therefore, the last four chapters of 2 Corinthians must form part of the "severe letter" written after Paul's "painful visit" to Corinth.[51]

The major alternatives are presented as (1), (2), and (3) in the following table:

	(1)	(2)	(3)
Letter A (Note, 1 Cor. 5:9)	lost	lost	a fragment preserved (2 Cor. 6:14–7:1)
Corinthians visit Paul at Ephesus; a letter received (1 Cor. 1:11; 16:17; 7:1)			
Letter B (Note, 2 Cor. 2:1ff.; 12:14; 13:1ff.) Paul goes to Corinth—"the painful visit"	1 Cor.	1 Cor.	1 Cor.
Letter C "the severe letter" (Note, 2 Cor. 2:4; 7:8)	lost	partially preserved (2 Cor. 10–13)	partially preserved (2 Cor. 10–13)
Paul leaves Ephesus; meets Titus with news from Corinth in Macedonia (2 Cor. 2:13; 7:13)			
Letter D "the thankful letter" (Note, 2 Cor. 1:11; 2:14; 8:16; 9:12, 15)	2 Cor.	2 Cor. 1–9	2 Cor. 1:1–6:13; 7:2–9:15

[50]Attention may be called to the ostensibly repetitious admonitions in chapters 8, 9 concerning "the collection," leading some scholars, upon insufficient grounds, to postulate that these chapters are fragments of two letters. E.g., J. Héring, *The Second Epistle of Saint Paul to the Corinthians*, trans. Heathcote and Allcock (1967), p. 65 [hereafter, *Second Epistle*]. Cf. Feine-Behm-Kümmel, *Intro.*, pp. 213f.

[51]Filson, *IB*, vol. 10, pp. 270f.; Lake, *Earlier Epistles*, pp. 154ff.; Strachan, *2 Corinthians*, pp. xvi ff; J. Héring, *Second Epistle*, pp. xi f.

The defenders of the unity of 2 Corinthians point to a number of difficulties inherent in the several partition theories. It is easy to exaggerate the contrast between the tone of the two major sections of 2 Corinthians, 1–9 and 10–13. But the chief difficulty lies in the unnatural interpretation that must be placed upon several passages referring to Paul's future plans. It seems logical to conclude that 2 Corinthians 12:14–18 was written after 2 Corinthians 8:16–24. Moreover, 12:14, 21 and 13:1 were written in *anticipation* of a visit; "the severe letter" as a *substitute* for one. The partition theorists have claimed that there are passages in 10–13 which point forward, and corresponding passages in 1–9 which point backward, to the *same* actions of Paul. But these statements are capable of more plausible interpretations on the assumption that 2 Corinthians is a unity as it stands. If 10–13 is a part of *Letter C* it is strange that the conditions Paul imposes for his next visit in these chapters do not include any reference to the offender whose action occasioned his "severe letter." The event which was the subject of the "severe letter" according to 2 Corinthians 2:3–5, 9, is not mentioned at all in 2 Corinthians 10–13.[52]

Final agreement will probably never be reached on these questions. Since the partition theories fall short of being convincing, it is perhaps best to conclude that "the previous letter" and "the severe letter" (*Letters A and C*) are lost to us, and that 2 Corinthians as we have it was composed by Paul as a single letter, though not without interruptions of time and mood, and some delays.

Divisons at Corinth and Paul's Opponents

Before a close analysis of 1 and 2 Corinthians is undertaken, another general problem should be faced. Almost every part of this correspondence reveals that the church at Corinth was seriously divided and that some of its members vigorously challenged Paul's authority. Therefore, a perennial question arises: Is it possible to describe the particular factions at Corinth and their distinguishing viewpoints and to identify the leaders and groups opposing Paul?

At the beginning of 1 Corinthians, Paul referred to the slogans of various persons, "I belong to Paul . . . to Apollos . . . to Cephas . . . to Christ." His words suggest to some readers that there were four, or at least three, distinct sects comprising the Christian community at Corinth; others interpret Paul's statements to mean only that there were quarrelsome groups within a single congregation.[53] Nowhere does the Apostle analyze the opinions of these partisans or directly attack their leaders and their doctrines. Paul acknowledged these persons only to teach that their schismatic spirit revealed a serious misunderstanding of the nature of the lordship of Christ and the Church's unity. His initial concern in

---

[52]McNeil, *Intro.*, pp. 139ff.; R. V. G. Tasker, *The Second Epistle of Paul to the Corinthians* (1958), pp. 30f. [hereafter, *2 Corinthians*]; Munck, *Paul*, pp. 168ff.; Heard, *Intro.*, p. 192. H. Windisch and others have advocated that 2 Cor. 10–13 preserves part of a letter written some while after 2 Cor. 1–9. L. Pherigo dates the final letter during Paul's imprisonment at Rome: "Paul and the Corinthian Church," *JBL* LXVIII (1949): 341ff. Cf. Feine-Behm-Kümmel, *Intro.*, pp. 212f.

[53]The existence of a "Christ party" is debatable. See Craig, *IB*, vol. 10, pp. 21f.; Hurd, *1 Corinthians*, 101ff. Cf. Munck, *Paul*, pp. 142f.; C. K. Barrett, "Christianity at Corinth, *BJRL* 46 (1964): 273ff.

this letter was to counter the argument of those who were claiming that his exposition of the gospel lacked intellectual challenge.

Some scholars have attempted to show that these particular groups are pre-supposed throughout the Corinthian letters. Thus, it is said, "the weak" referred to in 1 Corinthians 8 belonged to the "Cephas party"; those who denied a future resurrection of the dead (1 Cor. 15:12) belonged to the "Christ party"; and so on. Since there are large elements of conjecture in all such connections, many scholars have considered it futile to base interpretations of particular passages upon a partisan alignment. The enthusiastic endorsement of one missionary and the disparagement of others were but one expression of the schismatic spirit at Corinth. Other divisions in the church seem to have been caused by the social stratification of its membership; still others by the presence in the community of Gentiles and Jews representing various backgrounds.[54]

Opponents of Paul constituting the gravest challenge to his authority are most directly dealt with in 2 Corinthians. During his "painful visit" to Corinth, Paul suffered some serious abuse from one person in the church, and none of its membership arose to his defense.[55] Shortly afterward, the resistance to Paul at Corinth was strengthened by the arrival of persons who disputed vigorously Paul's authority. Since it is stated that these newcomers were of Jewish origin, it has been surmised by some readers that they were "Judaizers."[56] Claiming to be true apostles of Christ, or their representatives, and "servants of righteousness," they strongly opposed Paul's teaching that Gentile converts were wholly free from the requirements of the Mosaic Law.[57] Some have claimed that Paul's reference to "letters of recommendation" in 2 Corinthians 3:1 shows that these Judaizers came as official representatives from Judea. They had brought to Corinth letters of introduction from James and the church of Jerusalem.[58] The notice taken of Peter and "the brothers of the Lord" in 1 Corinthians 9:4ff. has been judged by some as evidence that a Judaizing element connected with Jerusalem was active in Corinth prior to the later arrival of these visiting brethren. In any event, sometime before the correspondence preserved in 2 Corinthians, Judaizing opposition to Paul at Corinth was intensified.[59]

The chief objection to this Judaizer theory is that circumcision is not alluded to in the Corinthian letters. In Galatians and Romans this was the issue in Paul's struggle with the Judaizers.[60] At Corinth would Judaizers have contented them-

[54]Craig, Beginning, pp. 7f.; Feine-Behm-Kümmel, Intro., pp. 200ff.

[55]2 Cor. 2:5ff.

[56]2 Cor. 11:22.

[57]Strachan, 2 Corinthians, pp. xxi ff.; Dibelius and Kümmel, Paul, pp. 137f.

[58]Strachan, 2 Corinthians, p. 80; Schoeps, Paul, pp. 78ff. Cf. Acts 15:1; Gal. 2:12.

[59]See Barrett, "Christianity at Corinth," note 53 above, pp. 286ff., who discusses with approval E. Käsemann's thesis that Paul's attack on "the superlative apostles" refers to the Jerusalem apostles. Barrett revives T. W. Manson's hypothesis that the Judaizers at Corinth, who did not require cir-cumcision of non-Jewish converts, were traveling missionaries who had strengthened the position previously advocated by members of the Cephas party (and by Peter himself?). Cf. Feine-Behm-Kümmel, Intro., pp. 209f.

[60]See below, pp. 420ff. and 440f.

selves with attacking Paul's authority and refrained from advocating their legalistic doctrines?

Perhaps the major alternative to the theory that Paul's opposition came from Judaizers is the opinion that his opponents were Christians whose background was Diaspora Judaism and whose understanding of the gospel was pre-Gnostic. Having received the Holy Spirit, some Jewish-Christians at Corinth were contending that they possessed "knowledge" (*gnosis*) and "spiritual gifts" which lifted them above other men who still "walked according to the flesh." Their pre-Gnostic version of Christianity was antilegalistic: no longer were they bound by the Torah and tradition; their emancipating slogan was, "all things are lawful." They were "spiritual men" (*pneumatikoi*).[61] According to this theory, "the superlative apostles" of 2 Corinthians 10–13 were anonymous visiting brethren who had aggravated this incipient tendency in the church to a pre-Gnostic distortion of the gospel, and downgraded the authority of Paul as one who "acted in a worldly fashion." The activity of these intruders brought to a climax a situation at Corinth which needed no further complication.

The existence in Corinth of a pre-Gnostic Judaism or Jewish–Christianity can only be a speculative hypothesis. The most that can be said with assurance is that Paul's opposition at Corinth came from Jewish–Christians, and that in the Apostle's opinion they "preached another Jesus." Paul does not say wherein their gospel differed from the early Christian *kerygma*. He was convinced by their arrogant actions as well as by their teachings that they were "false apostles" and "servants" of "Satan."[62] Since it is not possible to generalize concerning the form or forms of Corinthian Christianity, it is best to rely upon the immediate context of Paul's statements for a knowledge of the various positions taken by Christians at Corinth and the particular types of persons who opposed him.

The Content of the Letters

Much information can be gleaned from careful study of the letters themselves.

AN OUTLINE OF THE FIRST LETTER OF PAUL TO THE CORINTHIANS

A. Introduction, 1:1–9:
    1. The superscription, 1:1–3
    2. The thanksgiving, 1:4–9
B. Paul's instruction based on reports concerning abuses arising out of party strife, 1:10–6:20:
    3. Acknowledgment of factions, 1:10–12
    4. The primacy of Christ, 1:13–17
    5. "The wisdom of men" and "the foolishness of God," 1:18–31

---

[61] 1 Cor. 2:15–3:4; 4:8f.; 5:2a; 9:19ff.; 14:37ff.; 2 Cor. 10:2; 11:5f. See Lake, *Earlier Epistles*, pp. 222ff.; Munck, *Paul*, pp. 174ff.
[62] 2 Cor. 11:14f., 4.

6. Paul's first visit recalled, 2:1–5
7. God's wisdom taught by the Spirit, 2:6–3:4
8. Apostles are "fellow workmen for God," not rivals; only God can judge their work, 3:5–15
9. The saints are God's temple and possess all things, 3:16–23
10. Summary: the nature of apostleship; a personal appeal, 4:1–21
11. The report concerning sexual immorality and Paul's judgment concerning the case of incest, 5:1–5
12. The purity and separation of the Church vis-à-vis the world, 5:6–13
13. The report concerning litigation among members; Paul's counsel, 6:1–8
14. Summary: consecration and freedom from "law," 6:9–20

C. Paul's answers to questions raised in a letter from Corinth, and related matters, 7:1–16:12:

15. General teaching concerning the Christian understanding of marriage, 7:1–7
16. Advice to the unmarried and widows, 7:8–9
17. Counsel concerning separation and divorce, 7:10–16
18. Paul's rule is to maintain the *status quo*, 7:17–24
19. Reason for avoiding marriage, 7:25–35
20. The betrothed and asceticism, 7:36–38
21. Another word to widows, 7:39–40
22. The question concerning idol meats and idolatry; the Christian understanding of "knowledge" and of "love," 8:1–6
23. Avoid causing "the weak" to stumble, 8:7–13
24. The apostle's privilege: self-renunciation of his rights, 9:1–23
25. "The strong" must accept discipline and resist temptation; an example from scripture, 9:24–10:13
26. Summary: The meaning of the eucharist applied to the problem; conscientious scruples and neighbor love, 10:14–11:1
27. Worship: the veiling of women, 11:2–16
28. Worship: "the Lord's Supper"—abuses, and the tradition, 11:17–26
29. Summary: self-examination; self-judgment; self-restraint, 11:27–34
30. The question concerning spiritual gifts: one Spirit, a variety of gifts, 12:1–11
31. The body of Christ and its many members. 12:12–31a
32. The "more excellent way"—love, the *sine qua non*: the nature of love; its permanence; its superiority, 12:31b–13:13
33. Prophecy and speaking in tongues, 14:1–25
34. Summary: order in the church, 14:26–40
35. The tradition of the resurrection and its crucial significance, 15:1–19
36. The resurrection and the End, 15:20–28
37. "If the dead are not raised . . . ," 15:29–34
38. The resurrection body, 15:35–50
39. Assurance of immortality, and the lasting value of Christian work, 15:51–58

40. Instructions concerning "the contribution for the saints," 16:1–4
41. Paul's plans, 16:5–9
42. Instructions concerning Paul's fellow-workers, 16:10–12
D. The conclusion, 16:13–24:
43. Final exhortations, 16:13–18
44. Greetings, 16:19–20
45. Inscribed salutation with an imprecation; the advent prayer, 16:21–22
46. Benediction, 16:23–24

1 Corinthians was written to deal with a variety of problems deserving immediate attention. Paul had received disquieting news from Corinth through "Chloe's people," and perhaps others (B). Moreover, the church had written for his counsel (C). Since the organization of Paul's letter follows spontaneously along the lines suggested by the practical problems in hand, one looks in vain in it for an orderly exposition of the Apostle's gospel. It would be false, however, to suggest that the content of 1 Corinthians is "practical" rather than "theological." Few letters of the Apostle demonstrate as clearly that every part of Paul's moral instruction was related to some aspect of the Christian *kerygma*.[63]

We have seen that one cause of the divisions at Corinth arose from a misguided loyalty attached to various leaders (3). Apollos, who had been instructed by Paul's converts at Ephesus, had conducted a mission at Corinth in Paul's absence.[64] Some Christians there had championed the leadership of Apollos, and had compared his preaching with that of Paul to the latter's disadvantage.[65] Others had championed Peter. It is not possible to know whether or not Peter preached at Corinth; Paul himself may have told them about his special relation to Christ. Some deny that the words "I belong to Christ" referred to a fourth party at Corinth, but others believe its existence is implied from Paul's remark in 2 Corinthians 10:7. The "Christ party" probably was a group professing direct visions of Christ, an unbounded freedom resulting from their faith and baptism in his name, and repudiating all human leaders.[66]

With fine tact, Paul pointed to the error of his own champions (4). He had not spent his time in Corinth making Paulinists. He was indeed "the father" of the Corinthian church, but even the few persons he had baptized stood in no special relation to him.[67] Those who were initiated into the mystery religions might hold in reverence their priests or mystagogues, but it was not so, according to Paul's understanding, in Christianity. All Christian apostles were subordinate to Christ. They were not rivals but "fellow-workmen for God," and no man should attempt to pass judgment upon the relative values of their work (8).

The words of Paul in 1:17ff. were probably not directed solely against those who "belonged to Apollos." These partisans may have been chiefly responsible

---

[63]For brief summaries of the theology of Paul in 1 Cor., see Craig, *Beginning*, pp. 9f.; G. B. Caird, "Everything to Everyone," *Interpretation* XIII (1959): 387f.

[64]Acts 18:24ff.

[65]Apparently the apostles had done nothing to encourage this conflict, 1 Cor. 4:6; 16:12.

[66]See note 53 above.

[67]1 Cor. 4:15.

for criticizing Paul's lack of "wisdom," but there was a pervasive tendency to depreciate Paul's preaching, and he addressed his notes on "the foolishness of the *kerygma*" to the entire congregation.[68] No brief comment can exhaust the meaning of this remarkable passage (5). Paul presupposed a world view we identify as pre-Gnostic in his reference to "the rulers of this age." Yet the gospel of the crucified and risen Christ was not to be confused with the "wisdom" taught by other religions and philosophies of the age, whose representatives boasted that the esoteric knowledge they imparted was a powerful instrument for man's salvation. The Christian *kerygma* was a form of "wisdom" and "power," but it was a "mystery" revealed by the "Spirit which is from God" for the salvation of all men, whatever their intellectual capacities may be. All the same, only those enlightened by the Spirit could receive this gift. Therefore, truly "spiritual men" in the Church had no basis for intellectual pride. The "jealousy and strife" at Corinth indicated to Paul that his recent converts were still "of the flesh."[69]

The Apostle next comments on sexual problems (11). A notorious case of incest had been reported to him. It is not only the sin which shocked Paul but the condoning attitude of the church at Corinth. Paul's decision implied more than the separation of the offender from the Christian community, although this would surely be the practical result of the church's action. To be excluded from the church was tantamount to being cut off from the sphere of Christ's influence, and thrust back into Satan's dominion with dreadful, but not necessarily final, destructive consequences.[70]

There were many factors in the Corinthian environment which encouraged extramarital relations. Not only were there numerous brothels in the city to accommodate sailors, but the worship of Aphrodite, the goddess of love, led to intercourse with her "sacred" prostitutes. Since the Christian community could not isolate itself from Corinthian society and its influence, Paul insisted that it must maintain internal standards of purity and of discipline. It must judge the evil of its own members; God would judge those without (12).[71]

Paul's attack upon the sexual immoralities and debauchery at Corinth reveals a principal cause for the seriousness of the situation. Some Christians were not merely excusing extramarital relations as a common human weakness, but defending them (14). It was being said that physical actions like eating and drinking, involving the appetites of the body which perishes, would not affect the spirit of men. Paul countered this dualistic conception of the human personality by proclaiming the sanctity of the body. The new life of the Christian had been

[68] 1 Cor. 1:26f.; 2:1–3:3. Munck, *Paul*, pp. 143ff.

[69] 1 Cor. 2:6ff. R. M. Grant, *Gnosticism and Early Christianity*, pp. 157f., 175ff.; R. McL. Wilson, *Gnosis*, pp. 53ff.; Morrison, *Powers*, pp. 23f., 114ff.; C. K. Barrett, in "Christianity at Corinth", note 53 above, p. 275, distinguishes Paul's usage of "good and bad wisdom."

[70] Cf. Paul's comments concerning his threat to the whole congregation in his "severe letter," 2 Cor. 10:2, 13:7. Note Rom. 9:3; Gal. 4:8ff.; Rev. 2:5. Munck, *Paul*, pp. 189ff.; Barrett, *First Epistle*, pp. 125ff.

[71] The mention of the judgment leads to a digression in which Paul condemns Christians for legal actions against each other in the pagan courts, 1 Cor. 6:1–8.

purchased at great cost; the entire body of the believer was the temple of the Holy Spirit.

Paul's answer to certain questions raised in the letter from the Corinthians concerning marriage and celibacy reveal that there were persons in the church who took the opposite position from those who considered the sex act nonmoral or amoral. Ascetics were claiming that sex was inherently sinful. "Spiritual men" avoid marriage or, if married, depreciate coitus. Perhaps the slogan of this ascetic group was, "it is well for a man not to touch a woman (15)." [72]

Paul deals with this situation by first insisting that husbands and wives must not deny one another their conjugal rights, unless it be by mutual consent, and then only for a season lest Satan take advantage of their continence. Paul also asserted the positive value of marriage by referring to Jesus' commandment forbidding divorce (17). Moreover, he declared that Christian partners in marriages with pagans should not take the initiative in seeking separation; indeed the shared life might lead to the conversion of their mates. At the same time, Paul assured the Corinthian ascetics that celibacy was to be preferred to marriage. Indeed one gains the impression that Paul tolerated marriage because he disapproved so strongly of extramarital sexual relations. [73]

When Paul defended his views concerning the unmarried, he revealed his special reason for preferring celibacy to marriage (19). His words bear superficial resemblance to Stoic teaching concerning providence and apathy. But it was Paul's apocalyptic beliefs which led him to prefer the celibate ideal, beliefs which were hardly shared by the ascetics at Corinth. Since "the appointed time had grown very short" the Christian should give single-minded devotion to the Lord. As in the Thessalonian letters, so in 1 Corinthians, Paul proclaimed an interim ethic. [74] Paul's Christian apocalypticism also explains the "rule" which he applied generally to all his churches: the maintenance of the *status quo* in one's personal situation (18).

Other problems at Corinth grew out of the common belief in demons or spirits and in their harmful or beneficial influence. [75] In his answers to two questions from Corinth, Paul kept steadily in view the church as a close-knit fellowship which, nevertheless, could not avoid participation in the common life of the city.

As we have seen, animal sacrifice was practiced by others besides Jews in the Roman world. Among the Gentiles there were many private and public sacrifices to the gods. In neither case was the whole animal consumed by fire. Priests and worshipers received part of the sacrificial meat for their own consumption. Some worshipers used their portions for private banquets and sent out invitations, as

---

[72]The argument at this point may begin with Paul's agreement in principle with the ascetics as, in 6:12, he accepts the antilegalist's principle. But serious qualifications follow in both cases. See the valuable article by H. Chadwick, "All Things to All Men," NTS 1 (1955): 263ff.

[73]Note the grudging formula that "it is better to marry than to be aflame with passion," 7:9b.

[74]For a comparison between Essene and Pauline views concerning marriage, see F. M. Cross, Jr., *Ancient Library*, pp. 96ff., pp. 237f.

[75]Lake stresses the fact that the same general assumptions underlie passages in 1 Cor. which we identify as secs. 22–34 (*Earlier Epistles*, pp. 192ff.).

the following papyrus shows: "Antonious, son of Ptolemaeus, invites you to dine with him at the table of our Lord Sarapis."[76] Also, after public sacrifices arranged by city magistrates, the unburned sacrificial meat not given to priests was sold in the marketplace. Could Christians eat this idol meat in good conscience? Christians of Jewish background had obvious scruples against such a thing. The issue was complicated by the common belief that spirit powers, both good and evil, possessed men through the eating of food.[77]

Paul considered the problem from various angles (22-26). First, he agreed in principle with those at Corinth who denied the existence of the pagan gods. Theoretically, the question about what to do about "things offered to idols" was morally indifferent. But there were weaker brethren in the church, recent converts from paganism, who ate food "as really offered to an idol." Out of consideration for these persons Paul advised "the strong" to impose a voluntary limitation upon the exercise of their freedom. To encourage a brother to act against his conscience, even though one thinks his scruples absurd, is an evil which love would avoid. Whatever privileges "knowledge" brings, the violation of the commandment to love the brethren is not one of these. It is clear that whereas Paul shared the conviction of "the strong" concerning Christian liberty, he did not share their spirit.[78]

In appealing to his own example (24), Paul revealed his sensitivity to criticism and self-consciously expressed a principle which determined the special form of his defense of the Christian gospel and ethic: "I have become all things to all men, that I might by all means win some."[79] By thus adapting his counsel to the situation Paul left himself open to misunderstanding.[80] But, according to his own testimony, the Apostle deliberately adopted this flexible approach. It was for him a calculated risk. No interpreter of Paul can ignore this autobiographical clue, both to the working of the Apostle's mind and to his missionary strategy.[81]

Paul's allusion to the Exodus experience of the Israelites, and his curious haggadah concerning the "Rock which followed them" in their wilderness wanderings, may detract the modern reader from the course of the Apostle's argument.[82] At this place he reminds the Corinthians, who prided themselves that

---

[76]Cited from W. Barclay, *Letters to the Corinthians* (1957), p. 80.

[77]Lake quotes a comment of Porphyry preserved by Eusebius: ". . . most of all [evil spirits] delight in blood and impure meats, and enjoy these by entering into those who use them."

[78]The attentive reader may wonder why Paul did not invoke "the apostolic decree" prohibiting the eating of idol meat, especially since in Acts it is said that Paul delivered the decision of the conference to the churches established on the first journey (16:4). Possibly the subsequent action of the Judaizers led him to conclude that the decree had been written in bad faith, that he was no longer bound by it. But the decree was probably enacted after the Jerusalem Conference; see above, p. 365. Cf. Hurd, *1 Corinthians*, pp. 262ff.

[79]1 Cor. 9:19ff.

[80]Note 2 Cor. 1:13ff.; 5:11; Gal. 5:11.

[81]Chadwick, note 72 above, pp. 261ff. See Bornkamm, "The Missionary Stance of Paul in 1 Corinthians and in Acts," in Keck and Martyn, *Luke-Acts*, pp. 194ff. Bornkamm's interpretation of 1 Cor. 9:19ff. is sound but he draws too sharply the contrast between Paul's statement of his strategy and Paul's actions according to Acts.

[82]1 Cor. 10:1ff.

their conscience was enlightened and who believed that they were secure from infection by demons, that pride invites a fall. Furthermore, Paul argues that a person who sits at "the table of the Lord" cannot feast at the table of a pagan god, even though the so-called god is only an idol (26). Once more Paul's mystical faith that the believer is a member of Christ's body is introduced, and the connection of this idea with the bread of the Eucharist may point to the source of its inspiration.

Paul concluded this discussion of idol meats and idolatry with practical advice about what to do when a Christian is invited to a pagan home. He reminded his readers of their responsibility to avoid wherever possible giving offense to anyone, and appealed to his own conduct as the imitation of Christ.[83]

Paul turned next to deal with matters relating to public worship in the Corinthian church (27–34). His thought ranged over a number of local situations. But his principal concern was to answer the question concerning "spiritual gifts" and to place the phenomenon "speaking in tongues" in a context for its proper understanding.

Paul's Jewish predisposition, based upon a traditional understanding of Genesis 1 and 2, influenced his counsel concerning the veiling of women in public worship (27). Possibly he sought to discourage outbreaks of enthusiasm such as were common among the women worshipers of Dionysus, or criticisms from outsiders remembering the former status of some of the women converts.

For Paul, the subordination of woman to man was inherent in both the social order and the invisible power structure of the present age (note the reference to "the angels"). The obliteration of value distinctions between male and female in Christ did not affect the Apostle's belief that natural distinctions were established by God in creation. Also Paul's Christian hope, which included the conviction of an imminent end, may have determined his social conservatism.

The Apostle's words concerning the common-meal practices of the Corinthian church attract greater interest, principally because he refers to the liturgical formula of the Lord's Supper (28). But his concern of the moment was to rebuke the affluent in the church for their scandalous behavior at the community meals. If the Lord's Supper be turned into a picnic, revealing the greed and callous indifference of some members, the sacrament brings not divine blessing but judgment. The death memorialized at this Supper was at once the surrendering of Christ's life for man's salvation, and God's sentence of death upon man because of his sin. Thus whenever Christians receive the bread and cup in a proper manner they judge themselves guilty before God, accept afresh his verdict respecting their sin, and on faith receive divine forgiveness. Paul's reference to "discerning the body" has been understood either as a reference to Christ's presence in the bread and wine, or to the Church as Christ's body. Both meanings may be implicit.

---

[83]1 Cor. 10:23ff. That Paul followed Jesus in giving this counsel may be inferred from Mark 7:15, and from the agraphon noted above, p. 243. It is often concluded that Paul's counsel concerning idol meats is inconsistent. Some scholars believe that we have here a composite of two letters; Hurd argues that Paul sought to synthesize views expressed in his preaching and in his "previous letter," influenced by the apostolic decrees (Acts 15:19ff). See Barrett, *First Epistle*, pp. 16f., and loc. cit.

The assembly of Christians at Corinth for worship led to other disorderliness. Members were vying with one another, speaking in tongues and prophesying (30–34). Paul did not question the reality or validity of these spiritual gifts. But it is clear that he considered them relatively unimportant, especially when they were disruptive of community, led to private incommunicable teaching, and invited criticism from outsiders. This section has attracted an extraordinary interest because in the course of his discussion Paul developed his famous metaphor of the Church's unity as the body of Christ having many interdependent members (31), and composed his lyric description of enduring love (32).

Scholars have found near parallels to Paul's figure of the body and its members in both Greek and Jewish writings. Whatever the specific source, or sources, of Paul's symbolism—mythological or historical or a combination of both—his application is practical and apposite. The survival of the church at Corinth was threatened because some members—the prophets and the "spiritual"—considered themselves all-important and the rest nonessential. Paul declared that what is valued highest by God, and in the Church, may seem foolish to the world which commonly honors spectacular gifts in its leaders (cf. 1:26ff.). Mystical overtones have been detected in Paul's figure of the Church as Christ's body, but the emphasis here is upon the interdependence of the fellow members of Christ's visible body, the Corinthian congregation. God's gifts to this church were intended to serve the needs of the entire community rather than bring honor to isolated individuals.

Since love is not one of the "gifts" in chapter 12, and prophecy as "a higher gift" (12:31a) is discussed in chapter 14, some scholars have conjectured that the famous hymn extolling love (32) is an interpolation, perhaps written by Paul for another occasion. The location of the passage in 1 Corinthians is not inappropriate, however; in chapter 12 Paul stresses that the church is a community of persons whose fellow-feeling leads them to care for and fully share with each other, and at the beginning of the hymn on love the phenomena of speaking in tongues and prophesying remain in the foreground. Also, after his incomparable description of love's enduring qualities, Paul places in proper perspective the more ephemeral gifts of prophecy, tongues, and knowledge. The Corinthians had a too exclusive, too acquisitive, interest in these spectacular gifts; above all else they should aim to excel in love.

The teaching of Paul in 1 Corinthians concludes with a reminder of the essentials of the Christian *kerygma,* and with an exposition of the Christian hope of the resurrection of the body (35–39). Our attention has been repeatedly drawn to the opening statements of this classical passage. In it Paul declared that the validity of the entire structure of the *kerygma* rested upon a mighty act of God: Jesus had been raised from the dead. This event gave assurance that the eschatological victory of Christ had begun and that his reign must continue "until he has put all his enemies under his feet" and destroyed death.[84]

It is doubtful that any at Corinth denied this proclamation of the risen Lord, although aspects of the apocalyptic end-drama were puzzling. Some in the church,

---

[84]For a criticism of various contemporary readings of Paul's intention, see H. W. Boers, "Apocalyptic Eschatology in 1 Corinthians 15," *Interpretation* XXI (1967): 50ff.

probably Greek in background, may not have been able to conceive of any *bodily* form of life after death. This incredulity might have led them to deny the resurrection of dead men.[85] The world view of popular religions and philosophies envisioned the disembodied spirit of man passing through the planetary spheres, finally sloughing off every part of the temporal flesh-and-blood existence, even self-consciousness and reason. Paul acknowledged the element of truth in this Greek (or Gnosticizing?) tradition: "Flesh and blood cannot inherit the Kingdom of God."[86] But he went on to proclaim "a mystery": those who hope in Christ will not merely experience a passage from death to an eternal incorruptible state, but a change from a "physical body" to a "spiritual body." Paul seems to have associated this change with the coming of Christ.

Alternatively, the deniers of a future resurrection of the dead at Corinth may have been those "spiritual" Christians who understood one-sidedly Paul's preaching that believers in Christ have been raised with him.[87] If such were the situation, Paul would have wished to make clear that the new life in Christ, in which the power of his resurrection is being experienced, is nevertheless a life lived in hope of a final resurrection.[88]

The burden of Paul's teaching in the important passage concerning the nature of the resurrected body (38) is that there is both a radical difference and a real continuity between the human body that dies and the "body" that is raised. While Paul attempts to provide anologies from nature to support his position, he affirms that the paradoxical hope of receiving a "spirtual body" derives its reality and meaning from Christ's own resurrection. Paul's use of the term translated "immortality" is not to be confused with the commonplace belief in man's survival as a disembodied spirit. His expression "put on immortality" resembles superficially the language of the mystery religions, but Paul's teaching opposes the contemporary "gospels" of rebirth and deification.

The conclusion of 1 Corinthians contains brief exhortations and travel notes (D). At the time an overland trip to Macedonia seemed necessary and so Paul must delay coming to Corinth. Sometime between writing this and 2 Corinthians an emergency situation arose which led Paul to change his plans. The "painful visit," so-called, marked another phase in the fateful relation between the Apostle and the congregation at Corinth.

AN OUTLINE OF THE SECOND LETTER OF PAUL TO THE CORINTHIANS

A. Introduction, 1:1–11:

    1. The superscription, 1:1–2

[85]1 Cor. 15:12, 35. Cf. Justin Martyn, *Dial. with Trypho*, 80.
[86]1 Cor. 15:50.
[87]Rom. 6:5ff.; 2 Cor. 5:15; Gal. 2:19f.
[88]1 Cor. 4:8; 6:14f. See Barrett, *First Epistle*, pp. 347f. J. C. Hurd (*1 Corinthians*, pp. 282ff.) believes that Paul's earlier views and their later development contributed to this misunderstanding. Cf. J. M. Robinson, "Kerygma and History in the N.T.," *The Bible in Modern Scholarship*, ed. J. P. Hyatt (1965), pp. 121ff.; pp. 152ff.

2. The thanksgiving, 1:3–11: gratitude for God's consolation (3–7); for deliverance from death in Asia (8–11)

B. Paul's defense of his integrity, 1:12–2:11:
   3. Sincerity in act and word, 1:12–14
   4. Change of plans not an evidence of fickleness, 1:15–22
   5. Paul's delay, as the severe letter, explained as avoidance of another painful visit, 1:23–2:4
   6. The offender's punishment sufficient, 2:5–11
   7. Anxiety in Macedonia relieved by the coming of Titus, 2:12–17

C. The Apostle's ministry and message, 3:1–6:10:
   8. Letters of commendation, 3:1–3
   9. The ministry of the old and new covenants, 3:4–18
   10. The gospel enlightens all but the lost, 4:1–6
   11. Paul's humiliation has magnified God's power, 4:7–15
   12. The daily renewal of the inner man, 4:16–18
   13. The Spirit is a down payment of the Christian inheritance; the coming judgment of Christ, 5:1–10
   14. The constraining love of Christ, 5:11–15
   15. The new creation in Christ, 5:16–17
   16. The ministry of reconciliation, 5:18–21
   17. The paradoxes of the Apostle's experience, 6:1–10

D. An apostrophe: Paul's special appeal, 6:11–7:3:
   18. For large-heartedness, 6:11–13
   19. For consistency in faith and practice, 6:14–7:1
   20. For mutual confidence, 7:2–4

E. Paul reviews the situation prior to receiving the comforting news from Titus, 7:5–16:
   21. Paul's state before receiving encouraging news, 7:5–7
   22. The severe letter in retrospect, 7:8–13a
   23. Paul's comfort in the joy of Titus, 17:13b–16

F. The contribution for the poor in Jerusalem 8:1–9:15:
   24. The liberality of the Macedonians, 8:1–5
   25. The Corinthians are urged to complete their offering, 8:6–7
   26. Motives for giving, 8:8–15
   27. The sending of Titus and other delegates, 8:16–9:5
   28. The benefits of generosity, 9:6–15

G. Evidences of true and false apostleship, 10:1–13:10:
   29. Paul's weapons of warfare mighty through God, 10:1–6
   30. Paul's letters and actions consistent, 10:7–11
   31. Paul's sphere of authority includes Corinth, 10:12–18
   32. Paul jealously warns against beguiling preachers, 11:1–6
   33. Paul affirms his financial self-sufficiency, 11:7–12
   34. False apostles are ministers of Satan, 11:13–15
   35. Paul's credentials compared with those of "the superlative apostles," 11:16–12:10

36. The signs of Paul's apostleship, 12:11–21
37. Paul threatens not to spare the Corinthians, 13:1–10
H. Conclusion, 13:11–14:
    38. Final admonitions, 13:11–12
    39. Greetings from all the saints, 13:13
    40. Benediction, 13:14

Reconstructions of the course of events between the writing of 1 and 2 Corinthians must rely on speculation. But certain points seem clear. Timothy's return from Corinth, 1 Corinthians 16:10f., must have brought news of no improvement in the church. Soon afterward, Paul went directly to Corinth by sea. This journey, referred to in 2 Corinthians 2:1, is commonly called "the painful visit." It seems to have been a complete fiasco. One member of the Corinthian church rebelled against Paul's authority, and the congregation as a whole acted defiantly.

Upon Paul's return to Ephesus he wrote a third time to the Corinthians, sending the letter by Titus. This "severe letter" (so-called) was probably not preserved. Did the letter contain an ultimatum from the Apostle? Certainly he demanded the punishment of the rebel.[89] While awaiting the return of his fellow-worker, Paul suffered deep anxieties. Had he dealt too harshly with his converts? This fear and other misgivings were accompanied by threats to Paul's life. He left Ephesus sooner than he had planned. While at Troas, Paul was not able to go on with his work, although opportunities were given him to preach.[90] Taking leave of friends, Paul journeyed along the Egnatian Way, hoping to meet Titus with news from Corinth.

When Titus joined Paul, the Apostle learned that the Corinthians had been moved to grief and repentance by his severe letter. The offender had been punished by the congregation, although the specific action had occasioned some disagreement.[91]

Paul experienced great relief from his depression. As soon as possible he began a fourth letter to the Corinthians. He wrote in a reminiscent mood. The contrast of his states of mind when writing the "severe letter" and when receiving the report from Titus gave expression to a predominantly confident mood (7, 21). At the same time, there is a defensive undercurrent of anxiety which resonates throughout; an ambivalence of feeling, such as one also detects in the early chapters of 1 Thessalonians. In acknowledging his gratitude and confidence Paul makes frequent digressions to avoid misunderstandings, or else defensively to clarify conceptions of his own ministry.

The conventional "thanksgiving" (2) celebrates God's mercy and comfort made known to Paul as a sharer of the sufferings of Christ. Elsewhere Paul describes the vital union between the believer and his Lord, which faith establishes, as a

[89] Munck surmises that Paul, nearing despair, threatened to "deliver the church over to Satan" if the offender was not disciplined (*Paul*, pp. 190ff.). See note 70 above, p. 400.

[90] 2 Cor. 2:12f.

[91] 2 Cor. 2:6ff.

crucifixion with Christ.[92] This cannot mean that the sufferings of an apostle of Christ afford a complementary redemptive value, that alone the cross of Jesus is lacking efficacy.[93] Yet in Paul's mind the life of the Church, as Christ's body, is inseparably related to the eschatological events of Christ's death and resurrection: as founder of the Corinthian church, Paul is called to bear a special "affliction" on its behalf; as fellow-members of Christ's body, the Corinthians are themselves sharers of the same sufferings. Paradoxically, in the midst of these afflictions both share abundantly divine comfort. One finds in these words a profound theological context for the whole of 2 Corinthians.[94]

Vigorously defending himself, Paul declares that his dealings with the Corinthians had always been forthright and consistent (B). He was under compulsion to specify his legitimate claims since they were being disputed, to commend his actions which were made to appear vicious. Paul twice takes an oath supporting the truth of his statements.

While Paul's rehearsal of recent events here, and later in the letter (E), is an appeal to let bygones be bygones—the Apostle devoutly wished to put the dreadful crisis behind him—the possibility that the church at Corinth would fail to meet "the test" cannot be completely dispelled. As he launches a sustained defense of the source and nature of his ministry (C), Paul is haunted by thoughts of those who impugn his motives and question his credentials.[95]

Paul's comments on the ministries of the old and new convenants (9) emphasize the lasting splendor of the new age manifested in Christ as contrasted with the ephemeral, fading splendor of the revelation to Moses, whose authority is now superseded in the present age by the apostles and their ministry. Some interpreters consider that Paul is disputing here the visiting teachers alluded to in 2:17; 3:1, who, in their Judaizing zeal, were seeking to impose upon the Corinthians obedience to the Mosaic Law. But the thrust of the Apostle's words about the two dispensations (literally; "ministries") is not that the gospel abrogates the demands of the "written code," e.g., circumcision and food laws. He seems intent only in declaring that the transient glory of the old covenant has been surpassed by the glory of Christ proclaimed in the Apostle's *kerygma*. This passage, then, affords no substantial evidence for equating the activities of Paul's Jewish–Christian opponents in Corinth with those of the Judaizers in Galatia.

The undercurrent of defensiveness never far beneath the surface of Paul's statements of confidence, a confidence bolstered by Titus' assurance, erupts in the following section (10). The invisible world-rulers of this age reinforce the resistance of men to God's revelation in Christ, and his apostles contend with the same demonic forces seeking to frustrate their ministries. Yet in the face of such formidable and crushing opposition, Paul writes that he does not "lose heart."

[92]Rom. 6:6; Gal. 2:20.

[93]Cf. 1 Cor. 1:2, J. Héring, *Second Epistle*, p. 3.

[94]See the present writer's essay, "Aspects of Paul's Theology and Their Bearing on Literary Problems of Second Corinthians," in *Studies and Documents*, ed. J. Geerlings (1967), vol. XXXIX, pp. 95ff.

[95]2 Cor. 2:17; 3:1. G. Bornkamm considers 2:14–7:4 to be a secondary insertion and no part of "the thankful letter." *NTS* 8 (1962): 258ff.

In the consummation of the age now inaugurated, the "god of this world," and all other antithetical powers, will be subjugated by God, who will raise from the dead those persons belonging to the Lord Jesus. Just as Paul does not consider the benefits of his suffering and consolation apart from his Corinthian converts (1:6f.), he is not minded to think of his own salvation apart from theirs.[96]

Paul's description of the Christian's hope of inheriting "a house not made with hands, eternal in the heavens" has led some scholars to distinguish the eschatology expressed here from that set forth in 1 Corinthians and the Thessalonian letters.[97] The language contrasting the visible world with the perfect and enduring, invisible world, and his distinctions between the outward and inner man, do appear Greek. Nevertheless, Paul's rabbinical traditions and his apocalyptic eschatology remain in the background for correctly interpreting this passage.[98] The prospect of the full exposure of man's life "before the judgment seat of Christ" was an essential element in Paul's eschatology. He believed that no man is saved by his "works"—such an assurance was grounded solely in a faithful response to God's grace offered men in Christ—yet what man "has done in the body," his "work," must be, and certainly will be, submitted to Christ's judgment.[99]

One may be helped in understanding the conclusion of Paul's apology concerning his ministry as an apostle, under the imagery of "reconciliation," by reading without a pause 5:11–6:10 (secs. 14–17).[100] The grand themes developed in this passage catch our attention as, no doubt, they held Paul's. Note, however, should be taken of Paul's defensiveness: 5:12f. and 5:3f., 8. The Apostle is unable to free his mind of his detractors and their calumnies.

As at the creation, so in the time of Christ, all is the work of God, wrote Paul. The "new creation" is viewed by Paul against the background of man's revolt. God is declared to be the Reconciler—not the one to be reconciled—even though He is the one perennially opposed by men. The gospel of the death of Christ revealed to Paul the gravity of rebel man's situation, his banishment from God's presence, his subjection to God's wrath, as well as the wonder of God's reconciling grace.[101] Theologians find in Paul's statements *loci classicus* for discovering his doctrine of the atonement: What did Paul mean in saying: "he [Christ] died for all," or again, "for our sake he [God] made him [Christ] to be sin who knew no sin, so that in him we might become the righteousness of God"? A comparison with Paul's Letter to the Romans, especially 5:1ff., shows that the interpersonal imagery of enmity and reconciliation runs parallel in Paul's thought to his juridicial imagery of guilt and justification or vindication. In his application of both images Paul teaches his distinctive soteriology. In the Corinthian passage, however, the emphasis is not upon the meaning of God's action per se, but upon the agency

---

[96] 2 Cor. 4:11f., 14f.; Cf. 7:3.

[97] 2 Cor. 4:16ff.; 5:1ff. Cf. 1 Cor. 15:42ff.; 1 Thess. 4:14ff.; 2 Thess. 2:1ff.

[98] Héring, *Second Epistle*, pp. 34, 36ff.

[99] Cf. 1 Cor. 3:10ff.

[100] This brings the reader to the apostrophe (D), which contains the puzzling "insertion," 6:14–7:1.

[101] Cf. Rom. 1:18ff.; 5:12ff. See below, pp. 433f.

of the Apostle as "ambassador" for Christ. Paul offers the Corinthians no "theory" of the atonement. Rather he proclaims that the way of reconciliation has been provided for overcoming their estrangement.

Paul puts his battle-scarred life on the line, so to speak, to reinforce his written entreaties (17). Abused by men, at Corinth and elsewhere, the Apostle's participation in the afflictions of Christ are his substantial credentials. "Working together, with him [i.e., Christ] we entreat you . . . ."

As noted above, the poor connection of 6:14–7:1 in the context of this letter demands some explanation; however it is doubtful that a satisfactory explanation can be found. It cannot be denied that Paul's impassioned apostrophe, beginning at 6:11 and resumed at 7:2, is clumsily interrupted and that new subject matter is abruptly introduced. Yet Paul's letters contain numerous digressions and seemingly irrelevant asides, and 2 Corinthians, written during a greatly disturbed period, may contain more of the same. Already with 6:3 the emotional quality of Paul's entreaties disrupts the logical development of his ideas, and in recalling the dreadful vicissitudes and dramatic paradoxes of his life as an apostle, Paul may have been driven to abandon indirect discourse and resort to forthright exhortation. Perhaps it is too much, where such trauma of feeling is in evidence, to expect precise logical connections in Paul's correspondence. Possibly a loose connection may be found in free association with the following idea: openheartedness, i.e., uninhibited receptivity of persons with whom one has had differences, must not to be mistaken for a careless tolerance. In Corinth such openheartedness had led repeatedly to indiscriminate accommodation of Christian attitudes, beliefs, and behavior to those of "unbelievers."

The Apostle's long apology having ended in a flood tide of feeling, he returned to his reminiscence of the most recent crisis in his relations with the Corinthian congregation (E), the details of which we have already considered. Apparently this crisis had frustrated Paul's earlier plans for a collection of money from the Corinthians for the relief of impoverished Christians in Jerusalem.[102] Since Titus and two associates, who were to be the bearers of Paul's letter, were also being sent to assist the Corinthians in raising these relief funds, Paul writes to facilitate their work (F). Notice the variety of motives to which Paul appealed (26). Because he sought to remove all suspicion that these funds were being misappropriated, and because he spoke of desiring further proof of the Corinthian love, we may suspect that he was still uncertain of the church's attitude towards him.

After giving his counsel concerning the offering, Paul's thoughts naturally would have turned to his chief purpose in writing the letter, the preparation of the church for a third visit from the Apostle (G). If the unity of 2 Corinthians is assumed, we must ask why thoughts of this visit should have led Paul to conclude the letter as he did.

Trivial reasons have been given for his allegedly abrupt change of mood at 10:1, such as a sleepless night or an attack of indigestion. It is certainly wise to depend on clues provided by the letter itself rather than resort to mere fancies.

[102]See 1 Cor. 16:1ff.

Perhaps 2 Corinthians was written piecemeal, and several days passed before Titus and the other emissaries to Corinth took leave of Paul. Meanwhile bad news was received. Other Jewish–Christian apostles had come to Corinth, who were now claiming personal loyalty, superior knowledge, and demanding the church's support. By their preaching and other actions they seemed to be stirring up the dying embers of resistance to Paul.[103] Receiving such news as this, at the point of sending his thankful letter and his delegation to collect the Jerusalem offering, Paul was provoked to anger. The situation could become more critical than ever before. The Apostle was bound to assert his authority in no uncertain terms.[104]

Paul's ironic, sometimes bitter, words in the closing lines of 2 Corinthians have made varied impressions upon his readers. Since this is the most autobiographical passage in the Pauline Corpus, descriptions of the Apostle's personality have been drawn from it, some flattering, some derogatory. But no one is able to doubt the sincerity of Paul's love for these Christian people. He repeatedly wrote them to bear with him. It is certain that Paul suffered much from their vacillating attitudes toward him and from evidences of their serious misunderstanding of his message. He was unable to bring to maturity these "babes in Christ." Some of the same problems persisted for many years, as our later knowledge of this church reveals.[105] But the love of the "father" for these children, expressed in great tenderness and sharp rebuke, did not fail. He patiently provided them a secure foundation for their faith.

[103]Recall the discussion of the identity and intentions of these "superlative apostles," pp. 395ff.

[104]It is possible that whereas the news received was generally favorable, and the confidence of Titus had been contagious, the latter may have reported the various false accusations which had been believed by some about Paul. Now that Paul completes plans for his visit, and hears of the recent intruders, he is moved to make unequivocally clear his motives and the ground for his authority upon which he must stand. Other letters of Paul end with rebukes and warnings. Cf. Gal. 5:2; Tasker, *2 Corinthians*, pp. 32ff.; Munck, Paul, pp. 184ff.

[105]For a summary of evidence from 1 Clem. and other writings, see Moffatt, *1 Corinthians*, p. xxx.

chapter sixteen

THE GALATIAN
AND ROMAN LETTERS

The widespread ascendancy of the vegetation goddess, or earth mother, in the Hellenistic Age is evidenced by this relief from a Nabataean temple at Tannur. Atargatis was chief goddess of these people of the Transjordan; yet her powers were conceived to be those of Aphrodite, Demeter, Cybele and other goddesses of vegetation or fertility. (American Schools of Oriental Research and Dr. Nelson Glueck)

413

Claudius (A.D. 41–54) held by many contemporaries to be a weak, eccentric cripple, ranks as an outstanding emperor. Christian missions were aided by Claudius' extension of the Pax Romana in the eastern provinces. His friendship with Herod Agrippa I led him to protect Jewish rights; yet by placing Palestine under a Roman procuratorship, after the king's death, a nationalist reaction was caused. (Alinari)

Augustus (30 B.C.–A.D. 14) is represented in this sculpture as Pontifex Maximus, head of the Roman religion. Cast in this role, the emperor is pictured as the great restorer of Rome's moral and spiritual power. (Alinari)

PAUL'S Letter to the Galatians may have been written while the storm of controversy raged at Corinth. Perhaps a few months elapsed between its composition and the Letter to the Romans. If so, we possess two other writings which shed light upon this particularly crucial stage in the Apostle's career.[1] Yet the justification for grouping Galatians and Romans is not based solely upon these conjectures. More clearly than any other writings these letters, together, present the Apostle's distinctive exposition of the Christian *kerygma*—"the gospel according to Paul."

THE LETTER TO THE GALATIANS

Galatians was written in hot indignation. From beginning to end Paul vigorously defended his right to speak as an apostle commissioned by the Lord Jesus Christ, his independence of all human authority, and the total adequacy of his gospel and its moral dynamic for all men. As one reads the letter—if possible without interruption, which is its best introduction—several interrelated questions arise. Who were these Galatians? Can a place be found in the New Testament records for the establishment of churches by this name? Can we know the particular circumstances which led Paul to write this letter?

Answers to these questions must be drawn from Galatians and Acts but there is no consensus concerning them. With a few notable exceptions, scholars are fairly certain that the situation which prompted this impassioned letter can be identified. But there is no agreement as to the destination or date of Galatians. Fortunately it is not necessary fully to solve these critical problems in order to appreciate the essential meaning of this book, either in the early or the modern Church.

An Outline of the Letter of Paul to the Galatians

A. Introduction, 1:1–10:
  1. A superscription including a declaration of Paul's authority and independence as an apostle; an ascription of praise, 1:1–5
  2. An indignant statement concerning the apostasy of the Galatians in which the occasion for the letter is revealed, 1:6–9
  3. A defensive parenthesis, 1:10
B. Paul and Jerusalem: A personal apology (mostly narrative), 1:11–2:21:

[1]Feine-Behm-Kümmel, *Intro.*, p. 97.

4. Paul's gospel based on a revelation, 1:11–12
5. His early life opposed to the gospel and the Church, 1:13–14
6. His conversion isolated him from Jerusalem, 1:15–17
7. Except for a fifteen-day visit to Peter and James, Paul was for many years out of touch with Jerusalem, 1:18–24
8. After a lapse of fourteen years, another visit, 2:1–10: Paul submitted his gospel "to those who were of repute" (2); the incident concerning Titus (3–5); Paul's gospel not modified but recognized by the "pillars" (6–10)
9. Antioch and Jerusalem, 2:11–21: Paul's rebuke of Peter and Barnabas (11–14); the point of his altercation with Peter (15–21)

C. The gospel of justification by faith proclaimed in opposition to Judaizers (a vigorous polemic), 3:1–5:12:
10. The "foolish Galatians" are asked to recall their reception of the gospel, 3:1–5
11. As Abraham was justified by faith, so are his sons (the scripture supports experience), 3:6–9
12. Those who submit to a works-righteousness understanding of the law stand under its curse, from which Christ has redeemed men, 3:10–14
13. A promise given prior to the law cannot be annulled by it (a commonplace example is followed by a rabbinical interpretation of scripture), 3:15–18
14. The provisional character of the law as a means of salvation and its relation to the promise, 3:19–22
15. The law's custody prepared God's sons for the gospel; Abraham's offspring, inclusive of Jews and Gentiles, are "one in Christ Jesus," 3:23–29
16. Sons—not better than slaves while children—have received their adoption and are redeemed from the law through God the Father's own Son, 4:1–7
17. Would the Gentiles wish to return to their former bondage? 4:8–11
18. A parenthetical appeal: Paul recalls his presence and reception in Galatia; scorns the motives of Judaizers, speaks of his desire to return, 4:12–20
19. An allegory: Abraham's children by Hagar and Sarah contrasted, 4:21–5:1
20. An ultimatum, 5:2–12: the alternatives are circumcision—perfect obedience—vs. a faith response to the Spirit's appeal—the hope of righteousness (2–10); an angry aside (11–12)

D. The freedom of men who are led by the Spirit (mostly exhortation), 5:13–6:10:
21. Freedom issues in neighbor-love, not selfish indulgence, 5:13–15
22. Warfare between "the flesh" and "the Spirit," 5:16–18
23. The works of the flesh which forfeit the inheritance of the kingdom, 5:19–21
24. The fruits of the Spirit in men who have crucified the flesh, 5:22–25
25. Three special injunctions, 5:26–6:10: among Christians self-conceit, goading one another, and envy must be shunned (26); gentle forbearance must be practiced toward offenders, sympathy shown, self-knowledge and self-reliance must be sought (6:1–5); gifts must be liberally shared (6–10)

E. Concluding admonitions, 6:11-18:
  26. The "large letters" of Paul emphasize the nature of the Judaizer's threat, 6:11-16
  27. Paul's apostleship physically authenticated, 6:17
  28. Benediction, 6:18

There are several obscure passages in the Letter to the Galatians which are of historical importance and appear as roadblocks to the reader in following the course of Paul's apology. Hence the exposition of Galatians may be prefaced by a brief statement of its critical problems.

Historical Questions

Who were the "foolish Galatians"?[2] In the third and fourth centuries B.C., hordes of Celtic people invaded the Italian and Greek peninsulas. Eventually they were contained in the interior of Anatolia, where they built settlements. Chief among these were Pessinus, Ancyra, and Tavium. The Greek called these barbarians *Keltai* or *Galatae*. During the Roman conquests the territory of the Galatae was annexed and gradually extended. In 25 B.C. Galatia became an imperial Roman province. Its area included districts adjacent to the old kingdom of Galatia—Lycaonia and Pisidia—and parts of Phrygia and Cappadocia. Thus we can see that in Paul's day the term *Galatians* was ambiguous.

From ancient times to the present, many have believed that Paul addressed his letter to the people who were Galatians by racial heritage. In Acts 16:6 it is reported that Paul and his fellow missionaries "went through the region of Phrygia and Galatia." Again, on his next journey, Paul "went from place to place through the region of Galatia and Phrygia, strengthening all the disciples."[3] On the basis of these notes in Acts the assumption has been that Paul preached the gospel to the Galatian people during his "second missionary journey," having been frustrated in his attempt to proceed to Asia.[4] Churches were established at Pessinus and other settlements along the western border of the old kingdom of Galatia, perhaps at the chief city, Ancyra. An interval of three years may have elapsed before Paul's second visit to this region during the "third missionary journey." Several statements in the Galatian letter suggest that by this time disturbing symptoms of trouble had begun to appear.[5] Sometime later, when Paul was either at Ephesus or Corinth, news was received which prompted the Letter to the Galatians.[6]

Since the late eighteenth century this account of the origin of Galatians has come under attack sporadically. But at the turn of the present century Sir William

---

[2] Gal. 3:1.

[3] Acts 18:23.

[4] Acts 16:6. Cf. Gal. 4:13f.

[5] Gal. 4:13, 16, 20; 5:21 (1:9?).

[6] A classic statement of this theory is given in J. B. Lightfoot's, *Saint Paul's Epistle to the Galatians* (1905), pp. 1ff. More recently the tradition has been defended by Moffatt, Craig, Nock, Lietzmann, Dibelius, Schlier, and Goguel. See Feine-Behm-Kümmel, *Intro.*, pp. 191ff.

Ramsay, English archeologist and historian of the region of Asia Minor, persuaded numerous New Testament scholars that Paul's Galatian letter was written to the churches founded on his "first missionary journey"—Antioch, Iconium, Lystra, and Derbe.[7] This position became known as "the South Galatian theory"; the older view was called "the North Galatian theory." Some scholars refer to these opposing theories as "the province hypothesis" and "the territory hypothesis."

In defense of the South Galatian, or province, theory it is argued that Paul's allusions to geographical or political areas must not be made to conform to Luke's usage. The Apostle almost always names the Roman province in which his churches were located.[8] "Galatia" was the only inclusive term which could have been used to identify churches at Antioch, Iconium, Lystra, and Derbe. While it is not necessary to the South Galatian theory to show that Paul founded no churches in North Galatia, it has been observed that, contrary to his usual custom, the author of Acts mentions no cities in the travel notes of 16:6ff. and 18:23. In the latter passage it is said that Paul strengthened all "the disciples," not the churches.[9]

Other things are said to point to South Galatia as the destination of Paul's letter. In Galatians 2:9 and 13 Barnabas is mentioned as though he were known to the readers. According to Acts, Barnabas was with Paul on his mission in South Galatia but the two had parted company at the beginning of the next journey when, it is supposed, churches were established in North Galatia.[10] Some claim that churches in the more populous cities of South Galatia would have been subjected to the propagandizing activity of Paul's opponents from other places more than would those of the relatively inaccessible region of North Galatia.

A decision concerning the destination as well as the date of the Galatian letter depends upon the relation of Paul's visits to Jerusalem which are reported in Galatians 1-2 and Acts 9-15. While Galatians ought not to be forced into conformity with the secondary source, Acts, interpretations of Galatians are clearly affected by this problem.

If it is assumed that in Galatians 2 the Apostle is giving his report of the Jerusalem Conference, then it is obvious that Galatians was written after this meeting. But, as we have seen, this assumption is by no means universally held. If Paul's letter was addressed to North Galatian churches a preconference date is excluded; to South Galatian churches, any date after the "first missionary journey" is possible.

Some defenders of the South Galatian theory hold that Paul's letter was written

---

[7] W. M. Ramsay, *St. Paul the Traveller and Roman Citizen* (1896) and *A Historical Commentary on St. Paul's Epistle to the Galatians* (1900); E. D. Burton, *Epistle to the Galatians* (1921), pp. xxv ff. Foakes-Jackson and Lake, *Beginnings*, vol. V, pp. 224ff.; G. S. Duncan, *Epistle of Paul to the Galatians* (1934), pp. xviii ff. [hereafter, *Epistle of Paul*]; R. T. Stamm, *IB*, vol. 10, pp. 435ff.

[8] E.g., 1 Cor. 16:19; 2 Cor. 1:1; 8:1. Note however, Gal. 1:21, which refers to Syria in the narrower sense.

[9] Cf. Acts 14:23; 15:14; 16:5. Stamm, *IB*, vol. 10, p. 436. The efforts to establish from Acts 16, 18 that Paul did not visit the territory of Galatia but only "the Phrygian-Galatian country" are unconvincing; see Lake, *Earlier Epistles*, pp. 259ff. Cf. Burton, *Epistle to the Galatians*, pp. xxx ff.

[10] McNeile, *Intro.*, p. 145.

at this earliest possible date, shortly after his return to Antioch or even on his way there. At any rate, a preconference date affords the simplest explanation for Paul's silence concerning the position taken by Peter and James at the Conference and the "decree" accepted by Paul according to Acts 15. If this view is credible, Galatians becomes the earliest of Paul's letters, probably composed in A.D. 49.[11] No wonder Paul expressed surprise at the early defection of the churches in South Galatia. But this theory of the origin of Galatians appears to be stronger than it really is. While it is probable that the letter was written to the South Galatian churches, the sum total of the evidence points to Asia or Achaea and not Syria as the place of its origin, and to A.D. 56 not 49 as the time of its writing.

Another problem may be defined although its solution depends upon a detailed exposition of the letter. What were the objections of the troublemakers in Galatia? Most scholars agree that these troublemakers were "Judaizers," Jewish–Christians who taught that circumcision was essential to salvation and who declared that Christians were bound to observe the ceremonial laws of Moses; if not the whole Torah, at least some of its ritual features. In order to strengthen their position, the Judaizers were openly attacking Paul's credentials and the motives prompting his missions. They claimed that Paul was inevitably dependent upon the apostles of Jerusalem. He believed in the importance of circumcision; he had not required it of Gentile converts in Galatia only because he wished to launch a successful mission and to avoid persecution.

Some interpreters have thought that another group had become troublesome in the Galatian churches and that Paul's letter was directed against two fronts. Some Gentile converts were saying that Paul was not fully emancipated from Judaism. These persons represented the opposite pole from the others urging submission to the Jewish Law. They considered themselves above every law since they were "spiritual." [12] The identification of this group may remind the reader of the description of the *pneumatikoi* at Corinth. Indeed, one wonders if the arguments for their existence in the Galatian churches have not borrowed from the Corinthian letters. The "two-front theory" principally depends upon the concluding sections of Galatians.[13] It is not a necessary hypothesis, and it is unlikely that any evidence for the existence of radical "spirituals" among the Gentile Christians in Galatia can be deduced from the controversial sections of the letter.

Brief notice should be taken of a novel form of this theory, that Gentile Christians were provoking the Galatian controversy. It is claimed that a serious study of the Septuagint had persuaded some Gentile Christians that circumcision was necessary to salvation and that obedience to other Mosaic commandments would be pleasing to God. To support their position they were appealing to "the twelve,"

[11] A. E. Barnett, *The New Testament: Its Making and Meaning* (1946), pp. 25ff.; W. L. Knox, *Jerusalem*, pp. 80ff.; cf. ibid., p. 188, n. 14, and p. 227, n. 5; Duncan *Epistle of Paul*, pp. xxi ff. MacGregor, *IB*, vol. 9, pp. 198ff.

[12] J. H. Ropes, *The Singular Problem of the Epistle to the Galatians* (1929), develops the view advanced by W. Lütgert ten years earlier; Enslin, *Beginnings*, pp. 216ff. Cf. Feine-Behm-Kümmel, *Intro.*, pp. 194f.

[13] Gal. 6:1ff.

over the head of Paul, although they knew nothing about the Jerusalem apostles other than what Paul had told them.[14] According to this theory the Galatian heresy was an idealization of Judaism by Gentile converts to Christianity who were seeking to combine the Old Testament and the gospel. This theory cannot be supported by a careful analysis of Galatians.[15] Paul's understanding of the gospel and mission of the Church presented in Galatians cannot be sharply opposed to conceptions held by Peter, James, and other Jerusalem apostles.

Interpreting Galatians

In his salutation Paul wrote an unequivocal declaration of his apostleship and independence, suggesting at once that his detractors were attempting to subordinate him to others and derive his authority from them. The emphatic denial "not from men" should not be understood as meaning that he had derived nothing from those "who were apostles before" him. Paul made it clear that there was but "one gospel" from the beginning, and that the apostles were in full accord concerning its essentials.[16]

Dispensing with the customary "thanksgiving," Paul came directly to the point of his letter. He expressed dismay that the Galatian churches were "so quickly turning to a different gospel." The statement is not a decisive clue to the date or destination of the letter.[17] Paul's astonishment may spring from the fact that some of his churches had so readily succumbed to the Judiazers' teaching, when this was the very danger against which he had warned them. During a second visit Paul had pronounced a curse on any man who claimed that a message other than the one the Galatians had received was the gospel.[18]

The question interjected at this point reveals Paul's acute sensitivity to the charge that he was a publicity seeker (3). But without further delay, Paul reviewed his relations with the Jerusalem church. The Apostle's reference to his conversion attracts our attention. But the curious who wish to know "what really happened" are disappointed. Paul only said: it was "a revelation of Jesus Christ," and that his life as a Jew—as his first readers knew—had not disposed him towards Christianity (4–5). Like the great prophets of Israel, Paul spoke of his calling as antedating his birth—and, also echoing the oracles of the prophets, declared that when God's call came to him the purpose of his life had been revealed.[19]

[14] Munck, *Paul,* pp. 87ff. Munck proceeds from Gal. 6:13 which, he says, cannot refer to Jews or Jewish–Christians but only to Gentiles. M. Barth accepts Munck's position, "The Kerygma of Galatians," *Interpretation* XXI (1967): 131ff. See also Enslin, *Beginnings,* pp. 87ff.

[15] See M. Smith's trenchant criticisms of Munck's exposition of Gal. 2:1–10, "Pauline Problems," *HTR* L (1957): 107ff., especially, pp. 115ff.

[16] Gal. 1:7, 23f.; 2:9, 16. Cf. 1 Cor. 11:23; 15:1ff. Stamm, *IB,* vol. 10, pp. 453f., 461. J. T. Sanders, "Paul's 'Autobiographical' Statements in Galatians 1–2," *JBL* LXXXV (1966): 335ff.

[17] Stamm, *IB,* vol. 10, p. 450. Cf. Duncan, *Epistle of Paul,* pp. 19f.

[18] It is commonly conceded that Gal. 1:9 refers to a second visit, but could this mean his "return trip" (Duncan, *Epistle of Paul,* p. 19)? Could the Judaizers have moved in this quickly? See Burton, *Epistle to the Galatians,* p. 29.

[19] Cf. Gal. 1:15 and Jer. 1:4f.; Is. 49:1ff. Note the allusion in Acts 18:9 to Jer 1:8. Cf. Acts 26:12ff. and Is. 42:6ff.

Paul had not gone directly to Jerusalem after his conversion. It is not likely that he felt compelled to detail his itineraries. Even in the specific references—"after three years . . . after fourteen years"—he does not say from what points he reckons these intervals of time.[20] Paul wished to emphasize that there had been no need for him to consult the original apostles. He was not their emissary. Nevertheless they knew what he was doing and did not oppose him.[21] When he did revisit Jerusalem "after fourteen years" it was only "by revelation" that he was impelled to go up (8).

We must face again the question: Does Paul in Galatians 2 report the same meeting described in Acts 15? In the latter source Paul went up to Jerusalem as a commissioner of the church at Antioch. Galatians stresses Paul's independence, contradicting perhaps a delegate status. Yet in spite of this and other differences in detail, the circumstances of Galatians 2 and Acts 15 are so closely parallel that both would seem to be describing the Jerusalem Conference. The perplexity arises from Paul's statement that the authorities had "added nothing" to him at this time. The author of Acts was probably in error in connecting the decree of 15:19ff. with this Jerusalem Conference.[22]

The notice concerning Titus raises a question to which opposite answers are given. The obscurities in the Greek text may go back to a difficulty which faced Paul, not the copyist, in explaining this incident. Probably Paul's opponents had used the story of Titus as proof that Paul had submitted to authority in Jerusalem, and Paul had found the situation awkward if not embarrassing. Because of the behavior of certain Judaizers, Titus had voluntarily submitted to circumcision to avoid a scandal. But, Paul insisted in the letter, he had not submitted to these "false brethren," that is, in sacrificing his principle. It had only been a matter of expediency.[23] Titus had not been forced to have the operation. The incident does not prove Paul's subjection to Jerusalem. On the contrary, "the pillars" of the church had acknowledged the validity of his "gospel to the uncircumcised."

Are we now able to perceive who were the troublemakers? Paul's reference in 1:7 is not specific, but what of his words in chapter 2? Goguel surmised that "the ill-conceived irritation and bitter, almost scornful irony, with which he treated the pillars of the church" indicate that Paul "considered them responsible for what took place in Galatia."[24] Yet Paul's irony may be in his reference to the terms

[20]H. N. Ridderbos, *The Epistle of Paul to the Churches of Galatia* (1953), pp. 78ff. [hereafter, *Galatia*]. A few scholars place *within* the "fourteen years" Paul's great missions in the East, thus radically revising the traditional view that during this period Paul labored "in the regions of Syria and Cilicia" (Gal. 1:21. Cf. Acts 9:30; 11:25ff.). See J. Knox, *Chapters*, pp. 52ff.; C. H. Buck, Jr., "The Collection for the Saints," *HTR* XLII (1950): 1ff.; Ogg, *Chronology*, pp. 36ff.; G. B. Caird, *IDB*, vol. 1, pp. 606f.

[21]Sanders, note 16 above, pp. 339f.

[22]This plausible position is argued by Goguel, Cullmann, Dibelius, Kümmel, and Schlier; see above. Was the writer of Acts also mistaken in reporting that Paul was in Jerusalem with famine-relief funds (11:30, 12:25)? Feine-Behm-Kümmel, *Intro.*, pp. 196f. Or was the visit reported in Acts 9:26–30 not factual? Parker, "Once More, Acts and Galatians," pp. 179ff.

[23] Recall 1 Cor. 9:19ff., and Paul's position that one may voluntarily submit to the scruples of "the weak" without depending on them for salvation. Duncan, *Epistle of Paul*, pp. 41ff.; Lake, *Beginnings*, vol. V, pp. 196ff. Cf. Stamm, *IB*, vol. 10, pp. 470ff.

[24]Goguel, *Birth*, p. 313. Goguel admits that there are "only dark and obscure hints." See also C. K. Barrett, "Paul and the 'Pillar' Apostles," in *Studia Paulina* (honoring J. DeZwann, 1953), pp. 1ff.

of respect which his opponents in Galatia were using in their attempts to disparage his authority.

In the next section, Paul reports a sequel to the Jerusalem Conference (9). A few historians would place this incident at Antioch before the Conference, arguing that Peter and Barnabas would not have acted in this way after the decision reached in Jerusalem.[25] Others do not see how Paul could have ignored the decree so quickly and dared rebuke Peter and Barnabas for their vacillation. But the episode is intelligible as an aftermath of the Conference, especially if 15:19ff. was no part of its proceedings. The Conference had dealt with the crucial issue of circumcision and the Gentiles. But what of Jewish–Christians and the law? Were they released from its demands, especially the food laws which distinguished Jews of the Dispersion and prevented their absorption by paganism? The two issues were logically related, as Paul contended. But they probably arose separately. Luke may have failed to recognize this in retrospect.

However one deals with the historical problem, one can see that Paul appealed to the Antioch incident to prove his independence. And to clarify "the truth of the gospel" he proclaimed: that "a man is not justified (or made righteous) by works of the law, but through faith in Jesus Christ. . . ."[26] Paul referred to the Antioch incident to lead his readers into the heart of the gospel's message for all men, Gentiles as well as Jews. Having vindicated the divine origin of his apostleship and the legitimacy of his gospel, he turned to teach the truth of this universal gospel and to oppose its perversion by the Judaizers.

It is significant that Paul appealed first of all to the experience of his converts (10). But he took his case to the scriptures. It is apparent that the Judaizers had been defending their position by appealing to Genesis 17. God's promises to Abraham and to his offspring applied to Jews and to circumcised Gentiles only. Paul took his stand upon Genesis 15:6 and employed this text as the basis of a long and sustained argument which recalls other aspects of the Genesis story concerning Abraham as well as oracles from the Prophets. Paul was as eager as were his opponents to link the Christian gospel with God's former revelation recorded in the scriptures. He was certain that the good news that God justifies "men of faith" is implicit in the whole history of salvation.[27]

Paul's use of scripture may appear to some readers as not only obtuse but perverse, especially when he claims that God's promise made to Abraham's "offspring" referred to one, not to many.[28] Surely Paul knew a collective noun when he saw one. But underlying these rabbinical subtleties are convictions that combine to form a profound theology of history. The ideal of a holy people—the true offspring of Abraham—envisioned by the prophets of Israel under various images was not fully realized until the coming of the Messiah. But when "the time had fully come," Jesus in his own person fulfilled this ideal, and, through

[25] Duncan, *Epistle of Paul*, p. 40.

[26] On the meaning of Paul's terms, *righteousness* or *justification*, and *to make righteous* or *to justify*, vss. 16–21, see Romans 1:15ff. and 3:21ff.; below, pp. 431ff. and 437f.

[27] The excision of Gal. 3:6–9 from Marcion's canon is not surprising.

[28] Gal. 3:16 (cf. Gen. 22:17f. (LXX)); D. Daube, "The Interpretation of a Generic Singular in Galatians 3:16," *Jew. Quar. Rw.* 35 (1944): 227ff.

the gift of the Spirit, an ever-widening inclusive fellowship was being formed. The Church of Jesus Christ is the new Israel of God, the eschatological community, inheriting the promises of God unto the fathers. Paul quotes the Old Testament "to show that already in Israel (not only in the church) are found justification by faith, the promise as basis and scope of the law, and the covenant with the free children of God."[29]

But is not Paul's valuation of the Mosaic Law in Galatians almost wholly negative? Some interpreters have concluded that this is indeed so. All men who "rely on the works of the law" to merit God's blessing are under its curse.[30] It is declared that God's gift of the law, "four hundred and thirty years" after the promise to Abraham, certainly did not set aside the promise.[31] The law was provided to expose the sinfulness of God's people and to keep them dependent upon His gracious promise. Nevertheless, Paul writes that the law was not given directly by God, or it would have had the power "to make alive."[32] Instead the law had been given by angels and by the hand of an intermediary, Moses.[33] The law was a temporary and provisional means of discipline to bring men to Christ. Accordingly, believers in him are free from the tutelage of law; to seek salvation out of the law is to seek bondage.[34]

Although some interpreters of Galatians 3 view Paul's statements as primarily intended to depreciate the Mosaic Law, the thrust of Paul's argument is rather against those who misuse it by seeking to impose certain of its commandments or prohibitions upon Gentiles. The practical effect of this was to exclude some men from the covenant promises of God. Against the Judaizers, Paul fights for a community of God's people—his true "sons," "heirs according to promise"—in which none are excluded. In Galatians 3:26–4:7 Paul's intention is stated quite explicitly. For an understanding of Paul's evaluation of the law per se, one must also turn to certain of the Apostle's statements in his Letter to the Romans.[35]

If careful attention is given to Paul's use of another term, beginning with his important assertion in 2:16, further insight into the Apostle's specific concerns may be grasped. This term is *faith*, associated with Christ, whose name is written in the genitive case. In the RSV the Greek phrase is translated "faith *in* Christ,"[36] but it can equally well read "the faith of Christ," as other scholars have contended. One writer argues persuasively that Paul's thought, throughout this section of the Galatian letter—which is concerned with the relation between the Christian and the Mosaic Law—is influenced by his own and his reader's knowledge of transactions prescribed by Roman law for the transmission of inheritances.[37]

[29]M. Barth, note 14 above, p. 138. Paul's theology of history is more explicitly given in Rom. 9–11. See below, pp. 442ff.

[30]Gal. 3:10.

[31]Gal. 3:17f.

[32]Gal. 3:19a, 22.

[33]Gal. 3:19b–21. Cf. Acts 7:38, 58; Heb. 2:2; Deut. 33:2 (LXX); Jub. 1; Josephus, *Antiq.*, XV. v. 3.

[34]Gal. 3:24; 4:2.

[35]See below, pp. 440f.

[36]E.g., Gal. 2:15; 3:22; or "faith *in* the Son of God," 2:20.

[37]G. M. Taylor, "The Function of 'Pistis Christou' in Galatians," *JBL* LXXXV (1966): 58ff.

According to ordinary legal procedures, a testator assigned to a sole heir his legacy. In the testament, or covenant, provision was made for a *fidei commissum,* a trust which, when accepted by the sole heir, gave him the right to designate beneficiaries who would share this legacy, and who would thus themselves become heirs of the testator. Moreover, a Roman could, by his testament, adopt aliens or strangers so that in every sense they became sons and heirs. He could also provide testamentary "tutors" for them, as for his minor children designated beneficiaries, until the death of the sole heir, at which time the inheritance would be shared.

Paul's argument does seem to draw upon these analogies provided by Roman legal practices. He writes of Abraham and of his rightful descendants; of Christ as the sole offspring through whom God's blessing of Abraham comes to the Gentiles; of those who are heirs, yet subject to a tutelage until Christ accepts and fulfills the testamentary *fidei commissum* (summarily, the faith of Christ), whereby he makes them sons and heirs of the testator, i.e., God. Paul's primary use of the term *faith* is therefore analogous to the *fidei commissum* on which the testament or covenant is based and through which it is effectuated. This is the faith which Paul attributes to Christ, i.e., the faithful execution of his trust. But "faith" is used by Paul in other contexts—as in the case of Abraham in the past, and Christians in the present—to signify that trustfulness befitting those who have been chosen beneficiaries, who are "heirs according to promise." [38]

At 4:8 Paul appeals directly to his converts from paganism. He asked if they wished to become enslaved again "to the weak and beggarly elemental spirits" (17). Paul presupposed belief in invisible demons or world rulers, a commonplace, as we have seen, of the Greco-Roman world. Were the Judaizers in Galatia pandering to popular Gentile superstitions, claiming that adherence to Jewish dietary laws and the ritual calendar delivered men from the baneful influence of the spirit world? Tendencies towards syncretism were certainly present in Galatia. Was there an incipient Gnosticism in the Galatian Judaizers' doctrine? Some find evidence supporting an affirmative reply; others deny its sufficiency.[39]

An allegory based on the Genesis story of Abraham's sons follows an impassioned, personal appeal (18)[40], and provides a transition to Paul's moral exhortation. The controversial mood is sustained. The allegory introduces the theme of freedom and slavery by sharply contrasting two mutually exclusive ways of salvation (19). The responsible use of this freedom informs the admonitions of Paul which follow, which are concerned with those who are not under law but who are led by the Spirit (D). If this freedom is interpreted as the removal of all moral restraint, "the flesh" is given a base of operation for its works (23). But for Christians there is a law which must be kept: neighbor-love means that Christians are "slaves of one another."

[38] Ibid., pp. 67f. M. Barth (note 14 above, pp. 143f.) urges that the effort to make mutually exclusive Pauline faith and Jewish faith is misguided: "when Paul desires to illustrate what he means by faith he refers to O.T. passages."

[39] See F. R. Crownfield, "The Singular Problem of the Dual Galatians," *JBL* LXIV (1945): 491ff. Cf. Feine-Behm-Kümmel, *Intro.,* pp. 194f.

[40] See further, below, pp. 438f.

The demands of such a standard make it necessary that the man of faith surrender himself to the leadership of the Spirit, and that he make every effort to restrain his natural inclinations "to gratify the desires of the flesh." Love is a divine gift and cannot be self-cultivated. It is "the fruit of the Spirit," as are all of the moral characteristics of the Christian life (24).

Paul's argument in this hortatory section is a further attack upon the central problem in Galatia. One need not suppose that he has turned from the Judaizers to inveigh against another group. When first attacking the Judaizers Paul asked them: "Having begun in the Spirit are you now ending in the flesh?" Moreover, Paul's reference to those "who are spiritual" has no derogatory implication, and at the close of the letter Paul is still opposing those "who would compel" the Galatians to be circumcised and who thereby exalted "the flesh."[41]

The letter ends on a very personal note (E). We may reflect upon it in relation to the other personal appeals which break through Paul's argument toward the end of the doctrinal section (18, 20). The reader may have noticed that in these passages Paul's state of mind and manner of speaking are reminiscent of 2 Corinthians. In both letters the Apostle's estrangement from his churches led him to anguished expressions of emotion, to bitter irony, and to scornful reproach of his enemies. He contrasted sharply the reception which these churches had given him with their present attitudes, to their shame. He was much occupied with the mystery that spiritual strength is made perfect in weakness. In both letters Paul was forced to self-assertion.[42] When we consider these things, along with the similarities between Galatians and Romans which shall be shown presently, it is reasonable to conclude that Galatians was written during the Corinthian crisis. Henceforth Paul asked to be spared the anxiety caused by the backsliding brethren, the physical effects which his sufferings and persecution had had upon him.[43] If he must boast, he would boast of the things which showed his weakness. He would point to "the branding marks of Jesus," that were upon his body, for he is Christ's slave. Christ may do with him as he wills. Throughout the Letter to the Galatians, Paul exalted Christ and claimed a subservience to him alone.

THE LETTER TO THE ROMANS

The Setting of Romans in Paul's Career

The Letter to the Romans is, by common agreement, the most considered and systematic statement of Paul's gospel. Its great—many would say incomparably great—influence upon the history of the Christian Church is a matter of record. Because of this it is sometimes thought that Romans possesses a timeless quality. Yet the book is a genuine letter and not a theological treatise. Its exposition of

[41] Paul's contrast "flesh–spirit" superficially resembled the Orphic dualism, but probably presupposed the Hellenistic–Jewish way of stating the rabbinical doctrine of "the two impulses" which struggle in men. A. D. Nock, *St. Paul* (1938), pp. 166ff.; Stamm, *IB*, vol. 10, p. 560.

[42] See *IB*, vol. 10, p. 560; Stamm makes the most of these parallels.

[43] Cf. Gal. 6:17 and 2 Cor. 11:23ff.

the gospel reflects the controversies, pastoral problems, and spiritual experiences of its author.[44] A knowledge of the setting of Romans in Paul's career contributes much to its understanding.

Before reading Romans through one should examine its introduction, 1:1–15, and the personal notes at the end, 15:14ff., to observe the letter's testimony to its origin. For some while Paul's eyes had been turned toward Rome. He longed to preach there and to follow this visit with a mission in Spain. One may notice Paul's confession that he preferred the work of a pioneer evangelist to that of a pastor who must build on the work of other men. Indeed Paul would rather that others build on the foundations which he himself had laid, so that he might be free to press on to other places.[45] Before Paul could visit Rome, however, he had an obligation to discharge. He must deliver the contribution for the Christian poor in Jerusalem.[46]

Now this prospective journey to Jerusalem cannot be the one noted in Acts 18:22 for at that time the ministry of Ephesus lay before Paul. It must be the journey narrated in Acts 20, the object of which was delivery of the collection gathered among his Gentile churches.[47] It may be concluded, therefore, that Paul wrote the Letter to the Romans in Achaia, probably at Corinth during his "three-month" stay, before heading through Macedonia for Jerusalem.[48] According to our reckoning this would have been late in A.D. 56 or early in 57.

A reading now of Romans 16 reveals an item which confirms for some persons that Romans was written in Achaia. Paul commended to his readers Phoebe, a deaconess at Cenchreae, the port of Corinth. There are, however, some surprising features in this chapter. Could Paul, a stranger to Rome, have known more than twenty-six persons in its church? When Paul wrote 1 Corinthians from Ephesus, he sent greetings from "Prisca and Aquila together with the church in their house." Perhaps this point was not noticed, but examine 1 Corinthians 16:19 and Romans 16:5. Is it conceivable that within such a brief period this couple had returned to Rome, and that their house had become a gathering place for Christians? Another surprise is that "the dissensions and difficulties" referred to in Romans 16:17f. are not alluded to in chapters 1–15. Paul's warning against the creators of dissension sounds like the authoritative directive of a pastor to his people, hardly one written by a missionary to a church he had neither founded nor visited.[49] For these and other reasons many persons believe that Romans 16 was not a part of the letter written to the Romans. Rather it is an extant fragment

---

[44] ". . . so far as we know . . . [Paul] always took up his pen under the pressure of the urgencies of his mission. There is nothing in him of the academic theologian. The letter from Corinth to Rome is no exception to this rule." F. J. Leenhardt, *The Epistle to the Romans*, trans. H. Knight (1961), p. 14 [hereafter, *Romans*].

[45] How else can one explain 15:23a?

[46] Notice that Paul has double cause for misgivings, 15:31.

[47] Acts 24:17.

[48] Feine-Behm-Kümmel, *Intro.*, p. 220.

[49] For a concise account of the obscure origin of the Roman church, ibid., p. 217.

of what was probably a brief letter of commendation for Phoebe, and of greetings to friends, written from Corinth or Cenchreae to the church at Ephesus.[50]

The question of the integrity of Romans having been raised, brief notice must be taken of the curious textual variations in its last three chapters. The doxology, 16:25–27, appears at several different places in copies of the letter, while others omit it altogether. In the oldest Greek manuscript of Paul's letters, the third-century codex, Papyrus 46, the doxology follows 15:33. In other valuable manuscripts it stands after 16:23, or else after verse 24. Second-century Christian writers report that copies of the letter in Rome and in African churches contained only chapters 1–14.[51]

The conclusion is that this doxology was not written by Paul but by some editor. Perhaps it was composed as a suitable ending for the short form of the letter, or for chapter 16 if one can assume its separate existence. Beyond this conclusion, opinions may be grouped into two major alternatives. A few persons believe that Paul wrote the short letter, intending it for his churches in the East, and that he later edited a copy of it to be sent to Rome, with the additions at the end serving as "a covering letter."[52] It is more probable that Paul originally wrote one of the longer versions. The most plausible view is that Paul wrote chapters 1–15 to the Romans and that a copy of this letter, with its postscript chapter 16, was sent to Ephesus. The belief that Marcion was responsible for the short form of Romans has persisted. If he edited the text at Rome it is likely that he trimmed away 14:24–15:33. But the mutilation of the original text (with or without chapter 16) may be accounted for.[53]

Although some uncertainty remains concerning the exact content of Paul's letter, and whether or not he wrote it only for the Roman Christian community, the immediate purpose in sending this letter to Rome is clear. By means of it Paul announced his coming, explained the delay, and sought to gain the understanding of this important church, perhaps its assistance, prior to visiting Rome en route to Spain. Can one say more concerning the purpose of the Letter to the Romans? Some scholars have felt that the broad lines of Paul's theological argument suggest "other, more deeply lying foundations."[54] We press, then, beyond the relatively simple query "why did Paul send this letter to the Romans?" to the more difficult question "why did he write it in the way he did?"

The letter's testimony to Paul's lack of direct relationship to the church at Rome

[50] Knox, *Romans, IB,* vol. 9, pp. 365ff.; Enslin, *Beginnings,* pp. 262ff.; Leenhardt, *Romans,* pp. 26ff. For the retention of 16:1–23 as an integral part of the letter to the Romans, see C. H. Dodd, *The Epistle of Paul to the Romans* (1932), pp. xix ff., 234ff. [hereafter, *Romans*]; C. K. Barrett, *A Commentary on the Epistle to the Romans* (1957), pp. 281ff. [hereafter, *Romans*]; Feine-Behm-Kümmel, *Intro.,* pp. 224ff.

[51] Lake, *Earlier Epistles,* pp. 335ff.; T. W. Manson, *BJRL* 31 (1948): 224ff. Manson's evaluation of this evidence is summarized with approval (Munck, *Paul,* pp. 197ff.)

[52] Did the short letter omit references to Rome? See Lake, *Earlier Epistles,* pp. 362ff. Enslin, *Beginnings,* pp. 267f., supposes the letter to have been intended for the churches in Galatia.

[53] See Dodd, *Romans,* p. xvi. J. B. Lightfoot's suggestion that Paul later shortened his letter fails to account for the clumsy break at 14:23.

[54] Feine-Behm-Kümmel, *Intro.,* p. 220: A. Wikenhauser, *New Testament Introduction,* trans. J. Cunningham (1963), pp. 406ff.

makes it very unlikely that its subject matter stands in apposite relation to specific controversial issues within the Roman congregation. Only a few scholars today derive its purpose from this meager evidence.[55] Others have detected a defensively personal thrust in Romans and believe that Paul was moved at this time to write an impassioned apology for his life.[56] Still other scholars conclude that Paul composed this letter for the purpose of clarifying his principal convictions—for the benefit of the Romans and others—convictions which had been hammered out in the fires of controversy, convictions which needed to be drawn together in a constructive relation to one or more major truths of the gospel. Perhaps Paul realized that his opportunities for doing such a thing might be severely limited in the future.[57]

The history of this letter's interpretation shows that many generations of readers, especially since the Protestant Reformation, have tended to fix their attention upon its teaching concerning justification by faith interpreted in the context of an individual's experience. The significance of justification by faith for Christian theology has been very great indeed. Yet the result of this concentration of reader interest has been that segments of Romans have become somewhat tangential to its "main theme" containing, it is said, irrelevant or at least unnecessary excursues.[58]

One writer, noting this failure to discover a purpose for Romans sufficiently comprehensive to encompass the whole, calls the reader's attention to Paul's immediate purpose as providing the clue to the shape of his entire argument.[59] The extension of the Christian mission to Spain, beyond the "ecclesiastical province" centering in Jerusalem, created a new geographical orientation which Paul acknowledged, but also a theological problem which he perceived to be a major one. While preparing to take to Jerusalem the sum of money collected by his efforts among the Gentile congregations, Paul may have pondered whether such concrete manifestations of the Church's unity would any longer be possible between Christians so distant from one another that they might lose all contact. In proportion as the Church expanded it was threatened with the loss of its sense of unity. Anticipating this theological problem posed by his plan for the Spanish mission, Paul wrote to the most important church on the Western frontier declaring that the teaching at the very heart of the gospel—justification by faith—provided an affirmation of the Church's unity unbounded by time and space. From its very beginning the people of God was recruited by faith. Now through faith in Jesus Christ all men may benefit from the promises made to Abraham and

---

[55]Munck, *Paul*, p. 199, rightly emphasizes that it is profitless to draw a picture of situations in the Roman church from inferences in the letter which, for the most part, must be drawn from chapters 14–15. G. Bornkamm, "The Letter to the Romans as Paul's Last Will and Testament," *Australian Biblical Review* XI (1963): 4ff. Cf. Lake, *Earlier Epistles*, pp. 370ff.; Feine-Behm-Kümmel, *Intro.*, p. 221.

[56]E.g., A. Nygren, *Commentary on Romans*, trans. C. C. Rasmussen (1949), pp. 8f.

[57]T. W. Manson, J. Munck, see note 51 above. G. Bornkamm accepts with qualification, and further develops, Manson's thesis, see note 55 above.

[58]E.g., Rom. 5:12–21; 9–11 *et al.*

[59]Leenhardt, *Romans*, pp. 13ff.

to Israel. Yet Gentile believers must also clearly recognize that they belong essentially to the "trunk of the tree" which has borne them, so as to be able to acknowledge the unity and continuity of the people of God through its changing historical destinies.

It may seem passing strange that the purpose of a letter which does not contain the word *church* or specific references to unity should be defined as primarily an affirmation of the Church's unity. It would be well, however, for the reader of Romans to continue the search for some theme which pervades the whole. This letter has long suffered from interpreters who, for one good reason or another, have too narrowly limited their interest in its teaching, and then assumed that Paul's interest was likewise limited. Perhaps the Apostle's statement that the Christian gospel reveals "the righteousness of God" affords the surest clue to his overarching purpose in writing to the Romans.

An Outline of the Letter of Paul to the Romans

A. Introduction, 1:1–15:
    1. The superscription containing a credal statement, 1:1–7
    2. A thanksgiving including Paul's wish to visit Rome, 8–15
B. The gospel according to Paul, 1:16–15:13:
    3. The gospel reveals God's righteousness 1:16–17
    4. The righteousness of God manifested as judgment—the Gentiles, 1:18–32: those who reject the manifest knowledge of God are without excuse (18–23); idolatry and the resultant moral depravity of men (24–32)
    5. The righteousness of God manifested as judgment—self-styled "innocent critics," 2:1–16: morally upright men are condemned in their judgment of others (1–11); the impartiality of the divine retribution (12–16)
    6. The righteousness of God manifested as judgment—the Jew, 2:17–3:20: the privileges of Jews and their practices (17–24); circumcision and the mark of "a real Jew" (25–29); controversy concerning the advantages of the Jew (3:1–8); provisional summary of Paul's position (9–20)
    7. The righteousness of God manifested through the faithfulness of Christ— the justification of believing sinners, 3:21–4:25: justification defined (21–26); three inferences—boasting is excluded (27–28), the unity and universality of God established (29–30), the relation of law to the covenant of promise disclosed (3:31–4:25)
    8. The righteousness of God manifested in His salvation of men—the character of the new life in Christ, 5:1–8:39: justification and salvation (1–11); Adam and Christ—the corporate effects of sin and their remedy (12–21); death to sin and the law—three analogies (6:1–7:6); the law and the experience of deliverance from sin (7–25); new life in the Spirit and the assurance of ultimate salvation through God's love revealed in Christ (8:1–39)
    9. The righteousness of God manifested in His saving purpose in history, 9:1–11:36: Paul's anguish because of his unbelieving "kinsmen by race"

(9:1-5); Israel's apostasy, even if final, not a failure of God's purpose (6-13); God's election, even if arbitrary, not unjust (14-29); God's election not arbitrary (9:30-10:21); Israel's apostasy not final: there is a remnant chosen by grace (11:1-6), the remainder who stumbled are serving God's purpose of salvation (7-24), eventually all Israel will be saved (25-32); in praise of God's wisdom (33-36)[60]

10. The righteousness of God establishing right relations among men, 12:1-15:13: The basis of Christian morality (12:1-2); love among fellow-members of "the one body in Christ" (3-13); love of enemies (14-21); the relations of Christians to the State (13:1-7); the debt of love (8-10); the eschatological sanction (11-14); the relations of "the weak" and "the strong" in the Church (14:1-15:6); in the Church's unity, God is glorified (7-13)

C. Conclusion, 15:14-33:

11. Paul's work for God, 15:14-22
12. Paul's plans and God's will, 15:23-32
13. A benediction, 15:33

[D. Commendation of Phoebe; Greetings: Appeal and Warning; Benediction; Doxology (?), 16:1-27]

After introducing himself to the Roman church, Paul witnessed to his understanding of the essentials of the gospel (3). The whole letter is an explication of this testimony, but it contains certain ideas which merit clarification at the outset.

Interpreting Romans

Christianity was for Paul a dynamic religion. Its gospel was "the power of God working toward salvation." The realities signified by the terms—*salvation, to be saved*—held a more prominent place in Paul's thought than a statistical summary of their use in his letters may suggest.[61] In biblical and ancient Jewish traditions salvation had become increasingly an eschatological idea.[62] And thus it is in Paul's teaching. It remained a future hope. But true to the perspective of the Christian *kerygma*, Paul proclaimed that God's future was being anticipated in the present.[63] The gospel had proven to be the power of God put forth to bring salvation to every man.

Paul's distinctive synonym for salvation—distinctive, that is, in the early Church for it had deep scriptural roots—was "the righteousness of God." It is this which the gospel reveals. The modern reader may assume that Paul was affirming his

[60] The author gladly acknowledges his indebtedness to John Knox for his perceptive outline of Romans 9-11. Other parts of outline reflect the influence of Dodd's commentary, *Romans*, pp. ix ff.

[61] See the valuable exposition of Paul's thought under the concept of Salvation, C. A. A. Scott, *Christianity According to St. Paul* (1927).

[62] N. H. Snaith, *The Distinctive Ideas of the Old Testament* (1944), pp. 87-89 [hereafter, *Distinctive Ideas*]; A. Richardson, "Salvation," *IDB*, vol. 4, pp. 172ff.

[63] E.g., Rom. 5:9f.; 8:24; 10:9; 1 Cor. 1:18, 21; 3:15; 5:5; 15:2.

belief that God is a just being, that righteousness is one of his attributes. This commonsense inference is not to be rejected, yet it is important to know that in ancient Judaism the phrase connoted an active as well as a passive meaning. And the more the Jews looked toward "the end of the days" for the vindication of God, and of "the righteous" whom he approved, the more this active meaning of the term *righteousness* became associated with eschatology.[64]

Several passages in the prophets and Psalms of the Old Testament illustrate this theology of hope, that God will reveal his salvation, his righteousness:

> I [Yahweh] will bring near my righteousness [deliverance, RSV]
>   it is not far off,
> and my salvation
>   will not tarry;
> I will put salvation in Zion,
>   for Israel my glory.   Is. 46:13; cf. 51:5ff.; 56:1; 62:1.

> O sing to the Lord a new song,
>   for he has done marvellous things!
> His right hand and his holy arm
>   have gotten him salvation [victory, RSV].
> The Lord has made known his salvation [victory],
>   his righteousness has he openly shown
>   [he has revealed his vindication, RSV]
> in the sight of the nations.   Ps. 98:1f.

Within the eschatology of ancient Judaism, this thought of the revelation of the righteousness of God was associated with a day of judgment. When the coming manifestation of righteousness was celebrated, therefore, it was with assurance that God would bless "the righteous":

> O let the evil of the wicked come to an end,
>   but establish thou the righteous,
> Thou who triest the minds and hearts,
>   Thou righteous God.   Ps 7:9

Or again, in Ps. 31:1 the writer's plea, "in thy righteousness deliver me!" is accompanied by his faith that "the Lord preserves the faithful, but abundantly requites him who acts hautily."[65]

As we have seen, this belief in the imminence of divine judgment was especially prominent in Jewish apocalyptic writings. In them the faith of the Old Testament writers that the righteous would be vindicated by God in the coming judgment becomes intensely nationalistic.[66] But even more significant a development is the

---

[64] E. R. Achtemier, "Righteousness in the O.T." (esp. secs. 5–9), *IDB*, vol. 4, pp. 82ff. Dodd, *Romans*, pp. 12ff.; Bultmann, *Theology*, vol. 1, pp. 270ff.

[65] See also Ps. 17. Israel's faith was that Yahweh, as righteous judge, would restore the right of those who are deprived of it. Thus the revelation of God's righteousness would be the assertation of his power to accomplish this.

[66] Russell, *Jewish Apocalyptic*, p. 301. See above, pp. 78ff.

belief, persistently asserted, that God in judging man must surely vindicate Himself. In several apocalypses the revelation of the righteousness of God principally focuses upon the establishment of God's right, as sovereign ruler of all nations, a vindication of the trust of His faithful people in His right action and righteous judgments toward all men in their history.

The writers of 2 Baruch and 4 Ezra raised the question of the righteousness of God in the face of historical events which seemed to impugn it, and sought to defend his "righteous judgments." When Ezra is condemned for judging God, he is called upon both to give thanks for his place among the elect and not to doubt God's justice.[67] He also writes:

> [And yet] I will justify Thee, O God, in uprightness of heart,
> For in Thy judgments is Thy righteousness (displayed), O God . . .
> God is a righteous judge,
> And he is no respecter of persons.[68]

The writer of the Psalms of Solomon likewise defends the righteousness of God's judgment.[69] God's judgment which falls on every nation is just. But also that judgment which comes upon his own people: "behold, now, O God, Thou hast shown us Thy judgment in Thy righteousness."[70] In these contexts the righteousness of God is virtually synonymous with His faithfulness, His constancy.

Against this background of Jewish eschatology Paul's proclamation in Romans 1:17 and 18 is to be understood: "For in it [the gospel] the righteousness of God is being revealed . . . for the wrath of God is being revealed from heaven against all ungodliness and wickedness of men. . . ." In these statements Paul certainly claimed that the eschatological day of salvation and of judgment was no longer a future event only. Do historical considerations enable us to say more? What specific meanings are present in Paul's declaration that now "the righteousness of God has been manifested" (3:21)? Does Paul refer primarily to that righteousness which through Christ is given men by God, and which is now accounted valid before Him? Or does Paul chiefly proclaim how the righteousness which is God's is being manifested; how God's dominion as a Savior and Judge is being revealed to all mankind, in and through Jesus Christ? The alternatives have been often debated.[71] The present writer believes that the second expresses the central

---

[67] 4 Ezr. 7:17ff.; 8:37ff.

[68] 4 Ezr. 2:15ff; also, 2 Bar. 78:5; 1 En. 108:13.

[69] The verb *to justify* in Pss. of Sol. is plainly referred to God. "It is always the righteous who vindicates the sentence, judgments and name of God . . . ," G. Schrenck in *Theological Dictionary*, ed. and trans. Bromiley (1964), vol. II, p. 213.

[70] Pss. of Sol. 8:25; also 2:36ff; 8:38ff; 9:2f. Parallel ideas are found in Qumran writings; IQH ii, 24; IQS i, 26; xi, 14.

[71] E.g., note the recent articles by E. Käsemann, and R. Bultmann: Käsemann, "The Righteousness of God in Paul," *New Testament Questions*, pp. 168ff.; Bultmann, "Dikaiosune Theou," *JBL* LXXXII (1964): 12ff. The position defended in Bultmann's untranslated article is set forth in his *Theology*, vol. 1, pp. 270ff. See also J. Reumann, "The Gospel of the Righteousness of God," *Interpretation* XX (1966): 446ff. Arguments seeking to establish a single meaning for the term throughout Paul's letters are probably in error; but it is always pertinent to ask which meaning is *primary*.

motif in Paul's proclamation of the gospel. Paul does not *begin* with the question of how sinful men can be made or accounted "righteous," but rather how the right of God over his creation is being, and will yet be, realized in a manner consistent with his promises and covenant. For Paul, the Christian *kerygma* vindicated the judgments of God, past and present, and proclaimed his coming victory! All men, therefore, who accepted God's judgments proclaimed in the gospel as righteous judgments, and who acknowledged His claim upon them for believing obedience, received their vindication, and are given a share in His present and future victory.

The meaning of the crucial word *faith* is deepened in the course of the argument in Romans. But one should note that in the superscription Paul announced that his mission was "to win believing obedience . . . among all the Gentiles." [72] In his confessional statement (3), emphasis is placed on the fact that *all* men—not only the Jew to whom the gospel was first proclaimed, but also the non-Jew—are able to render this obedience that God requires. The power of God for salvation is available now to all men on equal terms: "to everyone who has faith."

Paul's appeal to the prophecy of Habbakuk 2:4 makes it plain that God's revelation in Jesus Christ had radically revised his understanding, both of the means whereby man may hope to obtain righteousness, and of the nature of saving faith. The oracle of the prophet—"the righteous shall live by faith"—was understood by rabbinical Judaism "as a comprehensive fulfillment of the commandments in meritorious faithfulness." [73] One Jewish sect in New Testament times understood the prophet's oracle to have an eschatological as well as a hortatory meaning. At first glance it may seem that the writer of the Qumran Habbakuk Scroll approaches the thought of Paul. For this writer, Habbakuk referred to "all those of the house of Judah *who live according to the Torah,* whom God will rescue from the place of judgment because of their labor and their faith in the teacher of righteousness."

Paul's teaching sharply contrasts with this. The righteousness of God was being manifested *apart from law,*[74] and those who are experiencing salvation "in the place of judgment" are not "the righteous" but sinners from among Jews and Gentiles. The writer of the Qumran commentary did teach that those who hope in God's vindication must have faith—faith in a person, the teacher of righteousness. But obedience to the Torah and the laborious discipline of the sect gave meaning to this saving "faith" in the teacher of righteousness. For Paul, reliance upon "the works of the law" was a flat denial of "faith in Jesus Christ." [75]

Once again, interpreters of Paul are presented with an ambiguous use of the genitive case. Should we read "faith in Jesus Christ" or "the faith of Jesus Christ," and accordingly what was Paul's primary reference when he used the single term

---

[72] Barrett's translation, *Romans,* p. 21.
[73] G. Schrenck in *Theological Dictionary,* vol. II, p. 187.
[74] Rom. 3:21a.
[75] Gal. 5:2ff.; Rom. 3:20. S. Johnson, "Paul and the Manual of Discipline," *JBL* XLVIII (1955): 160ff. Note IQS, xi, 12f.

faith? Perhaps one's answer should be deferred until the passage 3:21ff. is examined.[76]

Paul's exposition of the gospel begins, however, with Romans 1:18 (4), not with 3:21 (7). Paul did not write that "the wrath of God" was revealed before the gospel was proclaimed or received, or that it will be revealed only on the last day. "The wrath of God *is being revealed*," he wrote, here and now. The eschatological moment had come and, in accord with current Jewish eschatology, Paul believed that the wrath of God belonged to the same disclosure as His righteousness. God is now revealing his righteousness, Paul affirmed, by no longer withholding his wrath (4–6). God stood against men in their sin and was ready to save them. It is doubtful that Paul would have agreed with some of his modern interpreters who say that "the gospel proclaims not God's wrath, but his righteousness. . . ." Romans 1:18ff. may be correctly entitled: "The Gospel as God's Condemnation of Man."[77]

It is a testimony to Paul's Hellenistic–Jewish background, as well as to his allegiance to Christ as Lord, that he indicted Gentile society for its idolatry and saw in this the root of sexual perversions and other social vices (4).[78] The refusal to acknowledge God as God, to honor God, was essentially an idolization of self. As a result, men dishonor their own bodies. Worshiping beasts, men become like them. Paul also believed that God permitted this evil to bring its tragic consequences, for man's idolatry and vice could not be attributed to ignorance but to the defiance of His will.

Students of Paul's thought have quite naturally been attracted to the way in which Paul sought to establish the fact that all men were accountable to God for their behavior and stand under His judgment. Did Paul believe that all men know the claim of the divine Creator by the mere fact of their existence, that men have an innate consciousness of God's moral order? Does one find in Romans evidence for Paul's belief in a "natural" knowledge, or "general " revelation, of God? Perhaps the majority of Paul's readers have said yes. As a Hellenistic Jew, Paul had come under the influence of Stoic beliefs in natural law and in the universal phenomenon of man's moral consciousness or "conscience." Perhaps these beliefs (without some of the inferences drawn from them by the Stoics) had come to Paul through the Jewish "wisdom theology" of the period, which taught that the Torah had been both the plan and the instrument in God's creation of the world.[79] The Creation was conceived as a manifestation of God's Wisdom–Torah. Therefore some Gentiles could, and all others ought to, "do by nature what the law requires," since the Law was written on their hearts. "By their

[76] See below, pp. 438f.

[77] K. Barth, *A Shorter Commentary on Romans*, trans. D. H. van Daalen (1959), pp. 24ff. [hereafter, *Shorter Commentary*]. Barrett (*Romans*, p. 34): "the revelation of wrath . . . is a clear sequel of the revealing of God's righteousness."

[78] Wisd. of Sol. 14:12. Paul's statements throughout sec. 4 are paralleled at many points with this book of the Apocrypha.

[79] Davies, *Paul*, pp. 115ff., 165ff.

wickedness they suppress the truth" and bring upon themselves God's just judgment.

But this interpretation of Paul's argument is by no means self-evident to others. Paul wrote to Gentiles who had been confronted by the gospel. He declared that in the gospel there is revealed something that they did not already know, the objective fact that God had been declaring Himself unto men, that His will had been impinging upon human wills since the creation of the world. Now they could and must know, through the truth revealed in Christ, that as God's creatures they are accountable to Him.[80]

Neither way of explaining Paul's argument here is fully adequate. Although this indictment of Gentiles is grounded formally upon Paul's belief in man's natural knowledge of God and capacity to make moral judgments based upon the human situation, the starting point for Paul is the revelation of the truth about man revealed in Christ and His cross. That the gospel is Paul's norm of judgment throughout Romans 1–2 is evidenced when "the edge of the argument is turned, as it is at 2:16: God's judgment now, as at the last day, is a judgment through Christ."[81] Paul argued that only from the perspective of the gospel is the depth and seriousness of man's wrong fully exposed, and only its revelation of God's righteousness provides a basis for meeting the objections of any man who questions the rightness of God's judgments, who protests His justice. One thing seems certain, Paul was not advancing rational proofs for the existence of God in Romans 1–2. The prevalence in the Greco–Roman world of idolatry, not of atheism, is the human tragedy Paul deplores.

The Apostle evidently assumed that while some of his readers would join him in his condemnation of common social vices, they would fail to see that his indictment applied to themselves (5). But, said Paul, pious Jews (as well as Gentile moralists?) who pass judgment upon other men, "are doing the very same thing," glorying in themselves and not in God's grace towards sinners (6). Paul's words at this point concerning the coming "day of wrath" disclose once again his eschatological perspective. The judgment, like the salvation of God, is future, even though—or one might say because—it is being revealed in the present. The impartiality of God's judgment consists in the fact that all men are judged according to the light that has been given them. The Jew is not excused because he has the Law, nor the Gentile who disavows all knowledge of the truths which it teaches.

Paul knew that this position would not go unchallenged. He was bound to make clear his understanding of the teaching of scripture: God the creator of man is a righteous judge; he is no respecter of persons. When viewed from the perspective of the gospel, Israel's election and special privileges were fully consonant with this teaching. But at this place in the letter Paul only denied the common distortions of his position in this regard.[82] His immediate concern was to clinch the

---

[80] Barth, *Shorter Commentary*, pp. 26ff. Cf. E. Brunner, *The Letter to the Romans* (1959), pp. 16f. [hereafter, *Romans*]; Dodd, "Natural Law in the New Testament," *New Testament Studies*, pp. 140ff.

[81] W. Manson, "Notes on the Argument of Romans 1–8," in Higgins, *New Testament Essays*, pp. 154f.

[82] Rom. 3:1–8.

point: "there is no distinction . . ." between Jews and Gentiles, *insofar as their culpability is concerned*, ". . . since all have sinned and come short of the glory of God. . . ."[83]

In this summary statement we may be provided an important clue to Paul's conception of the nature of sin. So far he had said that man's sin consisted in his willful refusal to acknowledge God, in his false assumption that life is his own and not a gift of the Creator. This is man's essential sin, and from this disorientation all material sins arise. Paul had inherited these conceptions from Judaism. But as a Christian, Paul believed that the Creator had revealed "the light of the knowledge of the glory of God in the face of Christ."[84] Thus, when Paul declared that all men "fall short of the glory of God," he may have been saying that none reflect the glory of Christ's manhood, a nature faithfully submitted to the will of God, in obedience and in trust. When the Apostle affirmed that "all have sinned" he was not saying that all men are by nature evil, or that the best in every man is depraved. He was saying that, judged by Christ's likeness, all men are in fact sinners. It is the will of God that men conform to this standard; it is toward the attainment of this eschatological nature that He offers man His power unto salvation.[85]

Paul's deep pessimism concerning the possibilities of man apart from Christ is not to be attributed to his Jewish apocalypticism, but to his belief that the gospel had revealed the only means whereby right relations can be established between God and His estranged creatures, between man and his fellowmen: justification can be achieved only by God's "grace as a gift through . . . Jesus Christ." (7)[86]

The crucial term *justification* needs further clarification. What the verb *to justify* meant for Paul depended on its reference. With reference to God, it meant "to accept as righteous" His action or His judgments. With reference to men, *to justify* may mean "to make or declare righteous," or "to secure the vindication of someone." In the present context Paul does not claim that from the moment men are declared righteous they become, as we should say, virtuous or moral. He did not say that sinners are treated by God as if they are righteous (when in fact they are not). For Paul, God's justification of man—his act of making righteous—denoted a change in man's relation to God (and consequently to men), not a change in man's moral qualities. The believer is told that in the acknowledgment of his sin and of God's righteous judgment upon it, he is vindicated by God, his sins are not held against him. In the language of the lawcourt which Paul employed, the gospel proclaims the sinner's acquittal.

This justifying act of God is further described as "the redemption" and also as "an expiation by his (Christ's) blood to be received by faith." These two biblical terms—*redemption, expiation*—further emphasized the gratuitous nature of God's act, and point to the historic deed whereby this deliverance is accomplished. Both terms had special associations with Israel's deliverance from Egyptian bondage

---

[83] Rom. 3:23.
[84] 2 Cor. 4:6. Note also 3:17f.
[85] Col. 1:25ff.; 1 Cor. 11:1; 2 Cor. 3:17f.
[86] Note Paul's tautology—grace as a gift; "free for nothing," that is, from man's side.

by God's grace and power. *Expiation* may refer to the act of the priest on the day of atonement, the sprinkling of the lid or cover of the ark of the covenant with blood of the sacrificial animal. Symbolically this act was reminiscent of the great events revealing to Israel the divine mercy. It was a present and continuing means of receiving God's mercy and forgiveness. Paul's use of the image proclaimed that the cross of Christ was the place where God revealed His mercy. The shedding of the blood of Christ was the divine means whereby atonement was made for man's sin.[87]

The question is raised here whether man's "faith" is the principal reference when Paul writes of the instrument whereby God's justification of man is accomplished. According to the RSV, Paul wrote that the gospel manifested "the righteousness of God *through faith in Jesus Christ* for all who believe" (3:22). As noted above, throughout this passage, 3:21ff., Paul's emphasis is upon what God has accomplished through Christ, especially through his death. It is probable, then, that it is the faithfulness of Christ that is first of all being proclaimed, "the faith of Christ"—the fulfillment of his trust. In this context therefore, man's "faith" fundamentally consisted in an acknowledgment that God's judgment through Christ, upon any man in his sin, is indeed just.[88] No longer is man able to claim that his own acts are the basis upon which God will declare him "righteous" (3:20); the gospel calls upon men to believe in the efficacy of Christ's faith, in his "act of righteousness" (5:18), if they themselves are to be declared righteous by God. The gospel demonstrates that *God is righteous and that he declares righteous him who has faith in Jesus* (3:26).

The justification *of God* was probably still uppermost in Paul's mind when he asked his reader to consider three questions, all of which related God's justifying act in Christ to His former revelations to Israel.[89] God's deliverance of men, "on the ground of their faith" in Christ's faith, removed all cause for man's pride in his own moral achievements, all causes for interpreting God's favors as His favoritism, and, rather than destroying the authority of the Torah, established it.

Realizing that this final claim was far from self-evident, Paul introduced the case of Abraham which, as we learned from the Galatian controversy, had been thrown into his face as a witness against the truth of his gospel. But Paul had found that Abraham's story strengthened rather than weakened his position. Since much of the argument in this section of Romans parallels Galatians, no exposition of it will be undertaken here. Again Paul seems to draw upon Roman testamentary

---

[87] Barrett, *Romans*, pp. 77ff. Is Rom. 3:21–31 constructed around a pre-Pauline confessional formula? Several scholars think so, but its limits are in debate. See Reumann, "The Gospel of the Righteousness of God," note 71 above, pp. 432ff. Cf. C. H. Talbert, "A non-Pauline Fragment at Romans 3:24–26?" *JBL* LXXXV (1966): 287ff.

[88] See Rom. 4:1f., 9, 18f.; Rom. 8:3f. (also, Phil. 3:9). That the righteous man accepts *as righteous* the sentence of God is found in Jewish apocalypses, e.g., 4 Ezr. 10:16. It is an idea "in accord with the favorite usage of the rabbis." G. Schrenck in *Theological Dictionary*, vol. II, pp. 212f. See also note 38 above.

[89] Rom. 3:27ff.

law in defining concretely the nature of that faith appropriate to all who receive and inherit God's promises, and who are accounted righteous in His sight.

The next section (8) is introduced by a recapitulation and an *a fortiori* argument: *If* God has through Christ's death delivered us from the guilt and threatening consequences of sin and restored us to right relationship with himself, *how much greater* is the assurance that "we shall be saved by his (risen) life."[90]

Paul's exposition of the life "in Christ" (or "in the Spirit") follows the pattern of answering questions which are either implied or stated.[91] In the Adam–Christ typology, 5:12–21, Paul pursued further the question: how can *one* man's "act of righteousness" make it possible for *any* man to "rejoice in the hope of sharing the glory of God"? The discussion assumed the current Jewish belief that all men became subject to sin and death as the result of Adam's fall.[92] Sin existed in the world when the first man set himself against God, and its effects were continued and compounded "because all men sinned. . . ."[93] In the "Augustinian theology" of the Church, Paul is held responsible for the doctrine of sin as a hereditary disease. It is difficult to defend or deny this from the passage before us, for Paul limited himself to the thought of Adam as "a type" of unredeemed humanity and also of Christ. The fact that Paul said both things simultaneously makes it difficult to follow him. The differences brought to expression in the Adam–Christ anology are stressed particularly, for Paul does not view Christ as simply a better Adam who balances the effect of Adamic sin.[94]

Throughout the passage Paul is concerned chiefly with the corporate reality of sin, not with its origin. Since the life of man in society is corrupted by sin and death, salvation must consist in overcoming that "corporate wrongness which underlies individual transgression." This "social salvation" was now possible "in Christ"; through faith in him, men are lifted into a new order of life in which goodness is more powerful than evil, in its corporate as well as its individual manifestations.[95] The background of Paul's confidence is his conviction that in the life, death, and resurrection of Jesus Christ the Age to Come had dawned. Christ's coming had made possible for man a radically new order of life: "if anyone is in Christ *he is a new creation*."[96] Paul's Adam–Christ typology may have been influenced by current Jewish speculation about Adam as the first man, but elements in this speculation had been "demythologized" by the appearance in history of the Man of Heaven, Jesus of Nazareth, "the Son of man."[97]

"Where sin increased, grace abounded all the more." In writing this, Paul was

[90] Paul's figure of enmity-estrangement, followed by reconciliation-peace, in Rom. 5:1–11 closely parallels his thought in Rom. 3:21ff. See Barrett, *Romans*, pp. 107f.; Bultmann, *Theology*, vol. 1, pp. 285ff.

[91] Rom. 6:1, 15; 7:1, 7, 13. On the difficulty of finding a logical thread running through Rom. 5–8, see J. Knox, *IB*, vol. 9, pp. 450, 469f.

[92] Cf. 4 Ezra 3:21f.; 4:30.

[93] Rom. 5:12.

[94] Cf. 1 Cor. 15:22. See the valuable discussion on this section in Brunner, *Romans*, pp. 44ff.

[95] Dodd, *Romans*, p. 82.

[96] 2 Cor. 4:6; 5:17; Gal. 2:20; 5:14f.; 1 Cor. 14:20ff.

[97] Davies, *Paul*, pp. 37ff.; E. Best, *One Body in Christ* (1955), pp. 34ff.

reminded of a common objection to his doctrine that men are justified by God's grace: then "why not do evil that good may come?" This question was raised earlier and brushed aside with disgust. But now Paul faced it seriously.[98] The question was rooted in a serious misunderstanding both of the nature of saving faith and of the new life "in Christ." In his baptism the Christian renounced his past and its ways, as certainly as Christ's death had brought to an end one phase of his work. The believer's new life was a life risen with Christ.

This passage has attracted an unusual amount of interest and discussion for it sets forth Paul's view concerning baptism, as well as his conception of the "mystical" life *in Christ.* Some scholars have detected the influence of the mystery religions upon Paul's conception of an initiation by sacramental death and resurrection. It is indeed probable that Paul's language was shaped by a reaction to ideas of the pagan cults. But his teaching concerning the effect of Christ's death and resurrection originated in Jewish beliefs concerning the atoning value of the sufferings of the righteous—or of a representative "Righteous One"—which had found concrete fulfillment in the crucifixion and resurrection of Jesus the Christ.[99]

Moreover, baptism "in the name of Christ" derived its meaning for the early Church and for Paul from Christian eschatology. This is seen in the fact that the new life participated in the continuing realities of sin and death as well as in a victory which had overcome the dominion of both. At times Paul may seem to speak of the new life as did the initiates of the mystery cults: Christians are "dead to sin" and "alive to God in Christ Jesus"; they have crucified "the flesh." But the realism of the Christian *kerygma* is not lost sight of. Paul must exhort Christians against allowing sin to "reign" in their "mortal bodies." It was because the power of God for salvation had been anticipated in the believer's experience, not yet fully realized, that this paradoxical manner of speaking could not be avoided. For Paul the life in faith is never a self-assured possession. Yet when the Apostle speaks of "what the believer essentially is . . . he is always thinking of what he will be. The sureness of that future . . . enables him to refer to it as though it were an actual present fact."[100] But Paul was bound to acknowledge the reality of sin in himself and in every believer.

With Romans 7:7, Paul's thought progresses by means of another question: "What then shall we say, that the law is sin?" Earlier Paul had flatly stated that "through the law comes knowledge of sin."[101] He now supports this, saying that given the nature of men the effect of the law actually becomes an enticement to wrongdoing.

Paul's use of personal pronouns at this place has given rise to an unsettled controversy. Is he remembering his old life under the Torah, or is he speaking throughout, or at some particular place, of his present Christian experience? Those

[98]Note Rom. 3:8; 6:1ff.

[99]Barrett, *Romans,* pp. 122f.; Leenhardt, *Romans,* pp. 157f.; Cf. Bultmann, *Theology,* vol. 1, pp. 311f., 140ff.

[100]J. Knox, *IB,* vol. 9, pp. 480f. See Nygren, *Commentary on Romans,* pp. 239ff.; Barrett, *Romans,* pp. 129f.

[101]Rom. 3:20.

who defend the latter viewpoint stress Paul's use of present tenses, and notice that this passage falls within Paul's description of the new life in Christ.[102] But defenders of the alternative viewpoint argue that Paul could not have considered the life of peace and freedom in Christ to be beset by such torment.[103] Perhaps it is best to hold in abeyance one's decision in this matter until Paul's question has been considered: Is the law sin?

Paul answered negatively, by pointing to the positive value of the law. The failure of law is due to the nature of man. Since man rebels against external restraints, even the knowledge of God's commandments, which are "holy and just and good," sets up an intolerable tension between the will and the deed. Paul's poignant description of this split between intention and action needs no commentary. But the depth of the tragedy so described can be perceived when we remember what Paul has written elsewhere in Romans. His position may be summarized. The ineradicable problem of legalistic morality is that men tend to employ law for their own glory. Instead of being humbled by the commandments of God, they use them as the criteria for establishing their own righteousness.[104] Thus sin finds opportunity in the commandment, which promises life, and destroys man's life. Man's salvation lies not in reforming old laws or in discovering better ones, but in the obedience of faith, which is the submission to God's righteousness, established through the faithfulness of Christ.[105]

If in Romans 7 Paul wrote of his life under the law, he was not recalling his former attitudes, but the tragedy of a situation which became visible to him "only after he had attained the viewpoint of faith." Whatever frustrations the old Paul may have experienced, he had not realized the desperateness of his life under the law "until the message of grace hit its mark in him."[106] But is it not possible that Paul also described the life of the Christian as well, beginning perhaps with 7:14, the situation of the man dead to sin and yet alive to it? The Christian is being saved, but he is "saved in hope."[107]

It is this thought which underlies the poetic prose of Romans 8, for it was in the positive meaning of the Christian hope that Paul had found the way out of the subjective uncertainties of faith. There is a pathos in the recognition that these statements of assurance and certainty were written by Paul just before his fateful journey to Jerusalem. But in these words Paul exposed his innermost convictions. As C. H. Dodd has commented: "There is no arguing with such a certainty. Either you simply don't believe it or you recognize it as the word of God."[108]

The next section of the letter is a unit of thought which to some readers may

[102] J. Knox, *IB*, vol. 9, pp. 498ff.; Nygren, *Commentary on Romans*, pp. 287f., 296.

[103] Dodd, *Romans*, pp. 104ff.; Leenhardt, *Romans*, pp. 182f.

[104] Rom. 9:31f.

[105] Rom. 10:3f.; 3:22; 5:9. Paul's valuation of the Law in Romans is more positive than in Galatians; in Galatians the inadequacy of the Law for salvation is stressed; in Romans, salvation for those who transgress God's "holy" Law: Ridderbos, *Galatia*, pp. 20ff. Taylor, note 37 above, p. 60, n. 4; Bultmann, *Theology*, vol. 1, pp. 259ff.

[106] Bultmann, *Theology*, vol. 1, p. 266. Cf. Phil. 3:4ff.; Gal. 1:13f.

[107] Rom. 5:3ff.; 8:22ff.

[108] Dodd, *Romans*, p. 146.

seem an irrelevance (9). It is suggested that one may pass directly from 8:39 to 12:1 without being conscious of any omission. Interpreters who understand Romans as the gospel of salvation whereby individual men are delivered from sin and guilt, made righteous and engrafted into Christ by means of the spirit and faith, have the greatest difficulty finding a place for chapters 9–11 in this letter. But we have held that Paul is chiefly concerned in Romans to demonstrate that the gospel establishes the righteousness of God, his rightful dominion over the world—a revelation purposed to benefit "the Jew first" as well as "the Greek" (1:16f). Early in the letter Paul recognized that an objection could be raised, "that God is unjust" if, as Paul affirmed, he inflicts wrath "upon the Jews," upon the very people "entrusted with his oracles," attempting to live by His law and deriving their hope from it (3:5, 2). Paul abruptly repulsed this objection and went on to assert that every mouth protesting that God is unrighteous is, in fact, being silenced, for the gospel renders the whole world accountable to God (3:19f.). Only if God proves himself a just God and a Savior, only if God can "prevail when he is judged" (3:4), is there hope for man that he will be delivered from the wrongs he commits and suffers.

But how was Paul able to maintain God's righteousness in the face of his belief that Gentiles, who did not aspire to "righteousness," i.e., who did not acknowledge God's rightful dominion over His creatures, were being assured in the gospel of God's blessing; while many in Israel, laying claim to God's dominion by acknowledging his law, were being condemned? [109] What credibility could Paul hope to gain in claiming that God had revealed his righteousness in the gospel which, on the one hand, was being presented as something "promised beforehand through his prophets in the holy scriptures" [110] and yet, on the other hand, took away any special privilege for Israel and—as experience had shown—resulted in the exclusion of so many of God's chosen people?

The reader will find the suggested outline of Paul's defensive argument helpful. Viewing the chapters 9–11 as a whole, we may conclude that Paul saw two principles revealed in the history of salvation: selection and representation. God had chosen Israel to be His people and purposed through them to accomplish His salvation of men. But with the passage of time there had been an increasingly smaller number within Israel who truly represented this people of God in history. Then, with the coming of Christ, and with the formation of the "remnant chosen by grace" from among Jews and Gentiles, there had come into existence a community of men who responded to God's word with the faith of Abraham, and who therefore represented the true people of God. Because of these eschatological developments, and because of his belief in the triumphant power and love of God over all evil, Paul dared hope that when "the full number of the Gentiles come in" then "all Israel will be saved." Yet Paul was overcome with awe when he considered this "mystery," and prognostication gave place to praise.

Paul's letter was brought to a close with ethical teaching (10). This we have

[109] Rom. 9:30ff.
[110] Rom. 1:2; 3:21b.

PAUL'S CHRISTIAN INTERPRETATION OF HISTORY
(Romans 9-11 and related passages)

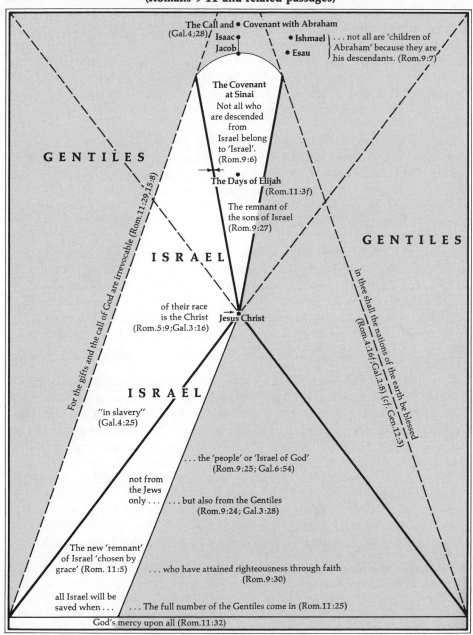

The Call and • Covenant with Abraham
(Gal.4;28)

• Isaac
Jacob

• Ishmael

• Esau

...not all are 'children of Abraham' because they are his descendants. (Rom.9:7)

The Covenant at Sinai
Not all who are descended from Israel belong to 'Israel'. (Rom.9:6)

GENTILES

The Days of Elijah
(Rom.11:3f)

The remnant of the sons of Israel
(Rom.9:27)

GENTILES

ISRAEL

For the gifts and the call of God are irrevocable (Rom.11:29,15:8)

of their race is the Christ
(Rom.5:9;Gal.3:16)

Jesus Christ

in thee shall the nations of the earth be blessed
(Rom.4:16f;Gal.2:8) (cf. Gen.12:3)

ISRAEL

"in slavery"
(Gal.4:25)

...the 'people' or 'Israel of God'
(Rom.9:25; Gal.6:54)

not from the Jews only...

...but also from the Gentiles
(Rom.9:24; Gal.3:28)

The new 'remnant' of Israel 'chosen by grace' (Rom. 11:5)

...who have attained righteousness through faith
(Rom.9:30)

all Israel will be saved when...

...The full number of the Gentiles come in (Rom.11:25)

God's mercy upon all (Rom.11:32)

seen was typical. But unlike the other letters, the exhortations in Romans were not prompted by the needs of a particular church. Some of this teaching was influenced by Paul's knowledge of the major problems which had arisen in his churches and his strategy in dealing with them. But much of it may have been drawn directly from his reflection upon "the mercies of God" revealed in the gospel, and the teaching of Jesus which he had received as a part of the Church's "tradition." Paul derived the essentially Christian moral attitudes from the gospel and showed how these might be applied to conduct both within and outside the Church.

How is the man who accepts as righteous the sentence of God upon his sinfulness, who believes that God has accounted him righteous because of his faith in the faithfulness of Christ—how is such a man to respond? Like the Old Testament prophets, Paul proclaimed that the only response acceptable to God is the offer of the self in obedience to God. Conformity to the divine will, not to socially acceptable patterns of behavior, is "the spiritual worship" of men who are in Christ.[111]

In the paragraph which follows, Romans 12:3ff., Paul's words recall those of an earlier letter addressed to the church from which he was now writing, Corinth.[112] The Christian's independence of moral judgment led neither to an irresponsible individualism nor to arrogance. He who is a fellow-member of the body of Christ must act accordingly. As in 1 Corinthians, Paul acknowledged that love is the most excellent of all gifts, that many of the attitudes which are characteristically Christian are the expression of love that is genuine, for the brethren and for the enemy.

It is difficult to understand Paul's counsel concerning the subjection of Christians to "the governing authorities."[113] Had the Apostle's own experiences conditioned him? Paul had traveled with comparative safety on land and sea, and sometimes he had escaped a lynching because of Roman law and order. Yet he also had seen the arbitrary and ruthless character of some governors, and he did not commend submission to the state for reasons of expediency, but "for the sake of conscience." Moreover, he appeals to the love commandment. Love required that men make every effort to "live peaceably with all men," and "vengeance" must be left to God.[114] But love also required more of the Christian, not less, than was required of patriotic, law-abiding citizens.[115] Paul had encountered civic irresponsibility in those who prided themselves in their freedom in Christ.

---

[111] Käsemann, New Testament Questions, pp. 188ff.

[112] Rom. 12:4ff.; 1 Cor. 12:12ff.

[113] The question concerning Paul's specific reference to "the governing authorities" (or "powers") has been vigorously and profitably discussed, raising the larger issue of Paul's views concerning the invisible spirits or demons ("principalities and powers," his usual terminology) and their relation to God and the redemptive work of Christ. See Morrison, Powers, pp. 11ff.

[114] Rom. 12:17ff.

[115] Rom. 13:8ff. Käsemann disputes the common views that Paul's teaching concerning subjection to civil magistrates should be "directly associated" either with his love ethic or with the "eschatological conclusion" in 13:11ff. (New Testament Questions, p. 199). But if, as he affirms, the whole section "stands under the sign of 12:1f.," the eschatological situation of the Christian is an underlying assumption.

The disclosure of Paul's eschatological sanction affords perhaps the principal clue to his counsel in this matter. But to some extent the interpreter must read between the lines. Did Paul associate the nearness of the end with the onslaught of demonic powers, and did he consider "the governing authorities" a restraining power, or their agents? [116] In any event, the Church must take advantage of limited opportunities to proclaim the gospel.

To the Galatians Paul had written that the Christian's special responsibility was toward "those who are of the household of faith." [117] So to the Romans, Paul's last exhortations appeal to the maintenance of love within the Church when conscientious differences of opinion arise. His advice to "the weak" and "the strong" in the Corinthian church should be remembered, but rather than pointing out to the Romans his own practice of avoiding giving offense to "the weak," Paul appealed to the example of Christ.[118]

The last words in the letter have to do with his own plans. But before disclosing these, Paul tactfully wrote:

> I myself am satisfied about you, my brethern . . . But on some points I have written to you boldly by way of reminder. . . ." [119]

In sum total these "points" give us one of the greatest letters ever written. In each generation Romans has served, "by way of reminder," to recall the Church to its reason for being—the proclamation of "the gospel of God."

[116] Cf. 2 Thess. 2:3ff.; 1 Cor. 2:5ff.; 5:1ff. (see above, pp. 391f., 400.); 1 Thess. 4:9ff.
[117] Gal. 6:10; 1 Thess. 4:9ff.
[118] Cf. Rom. 14:1–15:6 and 1 Cor. 8. See above, pp. 401f. It is important to recognize that Paul's principles are applicable to a restricted range of problems: Dodd, *Romans*, pp. 219f.
[119] Rom. 14:14f.

chapter seventeen

LETTERS FROM PRISON

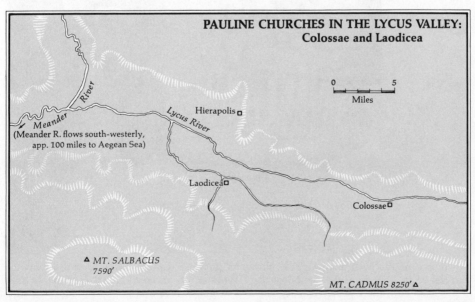

PAULINE CHURCHES IN THE LYCUS VALLEY:
Colossae and Laodicea

0   5
Miles

Meander River

Lycus River

(Meander R. flows south-westerly,
app. 100 miles to Aegean Sea)

Hierapolis

Laodicea

Colossae

▲ MT. SALBACUS
7590'

MT. CADMUS 8250' ▲

An image of the enthroned Cybele, Phrygian goddess (Magna Mater), whose worship flourished in Italy from the period of the Flavian emperors to the third century. At first a patrician cult, the Cybele-Attis legend of a woman's love and grief won the sympathy of the masses. (Alinari)

Although the pillory was used as punishment for slaves, the practical sense of the Romans inhibited cruelties to their *servi*. In the days of the Republic it was recognized that a slave had a soul, and he was permitted to adopt the cult of his choice. An edict from Nero's time charges the *praefectus urbi* to investigate complaints of slaves that their master's treated them unjustly. (British Museum)

At the outset the religion of Mithra, like the Christian, established itself among the lower classes. Probably through slaves it found its way into the Roman legions and finally into the court and educated society. The image of the bull-slaying became a familiar symbol of the dramatic "mystery" of Mithra, the Sun god. (Alinari)

P AUL, an ambassador and now a prisoner also for Christ Jesus." When these words were written, the Apostle's contact with Philemon and the church in his house was restricted to letter-writing and messages sent by a friend.[1] Three other letters of the New Testament were written, ostensibly by Paul, under similar circumstances: Ephesians, Philippians, and Colossians.[2] Ordinarily, readers of the so-called "Prison (or Captivity) Epistles" have pictured the Apostle languishing in a jail at Rome, awaiting the outcome of his appeal to Caesar. These writings—especially Ephesians and Philippians—have been considered his testaments, written at the end of his spiritual pilgrimage, his last witness to the Church before martyrdom.[3]

In recent times confidence in this picture has been shaken. The opinion prevalent today is that Paul did not write the Letter to the Ephesians. Also suspect in some quarters is the Letter to the Colossians. But Colossians, along with Philemon and Philippians, are probably genuine letters of Paul. Some persons today believe that one or all of the letters from prison may have been written at Ephesus, while a few favor Caesarea. Questions concerning the genuineness and occasion of the Prison Epistles are subjects for lively debate and cannot be lightly dismissed. If Ephesians or Colossians, or both, are denied Paul, then some features of the familiar outlines of Paul's theology must be sacrificed. Decisions concerning date also have important implications. If Ephesus is preferred to Rome as the place of writing, then the development in Paul's thought between the earlier and later letters (which are based on the traditional chronology) will have to be rejected.[4]

THE LETTER TO THE PHILIPPIANS

The Letter to the Philippians stands apart from the other three in the group. Colossians, Philemon, and—if written by Paul—Ephesians were sent by the same messenger. A perusal of their contents may suggest that all three were written within a few weeks. But Philippians was dispatched by another messenger under different circumstances.

---

[1] Phil. 9b. Also vss. 1, 10, 12, 23.

[2] Eph. 3:1; 4:1; 6:20; Phil. 1:7, 13f.; Col. 4:18 (9).

[3] Some persons enlarge this traditional picture to include 1, 2 Tim. and Titus. These writings imply developments which are difficult, if not impossible, to accommodate to a release and a second imprisonment at Rome (2 Tim. 1:16f.; 4:6, 16ff.). See below, pp. 506ff.

[4] Hunter, *Interpreting*, p. 66. See Dodd, *New Testament Studies*, pp. 67ff.

450

The Church at Philippi

In the early years of the Roman Empire few cities were as conscious of their importance as Philippi. In 42 B.C. this principal city of Macedonia was the scene of the critical battle which aligned Brutus and Cassius against the avengers of Julius Caesar, Anthony and Octavian. After the latter's victory, many soldiers were settled at Philippi. When Octavian, then Caesar Augustus, rebuilt the city he gave it the rank of "a colony"—a military outpost of Rome with special privileges for its inhabitants. The citizens of Philippi cultivated Roman manners, and Latin was the official language. As the first station on the Via Egnatia, the main highway leading from the east toward Rome, Philippi stood at an important crossroads. It was in close touch with the imperial capital, and also with the myriad influences resulting from its traffic with Asia Minor and Syria.[5]

The writer of the travel diary of Acts reports Paul's establishment of a Christian community at Philippi.[6] Historians of the Church have recognized this mission as Paul's first in the West. But perhaps one can detect in the Apostle's comment a consciousness of its special importance. He associated it with "the beginning of the gospel." This is an extraordinary phrase when one thinks of Paul's previous work, to say nothing of the earlier witness of the other apostles.

Luke passes over the development of the mission at Philippi and reports a series of incidents which brought it abruptly to a close.[7] Paul wrote to the Thessalonians shortly after this that he had "suffered and been shamefully treated at Philippi."[8] And so, we may believe, were Paul's converts after he left them. But the church maintained its life and did not forget "the partnership in the gospel" which its members shared with Paul. Nor did they forget him. Twice they sent supplies to support Paul's work, and they remembered him when he was at nearby Corinth.[9] In this connection, Paul's tribute to the generosity of the churches of Macedonia should be recalled.[10]

Perhaps as many as five years elapsed before Paul was able to revisit the Philippians. After his ministry in Ephesus, and in the midst of the Corinthian crisis, he undoubtedly went to Philippi. Perhaps he wrote the letter called 2 Corinthians there.[11] Beyond this, our knowledge of the church must be gleaned from allusions in the Letter to the Philippians. It would be fitting at this point to put aside this book and read the letter.

When the Philippians heard of Paul's imprisonment they sent a man named Epaphroditus to assist him and to deliver a gift of money. In part, Paul's letter is "a thank-you note," but the Apostle had much more to be grateful for than their gifts. One may notice the many expressions of Paul's affection for this church, and his joy in its progress. There are few references in the letter to individuals,

---

[5] F. W. Beare, *A Commentary on the Epistle to the Philippians* (1959), pp. 7ff. [hereafter, *Philippians*].
[6] Acts 16:9ff.
[7] Acts 16:16ff.
[8] 1 Thess. 2:2.
[9] Phil. 4:15f.; 2 Cor. 11:8f.
[10] 2 Cor. 8:1ff.
[11] 2 Cor. 2:4, 12f.; 7:5f.; Acts 20:3, 5.

but Paul does show deference to the leaders of the church, its "bishops and deacons," and he names a certain Clement and two women who had followed in the footsteps of Lydia and labored side by side with Paul in the gospel. It is evident that from Paul's viewpoint this letter was a poor substitute for a visit. He longed to see his dear friends at Philippi, and he planned to go to them as soon as possible.

The purpose of Philippians is so interwoven with the development of its thought that it may be examined in the course of an exposition of the letter. No neatly logical sequence of ideas can be traced in Philippians. "Paul writes out of a full heart, putting down his ideas as they come to him, and personal notices, outbursts of tenderness and thanksgiving, warnings, profound reflections are all mingled together." [12] Nevertheless, several divisions of the letter are discernible. An outline may assist in studying the contents.

An Outline of the Letter of Paul to the Philippians

A. Introduction, 1:1–11:
  1. The superscription, 1:1–2
  2. A thanksgiving containing Paul's expressions of affection, 1:3–8
  3. Prayer for the increase of the Philippians, 1:9–11
B. Paul reports his situation, 1:12–26:
  4. The by-products of his imprisonment in the local church, 1:12–18
  5. His only desire for deliverance is to serve the Church, 1:19–26
C. Paul's exhortations to unity, 1:27–2:18:
  6. An appeal for unity and courage while suffering for the sake of Christ, 1:27–30
  7. An appeal for unity in remembrance of Christ's divine condescension, 2:1–4
  8. A hymn to Christ—humiliation in death, exaltation by God as "Lord," 2:5–11
  9. An appeal for reverent and joyful obedience unto the End, 2:12–18
D. Plans concerning Paul and his workers, 2:19–30:
  10. Timothy to come soon; his worth is extolled, 2:19–23
  11. Paul to follow shortly, God willing, 2:24
  12. Epaphroditus, now recovered, to come at once; his service and courage are commended, 2:25–30
E. A fresh start in the act of saying farewell (Paul's warnings mingled with an apology for his life), 3:1–4:1:
  13. A violent warning against Jewish propaganda, 3:1–4
  14. Paul's renunciation of his own Judaism; his avowal of undying devotion to Christ, 3:5–16
  15. Paul warns the colonists of heaven against setting their minds "on earthly things," 3:17–4:1

[12] E. F. Scott, *IB*, vol. 11, p. 12.

F. Concluding admonitions, 4:2–9:
    16. Two feuding women are rebuked; help for them is implored, 4:2–3
    17. "Rejoice always"; let forbearance be known; find release from anxiety through prayer; an assurance, 4:4–7
    18. Pursue excellence, 4:8–9
G. Paul recalls the gifts of the Philippians, 4:10–20
    19. In acknowledging the church's concern, Paul speaks of his indifference to circumstance, of the secret he has learned, 4:10–13
    20. Paul invokes God's blessing upon a very special church, 4:14–20
H. Conclusion, 4:21–23:
    21. Greetings, 4:21–22
    22. Benediction, 4:23

The Place and Date of the Letter

The belief that Paul wrote Philippians from Rome draws principal support from its references to "the whole praetorian guard" and to "those of Caesar's household," and also to second-century Church tradition.[13] In recent times inscriptions and papyri have been discovered which prevent us from taking for granted the Roman provenience of Philippians. It seems that "the praetorium" was the government quarter in many important provincial cities, and that the expression "those of Caesar's household" referred to Rome's civil servants wherever situated.

Since scholars had already noticed several difficulties in the tradition that Philippians originated in Rome, the discovery of these inscriptions led to a thorough investigation of possible alternatives. It was recalled that in addition to his imprisonment at Philippi, the Apostle had been confined for two years at Caesarea.[14] Allusions in Paul's Corinthian correspondence also intimated one or more imprisonments during his ministry at Ephesus.[15]

The chief difficulty involved in the traditional view consists in the fact that Rome and Philippi were separated by a distance of nearly eight hundred miles, and Paul's letter implies that he had been in close communication with the Philippians for some while. Four trips between Paul's prison and the Macedonian city are suggested: the message of Paul's situation was sent and received at Philippi; Epaphroditus had come from the church to Paul; word was sent to Philippi that their messenger had been mortally ill; word had come back to Paul's prison revealing their anxiety. To these journeys should be added the prospective ones: Epaphroditus is being sent with Paul's letter; Timothy is to go to Philippi when Paul's situation is clarified, and then Paul hopes to visit Philippi himself. A one-way trip from Rome to Philippi would take over seven weeks. Approximately ten months would have been needed for the journeys which had already

[13] Phil. 1:12f.; 4:22. The Marcionite prologue to the letter, dating from the second century, reads: ". . . The Apostle praises them [the Philippians], writing to them from Rome, from prison, by Epaphroditus."

[14] Acts 24:22f., 27.

[15] 2 Cor. 1:8ff.; 11:23ff.; 1 Cor. 15:32.

taken place when Paul wrote Philippians. Once the Ephesian hypothesis is entertained, these difficulties are obviated. Ten to twelve days for travel between Ephesus and Philippi would suffice.

Other evidence has been claimed to support the new theory. Paul assured the Philippians that he would come to them if and when his release was obtained.[16] Acts reports that upon leaving Ephesus Paul went into Macedonia.[17] Some scholars have argued that 1:30 and 4:15f. imply that Paul had not been to Philippi since founding the church there. If Paul were writing from Rome this would not have been true. Moreover, when writing to the Romans Paul declared his intention to evangelize Spain. The Philippian letter gives no hint of this plan.

When Paul wrote Philippians he was contending with strong Jewish opposition.[18] According to Acts, this was Paul's situation at Ephesus.[19] But the same source reports that leaders of the synagogues in Rome had received Paul cautiously. It does not report that they persecuted him.[20] The letter reveals also that the Apostle was contending with strife among Christians.[21] Paul's speech to the Ephesian elders in Acts manifests his sensitivity to this problem at Ephesus.[22] If Romans 16 was addressed to the Ephesians, we have evidence that Paul's fears materialized.[23] Reference to Acts also discloses that Timothy was with Paul at Ephesus; no notice is taken of his presence in Rome.[24]

Other difficulties in the tradition of Roman origin relate to the gifts of the Philippians and their acknowledgment. In the letter Paul said that the Philippians lacked opportunity to help him over a period of time, and later revived their concern for him.[25] According to Acts, Paul visited Philippi twice after receiving the gifts at Corinth. Eight to ten years may have passed before his imprisonment in Rome. But if Philippians was written from Ephesus, then Paul's reference to the church's lack of opportunity and revival of interest implied no rude rebuke. The time interval is reduced to not more than three years, during which period Paul had been in Judea and Syria, and on the move "from place to place through the region of Galatia and Phrygia."[26] Epaphroditus arrived from Philippi laden with gifts shortly after the beginning of Paul's ministry in Ephesus, and the Letter to the Philippians was written sometime before 1 Corinthians, perhaps early in A.D. 55.[27]

---

[16] Phil. 2:23 (12:26f.).

[17] Acts 20:1f.

[18] Phil. 1:28f.; 3:2f.

[19] Acts 19:8f.; 20:19.

[20] Acts 28:17ff.

[21] Phil. 1:15ff.

[22] Acts 20:29f.

[23] Rom. 16:17ff. Note: "Andronicus and Junius . . . my fellow-prisoners" (v. 7).

[24] Acts 19:22; cf. 27:1ff.; Phil. 1:1; 2:19ff.

[25] Phil. 4:10.

[26] Acts 18:22f.

[27] Cf. Phil. 2:19ff. and 1 Cor. 16:5ff. The absence of any reference to the Jerusalem relief fund implies a date for Phil. before 1 Cor. (16:1). A full statement of the Ephesian theory is found in G. S. Duncan, *St. Paul's Ephesian Ministry* (1929). See also McNeile, *Intro.*, pp. 182ff.; J. H. Michael, *The Epistle of Paul to the Philippians* (1927), pp. xiii ff. [hereafter, *Philippians*]; F. C. Synge, *Philippians and Colossians* (1951), pp. 11ff.

The Ephesian origin of Philippians is not improbable.[28] But the theory is open to some serious objections. It cannot be established that Paul was imprisoned at Ephesus. Indeed the supposition that he was confined shortly after the work in Asia began may be nothing more than a conjecture framed to support the Ephesian origin of "the Prison Epistles." But granting the possibility, do the fragments of indirect evidence support a theory of an imprisonment of not less than three months' duration, under conditions permitting Paul to receive and dispatch messengers and letters? The only reference in the New Testament to a prolonged imprisonment allowing for such activities is the house arrest at Rome.[29]

The matter of distance is a formidable objection to the older view, but possibly too much is made of this point. Being a Roman colony, Philippi was in close communication with the capital and was connected with it by a good road affording overland travel in all seasons. Moreover, the number of journeys between Rome and Philippi, and the estimated time necessary for them, may have been exaggerated. The time could be cut in half if the Philippians heard of Paul's appeal to Caesar shortly afterwards and sent their help to Rome to meet him there.[30]

The absence of any notice of the mission to Spain is surely not an insuperable difficulty. Four or five years in prison was a sufficient setback to alter the Apostle's plans. He comments in the letter that he has learned to adjust to altered circumstance.[31] The arguments for the Ephesian hypothesis based on the improbability that both Jews and Christians opposed Paul in Rome are not strong. It is likely that the leaders of the synagogues opposed Paul once they became acquainted with his gospel and his influence. And Paul's Letter to the Romans (even without chapter 16) assumes both the independence of this church and its leaders and Paul's belief that the Christians at Rome would raise objections to his gospel.

From the teaching of Philippians very little, if anything, can be inferred as to its place and date of writing. Its similarities to Paul's early letters are not sufficiently close to prove that it belongs to the same period.[32]

When one has read all the arguments, he faces the inescapable conclusion that no open-and-shut case is possible. The vital question becomes, In which of the two settings do the mood and the situation of the Apostle seem to fit? The uncertainty of the answer should inhibit interpretations of Philippians based upon an imprisonment in one place or the other.

---

[28] The theory that Phil. was written from Caesarea is not equally probable, though it has the support of Lohmeyer and a few notable scholars. The difficulty of distance, Paul's relative safety at Caesarea (Acts 24:26), and the unlikelihood that Paul thought of an early visit to Philippi at this time militate against this alternative to Rome. Cf. Feine-Behm-Kümmel, *Intro.*, pp. 229ff., who conclude "that the probability of the Ephesian hypothesis is the slightest."

[29] Beare, *Philippians*, pp. 22f.

[30] Ibid., p. 19. Dodd, *New Testament Studies*, p. 97, n. 1.

[31] Phil. 4:11f.

[32] C. L. Mitton, *The Epistle to the Ephesians* (1951), pp. 114f., 330ff. Cf. Michael, *Philippians*, pp. xviiiff. It is sometimes argued that the Ephesian hypothesis is supported by the few authentic fragments of Paul's letters to Timothy in the Pastoral Epistles, but opinion is divided with respect to Phil. See P. N. Harrison, "The Pastoral Epistles and Duncan's Ephesian Theory," *NTS* 2 (1956): 250ff.

A Brief Exposition of the Letter

Evidence has been found leading some scholars to conclude that the Corinthian and Roman letters contain fragments of others. What of the letters from prison? Are there internal clues suggesting that Philippians may be a composite of two or more letters?

A recent partition theory may be cited. One scholar suggests that Philippians 4:10–20 preserves a letter of thanks (perhaps complete except for its salutation) acknowledging the gift brought to Paul by Epaphroditus; sections 1:1–3:1; 4:2–9 and 21–23 are a letter carried by Epaphroditus on his return to Philippi; and 3:2–4:1 is a fragment of a letter to the Philippians, of uncertain date, in which Paul warns against Jewish propaganda and shameful self-indulgence.[33] Arguments suggesting the alien character of 3:2–4:1 have plausibility. The abrupt transition at Philippians 3:1 has often perplexed its interpreters. But are Paul's words of thanks unsuited to the letter dispatched by Epaphroditus? The measure of disagreement in partitioning Philippians is far wider than in the case of 2 Corinthians. We have observed that abrupt changes of mood and style are not untypical of Paul. Should we be surprised to find them in a particularly personal letter?

There was no need to lay emphasis upon his apostleship in the superscription to this letter (1). Paul's authority was not disputed at Philippi. He simply identified himself with Timothy as "slaves of Christ." The special deference shown to "bishops and deacons" is noteworthy. But theories of Church polity rest insecurely upon this address.[34] Paul's words could mean "overseers and assistants." He may have remembered those men who administered the church's funds so liberally placed at his disposal.

The thanksgiving in Philippians is far more than a gesture of conventional piety (2). It bespeaks a deep affection freely given and received.[35] Paul's prayer for his friends held in mind "the day of Christ" (3). The hope of the believers was being fulfilled, but it was not yet completed.[36]

It is tempting to read between Paul's lines depicting his own situation (B). Is the main thought here that the gospel is being proclaimed at Rome, even though the publicity is of another sort than Paul had expected?[37] Uncertainty must remain. But we can account for Paul's vagueness. He did not wish to be unduly alarming. He wanted to emphasize the positive results of an imprisonment which might eventuate in his own death (4). Paul simply did not know what the outcome would be. At times he thought his deliverance likely and hopefully planned for the future;[38] at other times his death seemed imminent and he faced this prospect realistically. Paul was, as he wrote, "hard pressed between the two."[39]

[33] Beare, *Philippians*, pp. 1ff., 24ff., 100ff., 150f. Cf. E. J. Goodspeed, *An Introduction to the New Testament* (1937), pp. 90ff.; McNeile, *Intro.*, p. 179; Feine-Behm-Kümmel, *Intro.*, pp. 235ff.

[34] E. F. Scott, *IB*, vol. 11, p. 16; Beare, *Philippians*, pp. 49f.

[35] One may detect in Phil. 1:8 Paul's eagerness to include everybody in his affectionate embrace, those whom he must reprove and those he commends.

[36] Phil. 1:6, 10; 2:12f., 16; 3:12ff., 19f.

[37] E. F. Scott, *IB*, vol. 11, p. 7.

[38] Phil. 1:19, 22, 24ff.; 2:24.

[39] Phil. 1:22f.; 2:17; 3:10. Cf. 4:6ff., 11ff.

Why should Paul's imprisonment have given some men of good will boldness, while others sought by their preaching "to afflict" him? Paul's confidence had inspired the former to be more courageous. But one must speak less confidently concerning the preachers whose motives were mixed. The question involves Paul's situation. In any case, Paul did not psychoanalyze these brethren. He did not charge them with false teaching. What did it matter: "Christ is proclaimed; and in that I rejoice."[40]

Like Job, Paul was confident of his ultimate vindication.[41] Whether "salvation" was to be release from prison, or from life by death, Paul's thought was influenced directly by his eschatology (5). His only point in living now was the need of the churches; he yearned "to depart and be with Christ." There was some satisfaction that the choice was not his own. Paul's only anxiety was that Christ be honored, whether through a continuation of his ministry or through his martyrdom.[42]

The exhortations in Philippians emphasize the need for unity in the Church (C). Paul sensed first of all the disruptive power of fear (6). But he also recognized that selfishness and self-conceit insidiously destroyed the unity of a church, doing violence to love that is Christlike. It was usual for Paul to ground his ethical teaching in some aspect of the Christian *kerygma*. But this time he incorporated a poetic version of the story of salvation (8). The structure of the passage resembles a hymn:

> Though he was in the form of God,
> (He) did not count equality with God
> A thing to be grasped,
>
> But emptied himself,
> Taking the form of a servant,
> Being born in the likeness of men.
>
> And being found in human form
> He humbled himself
> And became obedient unto death
> (Even death on a cross).
>
> Therefore God has highly exalted him
> And bestowed on him the name
> Which is above every name
>
> That at the name of Jesus
> Every knee should bow,
> In heaven and on earth and under the earth,
>
> And every tongue confess
> That Jesus Christ is Lord
> To the glory of God the Father.

This hymn provides the sanction supporting Paul's exhortation to unity. A

[40] Phil. 1:18. Beare looks to Rome for the explanation (*Philippians*, pp. 59f.); Synge to Ephesus (*Philippians and Colossians*, p. 25). Michael catalogues a variety of explanations (*Philippians*, pp. 41f.).

[41] Phil. 1:19, possibly an echo of Job 13:16 (LXX).

[42] Phil. 1:21ff.

continuing Christological discussion has been provoked by this passage.[43] It probably prompted the Philippians to worship, not to debate and speculate. Yet questions of the hymn's origin and meaning relate to the important subject of the development of Christology in the early Church.[44]

Paul's exhortations often call to mind Old Testament scenes. The closing part of this section may have been influenced by Paul's recollection of Moses' charges to the children of God, and of temptations which beset Israel in their day of salvation (9).[45] There is an apparent paradox in the thought that men must work out their own salvation, for God is at work in them to will his good pleasure. Yet this was a succinct statement of Paul's belief in a divine providence which calls men to a serious life. The Christian calling is founded upon the grace of God, which, when apprehended, requires not less but more of men.[46]

When Paul noted future plans, it looks as though he intended to bring his letter to a close (D). But long postscripts are often incorporated in the body of Paul's letters. The prospective visits to Philippi were discussed above. It is interesting at this point to contrast Paul's lavish commendation of Timothy with the slur upon the rest (10). Would Paul have spoken so uncharitably of Christian leaders at Rome (or at Ephesus), especially after the magnanimity shown in the introduction of the letter? Perhaps he had asked several others to undertake the mission he was now entrusting to Timothy. Paul expected much of others while expecting the "impossible" of himself.

Paul's commendation of Epaphroditus may reveal the specific purpose of the letter (12). Did Paul fear that the church would think their emissary had been derelict in his duty? Was he writing to ensure Epaphroditus a cordial homecoming?[47] But why, one may ask, was Paul "less anxious" with Epaphroditus in Philippi than with him? The question may provide a clue to the abrupt transition at 3:1 and further unravel the purpose of Philippians. Several developments required the presence in Philippi of one of Paul's trusted fellow-workers who knew the community and its leaders.

Paul was angry when he lashed out against Jewish propaganda (13). Of course he did not have in mind all of his kinsmen by race. His choice of words reveals his contempt for the fanatics who, in their zeal for proselytizing, had preyed upon Paul's converts like scavenger dogs. When circumcision was made an end in itself, was it of greater religious value than other mutilations of the flesh? Paul's spiritualization of the Jewish rite is reminiscent of his words in Romans.[48] In contrast to those men who could pride themselves that the covenant sign was upon their flesh, Paul wrote of others whose only glory is Christ Jesus.

[43] For a discussion of the structure of the passage, see Beare, *Philippians,* pp. 74f. (also, pp. 1f.). R. P. Martin, *Carmen Christi* (1967); C. H. Talbert, "The Problem of Pre-existence in Philippians 2:6–11," *JBL* LXXXVI (1967): 141ff.; J. A. Sanders, "Dissenting Deities and Philippians 2:1–11," *JBL* LXXXVIII (1969): 279ff.

[44] See Anderson, *Jesus,* pp. 267ff., 278f., and literature noted. E. Käsemann, "A Critical Analysis of Philippians 2:5–11," *Journ. for Theo. and Church* 5 (1968): 45ff. Cf. C. H. Talbert, note 43 above.

[45] Cf. Deut. 31:25ff. and Phil. 2:15f., Beare, *Philippians,* pp. 88f. Note also 1 Cor. 10:1ff.; 2 Cor. 3:4ff.

[46] Phil. 2:12f. Cf. Rom. 8:26ff.; 1 Cor. 15:9f.; Gal. 2:19ff.

[47] Michael, *Philippians,* pp. 118f. Cf. E. F. Scott, *IB,* vol. 11, p. 70.

[48] Cf. Phil. 3:3 and Rom. 2:28f.

The contrast is wrought out in a passage which was a personal confession (14). If any man had grounds for "confidence in the flesh," Paul surely had. But his past, his "blameless" righteousness under the Law, had been renounced as amounting to nothing. The gospel had revealed "the righteousness of God," in the first instance, "through the faith of Christ," but received by Paul as "the righteousness from God [given men by God] that depends on faith." Paul affirmed once again what he had written in Romans: this gospel undercuts every reason for human pride.[49]

Paul's strong denial of his own perfection may sound to some readers like histrionic mock-humility.[50] But other letters of Paul reveal his conviction that the mark of Christian maturity is a frank recognition of one's own weaknesses and imperfections, and that it is developed through a vigilance which opposes self-conceit.[51] The Apostle's reference to the figure of his never-ending race led directly to another sharp warning. Paul always found persons who distorted his gospel of freedom from Law. Some claimed that Christians are free from sin; others found in his emphasis on freedom a sanction for self-indulgence or moral indifference. In Philippians as in Galatians, Paul balanced a warning against legalism with a warning against license. A graphic description is given of the materially minded man.[52] But in contrast to him a marvelous picture is drawn (15). The Christian's "commonwealth is in heaven." His mind cannot be fixed upon "earthly things." Perhaps Paul was thinking of the pride of the Philippians, living in an outpost of Rome, anticipating a visitation of Caesar their savior.[53]

One marvels at Paul's tactful approach to two quarrelsome women (16). He had spoken of his love for everyone in the church. He had dealt with their need for unity in Christ. And now, while rebuking the troublemakers, he commended them and asked someone—their "true yoke-fellow"—to help them.

The next two paragraphs appear to be a fresh attempt to bring the letter to a close (17–18). They are the words of a man reluctant to say good-bye for fear it may be his last. Paul cannot close without remembering especially the kindnesses of this church (19–20), but his words reflect a mood of resignation. His need is for peace and inner strength, not for gifts of money and more helpers. And Paul believed that God would supply these needs. It was not the serenity of the Stoics, nor their schooling in indifference to outward circumstance, which Paul had learned. He had discovered the secret of true contentment. Even when bound with chains, Paul was a man "in Christ."

THE LETTER TO PHILEMON

Let us view the remaining letters from prison in this order: Philemon, Colossians, Ephesians. It is easy to justify placing Colossians in the middle. Colossians

---

[49] Cf. Phil. 3:7ff. and Rom. 3:27ff. (v. 9). Should we say that traces of national pride remained in Paul's "subconsciousness"? See Davies, *Paul*, pp. 58, 68ff.

[50] Phil. 3:12ff.

[51] Note Phil. 2:3; Rom. 12:3, 16; 1 Cor. 1:28f.

[52] Phil. 3:19.

[53] Cf. Phil. 1:27 (literally, "behave as citizens worthy of the gospel").

is closely linked to Philemon in that both letters are sent by the same bearer and contain identical personal references.[54] But Colossians is also closely related to Ephesians, which will be discussed in Chapter 19. Again there is a common bearer. There is also a striking parallelism in language, style, and leading ideas which sets these two books apart from the rest in the collection.[55]

Colossians, then, stands in the key middle position. But there is value in studying these books from left to right. A decision relating to the origin of Philemon obviously affects one's judgment concerning the more substantial writing, Colossians, and, some would claim, by a chain of inferences, the Letter to the Ephesians. One can speak with greater assurance about the origin of Philemon than the others. Some words of John Knox bear this out:

> No reputable scholar doubts its authenticity [Philemon]. The little letter bears in itself every mark of genuineness. Its vocabulary and style are those of Romans, Corinthians, Galatians, and Philippians; and the personality of its author is unmistakable. Besides all this, the letter brings us a dramatic moment in the life of Paul which no later writer would have had either the skill or the motive to invent.[56]

An Outline of the Letter of Paul to Philemon

A. Introduction, 1–3:
  1. The superscription, 1–2
  2. A grace, 3
B. Thanksgiving, 4–7:
  3. Gratitude for Philemon's witness, 4–6
  4. Philemon's benefactions have brought Paul "much joy and comfort," 7
C. The request concerning Onesimus, 8–20:
  5. Paul rejects his right to command: prefers an appeal "for love's sake," 8–9
  6. The usefulness of Onesimus, 10–11
  7. Paul suppresses a reluctance to part with Onesimus, 12–14
  8. Providence turns evil into good, 15–16
  9. Charges, receipts, indebtedness, 17–20
D. The conclusion, 21–25:
  10. Paul's confidence that Philemon will do more than he asks, 21
  11. Plans for a visit, 22
  12. Greeting from Paul's friends, 23–24
  13. Benediction, 25

The Place and Time of Philemon

Where was Paul when he said good-bye to a slave named Onesimus and handed him over to Tychicus with this brief letter to Philemon? The traditional answer

---

[54] Cf. Col. 1:1, 7; 4:7ff.; Phil. 1:1f., 10, 23f.
[55] See below, pp. 463f.
[56] *IB*, vol. 11, p. 555.

has been, "At Rome." But we have seen that this judgment may have depended on two references in Philippians which do not bear the weight put upon them. Many scholars, including Professor Knox, who had devoted much study to Philemon, champion the Ephesian origin of the letter.

Several passages have been thought to support the new theory. Observe, first of all, that Philemon lived at Colossae, a town in the Roman province of Asia, about one hundred miles inland from Ephesus.[57] When Onesimus escaped, where would he most likely have run? To Ephesus, say the proponents of this theory, to the metropolis of his province rather than to faraway Rome. If Paul was at Ephesus, then his request to Philemon that a guestroom be prepared is a reasonable one. But if Paul was at Rome (planning a mission in Spain?) what would have been the point of such a request? Finally, two of Paul's friends, sending greetings to Philemon, were with him at Ephesus, while others had connections with this city, or the province of Asia. Only one of them, Luke, is definitely known to have been with Paul at Rome.[58]

The above arguments are not without merit, but they fall short of a demonstration. Surely a fugitive slave carrying stolen money might put as much distance as possible between himself and his master, especially since his apprehension would result in a severe flogging. Where could one get lost in a crowd better than in Rome? Paul's request for lodgings does not necessarily imply an early visit to Colossae. He may have intended to say no more than "keep the latch key out, I'll be along some day."[59] And finally, with respect to the group of friends, both Timothy and Aristarchus (who were with Paul at Ephesus) accompanied Paul on his journey to Jerusalem which resulted in the Roman imprisonment. Even if Timothy was not on shipboard with Paul he may have arrived at Rome a few weeks or months later. We should not expect such a detail to be recorded at the conclusion of Acts.[60]

The Letter to Philemon provides no compelling reasons for adopting the Ephesian hypothesis. Some passages in the letter are better suited to an imprisonment at Rome. Paul had known Philemon long enough to become attached to him as a "father," and as Paul wrote he needed him for a longer service during his "imprisonment for the gospel."[61] The provenience of Philemon must remain *sub judice*, at least until its companion letter is examined.

Interpreting the Letter to Philemon

After a reading of this brief letter, one may conclude that its purpose is self-evident. Yet its very brevity leaves many questions in our minds.[62] Philemon's

[57] See below, p. 464 and map, p. 447.

[58] Defenders of the Caesarea hypothesis appeal to Phil. 22ff. J. Knox, *IB*, vol. 11, 556; Dibelius and Kümmel, *Paul*, pp. 138ff.

[59] Beare, *IB*, vol. 11, p. 137; Dodd, *New Testament Studies*, p. 95.

[60] Dodd, *New Testament Studies*, pp. 92f.

[61] Phil. 10, 13.

[62] John Knox thinks that Onesimus belonged to Archippus, and that the letter was intended for

runaway slave had somehow come in contact with Paul. For the first time? Or had he known the Apostle before, while a slave in Philemon's service? In a moment of desperation had Onesimus looked for Paul? Had Epaphras led him to the Apostle? The raising of some questions is a mere pastime. But others lead to the purpose of the letter. It is well to keep two of these questions before us. What does Paul ask of Philemon? Upon what does he base his appeal?

Paul's approach was extremely tactful (3–4). He warmly acknowledged Philemon's reputation for faith and love of the brethren. He was, as Paul wrote, a refreshing person.[63] Paul's prayer was that Philemon's benefactions might result in bringing the two men into closer union with Christ.[64]

Paul had every reason to be tactful. He was asking Philemon to pardon a legally very serious offender. He was also asking to be excused the presumption of detaining Onesimus. Strictly speaking, Paul had defrauded his friend.[65] It was necessary to avoid every appearance of dictating to Philemon, lest his purpose in writing be defeated.

Paul was not self-conscious about his authority as an apostle. Our reading of his letters has surely confirmed this. Yet Paul chose to appeal to Philemon "for love's sake" (5). What did he want Philemon to do? Was Paul asking for Onesimus? Was he requesting Philemon to send him back his "child"?[66] Some of Paul's expressions suggest this. But can we be sure? The Apostle knew that Philemon could and might retain Onesimus (8).[67]

Does Paul ask for the slave's freedom? Not explicitly.[68] The important thing to notice is that Onesimus was sent home for the service of the gospel. Whether he remained with Philemon or returned to Paul, whether he remained in bonds or was set free, Paul asked that Philemon treat Onesimus as "a beloved brother." Philemon was to acknowledge the fact that a new relation existed between master and slave, not merely within the church, but with respect to law and social custom. Onesimus is "more than a slave," he is Philemon's brother—both as a man and as a Christian.[69]

Paul asked a lot of Philemon. Could he acknowledge this difference in fact as

---

him. It was sent via Philemon, perhaps the overseer of the Lycus valley churches living at Laodicea. He also suggests that "the letter from Laodicea" (Col. 4:16) is the canonical Philemon. Archippus is commanded at a congregational meeting to "fulfill the ministry . . ." i.e., to forgive Onesimus and send him back; *Philemon among the Letters of Paul* (1935), pp. 25ff. Cf. C. F. D. Moule, *The Epistles of Paul the Apostle to the Colossians and to Philemon* (1957), pp. 14ff. [hereafter, *Colossians and Philemon*].

[63] Phil. 7b. Note 20b.

[64] A paraphrase. The meaning of v. 6 is obscure.

[65] A papyrus fragment reveals that slave owners had redress before the law against persons harboring runaway slaves. See C. H. Dodd, *Abingdon Bible Commentary* (1929), p. 1292.

[66] Phil. 10, probably an indication that Onesimus had been converted while with Paul; cf. 1 Cor. 4:15.

[67] J. Knox believes that Paul asked for Onesimus, *IB*, vol. 11, pp. 566f.; also T. Preiss, *Life in Christ*, trans. H. Knight (1952), pp. 39f.

[68] ". . . no longer a slave" need not imply his emancipation. Cf. Gal. 3:27. The commentators are unsure of its meaning. Feine-Behm-Kümmel, *Intro.*, p. 246.

[69] Phil. 16b. This would seem to be the meaning of "in the flesh and in the Lord." Moule, *Colossians and Philemon*, p. 148.

well as in principle? Onesimus was now a man "in Christ." Could Philemon receive him as though Paul were coming to his home?

Paul seemed confident that he would—that Philemon would do even more than he asked—for Philemon owed Paul his Christian existence. The reader may notice Paul's play on the word "Onesimus" (useful or profitable) and observe his use of commercial formulae, the scribbling of his I.O.U. (9).[70] Could Paul count on Philemon's sense of humor? Or was he being careful to respect the rights, the liberty of Philemon?

The concluding words of the letter reminded his readers that the appeal was being made from prison. Like Onesimus, Paul and his associates did not know what the future held. But it mattered not. Like the slave, these men had found their freedom "in Christ Jesus."[71]

THE LETTER TO THE COLOSSIANS

The apparent close connection between Philemon and Colossians suggests that Paul wrote both letters. Yet some persons have had grave doubts. They consider that the type of error at Colossae hardly existed in Paul's lifetime; that the letter presents—in a distinctive style and manner—a view of Christ and the Church not developed in other letters of the Pauline collection (excepting Ephesians); and that its peculiar literary relation to Ephesians and earlier letters by the Apostle casts suspicion upon Pauline authorship. Accordingly, several alternative theories have been advanced, each claiming that Colossians is a pseudonymous writing. Some scholars hold that the writer of Colossians had access to several of Paul's letters and drew upon these to combat error at the Colossian church. Others conjecture that an authentic letter of Paul to the Colossians has been adapted by another person, in order to apply the authority of Paul's teachings to a new situation in the church.

How is one to decide? The issue depends mainly on the answer to two questions. First, do the verbal parallels or similarities between Colossians and earlier letters by Paul suggest that Paul wrote Colossians, or that someone composed it who had access to one or more of his letters? Second, is it probable that the type of error implied by Colossians appeared during Paul's lifetime and that Paul dealt with it (if it did arise) by developing the theological conceptions contained in this letter? Neither question can be answered simply; it cannot be denied that the origin of Colossians is a complex problem. For many persons, the scales teeter uncertainly. But, for the majority, they tip in favor of Pauline authorship.[72]

---

[70] Phil. 11. Also 20: "yes, brother, I want some 'profit' from you."

[71] For the intriguing theory that the slave Onesimus became a bishop, and also collected Paul's letters, see below, pp. 499f.

[72] The modern criticism of Colossians is concisely summarized in Beare's commentary, IB, vol. 11, pp. 143ff. See also, Feine-Behm-Kümmel, Intro., pp. 240ff. E. P. Sanders examines passages in Col. which appear to be verbatim or serial quotations from indisputable Pauline letters, or conflations thereof, and concludes that Paul did not write Col. as we have it: "Literary Dependence in Colossians," JBL LXXXV (1966): 28ff.; E. Lohse, "Pauline Theology in the Letter to the Colossians," NTS 15 (1969): 211ff.

If Paul wrote Colossians, then the traditional view of its Roman origin has high merit. To argue that Colossians was written at Ephesus involves more than the questionable assumptions noted in the study of Philemon. One must adopt an almost incredible hypothesis, that the conceptions of Christ developed in Colossians were of passing significance, of apologetic value only, for Paul. They do not appear in Romans, which sets forth a summary of the Apostle's gospel up to the time of its writing.[73] The curious affinities between Colossians and Ephesians may be discussed later. Contrary to the opinion of some, denial of the Pauline authorship of Ephesians is not sufficient to discredit Colossians. The relation between these writings is not circumstantially the same as between Philemon and Colossians.

The Church at Colossae

The ancient Phrygian settlement at Colossae had by Paul's time declined to the status of a small town.[74] It was situated on the Lycus River, a tributary of the Meander. Within a radius of twelve miles were the twin cities of Laodicea and Hierapolis, overshadowing Colossae in their significance. During most of the centuries of Roman rule, the district belonged to the province of Asia.

Apparently the founder of the churches in the Lycus valley was Epaphras.[75] He may have owed his conversion to Paul. In any event, he became a "beloved fellow-servant," whom Paul counted among his associates.[76] As Epaphras was a Gentile, one naturally concludes that his converts also were. Inferences from the Letter to the Colossians bear this out, but the district was not exclusively Greek.[77] Numerous Jews resided in the Lycus valley, and some of the churches' leaders may have been drawn from Gentile proselytes to Judaism or from the "God-fearers."

Paul had never visited Colossae. Epaphras had come to see him in prison, bringing news and affectionate greetings from his churches.[78] As a result of conversations with Epaphras, two letters were written by Paul: the canonical Letter to the Colossians and a lost writing, the Letter to the Laodiceans.[79]

The following passages drawn from Colossians disclose the controversial nature of the letter:

[73] Moule, *Colossians and Philemon*, pp. 13ff.; F. F. Bruce, *Epistle to the Colossians* (1957), pp. 170ff. Cf. Beare's cautious statements, *IB*, vol. 11, pp. 143ff. G. S. Duncan seems impressed with the objection based on Rom., but he now argues that Rom. was written early in the Ephesian ministry, *Exp. T.* 67 (1956): 163ff.

[74] Strabo, XII. 8. 13.

[75] Col. 1:7; 4:12f. For a sketch of the history of the Lycus valley churches, see J. B. Lightfoot, *Colossians and Philemon* (1875), pp. 1ff.

[76] Col. 1:7. The reading "on our behalf" is to be preferred. Note that the reference to Tychicus is identical, Col. 4:7.

[77] Col. 2:13; also 1:12, 21, 27.

[78] Col. 1:4, 7, 9, 23; 2:1.

[79] Col. 2:1; 4:16. E. J. Goodspeed supported Knox in identifying Philemon with this letter: *New Solutions to New Testament Problems* (1927), p. 51. Cf. Moule, *Colossians and Philemon*, pp. 17f.; Beare, *IB*, vol. 11, p. 239. For the identification of this letter with Eph., see below, p. 496 note 4.

> See to it that no one makes a prey of you by philosophy and empty deceit, according to human tradition, according to the elemental spirits of the universe, and not according to Christ. . . .
>
> Let no one pass judgment on you in questions of food and drink or with regard to a festival or a new moon or a Sabbath . . . let no one disqualify you, insisting on self-abasement and worship of angels. . . ." [80]

For a knowledge of the teaching being opposed by these admonitions we are dependent on inferences from Colossians. But our study of "the Gentile environment of Christianity" should enable us to understand better the nature of the danger confronting this church in the hinterland of Asia. After a first reading of Colossians one may find helpful the following brief analysis of the "philosophy" and discipline being urged upon the Colossian Christians. A study of the structure and contents of the letter will then lead to a greater appreciation of its marvelous apology.

The Erroneous Teaching at Colossae

The propagandists at Colossae may have described their teaching as "a philosophy" and also as a "tradition," claiming that it was a sophisticated system of thought sanctioned by antiquity.[81] A central position was given to invisible spirit-beings, twice referred to in Colossians as the *stoicheia* (the "elemental spirits of the universe").[82] These cosmic powers were also called "principalities and authorities." It was taught that together they constituted the *pleroma* (the "fulness," or full complement) of divine powers through whom God ruled the world. These powers were the means whereby divine revelation was given unto men; they controlled the ways of access whereby mortal men (or at least some men) ascended to their eternal destiny.

Essentially the propaganda at Colossae bears the characteristics of pre-Gnostic thought.[83] But we can go further and identify the system as a Jewish type of Gnosticism. The propagandists judged the piety of men by a legalism which reflects, at some remove, the Torah of Judaism. For them "questions of food and drink" were of great importance, as well as particular observances, "a festival or a new moon or a sabbath."[84] They also imposed ascetic practices which went beyond the requirements of the Law and the scribal traditions of Palestine. Perhaps a manual of discipline is implied in the reference to their commandments, "do not handle, do not taste, do not touch. . . ." We also learn that they sought to promote "rigor of devotion and self-abasement and severity to the body. . . ."[85]

---

[80] Col. 2:8, 16ff.

[81] See above, pp. 343f.

[82] Col. 2:8, 20. Cf. Gal. 4:8f.

[83] See above, pp. 347f. "It is still an open question whether the doctrines attacked by Paul in his letter to the Colossians . . . were types of Gnostic utterances or just syncretistic teachings in a more general sense." Van Unnik, *Newly Discovered Gnostic Writings*, p. 39.

[84] Col. 2:16.

[85] Col. 2:20ff. The asceticism of Qumran is suggested. Long ago J. B. Lightfoot suspected Essene

The relation of these legalistic and ascetic practices to the "philosophy" of the propagandists may be found in the belief that the Law was given by the angels. If so, they might have taught that the keeping of the Law was a form of self-abasement and veneration required by the angels.[86] The Colossian Christians were being offered a religion of knowledge which enabled men "to disarm the principalities and powers" of the invisible world, and also "to put off the old nature" and attain "fulness of life."

Had the erroneous teaching absorbed some of the aspects of the mystery cults which flourished in the region of Phrygia? An a priori probability may find support in Paul's reference to one propagandist who "took his stand on visions" (literally, "entered into what he had seen"). Some inscriptions from Asia Minor indicate that this expression was used in a technical sense by the mystery religions, describing the act following initiation whereby one entered the place of vision (the forbidden sanctuary?) to receive a revelation from the god.[87] Perhaps Epaphras had reported that one of the propagandists at Colossae boasted of his initiation into the higher mysteries. Paul's frequent use of his term "mystery" in this letter further suggests that the syncretistic error at Colossae derived some of its aspects from the mystery cults.[88]

AN OUTLINE OF THE LETTER OF PAUL TO THE COLOSSIANS

A. Introduction, 1:1–4:
  1. The superscription, 1:1–2
  2. The thanksgiving, emphasizing Paul's satisfaction in hearing of the progress of the Colossians, 1:3–8
  3. A prayer for the increase of the church ends with an affirmation of the eschatological victory, 1:9–14
B. Christ, the Mystery of God, 1:15–2:5:
  4. The Son and his relation to God (1:15a); the universe (15b–17); the Church (18)
  5. The Son as reconciler of all things (1:19–20); of the Colossians who were formerly pagan (21–23)
  6. Paul's office is to make known the mystery through sufferings for the sake of the church (1:24); through preaching Christ among the Gentiles (25–27); through the nurture of Christians (28–29)
  7. Paul's concern for the churches of the Lycus valley, 2:1–5; that they gain a full understanding of God's mystery—of Christ (1–3); resist "beguiling speech"; be established in the received faith (4–5)

---

influence at Colossae (*Colossians and Philemon*, pp. 83ff.). It is hardly possible to establish this hypothesis, but the Qumran discoveries prove the existence in Paul's day of a pre-Gnostic development within Judaism.

[86] F. F. Bruce, *Epistle to the Colossians*, p. 167. Moule is cautious, *Colossians and Philemon*, pp. 32f. Cf. Gal. 3:19.

[87] Beare, *IB*, vol. 11, pp. 138, 202ff.; however, the text of Col. 2:18 is obscure.

[88] Col. 1:26f.; 2:2f.; 4:3.

C. A human tradition contrasted with the tradition according to Christ, 2:6–3:4 (admonitions):
   8. The fullness of Christ, and of life in him, 2:6–10
   9. Buried and raised with Christ, 2:11–13a
   10. Christ's triumph in death, 2:13b–15
   11. The shadow of ritual; the substance that is Christ, 2:16–17
   12. Growth results from holding fast to Christ, not in asceticism and angel-worship, 2:18–19
   13. Ascetic taboos are a futile submission to vanquished spirits, 2:20–23
   14. Submit your minds to Christ who is your life, 3:1–4
D. The true discipline of men who declare the mystery of Christ, 3:5–4:6 (exhortations):
   15. The reformation of life, 3:5–17
   16. Household duties, 3:18–4:1; wives and husbands (18–19); children and parents (20–21); slaves and masters (3:22–4:1)
   17. A call to prayer, 4:2–4
   18. Behavior toward outsiders, 4:5–6
E. Conclusion, 4:7–18:
   19. Commendations of Tychicus and Onesimus, 4:7–9
   20. Greetings from Paul's associates, 4:10–14
   21. Personal greeting and final requests, 4:15–18a
   22. Benediction, 4:18b

In "the thanksgiving" Paul reported to the Colossians that the gospel, "the word of the truth," was everywhere "bearing fruit and growing," as it was among themselves (2). Already one detects the apologetic purpose of the letter. The propagandists were pressing upon the Christians their so-called true version of the gospel, proclaimed by Epaphras in its simplicity, a tradition with a universal appeal able to produce superior results. In his prayer for the church Paul desired that his readers recognize that this so-called "fulness of knowledge" or "spiritual wisdom" was not needed (3). God the Father had delivered them from "the dominion of darkness" and transferred them to "the kingdom of his beloved Son," in whom they had their "redemption."

The assurance which closes the first section proclaimed Christ "the beloved Son" of God the Father. Associated with this is a remarkable confessional statement concerning the significance of the Christian redeemer (B). Some scholars have suspected a later interpolation; the passage is unparalleled in Paul's writings. Alternatively, other scholars, noting the liturgical form and mythical content of the passage, conjecture that Paul, or an earlier churchman, took over a pre-Gnostic myth concerning the Heavenly Man who is also man's Redeemer, and composed a Christian hymn to Christ.[89]

Leaving open the questions of the source of these ideas, or an earlier form,

[89] E. Käsemann, "A Primitive Christian Baptismal Liturgy," *Essays*, pp. 149ff. See Beare, *IB*, vol. 11, pp. 162ff.; Moule, *Colossians and Philemon*, pp. 58ff.; J. M. Robinson, "A Formal Analysis of Colossians 1:15–20," *JBL* 76 (1956): 270ff. Feine-Behm-Kümmel, *Intro.*, pp. 241f. Cf. Heb. 1:1ff., and John 1:1ff.

we may say that there is no valid reason for assigning this passage to a later period. It is admirably suited to the purpose of Colossians and the development of its teaching. Either the author of Colossians composed the passage, or he adapted an earlier baptismal (?) hymn, to combat the specific danger facing the Lycus valley Christians. He reminded the church that its Lord is mightier than all cosmic powers and holds sway over them all.

Paul would not have been content merely to denounce the propagandists at Colossae. He had been ready to contend with the Judaizers in the Galatian churches on their own terms. And so, we may believe, Paul proclaimed Christ as the One who alone embraced in himself all the functions that were being falsely ascribed to "the elemental spirits of the universe." Christ bestowed upon his Church all the benefits of redemption being sought through the merely "human" traditions and profitless ascetic disciplines of the propagandists. Christ was the pre-eminent mediator between God and man (4); as One exalted above all "the authorities" by whatsoever name they were called, since they were a part of the created order, and derived their being from him. Moreover, as "the first-born from the dead," Paul proclaimed Christ the revealer and mediator in the new creation, especially with respect to the Church, the eschatological community—his body, of which he was the Head (5). Indeed, Paul affirmed that "all the fulness of God"—the full complement of divine powers—dwelt in Christ alone. The conclusion followed: the *stoicheia* possessed no power superior to, nor in any way qualifying, the power of the Christian redeemer.

Special interest has been shown in the writer's description of Christ "as the head of the body, the Church." Paul's use of the metaphor in 1 Corinthians and Romans differs from this, leading some scholars to deny Pauline authorship of Colossians. However, it is quite conceivable that the erroneous teaching in the church prompted Paul to extend his metaphor. The concept of Christ's headship over the Church stresses the dependence of all of its members upon Christ for life and power. In consequence "body" is used in correlation with "head" rather than (as in the earlier letters) with "spirit."

It is not possible to do justice to this passage—to the intrinsic wealth of its ideas—in a few sentences. We may conclude that under the pressure of the spurious claims being made by the propagandists at Colossae (and perhaps under the spell of a liturgy in praise of Christ) Paul was led to develop teachings which were implicit in his exposition of the *kerygma*. As in no previous situation, he was led to press beyond the thoughts of Christ's eschatological role in history to a proclamation of his pre-eminence in the order of Creation, to an acknowledgment that Christ's power to reconcile was not restricted to the Church, but was sufficient to reconcile everything that exists in the universe unto God.[90]

A strange statement appeared when Paul wrote to the Colossians about his

---

[90] Cf. 1 Cor. 2:6ff.; 8:5f.; Rom. 11:36; and Phil. 2:5ff. That Paul should have been influenced by ideas used by the Colossian propagandists, have taken up terms used by those against whom he argues, and consciously adapted them, is a probable assumption. See Chadwick, "All Things to All Men" (see p. 401, note 72), pp. 272ff.; Enslin, *Beginnings*, pp. 291f; F. F. Bruce, "St. Paul at Rome," *BJRL* 48 (1966): 282f.

work among the Gentiles, and of his concern for his readers (6–7). "In my flesh," he declared, "I complete what is lacking in Christ's afflictions. . . ." Paul's words elsewhere exclude one popular interpretation of this statement. It is incredible that Paul considered his sufferings to be vicarious in the sense of affording satisfaction for the sins of others.[91] The apologetic purpose of Colossians also excludes the notion that Paul's sufferings contributed to the effectiveness of Christ's sufferings. But it is consonant with Paul's thought that Christ continued to suffer in the Church, that the sum total of his sufferings were those of his Ministry, plus the sufferings of the members of his body, the Church.[92]

Paul described the gospel as "the mystery hidden for ages . . . but now made manifest"; and, again, he described it as the "mystery which is Christ in you, the hope of glory."[93] As in the pagan mystery cults, the term *mysterion* represented for Paul something given unto men through revelation. But the Christian "mystery" referred neither to an initiatory rite, nor to disclosed secrets which were to be withheld from the uninitiated. Rather, the mystery was to be proclaimed to every man. Its benefits were not restricted to the few persons who through cultic rites, ascetic discipline, mystical contemplation, or other means qualified themselves to receive the mystery. It was the Father who qualified believers in Christ "to share in the inheritance of the saints in light."[94] Therein was established a relation to one in whom men found "all the treasures of wisdom and knowledge" necessary to their salvation and to spiritual maturity.[95] For the Apostle, Christ *was* the Christian "mystery," but the mystery was also manifest in the life of men who were "in Christ."[96]

The heart of the *kerygma* proclaimed the death and resurrection of Jesus Christ, events which freed men forever from the ancient dread (9–10). No longer need they anxiously strive to secure their salvation through meticulous performance of "legal demands," to "disarm the principalities and powers" so-called. Such "human precepts and doctrines have the appearance of wisdom," Paul admonished his readers, "but they are of no value in checking the indulgence of the flesh."[97]

In this declaration Paul indicated the moral impotence of the propagandist's philosophy and practices, and introduced a series of moral exhortations which were intrinsic to his gospel (D). The form of this teaching was probably not original. A list of traits to be discarded like a filthy garment, others to be "put

---

[91] This passage has been used to defend the Roman Catholic doctrine of the "treasury of merits."

[92] Phil. 3:10; 2 Cor. 1:5; 12:9ff. See above, p. 408. Cf. Acts 9:4, 16. Possibly the Col. passage reflects Paul's belief that a certain quota of suffering was necessary (a Christian sublimation of the apocalyptic belief in the Messianic woes?). Cf. 2 Thess. 1:4ff.; 2:3a. Moule, *Colossians and Philemon*, pp. 76ff.

[93] Col. 1:25ff.

[94] Col. 1:12; cf. 2:18.

[95] Col. 2:2; 1:9ff.; 2:10, 19.

[96] Paul's use of "mystery" as a reference to God's eschatological act of salvation in Christ is "in agreement with 1 Cor. 2:1, 7." Feine-Behm-Kümmel, *Intro.*, p. 253.

[97] The reference to circumcision suggests that the propagandists were requiring it, not in order to contain Christianity within Judaism, as did the Judaizers in Galatia, but as one of the severities to the body (2:23) which attested a higher degree of piety. Cf. Col. 2:11ff. with Rom. 2:25ff. and Phil. 3:3; with Col. 2:12f. and 3:1ff., Rom. 6:1ff.

on," may have been compiled by the propagandists at Colossae (15). Similar lists were drawn up by contemporary Jewish rabbis and pagan moralists.[98] But in introducing the distinctive moral sanctions of the gospel, Paul charged these conventional ideas with new meaning and directed his readers to the source of power which enabled men to live by them.

The second table, the "household duties," is unique among Paul's letters (16). It has been compared with similar ones compiled by Jewish and pagan teachers, and by other early Christian writers.[99] The Christian tables are distinguished by their emphasis on the reciprocal nature of household rights as well as duties. This applied to wives, children, and slaves, not just to their social superiors. But the distinctive Pauline teaching, which transformed the conventional patterns of domestic morality, was that the Christian recognized that other persons are "in Christ."[100]

[98] Moule, *Colossians and Philemon*, pp. 126f.

[99] Peter 2:13ff.; Titus 2:1ff.; also Did. 4:9ff.; 1 Clem. 21:6ff.; Beare, *IB*, vol. 11, pp. 224ff.

[100] This unprecedented interest in domestic relations has been contrasted with 1 Cor. 7, and the thesis advanced that Paul's eschatological perspective had changed; see C. H. Dodd, "The Mind of Paul," *New Testament Studies*, pp. 109ff.; Beare, *IB*, vol. 11, p. 211, also p. 197. Cf. Moule, *Colossians and Philemon*, pp. 110f.; F. F. Bruce, *Epistle to the Colossians*, p. 257. It should be recalled that Paul had just written about a slave to a master, and to the church in Philemon's house.

part 3

CONFLICT AND CONSOLIDATION
IN THE POSTAPOSTOLIC AGE

chapter eighteen

CHRISTIANITY IN THE POSTAPOSTOLIC AGE

Roman Forum: Among the ruins of the Forum Romana are numerous monuments to the Roman Republic celebrating events paralleling the rise of Christianity, from the period of Augustus to the Emperor Hadrian. (Elliott Erwitt from Magnum)

The Arch of Titus erected in the Roman Forum by the Senate (c. A.D. 100) to commemorate victory in the war with the Jews (A.D. 66–70), which Titus concluded with the destruction of the temple in Jerusalem. (Anderson)

During the campaign against Judea led by Vespasian, he was proclaimed emperor (A.D. 70–79). Coins were issued throughout the empire boasting a Roman victory. This coin (enlarged) shows the portrait of Vespasian on the obverse; on the reverse, a Roman officer holding a commander's baton with one foot on a helmet stands guard over a crouching woman (the daughter of Zion) who weeps for her defeat. The palm tree symbolizes Judaea. *Judaea capta* reads "Vanquished Judea." (Bialik Institute)

Bas relief from the Arch of Titus, depicting the procession of the victorious Romans following their defeat of the Jews by Titus and his armies. Among the sacred objects looted from the temple in Jerusalem was the seven-branched menorah, representing the creation of the universe in seven days. (Alinari)

THE period which now comes under survey is as important as it is fascinating. With the exception of the genuine letters of Paul, and possibly the Gospel of Mark, all of the books of the New Testament were written after A.D. 65. Yet in spite of this apparent wealth of literature, the history of Christianity in the next half-century is shrouded in obscurity.

The four or five decades following A.D. 65 are commonly called "the postapostolic age," or the "precatholic period." The first description acknowledges the passing of "those who were from the beginning eyewitnesses and ministers of the word."[1] By A.D. 70 the chief apostles were dead, and the influence of the survivors was attenuated by the geographical spread of the gospel and the predominantly Gentile character of the churches. The term *precatholic* acknowledges an equally significant fact about this period. It was only well into the second century of the Christian Era that those forms of doctrine and organization prerequisite to the establishment of a "catholic" (universal) Church were achieved.[2]

We have studied the proclamation and pattern of teaching "declared at first by the Lord," and attested "by those who heard him."[3] We have followed Paul's vigorous advocacy of Christianity among the Gentiles, and examined his main writings. The question now becomes: What are the lines connecting this nascent Christianity and the ancient catholic Church of the second century?

The difficulty and perennial challenge of this question is partly due to the lack of a narrative sequel to the Acts of the Apostles. It might seem that adequate compensation for this lack is found in the more than a dozen New Testament books dating from this time. Yet critical scholars have not reached settled conclusions concerning the origins of the majority of these books. Consequently, all efforts to relate them to each other and to other Christian writings of the same general period are inevitably tentative. Some pieces of the "picture puzzle" are missing. Without these the existing parts do not form a wholly intelligible pattern.

Beyond question there were many Christians at this time who were not only able to write but were actively writing.[4] Yet their letters and tracts were intended to meet local or regional needs. They were certainly not considered components of a Christian canon of scripture. Later generations were not interested in preserving the writings that did survive from the earlier period. Some of them were stigmatized as heretical; others were inadequate for the current needs of the Church.[5]

[1]Luke 1:2.
[2]For the earliest use of the term *catholic*, see Ignatius, *Smyr.* 8:2.
[3]Heb. 2:3f.
[4]Cadbury, *IB*, vol. 7, pp. 32ff.
[5]M. H. Shepherd, Jr., "The Post-Apostolic Age," *IB*, vol. 7, p. 215.

Shall we abandon our study of the New Testament books as units, and from the various writings quarry material for constructing a history of Christianity in the postapostolic age? Some authors of books on the New Testament have followed this method. Passages have been selected from the New Testament, and from contemporary documents, which illustrate the principal interests and problems of second- and third-generation Christians. This material is then presented according to such various topics as the relation of the Christian movement to society and the state, the development of forms of organization, types of apology, and so forth.[6] From these authors one can learn much about the next half-century. In this chapter some of these developments affecting Christianity will be sketched.[7] But in the chapters which follow, the remaining canonical books will be studied as units. As in the previous sections, interest will center upon the special problems relating to the origin and interpretation of each.

THE POSITION OF CHRISTIANITY IN THE EMPIRE

It is possible that Paul's trial at Rome provoked a change in official and popular attitudes toward Christianity in the Roman world. The publicity and investigation caused by the Apostle's appeal to Caesar might have revealed that the movement was not a Jewish sect, and therefore not entitled to the privileges of a national religion.[8] Whatever its specific cause, Nero's massacre in A.D. 65 inaugurated an era of conflict between Christians and the state. Mark's Gospel indirectly witnesses to this troubled time. But the earliest Christian report is the noncanonical letter called 1 Clement. Writing from Rome to the Corinthian church around A.D. 96, Clement recalled the martyrdom of Peter and Paul:

> By reason of rivalry and envy the greatest and most righteous pillars [of the Church] were persecuted and battled to the death. . . . Peter who by reason of wicked jealousy, not only once or twice, but frequently endured suffering and thus, bearing his witness, went to the glorious place which he merited. By reason of rivalry and contention, Paul showed how to win the prize for patient endurance. . . . To the whole world he taught righteousness, and reaching the limits of the West he bore his witness before rulers. And so, released from the world, he was taken up into the holy place and became the greatest example of patient endurance.
>   To these men . . . there were joined a great multitude of the elect who by reason

---

[6]Works of this type, previously cited, are Craig, *The Beginning of Christianity,* and a newer study organized along the same lines, Kee and Young, *Understanding the New Testament;* also Goguel, *The Birth of Christianity.*

[7]For a review of modern literature and criticism, see S. Johnson, "The Emergence of the Christian Church in the Pre-Catholic Period," in *The Study of the Bible Today and Tomorrow,* ed. H. R. Willoughby (1947), pp. 329ff.; L. Goppelt, "The Existence of the Church in History," *Current Issues,* ed. Klassen and Snyder, pp. 193ff.

[8]Goguel, *Birth,* pp. 447f.; P. Carrington, *Early Christian Church,* vol. 1 (1957), p. 192. Reicke, *New Testament Era,* pp. 245ff.

of rivalry were victims of many outrages and tortures and became outstanding examples to us. . . .[9]

A common supposition is that this passage refers to Nero's massacre of Christians. The account of Tacitus is more circumstantial.[10] But neither Christian nor pagan sources provide an unequivocal explanation for Nero's action. Clement's insistence upon "rivalry and envy" suggests that conflict within the church at Rome was a contributing factor. Possibly Jewish denunciations are implied. If so, an attack upon Christianity at this time was part of a widespread concern to free Judaism from sectarian developments threatening the status of the nation in the Empire.

Nero's massacre does not seem to have touched off similar persecutions elsewhere. Yet wherever local officials and the populace were ill-disposed toward Christians, word of Nero's action would have encouraged denunciations and threats. Some scholars believe that the New Testament letter 1 Peter reveals that anti-Christian demonstrations did occur in Asia Minor in the following decades. Repercussions in Asia may provide the setting for the letters to the seven churches in the Revelation of John.[11]

Christian writers name Domitian (A.D. 81–96) as the next emperor to persecute Christians. 1 Clement may provide a contemporary witness. The letter begins: "Due, dear friends, to the sudden and successive misfortunes and accidents we have encountered. . . ." Clement's prayer, near the close of the letter, reads: "We ask you, Master, be our helper and defender. Rescue those of our number in distress . . . release our captives . . . Let all the nations know that you are the only God . . . Deliver us, too, from all who hate us without good reasons. . . ."[12]

According to the Roman historian Dio Cassius, Domitian slew "amongst many others" his cousin Flavius Clemens in his consulship, and arrested Clemens' wife, Domitilla, the emperor's niece. A charge of "atheism" was brought against them, "and on this many others who made shipwreck on Jewish customs were condemned, of whom many were put to death. . . ."[13] Some scholars, following Eusebius, hold that Domitilla was exiled at this time "because of her testimony to Christ."[14] It is interesting to think that Domitian's own niece had become a Christian. But the tradition is late and probably worthless.

Domitian was rigorous in his treatment of the Jews. He required them to pay the temple tax, which, after A.D. 70 had been diverted by Vespasian's order from the temple in Jerusalem to the temple of Jupiter in Rome. Financial shortages

---

[9] 1 Clem. 5:2ff. C. Richardson, Early Christian Fathers, vol. 1 (1953), pp. 45f. [hereafter, Fathers]. Note Ignatius, Eph. 12:2.

[10] See above, p. 196. Cf. M. Smith, "The Report about Peter in 1 Clement v. 4," NTS 7 (1960): 86ff.

[11] Goguel, Birth, pp. 524f.

[12] 1 Clem. 1:1; 59:4ff., Richardson, Fathers, pp. 43, 71f. Cf. E. T. Merrill, Essays in Early Christian History (1924), pp. 159ff.; Enslin, Beginnings, p. 313.

[13] Epitome, lxvii. 14. Cited from J. Stevenson, A New Eusebius (1957), p. 8. See also Suetonius, "Domitian," Lives of the Caesars, XV.

[14] H. E., III. 18. 4. Stevenson, A New Eusebius, p. 9. Cf. Reicke, New Testament Era, pp. 295ff.

plagued Domitian toward the end of his reign. Because of this he sought to impose the Jewish tax on as many as possible. It is reasonable to believe that persons who lived like Jews, such as God-fearers and some Christians, were subjected to denunciations and violence. They may have been victims of the strong measures taken against persons in high places who interested themselves in Jewish customs. Was it suspected that persons in this way were avoiding the cult of the emperor?

It was Domitian's open declaration of divine status and prerogatives which scandalized Jews and Christians. Coins struck by Domitian bear rude testimony to his claim to be "God the Lord." Many of these coins display the cult image of Domitian sitting in the holy place or on the throne of a god. In the new imperial temple at Ephesus a huge marble statue of Domitian became the focus of the emperor cult in Asia. Coins from Smyrna represent Domitian as father of the gods. An inscription from Laodicea glorifies the incarnate Jupiter in the doxology: "to Zeus the Supreme, the Savior, the Emperor Domitian." [15]

The strongest evidence for a recurrence of religious persecutions and martyrdoms under Domitian is the Revelation of John.[16] The Jewish apocalypse of 4 Ezra may reflect the revulsion of the synagogue also to the emperor's blasphemies, and the obstinate resistance of some Jews. At the same time, there is no evidence that Domitian issued an edict against either Christians or Jews as such.

From the reign of Trajan (A.D. 98–117) comes the first evidence that Christians were martyred simply upon their identification. Around A.D. 112, Pliny (the Younger) was sent to the province of Bithynia to reorganize its affairs. Excerpts from the governor's correspondence with Trajan read as follows:

> . . . In investigations of Christians I have never taken part; hence I do not know what is the crime usually punished . . . Meanwhile this is the course I have taken with those who were accused before me as Christians. I asked them whether they were Christians, and if they confessed, I asked them a second and a third time with threats of punishment. If they kept to it, I ordered them for execution; for I held no question that whatever it was they admitted, in any case obstinacy and unbending perversity deserve to be punished. There were others of the like insanity; but as these were Roman citizens, I noted them down to be sent to Rome.
>
> Before long . . . the mere fact that the charge was taken notice of made it commoner, and several distinct cases arose. An unsigned paper was presented, which gave the names of many. As for those who said that they neither were nor had ever been Christians, I . . . let them go, since they recited a prayer to the gods at my direction, made supplication with incense and wine to your statue . . . and moreover cursed Christ—things which (so it is said) those who are really Christians cannot be made to do. . . .

Trajan's reply:

> You have adopted the proper course, my dear Secundus, in the examination of the cases of those who were accused to you as Christians, for indeed nothing can be laid down as a general ruling involving something like a set form of procedure. They are not to be sought out; but if they are accused and convicted they must

[15] E. Stauffer, *Christ and Caesar,* trans. K. and R. Smith (1955), pp. 147ff.
[16] See below, pp. 556, 563f.

be punished—yet on this condition, that whoso denies himself to be a Christian, and makes the fact plain by his action, that is, by worshiping our gods, shall obtain pardon on his repentance, however suspicious his past conduct may be. Papers, however, which are presented unsigned ought not to be admitted in any charge, for they are a very bad example and unworthy of our time.[17]

Systematic measures to stamp out Christianity were not undertaken until the rule of Decius (A.D. 249–251). But from the time of Trajan the Church knew no security. The moderation of some officials availed little against the mounting tide of hostile public opinion.

JEWISH–CHRISTIANITY AND THE CONFLICT BETWEEN THE SYNAGOGUE AND THE CHURCH

We turn back to the martyrdoms of the apostles to recall the stoning of James in Jerusalem. In A.D. 62 the uneasy peace which existed between Jews and Christians in Judea was broken by action of the high priest, Annas. The one apostle who had done most to maintain peaceful coexistence met violent death. The record in Josephus of the stoning of James the brother of Jesus was noted in Chapter 10.[18]

Was Annas' action prompted by his jealousy of James' public favor? Probably so. But, for whatever cause, the decision of the Sanhedrin set aside the moderate counsel of Gamaliel and treated the head of the Church as a blasphemer.[19] The incident symbolized both a growing hostility between Jewish and Christian leadership in Jerusalem and the deterioration of the political situation. Zealot policies had gained the ascendancy and the disastrous war with Rome was imminent. In this chaotic time Christians were forced either to take sides or to abandon the city.[20] According to Eusebius, the Christians were led by a revelation to choose the latter alternative. Shortly before the siege of Titus they fled Jerusalem and sought asylum at Pella, a Gentile town of Perea. Most scholars believe that this tradition, also recorded by Epiphanius, is historical.[21]

The subsequent history of Palestinian Jewish–Christianity is obscure, both in its relation to Judaism, and in its relation to the Gentile churches. Some scholars have doubted that refugees of the early Church survived the catastrophe of A.D. 70.[22] But others have traced links between them and Jewish-Christian groups of a later time who lived in Judea, Syria, and Asia Minor. Most persons assume

---

[17] *Epistles*, X. 97, Stevenson, *A New Eusebius*, pp. 13f.

[18] *Antiq.*, XX. ix. i. Cited from Goguel, *Birth*, pp. 124f. Goguel also records the Hegesippus tradition preserved by Eusebius, and rightly dismisses it as containing many absurdities. See Shepherd, *IB*, vol. 7, p. 216. Cf. Carrington, *Early Christian Church*, pp. 190f.

[19] See above, pp. 154f.

[20] The anachronism reported in Matt. 23:35 and Luke 11:51 shows that the Zealots were not honored.

[21] *H. E.*, III. 5. 3. Elliott-Binns, *Galilean Christianity*, pp. 65ff. Cf. J. Munck, "Jewish–Christianity in Post-Apostolic Times," *NTS* 6 (1960): 130f.; also S. G. F. Brandon, *The Fall of Jerusalem and the Christian Church* (1951), pp. 168ff.

[22] See Munck, note 21 above; also Dix, *Jew and Greek*, pp. 63f.

that when peace was restored some of those who had fled to Pella returned to Jerusalem and lived there, at least until the time of Hadrian (A.D. 135).[23] Second-century fathers referred to Jewish–Christians called "Ebionites" (the poor). The first writer to mention them may be Justin Martyr.[24] Since later authors give the Ebionites other names, some scholars have concluded that the early title is itself an authentic link with the primitive Church in Jerusalem.[25] Others distinguish the Ebionites from a larger group referred to by Epiphanius as the "Nazarenes."[26]

Some of the refugees of A.D. 69 continued to live on the edge of Palestine. Here they were in close contact with several heretical Jewish sects, and were isolated from Christian churches. Some Qumran sectarians may have become converts at this time and introduced some of their doctrines and disciplines into the Jewish–Christian groups.[27] Did some of these people emigrate to Asia Minor and become the promotors of the teachings attacked by the authors of the "Pastoral Epistles," and by Ignatius?[28]

Other Jewish–Christians of Judea and Syria stood aloof from syncretistic tendencies. Perhaps the conservative tendencies of this remnant of the early Church found literary expression in the Gospel of Matthew and in the letters of James and of Jude. The letters will be discussed in a later chapter. But it should be recalled here that students of Matthew believe that Palestinian Jewish–Christian traditions are preserved in the material peculiar to the First Gospel.[29] Those who passed on these gospel traditions were bitterly hostile to Pharisees. Yet they were no less zealous in stressing the binding character of "the least commandments." They believed that Jesus had shown no interest in Samaritans and Gentiles. Accordingly they also shunned them. Some persons have attributed the strong eschatological emphasis in Matthew to the apocalypticism of Jewish–Christian prophets who in transmitting Jesus' teaching distorted it.[30]

Another Gospel provides evidence for the intensification of the struggle between Jews and Christians after the watershed of A.D. 70. In the Gospel of John the controversial material from Jesus' Ministry, and the story of his trial, emphasize the murderous opposition of Judaism to Christ. More strongly than in the Synoptic Gospels, "the Jews" are condemned for their rejection of him. It is probable that this viewpoint is reflected in Jewish–Christian sources underlying the Fourth Gospel.[31]

[23] Goguel, Birth, pp. 137f.; Carrington, Early Christian Church, pp. 410ff.

[24] Dial., XI. vii ff. Irenaeus identifies the sect advancing views similar to Justin's description as "the Ebionites," though his description varies somewhat, Adv. Haer., I.26; II.3, etc. Eusebius, H. E., III. 27. It should be recalled that some of the apocryphal gospels have been considered Ebionite targums of Matt., or of Matthean traditions.

[25] Cf., Gal. 2:10; Rom. 15:28. Weiss, Earliest Christianity.

[26] Dix, Jew and Greek, pp. 64ff., Shepherd, IB, vol. 7, pp. 215f. Cf. Goguel, Birth, pp. 141f.

[27] J. Danielou, The Dead Sea Scrolls and Primitive Christianity, trans. S. Attanasio (1958), pp. 122ff. [hereafter, Dead Sea Scrolls].

[28] See further, below, pp. 484f. and 509f.

[29] See above, pp. 202f., 211ff. and 288f.

[30] Heard, Intro., pp. 246ff.

[31] See further, below, pp. 579ff.

This section should be concluded with a word of caution. The antipathy to things Jewish shown in some Christian books of the postapostolic age reflects an internal and not merely an external conflict. Some heretical Jewish–Christianity undoubtedly originated in Gentile churches. To account for this, we need assume no connection with the primitive Christians of Jerusalem nor any direct influence of contemporary synagogues.[32]

DOCTRINAL DISPUTES IN POSTAPOSTOLIC TIMES

There are numerous references to "false" prophets and teachers in Christian writings of this period. Some historians speak of the rash of "heresies" which plagued the Church, yet the use of this term in its acquired sense is an anachronism. Until formal standards of orthodoxy were established, there was no basis for declaring "heretical" any particular type of teaching. It would be more correct to say that the second generation was characterized by an increasing number of schisms within the Church. "Sound doctrine" represented the beliefs of leaders of the stronger churches or, in some cases, the views of particular protagonists.

There is a classic statement that the early apostles went out "to the highways and hedges" and compelled people to come into the churches; the second generation had to contend with the result. Jesus' parable of the dragnet was preserved by Palestinian Christians of our period as descriptive of the church they knew: "the kingdom of heaven is like a net which was thrown into the sea and gathered fish of every kind . . . some good, some bad."[33]

What were the various beliefs and practices which brought from the faithful such anguished protests? Who were these "false teachers"? It is difficult to answer these questions. In our sources the schismatics are denounced. Their teachings are seldom refuted by argument. It is possible therefore to detect only a few of "the winds of doctrine" which were harassing the Church.

One controversy related to the interpretation of the scriptures and the authority of its interpreters. At this time "the scriptures" defined not only the Law, the Prophets, and the Writings but some books later to be declared apocryphal. The existing "Old Testament" constituted the final authority in the churches of this period.

There is an instructive passage in one of the letters of Ignatius, bishop of Antioch, written around A.D. 110:

> I urge you, do not do things in cliques, but act as Christ's disciples. When I heard some people saying, "If I don't find it in the original documents [the scriptures], I don't believe it in the gospel," I answered them, "But it *is* written there." They retorted, "That's just the question."[34]

Ignatius dismissed the problem by affirming Jesus Christ to be "the original documents." But until there was agreement upon authoritative Christian writings

---

[32] Munck's argument on this point is convincing (note 21 above), pp. 103ff.
[33] Matt. 13:47. Cf. 2 Tim. 2:20ff.
[34] *Philad.* 8:2ff. Richardson, *Fathers*, p. 110.

which set forth the relation of the *kerygma* to the Old Testament, there was bound to be a great variety of disparate opinions.

The basis of authority for particular interpretations was a closely related issue. Ignatius enforced his warnings against schism by declaring, "When I was among you I cried out, raising my voice—it was God's voice. . . ." Or again, in the same context, "It was the Spirit that kept on preaching in these words. . . ."[35] But it is likely that the bishop's antagonists, who "wanted in a human way" to mislead him, contended that the Holy Spirit validated their views.

Clement of Rome and the writer of 2 Timothy found the scriptures "profitable for teaching, for reproof, for correction, and for training in righteousness."[36] But the author of 2 Peter fulminated against "the ignorant and the unstable" who twisted the scriptures "to their own destruction" and imperiled the "stability" of the righteous.[37] And the writer of 1 John warned: "Beloved, do not believe every spirit, but test the spirits to see whether they are of God: for false prophets have gone out into the world."[38]

Until some court of appeal was set up, until the authority of the Spirit was related to the "received tradition," it was not possible to realize the ideal of "one faith." What criteria would be established for determining "the content of inspiration," and for "testing the spirits"?

Another area of doctrinal debate concerned the interpretation of Jesus Christ. We have observed the great variety of titles employed in the early Church to acclaim the eschatological significance of Jesus, in his Ministry and in his exalted state. Throughout the next generation certain of the earlier messianic categories were abandoned or limited in their use. "The Christ" became a mere appellate: "Christ Jesus" or "Jesus Christ." "Son of man" was almost exclusively restricted to the Gospel tradition, and in it to Jesus' sayings concerning his mission. "Servant" was limited to a liturgical mode of address.[39]

Other titles, however, emerged as a result of the impress of environmental factors upon the proclamation in the Hellenistic churches which used the Septuagint. When Caesar sought divine honors, Christ's role as *soter* (savior) was stressed. When philosophers and mystics spoke of the *logos* (word, thought) as mediating the life of the invisible world to men, Christ was proclaimed the revealing, redeeming Word. Forms of thought from the Hellenistic–Jewish "wisdom theology," employed by Paul, were further utilized in portraying Christ's role in Creation. Two New Testament books—the Gospel of John and Hebrews—developed along original and parallel lines the proclamation of Paul: Jesus Christ is God in his self-revelation.[40] In both books, as in Paul's writings, Jesus as "Son of God" and "Lord" are prominent conceptions. These titles from the received traditions were congenial to Hellenistic ways of thought.

[35] *Philad.* 6:7ff.
[36] 1 *Clem.* 13:1ff.; 2 Tim. 3:16.
[37] 2 Peter 3:14; also 1:20ff.; 1 Tim. 1:6f.
[38] 1 John 4:1.
[39] Note 1 *Clem.* 16; Bar. 5:2. Cullmann, *Christology*, pp. 78f. See above, p. 129.
[40] See further, below, pp. 509, 512f., 532ff., and 589ff.

Two dangerous tendencies affecting the exposition of the person of Christ developed in the period under survey. Pre-Gnostic thought in Syria and Asia Minor produced two forms of speculation which struck at the very heart of the *kerygma*. One denied the real humanity of Jesus; the other, his divinity. Some teachers in the churches held that Christ had been an angelic redeemer-god sent from the invisible overworld. He only seemed to be a man. This mythological view is known as *docetism*, a term derived from the Greek verb "to seem." Ignatius attacked the teaching of this devastating doctrine in the churches of Asia:

> Be deaf . . . when any one speaks unto you apart from Jesus Christ, who was of the race of David, the child of Mary, who was truly born, and ate and drank, was truly persecuted under Pontius Pilate, was truly crucified and died, before the eyes of those in heaven and those on earth and those under the earth; who was also truly raised from the dead, since his Father raised him up. . . .
>
> But if it be, as some godless men assert, that he suffered as a phantom only . . . then I lie against the Lord.[41]

New Testament books from the Johannine circle in Asia Minor opposed the denial of Christ's true humanity, revealing that this grievous error described by Ignatius persisted from an earlier time.[42]

Some words of Irenaeus may be cited as a description of a strange doctrine which also may be identified as a pre-Gnostic aberration. He wrote that a teacher named Cerinthus taught

> that the world was not made by the primary God, but by a certain power far separated from him . . . He represented Jesus as having not been born of a virgin, but as being the son of Joseph and Mary . . . After his baptism, Christ descended upon him . . . from the Supreme Ruler, and that then he proclaimed the unknown Father, and performed miracles. But at last Christ departed from Jesus, and that then Jesus suffered, and rose again, while Christ remained impassible, inasmuch as he was a spiritual being.[43]

Cerinthus shared the commonplace Hellenistic view that matter was evil. Therefore the creator of the world could not be the righteous "God of the Jews." In the same passage Irenaeus reported that the opinions of the Ebionites "with respect to the Lord are similar to those of Cerinthus."

Because Jesus suffered, said some Jewish–Christians, he was not divine. This was the reverse of the docetic error: because Jesus was divine, he did not suffer. But both schismatics claimed that some higher "power" was the real Christ. The one declared that the Spirit of the Lord (in the Jewish sense) lived within an uncommonly good man. The other clothed a heavenly power with the appearance of manhood.[44]

One other doctrinal dispute may be noted. It arose from the question of whether

---

[41] *Trall.* 9f. Stevenson, *A New Eusebius*, p. 47. See also Eph. 7:1ff.; *Smyr.* 1–7, *Mag.* 11. See also the apocryphal Gospel of Peter (ca. A.D. 125–150).

[42] See below, pp. 567, 569, and 589, 599.

[43] *Adv. Haer.*, I.21.

[44] H. M. Gwatkin, *Early Church History to* A.D. *313*, vol. 1 (1909), p. 11.

lapsed Christians should be readmitted to churches upon repentance. According to Matthew, the Jewish–Christians of Syria followed a procedure based upon a ruling of Jesus. A sinful brother was to be duly warned by the person against whom he had offended. If he refused to repent, the church was to warn him. If this ultimatum was ignored, he was to be treated "as a Gentile and a tax collector." The churches of Syria believed that they had received from the Lord the powers of binding and loosing, and that their decisions were ratified in Heaven.[45]

But what was to be done in the case of repentant apostates who had denied their Lord during persecutions, or who had reverted to their pagan vices? The writer of Hebrews flatly denied the possibility of a second repentance for persons who had "been enlightened," who had "tasted of the goodness of the Lord and the powers of the age to come."[46] But Clement and Hermas of Rome offered forgiveness to penitent Christians. In the Shepherd of Hermas, the Roman church was provided a "prophetic" supplement to the *kerygma*. Even those who had "blasphemed the Lord," and who "added to their sins wanton deeds and piled up wickedness" would be forgiven if they repented "with their whole heart." Nevertheless, the "revelation" to Hermas contained an ultimatum also. "For the Master has sworn to his elect . . . that if there still be sin after this day has been fixed [the day when the ultimatum was published?], they shall find no salvation; for repentance for the just has an end; . . . [whereas] the day of repentance for the heathen is open until the last day."[47]

MORAL PROBLEMS IN THE CHURCHES

After reading the letters of the New Testament from this period, a person might conclude that their writers were more concerned to denounce the lax morals of the "false teachers" than to expose their erroneous theology. But there are a number of hints that bad morals were attributed to bad theology and vice versa.

The two extremes in conduct which were evidenced in Paul's churches continued to disrupt the unity of later congregations: legalism and license. Under the pressure of pre-Gnostic ideas, some Christian teachers developed a rigorous code of morality combining Jewish legal practices and various ascetic disciplines imposed by pagan groups. "The Colossian heresy" was found by Ignatius to be troubling other towns in Asia Minor a half-century later:

> Now if anyone preaches Judaism to you, pay no attention to him. For it is better to hear about Christianity from one of the circumcision, than Judaism from a Gentile. . . .[48]

[45]Matt. 18:15ff. Note its similarity to the Qumran discipline both in the corporate procedure for restoring penitent members and the treatment of impenitents as outsiders. Cf. Tit. 3:10f., 1 John 5:16f.
[46]Heb. 6:4ff.; 10:26ff.; 12:16f.
[47]*Shep. of Her.*, II. ii. 1ff. K. Lake, *Apostolic Fathers* (Loeb Lib.), vol. 2 (1913), pp. 19ff.
[48]*Philad.* 6:1; Richardson, *Fathers*, p. 109.

> For if we still go on observing Judaism, we admit we never received grace . . .
> we must learn to live like Christians. . . . Get rid of the bad yeast. . . . It is mon-
> strous to talk Jesus Christ and live like a Jew. . . .[49]

Earlier the writer of the letters to Timothy opposed "the doctrine of demons"
which prohibited marriages and enjoined abstinence from certain foods and
rigorous "bodily training."[50]

As in Colossae, pre-Gnostic teachings continued to promote the opposite
extreme—profligate living. Some Christians claimed moral perfection by perverse
distortions of the doctrines of regeneration and of freedom from all law. Thus
they arrogantly did as they pleased and scorned their scrupulous brethren who
were of "the flesh." The writer of 2 Peter specifically declared that Paul's letters
and the scriptures generally were being exploited for the promotion of lawlessness.[51] Ignatius observed that the docetists in Asia Minor were denying the
distinctive moral injunction of the gospel by their careless disregard of the needs
of the brethren:

> Let no one be misled: [by speculations concerning] heavenly beings, the splendor
> of angels, and principalities. . . . Pay close attention to those who have wrong
> notions about the grace of Christ . . . and note how at variance they are with God's
> mind. They care nothing about love: they have no concern for widows and orphans,
> for the oppressed, for those in prison or released, for the hungry or thirsty.[52]

The same denial of the faith by unconcern for the brethren was observed at
an earlier time by the writer of the letters of John.[53]

The apocalyptic seer of the Johannine circle condemned the lawlessness caused
by the teaching of "the Nicolaitans."[54] Like the "spiritual" libertines in the
Corinthian church of Paul's time, the Nicolaitans claimed that the eating of idol
meats was a morally indifferent action.[55] From John's scornful comments it is
difficult to know what were the views of these troublemakers. But the cause of
his condemnation is evident. He was convinced that they had gone too far in
accommodating their conduct to pagan standards.[56] The writer of Jude excoriated
some Christians as thorough reprobates. They had rejected all authority and were
living "by instinct like irrational animals."[57]

The conclusion is unavoidable. Among second- and third-generation Christians
there were serious declensions from the moral ideals of the gospel. Some who
began in faith submitted again "to a yoke of slavery," and their legalism emptied
the cross of Christ of its power. Others used their Christian freedom "as an

[49] *Mag.* 8ff.; Richardson, *Fathers,* pp. 96f.
[50] 1 Tim. 4:1ff.
[51] 2 Pet. 3:15f.
[52] *Smyr.* 6:2; Richardson, *Fathers,* p. 114.
[53] 1 John 4:1. As in Matt., "lawlessness" in the church is condemned as sin, 1 John 3:4; 2:3ff. Cf.
Matt. 24:11ff.; 5:19; 13:41ff.
[54] Rev. 2:6, 14f., 20ff.
[55] Rev. 2:14. Cf. *Did.* 6:3.
[56] Craig, *Beginning,* p. 302; Goguel, *Birth,* pp. 409ff.
[57] Jude 4, 8; 2 Pet. 2:12.

opportunity for the flesh," and their liberty became a stumbling block to the weak. In the absence of the apostles' authority, some other means of enforcing discipline became imperative.

THE DEVELOPMENT TOWARD FORMAL ORGANIZATION

The organization of the earliest churches was characterized by spontaneity and variety. The intensity of the hope of Christ's coming in glory did not discount all efforts toward ordering the common life of the believers. The "apostles and elders" in Jerusalem met the needs of the Church as they arose, adapting the patterns of organization followed in the synagogues and in sectarian groups.[58] Nor was Paul's conviction that the End was imminent incompatible with his belief that there should be "order" in the churches.[59] To the Thessalonians, disturbed by eschatological excitement, Paul wrote: "We beseech you, brethren, to respect those who labor among you and who are over you in the Lord and admonish you, and to esteem them very highly. . . ."[60]

The earliest writing to give attention to types of the Christian ministry is 1 Corinthians.[61] In this letter the Apostle describes two series of God's gifts to the Church. First in importance are "apostles," "prophets," and "teachers." It is probable that these offices were primarily concerned with the transmitting of the Church's tradition, with explaining the relation of the gospel to the scriptures, with training new converts in the Church's pattern of teaching. The second series of offices includes "workers of miracle, healers, helpers, administrators, speakers in various kinds of tongues." Since Paul does not enumerate this series he probably considered that these "gifts" were suited to special needs and did not constitute indispensable ministries.[62]

The preeminent leaders in Paul's churches are variously designated in the sources. We have seen that he addressed "the bishops and deacons" of Philippi. According to Acts there were "elders" in Paul's churches of Asia Minor. The Ephesian elders are described as overseers or guardians (bishops) of the flock.[63]

The summary above emphasizes the looseness of organization in the earliest churches. Yet a strong sense of unity was not lacking. Christians in every place formed the people or saints of the Messiah living in the new Age. This eschatological conviction preceded the formation of individual churches.[64] In spite of Paul's recognition of schism in the body of Christ, he was convinced that Christians were united in Him, baptized by one Spirit. Believers in Christ were therefore fellow-members one of another.

[58] See above, pp. 140ff.
[59] 1 Cor. 14:26ff.
[60] 1 Thess. 5:12f.
[61] 1 Cor. 12:28ff.
[62] Cf. Rom. 12:6ff., where prophets and teachers are listed but another series of ministries follows.
[63] Acts 20:17, 28; 14:23. Cf. 1 Pet. 5:1ff.
[64] See above, pp. 119f. and 135f.

The literature of the postapostolic age reveals a loss of this sense of the existing unity of the Church. Ideally the Church is one, but instead of a conviction of its reality writers of this time yearned for unity. We have seen that Luke somewhat idealized the harmony of the earliest days. In his day "the company of those who believed" were not "of one heart and soul."[65] In the Gospel of John, Jesus prays for those who believe in him through the apostles' word, "that they may become perfectly one," not that they may remain united.[66] The author of Ephesians exhorts his readers to "be eager to maintain the unity of the Spirit." The purpose of the Spirit is that "we all *attain* to the unity of the faith. . ."[67] Acts, John, Ephesians— books written within a few years of each other—appeal to a divided Church to find its unity in the apostles' tradition and in the fellowship of the Spirit.[68]

The concept of "apostolicity" assumed a still greater importance at the turn of the century. Clement, rebuking the Corinthian church for deposing certain elders, claimed that the apostles had appointed their first converts "to be bishops and deacons of future believers." Moreover, Clement declared that provision was made by them for successors to these men.[69] Clement's description of the apostles' provisions is not altogether clear. Some claim that he affirmed a doctrine of "apostolic succession," that the elder-bishops of succeeding generations were to be ordained to their office by men who had themselves inherited by ordination the authority of the apostles. But other scholars are not sure that Clement's words are to be so understood.[70] In any case, it is clear that the views of the church at Rome had not become established at Corinth.

An interesting passage in the Didache (or, Teaching of the Twelve Apostles) reflects a reluctance to abandon the idea that Christian leaders should arise spontaneously under the influence of the Spirit. Yet the same passage acknowledges that "bishops" and "deacons" had by this time taken over the ministries earlier performed by "prophets" and "teachers," and that some of the temporary representatives of the older orders were charlatans. The Didache taught that only "genuine" leaders should be followed, whether these be visiting prophets or local appointees.[71]

Some interpreters of the Pastoral Letters of the New Testament declare that in them "the bishop" is distinguished for the first time from "elders" and "deacons." Paul's fellow-workers Timothy and Titus are represented as the

---

[65] Acts 4:32; 2:42, 44.

[66] John 17:20f., 23. See further, below, pp. 597f.

[67] Eph. 4:3, 11ff. Note especially v. 14. Cf. Rom. 12:4ff.

[68] E.g., Eph. 3:4f. (cf. Rev. 21:14). See further, below, pp. 502ff., 597, and 600. Matt. 16:18ff. should be recalled in this connection. Whatever the origin of this controversial saying, it attests the importance placed upon Peter and "the twelve" in the churches of Syria.

[69] 1 *Clem.* 42–44.

[70] Richardson, *Fathers*, pp. 63ff. The "pre-Catholicism" of Clement is supported by his comparison of the functions of the elder-bishop and the OT priests. R. M. Grant, *Intro.*, p. 408.

[71] *Did.* 10:7ff. The origin of the Didache and of its component parts is disputed. The view taken here is that the Didachist employed Syrian sources dating from the close of the first century, and that his method of inserting material *en bloc* makes it possible to extract the earlier from the later. See Richardson, *Fathers*, pp. 161ff. Goguel, *Birth*, pp. 267ff.

prototypes of these bishops, the emissaries of the apostles. By the time these letters were written, some churches had adopted a form of organization commonly known as "the monarchical episcopacy," that is, the rule of a single bishop over a church, with the counsel of elders and the assistance of deacons. Others believe that the texts of the letters do not support this hypothesis.[72]

The letters of Ignatius reveal that by A.D. 110 some of the churches in Syria and Asia Minor had moved a step further toward centralization of authority. There are no references to the submission of the bishop of a church to traveling emissaries of the apostles, or to anyone else. The Magnesian church is warned to respect the authority of their youthful bishop, Damas, "as they respect the authority of God."[73] In some churches, at any rate, the bishop had become the custodian of the apostolic tradition. He fulfilled in the local congregation the functions formerly served by prophets and teachers in the early Church.

At the same time, Ignatius associated elders and deacons with the bishop. The following passage shows the hierarchical yet coordinate authority of these offices:

> The deacons represent Jesus Christ, just as the bishop has the role of the Father, and the elders are like God's council and an apostolic band. You cannot have a church without these.[74]

This passage also discloses the conception which Ignatius held concerning the basis of authority of these offices. He does not here (or elsewhere) appeal to apostolic succession. He held a mystical view that the essential ministries of the Church "are the earthly antitype of a heavenly pattern."[75]

It should be noticed that in all of the sources from this time the independence of local churches was still the order of the day. Yet there are signs that the larger churches and the more prominent bishops were seeking to extend their influence. Clement, representing the church at Rome, sharply rebuked the church at Corinth; Ignatius, bishop of Antioch, admonished the churches of Asia; the "elder John" wrote to Gaius claiming authority over the local leadership of this church. At the same time, in their admonitions, these bishops or elders could rely only upon moral persuasion.[76]

While the development toward formal organization served as a rein upon those who threatened to divide the churches, it is probable that the strongest unifying influence was worship. As in apostolic times, Christian worship consisted in more than formal ceremonies. The author of Hebrews encouraged his readers not to neglect "meeting together." But formal assemblies and "praises of the lips" were not enough. The "sacrifices pleasing to God are that men not neglect to do good and to share what they have."[77]

One day in the week was especially significant. At the time of John's apocalyptic

[72]See further, below, p. 507.
[73]*Mag.* 2f.; 6:1. Also *Trall.* 7:1; 13:2; *Philad.* 7; *Poly.* 2:2.
[74]*Trall.* 3:1ff.; Richardson, *Fathers,* p. 99; cf. *Smyr.* 8:1f; *Mag.* 7:1.
[75]Richardson, *Fathers,* p. 76; R. M. Grant, *Intro.,* pp. 408f.
[76]1 *Clem.* 7:1ff.; Ignatius, *Trall.* 3:3f.; *Eph.* 3:1ff.; *Mag.* 12f.
[77]Heb. 10:23ff.; 13:15f. Also Jas. 1:26f. Cf. Ignatius, *Eph.* 13.

vision he knew that Christians everywhere were gathering for worship. It was the "Lord's Day," the first day of the week, the day of his resurrection.[78] Ignatius and the writer of the Didache also refer to the "Lord's Day." [79] Pliny's comment concerning Christian worship in Bithynia may be noticed in this connection:

> . . . on a fixed day [they] assemble before daylight and recite by turns a form of words to Christ as a god . . . they bound themselves with an oath . . . not to break their word. . . . After this was done, their custom was to depart, and to meet again to take food. . . .[80]

Some New Testament books from this period may contain prayers, hymns, and homilies used in the public worship of the churches at this time and earlier. We have commented upon the possibility that liturgical and lectionary influence determined to some extent the form of the Synoptic Gospels, and vestiges of hymns and formal confessional statements were found in the letters of Paul.[81] These influences are more evident in the latest New Testament books.

The reports which Pliny had received suggest that the Lord's Supper was still an actual meal at this time. This central cultic act of worship was called by several names: "the breaking of bread," [82] "the *agape*" (love-feast),[83] and "the *eucharist*" (thanksgiving).[84] The Gospel of John, which does not report the institution of the Lord's Supper, shows that its teaching gave significance to the partaking of food on all occasions.[85] From this and other writings we conclude that Christ's presence was felt at the love-feasts in the churches, and that by these gatherings the advent hope was kept alive in spite of the decline of apocalyptic enthusiasm.

As long as there were prophets in the churches, these men conducted the cultic meal according to the inspiration of the moment.[86] But with the passing of this order, it is probable that the leading elder-bishops presided. Since not all of these appointed officers had the gift of extempore prayer, models were devised for their use.[87] The earliest liturgical setting for the Eucharist is recorded in the Didache. The following prayer is prescribed for the conclusion of the meal:

> We thank you, holy Father, for your sacred name which you have lodged in our hearts, and for the knowledge and faith and immortality which you have revealed through Jesus, your child [or Servant]. To you be glory forever.
> Almighty Master, you have created everything for the sake of your name, and have given men food and drink to enjoy that they may thank you. But to us you

---

[78] Rev. 1:10.

[79] Ignatius, *Mag.* 9:1; *Did.* 14:1. Note the reference to "the eighth day," the day after the Jewish Sabbath, in *Bar.* 15:9.

[80] *Epistles*, X. 96. Stevenson, *A New Eusebius*, p. 14.

[81] See above, pp. 191, 208, 457f. and 467.

[82] *Did.* 14:1. Cf. Acts 2:24ff. See above, pp. 146ff.

[83] Note Jude 12.

[84] Ignatius, *Eph.* 13:1; *Philad.* 4; *Did.* 9f.

[85] See further, below, pp. 591ff.

[86] *Did.* 10:7. See also 1 Cor. 14:26ff.

[87] Craig, *Beginning*, pp. 280f.

have given spiritual food and drink and eternal life through Jesus, your child [or Servant].

Above all, we thank you that you are mighty. To you be glory forever.

Remember, Lord, your Church, to save it from evil and to make it perfect by your love. Make it holy and gather it together from the four winds into your Kingdom which you have made ready for it. For yours is the power and the glory forever.

Let Grace (Christ) come and let this world pass away.

Hosanna to the God of David!

If anyone is holy, let him come. If not let him repent.

Maranatha! Amen.[88]

The Didache also contains the earliest reference to a form for the administration of baptism in the Church, and comments on the preparations necessary for this rite. The importance of baptism did not diminish in the age following the apostles.[89]

Sometimes it is remarked that the leaders of the Church in the third and fourth generations were men of limited intelligence, and often quite pedestrian in the ways they met the challenge of their times. But theirs was a notable achievement. They formulated and secured safeguards for the tradition of the apostles. Yet they allowed for flexibility in the development of patterns of teaching and community life.[90] One Christian of the postapostolic age expressed the secret of this achievement. In spite of shocking divisions and moral lapses in the churches, the followers of Jesus and his apostles were guided by "the Spirit of truth." Unto ordinary men such as filled the churches, in those days as in the present, were declared "the things that are to come."[91]

[88]*Did.* 10. Richardson, *Fathers,* pp. 175f. "Servant" is to be preferred to "child" as the translation of *pais.* See above, p. 129.

[89]See Kee and Young, *Understanding the New Testament,* pp. 368ff.

[90]Shepherd, *IB,* vol. 7, p. 215; Craig, *Beginning,* pp. 303f.

[91]John 16:7ff.

chapter nineteen

WRITINGS FROM
THE PAULINE CIRCLE

Reconstruction of a room from a Roman villa: a *cubiculum* (bedroom) from a villa near Boscoreale, c. 40–30 B.C.; couch and footstool (with bone carvings and glass inlay), first century A.D.; part of a mosaic pavement, second century A.D. (The Metropolitan Museum of Art)

493

Realistic gravestone sculpture of a citizen and his wife, expertly portraying the matter-of-factness of Roman portraiture. (Ewing Galloway)

Statue of a lar, tutelary deity of the Roman household, and a guardian of travelers, of Etruscan origin. (The Metropolitan Museum of Art, Rogers Fund)

A Roman schoolboy arriving late for class and beginning to apologize is shown in this relief from a tomb at Neumagen (Gaul). (The Bettmann Archive)

THERE are some things in them hard to understand. . . ." The reference is to the Letters of Paul; the comment by the author of 2 Peter.[1] Many others in the postapostolic age and since have agreed. The misunderstandings, the distortions of his teaching, which Paul experienced persisted beyond his lifetime.[2] Although some have supposed that Paul was forgotten for a period, it is unlikely that this was ever the case in important areas of the Church. Second- and third-generation Christians drew inspiration from the story of his life, and his letters were copied and quoted as possessing unusual authority.[3]

In addition to Acts, several books of the New Testament witness to the influence of Paul after his martyrdom. Four of these will be studied in this chapter—Ephesians, 1 and 2 Timothy, and Titus. Some scholars list 1 Peter among the writings by Paulinists. Still others claim that the Gospel of John and Hebrews are Pauline books.

LETTER TO THE EPHESIANS

Ephesians is a theological tract having the formal appearance of a letter. It has been described as "the crown of Paulinism," for its writer reduced some of the principal ideas of the Apostle to a system dominated by a single theme. According to Church tradition, as we have seen, Paul wrote Ephesians from his Roman prison, shortly after Colossians. But many modern critics agree that Ephesians is a later work written by a Paulinist. In any event, the choice lies between Paul and someone well acquainted with his thought.

A completely satisfactory solution of the origin of Ephesians has not been reached. Indeed, arguments for and against Pauline authorship are so evenly matched that protagonists tend to overstate their cases and persuade others to the opposite opinion. Only a brief discussion of this perplexing critical problem is necessary.[4]

---

[1] 2 Pet. 3:16.

[2] Jewish–Christian opposition to Paul reached a zenith in the Pseudo–Clementines. See Hennecke and Schneemelcher, *New Testament Apocrypha*, vol. 2, pp. 71f., 103ff.

[3] Note Clement's comment, above, p. 477; McNeile, *Intro.*, pp. 328ff.

[4] Beare, *IB*, vol. 10, pp. 597ff.; E. Goodspeed, *The Meaning of Ephesians* (1933); Mitton, *The Epistle to the Ephesians* [hereafter, *Ephesians*]; *Studies in Ephesians*, ed. F. L. Cross (1956). Cf. F. J. A. Hort, *Prolegomena to St. Paul's Epistles to the Romans and Ephesians* (1895). Wikenhauser, *New Testament Introduction*, pp. 421ff.; R. M. Grant, *Intro.*, pp. 199ff.

The Problem of Authorship

There are fundamental differences in the style and language of Ephesians and those of the unquestionably genuine letters of Paul. The great sixteenth-century classicist Erasmus commented on the literary peculiarities of Ephesians. Those who can read Paul's letters in Greek are most sensitive to this, but the English reader can notice the differences in style between, let us say, the Corinthian letters and Ephesians. In the latter the sentences are long and involved, containing many participles, relative pronouns, and synonyms joined together. Paul's style has been likened to a cascade. It is quick, light, allusive. The style of Ephesians is more like a glacier—slow-moving, massive, majestic. Some have sought to account for this by noting the noncontroversial and meditative mood of Ephesians, as well as the devotional nature of its theme. Others have conjectured that Paul relied on a trusted helper to compose the final draft of the letter. All agree that the criterion of style must be employed with caution.[5]

The unusual vocabulary of Ephesians is another linguistic element of the problem. More than ninety words which are not found elsewhere in Paul's letters appear, and this novel vocabulary is akin to Christian writings after Paul. Common Pauline words are put together in unusual ways, and others are used with different shades of meaning.[6] Some persons consider that the subject matter of Ephesians is sufficient to explain these facts. But when it is observed that identical words, e.g., *mystery* and *fullness,* are used differently in Colossians and Ephesians—two letters composed at nearly the same time if both were written by Paul—there is reason to question the adequacy of such explanations.[7] Moreover, in no other letter does Paul depend so extensively upon reproducing ideas previously expressed in writing. Much weight is given to this evidence of literary dependence by those who view Ephesians as a pseudonymous work.[8] Some worthy disciple of Paul, it is claimed, created a mosaic of "tiny elements of tradition," and the result is a carefully worked-out theme. Of course, it can be shown that in his major letters Paul relied on tradition—hymnic fragments, primitive confessions, and the like. Yet the Apostle did not employ these pieces of tradition to help express his ideas, but to buttress them, just as he did with scriptural proof.[9]

Several theological aspects of Ephesians are important to the question of origin. In 1 Corinthians, Paul wrote that "no other foundation can any one lay than that which is laid, which is Jesus Christ." In Ephesians "the apostles and prophets" are called the foundation of the Church.[10] In the main letters of Paul, God is the reconciler of men, working through Christ. In Ephesians Christ is the reconciler, and the death of Christ, so central to Paul's gospel, is subordinated to his exaltation.[11] Peculiar to the Pauline letters is the declaration in Ephesians that

[5]McNeile, *Intro.,* p. 168; F. L. Cross, *Studies in Ephesians,* pp. 30f.
[6]Note the examples given by Beare, *IB,* vol. 10, pp. 598ff.; G Johnston, *IDB,* vol. 2, p. 109.
[7]Cf. Eph. 3:3ff. and Col. 1:26f. (1 Cor. 2:1); also Eph. 1:9; 5:32. Feine-Behm-Kümmel, *Intro.,* pp. 253f. See also, Eph. 1:23 and Col. 1:19; G. Johnston, "Ephesians," *IDB,* vol. 2, p. 110.
[8]Mitton, *Ephesians,* pp. 86ff. Tabular summaries in Johnston, *IDB,* vol. 2, pp. 110f.
[9]E. Käsemann, "Ephesians and Acts," in Keck and Martyn, *Luke–Acts,* pp. 288f.
[10]Cf. 1 Cor. 3:11; Eph. 2:20.

Christ "descended into the lower parts of the earth." [12] There is no suggestion of the coming of the Lord, whether soon or late.[13] For the author of Ephesians the object of Christ's Ministry had been to break down "the dividing wall of hostility" between Jew and Gentile.[14] As ardently as Paul longed for harmony between both ethnic groups in the churches, he did not speak of this as the primary object of Christ's mission. Some say that Paul developed in Ephesians some of the deeper implications of his earlier teachings. Others consider that this "unprecedented development," in certain instances, amounts to contradiction, providing a chief objection to apostolic authorship.[15]

Since there is every reason to believe that a Paulinist should have employed some of Paul's primary ideas, more weight must be given to lesser ideas which also reflect a changed perspective.[16] An example of a secondary idea would be the conception of Paul's mission recorded in Ephesians 3:4–13. The passage states that Paul was entrusted with a particular revelation, namely, that the Gentiles should be "fellow heirs, members of the same body [with Jews], and partakers of the promise in Christ Jesus through the gospel." According to Paul his fundamental revelation was that the principle of obedience to the Torah as a means of salvation was now set aside. The corollary of this proclamation was the admission of Gentiles into the Church. In Ephesians the means and the end are reversed. It is difficult to believe that Paul ever abandoned his conviction that the distinctive message entrusted to him was that "Christ is the end of the law." [17] The passage before us raises another suspicion. Would Paul have commended himself in this manner? The words are more easily suited to an admirer measuring the greatness of Paul's achievement. The attitude of the writer toward the "holy apostles and prophets" indicates that he was a recipient of the revelation given through them.

Any solution of the problem of authorship contains large elements of subjective feeling. Either Ephesians is an original, noncontroversial writing composed, in whole or in large part, by Paul shortly after Colossians (with a greater than usual reliance upon an amanuensis?); or it is the writing of a follower of Paul, whose mind was steeped in the language and thought of Colossians, and of other letters of the Apostle, but who was also a theologian in his own right. The cumulative weight of the internal evidence seems to support the latter alternative. The question is still in debate. Perhaps it will never be answered with certainty.

The Destination of the Letter

Two facts lead the majority of scholars to say that Ephesians was not written for the church at Ephesus, at least not exclusively for this Asian church. Several

---

[11] Cf. 2 Cor. 5:18ff.; Rom. 5:10f.; and Eph. 2:16. Also Col. 1:20; 2:13f.

[12] Eph. 4:9f. Cf. 1 Cor. 15:4f.; Rom. 10:6f.

[13] The consummation of the Church's hope "in the coming ages" is the perfecting of the unity of all things, including "the faith."

[14] Eph. 2:13ff. Mitton, *Ephesians*, pp. 20f.

[15] McNeile, *Intro.*, p. 172; cf. Mitton, *Ephesians*, p. 16f.; Feine-Behm-Kümmel, *Intro.*, pp. 254f.

[16] Beare, *IB*, vol. 10, p. 599.

[17] Rom. 10:4. Cf. Eph. 2:15.

of the best manuscripts omit the address "at Ephesus," as the editors of the RSV acknowledge.[18] Moreover, the absence of greetings and other personal notices is conspicuous. These facts defy explanation if the letter was addressed directly to a church in which Paul had labored for from two to three years. Some statements in Ephesians imply that its readers knew Paul only by reputation, and that the writer had hearsay knowledge of his readers' Christian witness.[19]

There are two principal explanations for these facts. A popular view is that Ephesians was composed as a circular letter to be carried from place to place by a single courier (Tychicus?). Perhaps the author left a blank space in the letter's superscription, expecting the reader to supply the appropriate address: "at Laodicea," "at Hierapolis," and so on.[20] The alternative to the circular letter theory is that a second-century scribe supplied the words, "at Ephesus," bringing the letter into conformity with its traditional title and the superscriptions of other Pauline letters. The original address was therefore "to the saints who are also faithful in Christ Jesus." This mode of address would be strange from Paul's pen; from a writer in the postapostolic age, appropriate. Nothing is certain about the destination of this letter except that it was not written for one church, at any rate not for the Ephesians alone.

The Occasion for the Writing of Ephesians?

The purpose of Ephesians will be considered along with an exposition of the letter. But brief notice should be taken of the view advanced by Edgar Goodspeed.[21] His position is that a Christian of Asia, long acquainted with the Letters of Colossians and Philemon, was prompted by the publication of Acts to look for other letters of the great Apostle. Acts led him to the Galatian churches, to Philippi, Thessalonica, Corinth, and Rome. Upon reading the letters found at these places, the collector was much impressed. Paul's letters transcended the temporal situations which occasioned them, and contained a message and admonitions relevant to his own day. He decided to make the collection available to the Church at large and, in order to focus the essential teaching of Paul, he composed an introduction in letter form. Thus Ephesians was written as a preface to the collection. Since the author knew Colossians best of all, its influence was outstanding, but he lifted from all of the letters typical ideas, organizing Paul's gospel around a theme of great significance for the Church. Goodspeed is attracted to the conjecture that the collector of Paul's letters and the author of Ephesians was

---

[18]Eph. 1:1. See Beare, *IB*, vol. 10, pp. 601f.; Feine-Behm-Kümmel, *Intro.*, pp. 248f.

[19]Eph. 3:1f.; 1:15; 4:21.

[20]J. A. Robinson, *St. Paul's Epistle to the Ephesians* (1909), pp. 11f. [hereafter, *Ephesians*]. Cf. F. L. Cross, *Studies in Ephesians*, pp. 14ff. Marcion's view that Eph. was the Letter to the Laodiceans has a few modern supporters, but it is improbable (McNeile, *Intro.*, pp. 176f.) Feine-Behm-Kümmel, *Intro.*, pp. 249f.

[21]In addition to *The Meaning of Ephesians*, see E. J. Goodspeed's *The Key to Ephesians* (1956) and *Christianity Goes to Press* (1940).

Onesimus, the erstwhile runaway slave, and at this time the bishop of the church at Ephesus.

The Goodspeed theory has several practical values. It reconstructs a set of circumstances and a motive for the writing of Ephesians by a Paulinist. It accounts for the literary influence of Colossians, and of other letters of Paul, upon Ephesians. It explains why Ephesians, although not by Paul, always had a place in the collection of his letters.[22] Some details of Goodspeed's theory, however, lack plausibility. Many scholars are persuaded that the letters of Paul were only gradually brought together into a single collection. Was Paul nearly forgotten, so that Acts and the publication of his letters rescued him from oblivion? Can the decisive influence of Acts upon the writer of Ephesians be established? Is it just to describe Ephesians as a mosaic of passages from Paul's letters, a brief summary of Paul's gospel, or to speak of its contents as a preface? These questions will be raised again after an exposition of Ephesians.

An Interpretation of the Letter

A date for the writing of Ephesians around A.D. 90 is consistent with the allusions to it in the writings of the Apostolic Fathers and with the supposed influence of Acts. Yet if 1 Peter reflects the influence of Ephesians, as many believe, Ephesians might be dated a decade earlier. The closeness of the author to Paul's situation supports a date not long after the Apostle's death. The affinities between Colossians and Ephesians point to the latter's composition in the province of Asia.

AN OUTLINE OF THE LETTER TO THE EPHESIANS

A. Introduction, 1:1–2:10:
   1. The superscription, 1:1–2
   2. A doxology, proclaiming the purpose of God to unite all things in Christ, and the benefits of believers, 1:3–14
   3. A prayer for the reader's enlightenment, passing into praise of the greatness of God's power, 1:15–2:10
B. An exposition of the unity of men in Christ, 2:11–23:
   4. The former hopeless state of the Gentiles, 2:11–12
   5. The reconciliation of Jew and Gentile "in one body through the cross," 2:13–18
   6. The household of God, 2:19–23
C. The mystery of Christ made known to Paul, 3:1–13:
   7. The revelation mediated through the "holy apostles and prophets": the Gentiles are fellow heirs of the promise, 3:1–6
   8. The plan: the Church is to make known to the invisible powers "the manifold wisdom of God," 3:7–13
D. Paul's prayer is resumed; a doxology, 3:14–21:

---

[22] Mitton, *Ephesians*, pp. 41ff., 50f.

9. Prayer for the readers' fulfillment, 3:14-19
10. In praise of the divine power and glory, 3:20-21

E. Exhortations to unity, 4:1-6:9:

11. A call to consecration, 4:1-6
12. God's various gifts intended for the unity and maturity of the saints, 4:7-16
13. Their former lives contrasted with their new natures, 4:17-24
14. A description of Christian behavior as the opposite of pagan immoralities, 4:25-5:20: specific commands (4:25-5:2); light opposes darkness (5:3-14); a summary (5:15-20)
15. Mutual subordination in the household of God, 5:21-6:9: the relation of husbands and wives is that of Christ and his Church (5:21-33); children and parents (6:1-4); slaves and masters (6:5-9)

F. Christian warfare, 6:10-18:

16. Be strong in the Lord, 6:10
17. Put on the whole armor of God, 6:11-17
18. Pray at all times, 6:18a

G. Conclusion, 6:18b-24:

19. Appeal for supplications for the saints, and for the writer, 6:18b-20
20. Commendation of Tychicus, 6:21-22
21. Benediction, 6:23-24

The first three chapters of Ephesians are a meditation in praise of God, beginning and ending in prayer (A-D). The letter's introduction has been likened to the flight of an eagle "rising and wheeling round, as though for awhile uncertain what direction in his boundless freedom he shall take." Just so the thought of the writer of Ephesians "ranges this way and that in the realm of the spirit, marking out no clear course, but merely exulting in the attributes and purposes of God."[23] The conviction which gives a unity to the whole is that there is a predestined purpose working in history, and beyond it, toward some marvelous, all-embracing goal. Christ has revealed the mystery of the divine will. Through Christ and his Church, God is accomplishing an ultimate unity, the reintegration of every conflicting, disintegrative force in the universe (2). Does the writer envision that in the end the judgment of wrath will be set aside?[24]

In the thought of the writer, God "the Father" is the absolute prototype of all authority. God's sovereignty was not for him an abstract concept, but a personal relation: "the Father of our Lord Jesus Christ."[25] This apprehension of God as "the Father" is the ground for the writer's belief in the primordial and predestined unity of Creation. Yet his emphasis is not placed upon some speculative, ideal unity, but upon the revelation of God's will toward unity, and of His power to achieve it, in historical events: the resurrection of Christ, and the union of formerly hostile segments of mankind in a visible community (3).

[23]Robinson, *Ephesians*, p. 19.
[24]Eph. 2:3; 5:6. G. Johnston, *IDB*, vol. 2, p. 113. Cf. Rom. 2:3ff.; 5:9.
[25]Eph. 1:3, 17. Also 2:18; 3:14f.; 4:6; 5:20; 6:23.

Since Ephesians declares that the Church is the primary stage in the accomplishment of the unification of the universe, its teaching concerning the nature and role of the Church merits special consideration. Let us notice, first of all, the author's mystical conception of the Church as the necessary complement of Christ. As the head of the Church, Christ is its "fullness"; but the Church as his body brings to completion the purposes conceived by Christ.[26] It is in accord with this belief that the writer prays that the Church's membership may be "filled with all the fullness of God," and that the perfected life of the Church may express the totality of God's purpose revealed in Christ.[27] This purpose is to be fulfilled when all things are united in Christ, and to that end all things are tributary to him who is the head of the Church.[28]

This mystical conception of the relation of Christ to his Church is set forth also in the hortatory section of Ephesians.[29] The writer's ideal of Christian marriage was that husbands and wives should conceive of their relations to each other in the light of the archetypal union existing between Christ and his bride, the Church. Three relations are treated as analogous in this passage, and its meaning is therefore not easy to follow: husband-wife, Christ-Church, person-body. But the emphasis throughout is upon the realistic, coordinate union between Christ and the Church. The exclusiveness of the physical-spiritual union of husband and wife provides a profoundly significant symbol of the unity existing between members of Christ's body and of the subjection of the Church to Christ as Lord.

The transcendental significance of the Church is most clearly taught in the idea that "through the church the manifold wisdom of God" is being made known to "the principalities and powers in the heavenly places."[30] Once again in a New Testament writing we encounter the world of pre-Gnostic thought. It is difficult to understand how the formation of the Church could be conceived as having some unprecedented effect upon the world rulers. But the writer believed that the unity of Jew and Gentile in one body gave prescience of the ultimate unity of "all things," heretofore unknown to men or to the world of spirits.[31] To persons intimidated by the vastness of the universe, and cowed by a fear of fateful determinisms of all kinds, this faith and hope are relevant. To men oppressed by the seeming insignificance of the Church, and wavering in their loyalty to its purposes, this message is invigorating.

Nevertheless, the mystical and transcendental significance of the Church was not the principal interest of the writer of Ephesians. He was concerned chiefly to proclaim the importance of the Church as the *historical* agency purposed by God to reconcile man to man and to lift the spirit of man into communion with

---

[26] Eph. 2:22f.

[27] Eph. 3:19. Cf. Col. 1:18f.; 2:9.

[28] In Eph. 2:23 the choice lies between the active or passive voice of the present participle of the verb "to fill." The latter is preferable. In God's ordering of events, Christ's work is "being filled," or fulfilled.

[29] Eph. 5:21ff.

[30] Eph. 3:10. This preoccupation may account for the writer's lack of explicit missionary interest in, or compassion for, "the sons of disobedience," 2:2f.; 4:17ff.

[31] Eph. 3:4; 2:1f.

the divine.[32] Now that Jews and Gentiles had been made one, there was no limit to the power of Christ the Reconciler. Through him all men could find a basis for unity; through him they might "have access in one Spirit to the Father." A new human type had been created by God in Christ which was not determined by national, cultural, or racial factors. This new man was not "Jew" or "Gentile," but "Christian" (B).

For the writer and his readers the time of "the holy apostles and prophets" appears to have ended.[33] The Christian faith is now being transmitted by evangelists, pastors, and teachers.[34] The interest of Ephesians in these charismatic ministries of the church, and the absence of any reference to "bishops," in contrast with the Pastoral Letters, suggests a "pre-Catholic" origin for Ephesians, yet a setting in which there was a keen yearning for ecclesiastical unity.[35] The author, however, does not attack errorists directly; rather, in keeping with the approaches of the writers of the Pastorals and the Fourth Gospel, he opposes them "with the fascinating phenomenon of the *una sancta apostolica.*"[36] Prominent attention is given to Christian baptism in Ephesians, which is to be expected in a Pauline writing, but what explanation is there for silence concerning the Lord's Supper?

The following comments concern the admonitions which conclude Ephesians (E–F). Moral exhortation is found early in the letter, when the Paulinist's predestinarian theme is given somewhat curious expression: "created in Christ Jesus for good works, which God prepared beforehand that we should walk in them."[37] Once again, the readers are urged to conform the pattern of their lives to the holy purpose which the Church was intended to serve. They should be eager to maintain within their fellowship that unity which God willed for His Creation (11). Christ had provided the Church with the essential gifts for the attainment of this end (12).

The midrash in Ephesians 4:8ff. is connected with the thought of Paul in Colossians 2:15, but the pre-Gnostic view, that the rulers of the heavenly spheres are by nature evil, is not found in the Paulines.[38] The writer of Ephesians took a further step in the direction of the developed Gnostic systems when he wrote that the Reconciler descended through the heavenly places, and ascended through the same spheres leading "the host of captives."[39] Yet the purpose of "the gnosis

[32] Beare, *IB*, vol. 10, p. 607. The writer of Eph. is definitely interested in "the redemptive-historical anchorage of the church." E. Käsemann, "Ephesians and Acts," in Keck and Martyn, *Luke-Acts*, p. 291.

[33] Eph. 3:5.

[34] Eph. 4:11f.

[35] Eph. 4:3ff.

[36] Käsemann, note 32 above, p. 292.

[37] Eph. 2:10; 1:4, 12. "Good works" (pl.) is a phrase avoided by Paul.

[38] In Col. there is no harm in the invisible powers, provided men do not worship them; in Eph. they are "the spiritual hosts of wickedness." Eph. 6:11f.; 2:2.

[39] Eph. 4:8ff. Two R. C. scholars have recently sought to establish the influence upon the writer of pre-Gnostic Jewish thought and modes of expression, closely paralleling the Qumran texts. Murphy-O'Connor, *Paul and Qumran*, pp. 115ff. and 159ff.

of redemption" in Ephesians was not the enlightenment of individuals. Christ's gifts were provided for the achievement of the corporate unity of his Church, "for the building up of the body of Christ . . . in love."

After sharply contrasting pagan and Christian morality, the writer solemnly warned his readers against relapsing into their "former manner of life" (13–14). His references to "the unfruitful works of darkness" done "in secret," and to the deceivers, suggest that the temptation toward impurity and other forms of self-indulgence came from within the Church and not only from pagan society.[40]

The ethical section of Ephesians concludes with a brief table of household duties modeled upon the conventional pattern of moral teaching in the Hellenistic Age, but especially upon Colossians. Particular stress was placed upon the mutual subordination of husbands and wives because, as we have noted, the writer saw in marriage a profound symbol of the nature of the Church.

The familiar passage depicting the Christian warrior in full armor has been described as a sublimation of the apocalyptic image of the final conflict (F). The evil day is no longer the apocalyptic "tribulation," but the present time; Christ is no longer conceived as the One who shall destroy evil with the fiery breath of his mouth.[41] But the Christian life is depicted, as in the whole of the New Testament, as an unremitting warfare against evil, for which struggle all the resources of the gospel are needed.

Is it possible to describe more specifically the circumstances leading to the composition of Ephesians? Goodspeed's thesis (noted above) has many advocates: the chief purpose of Ephesians was to serve as a prefatory statement, a general introduction to Paul's gospel, on the occasion of a major collection of Paul's letters. The present writer believes that a specific situation in the church, rather than a literary intention, provides a more plausible circumstance for the writing of Ephesians. Its author was probably faced with an attitude among Gentile Christians which Paul had anticipated, but which developed into a crisis only in the postapostolic age.[42] The writer knew of Gentile Christians who were disparaging the Jewish past of the Church. This past was represented by Jewish–Christians, the remnant of the Israel of God in and through whom the Christian Church held continuity with the people of the old covenant and the eternal promises of God. The author of Ephesians, doubtless a Jewish Christian himself,[43] met this situation by emphasizing that the Church's Lord had reconciled, in one body, Jew and Gentile. This fact gave prescience of a final integration of "all things" in Christ, and hope for the emergence of a truly universal Church.[44]

---

[40]Note Eph. 5:3ff. Cf. 1 John 1:6; John 3:20f.

[41]Eph. 6:13. Cf. 5:15.

[42]Cf. Rom. 11:17ff., and Paul's repeated emphasis: "the Jew first but also the Greek."

[43]Eph. 2:3, 11, 17. Beare, *IB*, vol. 10, p. 607.

[44]Feine-Behm-Kümmel, *Intro.*, p. 257, who cite approvingly the thesis of H. Chadwick. Käsemann's interpretation is similar, but Conzelmann thinks that the controversy was acute when Paul wrote Rom. 9–11, and that the writer of Eph. views the situation theoretically and from a distance (Keck and Martyn, *Luke–Acts*, pp. 291, 307f., and 315, n. 99).

THE PASTORAL LETTERS

Three letters of the New Testament are called "the Pastorals"—1 and 2 Timothy, and Titus. The original contents of these writings explain the derivation of this description. They were composed by a "pastor," that is, by one who had the concerns of a shepherd or caretaker; and the letters are addressed to pastors and deal with their various duties. The term *Pastorals* is at least as old as the eighteenth century, and although its appropriateness has been questioned, especially with respect to 2 Timothy, no better common designation has been suggested.[45]

The primary problem facing the interpreter is whether or not Paul was the Pastor. From the late second century until modern times, the assumption was that Paul's appeal to Caesar resulted in his acquittal. After his release he resumed missionary work in the East, and wrote 1 Timothy and Titus. He was arrested again and brought back to Rome. During this second imprisonment, and shortly before martyrdom, Paul wrote 2 Timothy. A critical examination of the letters demonstrates that this tradition cannot any longer be maintained. A full statement of the case is not necessary to feel the cumulative weight of the evidence against Pauline authorship.

The Problem of the Pastorals

The Pastorals are missing from Marcion's collection of the Paulines and also from the earliest codex, Papyrus 46. This evidence can be interpreted in several ways and is therefore inconclusive. It is almost certain that there are allusions to the Pastorals in the writings of the Apostolic Fathers which establish their origin before Marcion's time. It is quite possible, however, that Marcion's New Testament did not contain these letters. Since the ending of the papyrus codex is lost, nothing can be established by its omission of the Pastorals.[46]

It is the internal evidence that is decisive. The vocabulary and style of the Pastorals reflect a marked difference from the indisputably genuine letters of Paul, and point to a postapostolic provenience. More than a third of the words in the Pastorals are non-Pauline, and many Pauline terms are used differently. There are also at least 170 words in the Pastorals which are not found elsewhere in the New Testament.[47] The significance of this linguistic data can be seen best when the doctrinal connotations of the vocabulary are studied.

---

[45]P. N. Harrison, *The Problem of the Pastoral Epistles* (1921), pp. 13ff. [hereafter, *Pastoral Epistles*].

[46]D. Guthrie, *The Pastoral Epistles* (1957), pp. 13f. C. K. Barrett, *The Pastoral Epistles* (1963), pp. 1ff.; R. M. Grant, *Intro.*, p. 209. Cf. J. Knox, *Marcion and the New Testament* (1942), pp. 40ff.; B. S. Easton, *The Pastoral Epistles* (1947), pp. 30ff.

[47]P. N. Harrison's study of the vocabulary is the most complete (*Pastoral Epistles*). His conclusions are summarized and evaluated by F. D. Gealy, *IB*, vol. 11, pp. 360ff; also, J. C. Beker, *IDB*, vol. 3, p. 670. Harrison's statistical methods have been challenged, but his principal conclusions are widely accepted. See K. Grayston and G. Herdan, "The Authorship of the Pastorals in the Light of Statistical Linguistics," *NTS* 6 (1959): 1ff. Feine-Behm-Kümmel, *Intro.*, pp. 262ff. Cf. Guthrie, *Pastoral Epistles*, pp. 212ff., J. N. D. Kelly, *The Pastoral Epistles* (1963), pp. 21ff.

A consideration of the personal allusions in the Pastorals, and of the historical framework of the letters, reveals other aspects of the problem. The following passages should be noted: 1 Timothy 1:3; Titus 1:5 and 3:12; and 2 Timothy 1:8, 15ff., and 4:9ff. Although these passages have suggested the origin of the letters during Paul's imprisonments at Ephesus or at Caesarea, they demand the tradition of the Apostle's release and second Roman imprisonment if written by Paul.[48] Yet this assumption is not free of difficulties, even when all other elements in the problem are set aside. Is it conceivable that Paul should have urged Timothy to remain at Ephesus, and carefully instructed him concerning his mission there, and then commanded him to come to him at Rome? Again, Timothy is said to have witnessed Paul's sufferings at Antioch, Iconium, and Lystra, all of which occurred before Timothy became Paul's associate. If the personalia in the Pastorals are historical, it is more probable that the Pastor incorporated fragments of Paul's correspondence concerning events within the period covered by Acts. The "fragment hypothesis" will receive further notice below.

The theological outlook of the Pastor is an important element in the problem. Beyond question, some of Paul's distinctive teaching is set forth in the Pastorals, and the Apostle's gospel is the norm of "sound doctrine." But, as E. F. Scott has written, this manifest desire of the writer to think like Paul makes more significant his failure to understand several of Paul's key doctrines. "He does not know what Paul meant by the Law; he confuses Pauline faith with loyalty to a Church tradition; he forgets the central value which Paul attached to the Cross; he has nothing to say of the conflict between the flesh and Spirit; his thought is quite untouched by the Pauline mysticism."[49]

The Pastor's portrayal of the Christian's life as a life of "piety" is often contrasted with Paul's delineation of the moral qualities of the life "in Christ." "The assertion that the Pastorals contain a moralized version of Paulinism is not without foundation."[50] For Paul, "righteousness," as it pertained to the individual, denoted his new status or relation vis-a-vis God; "righteousness" in the Pastorals refers to a person's uprightness, his moral respectability, we might say. Is it possible that Paul should have laid stress upon the value of "good works" which sometimes appear in the Pastorals as ends in themselves?[51] Modern writers have referred to the "bourgeois" morality of the Pastorals. Words rarely used by Paul illustrate the appropriateness of this description, at least as a tendency: "sobriety," "a godly life," a "good conscience," are set forth as identifying marks of the Christian.

---

[48] Duncan, *St. Paul's Ephesian Ministry*, pp. 184ff. Cf. P. N. Harrison, "The Pastoral Epistles and Duncan's Ephesian Theory," NTS 2 (1956), and Duncan's reply, NTS, 3 (1957): 250ff. and 211ff. Cf also, Kelly, *Pastoral Epistles*, pp. 6ff., and Barrett, *Pastoral Epistles*, pp. 7ff. For difficulties inherent in the tradition of Paul's release, resumption of missions in the East, and second Roman imprisonment, see Feine-Behm-Kümmel, *Intro.*, pp. 265f.

[49] E. F. Scott, *The Pastoral Epistles* (1937), p. xxi. See the important discussion in Easton, *Pastoral Epistles*, pp. 22ff. The rejoinders of Guthrie, *Pastoral Epistles*, pp. 38ff., and of Kelly, *Pastoral Epistles*, pp. 16ff., are not persuasive.

[50] C. K. Barrett, *Pastoral Epistles*, pp. 25f.

[51] 1 Tim. 2:10; Tit. 2:14; cf. 1 Tim. 1:5.

It appears that in settling down in the world, churches Christianized some of the secular virtues.[52]

Another element in the problem is the Church situation reflected in the Pastorals. The leaders of the earliest churches, "the apostles, prophets, teachers," have been succeeded by the bishop and elders or by the elder-bishops—the point is debatable—and by the deacons. Moreover, the positions of "Timothy" and "Titus," and the prerogatives given them through their ordination by elders, suggest that they were bishops even though the title is not used. Probably the Pastor wished to avoid too glaring an anachronism in letters from "Paul" to his colleagues.[53] At any rate, the status which is held by "Timothy" and "Titus" is superior to the "elders" whom they appoint, supervise, and discipline. If "Timothy" and "Titus" were (monarchical?) bishops, then it follows that the Pastor himself assumed prerogatives later held by archibishops or the metropolitans. The form of the letters led him to employ the functional title *apostle*.[54] Since the term *bishop* is used invariably by the Pastor in the singular (the terms *elder* and *deacon* always in the plural) it may have been taken for granted that the monarchical episcopacy was the order in his churches. But as the Pastor was more interested in seeking qualified men than in justifying a particular type of ministry, we cannot be sure.

A survey of the contents of the letters reveals the extent to which the Pastor was preoccupied with attacking false teachings. But the only way he could cope with the situation was to contradict, denounce, and ridicule. Unlike Paul, who in Colossians offered a creative interpretation of the gospel to refute the distortions of pre-Gnostic speculations and asceticism, the Pastor resorted only to name-calling, and appealed to "the truth," "the good teaching," and the like.[55] His conservative mentality is shown in his concern that the deposit of faith be guarded. All in all, he represents a very different spirit from that revealed in the nine Paulines. Whether or not Ephesians was written by Paul, it is in every respect worthy of the Apostle. The same cannot be said of the Pastorals. Yet like the writer of Ephesians, the Pastor commended Paul to his churches as the great exemplar of Christianity, and in this he rendered a service of inestimable value.

The conclusion seems to be irresistible: 1 and 2 Timothy, and Titus, were written by a Paulinist who is known to us only through his letters. It is a safe surmise that he was a convert from Hellenistic Judaism and that, by the time of his writings, he held a position of eminence in the Pauline churches of Asia Minor.[56] There is no difficulty in the view that the Pastor chose to write under the pseudonym of "Paul." He was "fighting the good fight" in the Apostle's name. The only

[52]J. C. Beker, *IDB*, vol. 3, p. 675; Feine-Behm-Kümmel, *Intro.*, pp. 270f.

[53]Easton, *Pastoral Epistles*, p. 177.

[54]Gealy, *IB*, vol. 11, pp. 344f. Cf. Feine-Behm-Kümmel, *Intro.*, pp. 268f., who question the validity of this identification with a later office.

[55]1 Tim. 1:19; 3:9; 4:1; 2 Tim. 3:8; 4:7; Tit. 1:13. Also 1 Tim. 3:15; 4:3; 2 Tim. 2:15, 18; Tit. 1:14.

[56]See the interesting but unconvincing hypothesis that Luke was the framer of the Pastorals during Paul's last years, at the Apostle's behest and uncorrected by him: C. F. D. Moule, "The Problem of the Pastoral Epistles," *BJRL* 47 (1965): 430ff.

difficulty in the theory of pseudonymity concerns the Pauline personalia. Notice has been taken of the view that the Pastor built up his letters from fragments of the Apostle's personal correspondence with colleagues. This is an attractive but fanciful hypothesis.[57] The problem concerning the personalia is literary and historical, not moral. No agreement as to the identification or origin of "precious fragments" has been reached, and perhaps never will be. What "rings true" to one reader seems obvious "fiction" to another.[58] The significance of the matter can easily be exaggerated. In any event, the teaching of the letters is not by Paul but by a Paulinist.

The Date and Mutual Relation of the Pastorals

Although Titus stands after the two Timothys in the New Testament, this does not mean that it was written last. Those who hold that Paul wrote the letters in their entirety agree upon the following order: 1 Timothy—Titus—2 Timothy. Since there is no reference to persecution in 1 Timothy or Titus, they are usually dated before the winter of A.D. 64; 2 Timothy within the year.[59]

No agreement concerning the order and dates of the Pastorals has been reached among those who reject Pauline authorship. Many would reverse the position of the Timothys since, it is said, the opposition to the false teachers becomes progressively more intense as one reads 2 Timothy, then Titus, and then 1 Timothy. Following this sequence a development in Church organization has been detected, and a progressive lessening of interest in personal data concerning Paul.[60] But other readers have questioned the validity of these reasons, and observed the dramatic fitness of 2 Timothy as the concluding letter in the group.[61]

The dates of the three letters are determined chiefly by decisions concerning the so-called parallels in the writings of the Apostolic Fathers, and by the identification of the schismatic teaching which the Pastor opposed. The type of Church organization also has been used as a clue, some persons placing the Pastorals before, others after, the Letters of Ignatius (ca. A.D. 110). A choice lies between dating them within a decade on either side of A.D. 100, or later in the second century. The earlier dating is more probable than a date as late as A.D. 150, as conclusive evidence is lacking that the Pastorals were anti-Marcionite documents.[62] If dependency upon the Pastorals by Polycarp is supported by a study of his letter(s), then the Pastorals can hardly be dated after A.D. 125.

Interpretation of the Pastoral Letters

We shall follow here the order: 1 Timothy—Titus—2 Timothy.

[57] See Barrett, *Pastoral Epistles*, pp. 10f.; C. F. D. Moule, note 56 above, pp. 433f.

[58] See Moffatt, *Intro.*, pp. 403f.; Harrison, *Pastoral Epistles*, pp. 93ff.; C. A. A. Scott, *Christianity According to St. Paul*, pp. xxii f., 135ff. Guthrie, *Pastoral Epistles*, pp. 21ff. Cf. Enslin, *Beginnings*, pp. 306f.; Goodspeed, *Intro.*, pp. 340f.

[59] Gealy, *IB*, vol. 11, pp. 368ff.

[60] Easton, *Pastoral Epistles*, pp. 17ff. Moffatt, Goguel, and Harrison are also supporters of this order.

[61] E.g., the German scholars Dibelius and Jülicher.

[62] See below, p. 511; Gealy, *IB*, vol. 11, pp. 368f.; also 358ff.

An Outline of the First Letter of Paul to Timothy[63]

A. Introduction, 1:1–17:
1. The superscription, 1:1–2
2. The purpose of Timothy's ministry at Ephesus, 1:3–11
3. Thanksgiving for the grace of Christ toward Paul; the Apostle's witness; a doxology, 1:12–17
B. The charge to Timothy, 1:18–6:19:
4. Timothy's faith and good conscience contrasted with the attitudes of two other men, 1:18–20
5. Instructions concerning public prayers, 2:1–8
6. The demeanor of women at worship, 2:9–15
7. The qualifications of a bishop, 3:1–7
8. The qualifications of deacons, 3:8–13
9. The character of the Church, 3:14–16
10. Warnings against the ascetic "doctrines of demons," 4:1–5
11. The training and example of the "good minister of Christ Jesus," 4:6–16
12. Conduct toward persons of different ages and sexes, 5:1–2
13. Instructions concerning widows, 5:3–16
14. The remuneration, discipline, and selection of elders, 5:17–22
15. A caution against abstinence; proverbial sayings, 5:23–25
16. The behavior of a Christian slave, 6:1–2b
17. In identifying the marks of false teachers, the Pastor comments upon the perils of wealth, 6:2c–10
18. A charge to the "man of God," ending in an ascription of praise, 6:11–16
19. A warning to the rich leads to a description of true wealth, 6:17–19
C. Conclusion, 6:20–21:
20. A final appeal, 6:20–21a
21. A grace, 6:21b

Several features of the superscription of 1 Timothy imply non-Pauline authorship. The formal greeting would be odd if addressed by Paul to his intimate disciple. But as the introduction to a charge from a bishop to younger subordinates, the address is thoroughly appropriate. The words *God our Savior* are not paralleled in the main Paulines, and reflect the language of the postapostolic Church.[64]

The letter's first paragraph clearly reveals the Pastor's purpose (2). The Pauline gospel was being perverted by persons occupying themselves with "myths and endless genealogies," and claiming to be "teachers of the law." That this mythical speculation was of Jewish origin is explicitly stated in the Letter to Titus.[65] Some consider that the reference was to second-century Gnostic teaching concerning the emanations which proceed from God. But it is more probable that the Pastor scorned pre-Gnostic Jewish speculations involving a mystical or allegorical

---

[63]Cf. the suggestive outlines of the Pastorals proposed by J. C. Beker, *IDB*, vol. 3, p. 672, which emphasize their dominant themes: "the disruptive influences of the heretics, and efforts toward consolidating the church in opposition to heretics."

[64]Gealy, *IB*, vol. 11, pp. 377f.; Easton, *Pastoral Epistles*, p. 108.

[65]Tit. 1:14; 3:9. Note also 1:10.

interpretation of narrative portions of the Torah.[66] It is difficult to imagine Paul writing that the Law was not given for "the just" but only for "the ungodly and profane." Yet the Pastor's insistence reveals that a new type of ascetic legalism had arisen. He was confident that if Paul were living he would vigorously oppose it.

In the references to Paul which follow, one sees why the Pastor wrote in his name (3). For him, Paul was the foremost exponent of the Christian tradition. The saying in verse 15 is not an expression of Paul's, yet the Apostle surely would have approved his follower's impression of his witness.

Before proceeding to the particulars of his "charge," the Pastor stated the credentials of the ideal type of Church leader for the second generation (4). The apostles and prophets had selected promising men who had been ordained by the elders. The contrasting apostate leaders served as a warning to the faithless and erring. It is noteworthy that the power of excommunication was not delegated to "Timothy." As observed in the previous chapter, the postapostolic Church was loath to exercise such drastic discipline.

Because of the next paragraphs, and others like them, the Pastorals have been called "primitive church manuals with particular reference to church officers."[67] This description does not cover their contents nor suggest their principal interest. Yet the Pastorals contain some instructions regarding public worship, the qualifications (but not the specific functions) of church officers, and of other special groups within the Church, such as widows and slaves. "Timothy" was addressed as one in charge of public worship and he was told for whom, and in what manner, prayer was to be offered (5).

Paul restricted the freedom of women in public worship, even though he insisted upon their equality "in Christ."[68] The Pastor believed that women were disqualified from all public leadership (6). This was not an expediency, but the order of creation. By nature women were transgressors, easily deceived, and the young ones, especially, were too garrulous.[69] In the selection of widows for orders, strict standards of selection were enjoined.[70]

The Pastor took for granted that "Timothy" knew the status and functions of the bishop, the elders, and the deacons (7–8, 14). His concern was that only those persons be selected who had proven their moral stability, and who conformed to conventional standards of piety.[71] Also the officers must have no conscientious doubts concerning "the faith."[72] In the midst of this counsel relating to church officers, the Pastor gave his reasons for his concern. They may be summarized as follows: The Church must be ordered in its corporate life, not because this is an end in itself, but because it is "the pillar and bulwark of the truth" (9).

---

[66]McNeile, *Intro.*, p. 191; R. McL. Wilson, *Gnosis*, pp. 41ff. Cf. Easton, *Pastoral Epistles*, pp. 112ff.
[67]Enslin, *Beginnings*, p. 302.
[68]1 Cor. 14:32ff.; Gal. 3:28.
[69]Cf. 2 Tim. 3:6; 1 Tim. 5:11ff.
[70]1 Tim. 3:11; 5:9ff.
[71]Note this prior concern, 1 Tim. 3:3ff.; 8:12f.; 5:9f. Cf. Tit. 1:7f.
[72]1 Tim. 3:6, 9. Cf. Tit. 1:9; 2 Tim. 2:24.

The Church's purpose for being is to confess the mystery of Christ's Lordship over heaven and earth. (This is emphasized by the inclusion of a liturgical fragment.[73]) But the Church exists also as a defense and a security against destructive doctrine (10).

The Pastor did not for long refrain from attacking the false teachers. We are now informed that they advocated a rigorous asceticism. Paul counseled tolerance of "the weak" who held ascetic views concerning marriage and matters of diet. The Pastor allowed no such toleration. Even "Timothy" was not free to associate spiritual discipline with "the training table," not free to be a "teetotaler." [74] The pre-Gnostic notion that the "fleshly" appetites invariably were evil put the issue of asceticism for religious motives in a new context. If Paul had lived in these "later times," when the imminence of the End was no longer expected, would he have affirmed, without qualification, the positive value of life in this Age?[75] The Pastor thought so, provided Christians remained chaste, temperate, and void of greed, especially in money matters, and fulfilled their station in life and its duties.

The concluding appeal provides the most direct justification for describing as pre-Gnostic the teaching opposed by the Pastor (20). His antagonists laid claim to a *gnosis*. Some scholars have detected a reference in this passage to a lost book called "the Antitheses" which was written by Marcion and dealt with the "contradictions" between the Law and the gospel. But this is a slim basis for dating 1 Timothy around A.D. 150 or later. Throughout the letters the author displays a temperamental distaste for argument. One of the things that distressed him most was that the schismatics had "a morbid craving for controversy." [76]

An Outline of the Letter of Paul to Titus

A. Introduction, 1:1–4:
   1. The superscription containing a statement concerning Paul's credentials, 1:1–4a
   2. A grace, 1:4b
B. The purpose and conduct of Titus' ministry in Crete, 1:5–2:15:
   3. A recollection of the Apostle's instructions, with special reference to elders and the bishop, 1:5–9
   4. The activities and reputation of the Cretan false teachers, 1:10–16
   5. Regulations concerning the conduct of the minister and the congregation, 2:1–10

[73] This confession reflects other postapostolic writings. Cf. John 1:14; 3:13f.; 6:62f.; 16:28; 1 Pet. 3:18; Heb. 1:14ff. The first two lines present a theme similar to Rom. 1:3f.; however, the proclamation of the cosmic rule of Christ more nearly approximates Phil. 2:9ff., though it may represent a further development (Schweizer, *Lordship*, pp. 64ff.).

[74] 1 Tim. 5:3.

[75] Cf. the advice of the Pastor and of Paul concerning young widows, 1 Tim. 5:14; 1 Cor. 7:8f., 39f.

[76] 1 Tim. 6:3ff.

6. The training and behavior of persons who have seen manifested "the grace of God," 2:11–14
7. Summary concerning the general functions and status of Titus, 2:15
C. Christian conduct in a pagan society, 3:1–8a:
8. The Christian witness in the community, 3:1–2
9. Contrast between the Christians' former paganism and their present standing and future hope, 3:3–8a
D. Conclusion, 3:8b–15:
10. Good deeds attest sound doctrine; the lives of false teachers are "unprofitable and futile," 3:8b–9
11. A rule concerning the treatment of factious men, 3:10–11
12. Personal services requested, 3:12–13
13. The importance of "good deeds" stressed again, 3:14
14. Greetings and a grace, 3:15

The shortest of the Pastorals has the longest salutation. Its formal, liturgical character is incongruous in a personal letter. It reveals the Pastor's conception of his own ministry. He was entrusted with the apostolic *kerygma*. His right to command was given by the supreme commander (1). From the beginning the special emphasis of this letter is upon the inseparability of knowledge of the truth and true piety.

The author makes no effort to relate his addressee to the Titus of Paul's letters. It is profitless to seek a historical setting for the Cretan mission.[77] The ministry of "Titus" is a type of the successor to the apostles in any church: the work of the apostles was to be restored wherever deterioration had set in, and the Church was to be provided a qualified ministry (3).

The Pastor's contempt for "Cretans" and his refusal to counsel patience in dealing with them (4) may be compared with Paul's failure to castigate all Corinthians as sensuous merely because of their popular reputation. The writer's source of the generalization concerning Cretans was a popular tag attributed to Epimenides (ca. 500 B.C.), but the origin is uncertain of the proverb, "to the pure all things are pure. . . ."[78] Under the influence of pre-Gnostic ideas, the false teachers may have claimed that no action could defile those who had been enlightened, and the Pastor may have referred to their dictum in irony.

The instructions to Titus concerning various groups within the Church resemble closely those given in 1 Timothy (5–7). The rulings echo Paul's counsel, conditioned by the conventional moralism of the age, and introduce the distinctively Christian sanction for complete fidelity. The epithet "our great God and Savior Jesus Christ" drew the notice of early scribes of the letter, and it has continued to provoke theological discussion. The Pastor's ordinary practice was to write "God the Savior," and to refer separately to Christ.[79] Have we here an expression

[77] Gealy, *IB*, vol. 11, p. 525. Cf. Guthrie, *Pastoral Epistles*, pp. 183f.
[78] Cf. the saying of Jesus, Mark 7:14, cited by Paul, Rom. 14:14. Easton, *Pastoral Epistles*, p. 89.
[79] Cf. Tit. 1:3.f.; 2:10; 3:4, 6; 1 Tim. 1:1; 2:3; 4:10; 2 Tim. 1:9f. Also Jude 5; Luke 1:47.

framed, in the worship of the Church, as a reaction to the liturgies of the emperor cult and mystery religions?

Like Paul, the Pastor wrote concerning the moral responsibilities of Christians in a pagan society. Like Paul, he called his readers to a deepened appreciation of "the grace of God," and of the character of their new life and eternal hope, by reminding them of their former situation apart from faith in the gospel.[80] But the idea that by God's grace men are "trained to renounce" godless ways is not found in Paul. "In Paul grace is not educative but liberating": by it men are set free from "worldly passions."[81] Also, unlike Paul, the Pastor conceived of salvation as a past event, although still a matter of hope; and baptism as "the washing of regeneration" (C). This entire passage is instructive, as evidence of early Paulinism giving place to the theology of the later catholic Church.[82]

Titus ends on a note which dominates the Letter of James: true faith is known by its works, not its words. The times demanded this emphasis (10, 13).

An Outline of the Second Letter of Paul to Timothy

A. Introduction, 1:1–18:
    1. The superscription, 1:1–2
    2. A thanksgiving recalling Timothy's heritage, Paul's testimony and suffering; and containing an encouragement to Timothy, 1:3–14
    3. Some experiences of Paul in Asia, 1:15–18
B. The charge to Timothy, 2:1–4:5:
    4. Various analogies depicting the calling of the Church leader, 2:1–7
    5. Paul's gospel and personal witness recalled, 2:8–13
    6. Things to do and things to avoid, with special reference to promoters of controversy, 2:14–3:9
    7. Another reminder of Paul's life and persecutions, 3:10–13
    8. Another reminder of Timothy's heritage, especially his long acquaintance with the scripture, 3:14–17
    9. A summary of the charge emphasizing steadfastness, 4:1–5
C. Paul's farewell, 4:6–22:
    10. The reward of faithfulness: "the crown of righteousness," 4:6–8
    11. Paul's situation; personal requests; a statement of confidence ending in a doxology, 4:9–18
    12. Greetings and an urgent request, 4:19–21
    13. Benediction, 4:22

At its beginning 2 Timothy more closely corresponds in form to Paul's letters than do 1 Timothy and Titus (1–2). Yet the Pastor's vocabulary reveals striking differences.[83] Moreover, the bases upon which the addressee was given encour-

---

[80] Cf. 1 Cor. 6:11; Col. 1:21ff. (Eph. 2:11ff.).
[81] Barrett, *Pastoral Epistles*, p. 137. Cf. Tit. 2:11f.; Rom. 6:15ff.
[82] Note the implicit trinitarian teaching. C. A. A. Scott, *Christianity According to St. Paul*, pp. 175ff.
[83] Gealy, *IB*, vol. 11, pp. 460ff.

agement suggest that "Timothy" typified the leadership of a later generation (the third?). He is summoned to be loyal to a faith which was not new in his time. It was an established "pattern of sound words," espoused by his family, by the great Apostle Paul, and tested by much suffering. As Timothy had been properly ordained, he could expect the powerful guidance of the Holy Spirit.

Loyalty to the gospel of the martyred Apostle is the keynote of 2 Timothy. Various teachings of the Apostle are utilized by the Pastor, but in his summary of the effect of "the appearing of our Savior Christ Jesus," there is reflected the language generally used by the Hellenistic church in its worship.[84]

The allusions to the widespread defections from Paul in Asia, with the notable exception of "the household of Onesiphorus," constitute a problem for interpreters, whether or not Pauline authorship is claimed (3). Assuming that the writer was a Paulinist, the reference may have been to his own experiences in prison. Or the Pastor may have pictured the loneliness and repudiation, which Paul was known to have suffered, in order to enforce his appeal. Timothy was entrusted with a gospel that had been valiantly defended. Thus Timothy should expect his "share of suffering" and, to fulfill his ministry, devote himself to his calling as Paul had. He must not weaken, however hard the struggle. Above all, he must "remember Jesus Christ . . ." and the promises of the *kerygma* confessed by the Church. Paul's witness led men to his Lord (5).

The reference to Hymenaeus and Philetus as men who held that "the resurrection is past already" is intriguing.[85] Were these schismatics denying the Church's proclamation concerning the general resurrection, and teaching that faith and baptismal regeneration directly mediated the new life of eternity? The realistic future eschatology of "the faith" must not be abandoned.

It is somewhat surprising to find in the Pastorals the following injunction: "the Lord's servant must not be quarrelsome, but kindly to everyone, an apt teacher, forbearing, correcting his opponents with gentleness."[86] Should we conclude that the writer was not able to follow the counsel he gave others? Perhaps a distinction was made between the treatment of various types of opponents. In dealing with those errorists who threatened the survival of the Church and its gospel, the Pastor followed the mores of his time and attacked them in much the same way the popular philosophical schools denounced one another, ascribing all the vices of contemporary society to them.[87]

The warnings in 2 Timothy concerning the rebellion "in the last days" superficially resemble a passage in 2 Thessalonians, and those in other Christian writings, concerning the tribulation preceding the End.[88] But the apocalyptic ideas have been significantly transformed. According to the Pastor, the "rebellion" had already begun. The future tense of apocalyptic prediction—the literary device of pseudonymity to describe post-Pauline conditions—was not consistently retained.

[84]Easton, *Pastoral Epistles*, pp. 40f.; Scott, *Christianity According to St. Paul*, pp. 93ff.
[85]2 Tim. 2:16ff.
[86]2 Tim. 2:24.
[87]2 Tim. 2:16; 3:2ff., J. C. Beker, *IDB*, vol. 3, p. 672.
[88]2 Tim. 3:1ff. Cf. 2 Thess. 2:1ff.; Mark 13; Acts 2:17ff.

Nor was the exposure of corruption thought to be coincident with the coming of Christ as judge. It was the triumph of orthodoxy over "counterfeit faith." Even when the Pastor warned that "evil men and imposters would go on from bad to worse," there was no reference to signs of the End. The only antidote to this distressing prospect was that the faithful, under the leadership of "Timothys" who followed the example of the Apostle, would continue in what they "have learned and have firmly believed." They would find in inspired scripture their equipment "for every good work" (7–8).

The need for steadfastness did recall the advent hope of the Church. But the Pastor's charge pointed backward to the ordination liturgy, rather than forward to a fearsome, imminent event (9).

Readers will not agree concerning the letter's farewell (10). Some will say that Paul certainly wrote it. Others will consider this incredible, and say that it is the Pastor's loving tribute to his hero. In either case, these celebrated words are no less impressive, as a reminder of Paul's greatness and of the contagion of his hope.

The personalia which bring the letter to a close are somewhat anticlimactic (11–12). Many readers are convinced that the Pastor has tacked onto his writing a precious fragment of a letter written by Paul on the eve of his martyrdom. There is no completely satisfactory explanation for the origin of this passage. But the preoccupation of "Paul" with his own discomforts, and with the deceitfulness of men, does not conclude the letter. The last word is the witness of hope and praise.

chapter twenty

FIVE "OPEN LETTERS"
TO CHRISTIANS

The Roman Colosseum, famous public work of, and monument to, the Flavian emperors. (ENIT)

517

Sestertius of Trajan (98–117 A.D.): Emperor's head on the obverse; reclining figure on the reverse is a river god, probably celebrating Trajan's improvement of Rome's water supply. (The Chase Manhattan Bank Money Museum)

Marble bust of the emperor Trajan. Much of Trajan's reign was spent in defensive warfare and conquest, and in coping with provincial mismanagement. Pliny's letters to Trajan describe the situation in Bithynia and, in one, he reports on Christians in this province. (British Museum)

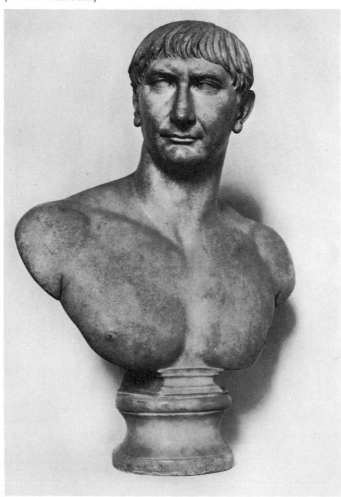

The letter to the Hebrews: Third or fourth century Greek papyrus, showing text of Hebrews 12:1–11 (col. 68) of ms. (British Museum)

F ROM the early fourth century to the present time, seven letters of the New Testament have been known as "General (or Catholic) Epistles": James, 1 and 2 Peter, 1, 2, and 3 John, and Jude. This description identifies writings intended for the whole Church, or at least for large groups of Christians in various places. The "open letter" may be suggested as a modern equivalent for the ancient "Catholic epistle."[1]

Only four of the General Letters will be discussed in this chapter. The three Letters of John will be considered in the next, along with another writing from "the Johannine circle." But to the four brief writings which remain a longer one shall be added, the Letter to the Hebrews. For many centuries Hebrews was included in the Pauline corpus. It was assumed that the Apostle was its author. But the writing does not profess to be by Paul, and it is certain as any conclusion drawn from the internal evidence can be that Paul did not write it. Hebrews has sometimes been called a "general letter," and so it is appropriate to include it here. In many respects, however, Hebrews is a unique document.

There is no satisfactory arrangement of the General Letters along chronological lines, and Hebrews has been dated as early as A.D. 60 or as late as 110. If priority is given the most important of the books under consideration, there can be no doubt that 1 Peter and Hebrews should be discussed first.

THE FIRST LETTER OF PETER

The general character and purpose of this little book can be briefly stated. It is an open letter ostensibly addressed to the Christians residing in five provinces of Asia Minor who were being disturbed by the unwelcome attentions of government officials and by the scorn and abuse of their non-Christian neighbors. The purpose of the writer was to recall to his readers the resources of the Christian gospel and to rally their courage and hope. The result was that the whole Church received a very appealing and beautiful book as a priceless legacy. It is easy to see why 1 Peter is a favorite among Christians today. As one commentator observes, "this gallant and high-hearted exhortation breathes a spirit of undaunted courage and exhibits as noble a type of piety as can be found in any writing of the New Testament outside the gospels."[2]

The letter was composed in Peter's name. "Silvanus," called by the author "a

---

[1] Enslin, *Beginnings*, pp. 317f., shows that "catholic epistles" was used also as a synonym for canonical writings.

[2] J. W. C. Wand, *The General Epistles of St. Peter and St. Jude* (1934), p. 1.

faithful brother," seems to have had some part in writing or delivering the letter.[3] A cursory examination of the content of 1 Peter may lead to the conclusion that no outstanding critical problems are found in it. But this is not the case. The letter has given rise to a series of vexing questions concerning which there have been strong differences of opinion.

The Authorship of the Letter

By the time the word *canonical* was applied to Christian writings, 1 Peter held an undisputed place on the list.[4] There is, however, less evidence for its use in the Church of the West than for its use in that of the East. In his writing "Against Heresies," Irenaeus introduced a quotation from 1 Peter with the formula, "Peter says in his epistle, 'whom though you see him not. . . .'"[5] Eusebius, who noticed its use by Irenaeus, reported also that Papias knew Peter's "former epistle."[6]

In writings of the Church before A.D. 150 there are no references to a letter written by Peter. But many scholars have detected allusions to 1 Peter in Polycarp's Letter to the Philippians, bearing out a statement by Eusebius that this apostolic father had used it.[7] A few persons claim that Clement, Barnabas, and Hermas knew 1 Peter, but the evidence is inconclusive. There are possibly echoes of 1 Peter in "the Gospel of Truth," recently discovered at Nag–Hammadi and attributed to Valentinus before A.D. 145. The New Testament letter 2 Peter refers to the existence of an earlier letter bearing Peter's name, but the date of 2 Peter is not certain.[8]

The traditional attribution of 1 Peter to the disciple of Jesus has been seriously challenged in modern times because of evidence in the letter which seems to discredit it. First of all, 1 Peter was written "in fluent and idiomatic Greek, much better than that of Paul, and the Biblical quotations show an intimate knowledge of the Septuagint."[9] This is hard to tally with the view that an "uneducated," Aramaic-speaking Galilean fisherman wrote it. In the second place, it is said that the letter discloses the writer's dependence upon Paul. Not only does he reflect Paul's ideas, he seems to depend on some of the collected letters of the Apostle, certainly Romans and probably Ephesians.[10]

A third objection to Petrine authorship arises out of the conviction that the

[3]1 Pet. 5:12.

[4]The absence of 1 Pet. in the Muratorian Canon is no exception. The extant text of this list is fragmentary.

[5]*Adv. Haer.*, IV. ix. 2. Also V. vii. 2.

[6]*H. E.*, III. 39. 17.

[7]Ibid., IV. 14.

[8]See below, pp. 543f. For an evaluation of the use of 1 Pet. in the ancient Church, see McNeile, *Intro.*, pp. 335ff.; W. C. van Unnik, "First Letter of Peter," *IDB*, vol. 3, pp. 760f.

[9]Heard, *Intro.*, p. 169; F. W. Beare, *The First Epistle of Peter* (2d ed., rev., 1958), pp. 25ff. [hereafter *1 Peter*].

[10]W. Sanday and A. C. Headlam, *The Epistle to the Romans* (5th ed., 1902), pp. lxxiv ff.; C. L. Mitton, "The Relationship between 1 Peter and Ephesians," *JTS* I, n.s. (1950): 67ff.; Goodspeed, *Intro.*, pp. 273f.

letter lacks the personal quality one would expect if written by an intimate disciple of Jesus. Unlike the Apostle, the writer of 1 Peter is said to be self-effacing to the point of being colorless.[11] A fourth objection relates to the historical situation implied by several statements in 1 Peter, but especially in the following: ". . . if one suffers as a Christian, let him not be ashamed, but under that name let him glorify God."[12] As we have seen, there is no direct evidence that the mere confession of the name constituted a crime against the state until the time of Trajan. Pliny's letter to the emperor, sent from one of the provinces to which 1 Peter was addressed, has been considered by many scholars crucial evidence for a second-century dating of the letter.[13]

Furthermore, it should be noted that some critics judge that the form and the tone of 1 Peter reflect developments more compatible with the postapostolic age than with Peter's lifetime. Form critical studies have identified the principal contents of 1 Peter as a traditional charge and instructions given converts at the time of their baptism.[14] The tone of the letter is said to reflect a "central" churchmanship and theological conceptions which had not developed during Peter's time.[15]

Such formidable objections as these cannot be dismissed lightly. But some defenders of the tradition believe that several of the real difficulties have been exaggerated, that some of the objections have no validity, and that other important evidence has been overlooked. With regard to the letter's excellent Greek, many admit that if one must claim that Peter wrote without help, the tradition would have to be abandoned. But the author of 1 Peter explicitly says "by Silvanus . . . I have written briefly to you."

The Silvanus hypothesis may be used to remove other objections. In all probability, Peter's amanuensis was the same Silvanus named with Paul and Timothy as a writer of the letters to the Thessalonians, and called "Silas" in Acts. Thus the "Paulinism" of 1 Peter can be explained. Recognizing his own unfamiliarity with the language of his readers and placing confidence in his experienced helper, the Apostle gave Silvanus considerable freedom and scope in interpreting the gist of his own ideas. It is more probable that the Pauline language, so-called, represents only a common theological heritage.[16]

The third objection is often flatly denied. Readers are directed to passages in 1 Peter which allude to events from Jesus' life and to his teachings.[17] It is evident that this criterion of authorship is subjective. Do such references to the Ministry as the letter contains imply intimate acquaintance with Jesus, or with the traditions of the Church concerning him? One may observe that opposite conclusions

[11]McNeile, *Intro.*, p. 216; M. Dibelius, *A Fresh Approach to the New Testament and Early Christian Literature* (1936), pp. 24f.

[12]1 Pet. 4:15; also 5:8f.

[13]Beare, *1 Peter*, pp. 13ff.

[14]See further, below, pp. 525f.

[15]Beare, *1 Peter*, pp. 16ff., 31ff.

[16]E. G. Selwyn, *The First Epistle of St. Peter* (2d ed., 1947), pp. 7ff. [hereafter, *1 Peter*]; Hunter, *IB*, vol. 12, p. 78; van Unnik, *IDB*, vol. 3, pp. 763f.; B. Reicke, *Epistles of James, Peter and Jude* (1964), pp. 69ff. [hereafter, *James, Peter and Jude*]. Cf. Beare, *1 Peter*, pp. 28f., 182f., 188ff.

[17]E.g., Selwyn, *1 Peter*, pp. 23f., 365ff.

have been drawn by scholars from the writer's failure to exploit the personal relation of Peter to Jesus.[18]

The fourth objection is rebutted by saying that most of the references to "sufferings" in the letter imply no more than the public hatreds and abuses which were the common lot of Christians from the very earliest days. Even if some passages are taken as references to persecutions by the state, the evidence is inconclusive that Christians were never punished "for the name" before the time of Trajan. We cannot infer from the letter to what extent, if at all, official punitive measures had been taken by this time in Asia Minor.[19]

Neither side in this debate has been convinced by the arguments of the opponents. Some scholars have felt that the impasse is due to the fact that two improbable theories have been opposed to each other. A third alternative is proposed: 1 Peter was not written by the Apostle but by a representative of the church at Rome late in the period of Domitian. E. J. Goodspeed's account of the origin of 1 Peter has some original features, but we may take it as representative of this view.[20] Domitian's time, Goodspeed asserts,

> supplies everything necessary to the understanding of the letter: Hebrews has challenged the Roman church to become the teacher of the churches;[21] . . . Revelation has created a dangerous moral situation in the church in the chief Christian center of Asia Minor—the danger that the church while meeting persecution heroically might nevertheless be betrayed into the very human error of hating its enemies;[22] the Pauline corpus has exhibited Paul as a writer of letters to churches (*and as the advocate of a more moderate position towards the state*),[23] and Ephesians has shown the possibilities of the encyclical; the Roman church has another great name at its command, in its patron Peter . . . and for whom it can claim to speak just as authentically as Ephesus in the Revelation spoke for Christ . . . After Revelation and Hebrews, 1 Peter became almost a necessity. We may therefore confidently date 1 Peter about A.D. 95, soon after the appearance of Revelation and Hebrews and very near in date to 1 Clement, another product of the same movement in the same church.[24]

Goodspeed's view is a neat—some would argue, too neat—solution of the problem, supplying a motive for pseudonymity. It suffers from the same difficulty facing all efforts to situate 1 Peter in the late nineties: the evidence that Domitian persecuted Christians *for the name* is extremely tenuous, perhaps nonexistent. Instead of breaking the critical impasse, some have concluded that the proposal of the date under Domitian "combines all the difficulties of the other views." [25]

[18]Cf. van Unnik (*IDB*, vol. 3, p. 763) and Feine-Behm-Kümmel, *Intro.*, p. 298.

[19]Ibid., pp. 52ff.; McNeile, *Intro.*, pp. 221f.; Hunter, *IB*, vol. 12, pp. 79f.; van Unnik, *IDB*, vol. 3, p. 762.

[20]Goodspeed, *Intro.*, pp. 265ff.

[21]Heb. 5:12.

[22]See below, p. 562.

[23]Cf. Rom. 13:1ff. and 1 Pet. 2:13ff., 4:15. Italics mine.

[24]Goodspeed, *Intro.*, pp. 283f.

[25]K. Lake, *An Introduction to the New Testament* (1937), pp. 166f. [hereafter, *Intro.*]; Beare, *1 Peter*, p. 13; Reicke, *James, Peter and Jude*, pp. 71f. Cf. Feine-Behm-Kümmel, *Intro.*, pp. 298f.

At the present time there does not seem to be a completely satisfactory account of the origin of 1 Peter, although the evidence seems to favor pseudonymous authorship and a placing of the letter in the days of Trajan. By this time Christians of Asia Minor knew that Peter was long since dead. "They would recognize the pseudonym for what it was—an accepted and harmless literary device, employed by a teacher who is more concerned for the Christian content of his message than for the assertion of his own claim to authority."[26]

Interpreting 1 Peter

The letter is addressed from "Babylon."[27] Some have taken the term to apply generally to the Church in exile, recalling the letter's initial reference to Christians as "exiles of dispersion." But the author represented the authority and conveyed the greetings of a particular church. It is far more likely that "Babylon" stands for Rome than for the ancient city of Mesopotamia, or the Roman frontier post on the Nile.[28] The Christian use of Babylon as a code word for Rome is attested by the book of Revelation.[29]

AN OUTLINE OF THE FIRST LETTER OF PETER

A. 1. The superscription, 1:1–2
B. The blessings of those who have been born anew to a living hope, 1:3–12:
    2. Praise to God for the resurrection of Jesus Christ, and for the Christian's inheritance, 1:3–5
    3. The joy of Christians enduring sufferings has its origin in their love of Christ and their hope in him, 1:6–9
    4. The prophets of Israel and the gospel, 1:10–12
C. An exhortation to holy living, 1:13–2:3:
    5. The Christian calling—conformity to the holiness of God, 1:13–16
    6. Its basis—the sacrificial death and glorification of Christ, 1:17–21
    7. The purity of Christians a product of the eternal word of God which in turn produces "a sincere love of the brethren," 1:22–25
    8. A call to renounce various evils, and to "grow up to salvation," 2:1–3
D. The nature of the Church, 2:4–10:
    9. The Church as God's true temple; its people a holy priesthood, 2:4–5
    10. Christ, the cornerstone or stumbling-stone: testimonies from the Old Testament, 2:6–8
    11. The privileges and responsibilities of God's people, 2:9–10
E. A code of good conduct to be maintained among the Gentiles, 2:11–4:11:

---

[26] Beare, *1 Peter*, p. 29.
[27] 1 Pet. 5:13.
[28] Heard, *Intro.*, pp. 171f.; G. T. Manley, "Babylon on the Nile," *Evang. Quar.* XVI (1944): 138ff.; cf. van Unnik, *IDB*, vol. 3, p. 764.
[29] See below, pp. 563f.

12. A brief exhortation to Christian integrity as a means of allaying suspicion and testifying to Christ, 2:11–12
13. The duties of Christian citizens, 2:13–17
14. Christian slaves and the call to imitate Christ, 2:18–25
15. Christian wives and husbands, 3:1–7
16. A summary of typical Christian attitudes, supported by Psalm 34, 3:8–12
17. Attitudes of Christians when suffering for righteousness' sake, 3:13–17
18. The example of Christ, whose death and resurrection brought benefits, represented in the believer's baptism, which are cosmic in their range and significance, 3:18–22
19. A renewed exhortation to holy living and to a renunciation of former pagan practices, in view of the coming judgment, 4:1–11

F. "The fiery ordeal" poses a serious challenge, 4:12–19:
20. Those who share Christ's sufferings can anticipate joyfully sharing in his glory, 4:12–14
21. Shame accompanies suffering for evil-doing, but sufferings "under the name" glorify God, 4:15–16
22. The time of judgment, 4:17–19

G. The conclusion, 5:1–14:
23. Exhortations concerning the elders, 5:1–5
24. Admonitions to humility, patience, perseverance, 5:6–11
25. The closing and greetings, 5:12–14a
26. A grace, 14b

The reader may notice that with 4:12 the letter seems to take up afresh the theme of suffering (F). This verse marks a natural division, and several theories concerning the sources and form of the letter's contents make it a point of departure. Some have held that 1 Peter 1:3–4:11 reproduces a sermon to which someone has added an epistolary beginning and ending. The body of the letter contains many liturgical expressions and other signs pointing to the origin of its material in services of public worship. Several persons, following the suggestion of a German scholar, have developed a theory that the pattern of an actual baptismal service is followed from the prayer which opens the letter, with its stress on the certainties of salvation, through the instruction, to the administration of baptism (after 1 Peter 1:21). At this point in the letter the tenses change. "Having purified your souls . . ." marks the continuation of the service with exhortations, hymns, a revelation through a prophet, and a closing prayer. It has been suggested also that the section 4:12–5:11 reproduces a closing service for the entire congregation. Hence the reference to sufferings which the newly baptized, with the entire fellowship, are now called upon to endure.[30]

These various theories which account for the form of 1 Peter as a transcript of a baptismal service in progress must supply the numerous rubrics of the liturgy and homily which are, of course, missing from the text of the letter. The imagination of some scholars has been given free play in reconstructing liturgical proce-

---

[30] Beare, *1 Peter*, pp. 6ff., 192ff.

dures and in providing a setting in worship for exhortations and admonitions which have a more general application.[31] With good reason, one scholar comments, "I do not find it easy . . . to conceive how a liturgy-homily, shorn of its 'rubrics' . . . but with its changing tenses and broken sequences all retained, could have been hastily dressed up as a letter and sent off (without a word of explanation) to Christians who had not witnessed its original setting."[32]

On the more probable assumption that 1 Peter is a genuine letter, written specifically for the communities indicated in its superscription, it has been conjectured that its brokenness reveals that two letters have been welded together. The author may have written 1 Peter 1:1–4:11, with a closing greeting to some churches where persecution was still only a possibility, and 1:1–2:10 and 4:12–5:14 to other churches where persecution was severe. Later, when the apostolic writings were being collected, "the two 'insets' were copied continuously, one after the other, within the common framework of salutation and farewell."[33] Since such an editing process has left no textual evidence, as in the case of the Roman letter (a close parallel), it is perhaps more satisfactory to consider 4:12–5:11 as a recapitulation.[34] The writer wished to emphasize certain points in his exhortation in view of the impending threat to the entire region.

Two themes of the letter's exhortation are the necessity of patient endurance of suffering, since it is a sign of the coming blessedness of the people of God;[35] and the practical value as well as the theological mandate of a Christian's "good behavior."[36] By means of these things the followers of Christ (note 2:21) continually glorify God.[37]

The First Letter of Peter is unquestionably a writing of great power and effectiveness, whoever its author may have been. If it is considered a pseudonymous writing originating in the Church at the beginning of the second century, it furnishes further evidence of the influence and diffusion of Paul's interpretation of the gospel, and significant clues to the life of Christians in Asia Minor in the postapostolic age. If it is accepted as a writing of Silvanus expressing Peter's ideas and exhortations, 1 Peter "is an invaluable piece of evidence for the apostolic approval and support of the main lines of Paul's teachings. Although we have Paul's own word for this, it has often been challenged."[38] Whether written by

---

[31] W. C. van Unnik, "The Teaching of Good Works in 1 Peter," *NTS* I (1955): 92ff.; *Exp. T.* LXVIII (1956): 79ff.; C. F. D. Moule, "The Nature and Purpose of 1 Peter," *NTS* 3 (1956): 1ff.

[32] Moule, note 31 above, p. 4.

[33] Ibid., p. 7ff.

[34] See the arguments for the essential unity of 1 Pet. in composition and theme, Feine-Behm-Kümmel, *Intro.*, pp. 295f. B. Reicke suggests that with 4:7ff. the writer's interest turns from the newly baptized, only, to the whole congregation (*James, Peter and Jude*, pp. 74f.).

[35] 1 Pet. 1:8, 13; 4:1, 13; 5:8.

[36] See 1 Pet. 2:14f.; 3:1 and 10ff.

[37] E.g., 1 Pet. 2:9; 4:16.

[38] Heard, *Intro.*, pp. 174f. The Pauline aspects of the letter can be exaggerated. The great ideas in 1 Pet. "are not mere copies or repetitions" of those found in Paul's letters, "but rank alongside those of the apostle to the Gentiles." (van Unnik, *IDB*, vol. 3, p. 765). E.g., the clear allusions in 1 Pet. to baptism, its echoes of Lord's Supper observances, afford a more explicitly sacramental basis for ethical teaching than one finds in Paul's letters. See the abstract of A. R. Jonsen's thesis, *NT Abstracts* 8 (1964): 399f.

Peter or in his name, the letter is, as John Calvin said, "truly worthy of the chief of the Apostles, full of apostolic authority and majesty."

THE LETTER TO THE HEBREWS

The first known writer to refer to Paul's authorship of the book called "Letter to the Hebrews" noticed its differences from other letters attributed to the Apostle. Clement of Alexandria (ca. 150–215) surmised that Luke had translated into Greek a letter written by Paul in Hebrew. Another Alexandrian, Origen (ca. 180–250), said that someone who knew Paul must have written down the Apostle's thoughts at a later time. According to Eusebius, Origen knew of traditions from an earlier period ascribing Hebrews to Clement of Rome, as well as to Luke. But Origen's own, oft-quoted judgment on this question was, "in truth, God knows." [39]

Hebrews was written at least a century before Origen. Passages from it are echoed in 1 Clement, and possibly in the Shepherd of Hermas. But the fact remains that the earliest direct evidence from Rome assigning the authorship of Hebrews to Paul and according it canonical status dates from the middle of the fourth century. It is not surprising that there is a variety of opinion among modern scholars concerning the origin of this book. [40]

The Problem of Authorship and Date

Hebrews has been called "the riddle of the New Testament." Roman Catholic scholars are unable to surrender the tradition that its thought is Pauline, but many follow the lead of Origen in advocating a theory of mediate authorship. The overwhelming majority of Protestant scholars deny Hebrews to Paul on the grounds of its style and language, its thought forms and doctrines, and the situation of the readers which the book presupposes. The ancient guessing game is still being played, but many have adopted Origen's sensible conclusion: the writer's identity is not likely to be known this side of divine omniscience. He was certainly a Christian, probably a convert from Hellenistic Judaism. But statements concerning the author are merely inferences drawn from the writing.

Only a few parts of "the riddle" have been solved. The book cannot have been a translation from Hebrew or Aramaic. Its Greek is evidently original, of high literary quality. [41] Moreover, many are agreed that Hebrews should be classed as a homily or sermon and not, properly speaking, a letter. It is true the book ends like a letter, a fact which can be variously explained. But Hebrews is "a

[39] Eusebius, *H. E.*, VI. 14. 2ff.; VI. 25. 11ff. The evidence is ably summarized by T. W. Manson, "The Problem of the Epistle to the Hebrews," *BJRL* 32 (1949): 1ff.; the relevant texts are cited by A. C. Purdy, *IB*, vol. 11, pp. 581ff.

[40] Feine-Behm-Kümmel, *Intro.,* summarize Protestant and Roman Catholic positions concerning the tradition of Pauline authorship, p. 276; F. F. Bruce, *The Epistle to the Hebrews* (1964), pp. xxxv ff. [hereafter, *Hebrews*]; also, "Recent Contributions to the Understanding of Hebrews," *Exp. T.* 80 (1969): 260ff.

[41] R. M. Grant, *Intro.,* p. 216.

have suggested that the author directed his exhortation to Jewish–Christians of the Essene type. Like the Essenes, this group represented Jewish particularism in an acute form; conceived of the Messiah's functions along priestly lines; engaged in speculations concerning the angels and the relation of Moses to messianism; and interpreted the scriptures allegorically.[51]

Obviously a decision from among this wide number of proposals rests upon a detailed exposition of the text of Hebrews.

The Problem of the "Epistolary Ending"

When the internal evidence of Hebrews is weighed, the scales are often tipped by a decision concerning its final section. The relation of the closing verses to the whole book is not merely a literary problem.

The first alternative is that the author wrote his homily with a definite group in mind. For these persons the notes were appended. A second is that the author originally composed his homily and, at a later time, added an epistolary ending. Two reasons have been given for this afterthought. Perhaps he wished to publish his work as a pseudonymous writing, as a Pauline letter; or he decided to send the homily, which had been prepared for another purpose, to a special group. A final alternative is that Hebrews 1–12 (or 1:1–13:17?) formed the original book. Someone else tacked on the ending to give the whole "the stamp of Pauline authority."

The absence of any textual evidence makes highly speculative the three hypotheses which reject the unity of Hebrews. The theory of a pseudonymous writing, whether simulated by the author or someone else, raises the difficulty of the omission of Paul's name in the salutation. The improbability that an opening address was ever affixed to Hebrews is another objection to this theory.

The view that the ending was tacked on by someone else has greater plausibility, especially since verbal parallels to Paul's letters have been noted in this section, and not in the rest of the book.[52] But the most probable explanation is the first. The author wrote the homily for a group whose needs he knew well. The book is not impersonal. The exhortation is direct throughout.[53] The author's failure to deal directly with local matters in the course of his argument gives plausibility to the view that his writing was intended as an "open letter." Such a carefully constructed and composed argument was not written merely for a small group of the author's friends.

---

[51] See Schubert, *Dead Sea Community*, pp. 157ff., who cites the research of the Jewish scholar, Y. Yadin; J. Danielou, *Dead Sea Scrolls*, pp. 111f., who cites a German study by H. Braun. The Qumran midrash, 4Q Flor., with its exposition of Gen. 14:18ff., is evidence adduced to support this association. See J. A. Fitzmyer, *Cath. Bib. Quar.* 25 (1963): 305ff.

[52] Enslin, *Beginnings*, pp. 314f.; McNeile, *Intro.*, 230; A. C. Purdy, *IB*, vol. 11, pp. 591f.

[53] See F. V. Filson, *Yesterday: A Study of Hebrews in the Light of Chapter 13* (1967), who argues that the "key themes" in chapter 13 agree with the extensive hortatory passages in chapters 1–12; Feine-Behm-Kümmel, *Intro.*, p. 270.

An Interpretation of the Letter

Some perception of the structural unity of this book is prerequisite to its understanding.

AN OUTLINE OF THE LETTER TO THE HEBREWS[54]

A. Introduction, leading up to the central thesis, 1:1–4:16:
  1. The Son of God, heir of all things and the final revealer of God's purpose in creation and redemption, has performed the high priestly act of making purification for sins, 1:1–3
  2. The uniqueness of the Son in comparison with the angels, 1:4–14
  3. Exhortation: the danger of neglecting the superior revelation, 2:1–4
  4. The scriptures witness to a temporary subordination of the Son to the angels, that through suffering and death he might become "the pioneer" of man's salvation, and have sympathy with men as their high priest, 2:5–18
  5. Exhortation: the scriptures attest the superiority of the Son over Moses the servant; Moses' faithfulness a type of the Christian's calling to be faithful, 3:1–6
  6. Exhortation: refuse not to hear today the voice of God in the gospel of his Son; let none fall as did Israel in the day of provocation, 3:7–4:13
  7. The central thesis is stated with an accompanying exhortation: the exalted Son, having been tempted as we are, is able to sympathize with human weaknesses; therefore, boldly approach the throne of grace, 4:14–16
B. Preliminary development of the central thesis, 5:1–6:20:
  8. The nature of the Son's office as "priest forever, after the order of Melchizedek": his functions and his qualifications, 5:1–10
  9. Exhortation: pay heed to this difficult doctrine, 5:11–6:20: a rebuke for the reader's lack of development (5:11–6:3); a warning that no second repentance is possible (6:4–8); an encouragement—God will not overlook their witness (6:9–12); an assurance—the certainty of God's sworn promise (6:13–20)
C. Extended treatment of the central thesis: an explication of Christ's high priesthood and mediation of the new covenant, 7:1–10:18:
  10. Melchizedek, the type of the perfect high priest, 7:1–3
  11. This priesthood superior to the Levitical, 7:1–28: Abraham recognized Melchizedek's superiority (7:4–10); since the priesthood is related to the Law, both fail and fall together (7:11–19); unlike the appointment of the Levitical priests, the surety of a better covenant is confirmed by a divine oath (7:20–22); only the true priest holds his office permanently (7:23–25); only the true priest is sinless (7:26–28)

---

[54] In outlining the contents of Heb., two works were found to be especially suggestive: McNeile, *Intro.*, pp. 225ff., and T. W. Manson, "The Problem of the Epistle to the Hebrews," *BJRL* 32 (1949): 6ff.

12. Christ's ministry in the "heavenly sanctuary" effectively mediates the new covenant of promise, 8:1–10:18: the point is stated summarily and defended from prophecy (8:1–13); the earthly sanctuary a type of the heavenly—the place (9:1–5) and the ritual culminating in the day of atonement (9:6–7); the inadequate results (9:8–10); Christ's fulfillment "once for all" summarized (9:11–15); both covenants established by the shedding of blood, but Christ's sacrifice the better one (9:16–28); Jesus came into the world not to offer animal sacrifices but to fulfill the divine will; his heavenly exaltation; the witness of scripture (10:1–18)

D. Extended development of the hortatory implications of the great salvation, 10:19–12:29:

13. Exhortation: avail yourselves fully of "the new and living way" while there is still time, 10:19–25

14. The fearful prospect of the judgment for those who "sin deliberately," 10:26–31

15. Encouragement: a recollection of "the former days" should be a spur to fresh resolves and to endurance; the promise of the scriptures, 10:32–39

16. Expectant faith, the correlative of God's promise and its fulfillment, 11:1–12:3: the nature of faith (11:1–3); the exemplars and heroes of faith (11:2–30); the fulfillment of "the things hoped for" shared by the faithful of all ages (11:39–40); motives for patient faith (12:1–3)

17. The divine discipline of sons, 12:4–13

18. Exhortation: cultivate the Christian virtues; unlike Esau, despise not your inheritance, 12:14–17

19. Summary: apocalyptic fulfillment—assurances and threats, 12:18–29

E. Closing exhortations, 13:1–17:

20. Maintain brotherly love, sexual purity, freedom from greed; the Lord is our helper, what more do we need? 13:1–6

21. The example of former leaders, and of Christ—man's eternal contemporary; follow Christ though it mean social ostracism, 13:7–16

22. Concerning the church's present leadership, 13:17

F. The epistolary ending, 13:18–25:

23. Personal requests, 13:18–19

24. Benediction, 13:20–21

25. Final appeal; greetings; a grace, 13:22–25

In few books of the New Testament does understanding of any part depend so much upon the recognition of its relation to the whole. The argument of Hebrews is carefully developed, apparently along the lines of a classical Hellenistic model. The central thought of Hebrews is the finality of the revelation in Jesus Christ the Son of God. But exhortations belong to the "warp and woof" of this doctrinal pattern. At the end of the writer's introduction, the explanation for this correlation is given (9): the discouragement and indifference of the letter's recipients, which were leading them to the brink of apostasy, arose from their inadequate understanding of the meaning of Jesus Christ.

In the development of his thesis, the writer presented Jesus Christ as the great High Priest, the mediator of the new covenant, and as the one, sufficient sacrifice for sins (C). Throughout this section the absolute superiority of Christ's priesthood and sacrifice are variously contrasted with the imperfect and provisional Levitical cultus established according to the scriptural pattern. The extended development of the author's "word of exhortation" (D) contains many references to the foregoing doctrine and to threats and promises of the scriptures. The homily closes with ethical admonitions concerning the Church's life, personal and corporate (E).

Many interpreters have concluded that Hebrews presents a radical modification of the *kerygma* of the early Church. Instead of the familiar contrast between the present and future Ages, the writer worked with a contrast between coexisting worlds—the material and the heavenly. Like Philo and the author of the Wisdom of Solomon, the author of Hebrews interpreted the past and present alike in terms of the philosophy that the phenomenal is but an imperfect, shadowy transcript of what is eternal and real. The author was familiar with the eschatology of the primitive Christian confession. This cannot be denied. But, it is said, his acknowledgment of the received traditions was formal, and "hardly consonant with his deepest thought." Not only had the author derived his idea of the heavenly counterparts from contemporary Platonism, but he developed his argument by using Greek methods to allegorize the scriptures.[55]

There can be no denying that Hebrews often closely parallels Hellenistic thought, especially the type found in writings associated with Alexandria of Egypt. But it is doubtful that the author abandoned the perspective of the Christian *kerygma*, either consciously or unconsciously. As one writer has said, "the moral earnestness of Hebrews is reinforced by eschatological considerations, outspoken, and often quite primitive in form."[56] He shared the characteristically Christian conviction that some eschatological events had already taken place though others remain in the future as objects of hope.

A close examination of the author's interpretation of the Septuagint reveals that the resemblance to Greek methods of allegorizing classical documents is more apparent than real. This may be shown by viewing interpretations of the same Old Testament passages by Philo and by the author of Hebrews. The latter writer always insists upon the reality of events in time "with objective and corporate consequences"; Philo writes "either of the timeless reality of heaven or of subjective religious experience."[57] Philo's Melchizedek-figure is the personification of a mediating principle. His high priest hovers between the real and phenomenal worlds. In Hebrews, Jesus is portrayed as the historical fulfillment of the eschatological drama of redemption. The High Priest, after the order of Melchizedek in his uniqueness, made atonement for the sins of men in a concrete, unrepeatable,

[55] Moffatt, *Hebrews*, pp. xxxi ff.; Feine-Behm-Kümmel, *Intro.*, pp. 277f.

[56] C. K. Barrett, "The Eschatology of the Epistle to the Hebrews," in Davies and Daube, *Background*, pp. 363ff., 391. See also L. O. Bristol, "Primitive Christian Preaching and the Epistle to the Hebrews," *JBL* 68 (1949): 89ff.; W. Manson, *Hebrews*, pp. 9, 47ff., 184ff.; R. V. G. Tasker, *The Gospel in the Epistle to the Hebrews* (1950).

[57] Barrett, note 56 above, p. 389. Cf. R. M. Grant, *Intro.*, p. 219.

historical deed. Thus, for the author of Hebrews, "Jesus" does not personify a mediating principle which, when apprehended by the mind, procures a safe passage through the heavenly spheres. He had been a man who learned obedience to God and sympathy for the needs of men through the things that he suffered. His death was not given as a paradigm of the spiritual sacrifices which men must make from time to time to attain their salvation. His real death was a vicarious sacrifice, offered "once for all," which cannot, and need not, be repeated.[58]

We may conclude that the historical and eschatological realism of the author preserved his interpretations of scripture from becoming merely allegorical. He found types and parables of the gospel's witness to Christ in the haggadah and the halakah of the Torah. His interest in the Prophets and the writings was equally intense. Yet his perspective upon the scriptures was the perspective of the *kerygma:* the divine promises were being fulfilled "in these last days."[59] No more than Paul does the author of Hebrews transform the primitive gospel into a *gnosis* of redemption.

Many features of Hebrews which scholars have attributed to Platonism, or— more proximately—to Philonism, probably were derived from the apocalyptic imagery that was intrinsic to the early Christian proclamation. In his homily the writer employed this symbolism primarily to enable his readers to understand the moral implications of the *kerygma*. Perhaps his distinctive exposition of the gospel had been formulated earlier in the interests of a Christian apology. The writer's experience may have shown him that many persons failed to see the relevance of the gospel, supposing its apocalypticism to be either crude or fantastic. He sought to overcome such obstacles to faith by developing those elements in Christian apocalypticism that the philosophically minded could understand. To this extent the author of Hebrews set forth the gospel in a new idiom. But there is the same gospel in Hebrews that is proclaimed everywhere in the New Testament.

Certain passages in Hebrews will always be popular reading for Christians; for example, its portrayal of the humanity and sympathy of Christ, its roll call of the heroes of faith. Yet Hebrews will never be a popular book. The argument deals with archaic and even repulsive practices, and seems singularly irrelevant. Nevertheless, the writer's mode of thought has a perennial appeal for certain types of mind, and again and again the modernity of his ideas has been recognized. This comes as a confirmation of the author's own conclusion: "Jesus Christ is the same yesterday and today and forever."[60]

THE LETTER OF JAMES

One of the most disputed writings of the New Testament is the Letter of James. Both liberal and conservative critics are divided among themselves concerning

[58] Barrett, p. 388; also pp. 366ff., 373ff.

[59] Heb. 1:2.

[60] Heb. 13:8. Note F. F. Bruce's summary of points made by the author which hold special relevance (*Hebrews*, pp. xi f.).

its authorship and date and its setting in the historical development of Christianity. More importantly the religious value of James is often disparaged. Some say that it presents an interpretation of the gospel which was repudiated by Paul or, if written after Paul, contradicts or qualifies the Apostle's teaching. It is well known that Martin Luther questioned the theological value of James and referred to it as "a rather straw-like epistle," though he conceded that it contained "many good sayings." [61]

The modern reticence concerning James may have been felt in the ancient Church. Recent researchers have detected allusions to James in 1 Clement and in the Shepherd of Hermas, but the judgment of Eusebius in the fourth century still holds true: "Certainly not many of the ancients have mentioned it." No writer before Origen is known to have attributed the book to James, "the Lord's brother," and Origen's position toward its authority was somewhat vacillating. A century later, Eusebius placed James among the "disputed books." For knowledge of its origin we are dependent upon the letter itself.[62]

AN OUTLINE OF THE LETTER OF JAMES

A. Introduction: the trials of life and the perfecting of pure religion, 1:1–27:
    1. The superscription, 1:1
    2. Only the tested faith is perfect and complete, 1:2–4
    3. Only those who pray for wisdom with faith will receive it, 1:5–8
    4. Only the lowly and steadfast, among either the poor or the rich, will receive "the crown of life," 1:9–12
    5. Only by one's own desire is a person tempted to do evil; every "good endowment" is from "the Father of lights," 1:13–17
    6. Only moderation in speech and meekness enable "the word of truth" to increase, 1:18–21
    7. Only those who persevere "in doing the word" shall be blessed, 1:22–25
    8. Only those who bridle their tongues escape self-deception and vanity, 1:26
    9. The marks of "religion that is pure and undefiled," 1:27
B. Concerning right relations with men and with God, 2:1–5:6:
    10. Partiality towards the rich is contrary to the gospel, especially its "royal law," 2:1–13
    11. "Faith by itself, if it has no works, is dead," 2:14–26
    12. No one can be a perfect man, much less a teacher, who cannot curb his unruly tongue, 3:1–12
    13. "Friendship with the world" and its consequences, contrasted with "the wisdom that is from above," 3:13–4:6
    14. An appeal: submit to God in repentance and humility, 4:7–10

[61] See R. V. G. Tasker, *The General Epistle of James* (1956), for a concise review of Roman Catholic and Protestant attitudes to James, pp. 13ff. [hereafter, *James*].
[62] Eusebius, *H. E.*, II. 33; Origen, *Rom.* 6. 286.

15. Concerning evil-speaking, the law, and the judgment, 4:11–12
16. An apostrophe: the folly of man, 4:13–5:6
C. Conclusion: concerning the need for patience and fellow-feeling in suffering, 5:7–20:
17. The eschatological sanction, 5:7–12
18. The fellowship of the saints; the value of prayer, especially in healing the sick, 5:13–18
19. The spiritual rewards for reclaiming a wanderer, 5:19–20

The Character of the Book and Its Origin

Apart from its superscription, James does not read like a letter. The writer identifies himself as James and he appears to be a Christian leader. Yet the address of the book is completely impersonal, and there are no direct references to the situation of the recipients or the author's relation to them. We have noticed that Hebrews does not have a letter's beginning; James does not have its usual ending. Outlines of the book, including the one above, can only identify its miscellaneous topics and call attention to its principal themes. If there is a unity in James, it is found in the writer's practical purpose, not in its subject matter.[63]

For James, faith had to be expressed in good works or its profession was seriously suspect. Apparently this writer was convinced that many Christians in the Church of his day were smugly complacent, in their conformity to the world and its ways, and indifferent to the needs of their brethren. James wrote not to instruct persons in the faith, but to exhort them to recognize its plain moral obligations.

Several features of this book have suggested an early, Palestinian origin. Its Jewish tone has given currency to a theory that its ideas were originally written in a book by a Jew named "Jacob." Some Christian editor interpolated a few references to Jesus Christ and produced the canonical book. This theory can be maintained only by drastically underestimating the contributions of the Christian editor. The doctrinal presuppositions of the writer are scarcely disclosed, but one finds in James references which certainly imply ascription to the Christian *kerygma*, not to Judaism. The whole discussion concerning faith and works assumes a debate among Christians, not Jews.[64]

Many studies of James refer to the "primitive simplicity" of its Jewish–Christianity. The author's religion is said to be a religion of the Law, purified by the influence of Jesus' teachings but unaffected by the theology set forth in the letters of Paul and other later books. For some modern critics this evidence confirms the Church's tradition that the book was written by James the Lord's

---

[63] B. S. Easton, *IB*, vol. 12, pp. 9f., Enslin, *Beginnings*, p. 330. R. M. Grant, observing that sections of the "letter" reveal a rhetorical skill, suggests that James is an unfinished collection of materials useful to teachers in the Jerusalem church (*Intro.*, pp. 220f.). Cf. Reicke, *James, Peter and Jude*, pp. 6f.

[64] Feine-Behm-Kümmel, *Intro.*, pp. 287f. Note that the royal "law" of love is described as the "law of liberty," Jas. 2:8, 12; cf. Gal. 5:13f.; 2 Cor. 3:14–17.

brother, or at least supports a theory of mediate authorship.[65] A few scholars believe that James was written by some teacher in a Galilean community of Christian Jews.[66]

There are features of James which render implausible these accounts of its origin. The author's moral exhortations are presented in typical Hellenistic forms. The book is written in prose, in the second person used by writers of popular moral tracts, and its illustrations and style often resemble the Stoic–Cynic diatribe. The author was able "to write easily and fluently in Greek," and to employ various rhetorical devices utilized in Hellenistic literature.[67] He was familiar with the terminology and content of Stoic ethics. There are echoes in James of the Septuagint and of Jewish wisdom books of Hellenistic Judaism. Such signs of "the Greek shape" of James indicate that its author's background was Diaspora Judaism but this is not undisputed.[68] The same literary features, however, make incredible the theory that the canonical book is a translation from Aramaic or from the colloquial Greek of Palestine.

Reminiscences in James of Jesus' teaching, which the reader may have noted, are sometimes said to support a Palestinian provenience and the tradition concerning its authorship. It may be argued that a brother of Jesus, writing before A.D. 62, the date of James' martyrdom, would not have failed to witness to his death and resurrection, or to other events from the Ministry. But an alternative defense of the primitive Palestinian origin of this teaching is that only some of this tradition may have been derived from the Apostle James.

The sum total of the internal evidence supports the view that James is a pseudonymous writing. Jerome reported that this belief was "not uncommon" in the ancient Church, and 2 Peter and the Pastoral Letters provide New Testament parallels. The choice of James as the patron of the book may be explained in the same way one explains the Pastor's use of Paul's name and apostolic authority.

Two facts weigh heavily in favor of a postapostolic dating of James—the nature and form of its moral aphorisms, and the absence of early information concerning the letter and the shyness of the Church in accepting its authority. The date and place of the writing of James are hidden in the obscurity of the record of Jewish–Christianity after A.D. 70.

A Brief Interpretation of the Letter

The address—"to the twelve tribes in the dispersion"—is a figurative one (1). The author applied a bold metaphor to the Christian communities scattered

[65] Tasker, *James*, pp. 20ff.; T. W. Manson, *Companion*, pp. 118f.; Heard, *Intro.*, pp. 164ff. T. H. Gaster claims that the Qumran scrolls "open a window upon the little community of Jewish–Christians clustered around James in Jerusalem . . . the urban brethren of the hardier souls that betook themselves to Qumran . . ." (*Dead Sea Scriptures*, pp. 15ff.).

[66] Elliott-Binns, *Galilean Christianity*, pp. 45ff., who also refers to the views of the French scholar, Jean Reville.

[67] Easton, *IB*, vol. 12, pp. 4, 6; Enslin, *Beginnings*, p. 332; McNeile, *Intro.*, p. 204. Cf. Tasker, *James*, pp. 29f.

[68] Feine-Behm-Kümmel, *Intro.*, p. 290. Cf. R. M. Grant, *Intro.*, p. 222.

throughout the Empire. Would James of Jerusalem have identified the Church as the new Israel?

Moffatt's paraphrase brings out the wordplay which introduced the writer's exhortations: "Greeting. *Greet* is as pure joy. . . ." (2). Like the Stoics, James taught that the trials of life are not evils to be avoided. Rather they are character-building experiences to be accepted joyfully. The author was more directly influenced by the common Christian teachings than by Stoicism, but he found elements of the latter congenial.[69] The letter's references to "trials" and to "sufferings" are too slight to show their external causes. "Trials" also refer to inner constraints, to "temptations."[70]

The connection of the next exhortation may be found in the author's recognition that the capacity of Christians to endure trials is proportionate to their dependence upon divine wisdom. Yet, again, a single word may provide the only link: lacking . . . lack (3).

From the beginning of the book the author reveals his "pet peeve": the double-minded man, that is, the Christian whose profession of piety is insincere. Formal prayers have no results at all; the prayer of the truly righteous man has powerful effects.[71] In the thought of James, "wisdom" and "righteousness" are inseparable, as in the Wisdom Literature of Judaism.[72]

Another animus of James is introduced: his contempt for selfish, rich Christians, especially the social snobs among them. But James does not dwell upon this subject. He was anxious to assure his readers that God rewards those who endure trials, and that trials cannot be interpreted as God's attempt to break down faith (4–5).

The thought of God's "gifts" may have suggested to James the "perfect gift" of the new creation. The writer's references to "the word of truth," and to God's people as "a kind of first fruits," derive ultimately from the scriptures. But his further description of "the word" discloses his Christian presuppositions. The word implanted in the reader's heart is the gospel which is powerful unto salvation.[73]

The rebuke of the quick-tempered and thoughtless in speech becomes more direct later in the letter.[74] Its connection here with the writer's doctrine of regeneration reflects again his basic concern that Christians be morally sound: the implanted word needs clean soil in which to grow (6, 8). This idea is given further application in the admonition against only hearing the word and not doing it (7). The use of the metaphor of the mirror as a device useful to self-knowledge was a commonplace among Greek moralists.[75]

[69] Cf. 1 Pet. 1:6f.; 4:12f.; Rom. 5:3f. Seneca. *Epis. XXIII, De Prov.* 4.

[70] Jas. 1:12f.; 5:10, 13.

[71] Jas. 1:6f.; 5:16b. Cf. Mark 11:23 and pars.

[72] The influence of the Jewish Wisdom Books is evident throughout; for "the crown of life" cf. Wisd. of Sol. 5:15f. (also 2 Tim. 4:8; 1 Pet. 5:4; Rev. 12:3); for the idea that temptation cannot be sent from God, cf. Ecclus. 15:11f. (1 Cor. 10:13).

[73] Jas. 1:21. Cf. Rom. 10:8f.; 1 Pet. 1:23; 2:1f.

[74] Jas. 1:26; 3:1ff.

[75] J. Moffatt, *The General Epistles* (1928), pp. 26f.

James defined the marks of true religion as public charity and personal purity (9). Thoroughly Jewish is this close association of the idea of "defilement" with belief that self-knowledge depends upon the study and practice of "the perfect law." But it is evident that the writer's ideal of "unstained" religion was ethical rather than ceremonial. Nothing is said in James concerning the necessity of pious acts like fasting, public prayers, and the like. These are not the "works" to which he refers. The accounts in Acts concerning James and the Jewish–Christians in Jerusalem suggest that they neither perceived nor practiced this distinction. The admonition that Christians should avoid the contamination of the world is repeated later in the letter, but in neither place does the author say how this is to be accomplished.[76]

From this point on in James, one can detect very little if any logical relation of its sections. Only two of its themes will be given special consideration in the following paragraphs: the writer's reproofs of "the rich" (10, 16); and his teaching concerning faith and works, the law, and judgment (11, 14–15).

The passages concerning the rich raise a serious objection to an early, Jerusalem origin of the book. It is true that the writer's tendency to equate the pious and the poor reflects the perspective of Palestinian Judaism. But it is highly doubtful that there were rich members in the Jerusalem church in sufficient number to call forth the reproofs of James. One may recall the Pastor's charge to Timothy with reference to the "haughty" members of the postapostolic Church who were "rich in this world."[77]

To the writer of James, partiality toward rich people was especially obnoxious in public assemblies devoted to the worship of "the Lord of glory." He reflected the teaching of Jesus and the whole Church when he recognized in such discrimination a serious breach of "the royal law." In the Christian fellowship all men were "neighbors" regardless of the social and economic distinctions of society. But James was not content to say that rich and poor should be treated alike. He had special words of condemnation for the rich. He accused them of exploiting the poor, of being insensitive to the needy. Because of their attachments to wealth they suffered the illusion that they were secure to make whatever plans they might wish. It is refreshing to find in the New Testament an echo of the voices of the great prophets of Israel. Yet James did not glorify poverty as such. The "lowly brother," not merely the poor Christian, may boast in God's exaltation.

Some scholars believe that James misread the position of Paul set forth in his letters, especially in Romans.[78] Did James suppose his argument to be at cross-purposes with Paul? The evidence is not sufficient to prove a literary influence of Paul upon James. But a pre-Pauline date for James is not the most satisfactory explanation. It was only with Paul that the antithesis "faith not works" entered Christianity. With many interpreters, we may say that James was attacking a perversion of Paul's doctrine of justification by faith. Such perversions occurred

[76] Jas. 4:4ff.

[77] 1 Tim. 6:10, 17ff.

[78] Goodspeed, *Intro.*, p. 291; R. H. Fuller and G. E. Wright, *The Book of the Acts of God* (1957), p. 327.

during Paul's lifetime and, according to the writer of 2 Peter, continued to plague the Church in postapostolic times.[79]

The wrong impression that James opposed Paul may result from a failure to recognize the different connotations of their words. The same terms could be used differently by the two authors because their situations were different. By "works" Paul meant acts of obedience to the moral and ritual requirements of the Torah. James clearly implied that the essential "works" are acts of disinterested love for one's neighbor in need. By "faith," pure and simple, James meant an intellectual assent to certain doctrines, such as the belief that God is one.[80] Such "faith" could be either sincere or feigned. For Paul, "faith" was a personal response to God revealed in Christ, establishing a relation in which genuine obedience became possible for the first time. What James derided as a feigned faith, or "dead faith," Paul would have said was not Christian faith at all.[81]

Faith was essential to both, and to both love of one's neighbor was the necessary consequence and proof of faith. Doubtless, Paul would have preferred to speak of Christian acts of compassion as the "fruits" of the Spirit, but he would have had no substantive quarrel with James. The fact that James could speak of "works" as the mark of a Christian shows that the problem of the relation of the Jewish Law to Christian faith no longer existed.

Even though all this is conceded, it cannot be said that James' position represents an adequate restatement of Paul's great doctrine. The Apostle, as we have seen, placed the reality of justification at the very moment a person responded in faith to the *kerygma*. The believer in Christ anticipated in the present time God's final judgment and salvation. James does not seem to have grasped the full measure of God's gift in Christ. He could speak of the Christian's hope of "righteousness" as the harvest of the good life.[82] Nevertheless, one wonders if it was any part of James' purpose either to qualify or to defend Paul's doctrine. The practical tone of the entire letter reveals his primary concern: the exposure of the moral sterility of Christians whose faith is mere talk. James' grasp of the theological significance of the gospel may have been deficient, but his stern insistence upon the obedience of faith provided a wholesome antidote to all evangelicalism that would save its own soul while it lets a brother suffer the want of life's elemental needs.[83]

---

[79] Rom. 6:1ff.; Gal. 5:1ff.; 2 Pet. 3:14f.; Goguel, *Birth*, pp. 374ff.; Enslin, *Beginnings*, pp. 330f.; Easton, *IB*, vol. 12, p. 41.

[80] Jas. 2:19.

[81] Jas. 2:20, 26.

[82] Jas. 3:17f. Note also 2:5. See the discussion of "the theological problem," Feine-Behm-Kümmel, *Intro.*, pp. 291f.

[83] Hunter, *Interpreting*, p. 120. C. E. B. Cranfield observes that "a hostile, contemptuous, or patronising attitude" to James has obscured the "sober truth" that what one finds in the letter "is no untheological moralism but a faithful—though, for a special purpose, oblique—proclamation of the gospel of Christ," extraordinarily relevant for the Church in the later half of the twentieth century. "The Message of James," *Scot. Journ. of Theo.* 18 (1965): 182ff. and 338ff.

THE LETTER OF JUDE

Jude is another General Letter which more appropriately may be called a tract. The brevity of Jude is not the chief cause of uncertainty concerning its origin and value. The author suppressed a desire to write concerning the Church's "common salvation" and in so doing veiled his particular understanding of the gospel from later readers. He wrote, as he says, to attack certain "ungodly persons." Apparently he felt no need to refute their teaching. He only vituperates against them.[84]

The superscription identifies the author as Jude [Judas], "the brother of James," and therefore of Jesus. But it is most unlikely that this Jude wrote the tract, or that the association of the book with "founder's kin" resulted in its preservation. According to some scholars, the words "the brother of James" were added by a later scribe. Others suggest that the tract first circulated under the name of "Judas [son] of James," who was one of "the twelve."[85] The majority of critics hold that Jude is patently a pseudonymous writing, and that probably it was recognized as one from the beginning.

Two facts support the postapostolic origin of Jude: the author's references to "the predictions of the apostles" and to the imperative need that the lives of Christians be established on "the most holy faith," and the affinities of Jude with the Pastoral Letters and, possibly, with 1 John. In the first place it seems evident that neither the author nor his readers belonged to the first generation of Christians. The second fact, that there is close affinity with other writings of the postapostolic period, is established less securely since it is difficult to determine the nature of the false teaching opposed by Jude.[86]

The use of Jude by the author of 2 Peter supports a date for the writing of Jude before A.D. 150.[87] If there are echoes of Jude in the Didache or in Polycarp's correspondence, then its composition may be as early as A.D. 100. The identification of the locality of the author or his first readers is mere guesswork.[88] The historical importance of this letter, as of 2 Peter, lies in the evidence it affords that radical differences in theology and ethics forced the churches "to establish the 'apostolic' norms of canon, tradition and authoritative interpretation" of the faith.[89]

---

[84]Jude 3f.

[85]Goodspeed, *Intro.*, pp. 348f. Cf. Luke 6:16; John 14:22. B. H. Streeter's view that the author was Jude, the third bishop of Jerusalem ca. A.D. 125, is given in *The Primitive Church* (1930), pp. 178ff. For a defense of the traditional view, see Heard, *Intro.*, pp. 215ff. Cf. McNeile, *Intro.*, p. 243.

[86]Cf. Jude 17; 1 Tim. 5:1; 2 Tim. 3:1, 4:3 (Acts 20:29f.; Mark 13:6). The Pastor writing in Paul's name can make these his own predictions; the writer of Jude does not carry the impersonation as far. With Jude 20, cf. Polycarp, *Phil.* 3:2.

[87]For arguments supporting the reverse of this common view of dependence, see Reicke, *James, Peter and Jude*, pp. 189f., who conjectures that both letters derive from a common tradition. Cf. J. C. Beker, "Second Letter of Peter," *IDB*, vol. 3, p. 768.

[88]For a summary of the earliest notices of Jude in Church traditions, see A. E. Barnett, *IB*, vol. 12, pp. 317f.

[89]J. C. Beker, "Letter of Jude," *IDB*, vol. 2, p. 1009.

AN OUTLINE OF THE LETTER OF JUDE

A. Introduction, 1–4:
   1. The superscription, 1–2
   2. The exigency prompting the letter: the insinuation into the Church of "ungodly persons," 3–4
B. The false teachers: their character briefly described; their doom foretold, 5–16:
   3. Examples from the scriptures of the punishment of rebels, 5–7
   4. The errorists are portrayed and denounced, 8–13
   5. Apocalyptic writings prophesy their judgment, 14–16
C. The "most holy faith," the sure foundation, 17–23:
   6. The apostles foretold the coming of these "scoffers," 17–19
   7. The Christian's defenses, 20–21
   8. Pity the errorists, but do not let their immoralities lead to compromises, 22–23
D. A doxology, 24–25

While the salutation of Jude offers no proof of the influence of Paul upon the author, the Apostle's letters provide the most articulate commentary upon it (1). The writer's appeal that his readers "contend for the faith" shows that he was convinced that there was such a thing as a common Christian tradition. Certain "ungodly persons," however, were perverting this gospel "into licentiousness." Either because of their actions, or in addition to them, they were denying the Church's "only Master and Lord Jesus Christ." It is doubtful that these errorists can be shown to have advocated Gnostic views, or docetism in particular, but Jude provides further evidence of "lawlessness" in the postapostolic Church, and pre-Gnostic views may be detected in some oblique references in the letter.[90]

As a proof of the gravity of the errorists' situation, Jude recalled the testimony of the scriptures concerning God's severe judgment upon rebels (3). Jude's reference to the presumptuous angels, and their imprisonment "in the nether gloom" until judgment day, echoes 1 Enoch and possibly the Book of Jubilees.[91] Two or three passages in Jude refer to the sexual immoralities of the persons he condemns. It may be that they were justifying their actions by speculations concerning the angels.[92] In any case, Jude's primary purpose was to warn that those who have been saved by the gospel may fall into sin and be hopelessly lost (4).

We have seen that several books in the New Testament refer to a popular belief that the Law of God had been mediated by angels. Jude implied that faithful angels also sought to ensure that men honor it. But the errorists were rejecting all authority and reviling "the glorious ones." Like "irrational animals" their

---

[90]Goguel, *Birth*, p. 419; Goodspeed, *Intro.*, pp. 345f.; Enslin, *Beginnings*, p. 336; J. C. Beker, *IDB*, vol. 2, p. 1010f.; Feine-Behm-Kümmel, *Intro.*, p. 300. R. M. Grant, *Intro.*, pp. 227f.

[91]Gen. 6:1ff. Cf. 1 En. 10:41ff.; 12:4ff. Bk. of Jub. 5:6 (cf. 1 Pet. 3:19f.).

[92]Goguel, *Birth*, p. 420. Cf. Reicke, *James, Peter and Jude*, pp. 202f., 213, who argues that the rebels were anarchistic and antinomian, setting aside the constituted authorities in the church and claiming special knowledge and wisdom.

knowledge was limited to the things of sense. Jude's reference to the selfish carousings of the errorists at the Church's love-feasts reminds us of Paul's rebuke of certain Christians at Corinth for similar actions.[93]

The thought of the impending doom of the errorists led Jude to recall the picture of the final judgment in 1 Enoch.[94] The writer's effective use of scripture and his original application of its vivid imagery deserve notice. But the reader is not impressed by Jude's "name-calling."

Perhaps there are two values preserved in this little book. The inspirational phrases of its noble doxology (D) somewhat redeem the vitriolic quality of the writer's polemics. And the insistence of the writer that the Church's security against error rests upon the grace of God and the *kerygma* it has received is the more impressive when we realize that persons of the temper of Jude contended for it. There was "a faith which was once for all delivered to the saints," as we have seen—not a fully articulated system of doctrine, but faith in Jesus as the one by whom man's salvation was inaugurated and was to be consummated. That the "most holy faith" survived such pettiness and licentiousness within the Church, as well as attacks from without, is cause for wonder.

THE SECOND LETTER OF PETER

Scarcely an independent scholar maintains that Jesus' disciple from Galilee composed the letter called 2 Peter. This writer's art has not hidden the conventional marks of a pseudonymous writing of the second-century Church. Ancient Church tradition contains no evidence of the existence of this letter before the Dialogue written by Justin Martyr around A.D. 155. And it is not certain that Justin refers to 2 Peter. Its admission into the New Testament as a canonical writing was certainly later. Notable exceptions were still being taken to its authenticity in the lifetime of Jerome.[95]

The writer claims the name and authority of "Simon Peter." He refers to the Apostle's presence on "the holy mountain" of Jesus' transfiguration and to Jesus' prediction concerning his death. But his knowledge of Peter and of these things was derived from the Church's traditions.[96] His reference to "our beloved brother Paul" is also a device of pseudonymity. When 2 Peter was written, collections of Paul's letters were being used and accorded canonical authority.[97]

The secondary character of 2 Peter is revealed most clearly in the passages which seem to have been lifted by its author from Jude. Besides padding his source, he has changed Jude's present tenses into future, and removed the reference to Enoch, other marks of a pseudonymous writing.[98] Since there were being cir-

[93] Cf. Jude 12; 1 Cor. 11:17ff. Whether the errorists had been separated or withdrawn from the congregations they were influencing is not clear. See especially v. 12.

[94] Jude 14f. (1 En. 1:9).

[95] Barnett, *IB*, vol. 12, p. 163.

[96] 2 Pet. 1:18; 1:14 (Mark 9:2ff. and pars.; John 21:18f.).

[97] 2 Pet. 3:15f.

[98] Cf. 2 Pet. 2:1–8; 3:1f. and Jude 4–19. It is unlikely that the short tract by Jude would have contained extracts from 2 Pet. Feine-Behm-Kümmel, *Intro.*, p. 303. Cf. Reicke, note 87 above.

culated at the time at least two writings attributed to Peter—an apocalypse and a gospel—there is no difficulty in accounting for the origin and survival of a pseudonymous letter.[99] The writer of 2 Peter need not be charged with lacking integrity. He sought to discredit views which he sincerely believed were opposed to the apostles' proclamation. As defender of the faith, i.e., the Church's doctrinal tradition, against error, the author stands in the shadow of the Prince of the Apostles.[100]

A date for 2 Peter sometime within the period A.D. 125 to 150 commands the widest assent among scholars. Any date up to the third century is possible, but an early second-century dating is more probable. The purpose of this letter and, to some extent, the views of the adversaries attacked will be disclosed in its reading and exposition.

An Outline of the Second Letter of Peter

A. Introduction, 1:1–21:
   1. The superscription, 1:1–2
   2. The Christian's privileges: the enabling power; the call; the promises, 1:3–4
   3. The Christian's responsibilities: to confirm the call and election, 1:5–11
   4. Peter recalls his witness concerning these things, 1:12–21
B. The false teachers: their general character described; their doom solemnly foretold, 2:1–22:
   5. A statement concerning the antecedents of the false teachers, and the consequences of their "destructive heresies," 2:1–3
   6. Examples from the scriptures of the punishment of rebels, 2:4–10a
   7. The errorists are portrayed and denounced, 2:10b–22
C. The defense of "the promise of his coming," 3:1–13:
   8. Prophecy and the apostolic witness are recalled, 3:1–2
   9. The scoffers' taunt and their claim, 3:3–4
   10. Things have not, and will not, "remain the same": the flood a type of the coming judgment, 3:5–7
   11. The Day of the Lord: reasons for patience and repentance, 3:8–10
   12. Summary: the Lord's promise and its implications for the Church, 3:11–13
D. Conclusion, 3:14–18:
   13. The exhortation of Peter is supported by Paul "in all his letters," but the latter's difficult doctrines are being distorted, 3:14–16
   14. A final warning and admonition, 3:17–18a
   15. A doxology, 3:18b

Perhaps Luke's reference to Simon (Symeon), in connection with the issuance of the Apostolic Decree, provided the precedent for the superscription of

---

[99] James, *Apocryphal New Testament*, pp. 505ff. See also "The Preaching of Peter," ibid., pp. 16ff., and "The Acts of Peter," ibid., pp. 300ff.

[100] Enslin, *Beginnings*, p. 340f.; E. Käsemann, "An Apologia for Primitive Christian Eschatology," *Essays*, pp. 177f.

2 Peter.[101] Later generations, possessing the Apostle's faith, have an imperative responsibility for guarding and defending it. In our study of the Pastorals we observed the tendency in the postapostolic Church to refer to Jesus as God as well as Savior (1).[102]

It is probable that the early reference to the "knowledge of God" was more than a liturgical formula for the writer of 2 Peter.[103] Had *gnosis* become a technical religious term in our writer's circle? As we shall see, it is possible that *Gnostic* may be the label we should apply in describing the writer's principal adversaries. According to the teaching of 2 Peter, a personal acknowledgment of the truth revealed in "Jesus our Lord," not mystical or mythical speculation, makes for sound and steady growth in all things pertaining "to life and godliness." Only by such means are men enabled to "become partakers of the divine nature" (2–3).

Two incidents relating to Peter are introduced by the writer to support the adoption of the Apostle's name (4). The parallels in 2 Peter to Jude need not detain us (B). Apparently our writer felt that Jude's description of false teachers was a "classic," and, in a general way, suited his adversaries. But one wonders if he fully understood his source? The reader finds difficulty in following the thought of 2 Peter without turning to Jude.[104] The emphasis on the moral accountability of the errorists in 2 Peter is noteworthy. Are the author's words at this place a homiletical application of a saying traditionally ascribed to Jesus? [105]

The appeal of Jude to the witness of the apostles is broadened to include "the holy prophets."[106] By this time the Christian prophets were figures of the past.

Is it possible to identify the particular errorists attacked by the writer of 2 Peter? A certain answer to this question is precluded by the fact that the teaching and tactics of his adversaries are not described directly. Did the writer simply assume full knowledge on the part of his readers, or did he wish to avoid drawing attention to the specific views of the troublemakers for fear of enticing insecure Christians into their camp? Several students of the second-century Gnostic systems have detected in the writer's vocabulary, and oblique comment, typical Gnostic teachings. It is said that "the kerygma of the Gnostics percolates at times through the abusive language" of the letter.[107] The "destructive heresies" of those who are attacked resemble features of "developed Gnosticism." Men are offered "freedom" from "the defilements of the world." A bold defiance of the angelic powers is encouraged, as though men are no longer subject to them, or for that matter, to any established authority.[108] This alleged freedom from the flesh had tended toward libertinism and self-centeredness or greed.[109] Some scholars have inferred from the writer's reference to the perversion of Paul's writings that these Gnostics

[101]Cf. Acts 15:14; Barnett, *IB*, vol. 12, p. 167.
[102]Tit. 2:11f. Also John 20:28; Ignatius, *Eph.* 1:1; 18:2.
[103]2 Pet. 1:3, 8; also 2:20f.; 3:18.
[104]McNeile, *Intro.*, pp. 248f.
[105]2 Pet. 2:20ff. Cf. Matt. 12:43ff.; Luke 11:24ff. (Q).
[106]2 Pet. 3:2; Jude 17.
[107]J. C. Beker, *IDB*, vol. 3, p. 769; Käsemann, *Essays*, pp. 170f.
[108]2 Pet. 2:1ff., 10, 18f.
[109]2 Pet. 2:12f., 18.

were "closely linked to the Marcionite wing of the movement."[110] This is admittedly quite speculative. It is of more importance to an understanding of the letter that the errorists are identified as Gnostics or pre-Gnostics because the primitive Christian eschatology no longer held any meaning for them.[111]

The next section of the letter discloses that it was this particularly distressing error which the writer seeks to rebut (C). His adversaries were scornfully repudiating the early Christian's belief in Christ's return, his Parousia. We have seen that at Thessalonica the delay of Christ's (second) coming caused anxious fears. Paul wrote to assure this church that its dying members would share in the Lord's coming victory. The writer of 1 Peter, as our author noted, had also dealt with the perplexity that some Christians felt because of the delay.[112] Other writings of the postapostolic age imply that at least in limited circles the hope of the near advent of Christ had waned. The apocalyptic visions of the early Church were retained, but sometimes in a formal and much attenuated form. The Second Letter of Peter provides the earliest certain evidence from the New Testament that in some churches the advent hope was being denied. Our writer knew Christians who scoffingly denied the reality of "the promise of his coming," not only because of its unfulfillment, but also because they believed in the constancy of the physical laws of the universe (9).

The writer vigorously attacked this skepticism. He denied that all things "have continued as they were from the beginning of creation" (10), and he reasserted and re-emphasized the apocalyptic message of the early Church (11). The biblical account of the flood in the days of Noah proclaimed the truths that the universe was subject to the rule and the judgments of God, and that the ungodly perish. Our writer's restatement of the traditional hope of the Church contains two distinctive aspects. Instead of emphasizing the suddenness and unpredictability of the Lord's last day, he called to mind the scriptural teaching that God's time scheme differed from clock-time. He also stressed the catastrophic nature of the End. Alone among the New Testament writers, the author of 2 Peter employed an apocalyptic symbol reminiscent of the Stoic doctrine of world conflagration (11–12).[113]

That the writer in this restatement remained true to the hope embedded in the primitive Christian eschatology has been denied. It is claimed that the early expectation of God's triumph through Christ is replaced by a proclamation of the apotheosis of the pious man, destined to become partaker "of the divine nature," rewarded for his righteousness, and escaping the destruction of the wicked. The writer's thought, it is said, "marks the relapse of Christianity into Hellenistic

---

[110]J. C. Beker, *IDB*, vol. 3, p. 769.

[111]Käsemann, *Essays*, pp. 171f.; C. H. Talbert, "II Peter and the Delay of the Parousia," *Vigiliae Christianae* 20 (1966), argues that in its "testament" form this letter aims to foretell the emergence of error after the death of Peter and to appeal to apostolic authority as a defense against some Christian sects denying the Church's conviction of a Parousia judgment.

[112]2 Pet. 3:1ff. (1 Pet. 1:3ff.; 4:5ff.).

[113]Is. 66:15f.; Joel 2:30 (Acts 2:19f.); Dan. 7:9f.; 1 En. 83:3ff.

dualism'': this version of the Christian *kerygma* offered man a way of escape from the corrupt world and safe transit to the eternal realm.[114]

Although it must be conceded that the writer's teaching contains contradictory elements, this reading of the eschatology of 2 Peter, as nearly indistinguishable from Gnosticism, seems to be one-sided. The writer's hope reflects—at some remove it is true—the same tension between the "now" and the "not yet" present in the early *kerygma*, and his moral imperatives, as in Paul's letters, are based upon the indicatives of the gospel.[115]

Some readers will doubtless conclude that the theology and manner of defense adopted by the writer of 2 Peter leave much to be desired, and find his apocalyptic literalness unappealing. Yet, his moral admonitions which were prompted by a steadfast hope, maintained in the face of widespread skepticism, eventually won for this book a place among the Christian scriptures.

[114] 2 Pet. 1:4. Käsemann, *Essays*, pp. 178ff.
[115] J. C. Beker, *IDB*, vol. 3, pp. 769.; R. M. Grant, *Intro.*, pp. 230f.

chapter twenty-one

WRITINGS FROM
THE JOHANNINE CIRCLE

Ruins of the Palace of Domitian (emperor A.D. 81–96) on the Palatine (central section, west view). (Rev. Dr. Raymond V. Schoder, SJ)

Bust of Domitian. Roman senatorial, Greek and Christian writers of antiquity damned
Domitian as a tyrant because of alleged attacks upon the aristocracy, Hellenism, and the
Church. Modern scholars have difficulty assessing his accomplishments and failings
objectively. Domitian's policies were generally intelligent, favorable to the middle class,
until he lost control in the final years of his reign. During this time the cult of Domitian
was augmented in the province of Asia. (Alinari)

Reproduction of a woodcut by Albrecht Dürer (1471–1528) entitled "Four Horseman of the Apocalypse." (By permission of the Ackland Art Center, University of North Carolina, Chapel Hill)

FIVE New Testament books are ascribed by tradition to John the Son of Zebedee, one of Jesus' original disciples. Irenaeus, bishop of Gaul, voiced this belief in his church, and in other places, at the close of the second century with respect to the Gospel, Revelation, and the first two letters of John.[1] To Irenaeus also we trace the information that "John the disciple of the Lord" bore faithful witness to the apostolic tradition in the church at Ephesus "until the time of Trajan."[2]

Apparently the letters of John gained acceptance with greater difficulty than the Gospel. The earliest explicit reference to 3 John, as a writing of doubtful authenticity, dates from the first half of the third century.[3] During the fourth century, however, Jerome's advocacy led to the canonization in Rome of all three letters; and in the East, Cyril and Athanasius supported belief in their apostolic authorship, an opinion which ultimately prevailed.

Questions relating to the origin of the Johannine writings are complicated by the fact that the internal evidence is not direct. Only the Revelation gives its writer's name, and that simply as John. The Gospel and 1 John are anonymous writings. The lesser letters, 2 and 3 John, were composed by a writer or writers identified simply as "the Elder."

The view taken in this chapter is that whatever conclusions may be reached concerning the authorship of the Johannine books, the tradition is probably correct which associates all five with a church or churches in Asia. Their literary, historical, and theological affinities are striking, in spite of their differences. They are all associated with the testimony of the Apostle John. Thus they may be called, "writings from the Johannine circle."

THE MARTYRDOM TRADITION

Conflicting traditions have survived concerning the later life of the Apostle John. The testimony of Irenaeus has little earlier support, and there are reports which some scholars consider sufficient to discredit it. According to Mark, Jesus forewarned the sons of Zebedee that they would suffer as he must suffer.[4] An

---

[1]Muratorian canon; Clement of Alexandria, Strom., III.5.45 (Eusebius, H. E., VI.14.7); Origen (Eusebius, H. E., VI.25.9f.). Irenaeus quotes from 1 and 2 John as though they were a single letter, Adv. Haer., III.15.5–8.

[2]Eusebius, H. E., III.23, cites the apology of Irenaeus. The original sources are Adv. Haer., I.9.3; II.22.5; III.3.4, 17.5–8; V.33.3.

[3]C. H. Dodd, The Johannine Epistles (1946), pp. xi ff.

[4]Mark 10:39.

epitomist of a church history written by Philip of Side (fifth century) gives the following quotation: "Papias in his second book says that John the Divine and James his brother were killed by Jews." In the writing of another, Georgius Monachus (ninth century), a similar reference to Papias is found. Two lists of Christian martyrs, one dated around A.D. 411, the other around 505, imply that John suffered the same fate as his brother James, perhaps at the same time. It should be recalled that Acts reported that James was put to death by Herod (Agrippa I, A.D. 41–44).[5]

These records are interpreted as having cumulative force or no value at all. Some scholars say that it matters not whether Mark's saying of Jesus is a genuine prediction or a prophecy after the event. It would not have been recorded if it had not been fulfilled. Other scholars have replied that the passage in Mark can be used as proof that both James and John were martyred only if it is a prophecy after the event. But it cannot be considered such unless independent evidence can be produced. The so-called "evidence" is not worthy of consideration, therefore the argument is a circular one. Neither Philip nor Georgius was an accurate historian, and both Eusebius and Irenaeus had read the works of Papias. The martyr lists may be based on nothing more than an interpretation of Mark's passage. They hardly provide the necessary independent witness.

It seems that a conclusion must rest upon a choice between the truthfulness of Irenaeus and Eusebius on the one hand or the accuracy of Philip and Georgius on the other. If this is so, then credit should be given the earlier writers. It cannot be said that the martyrdom tradition disposes of the apostolic authorship of any of the Johannine writings. Yet it is evident that the testimony concerning John's last days is severely limited and equivocal.[6]

THE REVELATION TO JOHN

The book of Revelation is one of the least read and the most misunderstood writings of the New Testament. Many Christians do not know what to make of it; a few make of it entirely too much. The book is commonly called "Revelations." This is an accurate description if it applies to the many visions of its author. But the title is singular, not plural. This in itself identifies the peculiar literary genre of the work. Unlike many writings of its type, however, Revelation is not a pseudonymous book. It contains a new message given to a contemporary seer under the authority of his own, not another's, name. And it begins with a series of short letters. But otherwise Revelation is a typical *apocalypse*.[7] This fact should

---

[5]C. K. Barrett, *The Gospel According to St. John* (1955), pp. 86f. [hereafter, *St. John*].

[6]McNeile, *Intro.*, pp. 287ff.; J. H. Bernard, *The Gospel of John* (1928), vol. I, pp. xxxvii ff. Cf. R. H. Charles, *The Revelation of St. John* (1920), vol. I, pp. xlv ff. [hereafter, *St. John*]. For a brief discussion of the obscure history of the church at Ephesus, see Lake, *Intro.*, pp. 173ff.

[7]An exception to this common view is expressed by J. Kallas, who argues that the writer has a nonapocalyptic eschatology and explanation of suffering, "The Apocalypse—An Apocalyptic Book?" *JBL* LXXXVI (1967): 69ff.

prevent the serious reader from being misled by some interpretations which have been imposed upon it.

That some modern Christians should find Revelation distasteful is not surprising. By the end of the second century its authority was generally acknowledged. But the voice of the Church was not unanimous.[8] The book's popularity with many raised the doubts of a few. It was as eagerly received by millenarians of the second as of the twentieth century, lusting for the pleasures of "reigning on the earth a thousand years" with Christ.[9] Some leaders of the ancient Church rejected the authority of this doctrine. It should be noted also that Marcion was repelled by its Jewish character and therefore denied to Revelation an apostolic authority.[10] His followers are still among us. The Church of the West rose to the defense of the book. But not all misgivings were allayed by official declarations. The great Jerome expressed his personal doubt about its canonical standing, and, later, Protestant reformers did the same.

Christians at Alexandria in the third century found no great difficulty with the teaching of Revelation. This ease probably was due to the tendency within this church to interpret scripture allegorically. Origen, a forthright foe of millenarianism, rejected a literal interpretation and exercised his ingenuity to recover the spiritual (allegorical) meaning of Revelation. The book still suffers from Origenesque interpretations. It is a well-known fact that Dionysius, bishop of Alexandria (A.D. 247–264), was the first serious scholar to argue that Revelation could not have been written by the same hand as the Fourth Gospel. Its style, grammar, and ideas were not those of the fourth evangelist. Since the bishop accepted the apostolic authorship of the Gospel, he was bound to deny it to Revelation. Eusebius, who reported the bishop's views, found them convincing. He suggested that Revelation was written by a certain John, "the elder" of Ephesus, of whom Papias had written. The historian adopted an indecisive position; Revelation could be accepted or rejected as scripture "as may seem proper."[11] Unfortunately the attitude of Eusebius has been the practical position of many in the Church since his time. It can be said also that the "higher criticism" of Dionysius clearly adumbrated the "critical orthodoxy" of modern scholars.

Before turning from this brief review of the reception accorded Revelation, notice may be taken of ancient traditions concerning the date and circumstances of its composition. The earliest authorities are almost unanimous in assigning Revelation to the last years of Domitian's reign. Somewhat later, a few others thought the situation implied the reigns of Claudius, Nero, or Trajan.[12] It is not possible to say whether any of these traditions are based on evidence independent of the book. A similar spread of opinion has resulted from modern analyses of

[8] Charles, *St. John*, vol. I, pp. c ff.; McNeile, *Intro.*, p. 263.

[9] Rev. 20:1ff. The first millenarians were the Montanists, a widely influential heretical group in Phrygia around A.D. 150.

[10] Tertullian, *Adv. Marc.*, IV.5; also III.14.

[11] Eusebius, *H. E.*, III.39.6; also III.24.18 and 25.4. For the traditional story of the Apostle's exile to Patmos, III.18 and 20; also Tertullian, *De praescrip. Haer.*

[12] Charles, *St. John*, vol. I, pp. xci ff.

its content. But contemporary as well as ancient authorities tend to agree that Revelation was written in the final phase of Domitian's rule.[13]

The Witness of the Apocalypse to Its Origin

Four times the author of Revelation called himself "John."[14] He wished to be known to his readers as God's "servant," and their "brother," sharing "in Jesus the tribulation and the kingdom and the patient endurance." It is doubtful that John's words claim an official position; it was enough that he had heard and seen "the revelation of Jesus Christ." Nevertheless, from the conclusion of the book, it is clear that he considered himself a Christian "prophet," and his message, "words of the prophecy,"[15]

In the light of the internal evidence, modern scholars do not hesitate to reject the equivocal witness of the second century concerning the apostolic authorship of Revelation. But this judgment rests upon broader consideration than the writer's references to himself. The general thought, vocabulary, and style of Revelation set it apart from the Fourth Gospel. One scholar summarizes the case in the following words:

> In the Revelation God's love is mentioned once, his fatherhood not at all, and the material imagery of the Revelation is in sharp contrast to the mysticism of the gospel. Many of the specially characteristic words of the gospel are absent from the Revelation, e.g., truth, or used in a different sense, e.g., light, only with a physical meaning; different Greek words are employed in the two books for "the Lamb." The style of Revelation is barbarous, and only consistent with a very imperfect knowledge of Greek grammar.[16]

Obviously these negative judgments carry greater weight with those who hold that John the Apostle wrote the Fourth Gospel or that his typical witness is reported therein. Otherwise some may feel that the disciple's Galilean background could account for the form and content of Revelation. Yet the absence of any trace of the writer's association with Jesus in his Ministry, and his reference to "the twelve apostles of the Lamb," to mention but two considerations, make this surmise extremely improbable.[17] There were many persons named John in the early Church. An inspired writer such as this one might easily have been mistaken for the Lord's disciple with the same name, at a time when the sanction of apostolic authority was sought and Revelation was a controversial document. For those seeking a designation for the author more suggestive than "St. John the Divine," "John the Seer" may serve.

References in Revelation to its date and to the circumstances of its writing should now be noted. Some passages imply a date before the fall of Jerusalem.

[13] See further, below, pp. 556f., and 563.

[14] Rev. 1:1, 4, 9; 22:8.

[15] Rev. 22:6f., 9f., 18f.

[16] Heard, *Intro.,* p. 239. The comparative studies of R. H. Charles established beyond reasonable doubt a different authorship (*St. John,* vol. I, pp. xxxix ff.).

[17] Rev. 21:4. McNeile, *Intro.,* pp. 264f.

In one of these the temple is pictured as still standing. This may be no more evidence for a date before A.D. 70 than references to the Jerusalem cultus in Hebrews and in other postapostolic writings.[18] The figure of the woman whose child had been exalted to heaven fleeing "to the place where she is to be nourished for a time . . ." has been considered an image of the flight of the Jerusalem church to Pella.[19] Some have thought that the five fallen "kings" refer to Roman emperors, reckoning from Augustus. The king "who is" may therefore be Vespasian (A.D. 69–79).[20] But references such as these may only indicate that the author incorporated earlier materials. There are other signs that he had used sources.

In its completed form Revelation probably originated in the closing years of Domitian's reign. Internal evidence supports this ancient Church tradition. The deterioration of the early zeal of the church at Ephesus, and the situation at Sardis and Laodicea, point to a time some while after Paul's lifetime. The church at Smyrna was nonexistent in Paul's day.[21] The trouble being caused by the Nicolaitans, discussed in Chapter 18, seems to root in a lawlessness of the type rebuked by the writers of Jude and 1 John.

The most crucial evidence is provided by the writer's visions of the beasts from the sea and from the earth.[22] Some have too quickly concluded that these are transparent pointers to the emperor cult in Asia during Domitian's rule. But we have seen that evidence more nearly contemporaneous than these traditions concerning Revelation cast shadows of doubt about Domitian's policies and attitudes toward Christians.[23] There is of course no evidence before Domitian of state persecutions in Asia, and Domitian does seem to have pressed Caesarworship in this province. But this of itself does not preclude an earlier date for Revelation. The writer's fears and hatred of Rome, to say nothing of his prophetic insight, are sufficient to explain his conviction that its authorities were determined to annihilate worship of the true God.[24] Nevertheless, the evidence presented in the previous paragraph cannot be dismissed. Interpreters also must reckon with the influence upon the author of a popular bogey that Nero was not dead. It is said that after A.D. 88, but not before, the current form of this legend was that Nero would reappear as a beast from the abyss.[25] Accordingly, two large sections of Revelation may be assigned to the later half of the reign of Domitian (A.D. 81–96).

Any discussion of the circumstances surrounding the origin of Revelation must do justice to the writer's own account. He was alarmed because of the spiritual sickness of Asian Christians. But this was not the chief cause of his writing. Like a true prophet he was compelled by the Spirit to proclaim those things which

---

[18] Rev. 11:1f. See above, p. 528.

[19] Rev. 12:13ff.

[20] Rev. 17:10. McNeile, *Intro.*, pp. 361f. Cf. Enslin, *Beginnings*, pp. 365ff.

[21] Rev. 2:8ff. Polycarp, *Phil.*, XI. Charles, *St. John*, vol. I, p. xciv.

[22] Rev. 13:1ff. Note also 2:13.

[23] See above, pp. 478f.

[24] Enslin, *Beginnings*, p. 364f.

[25] Rev. 13, 17. McNeile, *Intro.*, p. 262; Charles, *St. John*, vol. I, p. xcv.

would "soon take place." How far the contents of Revelation reflect John's ecstatic experiences on Patmos cannot be said.[26] But at least three external influences upon the form of his message have been detected: the Old Testament, contemporary Jewish apocalypses, and the worship of the Christian Church. These three factors deserve brief comment.

Revelation contains over five hundred allusions to the Old Testament. The writer has reminted much of the imagery of scripture in presenting his visionary experiences.[27] But even more important may have been the influence of several Jewish apocalypses which were currently in circulation. Many scholars claim that the writer has borrowed extensively from these. One "school" contends that the bulk of Revelation reproduces one or more of these Jewish tracts. But not many have been persuaded that the "seer" is only an "editor." The Christian aspect of Revelation cannot be reduced to a prologue, epilogue, and a few interpolations.[28]

In recent times attention has been given to the impress of Christian liturgy upon the Seer's mental processes. One writer has said, "It is as if the author, cut off from the Church's worship on the Lord's day, meditates upon its offering of praise and thanksgiving which is counterpart of the heavenly liturgy."[29] The prayers and other liturgical materials in Revelation have been used as sources for reconstructing the worship in the postapostolic Church.[30]

A Brief Interpretation of Revelation

The suggestion that the book should be read in its entirety has been delayed. This was inevitable. No book of the New Testament makes such demands upon its reader; no book so much requires a critical introduction. At the same time, it is quite impossible to learn the message of Revelation from secondary sources. One must view with his own eyes this vast, fantastic panorama, even though one needs a guide map.

Unfortunately the reader does not find general consent as to the plan of the book.[31] In part this lack is due to two or more conceptions of its disordered content. On the one hand, some interpreters assume that its visions follow a consecutive, temporal series. If the text of the book does not display consistency, one must suppose either its dislocation or the hand of an editor, or both. Only by critical restoration can the progress of the Seer's thought be recovered.[32] On the other hand, many interpreters—perhaps the majority—believe that the Seer

[26]Rev. 1:9ff.

[27]R. H. Preston and A. T. Hanson, *The Revelation of St. John the Divine* (1949), pp. 34ff., and throughout the commentary [hereafter, *St. John the Divine*].

[28]Hunter, *Interpreting*, pp. 100f.; Lake, *Intro.*, p. 178.

[29]Fuller and Wright, *Book of the Acts of God*, pp. 335f.

[30]L. Mowry, "Revelation 4–5 and Early Liturgical Usage," *JBL* LXXI (1952): 75ff.

[31]See the various outlines reported in McNeile, *Intro.*, pp. 254ff; J. W. Bowman, "Book of Revelation," *IDB*, vol. 4, pp. 64ff.

[32]E.g., Charles, *St. John*, vol. I. pp. xxv ff. See the elaborate rearrangement proposed by John Oman in McNeile, *Intro.*, pp. 257ff.

adopted some scheme of recapitulation. His visions are often parallel, repeating in various imagery the three conventional stages of the apocalyptic drama: the period of catastrophies on earth and in heaven; the coming of Christ to destroy the powers of evil; the final judgment with its eternal rewards and penalties.[33] A third group of interpreters say that the book defies structural analysis, believing that the author was not interested in these matters. As in some modern impressionistic paintings, the viewer must not expect logical patterns but seek to appreciate the kaleidoscopic nature of Revelation's many-splendored vision.

An Outline of the Revelation to John

A. Prologue, 1:1–20:
   1. A solemn superscription including a beatitude, 1:1–5a
   2. In praise of the risen Christ, 1:5b–6
   3. A solemn declaration: behold, he is coming, 1:7–8
   4. The revelation to John, 1:9–11
   5. The initial vision, 1:12–20
B. Letters to the seven churches, 2:1–3:22:
   6. Ephesus, 2:1–7
   7. Smyrna, 2:8–11
   8. Pergamum, 2:12–17
   9. Thyatira, 2:18–29
   10. Sardis, 3:1–6
   11. Philadelphia, 3:7–13
   12. Laodicea, 3:14–22
C. A vision of heaven, 4:1–5:14:
   13. The throne of the eternal God surrounded by his worshipers, 4:1–11
   14. The vision of Christ the conqueror—who is given the scroll with the seven seals, and worshiped with God, 5:1–14
D. The effect on earth of the opening of the seven seals, 6:1–8:1:
   15. The four seals and the four horsemen, 6:1–8
   16. The fifth seal and the cry of the martyred saints, 6:9–11
   17. The sixth seal: some brighter phases of the eschatological drama are anticipated, 6:12–7:17: the day of wrath and its universal terrors (6:12–17) contrasted with the "sealing" of the saints and their rapture (7:1–17)
   18. The seventh seal: silence in heaven, 8:1
D. A vision of the seven trumpeting angels who stand before God, 8:2–11:19:
   19. The ministry of the angels at the altar of heaven, 8:2–6
   20. At the sound of the trumpets of four angels, the earth is partially destroyed, 8:7–13

---

[33] M. Kiddle, *The Revelation of St. John* (1940), pp. xxix f. Cf. Preston and Hanson, *St. John the Divine*, pp. 17ff., and A. M. Farrar, *A Rebirth of Images* (1949); both commentaries hold that the author's thought moves in a series of cycles. The latter finds keys to the structure of Rev. in the numbers, the Jewish liturgical year, and the signs of the zodiac; Bowman (note 31 above) perceives influences of the Jewish temple and Greek–Roman stage furnishings.

21. At the sound of the fifth angel's trumpet, demonic locusts are unleashed (the first of three woes), 9:1–12
22. At the sound of the sixth angel's trumpet, the second woe (again, brighter phases of the eschatological drama are anticipated), 9:13–11:14: four militant angels and their cavalry are released, bringing to the earth three plagues (9:13–19); the unrepentant survivors (9:20–21); the cosmic angel appears (10:1–7); the seer eats the scroll from the angel's hand (10:8–11); the measuring of a part of the temple and the two mighty witnesses (11:1–6); the death and resurrection of the witnesses and their final bliss, the terror of their foes (11:7–14)
23. At the sound of the seventh angel's trumpet, the announcement of the end brings joy in heaven and cosmic repercussions (the third woe), 11:15–19

E. Seven visions concerning the dragon and his emissaries, and the Messiah and his Church, 12:1–15:4:
   24. First vision: the heavenly mother and the dragon; the birth of the heavenly child; the dragon is thwarted, 12:1–17
   25. Second vision: the rise of the beast from the sea invested with the dragon's power; his blasphemy and his reprobate worshipers, 13:1–10
   26. Third vision: the delegated power of the second beast "from the earth"; his persecutions, 13:11–18
   27. Fourth vision: the conquering Lamb and the "redeemed from the earth," 14:1–5
   28. Fifth vision: the angel with the "eternal gospel," followed by two angels of woe; a beatitude for the martyrs, 14:6–13
   29. Sixth vision: "one like a son of man," and the angels of wrath, 14:14–20
   30. Seventh vision: after the final judgment, the triumphant songs of Moses and the Lamb, 15:1–4

F. Visions concerning the seven bowls full of the wrath of God, 15:5–16:21:
   31. The opening of the temple of heaven, 15:5–16:1
   32. First bowl: the plague of sores upon the worshipers of the beast, 16:2
   33. Second bowl: plague of the sea turned to blood, 16:3
   34. Third bowl: plague of the rivers and springs, 16:4–7
   35. Fourth bowl: plague of fierce heat, 16:8–9
   36. Fifth bowl: plague of darkness upon the kingdom of the beast, 16:10–11
   37. Sixth bowl: plague of drought prepares for "the kings from the east" and for Armageddon, 16:12–16
   38. Seventh bowl: plague of cosmic upheaval, 16:17–21

G. Visions of the judgment upon Babylon, 17:1–19:10:
   39. The great harlot is depicted, 17:1–6
   40. The scene is interpreted, 17:7–18
   41. Vision of the angel announcing Babylon's fall, 18:1–3
   42. A dirge and taunt song over Babylon, 18:4–20
   43. Vision of the millstone, and the violent overthrow of Babylon, 18:21–24
   44. The mighty voice of the heavenly multitude exults in the divine deliverance and worships God, 19:1–8

Church of God.[34] The letters contain more than deprecations, however, for eternal rewards are promised to the martyrs.[35]

The writer's vision of heaven (C) is a *sursum corda*. The persecuted Church must look up to the awful majesty of God the Creator. Just as Paul wrote, Christians set their minds "on the things that are above where Christ is. . . ."[36] Without this vision, faith cannot endure. Two features of John's symbolism may attract the reader, his "celestial mathematics," and his bizarre mythological beasts. Biblical and ancient Jewish tradition provide the safest contexts for interpreting this symbolism. For example, the Lamb with horns is derived from the horned ram of several Jewish apocalypses.[37] But behind the figure of "the Lamb that was slain," whose blood ransoms men for God, is surely the event of the crucifixion as understood in the light of Isaiah 53. The early Christian use of the Passover lamb as a type of the cross of Christ further enriched this imagery.[38] When God's judgments are in the world, the new Israel can expect divine protection.

A description of the woes preceding the End was a familiar apocalyptic feature, as we have seen (D). John developed this pattern in a distinctive way. Just as the reader is led to expect the opening of the final "seal," a new sequence of woes is initiated; before the last angel's trumpet sounds, another dreadful series begins. In the outline the proposal is made that at such places the writer has anticipated the brighter side of the judgments of God to hearten his readers.[39] We need not dwell upon these repetitious passages. Sufficiently mystifying to need commentary are the related scenes.

The obscurity of John's symbolism troubles us less than his morbid, pitiless preoccupation with scenes of punishment. Our moral consciousness, not our reason, is repelled. When we read that the opening of the seals by Christ brings war, civil dissension, famine, and other disasters; the prayer of the martyrs for blood revenge; and the dreadful series of woes, repeated thrice, we may ask: To what extent is Revelation "a Christian book"? Many have pondered this question. With regard to the wrath of God and the fearful prospect of judgment, the writer does not depart from the teaching of the New Testament generally.[40] When we read these disaster scenes we should not overlook the fact that Revelation was written to encourage persecuted Christians living in disastrous times, not to frighten pagans into repentance. Furthermore, the petition of the martyrs is more than an impatient cry for revenge; it is "a heartfelt self-identification with the purpose of God, imperfectly expressed, no doubt, but in essence identical with the prayer 'Thy kingdom come.' "[41]

---

[34] E. F. Scott, *The Book of Revelation* (1941), p. 61.

[35] W. Barclay, *Letters to the Seven Churches* (1957).

[36] Col. 3:1ff.

[37] Rev. 6:16; 7:17; 14:1ff.; 17:14; 22:1ff Cf. En. lxxxix ff.; Test. XII Pat.; Jos. xix. 8.

[38] Cf. 1 Cor. 5:7, and, especially, John 19:31ff.

[39] Cf. 2 Thess. 1:5ff.; 2:9ff. Also John 17:33. C. B. Caird, *The Revelation of St. John the Divine* (1966) pp. 82f. [hereafter, *Revelation*].

[40] Ibid., pp. 292ff.; W. Klassen, "Vengeance in the Apocalypse of John," *Cath. Bib. Quar.*, 28 (1966): 300ff. Cf. Kallas, note 7 above, pp. 74ff.

[41] Fuller and Wright, *Book of the Acts of God*, p. 337; see also Preston and Hanson, *St. John the Divine*, pp. 29ff.

Nevertheless, while these and other things can be said, the fact remains that John's vindictiveness is reminiscent more of Qumran's spirit than of Jesus'.[42] But Christians have the Sermon on the Mount to purge Revelation of its dross. Some persons value Revelation as though it contained the whole gospel; others see no gospel in it. But there is another point of view, that which acknowledges Revelation to be an essential part of the gospel but by no means the whole of it.[43]

Our attention may now be directed to the seven visions concerning the dragon and his agents (E). In these scenes we see the conflict between Christianity and the dread forces of evil in a historical setting. Some of these scenes may be called "flashbacks." The birth of the heavenly child and the murderous attack of the dragon may have intended a transparent disguise of the birth of Jesus to Mary, and Herod's threat to his life (24). In the Apocalypse, events on earth have their counterparts in heaven. But it is more probable that the "woman clothed with the sun" is a symbol throughout of the Church.[44] Like Paul and the writer of Hebrews, John recognized the continuity between Israel and the Church. From the womb of Israel the Christ was born. In either case, the deliverance of this child from death surely symbolized the resurrection and heavenly exaltation of Christ. The war fought in heaven and also on earth represented John's adaptation of the teaching found in Paul's letters and elsewhere. The triumph of Christ resulted in the fall of the demonic powers but not their final conquest.[45]

The visions of the beasts are companion pieces (25–26). The blasphemous monster from the sea probably suggested Domitian, or the representative of his imperial power in Asia, as noted above. The second beast symbolized the imperial priesthood or, more inclusively, the local government which vigorously fostered the emperor cult in Asia. Some commentators have detected an evil parody in these pictures. The dragon and the two beasts war in concert against God's Lamb and the divine Spirit incarnate in the Church. In John's day men worshiped the god of power incarnate in the Roman emperor and the State, rejecting the true trinity. The vision which pictures the conquering Lamb as the one who accepted suffering, instead of inflicting it upon men, provides welcome relief from the woeful scenes of judgment (27); likewise, the vision of the universal proclamation of "an eternal gospel," and the coming of "one like unto a son of man" (28–30). But in these brighter scenes all darkness is not dispelled, nor do the songs of the saved drown the woeful dirges. John believed, in company with other writers of the New Testament, that judgment attends the heralding of the good news for men who will not receive it.[46]

John's lurid tapestry of the judgment is further embroidered by the visions of the seven bowls outpoured, leading up to the fall of "Babylon" as a symbol for Rome's tyrannical power structure. These scenes are richly interwoven with Old Testament symbolism and language (39–44). In the explanation of the vision

[42] Cf. Klassen, note 40 above.

[43] See Feine-Behm-Kümmel, *Intro.*, pp. 331ff.

[44] Ibid., p. 92; Caird, *Revelation*, p. 149. Cf. M. Rist, *IB*, vol. 12, pp. 363, 452ff. For an account of the origin of this "international myth," these and other commentaries should be consulted.

[45] Rev. 12:7ff.; Col. 2:15 (Gal. 4:3ff.?). See also Luke 10:17.; John 12:31f.

[46] Rom. 10:15ff.; Heb. 2:2ff.; John 3:17ff.

of "the great harlot [the goddess Roma?]," the beast from "the bottomless pit" is recalled and his destined fate announced (40). The revelation to John of this "mystery" is not altogether clear to his modern reader, for there is a confluence of references, literary and historical, and the symbolism is complex.[47] By such means, however, John assured his readers that, in the clash of powers in history, the Lamb was destined to conquer. "Another angel" then appeared to chant a dirge announcing Babylon's doom (41–42). Zeal for the vindication of God's righteousness led John to echo the taunt songs of the Old Testament prophets. Other New Testament writings do not allow the Christian to believe that God exacts double punishment for sin. It is possible though not probable that one New Testament book was written to correct the effect of these impassioned songs of hatred against Rome.[48]

The seven visions which follow proclaim a temporary check upon Satan's power to deceive men, an interregnum of the Messiah, a world conflict and the consigning of Satan to a place of eternal torment, judgment day, and the beginning of the eternal reign of God and the elect (H). Some of these scenes appear to be a gathering up of earlier ideas, in anticipation of the last "last things."[49] The Gog and Magog theme, which is derived from Ezekiel, recalls Armageddon (50).[50] The beasts are again disposed of; not finally, but their doom is announced. The thousand-year reign of Christ on earth is interposed. With John's development of the simpler patterns of doomsday one should compare several first-century Jewish apocalypses which also depict a temporary messianic kingdom as the prelude to the Age to Come.[51] While John's interest centered chiefly upon the ultimate, not this penultimate, kingdom, one cannot conclude that John was unwillingly a captive to traditional beliefs. The millennium was deliberately introduced to encourage a martyr church. The repeated attempts which have been made to literalize this fleeting vision and to fit it into the calendar time of the future have led to nothing but confusion and vexation.[52]

The imagery of John's vision of the last judgment (51) stresses his belief that nothing—absolutely nothing—in the created order escapes the divine scrutiny; nothing remains beyond the reach of God's power. Death and Hades release their captives at God's command, and the final frustrations to the fulfillment of the purpose of the Almighty are removed. Whatever uncertainty may have lingered in the mind of Paul, John was no believer in universal salvation.

John's picture of the fate of the damned has been contrasted unfavorably with the mythologies of the End described by prophets of other religions. Yet his vision

[47]E.g., see the difficulties facing the reader in identifying the apparently straightforward reference to the seven kings, Rev. 17:10f. Caird, *Revelation*, pp. 217ff.

[48]See above, p. 523.

[49]Some scholars find it necessary to resort to displacement theories to understand Rev. 20–22. See Preston and Hanson, *St. John the Divine*, pp. 129ff.

[50]Ezek. 29:17ff. Cf. Rev. 16:16.

[51]2 Esd. 7:27ff. Cf. 2 En. 33:2 (of very questionable date). See above, pp. 87f., and the helpful comment by M. Rist, *IB*, vol. 12, pp. 518f.

[52]For a judicious discussion of this problematical passage, see Caird, *Revelation*, pp. 248ff.

of the holy city is without parallel for the sublimity of its themes (52–57). Exploiting the rich and complex symbolism of the Old Testament to describe the new Jerusalem, he ends by stressing the Christian's attainment of the ultimate blessedness: God's "servants shall worship him; they shall see his face. . . ."[53] The power of these visions to move the spirit of men is enshrined in the world's great art. Prosaic commentary runs the risk of botching the effect of this vivid canvas. John's "new Jerusalem" is not conceivable; it is only imaginable.

THE THREE LETTERS OF JOHN

That 1, 2, and 3 John share a similar background is rarely questioned today. We may assume therefore that in considering questions relating to their origins the three writings should be mutually illuminating.

Second and Third John are accurately described as letters. But 1 John has none of a letter's characteristics. Its author may have intended one, but it is probable that he composed a sermon or pastoral homily for the instruction of several groups of Christians.

What can be learned about the origin of the Johannine letters, their purposes, destinations, and dates? In the two brief letters, but not in the homily, the writer calls himself "the Elder." Nothing is said about his position or relation to his readers. Apparently he exercised some authority over a group of churches and their elders. Third John is the most personal of the three.

AN OUTLINE OF THE THIRD LETTER OF JOHN

A. Introduction, 1–4:
  1. Superscription and greeting, 1–2
  2. Expression of joy upon hearing the good report concerning Gaius, 3–4
B. Commendations, 5–8:
  3. Of Gaius, for his "service to the brethren," 5–6
  4. Of the deserving brethren, 7–8
C. The insubordination of Diotrephes, 9–12:
  5. The offenses of Diotrephes are described, 9–10
  6. Counsel to imitate the good; a test of a godly man, 11–12
D. Conclusion, 13–15:
  7. Reasons for brevity, 13–14
  8. Greetings, 15

Was "the Elder" one who was known among his friends as "the old man," or was he simply one of a body of recognized leaders in a particular church? The superscription itself reveals nothing, but the writer's commendations of Gaius and others do. It is clearly implied that the traveling missionaries are under the

[53]Rev. 22:4.

supervision of the writer and that he feels justified in calling upon a group of churches to receive them and to provide for their keep.[54]

A certain Diotrephes, however, had boycotted the Elder and his emissaries. His opposition had led him to speak slanderously of the Elder and to seek to exclude from the church any persons who welcomed his missionaries (5).

The Elder does not directly accuse Diotrephes of erroneous teachings. He attributed his insubordination to personal ambition. Perhaps Diotrephes is to be regarded as a forerunner of the presiding bishop whose office is recognized in the letters of Ignatius, or as "the kind of upstart whose ambition made the emergence of the Ignatian bishop inevitable."[55] But may one surmise that the cause for the altercation ran deeper? Both the extreme measures taken by Diotrephes and the tenor of the Elder's rebuke suggest that something more than personal rivalry led to the rift. Did sharp doctrinal differences exist between the two concerning the gospel?[56] Perhaps 2 John may provide clues for an answer.

AN OUTLINE OF THE SECOND LETTER OF JOHN

A. Introduction, 1-3:
    1. The superscription, 1-3
B. The summons to follow the truth, 4-6:
    2. An expression of joy that some are following the truth, 4
    3. An appeal for loyal compliance, 5-6
C. The deceivers and instructions concerning them, 7-11:
    4. Their doctrine of Christ, 7
    5. Warning against defection, 8
    6. A test of a godly man, 9
    7. No hospitality for the deceivers, 10-11
D. Conclusion, 12-13:
    8. Reasons for brevity, 12
    9. Greeting, 13

The letter before us was written by the Elder to the Church. This use of the feminine singular—"the elect (lady)"—is found in one New Testament writing, but numerous parallels are given in the literature of the period.[57] The closing greeting of the letter, and the author's use of the second person plural from verse six, confirms that the address is a thin disguise for a pastoral letter to Christian congregations.

The emphasis on the word *truth* in the superscription suggests that the letter was prompted by a threat to it; "all who know the truth" distinguish true from

---

[54]Cf. Matt. 10:8; 1 Cor. 9:1ff. Recall the evidence provided by *Shep. of Her.* and the *Did.* of trouble caused by such itinerant ministers in the postapostolic age (see above, pp. 488f.).

[55]C. B. Caird, "Letters of John," *IDB*, vol. 2, p. 950. See above, p. 489.

[56]For a summary of various attempts to reconstruct the situation in the church, see Feine-Behm-Kümmel, *Intro.*, p. 314. See further, below, p. 569.

[57]1 Peter 5:13. Cf. Gal. 4:21ff., Bar. 4f. For Hellenistic parallels, Dodd, *Johannine Epistles*, pp. 144f.

false believers. Unlike 3 John, this letter explicitly declared that erroneous doctrine had created a schism in the Church. The troublemakers are "men who will not acknowledge the coming of Jesus Christ in the flesh" (4). They were, as we have characterized such teaching," docetists." They denied the reality that Christ had been a human being. Apparently these docetists considered their teaching a superior understanding of the gospel. They had "gone out into the world" to proclaim their "progressive" views, and they had clashed with the Elder and his missionaries. From the latter's point of view, the docetists were not teaching a mature understanding of the faith; they were impostors. Anyone who held these views was, in fact, "the antichrist," and his so-called advanced teaching was a serious departure from "the truth" which could result only in a loss of the divine fellowship and the Christians' reward (5–6).

This short letter implies that the errorists had not as yet reached "the elect lady and her children" (7). The Elder forewarned the Church to insure a quarantine against docetism. The emphasis of the letter upon the Christian commandment to "follow love" suggests that the docetists were violating the law of Christ by their divisive spirit or by their indifference to the needs of the brethren.

Some scholars see unmistakable evidence in 2 John that the aberrant teaching under attack was a Gnostic or pre-Gnostic version of Christianity which taught "salvation by esoteric knowledge," excited "an enthusiasm devoid of moral concern," and nourished "a spirituality contemptuous of things material."[58] Because of their depreciation of matter, as incapable of mediating the divine, these Gnostics threatened belief in the humanity of Christ and the redemptive power of his real death. Since this erroneous teaching combatted in 2 John had produced an heretical Christology, it is claimed that "we have to do here with a developed form of Gnosticism."[59] Of this one cannot be sure, but further evidence for identifying the specific content of the teaching of the Elder's opponents may be found in the "larger letter" of John.

An Outline of the First Letter of John

A. Prologue, 1:1–4:
    1. Testimony to the gospel, 1:1–2
    2. The author's purpose, 1:3–4
B. Fellowship with God: the test of behavior, 1:5–2:17:
    3. Those who walk in the light (that is, who have fellowship with God, who is light) live according to the truth and are cleansed from all sin, 1:5–7
    4. Those who are free from all sin are those who confess sin, relying upon him who is the expiation for sins, 1:8–2:2
    5. Only those who keep God's commandments know him, 2:3–6
    6. The application of the test to the reader's situation, 2:7–17

[58] C. B. Caird, *IDB*, vol. 2, p. 947.

[59] Feine-Behm-Kümmel, *Intro.*, p. 310; Cf. R. McL. Wilson, *Gnosis*, p. 42. Unconvincing efforts have been made to identify John's opponents as Cerinthian, see above, p. 484.

   C. Fellowship with God: the confessional test, 2:18–27:
      7. The "many antichrists" are harbingers of "the last hour," 2:18
      8. The departure of the antichrists validates the test, 2:19–21
      9. The confession, 2:22–25
     10. The assurance of those who are being taught the truth and who are not deceived by the lie, 2:26–27
   D. The development of the two tests and their relationship, 2:28–3:24:
     11. The behavior of the children of God in view of Christ's [second] coming, 2:28–3:3
     12. The children of God and of the devil: the opposite tests of "lawlessness" and "doing right," 3:4–10
     13. Abiding in death and in eternal life: the opposite tests of hatred and love, 3:11–18
     14. The test of confidence before God, 3:19–22
     15. Summary: the two basic tests restated; the assurance of the Spirit, 3:23–24
   E. The test of the Spirit: the confession that Jesus Christ has come in the flesh, 4:1–6:
     16. False prophets and the spirit of error, 4:1–3
     17. Those possessed of the true Spirit overcome the world, 4:4–6
   F. The interrelation of the tests of behavior and confession; the assurances of the children of God, 4:7–5:13:
     18. The command to love is based on the revelation of love, 4:7–12
     19. The assurance of the Spirit is voiced in the confession that Jesus is the Son of God, 4:13–16
     20. The assurance in the day of judgment: love casts out fear, 4:17–18
     21. Summary: the test for the reality of faith is love of the brethren; the assurance of victory over the world, 4:19–5:5
     22. The witness of the Spirit is the testimony of God, 5:6–13
   G. Epilogue, 5:14–21:
     23. Concerning petition and intercession, 5:14–17
     24. The Christian certainties, 5:18–20
     25. A postscript, 21

The reader of 1 John may wonder if the author was guided by any plan in writing his homily. The metaphor of the spiral has been suggested. In the course of developing a theme the author sometimes brings us back to the starting point; almost, but not quite, for there is a slight shift which provides a transition to a fresh theme; or some theme which has been enunciated earlier is taken up again from a slightly different angle.[60] Scholars agree on the main divisions of the letter but there are wide variations within these. The above outline calls attention to two major tests of "the truth"—the one, doctrinal, the other, ethical—which are the foci of 1 John.[61]

---

[60] Dodd, *Johannine Epistles.*, pp. xxi f.

[61] McNeile, *Intro.*, pp. 300ff.; cf. Feine-Behm-Kümmel, *Intro.*, pp. 306f.; also pp. 308f., for unsatisfactory attempts to explain the homily as the author's revision of an original, earlier writing.

One scholar has suggested that the nature of the writer's opposition is revealed in his warnings against taking seriously certain claims that were being made. These passages begin with the conditional clause: "if we say that . . ."[62] Some persons were evidently boasting a special *gnosis* as well as love of God, and an especially intimate relation to Him which set them above good and evil. It is also reasonable to suppose that the strange word *chrism*, or "unction," which is twice used to describe the gift of the Spirit, found its way into the letter because John's opponents used it to describe their own unique spiritual endowment.[63]

Reference is made to the many "false prophets" who have "gone out into the world." Surely these are the same persons described as "the deceivers" in 2 John.[64] The writer exposes their error by countering it in his solemn confession: "every spirit which confesses that Jesus Christ has come in the flesh is of God." A second test also recalls 2 John: those who "follow love" are of God and therefore are to be received into the Church's fellowship.[65]

A view of the relation of 1 and 3 John is likewise illuminating. In 3 John we read of the efforts of Diotrephes to put out of the church persons who, in the Elder's judgment, "follow the truth." In churches where the Elder's influence was strong, the reverse situation had obtained. Thus in 1 John it is reported that the errorists had withdrawn. Again, the Elder's maxim stated in 3 John—"he who does good is of God; he who does evil has not seen God"—receives full exposition in the homily before us.[66]

The following conclusions seem to be warranted. The Elder composed all three writings. 1 John was probably a homily written for the churches within his sphere of influence, to be carried by the traveling missionaries under his supervision. On one of these trips, 2 John was dispatched to warn a particular house-church against the activities of a rival missionary group with Gnosticising tendencies, espousing the docetic doctrine and acting in an uncharitable way toward their fellow Christians, especially to the Elder's partisans. On this trip also 3 John may have been sent to encourage "the beloved Gaius" to maintain his loyalty, and to inform him about the particularly offensive actions of Diotrephes. As 2 and 3 John have almost identical conclusions, it is likely that they were dispatched together.[67] Since 2 John provided information about the errorists, perhaps the writer felt no need in the letter to Gaius to refer to the doctrinal root of the trouble. First John reveals what manner of man the Elder was.

Into what geographical and temporal setting can these situations be placed? The earliest evidence for the existence of the Johannine letters is given in writings originating in the province of Asia—Polycarp's Letter to the Philippians, and the works of Papias.[68] This fact alone has been taken to associate with Asia the

---

[62] E.g., 1:6, 8; 2:4, 6; 4:20. C. B. Caird, *IDB*, vol. 2, p. 947.

[63] Ibid, p. 947.

[64] 1 John 4:1f. Cf. 2 John 7.

[65] 2 John 5f., 10. Cf. 1 John 3:10, 14f., 23.

[66] 3 John 11b; 1 John 3:4ff.

[67] A. N. Wilder, *IB*, vol. 12, p. 210. Cf. Dodd, *Johannine Epistles*, who holds that 3 John dealt with "an entirely different situation" considerably later than 1 and 2 John (p. lxvi).

[68] Eusebius, *H. E.*, III.39.3f. Dodd, *Johannine Epistles*, pp. 155f.

churches and persons revealed in the Johannine letters. The probability finds support in the special use of the title "Elder" in this region. In the apologetic writing of Irenaeus, who came from Asia, this phrase appears— "the Elders, disciples of the Apostles." As we have observed earlier, Eusebius reported that Papias made reference to "the Elder," or to a certain John who, as "the Elder," was to be distinguished from John the Apostle.[69]

Whether the writer of the Johannine letters was this man to whom Papias referred can only be guessed. In any case, it is certain that there was a time in the churches of Asia when certain persons could have written under the title "the Elder," as mediators of the apostolic tradition, without needing to add their names or any other signs of authority.

The dating of the Johannine letters can only be approximate. The few notices in the ancient Church make a time beyond A.D. 140 unlikely. It is not probable that after the reign of Trajan (A.D. 117) there were still men in the churches of Asia who would be called "the Elders." The organization of the churches in the Elder's neighborhood appears to antedate the situation presupposed by Ignatius, and corresponds to the situation at Corinth when Clement of Rome wrote to this congregation (A.D. 96). There are, however, no signs of persecution in the Johannine letters, which prevents the location of them in the period of crisis reflected in Revelation. The erroneous teaching attacked in 1 and 2 John affords little help because of the obscurity surrounding the rise of docetism.

A date for all three writings around the turn of the second century is consistent with the above evidence, such as it is. But the question of the date, as well as of the authorship, of the Johannine letters relates to another: What is the connection between the Johannine letters and the Fourth Gospel? To this work we turn in the final chapter.

[69] See above, p. 554.

chapter twenty-two

THE GOSPEL
ACCORDING TO JOHN

Fresco picturing Jesus and the Samaritan woman by the well (John 4), found on the walls of a Christian catacomb under a street near the Via Latina, Rome. (Wide World Photo)

The Gospel of John was early associated with the eagle, one of the "four living creatures" of the Apocalypse to John (4:6ff). The eagle may have symbolized the heavenly source of the gospel, or the conviction of its early readers that their thoughts soared upward in contemplation of the divine nature of Jesus. From the Book of Cerne. (The University Library, Cambridge, England.)

Recto of a Greek Papyrus fragment (P. Ryl. Gr. 457) with a portion of the text of John 18:31–33. (Courtesy of John Rylands Library, Manchester, England.)

The Codex Sinaiticus is a fourth century Greek manuscript containing the whole of the New Testament, two writings of Apostolic Fathers, and much of the Old Testament. This picture shows the conclusion of the Gospel of John. The text is written in large Greek capitals on vellum; its four-columned pages are 15″ x 13½″. (British Museum)

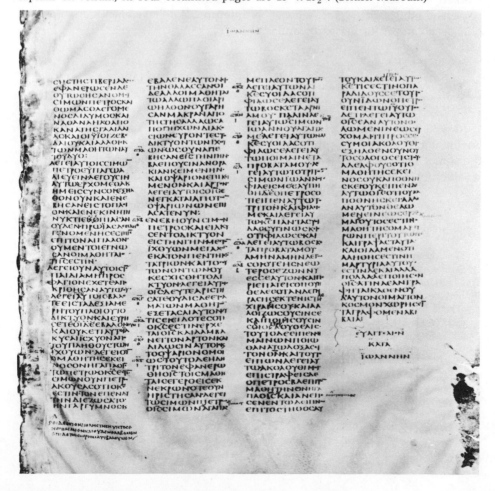

RECENT criticism of the Fourth Gospel of the New Testament has produced a bewildering assortment of books and research articles.[1] More significant than the variety and quantity of this literature is the fact that since World War II several major works have been published which advance new, comprehensive "solutions" to the "Johannine problem"—solutions to questions concerning the origin of the Fourth Gospel, explaining the complexities of its distinctive form, content, and purpose.[2] Perhaps a time has arrived for a fresh assessment of the Fourth Gospel, for a rediscovery of the teaching of one of the two greatest interpreters of Christianity in its first century. This prospect has engaged the mature reflections of some of the most productive New Testament scholars of this century. Yet they have worked in relative isolation and their accomplishments have not established a consensus.[3] Instead, several "schools" of interpretation have emerged to spur on other scholars to further explorations.

THE PROBLEM OF ORIGIN

Ancient Church Tradition Concerning John

As noted in the last chapter, the Church at the close of the second century taught that the Fourth Gospel had been written by the disciple of Jesus, John the son of Zebedee. We have also seen that Irenaeus was the star witness to this tradition. Following his comments concerning the origin of the other three Gospels, Irenaeus wrote:

> Afterwards John, the disciple of the Lord, who also reclined on his bosom, published his gospel, while staying at Ephesus in Asia.[4]

[1] W. F. Howard, *The Fourth Gospel in Recent Criticism and Interpretation*, rev. C. K. Barrett (4th ed., 1955) [hereafter, *Recent Criticism*]; Hunter, *Interpreting*, pp. 78ff., updated by the author's article, "Recent Trends in Johannine Studies," *Exp. T.* LXXI (1960): 164ff. The present writer assesses recent contributions to "The Search for the Theology of the Fourth Evangelist," in the *Journ. AAR* XXXV (1967): 3ff.

[2] C. H. Dodd, *The Interpretation of the Fourth Gospel* (1953) [hereafter, *Fourth Gospel*]; idem., *Historical Tradition in the Fourth Gospel* (1963) [hereafter, *Tradition*]; R. Bultmann, *Theology*, vol. 2; idem., untranslated German commentary in several editions since 1941; C. K. Barrett, *St. John*; R. Schnackenburg, *The Gospel According to St. John*, trans. K. Smyth (1968) [hereafter, *St. John*]; R. E. Brown, *The Gospel According to John, Anchor Bible*, vol. 29 (1966), vol. 29A (1970) [hereafter, *John, AB*].

[3] J. A. T. Robinson defines a critical consensus "The New Look on the Fourth Gospel," *Twelve New Testament Studies* (1962), pp. 94ff.; but serious differences among scholars are expressed: "the Gospel as a whole remains an enigma," E. Käsemann, *The Testament of Jesus*, trans. G. Krodel (1968), pp. 1f.; J. L. Martyn, *History and Theology in the Fourth Gospel* (1968), pp. xv ff. [hereafter, *History and Theology*].

[4] *Adv. Haer.*, III. 1.1, quoted by Eusebius, *H. E.*, V. 8. 4. See above, p. 186.

It should be recalled that the bishop of Gaul had come from Ephesus. As a youth he had heard Polycarp, and Polycarp (so Irenaeus says) had known John in Ephesus. This account is credible, although it was based upon the memories of youth, and the bishop was not always accurate in his accounts of the Apostolic Fathers.[5]

There are other considerations, however, of importance. Ignatius in writing to Christians at Ephesus did not mention John's connection with them, although he emphasized their close relation to Paul. Also there is no reference to the Gospel of John in Polycarp's Letter to the Philippians, although he quoted from 1 John. Justin Martyr, who possibly knew the Gospel, did not mention it, although he ascribed Revelation to the Apostle John. The argument from silence is always precarious, but in this instance the absence of references to the Gospel in writings which should be expected to contain them is perplexing, if the work was published with the full authority of apostolic authorship.[6] As one scholar has commented, "No theory about the Gospel that fails to give an explanation of the phenomena presented by the writings of Ignatius, Polycarp, and Justin has much chance of survival."[7]

Some Christians in the early second century rejected the apostolic authority of the Gospel. Irenaeus noted that certain persons disapproved its teaching concerning the Holy Spirit.[8] Epiphanius referred to a group, perhaps the same persons, ascribing the Gospel and Revelation to Cerinthus, a Gnostic teacher. Epiphanius called them the *Alogi* (anti-Word, or irrational, men).[9] The views of the Alogi may prove nothing more than their critical incompetence, but the fact that the authority of the Fourth Gospel could be openly challenged by Christians at this time throws some suspicion upon the direct value of the Johannine tradition cited by Irenaeus.

Before examining the witness of the Gospel to its origin, notice should be taken of the popular account received by the Church concerning the circumstances leading to its writing. Eusebius quotes Clement of Alexandria as having said:

> . . . last of all, John, perceiving that the external facts had been made plain in the gospel, being urged by friends, and inspired by the Spirit, composed a spiritual gospel.[10]

---

[5] Eusebius, *H. E.*, IV. 14. 3ff. and V. 20. 9f. Irenaeus may have been a boy of fifteen or so when Polycarp was martyred (ca. A.D. 155). Polycarp was born in A.D. 65. If the disciple John lived in Ephesus "until the time of Trajan," Polycarp could have been his associate for a few years. For a clear statement of the discrepancies between Irenaeus' report of Papias' knowledge of the Gospel of John and Papias' own words, see Feine-Behm-Kümmel, *Intro.*, pp. 170ff.

[6] See *The New Testament in the Apostolic Fathers*, Oxford Soc. of Hist. Theo. (1905); also J. N. Sanders, *The Fourth Gospel in the Early Church* (1943), pp. 27ff.

[7] T. W. Manson, "The Gospel of John," *BJRL* 30 (1947): 312f.; cf. B. F. Westcott, *The Gospel According to John* (1903), p. lxii [hereafter, *John*].

[8] *Adv. Haer.*, III. 11. 9.

[9] John 1:1: "In the beginning was the 'logos'"; Epiphanius, *Panarion haer.*, LI. 2f.

[10] Eusebius, *H. E.*, VI. 14. 7. Cf. the more circumstantial account in the Muratorian canon, which reports that John was urged to write by his "fellow disciples and bishops," who then certified his work. See Feine-Behm-Kümmel, *Intro.*, pp. 168f.

This statement has attracted much interest. Modern criticism seems to have established at least two aspects of this "precritical judgment," that John is the latest and the most theologically developed of the Gospels.

AN OUTLINE OF THE GOSPEL ACCORDING TO JOHN[11]

A. Introduction, 1:1–51:
   1. The prologue, 1:1–18
   2. The testimonies of John the Baptist and of the disciples, 1:19–51
B. The Book of the Signs, 2:1–12:50:
   3. First episode—the new beginning, 2:1–4:42: the sign at Cana (2:1–11); the cleansing of the temple (2:12–25); first discourse—the conversation with Nicodemus (3:1–21); an appendix (3:22–36); second discourse—Jesus' conversations with the woman of Samaria, and the disciples (4:1–45)
   4. Second episode—the life-giving word, 4:46–5:47: the second sign at Cana (4:46–54); the healing at Bethzatha Pool (5:1–9); discourse on Christ's power to give life and to judge (5:10–47)
   5. Third episode—the bread of life, 6:1–71: the feeding of the five thousand (6:1–15); Jesus comes to the disciples on the sea (6:16–21); conversation concerning the true bread (6:22–59); appendix (6:60–71)
   6. Fourth episode—light and life, 7:1–8:59: introduction (7:1–10); conversations during the feast of tabernacles (7:11–8:59)
   7. Fifth episode—judgment by light, 9:1–10:42: the healing of the man born blind (9:1–7); a trial scene (9:8–34); a dialogue passing into the discourse on the shepherd and the flock (9:35–10:21); appendix (10:22–42)
   8. Sixth episode—the victory of life over death, 11:1–54: the raising of Lazarus from the dead (11:1–44); appendix (11:45–54)
   9. Seventh episode—life through death, the meaning of the cross, 11:55–12:50: the anointment at Bethany (11:55–12:11); the triumphal entry (12:12–19); the approach of the Greeks (12:20–26); judgment by the word (12:27–50)
C. The Book of the Passion–Resurrection, 13:1–20:31:
   10. The farewell discourses, 13:1–17:26: washing the disciples' feet; the betrayal foretold (13:1–30); dialogue on Christ's departure and return (13:31–14:31); discourse on Christ and his Church (15:1–16:33); the prayer of Christ (17:1–26)
   11. The passion narrative, 18:1–19:42: the arrest (18:1–11); trial before the high priest, Peter's denial (18:12–27); the examination before Pilate (18:28–19:16); the crucifixion (19:17–30); the burial (19:31–42)
   12. The resurrection narrative, 20:1–31: the finding of the empty tomb (20:1–10); the appearance of Jesus to Mary (20:11–18); the appearance

---

[11] The writer acknowledges his indebtedness to C. H. Dodd for this outline of the structure of the Gospel, especially of its "Book of the Signs."

to the disciples· without Thomas (20:19–25); the appearance to the disciples with Thomas (30:26–69); the purpose of the Gospel (20:30–31)
[D. Conclusion, 21:1–25:
 13. The appearance beside the Sea of Tiberias, 21:1–23
 14. A testimonial, 21:24–25]

The Witness of the Gospel to Its Origin

The reader of John may conclude from the prologue that its author was an eyewitness to Jesus' Ministry. Since the Gospel is anonymous, inquiries have focused upon the identity of disciples who are mentioned but not named. Most important of these is the man described as "the disciple whom Jesus loved."[12] The phrase suggests one of Jesus' intimate followers. According to the synoptic tradition, these would have been Peter, and Zebedee's sons, James and John. Since James was killed by Herod, and Peter is distinguished in the narrative from "the disciple whom Jesus loved," John alone remains. The sons of Zebedee are never named in the Gospel. Surely one may say that the "beloved disciple" was John. Is he not also "the other disciple" closely associated with Peter in the Gospel?[13]

Some interpreters, following this reasoning, have observed other evidence which suggests that the author must have been a Palestinian Jew. He knew the geography and customs of the region, and the religious beliefs and ordinances of its people. Besides, it is said, there is an Aramaic quality about the Greek of the Gospel.[14]

These considerations were used by conservative scholars at the turn of the present century to support the traditional ascription of the Gospel of John to Jesus' disciple. More recently, some have claimed that archeological discoveries provide a broader confirmation for the Palestinian provenience of its traditions; more especially, its words and ideas have a close affinity with those of the Qumran scrolls.[15]

But the reader may have observed other aspects of the Gospel not favorable to the traditional account of John's origin. Chief among these is the striking difference between the portraits of Jesus in John and in the Synoptic Gospels. At first sight, the four Gospels have much in common. Jesus' Ministry opens with the testimony of John the Baptist. Twelve disciples are called. There is a popular ministry in Galilee, during which time Jesus performed many cures. He fed five thousand by the lake, and at night came to his disciples on the water. Jesus' popularity declined, but Peter confessed him to be the Holy One of God. There is then a transposition of the Ministry from Galilee to Judea. The passion and

---

[12] John 13:23; 19:26f.; see also 18:15f.; 20:2 (1:34ff.?). Cf. Acts 3:1ff.; Luke 22:8; Gal. 2:9.

[13] For a judicious discussion of the arguments for and against the identification of the "beloved disciple" with John, which favors it, see R. E. Brown, *John, AB*, vol. 29, pp. xcii ff. Cf. Feine-Behm-Kümmel, *Intro.*, pp. 165ff.

[14] See especially Westcott, *John, Intro.*; Black, *Aramaic Approach*, pp. 272ff.

[15] W. F. Albright, "Discoveries in Palestine and the Gospel of St. John," in Davies and Daube, *Background*, pp. 153ff. Hunter, "Recent Trends," note 1 above, pp. 165ff.; Brown, *John, AB*, vol. 29, pp. lxii ff.

resurrection narratives in all the Gospels have much the same pattern. It is not surprising that John should supplement the synoptic tradition at various points.

There are, however, remarkable differences. In John, Jesus is publicly proclaimed the Messiah at the outset of his Ministry. Does this not contradict the whole plan of the Ministry according to Mark? There are no baptism or temptation narratives in John; no proclamations of the near advent of the kingdom of God. There are no demon exorcisms. This is strange, since Mark reported that the ministry in Galilee was characterized by preaching in the synagogues and "casting out demons."[16] The early dating of the cleansing of the temple is surprising. In Mark this incident aroused the fury of the Sadducees and led to Jesus' crucifixion. But in John the provocative event is the raising of Lazarus, a story which is missing from the Synoptic Gospels.[17] Jesus' frequent visits to Jerusalem may be contrasted with the Synoptists' account of a single fateful journey.

Careful comparisons of similar incidents reveal that John's versions often reflect a later stage in the transmission of the traditions of the Ministry. This is not always the case. As an example, the reader may compare John's account of the healing of the official's son with the healing of the centurion's servant in Matthew and Luke.[18] Also, closer investigation of the concluding narratives in all four Gospels reveals that John stands apart from the rest. This was pointed out in our attempt to reconstruct the Ministry.

The same divergencies are found when the teaching of Jesus in John is compared with the threefold synoptic tradition. There are no parables in the Fourth Gospel, and the themes and the style of Jesus' discourses are unlike those of the other Gospels. These differences can be exaggerated, but there is a notable absence in John of Jesus' teaching in short, pictorial, and concrete words, so familiar to the reader of the Synoptic Gospels. Instead, in the discourses attributed to Jesus, the diction resembles that of the writer of 1 John.

Some scholars minimize these difficulties by emphasizing the fragmentary character of the Synoptic Gospels and the special purposes which informed the evangelists' selections of traditional materials. They have preferred John's plan of the Ministry and have found an emphasis upon the public teaching of Jesus in the synoptic sources, and upon Jesus' private instruction of the Twelve in the great discourses of John.[19] It should be noticed that the fourth evangelist seems to exclude this popular means of harmonizing.[20] Most modern critics agree that comparative studies of the Gospels make it very improbable that the Fourth Gospel, at least in its present form, should be regarded as the writing of Zebedee's son.[21] But a decision concerning John's relation to the canonical Gospel must depend upon additional considerations. In the next section we shall ask whether

---

[16] Mark 1:39.

[17] John 11:1ff. Note vss. 47ff.; also 12:9ff., 17ff.

[18] John 4:46ff. Cf. Matt. 8:5ff., Luke 7:1ff. (Q).

[19] Westcott, *John*, pp. clvi–clxx ff.

[20] John 18:19ff.

[21] McNeile, *Intro.*, pp. 270ff.; Enslin, *Beginnings*, pp. 438ff.; R. H. Strachan, *The Fourth Gospel* (3d ed., 1941), pp. 1ff. These books are especially helpful in setting forth the differences.

or not it is possible to reconstruct several stages in the composition of John's Gospel.

Indirect evidence of the Gospel that sometimes has been used to buttress the tradition of John's authorship probably points to a final composition at some remove from eyewitness testimony. Such familiarity as the author shows with Palestinian conditions could easily have been derived from his sources. The fourth evangelist held a detached attitude to "the Jews" and "their Law."[22] The so-called eyewitness scenes are problematical. Sometimes they reflect the more circumstantial narratives of a developed tradition while others seem relatively undeveloped. At some places the narrative may be attributed to the writer's dramatic skill: were eyewitnesses present when Jesus talked with the Samaritan woman, or conversed with Pilate?[23] It is evident that those who first commended this Gospel identified the "beloved disciple" with John. But if Zebedee's son had authored this Gospel, would he have referred to himself as "the disciple whom Jesus loved"?[24]

Questions Concerning the Sources and Composition of John's Gospel

Many scholars have held that the fourth evangelist's dependence upon one or more of the Synoptic Gospels renders improbable the apostolic authorship of John. The question of literary dependence does have this, and other, important implications and has been carefully examined.[25] Comparative studies in the modern period led first to a majority opinion that John knew one or more of the other Gospels. In recent decades this hypothesis has been challenged repeatedly.[26] John, some have said, had access to an independent tradition; others conclude that he drew independently upon traditions similar to those used by the Synoptics, at least by Mark and Luke.

It does not seem that John's many differences from the Synoptics can be explained satisfactorily by a theory of either deliberate change or misunderstanding, or both.[27] Moreover, the similarities between John and Mark, or Luke, reveal that John did not follow his alleged sources consistently. Some scholars still appeal to the few narrative sequences and striking "verbal reminiscences" which are found in the same order in John, as sufficient evidence supporting the hypothesis that John had read Mark or Luke, or both.[28] In view of the extensive differences, however, neither these narrative sequences nor the

---

[22] John 8:17; 10:34.

[23] John 4:7ff., 27; 18:33ff.

[24] John 21:20f.

[25] Barrett, *St. John*, pp. 14ff.; Howard, *Recent Criticism*, pp. 128ff.

[26] P. N. Gardner-Smith, *St. John and the Synoptics* (1938); Dodd, *Tradition*; Brown, *John, AB*, vol. 29, pp. xliv ff.; Bultmann, *Theology*, vol. 2, p. 3.

[27] This is illustrated in the commentary of E. Titus, *The Message of the Fourth Gospel* (1957) [hereafter, *Message*]. It is difficult to believe that John corrected and supplemented the Synoptics by somewhat randomly adding to, subtracting from, or otherwise changing their text.

[28] E.g., Barrett, *St. John*, pp. 34ff.

linguistic parallels establish literary dependence. It is more probable that similar narrative traditions underlie the Gospels, which reported identically some sequences from the Ministry of Jesus. Cross-influence from the Synoptics upon copies of John's Gospel may explain the "verbal reminiscences" better than a theory that John quoted somewhat eclectically, perhaps from memory only.[29]

According to some scholars, the Fourth Gospel manifests the influence of the collected letters of Paul. Others assume a dependence upon Pauline Christianity that is less direct.[30] Resemblances to Paul's teaching, however, are more likely to be explained as an independent development of a common, earlier tradition. Only with caution should Paul be used to interpret John.[31]

A closer relation exists between the Fourth Gospel and the other Johannine writings of the New Testament. Many scholars believe that a comparison of the words and ideas of the Johannine letters and the Gospel demonstrates common authorship.[32] We have seen that the writer of the second and third letters refers to himself as "the Elder" (presbyteros).[33] Defenders of the apostolic authorship of the Gospel, and of one or more of the letters in the ancient Church, apparently saw no difficulty in the identification of Zebedee's son as "the Elder." Some modern critics however, take a clue from a statement attributed to Papias which seems to distinguish the John who is named with others of the twelve disciples, from another "disciple" who is called "the elder John."[34] This Elder John, it is conjectured, composed the letters and the Gospel; or, if not the Gospel in its original form, one of its major recensions.[35]

Common authorship of the Gospel and letters, upon which these speculations must depend for their plausibility, is denied by other scholars on the ground that there are significant differences in the vocabularies and theologies of these books.[36] While it may be said with confidence that the author of the letters, and the author or authors of the Fourth Gospel, belonged to the same "circle" or "school," doubt remains concerning identity of authorship. Recent studies of the Gospel have stressed the independence and originality of the fourth evangelist as an interpreter of Jesus Christ. There is no book in the New Testament quite like it.

[29] Brown, John, AB, vol. 29, pp. xlvi f.; cf. Feine-Behm-Kümmel, Intro., p. 144f.

[30] Goodspeed, Intro., pp. 311f.; E. C. Colwell and E. Titus, The Gospel of the Spirit (1953), pp. 42ff.; cf. Goguel, Birth, pp. 323, 349ff.

[31] Dodd, Fourth Gospel, pp. 5f.; Bultmann, Theology, vol. 2, pp. 6ff.

[32] A. E. Brooke, The Johannine Epistles (1948), pp. 1ff.; W. F. Howard, "The Common Authorship of the Johannine Gospel and Epistles," JTS LVIII (1947): 12ff. (reprinted in Howard, Recent Criticism, pp. 282ff.).

[33] 2 John 1; 3 John 1.

[34] Eusebius, H. E., III. 39. 3ff. Note that Papias' statement is susceptible to differing interpretations (Barrett, St. John, pp. 88ff.); cf. Brown, John, AB, vol. 29, pp. xc ff.

[35] Ibid., p. ci, Brown posits that "one particular disciple" of John, Zebedee's son, "gave shape to the stories and discourses now found in the Fourth Gospel." Although Brown gives no name to this disciple-evangelist, he acknowledges that "some may be attracted by the hypothesis" of John the Elder. Feine-Behm-Kümmel, Intro., p. 173, entertain the probability, and cite its supporters; Barrett (St. John, p. 92) seems to exclude the possibility.

[36] C. H. Dodd, "The First Epistle of John and the Fourth Gospel," BJRL 21 (1937): 129ff.; Brooke, Johannine Epistles, pp. xlvii ff.; A. N. Wilder, IB, vol. 12, pp. 214f.; C. B. Caird, IDB, vol. 2, pp. 950ff.

If, then, the origin and special characteristics of John cannot be explained satisfactorily by references to other canonical writings, is it possible to identify special sources and literary influences which shed light upon the "Johannine problem"? The search for answers to this question has led to two types of research. One, literary features of the Gospel have led some scholars to posit earlier, diverse sources (otherwise unknown), and to reconstruct several stages in the revision and editing of the Gospel. Two, an examination of extant, non-Christian writings has encouraged some modern historians to re-create the cultural setting of the Gospel and its first readers and, from this perspective, to explain its special purpose. The remainder of this section will focus upon the allegedly complex literary history of the Fourth Gospel; the next section will consider problems relating to a recovery of its original environment.

In 1960 one scholar, reviewing recent criticism of John's Gospel, observed that interest seemed to have waned "in reshuffling the leaves of the Gospel to secure an allegedly better order, or in trying to separate off a hypothetical 'original' from the work of various redactors."[37] This may be an adequate summary respecting recent British scholarship, but not German and American research. The theories of Rudolf Bultmann concerning the composition of the Fourth Gospel, set forth in the successive editions of his influential commentary on John, have continued to focus attention upon the *aporias,* i.e., the "unsolved difficulties" present in the text of the Gospel.

Many scholars before Bultmann had observed that John's narrative and discourses are not developed in a logical, orderly fashion. There are numerous disjunctions or awkward connections in the text. These had been explained in a variety of ways: either the evangelist failed to edit carefully his source or sources, or left his Gospel unfinished; or his work underwent a process of redaction and interpolation; or the Gospel's original order has been obscured by accidental displacements and clumsy rearrangements.[38]

Bultmann's reconstruction of the composition history of John's Gospel contains variations of these earlier theories and follows several steps, which may be described briefly. We may note, first of all, that he removes textual glosses which are attributed to late copyists, rather than to the evangelist or to one or more early redactors of his work.[39] Bultmann's criticism of the language, style, and methods of the evangelist then enables him to separate the author's writing from several hypothetical sources he employed. Bultmann is convinced that he can distinguish the evangelist's theology from ideas more or less clearly discernible in these sources.

Bultmann hypothesizes three major, pre-Johannine literary sources:[40] (a) the

---

[37] Hunter, *Recent Criticism,* p. 164.

[38] See, Feine-Behm-Kümmel, *Intro.,* p. 141.

[39] John 7:53–8:11 (note RSV); 5:4; 6:23; 13:10; 14:30; 16:16; also 2:15; 4:1, 11; 22:20. In support of the first six passages, Bultmann can appeal to textual variations among ancient mss.

[40] For brief descriptions of Bultmann's source theories, see D. M. Smith, Jr., *The Composition and Order of the Fourth Gospel* (1966), pp. xiii f. [hereafter, *Fourth Gospel*]; Brown, *John, AB,* vol. 29, pp. xxix f.

document underlying the prologue, which was also used as a basis for many of the discourses in the Gospel. Bultmann calls this source the "revelation-discourses." Telltale marks of identification are its distinctively poetic structure, the Semitic quality of its language, and its Gnostic mythological motifs. (b) Another major document is the source from which was derived most of the miracle stories found in John 1–12. Evidence of this narrative tradition is found in the enumeration of "signs" in John 2:11 and 4:54, and in the statement, John 20:30–31, which stood at its conclusion. Semitic influences also identify this document, which Bultmann designates the "sign-source." (c) A third written source underlies the passion-resurrection narrative, John 18–20. The style of this source is not as clearly defined, but Bultmann claims that the evangelist's and redactors' additions are evident, and that unusual terms, inconsistencies in the narrative, and so on, reveal a source that was only partially edited.

Bultmann does not claim certainty for his source theories. Yet it is evident that in assigning passages in John to these various documents, and exhibiting the use which the evangelist has made of them, he has taken a crucial step in interpreting the Gospel.

Perhaps Bultmann's so-called "sign-source" hypothesis is the most plausible of his several source theories. Many scholars who consider that the existence of such a source is probable are reluctant, however, to identify its precise content, viewpoint, and limits.[41] One scholar, extending this hypothesis, states that John's miracle source also contained a passion-resurrection story, and that this primitive written gospel, used by the evangelist, can now be reconstructed.[42] While there is strong probability that some written, as well as oral, traditions were used by John (as by the writers of the other Gospels), this effort to reconstruct a gospel-like document underlying John becomes too speculative a basis for gaining access to the evangelist's interpretation of Christ. The important question is, of course, what the evangelist wanted to say to readers, and to this end it is likely that he thoroughly assimilated nearly all of his source materials and pressed them into the service of his intention.

Bultmann's stylistic criteria for separating the evangelist's writing from his sources have been sharply contested. Shortly before the completion of Bultmann's commentary, Eduard Schweizer published the results of his detailed study of the literary characteristics of the Johannine books. Applying his linguistic data to the Fourth Gospel, Schweizer concluded that no continuous sources could be distinguished from the evangelist's work on the bases of stylistic criteria. Other scholars extended Schweizer's critical methods and raised serious questions concerning Bultmann's applications of his criteria.[43] Bultmann believes that such unity as the Gospel manifests is due to the evangelist's imitation of the stylistic characteristics of his sources. While this possibility cannot be denied, it is difficult to

---

[41] Schnackenburg, *St. John*, vol. 1, pp. 64ff.; Brown, *John*, AB, vol. 29, p. 195; Smith, *Fourth Gospel*, pp. 110f.

[42] R. Fortna, *The Gospel of Signs: A Reconstruction of the Narrative Source Underlying the Fourth Gospel* (1969).

[43] Smith, *Fourth Gospel*, pp. 64ff.

believe that such editing could have resulted in a random distribution throughout the sources of the stylistic characteristics such as Schweizer and others have adduced. If, indeed, the evangelist assimilated the matter of his sources to his own style, does it not follow that the task of source criticism becomes problematical and its results highly questionable?[44] One scholar has shown that when John uses a source we can check on, namely, the Old Testament, he accommodates everything to his own purposes.[45]

The novelty of Bultmann's redaction hypothesis consists in his claim that the same editing process accomplished several things: notes left by the evangelist in some disarray were rearranged; certain additions were made to conform the evangelist's teaching to a later Christian orthodoxy; and an appendix was added to the Gospel, chapter 21.

Bultmann's major restorations of the original order of the evangelist's "notes" are based on the following considerations: (a) According to John 6:1, "Jesus went to the other side of the Sea of Galilee"; but according to the preceding chapter he was in Jerusalem. If chapters 5 and 6 are transposed everthing falls into place. (b) Likewise, John 7:15–24 is incomprehensible in its present location; it belongs with the discourse in chapter 5, perhaps as its conclusion; therefore 7:25ff should follow 7:1–14. (c) John 10:19–21 must be the ending of chapter 9; while 10:1–18 belongs with 10:27–29. (d) John 12:44–50 has no relation to its context; it too goes with chapter 9. (e) Something is wrong with the order of John 13–17, for although 14:30–31 leads to the passion narrative ("Rise, let us go hence"), three chapters of discourse follow. Chapters 15–17 must therefore originally have preceded 13:36–14:31.[46]

Bultmann's theory of accidental dislocation, like those of others, is surely not fantastic. Loose sheets of a book (unfinished?) could conceivably have become misplaced, and an editor-disciple may not have restored them to their proper order. But one must view with skepticism the proposed rearrangements. Some of Bultmann's alterations "improve" connections, others create new difficulties. All rearrangements must depend upon some doubtful assumptions: that the critic is able to restore the "original" while the hypothetical disciple-editor was not; that the evangelist's narrative-discourse sequences were written in a logical, orderly way, and that his purpose required that he adhere to precise chronological and geographical connections. With good reason many interpreters have preferred to read the Gospel in its present order, to see if sense can be made of it; then if insuperable difficulties are encountered one may resort to conjectural alteration.[47]

Bultmann's assumption that the evangelist was a consistent, as well as an original and independent, thinker leads him also to identify four major types of "ecclesiastical redaction": (a) ideas relating to a sacramental appropriation of the

[44]Ibid., p. 108.

[45]C. Goodwin, "How Did John Treat His Sources?" *JBL* LXXIII (1954): 61ff.

[46]These points are summarized in R. M. Grant, *Intro.*, pp. 155f. For a more detailed summary and criticism, see Smith, *Fourth Gospel*, pp. 116ff.

[47]Barrett, *St. John*, pp. 18ff.; Feine-Behm-Kümmel, *Intro.*, pp. 146f.

saving work of Christ;[48] (b) passages proclaiming a futurist eschatology in terms of Jewish–Christian apocalypticism;[49] (c) verses harmonizing John's Gospel with the Synoptics;[50] and (d) statements laying claim to apostolic and eyewitness authority.[51]

In developing this intricate redaction theory Bultmann assumes a heavy burden of proof. Having followed his analysis of most of the theologically suspect passages, the present writer concludes that Bultmann's contentions fall short of being convincing. John's sacramental interest is far too pervasive to be eliminated by the excision of the passages Bultmann denies to him. The problem of the juxtaposition of a realized and a futurist eschatology in the Gospel may be solved in other, more probable, ways than by Bultmann's resolution in removing the tension. The remainder of the miscellaneous material assigned to ecclesiastical redaction appears neither to be consistent nor to justify the motives that are alleged for it.

A more tenable alternative to Bultmann's theory is this, that the evangelist was himself the principal "ecclesiastical editor" of Johannine traditions. However uncertain our knowledge of the provenience of the sources used, and however obscure the circumstances surrounding the composition of this Gospel, it seems clear that its author assimilated congenial materials, adapting them to his special purposes.[52] The excision from the text of the several passages which may be attributed, with some confidence, to redaction by other hands (e.g., chapter 21) affects but slightly the task of interpreting the Gospel's teaching.[53]

Exploring the Cultural Background of John's Gospel in Search of Purpose

For an understanding of the evangelist's purpose, the importance of his own statement cannot be overemphasized.[54] Nevertheless, these words provide a starting point for, not the conclusion of, discussion. Was the Gospel written to confirm and instruct Christians, or to convert unbelievers? Is the confession, "Jesus is the Christ, the Son of God," stressed because other, less satisfactory titles were

---

[48] E.g., 6:51c–58; 3:5 ("water and . . ."); 19:34b–35. The term *ecclesiastical redaction* implies that theological revision was necessary to make the Gospel conformable to the Church's "sound doctrine." It is evident that the identification of such passages depends primarily on ideological rather than stylistic or contextual analysis.

[49] E.g., John 5:28–29; 6:39, 40, 44, 54; 12:48.

[50] E.g., John 1:22–24, 27; 3:24; 20:9.

[51] E.g., John 19:35; ch. 21.

[52] The stylistic objections against Bultmann's source theories are inapplicable when it is supposed that the edited material is introduced by the evangelist.

[53] Note here the interesting hypothesis of multiple authorship proposed by R. E. Brown (*John, AB*, vol. 29, pp. xxxiv ff.) to explain "the substantial unity of the Gospel" while taking into account "the various factors" which militate against the tradition of single authorship. Cf. Barrett, *St. John*, pp. 113f.

[54] John 20:30f.

being given to Jesus? Was his divine sonship being inadequately or wrongly conceived? Moving from this statement to a search for the intention implicit in the Gospel as a whole, several alternatives have been proposed.[55] John's purpose, according to many interpreters, was missionary, but those who share this conviction are divided as to whether the Gospel was written to win Gentiles, or Jews of the Diaspora, to belief in Jesus as Messiah. Others have detected in the Gospel a strong polemical thrust. Some believe the front was directed against the disciples of John the Baptist, who were excessively venerating the martyred prophet; others perceive that Judaism was the target of John's polemic, that he aimed to refute serious charges being made in the synagogues against Christianity.

It may not be necessary to choose among these alternatives. There is in John a strong emphasis upon the inclusive, universal purpose of the Christian gospel, and apologetic motifs are found throughout. A determination of John's purpose of purposes depends to some extent upon one's judgment concerning the specific background of John's first readers, which will be discussed below. The present writer believes, however, that the internal evidence reveals that the Gospel was written primarily for Christians, not for outsiders.[56] John was written to encourage Jesus' disciples to persist in their belief that he was and is, indeed, the Christ, the Son of God; to be assured of their life in him; to continue in his "word," and be guided into all the truth. Of course, as beneficiaries of the gospel of Christ, his disciples are sent into the world to witness against it, but also to bring to the world that knowledge which is eternal life.

Recent studies of John's Gospel have considered its purpose from the perspective of the evangelist's intellectual environment, in the hope of discovering the origin of his theological language, and the religious needs of the Gospel's first readers. Is it possible to recover the cultural milieu of the Fourth Gospel? It stands to reason that the evangelist had some particular type or class of readers in mind and that he selected and interpreted his materials for their instruction.

Earlier studies relating to the non-Christian background of the Gospel laid stress upon its Greek character. The conclusion was reached that John was "the Gospel of the Hellenists."[57] The following statement emphasizes some elements in this point of view:

> . . . the thoroughly Greek character of the thought and interest of the Gospel, its literary (dialogue) cast, its thoroughly Greek style, its comparatively limited use of the Jewish scriptures (roughly one-fifth of Matthew's), its definite purpose to strip Christianity of its Jewish swaddling clothes, its intense anti-Jewish feeling, and its great debt to the mystery religions—combine to show that its author was a Greek [sic] not a Jew. In the Gospel of John the Greek genius returns to religion.[58]

[55] Feine-Behm-Kümmel, *Intro.,* pp. 161ff.

[56] F. Hahn, *Mission in the New Testament,* trans. F. Clarke (1965), pp. 152ff.; Brown, *John, AB,* vol. 29, pp. lxvii ff.

[57] The title of an influential book by B. W. Bacon, published in 1933. See also E. C. Colwell, *John Defends the Gospel* (1936).

[58] Goodspeed, *Intro.,* pp. 314f. Schweitzer, *Mysticism of Paul,* pp. 349ff.

This opinion was not destined to sweep others from the field. Before the discovery of the Qumran scrolls there were scholars who affirmed that the thought of the fourth evangelist was more directly influenced by the Old Testament and rabbinic Judaism than by Hellenism. The conviction of the Palestinian provenience of some of John's sources kept the question open. Since the Qumran discoveries, a stronger case can be made for the essentially Jewish background of the author's words and ideas. As one reporter has observed, "the Scrolls show that we do not need to look outside Palestinian Judaism for the soil in which the Johannine theology grew." [59]

The question of the background of the Gospel is complicated by the fact that Hellenism and Judaism do not identify mutually exclusive cultures in a period when Oriental and Western ideas and modes of thought had met and intermingled. Some interpreters are convinced, after a wide canvass of non-Christian writings, that John's Gospel manifests affinities with a variety of literatures. Need one choose between Jew or Greek? Interesting parallels to passages in John have been found in the rabbinical and sectarian Judaism of Palestine, and in Philo's writings and other Hellenistic–Jewish books. Moreover, John's thought has been judged akin to a type of religious thought found in the Hermetic tractates, as well as to the Stoicized–Platonism of popular philosophy. Thus it is claimed that the vocabulary and thought forms of John's Gospel were familiar to Jews and non-Jews of various places, who seemed to share a common universe of discourse. John's purpose led him to translate the Palestinian, Aramaic gospel of Jesus and the early Church, with its biblical and ancient Jewish language and imagery, into the meaningful idiom of another age and a more expansive cultural environment. He chose aspects of Jewish–Christian teaching which had Hellenistic parallels, and by this means established bridges between apparently antagonistic "worlds" of thought.[60]

Others have rejected this broad, general view and claimed that it is possible to define with greater specificity and clarity the contours of John's immediate environment. As early as 1925, Bultmann's studies of the Fourth Gospel had led him to Ignatius and to the Odes of Solomon—evidences of early Syrian Christianity, and also to certain texts preserved by a Mandean sect which has survived to the modern era. These sources seemed to provide the most direct access into the Gnostic, mythological world of ideas presupposed by John. Bultmann conjectured that a pre-Christian Gnostic movement had originated in Persia, spread westward, and influenced Jewish and pagan groups in Syria and Judea.[61] Perhaps John himself was an ex-Gnostic. At least one of his major sources, the "revelation discourses," was Gnostic and was "Christianized" by John.

---

[59] M. Burrows, *D.S.S.*, pp. 339f. See R. E. Brown in Stendahl, *Scrolls*, pp. 183ff.; O. Cullmann, "A New Approach to the Interpretation of the Fourth Gospel," *Exp. T.* LXXI (1959): 8ff., 39ff.; J. A. T. Robinson, "The Destination and Purpose of St. John's Gospel," *NTS* 6 (1960): 117ff.

[60] Dodd, *Fourth Gospel*, Part I: "Background"; Barrett, *St. John*, pp. 22ff., 107f.; W. F. Howard, *IB*, vol. 8, pp. 452ff. For the alleged Stoic parallels, see Strachan, *Fourth Gospel*, pp. 42ff. Note R. E. Brown's reservations concerning Hellenistic influences apart from those derived from Judaism (*John, AB*, vol. 29, pp. lvi ff.).

[61] Feine-Behm-Kümmel, *Intro.*, p. 156.

This effort to characterize John's thought as an interaction with Oriental Gnosticism, and to reconstruct its background from a curious miscellany of texts, some dating from a much later time, seemed farfetched to many scholars.[62] The relevance of the Mandean texts has appealed to few interpreters of John. But the amazing discoveries in the 1940s at Qumran and Nag–Hammadi led to a closer examination of the alleged Gnostic background of the Fourth Gospel. While Qumran provided evidence for, what some have called, a pre-Christian, Gnosticizing Judaism, Nag–Hammadi revealed an early Christianity with Gnostic tendencies, reflecting both Jewish and non-Jewish ideas and motifs.

As noted above, the publication of Qumran fragments had early led several scholars to affirm that they provided striking affinities with the Johannine books. Similar to the statement we have cited is the following: "In these new texts we get to lay hold upon the native soil of John, and this native soil is . . . a Palestinian–Jewish sectarian piety of Gnostic structure."[63] A few scholars now claim that the fourth evangelist was influenced directly by the teachings of the Qumran community, but more seem content to say that John manifests familiarity with *the type of thought* exhibited in the scrolls. A representative of this group has written "that for *some* features of Johannine thought and vocabulary the Qumran literature offers a closer parallel than any other contemporary or earlier non-Christian literature either in Judaism or in the Hellenistic world."[64]

Although the present state of our knowledge makes it impossible to do more than approximately delimit the cultural background of John, many scholars are prepared to acknowledge affinity between John and pre-Gnostic thought. We have seen that the writer of the Johannine letters was combating some Gnosticizing tendencies known to him in several Christian communities.[65] Even though one may only say with certainty that the fourth evangelist belonged to the same circle as the letter writer, it is probable that he was acquainted with the ideas and behavior attacked in them.

The outstanding problem concerns the conclusions to be drawn from the alleged "Gnostic terminology" of the Fourth Gospel.[66] Should one conclude that John's thought world was broadly representative of the syncretistic culture of his period, and that his language was later borrowed by Gnostics and invested by them with specifically Gnostic connotations (Gnostic *use* of a document does not make the document itself "Gnostic")?[67] Or, alternatively, should one conclude that John consciously attacked pre-Gnostic tendencies in the churches of his time, using the language employed by these errorists to repudiate the points of view expressed therein?[68] "That there exists a relation of some kind between the Fourth Gospel

[62] Ibid., p. 158.

[63] K. G. Kuhn, quoted in Feine-Behm-Kümmel, *Intro.,* p. 156. See also F. M. Cross, Jr., *Ancient Library,* pp. 215f. Cf. H. Teeple, "Qumran and the Origin of the Fourth Gospel," *Nov. Test.* IV (1960): 6ff.

[64] Brown, *John, AB,* vol. 29, pp. lxiii. Note Kümmel's theory that John was influenced by another Jewish–Gnostic sectarian group "on the edge of Palestinian Judaism," whose thought world was more strongly mythological than Qumran's (Feine-Behm-Kümmel, *Intro.,* pp. 160f.).

[65] See above, pp. 567ff.

[66] R. McL. Wilson, *Gnosis,* pp. 45ff.

[67] Dodd, *Fourth Gospel,* pp. 97, 102; Brown, *John, AB,* vol. 29, pp. lxxx ff.

[68] Barrett, *St. John.,* pp. 116f.; Feine-Behm-Kümmel, *Intro.,* pp. 160f.

and non-Christian Gnosticism is scarcely open to question; exactly what this relation is, is one of the most disputed problems in current New Testament scholarship."[69]

The picture is a confusing one. But several important gains may be noted. No longer can John's Gospel be considered "an acute Hellenization" of the *kerygma* of the early Church, far removed geographically and culturally from the Palestinian world of Jesus and his first interpreters. Nor can the comprehension of John's theology be limited to a narrowly defined, esoteric group. Apparently John was sensitive to important currents of thought, widely influential in his age, but also not alien to ancient Palestinian Judaism or early Jewish–Christianity. One must be wary, then, of all efforts either to reduce everything in the Gospel to a single, pre-existing pattern of ideas, or to claim a late, extra-Palestinian provenience for Johannine tradition. And, finally, it should be stressed that the more thorough the comparisons between John's Gospel and the relevant literatures, the more impressive is the evidence for the originality of the evangelist's theology, for its specifically Christian content.[70]

Date and Place of Writing

Until recent times the consensus had been that the Gospel was written around A.D. 100. It is doubtful that the shifting winds of opinion have shaken this position. In the nineteenth century some argued that John appeared in the later half of the second century. The discovery of papyrus fragments containing parts of the text of the Gospel excludes this possibility.[71] If one could be certain as to whether or not Ignatius knew the Gospel (ca. A.D. 110); if the date of Heracleon's commentary could be fixed; if the relation between the Gospel and 1 John were established, definite clues would be provided. But in the present state of knowledge we are faced with a string of uncertainties.

The place of the Gospel's origin is likewise uncertain. Three cities have been suggested: Ephesus, Antioch of Syria, and Alexandria. Although the claims of Alexandria have been somewhat strengthened by the recent discoveries at Nag-Hammadi, Ephesus remains the most likely place.[72] Until further evidence comes to light, we must content ourselves with the realization that "it is more important to understand the theological task achieved by the Fourth Evangelist than to know his name, and to know the materials with which he worked, and the way he used them, than to know the date and place at which he wrote."[73]

---

[69] Barrett in *Current Issues,* ed. Klassen and Snyder, p. 210.

[70] An important example is given in Bultmann's commentary which interprets the Gospel against the background of Gnosticism, but which shows "that at every crucial point the Gospel is in tension with the Gnostic point of view, indeed repudiates it." Neill, *Interpretation of the New Testament,* p. 310.

[71] Papyrus Egerton 2 and the Rylands fragment (P52).

[72] Howard, *IB,* vol. 8, p. 441; Brown, *John, AB,* vol. 29, pp. ciii f.; Barrett, *St. John,* pp. 109f.

[73] Barrett, *St. John,* p. 108. See the writer's valuable exposition of John's theology, pp. 56ff. Cf. Bultmann, *Theology,* vol. 2, pp. 15ff.; Goguel, *Birth,* pp. 347ff.; W. F. Howard, *Christianity According to St. John* (1946) [hereafter, *Christianity*]; Brown, *John, AB,* pp. cv ff.

INTERPRETING THE FOURTH GOSPEL

Introduction

John's approach to the Ministry of Jesus was not through Bethlehem but through the conceptual world familiar to his readers. "In the beginning was the *Logos* . . ." (1). This Greek term is found in numerous Jewish and pagan writings of the period. Its literal meaning is "word," but *logos* signified both the word in the mind—thought or reason—and the spoken word—purpose expressed, or fulfilled, hence, the deed. To the Greek-speaking convert from Judaism, the first statements in the Gospel recalled the miracle of creation, and the prologue stood as a concise summary of God's revelation in Israel's history through Moses and the prophets. "By the word of the Lord the heavens were made, and all their host . . ." proclaimed the Psalmist, and in the Wisdom books, "Wisdom" was the active agency of God in creation, in redemptive history and in judgment, paralleling the activity of the *Logos* in John's prologue.[74] A Gentile convert might have been reminded not only of the Septuagint but of a popular belief of Hellenistic writers that ultimate reality can be designated *logos*, reason, and that man's capacity for rational thought renders intelligible the invisible and material worlds.[75] To Christian readers, of whatever background, the same statements could have been understood as an original proclamation of the *kerygma*: in the fullness of time God had revealed his purpose in a historical deed: the gospel of Christ is the Word.[76]

"And the logos *became flesh*. . . ." With this declaration John's prologue reached its climax. Although some readers see references to Christ's Ministry earlier, this statement celebrates the miracle of the incarnation. A man "sent from God" had not merely spoken the word of the Lord; he was himself the Word. To the convert from Judaism, the evangelist offered reassurance. This is he "of whom Moses in the Law and also the prophets wrote."[77] To the reader nurtured in the confidence that the mind or spirit of man was susceptible to a saving knowledge of truth, John declared: The life-giving Light has dawned, but not through speculative thought or mystical contemplation. "No one has ever seen God; the only Son, who is in the bosom of the Father, he has made him known."[78] The knowledge of the eternal world could not be mediated adequately through abstract principles or myths, but only through a deed, through the personal history of a man. No phantom God, this man of Nazareth. "The word became *flesh*." And to this truth the Church continued to bear witness, John said, in opposition to docetic tendencies. "We have beheld his glory. . . ."[79]

The virtual omission of the term *logos* from the remainder of the Gospel raises

[74] Ps. 33:6f.; Prov. 8:22ff.; Ecclus 1:1; 24:3ff.; Wisd. of Sol. 7; 9.

[75] Read John 1:1–5 substituting "it" for the personal pronouns "he" and "him," R. M. Grant, *Gnosticism and Early Christianity*, pp. 116f.

[76] Cf. 1 Cor. 1:23; Gal. 3:1; Acts 2:36. Barrett, *St. John*, pp. 127ff.

[77] John 1:41, 45, 49.

[78] John 1:9f., 18.

[79] John 1:14, 16. This emphasis upon "flesh" is so understood by most interpreters. E. Käsemann, who attributes a "naive docetism" to the evangelist, says that 1:14 means nothing more than that the divine word descended into the world of men (*Testament of Jesus*, pp. 9, 12f.).

an important question: Was the prologue integrally related to the Gospel, or was it added as an afterthought? Many scholars, observing its unique poetic structure with prose interpolations, and several theological concepts which are not developed in the Gospel, are convinced that John 1:1–18 was not originally the work of the evangelist. Perhaps he has adapted an earlier hymn, composed by another from the Johannine circle.[80] It is true that some of the concepts in the prologue do not reappear in the Gospel. Especially noteworthy is the term *logos* itself. A probable explanation for this is that *logos* was abandoned because John did not wish the reader to interpret Jesus from the standpoint of the term with its manifold associations. Rather he intended that the *logos* idea be understood in the light of the Ministry of the Revealer. The principal motifs of the prologue are threaded through the whole Gospel: light-darkness, life coming into the world, witness-belief, to receive, to be born of God, truth, the only Son. These ideas are themes of the Gospel which, in narrative and discourse, are inseparable from the life story of the Word-made-flesh.

The story of Jesus' Ministry begins with the witness of John the Baptist proclaimed on three days, days which have a programatic rather than a chronological significance. This narrative sequence develops the initial statement concerning the Baptist in the prologue.[81] In the remainder of chapter 1 a typical theological conviction of the evangelist is presented: realities which were manifested on particular occasions from the Ministry, according to the other Gospels, are proclaimed as having been revealed throughout Jesus' history. The evangelist has the Baptist proclaim the saving benefit of Christ's cross; on the occasions of the call of the first disciples, they summarize the whole meaning of their discipleship. A synopsis is given here of "the gradual increase in [the disciples'] understanding that took place throughout the ministry of Jesus and after the resurrection."[82]

This proleptic perspective also provides a basis for the juridical development of John's Gospel. In the Synoptics, Jesus' trials take place on the eve of his death; in the Acts, those of his disciples, following their witness to his resurrection. Throughout John's account of the Ministry men seek to bring Jesus to trial; they pass judgment upon any person or anything purporting to witness to the truth. There are, of course, climactic "trial scenes" in the Gospel. For example, Jesus adduces a series of witnesses to the truth of his revelation, and Pilate judges Jesus.[83] There is irony in both situations: men, not Jesus, are being tried. But the point now stressed is the presence of legal terminology throughout John. It has been observed that "the Gospel opens with a trial and John the Baptist under interrogation."[84]

---

[80]Brown, *John AB*, vol. 29, pp. 18ff.; Bultmann's theory of a non–Christian Gnostic hymn is not credible: see Smith, *Fourth Gospel*, pp. 60ff., 113.

[81]John 1:6–8, 29, 35.

[82]Howard, *Christianity*, pp. 26f. See the perceptive comments on John's use of temporal expressions, "now," "before," "a little while," "in that day," etc., by which means the evangelist distinguishes but also makes correlative "the time of Jesus" and "the time of the Church," in N. Dahl, "Johannine Church and History," *Current Issues*, ed. Klassen and Snyder, pp. 125f. J. L. Martyn, *History and Theology*, acknowledges the same phenomena as the two stages or levels of John's drama.

[83]John 5:31ff.; 18:28ff.

[84]Brown, *John, AB*, vol. 29, p. 45; Dahl, note 82 above, pp. 137ff.

The Book of the Signs

Following the suggestion of several interpreters, chapters 2 through 12 have been designated the "Book of the Signs" (B).[85] The word *sign* is used seventeen times by the evangelist to designate actions of Jesus, some of them miraculous, others nonmiraculous.[86] There are repeated references also to "the works" of Jesus.[87] His actions seem to be regarded as parables, directing the attention of men to some significance beyond the happenings as such, a significance which only men of faith can properly understand. It is probable that this use of the terms *signs, works,* is derived from the Old Testament. Like the "signs" performed by the prophets, Jesus' actions were more than illustrations of ideas; they anticipated events that were to take place. Jesus' signs are therefore not to be interpreted independently. They all point to a forthcoming event—the cross, which was his glorification, and the revelation of the Father's glory.[88]

The first episode contains two narratives (3). The first is explicitly called a sign, but the second is implicitly one. Considered separately, as events from the Ministry, these stories bristle with problems. The story of the water changed to wine is a celebrated stumbling stone. Would Jesus have acted in this way? The story of the cleansing of the temple raises other historical problems. It is as difficult to believe that Jesus would have prejudiced the authorities against himself at the beginning of the Ministry, as that he cleansed the temple twice. But the evangelist's special interests often render profitless and distracting a concentration upon such matters. If the grouping of stories epitomized some central and abiding truth about the Ministry, it mattered not to John that they were uprooted from their setting in life. If by altering the detail of some traditional story its implicit meaning was rendered clearer, can one properly speak of John's version as "fictional," as "a falsification of history"? One passage in the Fourth Gospel reveals how the mind of the evangelist worked in selecting and reporting incidents from the Ministry: the received traditions had been illumined by the testimony of the apostolic Church and the interpreting spirit of God.[89] None of the evangelists was interested in reporting bare facts concerning Jesus, but John's interest in the significance of Jesus' acts was more intense and sustained than that of the others. At every point he sought to grasp the Spirit-filled meaning of the facts relating to Christ so that his readers might have "life in his name."

A general observation may be made concerning John's predominant interest in the miracle tradition of the gospel. Each "sign," as the first makes quite explicit, manifests the glory of Jesus.[90] One scholar has rightly observed that John's concern

---

[85] Dodd, *Fourth Gospel,* pp. 297ff.; R. M. Grant, *Gnosticism and Early Christianity,* pp. 16, 18; Brown, *John, AB,* vol. 29, pp. cxxxviii f.

[86] John 2:11; 3:3; 6:14, etc.

[87] John 5:36. Note the equation, signs=works, in 6:20.

[88] Barrett, *St. John,* pp. 63ff. Perhaps it matters not whether the "signs" describe events as they actually happened. What does matter is that the signs reveal some aspect of the cross of Christ. Note John 2:4b. Jesus' "hour" is the crucifixion, the moment of his deepest humiliation, but also of his glorification. Cf. 7:1ff., 30; 12:27ff.; 13:1; 17:1. Of course, the evangelist built his narratives and discourses on what he believed to be real history.

[89] John 16:13f. Hunter, *Interpreting,* pp. 89ff.; Heard, *Intro.,* p. 95.

[90] See further below, p. 599.

is "everywhere apparent that Christ himself may not be overshadowed by any-thing . . . Jesus alone is the true divine gift to which all other gifts can and should only point . . . Johannine criticism of miracles begins and ends where Jesus himself is sought, or forgotten, *for the sake of his gifts.*" [91]

Assuming that John's Christian readers may have had diverse origins, what possible range of meanings would the "signs" at Cana and in the temple signify? In the Dionysiac "mystery" it was claimed that the god Dionysus transformed water to wine. Certain Hellenistic authors had "spiritualized" this pagan mythol-ogy. Wine signified divine inspiration, a *living* water bestowing life and truth.[92] Perhaps John's story proclaimed that only Jesus could truly give this benefaction. Man's quest for a life-giving draught, for a blissful immortality, could not be satisfied through mythical ritual or mystical ecstasy but only by a faith union with the crucified and risen Son of God. A reader of Jewish background could hardly fail to see in the water which was transformed by Christ a symbol of the religion of ceremonial and law.[93] By contrast, the wine provided by the Son of God symbolized the religion of the Spirit, the glad fulfillment of eschatological expectations. Christians familiar with the teachings of Jesus set forth in several similes preserved in the synoptic tradition, would also see the story as an acted parable: The gospel is the new wine which "the friends of the bridegroom" receive with incomparable joy.[94]

The work begun in Galilee was completed in Jerusalem. Like Luke, John seems to have epitomized the rejection of Jesus by bringing forward an incident from the Ministry. The story of the cleansing of the temple complements the sign at Cana: Christ not only perfected Judaism by transforming the old into something new, his coming resulted in judgment upon the old. The glory of God appeared in the temple to pass judgment upon its cultus and to render it obsolete. "He came to his own home, and his own people received him not." [95]

The first episode is further developed by means of two discourses. Throughout the Book of the Signs the evangelist interprets traditional stories and sayings of Jesus by means of discourses. The dialogue of chapter 3, which passes into a monologue, emphasizes the necessity of regeneration. In chapter 4, narrative and discourse affirm that the new life which faith in Christ produces is a continuing experience since it is eternal.

In the hope of Israel and the early Church, the transformation of human nature was associated with "the new heavens and the new earth." The early Christians were of the belief that men could enter now into the experience of that eschato-logical life, through faith in Christ and through the power of the Holy Spirit. The Age to Come had supervened upon the present age. The apocalyptic imagery was more or less adequate to express this paradoxical idea. In the Fourth Gospel

[91] See 2:11; 4:48, 53; 6:26ff. Käsemann, *Testament of Jesus*, pp. 19f. Italics mine.

[92] Barrett, *St. John*, p. 157.

[93] John 2:6. Cf. 4:12f., Dodd, *Fourth Gospel*, pp. 311f.

[94] E.g., Mark 2:19ff. and pars.

[95] John 2:13ff. (1:11). Cf. Mark 11:15ff. and pars. In John, Jesus' "country" is "the land of Judea." Cf. John 4:43ff. (3:22) and Mark 6:1ff. For this reason, perhaps, the temple scene, rather than the rejection at Nazareth, symbolized the failure of Jesus' "own people" to receive him. Cf. Luke 4:16ff.

both present and future aspects are retained, but it is clear from chapter 3 onward where the evangelist has placed the emphasis. "The hour is coming and *now is*." [96] Belief in Jesus Christ as the Son of God in the present was inseparably connected with the final transformation of human nature. The hope, which was even now being realized, anticipated an ultimate fulfillment. Conversely, a rejection of Christ brought the present life of men under God's final judgment.

In offering his interpretation of the *kerygma*, John employed concepts familar to Christians drawn from backgrounds other than Palestinian Judaism, although he may have assumed this origin for most of his readers. The term *the kingdom of God* was not the most familiar expression of Israel's hope, and the idea that a man must "be born again [or from above]" in order to have "eternal life" was a popular conception. The problem of Nicodemus was common to all men whose thought was influenced by pre-Gnostic dualisms: "How can this be?" How can any man, a prisoner of the lower world ("that which is born of flesh is flesh"), enter the world of light and life ("that which is born of spirit is spirit")? [97] We have observed that many religions and philosophies of the Greco–Roman world, not all which can be considered Gnostic, sought to overcome, or at least to bridge, this radical dualism and to give to men assurance of their eternal life. Like many persons, John believed that men were the children of God, potentially the inheritors of eternal life, and that eternal life must be received as a gift of God. Only through some revealer of God did men receive the power to become children of God. But contrary to popular belief, John affirmed that men could not fan to flame the sparks of divinity within, through participation in some "mystery," or through mystical self-transcendence. "Unless one is born of water and the Spirit he cannot enter the kingdom of God." [98]

The phrase just cited probably referred to Christian baptism, the sacrament of belief in "the name of Christ." The appendix to this discourse supports this assumption. [99] The Christian sacraments are not explicitly described in the Fourth Gospel; Jesus does not institute them. But baptism is presupposed in chapter 3, as is the Eucharist in chapters 6 and 15, and the sacraments possibly appear as subordinate themes elsewhere. Various reasons have been given for John's failure to deal explicitly with the sacraments of the Church. [100] In any case, he was less interested in the Church's acts of worship than in the Person and the deed giving them meaning. The acts themselves did not mediate "heavenly things"; only the one who had "descended from heaven" could do this. [101] Not the lifting up of "the host," but the exaltation of the Son of man upon the cross and through the resurrection brought eternal life to the believer. [102]

It is not possible within the limits of this chapter to comment upon the entire

[96] John 4:23; 5:25, etc.

[97] John 3:6.

[98] John 3:5; 1:12f.

[99] John 3:22ff.; Dodd, *Fourth Gospel*, pp. 309f. See the discussion in R. E. Brown, *John*, *AB*, vol. 29, pp. 141ff.

[100] Ibid. (Brown), pp. cxi ff.; Barrett, *St. John*, pp. 69ff. Cf. Titus, *Message*, pp. 26, 96ff.; Bultmann, *Theology*, vol. 2, pp. 58f.

[101] John 3:13f., 27, 31; 4:24; 6:32f., 50f., 63.

[102] John 3:14; 12:32.

sequence of episodes in the Book of the Signs, or to do justice to the progress of the evangelist's thought throughout. Only two other episodes will be considered, the second and the sixth.

The discourse which follows Jesus' healing of the official's son and the sick man at Bethzatha Pool turns upon the basic question of Jesus' authority (4). His violations of the Sabbath are not the matter discussed, but the real issue underlying such actions. In them, it was said, Jesus made himself "equal with God."[103]

The evangelist affirmed that the continuity and unity of action between the Father and the Son resulted from the latter's humble submission to the Father's will. Jesus exercised no independence of judgment; he was at all times subservient to the one "who sent him."[104] Yet because of this complete dependence, the Father committed to the Son divine prerogatives: the authority to bestow life and to judge men. As one who exercised these divine powers, Jesus deserved the highest honors which men could bestow upon him. Thus to refuse to honor the Son is to dishonor the Father.

The discourse deals also with the witnesses to Jesus' authority.[105] The Son did not bear witness to himself. The Father bore witness to the Son in ways which He Himself had appointed: John the Baptist had been sent to bear witness to Jesus; the works done by Jesus in the Father's name bore him witness; the scriptures, rightly understood, testified to his authority.

In the conclusion of this discourse the blindness of unbelief is attributed to man's estrangement from God.[106] The way of faith was denied those who did not have the word (logos) within, or "the love of God within," or who did not seek His glory. As the scriptures testified, Israel was called to be "the son of God," to live the life of obedient trust in God as Father. This life Jesus lived. Therefore, John proclaimed, he was "the Son of God."

It may be concluded that the evangelist asserted his faith in the equality of the Father and the Son in the strongest possible way. Yet he insisted that Jesus exercised divine functions because there had been in him a deliberate purpose to subordinate his will to God. This subordination was so complete and perfect that there existed between the Father and the Son, throughout the latter's Ministry, a unity of purpose and action. Thus for men to see Jesus was to see the Father.[107] Other men may be called "the children of God"; there has been only one Son.[108]

No discourse is appended to the narrative in the sixth episode of the Book

[103] John 5:18.
[104] The authority of Jesus, like that of Israel's prophets, was a delegated authority. See the discussion of important similarities and differences between Jesus and the prophets, Dodd, *Fourth Gospel*, pp. 255ff.
[105] John 5:31ff.
[106] John 5:42ff. Cf. 10:24ff.
[107] John 14:8ff. Cf. 10:30ff.
[108] It is no accident that the evangelist does not call believers "sons" of God, but "children." Paul preserved the same distinction, speaking of believers as sons by adoption, or as servants who become sons only through grace. Rom. 8:14ff., 23; Gal. 4:3ff.

of the Signs (8). Instead, every feature of the story is weighted with meaning. Whatever the form of the tradition underlying it, the entire episode was rewritten by the evangelist to epitomize the theological significance of the Ministry. The true meaning passed beyond the miracle itself and arose out of the event toward which it pointed—the death and resurrection of Jesus.[109] But the miracle was related also to an event which, for the reader, remained an outstanding promise: "He who believes in me, though he die, yet shall he live."[110] It is noteworthy that in the appendix to this episode the Jewish Council assembled to lay plans for putting Jesus to death. Here, as elsewhere, John taught that the sacrifice of Jesus' life made possible a resurrection.

The proclamation that Jesus is the giver of life moves along two planes in the Lazarus episode. The miracle anticipated the final resurrection of the dead from their graves. The story was thus a sign of that resurrection through which men pass from physical existence into life that is eternal. But the narrative also laid stress upon the faith that Jesus possessed the power to make alive *before* the last day. Several commentators have noticed the correspondence between the word of Christ in John 5:28 and his action in the raising of Lazarus:

Those who are in the tombs . . .	He found Lazarus in the tomb (11:17, 38)
will hear his voice . . .	he cried with a loud voice, (11:43)
and come out (5:28)	the dead man came out . . . (11:44)

One writer has concluded that the evangelist "has taken an event associated with the 'last day,' and transplanted it into the historic ministry of Jesus, thus making it a 'sign' of the life-giving which that ministry (when consummated) brought into effect."[111] To the evangelist was it no less a miracle that believers in Jesus Christ "*have passed* from death to life" than that the body of a dead man should have been revivified? If, upon the testimony of the Gospel and the Church, the possibility of this new birth seemed fanciful would people become convinced "if someone should rise from the dead"?[112]

Passion and Resurrection Narratives

It can be said that in John the Book of the Passion-Resurrection (C) does not begin with the betrayal of Judas and the arrest of Jesus, but with "farewell discourses." Chapter 12 marks the end of the Judean ministry and the beginning of the Passion. Instead of appending discourses to single incidents from the narrative, as in the preceding section, the evangelist interpreted the whole story beforehand. He therefore allowed the moving drama of the last week of Jesus'

[109] John 11:4, 25. It is probable that the remark of Thomas, v. 16, refers to Jesus' death also.
[110] John 11:23ff.
[111] Dodd, *Fourth Gospel*, p. 366.
[112] Luke 16:31.

life to make its maximum impact upon the reader.[113] Yet in composing the farewell discourses, the evangelist was motivated by historical as well as by theological considerations. According to the earlier Gospels, Jesus devoted himself to death *before* his trials and crucifixion.

In the dialogue with Nicodemus it was proclaimed that the love of God prompted the gift of Christ to the world. It is noteworthy that after John described the manner in which this gift was given and received by men, he returned to the theme of divine condescension. The love of the Son for the Father led him to "lay down his life"; the Father loved the Son because of his willing and perfect obedience. It is now proclaimed that the object of this mutual love of the Father and the Son was the revelation of the divine love for men.[114] The farewell discourses range over many subjects but there is one dominant note throughout, which is concisely stated in the words: "As the Father has loved me, so have I loved you; abide in my love."[115]

In the episode which provides the setting for the farewell discourses it is made evident that the "mysticism" of the evangelist cannot be associated with other religions of the period which could be described as mystical. In becoming the objects of divine love, the disciples of Jesus were bound together into a community with a mission to the world. They were governed by a new commandment. By this shall men know the disciples of Jesus, that they "love one another." The distinguishing mark of the new life into which men were brought by virtue of Christ's death and resurrection was a love for the world which continued in the disciples, after the example of their "Teacher and Lord."[116]

It is probable that John 13:31 to 14:31 forms a unity. The dialogue throughout is concerned with the "going" and "coming" of Jesus, his departure from the disciples and his return. According to some scholars, the evangelist employed the traditional hope of Christ's (second) coming as the point of departure for a radical reinterpretation of the Gospel. John taught that Christ's death on the cross *was* his ascent to the Father (corresponding to the image of the heavenly session at God's right hand), and his return to his disciples after death (closely associated, if not identified, with the coming of the Holy Spirit) *was* the second advent.[117] Yet it is more probable that the difference between the eschatology of the Synoptic Gospels and of the Fourth Gospel is to be explained as a difference of emphasis, not of substance. Jesus not only promised his disciples that he would go to prepare a place for them, but also that he would come again to receive them unto himself. This is not the same as his abiding presence.[118]

The conclusion of chapter 14 reads like a conclusion to "the farewell discourses." For this reason some interpreters have considered that these verses have

---

[113] A few notes are introduced to point to the fact that in the cross the Ministry was fulfilled, e.g., 18:14, 32; 19:24, 28.

[114] John 13:1; 3:16f.; 10:17; 16:27f.; 17:23ff.

[115] John 15:9.

[116] John 13:13ff.; 14:21; 15:12, 17. Cf. Mark 10:43ff.

[117] Dodd, *Fourth Gospel*, p. 395.

[118] John 14:3; 17:24. Barrett, *St. John*, pp. 56ff. E. Schweizer, "Orthodox Proclamation," *Interpretation* VIII (1954): 387ff.; Wilder, *New Testament Faith for Today*, pp. 147ff.

been displaced. Others note the parallelism between sections 13:31 to 14:31 and chapters 15 to 17, and conjecture that alternate versions of the same discourse have been juxtaposed. But the concluding words may only emphasize Jesus' acceptance of his destiny. He went forth to meet the adversary, not because he could not do otherwise, but because his love for the Father and for men led him to "do as the Father commanded." There is no movement to another place, but perhaps a change in temporal perspective is suggested.[119] The next discourse concerns Christ and his Church more than the previous one. The theological situation is focused more clearly beyond the cross, although the setting is still the eve of the crucifixion.

The passages in chapters 14 to 16 which tell of the coming of the *Paraclete* merit close attention. It is difficult to translate this Greek term in the contexts John uses it.[120] The *Paraclete* will be a *witness* in Jesus' defense, and a *spokesman* for him, continuing Jesus' "suit" with the world. The *Paraclete* is also to be a *consoler* of the disciples in Jesus' absence. Moreover, he is to be their teacher and guide— perhaps these functions may be expressed in the term *helper*.[121] Different inter- pretations have been given of the relation of the *Paraclete* to Jesus, on the one hand, and to the Holy Spirit, on the other. In 14:26, Jesus speaks of sending "another *Paraclete*." The close parallelism between the work of Jesus and the work of the *Paraclete*, and their corresponding relations to the disciples and the world, suggests that for John, Jesus continues his presence and ministry as the *Paraclete* in those who love him and keep his commandments. But as a spiritual presence, invisible to the world, but witnessing against it in and through the disciples' witness, the *Paraclete* is "the Spirit of Truth" or "Holy Spirit."[122] In the teaching of the evangelist, Jesus' promised coming is therefore partially fulfilled in the sending of the Spirit/*Paraclete*. By such means, Jesus "abides" with his own who are in the world, while yet present with the Father. The presence of Jesus with his disciples is not a substitute for, or in opposition to, the final coming of Jesus. But a greater emphasis is placed upon the former in the Fourth Gospel.

The prayer of Christ in chapter 17 stands as more than a summary of the teaching of the Gospel, more than a discourse on the mission of the Church obedient to its Lord. This prayer represents the movement of Christ toward God, an equivalent of the narrative of the ascension in Luke–Acts. It is the most impressive statement in the Gospel that the death of Jesus became the means whereby God's glory was manifested unto men.

The prayer discloses five divisions. In the first, Jesus prayed that the hour that had come (the hour of his death) might be the means of God's glorification, of bringing eternal life unto men, of reuniting the Son with the Father. The delegated work had been accomplished.[123] In the second division, the Ministry of Jesus and

---

[119] Dodd, *Fourth Gospel*, pp. 406ff.

[120] John 14:16f., 25; 15:26; 16:7–11, 13–15.

[121] R. E. Brown, "The Paraclete in the Fourth Gospel," *NTS* 13 (1967): 113ff.; Martyn, *History and Theology*, pp. 135ff.

[122] John 14:17 (16:13); 14:26.

[123] John 17:1–5.

its results (as set forth in John) are briefly summarized.[124] In the third division, Christ prayed for his disciples. He foresaw their situation in the Church after his departure and interceded in their behalf.[125] In the fourth division, Christ's prayer expressed his concern for all those persons who were to believe in him through the apostles' testimony. He prayed for their unity as a means of bringing to the world faith and experience of the love of God.[126] And last, Christ prayed for a final union of believers with himself in the presence of the divine glory.[127]

Divisions three and four may be singled out for comment. It may come as a surprise, if not an offense, that Christ should say: "I am not praying for the world but for those whom thou hast given me. . . ." Apparently the evangelist shared the belief of his period that "the world" was a realm of darkness under the control of the "rulers of this age."[128] Accordingly, those who "belonged" to the world not only did not know God but were alienated from him. Yet unlike many teachings of this time, the imprisonment of men in their darkness was not conceived as a consequence of their birth as mortals or of ignorance of their true natures. Because their deeds were evil, men loved the darkness, rather than the light which surrounded them.[129] Self-knowledge, or knowledge of the overworld of light and life, were not sufficient to overcome this darkness. Only because "the world" is the object of God's love, only because God gave his Son and the Son laid down his life, had men access to the truth that set them free from sin and death.[130] Christ's prayer for the disciples was that they might be enabled to fulfill their mission: to show forth to the world the divine love for the world. In this knowledge alone there was eternal life.[131]

Much interest has rightly centered upon Christ's prayer for the Church. The following ideas are expressed: It is the glory of the Church that it should express in its fellowship a token of that love which unites the Father and the Son; not until the Church becomes "perfectly one" can the world know God's purpose of love in sending the Son; the triumph of the Church's mission in the world goes hand in hand with the perfecting of the unity of the Church. At this place the reader is reminded of the portrayal of the nature and destiny of the Church in the Letter to the Ephesians.[132]

The kingship of Christ is a central aspect of the story of the passion in the Fourth Gospel.[133] Jesus went to his cross just as a king goes to his throne (11). There is a characteristic irony in the emphasis of this Gospel that Jesus was "the King of Israel," since "the Jews" would have none of him. Yet the scene in Pilate's

---

[124] John 17:6–8.
[125] John 17:9–19.
[126] John 17:20–23.
[127] John 17:24ff.
[128] John 12:31; 14:30; 16:11. Cf. 1 John 5:19.
[129] John 1:4f., 9f.; 3:19ff.
[130] John 3:16f.; 8:31ff.
[131] John 17:3; 17:17ff.
[132] Opinions have differed widely concerning John's conception of the Church and its mission vis-a-vis "the world." See R. E. Brown, *John, AB,* vol. 29, pp. cv ff.; Käsemann, *Testament of Jesus,* pp. 27ff.
[133] John 1:49; 12:13, 15; 18:33, 39; 19:3, 14f., 19ff.

court makes it evident that Jesus' kingship could not be interpreted along national or merely this-worldly lines. His sovereignty lay in his witness to the truth. The allegiance which he claimed was that of obedience to truth.[134]

The evangelist emphasized that the death of Christ was a voluntary act. When the soldiers came, he gave himself up; when death approached, the initiative again was taken by Jesus.[135] He defended himself when falsely accused. But it is probable also that the evangelist, like Luke, wished to stress Jesus' innocence.[136] One notices that in the action taken against Jesus, the Romans were involved from the beginning. Perhaps John sought in this way to emphasize that the whole "world" was aligned against him.

The word of Jesus from the cross, "I thirst," is reported as the fulfillment of scripture.[137] It is probable that John included this notice of Jesus' physical sensation to combat docetic tendencies in the Church of his time. If John knew of Jesus' cry of dereliction from the cross, he omitted it. This report might have been interpreted as the abandonment of God, leaving Jesus to die—not "the Christ," but merely a man. Instead of the word Mark reports, John wrote: "It is finished." On the cross Jesus' "work" was accomplished.[138]

One interpreter of the Gospel, who rightly stresses its theme of the glory of Jesus, comments that one is tempted to regard John's story of the Passion "as being a mere postscript which had to be included because John could not ignore this tradition nor yet could he fit it organically into his work."[139] On the contrary, the present writer agrees with another who writes "that the Passion narrative and Resurrection come last in John because they are the climax of his thought, as they are the climax of the Ministry of Jesus. The death of Jesus was the hour of glorification, when all the signs of his life were sealed by death, the ultimately real sign. It was the natural culmination of John's work. The meaning of the cross and resurrection set forth *spiritually* in chapters 14–17 has validity only because Jesus did *actually* die and rise again."[140]

One of the most striking features of John's Easter Story is his report that Christ's ascension and gift of the Holy Spirit were the immediate sequel to the cross. But was not Jesus' ascent to the Father coincident with his being lifted up upon the cross? Once again we see the evangelist's lack of interest in temporal connections. His concern was that events not be separated which derive their meaning from Jesus' acts of self-oblation. It should be noticed also that the shepherd who lay down his life for the sheep was not long separated from his flock. Christ did not leave desolate his own.[141] From the day of his victory he gave to them, as he promised, the Holy Spirit that he might abide with them forever.[142]

---

[134] John 18:33ff.

[135] John 18:4ff.; 19:17 (cf. Mark 15:21); 19:28, 30.

[136] John 18:19ff., 33ff.; 19:10ff.

[137] John 19:28. See also 11:33ff.; 12:37; 18:21.

[138] John 19:30. The same word is used in 17:4; 4:34.

[139] Käsemann, *The Testament of Jesus*, p. 7.

[140] Davies, *Invitation*, p. 482.

[141] John 14:18; 10:12f.

[142] John 20:19, 22; 14:16; F. W. Beare, "The Risen Jesus Bestows the Spirit," *Can. Journ. of Theo.* IV (1958): 95ff.

Notice how pervasively there is woven into the narratives of the appearances of the risen Christ the motif of "seeing and believing." There is no depreciation of the eyewitness testimony, as the emphasis upon the "many signs" makes clear. It was no less important for John that Jesus really died and was raised from the dead as that the "word became flesh" and dwelt among men. Accordingly, the evangelist emphasized the testimony of Peter, "the disciple whom Jesus loved," Mary Magdalene, the other disciples, and Thomas. Yet in the stories of Mary and of Thomas, John claimed that the privilege of sight was not all-important. There was, after all, a relative value to the postresurrection "appearances," for those who witnessed them as for those who did not and cannot. Evidence of the risen Christ must be received and appropriated by faith, not simply observed.

Unquestionably the evangelist believed that the first witnesses stood in a unique, unrepeatable position. It was of crucial importance that their words be true. Nevertheless, through their faith the successors of the apostles were united with the eyewitnesses: "We have beheld his glory. . . . Blessed are those who have not seen and yet believe." [143]

There were no days of anxious waiting for the disciples, no long separation from their Lord. But Mary was not permitted to cling to her departed "Master," to cling to the Jesus of the past. Thomas was invited to lay hold of the risen Christ. It was no longer the Word become "flesh" before whom Thomas bowed in adoration. It was the Son, existing in unity with the Father, now "with God," or simply, God. The disciple had perceived in the Jesus of history his "Lord," his "God." [144]

[143] John 1:14ff.; 20:29.
[144] John 20:28.

BIBLIOGRAPHY

1. Bartsch, H. W., ed., *Kerygma and Myth*, trans. R. H. Fuller, 1954.
Beare, F. W., "Canon of the N.T.," *Interpreter's Dictionary of the Bible*, Vol. I, 1962.
Braaten, C. E., *New Directions in Theology Today: History and Hermeneutics*, Vol. II, 1966.
————, and Harrisville, R. A., eds., *Kerygma and History*, 1962.
Bultmann, R., *Existence and Faith*, trans. S. M. Ogden, 1960.
Dodd, C. H., *The Bible Today*, 1947.
Ebeling, G., *Word and Faith*, trans. J. W. Leitch, 1963.
Feine, P., and Behm, J., *Introduction to the New Testament*, 14th rev., ed. W. G. Kümmel, trans. A. J. Mattill, Jr., 1966.
Grant, R. M., *A Historical Introduction to the New Testament*, 1963.
Käsemann, E., *Essays on New Testament Themes*, trans. W. J. Montague, 1960.
Kegley, C. W., ed., *Theology of Rudolf Bultmann*, 1966.
McNeile, A. H., *An Introduction to the Study of the New Testament*, rev. ed., C. S. C. Williams, 1953.
Metzger, B. M., *The Text of the New Testament*, 1964.
Parvis, M. M., "Text, N.T.," *Interpreter's Dictionary of the Bible*, Vol. IV, 1962.
Robinson, J. M., and Cobb, J. B., Jr., eds., *New Frontiers in Theology, The New Hermeneutic*, Vol. II, 1964.
Stendahl, K., "Biblical Theology, Contemporary," *Interpreter's Dictionary of the Bible*, Vol. I, 1962.

2. Cadbury, H. J., *The Book of Acts in History*, 1955.
Denny, J., *Jesus and the Gospel*, 1908.
Grant, F. C., *The Gospels: Their Origin and Their Growth*, 1957.
Keck, L. E., and Martyn, J. L., eds., *Studies in Luke-Acts*, 1966.
Schweitzer, A., *The Mysticism of Paul the Apostle*, trans. W. Montgomery, 1931.

3. Allegro, J. M., "Further Light on the History of the Qumran Sect," *Journal of Biblical Literature*, Vol. LXXXV (June, 1956).
Barrett, C. K., ed., *The New Testament Background: Selected Documents*, 1957.
Barthelemy, D. and Milik, J. T., *Qumran Cave I: Discoveries in the Judean Desert*, Vol. I, 1955.
Brownlee, W. H., "The Habbakuk Midrash and the Targum of Jonathan," *Journal of Jewish Studies*, Vol. VII, Nos. 3–4 (1956).
————, "The Historical Allusions of the Dead Sea Habakkuk Midrash," *American Schools of Oriental Research*, No. 126 (April, 1952).
————, "Mohommad ed-Deeb's Own Story of His Scroll Discovery," *Journal of Near Eastern Studies*, Vol. XVI, No. 4 (Oct., 1957).
Burrows, M., *The Dead Sea Scrolls*, 1955.
————, ed., *The Dead Sea Scrolls of St. Mark's Monastery*, American Schools of Oriental Research, Vol. I, 1950; Vol. II, 1951.
Charles, R. H., *Apocrypha and Pseudepigrapha of the Old Testament*, Vols. I and II, 1913.
Cross, F. M., Jr., *The Ancient Library of Qumran and Modern Biblical Studies*, rev. ed., 1961.
Danby, H., trans. and ed., *The Mishnah*, 1933.
Dupont-Sommer, A., *The Jewish Sect of Qumran and the Essenes*, 1954.
Easton, B. S., *Christ in the Gospels*, 1930.
Enslin, M. S., *Christian Beginnings*, 1938.
Gaster, T., *The Dead Sea Scriptures in English Translation*, 1956.
Grant, F. C., *Ancient Judaism and the New Testament*, 1959.
————, *The Economic Background of the Gospels*, 1926.
Grollenberg, L. H., ed., *Nelson's Atlas of the Bible*, 1957.
Klausner, J., *Jesus of Nazareth*, trans. H. Danby, 1929.
————, *The Messianic Idea in Israel*, trans. W. F. Stinespring, 1955.
Marcus, R., "Pharisees, Essenes, and Gnostics," *Journal of Biblical Literature*, Vol. LXXIII, 1954.
Milik, J. T., *Ten Years of Discovery in the Wilderness of Judea*, 1959.

Moore, G. F., *Judaism in the First Centuries of the Christian Era*, Vols. I–III, 1927.

Pfeiffer, R. H., *History of New Testament Times*, 1949.

Reicke, B., *The New Testament Era*, trans. D. E. Green, 1968.

Sandmel, S., *A Jewish Understanding of the New Testament*, 1956.

Schubert, K., *The Dead Sea Community*, trans. J. W. Doberstein, 1959.

Smith, M., "The Dead Sea Sect in Relation to Ancient Judaism," *New Testament Studies*, Vol. VII, 1961.

Thompson, J. A., *Archeology and the Pre-Christian Centuries*, 1958.

Vermes, G., *Discovery in the Judean Desert*, 1956.

Wilson, E., *The Scrolls from the Dead Sea*, 1955.

Wright, G. E. and Filson, F. V., *The Westminster Historical Atlas to the Bible*, rev. ed., 1956.

Zeitlin, S., *The Rise and Fall of the Judean State*, 1962.

4.   Brownlee, W. H., "A Comparison of the Covenanters of the Dead Sea Scrolls with Pre-Christian Jewish Sects," *Biblical Archaeologist*, Vol. XIII, 1950.

Bruce, F. F., *Second Thoughts on the Dead Sea Scrolls*, 1956.

Burrows, M., *The Dead Sea Scrolls*, 1955.

————— , *More Light on the Dead Sea Scrolls*, 1958.

Charles, R. H., *Religious Development Between the Old and New Testaments*, 1914.

Cross, F. M., Jr., *The Ancient Library of Qumran and Modern Biblical Studies*, rev. ed., 1961.

Danby, H., trans. and ed., *The Mishnah*, 1933.

Enslin, M. S., *Christian Beginnings*, 1938.

————— , "New Testament Times, II. Palestine," *Interpreter's Bible*, Vol. VII, 1957.

Farmer, W. R., *Maccabees, Zealots and Josephus*, 1956.

Fritsch, C. T., *The Qumran Community*, 1956.

Fuller, R. H., *The Foundations of New Testament Christology*, 1965.

Gerhardsson, B., *Memory and Manuscript*, 1961.

Jeremias, J., *Jerusalem in the Time of Jesus*, trans. F. H. and C. H. Cave, 1969.

Johnson, S., *Jesus in His Homeland*, 1957.

Klausner, J., *Jesus of Nazareth*, trans. H. Danby, 1929.

————— , *The Messianic Idea in Israel*, trans. W. F. Stinespring, 1955.

Manson, T. W., *Servant-Messiah*, 1953.

Milik, J. T., *Ten Years of Discovery in the Wilderness of Judea*, 1959.

Moore, G. F., *Judaism in the First Centuries of the Christian Era*, Vols. I–III, 1927.

Oesterley, W. O. E., *The Jews and Judaism During the Greek Period*, 1941.

Pfeiffer, R. H., *History of New Testament Times*, 1949.

Rabin, C., *Qumran Studies*, 1957.

Reicke, B., *The New Testament Era*, trans. D. E. Green, 1968.

Rowley, H. H., *The Relevance of Apocalyptic*, rev. ed., 1955.

Russell, D. S., *The Method and Message of Jewish Apocalyptic*, 1964.

Schubert, K., *The Dead Sea Community*, trans. J. W. Doberstein, 1959.

Stendahl, K., ed., *The Scrolls and the New Testament*, 1957.

van der Ploeg, J., *The Excavations at Qumran*, trans. Kevin Smyth, 1958.

Wilder, A. H., *Eschatology and Ethics in the Teaching of Jesus* rev. ed., 1950.

Winter, P., *On the Trial of Jesus*, 1961.

Zeitlin, S., *The Rise and Fall of the Judean State*, 1962.

5.   Barrett, C. K., *Luke the Historian in Recent Study*, 1961.

Black, M., *Aramaic Approach to the Gospels and Acts*, 2d ed., 1954.

Cadbury, H. J., *Acts, Interpreter's Dictionary of the Bible*, Vol. I.

————— , *The Making of Luke-Acts*, 1927.

————— , *Style and Literary Method of St. Luke*, 1920.

Conzelmann, H., *The Theology of St. Luke*, trans. G. Buswell, 1960.

Dibelius, M., *Studies in the Acts of the Apostles*, trans. M. Ling, 1956.

Feine, Paul, and Behm, Johannes, *Introduction to the New Testament*, 14th rev., ed. W. G. Kümmel, trans. A. J. Mattill, Jr., 1966.

Foakes Jackson, F. J., and Lake, K., *Beginnings of Christianity*, 1932.

Heard, R. G., *An Introduction to the New Testament*, 1950.

Hobart, W. K., *The Medical Language of St. Luke*, 1882.

Hunter, A. M., *Interpreting the New Testament 1900–1950*, 1951.

Käsemann, E., *Essays on New Testament Themes*, trans. W. J. Montague, 1960.
Keck, L. E. and Martyn, J. L., eds., *Studies in Luke-Acts*, 1966.
Knox, W. L., *The Acts of the Apostles*, 1948.
Macgregor, G. H. C., "Acts," *Interpreter's Bible*, Vol. IX.
Martin, R. A., "Evidence of Aramaic Sources in Acts I-XV," *New Testament Studies*, Vol XI, 1964.
Munck, J., *Acts, Anchor Bible*, Vol. XXXI, 1967.
Riddle, D. W., and Hutson, H. H., *New Testament Life and Literature*, 1946.
Rohde, J., *Rediscovering the Teaching of the Evangelists*, trans. D. Barton, 1968.
Russell, H. G., *Harvard Theological Review*, Vol. XLVIII, 1956.
Torrey, C. C., *The Composition and Date of Acts*, 1916.
van Unnik, W. C., "The 'Book of Acts' The Confirmation of the Gospel," *Novum Testamentum* Vol. IV, 1960.
Williams, C. S. C., *The Acts of the Apostles*, 1957.
————, *Expository Times*, Vol. LXIV, 1953.
Winn, A. C., "Elusive Mystery: The Purpose of Acts," *Interpretation*, Vol. XIII, No. 2 (1959).

6. Barrett, C. K., *The Holy Spirit and the Gospel Tradition*, 1947.
Betz, Otto, *What Do We Know About Jesus?*, 1968.
Black, M., *Aramaic Approach to the Gospels and Acts*, 2d ed., 1954.
Brownlee, W. H., "Messianic Motifs of Qumran and the New Testament," *New Testament Studies*, Vol. III, 1956.
Bruce, F. F., *Second Thoughts on the Dead Sea Scrolls*, 1956.
Bultmann, R., *Theology of the New Testament*, trans. K. Grobel (2 vols). 1951.
Conzelmann, H., *The Theology of St. Luke*, trans. M. Ling, 1956.
Cullmann, O., *Baptism in the New Testament*, 1950.
————, *Christ and Time*, trans. F. V. Filson, 1950.
Daube, D., *The New Testament and Rabbinic Judaism*, 1956.
Davies, W. D., *Invitation to the New Testament*, 1966.
————, *Paul and Rabbinic Judaism*, 1948.
————, and Daube, D., eds., *The Background of the New Testament and Its Eschatology*, 1956.
Dibelius, M., *Studies in the Acts of the Apostles*, trans. M. Ling, 1956.
Dix, G., *Jew and Greek: A Study in the Primitive Church*, 1953.
Dodd, C. H., *According to the Scriptures*, 1952.
————, *Apostolic Preaching and Its Developments*, 1936.
Filson, F. V., *Jesus Christ the Risen Lord*, 1956.
Flender, H., *St. Luke, Theologian of Redemptive History*, trans. R. H. and I. Fuller, 1967.
Foakes Jackson, F. J., and Lake, K., *Beginnings of Christianity* (5 vols.), 1932.
Foerster, W. and Quell, G., "Kyrios," in *Theological Dictionary of the New Testament*, trans. and ed. G. W. Bromiley, Vol. III, 1965.
Fuller, R. H., *The Foundations of New Testament Christology*, 1965.
Goguel, M., *The Birth of Christianity*, trans. H. C. Snape, 1953.
Hooker, M. D., *Jesus and the Servant*, 1959.
Klausner, J., *The Messianic Idea in Israel*, trans. W. F. Stinespring, 1955.
Knox, W. L., *The Acts of the Apostles*, 1948.
Lake, K., *The Earlier Epistles of St. Paul*, 1919.
Macgregor, G. H. C., "Acts," *Interpreter's Bible*, Vol. IX.
Martin, R. A., Syntactical Evidence of Aramaic Sources in Acts I-IX," *New Testament Studies*, Vol. XI, 1964.
Nock, A. D., *Early Gentile Christianity and Its Hellenistic Background*, 1964.
O'Neill, J. C., *The Theology of Acts in Its Historical Setting*, 1961.
Perrin, N., *Rediscovering the Teaching of Jesus*, 1967.
Rawlinson, A. E. J., *The New Testament Doctrine of the Christ*, 1926.
Rohde, J., *Rediscovering the Teaching of the Evangelists*, trans. D. Barton, 1968.
Schlatter, A., *The Church in the New Testament Period*, trans. P. Levertoff, 1955.
Schubert, K., *The Dead Sea Community*, trans. J. W. Doberstein, 1959.
Schweizer, E., "Discipleship and Belief in Jesus as Lord from Jesus to the Hellenistic Church," *New Testament Studies*, Vol. II, 1955.
————, *Lordship and Discipleship*, 1960.
Tödt, H. E., *The Son of Man in the Synoptic Tradition*, trans. D. M. Barton, 1965.
Williams, C. S. C., *The Acts of the Apostles*, 1957.

van Unnik, W. C., "The Book of Acts: The Confirmation of the Gospel," *Novum Testamentum*, IV (1960).

Weiss, J., *History of Primitive Christianity*, trans. and ed. F. C. Grant, 1937; reprinted, *Earliest Christianity*, 1959.

Zimmerli, W., and Jeremias, J., *The Servant of God*, trans. H. Knight and others, 1957.

7.   Barrett, C. K., *Luke the Historian in Recent Study*, 1961.

Brown, R. E., "The Unity and Diversity in New Testament Ecclesiology," *Novum Testamentum*, Vol. VI, 1963.

Bultmann, R., *Theology of the New Testament*, trans. K. Grobel (2 vols.), 1951.

Craig, C. T., *The Beginning of Christianity*, 1943.

Cross, F. M., Jr., *The Ancient Library of Qumran and Modern Biblical Studies*, rev. ed., 1961.

Cullmann, O., *Peter*, 2d ed., trans. F. V. Filson, 1962.

Dix, G., *Jew and Greek: A Study in the Primitive Church*, 1953.

Elliott-Binns, L. E., *Galilean Christianity*, 1956.

Foakes Jackson, F. J., and Lake, K., *Beginnings of Christianity* (5 vols.), 1932.

Goguel, M., *The Birth of Christianity*, trans. H. C. Snape, 1953.

Goodspeed, E., *The Twelve*, 1957.

Jeremias, J., *The Eucharistic Words of Jesus*, trans. A. Ehrhardt, 1955.

Keck, L. E., and Martyn, J. L., eds., *Studies in Luke-Acts*, 1966.

Knox, W. L., *St. Paul and the Church at Jerusalem*, 1925.

Lietzmann, H., *The Beginnings of the Christian Church*, trans. B. L. Woolf, 1937.

———, *Mass and Lord's Supper*, trans. D. H. G. Reeve, 1953.

Manson, T. W., ed., *A Companion to the Bible*, 1946.

Munck, J., *Acts, Anchor Bible*, Vol. XXXI, 1967.

———, *Paul and the Salvation of Mankind*, trans. F. Clarke, 1959.

Reicke, B., *The New Testament Era*, trans. D. E. Green, 1968.

Schlatter, A., *The Church in the New Testament Period*, trans. P. Levertoff, 1955.

Simon, M., *St. Stephen and the Hellenists in the Primitive Church*, 1958.

Stendahl, K., ed., *The Scrolls and the New Testament*, 1957.

Taylor, V., *The Gospel According to Mark*, 1952.

Weiss, J., *History of Primitive Christianity*, trans. and ed. F. C. Grant, 1937; reprinted, *Earliest Christianity*, 1959.

Williams, C. S. C., *The Acts of the Apostles*, 1957.

8.   Allegro, J. M., "Fragments of a Qumran Scroll of Eschatological Midrashim," *Journal of Biblical Literature*, Vol. LXXVII, Part 4 (1958):350ff.

Anderson, H., *Jesus and Christian Origins*, 1964.

Baillie, D. M., *God Was in Christ*, 1948.

Beasley-Murray, G. R., *Jesus and the Future*, 1954.

Betz, Otto, *What Do We Know About Jesus?*, 1968.

Brown, J. P., "An Early Revision of the Gospel of Mark," *Journal of Biblical Literature*, Vol. LXXVIII, Part 3 (1959).

Bultmann, R., *The History of the Synoptic Tradition*, trans. J. Marsh, 1963.

———, "A New Approach to the Synoptic Gospels," *Journal of Religion*, Vol. V, No. 6 (1926).

———, *Theology of the New Testament*, trans. K. Grobel (2 vols.), 1951.

Cranfield, C. E. B., "St. Mark 13," *Scottish Journal of Theology* 6–7 (1953–54).

Creed, J. M., *The Gospel According to St. Luke*, 1950.

Cross, F. M., Jr., *The Ancient Library of Qumran and Modern Biblical Studies*, rev. ed., 1961.

Davies, W. D., "Reflections on a Scandinavian Approach to 'The Gospel Tradition'," *Novum Testamentum Suppliment*, Vol. VI, 1962.

——— and Daube, D., eds., *The Background of the New Testament and Its Eschatology*, 1966.

Dibelius, M., *From Tradition to Gospel*, trans. B. L. Woolf, 1934.

———, *Studies in the Acts of the Apostles*, trans. M. Ling, 1956.

Dodd, C. H., *About the Gospels*, 1950.

———, *According to the Scriptures*, 1952.

———, *Gospel and Law*, 1951.

———, *New Testament Studies*, 1953.

Easton, B. S., *The Gospel Before the Gospels*, 1928.

Farmer, W. R., *The Synoptic Problem*, 1964.

Feine, Paul, and Behm, Johannes, *Introduction to the New Testament*, 14th rev., ed. W. G. Kümmel, trans. A. J. Mattill, Jr., 1966.

————, *Interpreting the Miracles*, 1963.
Fuller, R. H., *The Mission and Achievement of Jesus*, 1954.
Gerhardsson, B., *Memory and Manuscript*, 1961.
Gilmour, S. McL., *Luke, Interpreter's Bible*, Vol. VIII.
Goguel, M., *The Birth of Christianity*, trans. H. C. Snape, 1953.
Grant, F. C., ed., *Form Criticism: A New Method of New Testament Research*, 1934.
————, *The Gospels: Their Origin and Their Growth*, 1957.
Grobel, K., "Form Criticism," *Interpreter's Dictionary of the Bible*, Vol. II.
Harnack, A., *Sayings of Jesus*, trans. J. R. Wilkinson, 1908.
Heard, R. G., *An Introduction to the New Testament*, 1950.
Higgins, A. J. B., ed., *New Testament Essays*, 1959.
Hunter, A. M., *The Work and Words of Jesus*, 1950.
Jeremias, J., *The Parables of Jesus*, trans. S. H. Hooke, rev. ed., 1962.
Knox, W. L., *Sources of the Synoptic Gospels*: Vol. I. *Mark*, 1953.
————, *Sources of the Synoptic Gospels*: Vol. II, *St. Luke and St. Matthew*, 1957.
Kümmel, W. G., *Promise and Fulfillment*, trans. D. Barton, 1957.
Lightfoot, R. H., *The Gospel Message of St. Mark*, 1950.
Manson, T. W., *The Sayings of Jesus*, 1949.
————, *The Teaching of Jesus*, 2d ed., 1935.
Manson, W., *Jesus the Messiah*, 1946.
Minear, P., "Form Criticism and Faith," *Religion in Life*, Vol. XV, No. 1 (1945).
Nineham, D. H., ed., *Studies in the Gospels*, 1955.
Oxford Studies in the Synoptic Problem, 1911.
Pannenberg, W., *Jesus—God and Man*, 1968.
Perrin, N., *Rediscovering the Teaching of Jesus*, 1967.
Perry, A. M., "The Growth of the Gospels," *Interpreter's Bible*, Vol. VII.
————, *The Sources of Luke's Passion Narrative*, 1920.
Piper, O., "The Origin of the Gospel Pattern," *Journal of Biblical Literature* Vol. LXXVIII, Part 2 (1959).
Richardson, A., *The Miracle-Stories of the Gospels*, 1941.
Riesenfeld, H., "The Gospel Tradition and Its Beginnings," *Studia Evangelica*: Bd. 73.
Simpson, R. T., "The Major Agreements of Matthew and Luke against Mark," *New Testament Studies* Vol. XII, 1966.
Smith, M., "A Comparison of Early Christian and Early Rabbinic Tradition," *Journal of Biblical Literature*, Vol. LXXXII, 1963.
Streeter, B. H., *The Four Gospels*, 1924.
Taylor, V., *The Formation of the Gospel Tradition*, 1935.
————, *The Gospel According to Mark*, 1952.
————, "Theologians of Our Times," *Expository Times*, Vol. LXXIV (1962–63): 77ff., 262ff.
Tödt, H. E., *The Son of Man in the Synoptic Tradition*, trans. D. M. Barton, 1965.
Winter, P., *On the Trial of Jesus*, 1961.

9.   Anderson, H., *Jesus and Christian Origins*, 1964.
Bacon, B. W., *Studies in Matthew*, 1930.
Baltzer, K., "The Meaning of the Temple in the Lukan Writings," *Harvard Theological Review*, Vol. LVIII, 1965.
Bornkamm, G., Barth, G., and Held, H. J., *Tradition and Interpretation in Matthew*, trans. P. Scott, 1963.
Bultmann, R., *The History of the Synoptic Tradition*, trans. J. Marsh, 1963.
Burkill, T. A., *Mysterious Revelation*, 1963.
Burkitt, F. C., *Gospel History and Its Transmission*, 1906.
Cadbury, H. J., *The Making of Luke-Acts*, 1927.
Clark, K., "The Gentile Bias in Matthew," *Journal of Biblical Literature*, Vol. LXVI, 1947.
Conzelmann, H., *The Theology of St. Luke*, trans. G. Buswell, 1960.
Creed, J. M., *The Gospel According to St. Luke*, 1950.
Cullmann, O., *The Early Church*, trans. S. Godmann, 1956.
————, *Peter*, 2d ed., trans. F. V. Filson, 1962.
Davies, W. D., *Invitation to the New Testament*, 1966.
————, and Daube, D., eds., *The Background of the New Testament and Its Eschatology*, 1956.
Dodd, C. H., *New Testament Studies*, 1953.
Enslin, M. S., *Christian Beginnings*, 1938.

Gibbs, J. M., "Purpose and Pattern in Matthew's Use of the Title 'Son of David'," *New Testament Studies* Vol. X, 1964.

Gilmour, S. McL., "A Critical Examination of Proto-Luke," *Journal of Biblical Literature*, Vol. LXII, 1948.

Grant, F. C., *The Gospels: Their Origin and Their Growth*, 1957.

Guy, H. A., *The Origin of the Gospel of Mark*, 1955.

Heard. R. G., *An Introduction to the New Testament*, 1950.

Hore, D. R. A., *The Theme of Jewish Persecution of Christians in the Gospel According to Matthew*, 1968.

Hunter, A. M., *The Message of the New Testament*, 1944.

Keck, L. E., "The Introduction to Mark's Gospel," *New Testament Studies*, Vol. XII, 1966.

Kilpatrick, G. D., *The Origin of the Gospel According to St. Matthew*, 1946.

Knigge, H. D., "The Meaning of Mark," *Interpretation*, Vol. XXII, 1968.

Lightfoot, R. H., *The Gospel Message of St. Mark*, 1950.

Loisy, A. F., and Bacon, B. W., *The Gospel of Mark*, 1925.

Rawlinson, A. E. J., *The Gospel According to St. Mark*, 1949.

Manson, T. W., *The Sayings of Jesus*, 1949.

Marxsen, W., *Mark the Evangelist*, trans. R. Harrisville, 1969.

McNeile, A. H., *An Introduction to the Study of the New Testament*, rev. ed., ed. C. S. C. Williams, 1953.

Moffatt, J., *Introduction to the Literature of the New Testament*, 1918.

Moule, C. F. D., *The Birth of the New Testament*, 1962.

————, *The Phenomenon of the New Testament*, 1967.

Nineham, D. H., ed., *Studies in the Gospels*, 1955.

Oliver, H. H., "The Lucan Birth Stories and the Purposes of Luke-Acts," *New Testament Studies*, Vol. X, 1963.

Perrin, N., *Rediscovering the Teaching of Jesus*, 1967.

————, *What is Redaction Criticism?*, 1969.

Perry, A. M., *The Sources of Luke's Passion Narrative*, 1920.

Rawlinson, A. E. J., *St. Mark*, 1925.

Robinson, J. M., *The Problem of History in Mark*, 1957.

Robinson, W. C., Jr., "The Theological Context of Luke's Travel Narrative (9:51ff.)," *Journal of Biblical Literature*, Vol. LXXIX, 1960.

Rohde, J., *Rediscovering the Teaching of the Evangelists*, trans. D. Barton, 1968.

Schweitzer, A., *Quest of the Historical Jesus*, trans. W. Montgomery, 1911.

Stendahl, K., *The School of St. Matthew*, 1954.

Strecker, G., "The Concept of History in Matthew," *Journal of the American Academy of Religion*, 1967.

Streeter, B. H., *The Four Gospels*, 1924.

Taylor, V., *Behind the Third Gospel*, 1926.

————, *The Gospel According to Mark*, 1952.

Weiss, J., *History of Primitive Christianity*, trans. and ed. F. C. Grant, 1937; reprinted, *Earliest Christianity*, 1959.

Winter, P., "On Luke and Lucan Sources," *Zeitschrift für die neutestamentliche Wissenschaft und die Kunde der älteren Kirche*, Vol. XLVII, 1956.

————, "The Treatment of His Sources by the Third Evangelist in Luke XXI-XXIX," *Studia Theologica*, Vol. VIII, 1955.

Wrede, W., *The Messianic-Secret in the Gospels*, 1901.

10.   Anderson, H., *Jesus and Christian Origins*, 1964.

Barrett, C. K., "New Testament Eschatology," *Scottish Journal of Theology*, Vol. VI, 1953.

Bornkamm, G., *Jesus of Nazareth*, trans. I. and F. McLuskey, 1960.

Borsch, F. H., *The Son of Man in Myth and History*, 1967.

Braaten, C. E., and Harrisville, R. A., eds., *The Historical Jesus and the Kerygmatic Christ*, 1964.

Brown, R. E., "After Bultmann, What?" *Catholic Biblical Quarterly*, Vol. XXVI, 1964.

Bultmann, R., *Existence and Faith*, trans. S. M. Ogden, 1960.

————, *The History of the Synoptic Tradition*, trans. J. Marsh, 1963.

Caird, C. B., "Chronology of the New Testament," *Interpreter's Dictionary of the Bible*, Vol. I.

Cobb, J. B., Jr., "The Post-Bultmannian Trend," *Journal of Bible and Religion*, Vol. XXX, 1962.

Craig, C. T., "The Proclamation of the Kingdom," *Interpreter's Bible*, Vol. VII.

Cullmann, O., "The Gospel of Thomas and the Problem of the Age of the Tradition Contained Therein," *Interpretation*, Vol. XVI, 1962.

Dodd, C. H., *Gospel and Law*, 1951.
———, *Parables of the Kingdom*, 1936.
Doresse, J., *The Secret Books of the Egyptian Gnostics*, trans. P. Mairet, 1960.
Dunkerley, R., *Beyond the Gospels*, 1957.
Ebeling, G., *The Nature of Faith*, trans. R. G. Smith, 1961.
Fuller, R. H., *The Foundations of New Testament Christology*, 1965.
———, *The New Testament in Current Study*, 1963.
Fuchs, E., *Studies of the Historical Jesus*, trans. A. Scobie, 1964.
Grant, F. C., *The Gospel of the Kingdom*, 1940.
Grant, R. M., "Two Gnostic Gospels," *Journal of Biblical Literature*, Vol. LXXIX, 1960.
Goguel, M., *The Life of Jesus*, trans. O. Wyon, 1933.
Guillaumont, A., Puech, Quispel, et al., trans., *The Gospel of Thomas*, 1959.
Harvey, Van A., "The Historical Jesus, the Kerygma, and Christian Faith," *Religion in Life*, Vol. XXXIII, 1964.
Hastings, J., *Dictionary of the Bible*, Vol. I, 1904.
Hennecke, E. and Schneemelcher, W., *New Testament Apocrypha*, 1963.
Higgins, A. J. B., ed., *New Testament Essays*, 1959.
Hunter, A. M., *The Work and Words of Jesus*, 1950.
James, M. R., trans., *Apocryphal New Testament*, 1924.
Jeremias, J., *The Eucharistic Words of Jesus*, trans. A. Ehrhardt, 1955.
———, *Unknown Sayings of Jesus*, 1957.
Kasemann, E., *Essays on New Testament Themes*, trans. W. J. Montague, 1960.
———, *New Testament Questions of Today*, trans. W. J. Montague, 1969.
Klausner, J., *Jesus of Nazareth*, trans. H. Danby, 1929.
Koester, H., "Gnomai Diaphorai," *Harvard Theological Review*, Vol. LVIII, 1965.
Kümmel, W. G., *Promise and Fulfillment*, trans. D. Barton, 1957.
Schweitzer, A., *Mystery of the Kingdom of God*, trans. W. Lowrie, 1950.
Lundström, G., *Kingdom of God in the Teaching of Jesus*, trans. J. Bulman, 1963.
Manson, T. W., ed., *A Companion to the Bible*, 1946.
McArthur, H. K., "The Dependence of the Gospel of Thomas on the Synoptics," *Expository Times*, Vol. LXXI, 1960.
McCrown, C. C., "Jesus, Son of Man; A Survey of Recent Discussion," *Journal of Religion*, Vol. XXVIII, 1948.
Montefiore, H., "A Comparison of the Parables of the Gospel according to Thomas and of the Synoptic Gospels," *New Testament Studies*, Vol. VII, 1960–61.
Neill, S., *Interpretation of the New Testament*, 1964.
Ogg, G., *Chronology of the Public Ministry of Jesus*, 1940.
Parker, P., "The Meaning of Son of Man," *Journal of Biblical Literature*, Vol. LX, 1941.
Perrin, N., *Kingdom of God in the Teaching of Jesus*, 1963.
Richardson, A., ed., *Theological Word Book*, 1950.
Reicke, B., *The New Testament Era*, trans. D. E. Green, 1968.
Robinson, J. A. T., *Jesus and His Coming*, 1957.
Robinson, J. M., *A New Quest of the Historical Jesus*, 1959.
———, "The Recent Debate on the New Quest," *Journal of Biblical Religion*, Vol. XXX, 1962.
Schweitzer, A., *Out of My Life and Thought*, 1933.
———, *Quest of the Historical Jesus*, trans. W. Montgomery, 1911.
Schweizer, E., "The Son of Man," *Journal of Biblical Literature*, Vol. LXXIX, 1960.
———, "The Son of Man Again," *New Testament Studies*, Vol. X, 1962–63.
Sharman, H. B., *Son of Man and Kingdom of God*, 1943.
Strecker, G., "The Passion and Resurrection Predictions in Mark's Gospel," *Interpretation*, Vol. XXII, 1968.
Taylor, V., *The Life and Ministry of Jesus*, 1955.
Teeple, H. M., "The Origin of the Son of Man Christology," *Journal of Biblical Literature*, Vol. LXXXIV, 1965.
Tödt, H. E., *The Son of Man in the Synoptic Tradition*, trans. D. M. Barton, 1965.
van Unnik, W. C., *Newly Discovered Gnostic Writings*, trans. H. H. Hoskins, 1960.
Wilder, A., *New Testament Faith for Today*, 1955.

11. Betz, O., *What Do We Know About Jesus?*, 1964.

Branscomb, H., *Jesus and the Law of Moses*, 1930.
Bultmann, R., *The History of the Synoptic Tradition*, trans. J. Marsh, 1963.
————, *Jesus and the Word*, trans. L. P. Smith and E. H. Lantero, 1934.
Bundy, W. E., *Jesus and the First Three Gospels*, 1955.
Burrows, M., *More Light on the Dead Sea Scrolls*, 1958.
Cadbury, H. J., *What Manner of Man*, 1947.
Craig, C. T., *The Beginning of Christianity*, 1943.
Danby, H., trans. and ed., *The Mishnah*, 1933.
Daube, D., *The New Testament and Rabbinic Judaism*, 1956.
Davies, W. D., *Torah in the Messianic and/or Age to Come*, Journal of Biblical Literature Monograph Series, 1952.
Dodd, C. H., *Parables of the Kingdom*, 1936.
Enslin, M. S., "Once Again: John the Baptist," *Religion in Life*, Vol. XXVII, 1958.
Ferris, F., *The Story of Jesus*, 1953.
Fuller, R. H., *Interpreting the Miracles*, 1963.
————, *The Mission and Achievement of Jesus*, 1954.
Hunter, A. M., *The Work and Words of Jesus*, 1950.
James, M. R., trans., *Apocryphal New Testament*, 1924.
Jeremias, J., *The Parables of Jesus*, rev. ed., trans. S. H. Hooke, 1962.
Käsemann, E., *Essays on New Testament Themes*, trans. W. J. Montague, 1960.
Kraeling, C. H., *John the Baptist*, 1951.
Kümmel, W. G., *Promise and Fulfillment*, trans. D. Barton, 1957.
Manson, T. W., *Servant-Messiah*, 1953.
————, *The Teaching of Jesus*, 2d. ed., 1935.
Manson, W., *The Gospel of Luke*, 1930.
Moore, G. F., *Judaism in the First Centuries of the Christian Era* (3 vols.), 1927.
Munck, J., *Acts, Anchor Bible*, Vol. XXXI, 1967.
Pannenberg, W., *Jesus—God and Man*, 1968.
Perrin, N., *Kingdom of God in the Teaching of Jesus*, 1963.
————, *Rediscovering the Teaching of Jesus*, 1967.
Rawlinson, A. E. J., *St. Mark*, 1925.
Richardson, A., *The Miracle-Stories of the Gospels*, 1941.
Robinson, J. A. T., "Elijah, John, and Jesus . . ." *New Testament Studies*, Vol. IV, 1958.
Schubert, K., *The Dead Sea Community*, trans. J. W. Doberstein, 1959.
Stendahl, K., ed., *The Scrolls and the New Testament*, 1957.
Taylor, V., *The Gospel According to Mark*, 1952.
Turner, H. E. W., *Jesus, Master and Lord*, 1954.
Wilder, A., "The Sermon on the Mount," *Interpreter's Bible*, Vol. VII.
————, *Eschatology and Ethics in the Teaching of Jesus*, rev. ed., 1950.
Windisch, H., *The Sermon on the Mount*, trans. S. McL. Gilmour, 1951.
Winter, P., *On the Trial of Jesus*, 1961.

12. Barrett, C. K., *Jesus and the Gospel Tradition*, 1967.
Bornkamm, G., *Jesus of Nazareth*, trans. I and F. McLuskey, 1960.
Bultmann, R., *The History of the Synoptic Tradition*, trans. J. Marsh, 1963.
————, *Jesus and the Word*, trans. L. P. Smith and E. H. Lantero, 1934.
————, *Theology of the New Testament*, trans. K. Grobel (2 vols.), 1951.
Bundy, W. E., *Jesus and the First Three Gospels*, 1955.
Cadoux, C. J., *The Historic Mission of Jesus*, 1941.
Craig, C. T., "The Identification of Jesus with the Suffering Servant," *Journal of Religion*, Vol. XXIV, 1944.
Cullmann, *The Christology of the New Testament*, trans. S. C. Guthrie and C. A. M. Hall, 1959.
Filson, F. V., *A New Testament History*, 1964.
Fuller, R. H., *The Foundations of New Testament Christology*, 1965.
————, *The Mission and Achievement of Jesus*, 1954.
————, "The Virgin Birth: Historical Fact or Kerygmatic Truth?," *Biblical Research*, Vol. I, 1965.
Gardner-Smith, P., *The Christ of the Gospels*, 1938.
Goguel, M., *The Life of Jesus*, trans. O. Wyon, 1933.

Higgins, A. J. B., ed., *New Testament Essays*, 1959.
Hooker, M. D., *Jesus and the Servant*, 1959.
———, *The Son of Man in Mark*, 1967.
Jeremias, J., *The Eucharistic Words of Jesus*, trans. A. Ehrhardt, 1955.
———, *Jesus' Promise to the Nations*, 1958.
———, *The Prayers of Jesus*, 1967.
Johnson, S., *Jesus in His Homeland*, 1957.
Käsemann, E., *Essays on New Testament Themes*, trans. W. J. Montague, 1960.
Knox, W. L., *Some Hellenistic Elements in Primitive Christianity*, 1944.
Kümmel, W. G., *Promise and Fulfillment*, trans. W. Barton, 1957.
Lampe, G. W. H. and MacKinnon, D. M., *The Resurrection*, 1966.
Machen, J. G., *The Virgin Birth of Christ*, 1932.
Manson, T. W., ed., *A Companion to the Bible*, 1946.
———, *Servant-Messiah*, 1953.
———, *The Teaching of Jesus*, 2d. ed., 1935.
Manson, W., *Jesus the Messiah*, 1946.
Marshall, I. H., "The Synoptic Son of Man Sayings in Recent Discussion," *New Testament Studies*, Vol. XXII, 1966.
Marxsen, W., et al., *The Significance of the Message of the Resurrection for Faith in Jesus Christ*, ed. C. F. D. Moule, 1968.
Minear, P., "The Interpreter and the Nativity Stories," *Theology Today*, Vol. VII, 1950.
Nineham, D. H., ed., *Studies in the Gospels*, 1955.
Otto, R., *The Kingdom of God and the Son of Man*, 1938.
Oxford Studies in the Synoptic Problem, 1911.
Price, J. L., "The Servant Motif in the Synoptic Gospels," *Interpretation*, Vol. XII, 1958.
Rawlinson, A. E. J., *St. Mark*, 1925.
Richardson, A., ed., *Theological Word Book*, 1950.
Schweizer, E., *Lordship and Discipleship*, 1960.
———, "The Son of Man," *Journal of Biblical Literature*, Vol. LXXIX, 1960.
———, "The Son of Man Again," *New Testament Studies*, Vol. X, 1962.
Strecker, G., "The Passion and Resurrection Predictions in Mark's Gospel," *Interpretation*, Vol. XX 1968.
Taylor, V., *The Gospel According to Mark*, 1952.
Tödt, H. E., *The Son of Man in the Synoptic Tradition*, trans. D. M. Barton, 1965.
Simpson, D. C., ed., *Old Testament Essays*, 1927.
Winter, P., *On the Trial of Jesus*, 1961.
Zimmerli, W. and Jeremias, J., *The Servant of God*, trans. H. Knight and others, 1957.

13. Barrett, C. K., ed., *The New Testament Background: Selected Documents*, 1957.
Beare, F. W., "Greek Religion and Philosophy," *Interpreter's Dictionary of the Bible*, Vol. II, 1962.
Bevan, E., *Later Greek Religion*, 1950.
Bultmann, R., *Primitive Christianity*, trans. R. H. Fuller, 1956.
Cullmann, O., *The Early Church*, trans. S. Godmann, 1956.
Cumont, F. V. M., *The Oriental Religions in Roman Paganism*, 1911.
Davies, W. D., *Paul and Rabbinic Judaism*, 1948.
———, and Daube, D., eds., *The Background of the New Testament and Its Eschatology*, 1956.
Dodd, C. H., *The Interpretation of the Fourth Gospel*, 1953.
Doresse, J., *The Secret Books of the Egyptian Gnostics*, trans. P. Mairet, 1960.
Festugiere, A. J., *Personal Religion among the Greeks*, 1954.
Grant, F. C., *Ancient Roman Religion*, 1957.
Grant, R. M., *Gnosticism and Early Christianity*, 1959.
———, "Gnosticism," *Interpreter's Dictionary of the Bible*, Vol. II, 1962.
Grant, F. C., *Hellenistic Religion*, 1953.
Jonas, H., *Gnostic Religion*, 1958.
Klassen, W., and Snyder, G. F., eds., *Current Issues in New Testament Interpretation*, 1962.
Lietzmann, H., *The Beginnings of the Christian Church*, trans., B. L. Woolf, 1937.
Morrison, C. D., *The Powers That Be*, 1960.
Nilsson, M. P., *Greek Piety*, 1948.

Nock, A. D., *Conversion*, 1933.

Pfeiffer, R. H., *History of New Testament Times*, 1949.

Riddle, D. W. and Hutson, H. H., *New Testament Life and Literature*, 1946.

Rose, H. J., *Religion in Greece and Rome*, 1959.

Schoeps, H. J., *Paul: The Theology of the Apostle in the Light of Jewish Religious History*, trans. H. Knight, 1961.

Tarn, W. W., and Griffith, G. T., *Hellenistic Civilization*, 3rd ed., 1952.

van Unnik, W. C., *Newly Discovered Gnostic Writings*, trans. H. H. Hoskins, 1960.

Wilson, R. McL., *Gnosis and the New Testament*, 1968.

14. Bruce, F. F., *Commentary on the Book of Acts*, 1956.

———, "St. Paul in Rome," *Bulletin of the John Rylands Library* 46 (1964).

Cadbury, H. J., *The Book of Acts in History*, 1955.

Caird, C. B., "Chronology of the N.T.," *Interpreter's Dictionary of the Bible*, Vol. I, 1962.

Craig, C. T., *The Beginning of Christianity*, 1943.

Dibelius, M., *Studies in the Acts of the Apostles*, trans. M. Ling, 1956.

———, and Kümmel, W. G., *Paul*, trans. F. Clark, 1953.

Dodd, C. H., *The Meaning of Paul for Today*, 1920.

Flender, H., *St. Luke, Theologian of Redemptive History*, trans. R. H. and I. Fuller, 1967.

Foakes-Jackson, F. J., and Lake, K., *Beginnings of Christianity* (5 vols.), 1932.

Gärtner, B., *The Areopagus Speech and Natural Revelation*, 1955.

Haenchen, E., "'We' in Acts and the Itinerary," *Journal for Theology and the Church*, ed. R. W. Funk, Vol. I, 1965.

Higgins, A. J. B., ed., *New Testament Essays*, 1959.

Hurd, J. C., Jr., *The Origin of 1 Corinthians*, 1965.

Keck, L. E., and Martyn, J. L., eds., *Studies in Luke-Acts*, 1966.

Kee, H. C., and Young, F. W., *Understanding the New Testament*, 1957.

Knox, W. L., *The Acts of the Apostles*, 1948.

Macgregor, G. H. C., "Acts," *Interpreter's Bible*, Vol. IX.

Munck, J., *Paul and the Salvation of Mankind*, trans. F. Clarke, 1959.

Ogg, G., *The Chronology of the Life of Paul*, 1968.

Parker, P., "Once More, Acts and Galatians," *Journal of Biblical Literature*, Vol. LXXXVI, 1967.

Weiss, J., *History of Primitive Christianity*, trans. and ed., F. C. Grant, 1937; reprinted, *Earliest Christianity*, 1959.

Williams, C. S. C., *The Acts of the Apostles*, 1957.

Wood, H. G., "The Conversion of St. Paul," *New Testament Studies*, Vol. I, 1955.

15. Barclay, W., *Letters to the Corinthians*, 1957.

Barrett, C. K., "Christianity at Corinth," *Bulletin of the John Rylands Library* 46 (1964).

———, *The First Epistle to the Corinthians*, 1968.

———, ed., *The New Testament Background: Selected Documents*, 1957.

Beare, F. W., *St. Paul and His Letters*, 1962.

Boers, H. W., "Apocalyptic Eschatology in 1 Corinthians 15," *Interpretation*, Vol. XXI, 1967.

Bradley, D. G., "The Typos as a Form in the Pauline Paraenesis," *Journal of Biblical Literature*, Vol. LXXII, 1953.

Bristol, L. O., "Paul's Thessalonian Correspondence," *Expository Times*, Vol. LV, 1944.

Burkitt, F. C., *Christian Beginnings*, 1924.

Caird, C. B., "Chronology of the N.T.," *Interpreter's Dictionary of the Bible*, Vol. I, 1962.

———, "Everything to Everyone," *Interpretation*, Vol. XIII, 1959.

Chadwick, H., "All Things to All Men," *New Testament Studies*, Vol. I, 1955.

Cross, F. M., Jr., *The Ancient Library of Qumran and Modern Biblical Studies*, rev. ed., 1961.

Cullmann, O., *Christ and Time*, trans. F. V. Filson, 1950.

Deissmann, A., *St. Paul*, trans. L. R. M. Strachan, 1912.

Dibelius, M. and Kümmel, W. G., *Paul*, trans. F. Clark, 1953.

Dodd, C. H., *Gospel and Law*, 1951.

Frame, J. E., *Epistles of Paul to the Thessalonians*, 1924.

Grant, R. M., *Gnosticism and Early Christianity*, 1959.

Heard, R. G., *An Introduction to the New Testament*, 1950.
Hering, J., *The Second Epistle of Saint Paul to the Corinthians*, trans. Heathcote and Allcock, 1967.
Hurd, J. C., Jr., *The Origin of 1 Corinthians*, 1965.
Hyatt, J. P., ed., *The Bible in Modern Scholarship*, 1965.
Knox, J., *Chapters in a Life of Paul*, 1950.
Lake, K., *The Earlier Epistles of St. Paul*, 1919.
Lietzmann, H., *The Beginnings of the Christian Church*, trans. B. L. Woolf, 1937.
Manson, T. W., ed., *A Companion to the Bible*, 1946.
McNeile, A. H., *An Introduction to the Study of the New Testament*, rev. ed., ed. C. S. C. Williams, 1953.
Moffatt, J., *The First Epistle of Paul to the Corinthians*, 1938.
Morrison, C. D., *The Powers That Be*, 1960.
Munck, J., *Paul and the Salvation of Mankind*, trans. F. Clarke, 1959.
Murphy-O'Connor, J., ed., *Paul and Qumran*, 1968.
Ogg, G., *The Chronology of the Life of Paul*, 1968.
Price, J. L., "Aspects of Paul's Theology and Their Bearing on Literary Problems of Second Corinthians," in J. Geerling, ed., *Studies and Documents*, Vol. XXXIX, 1967.
Schoeps, H. J., *Paul: The Theology of the Apostle in the Light of Jewish Religious History*, trans. H. Knight, 1961.
Strachan, R. H., *2 Corinthians*, 1953.
Tasker, R. V. G., *The Second Epistle of Paul to the Corinthians*, 1958.
Wilson, R. McL., *Gnosis and the New Testament*, 1968.
Windisch, H., "Paul and the Corinthian Church," *Journal of Biblical Literature*, Vol. LXVIII, 1949.

16. Achtemeier, E. R., "Righteousness in the O.T.," *Interpreter's Dictionary of the Bible*, Vol. IV, 1962.
Barnett, A. E., *The New Testament: It's Making and Meaning*, 1946.
Barrett, C. K., *A Commentary on the Epistle to the Romans*, 1957.
————, "Paul and the 'Pillar' Apostles," in *Studia Paulina* (honoring J. De Zwann), 1953.
Barth, K., *A Shorter Commentary on Romans*, trans. D. H. van Daalen, 1959.
Barth, M., "The Kerygma of Galatians," *Interpretation*, Vol. XXI, 1967.
Best, E., *One Body in Christ*, 1955.
Bornkamm, G., "The Letter to the Romans as Paul's Last Will and Testament," *Australian Biblical Review*, Vol. XI, 1963.
Brunner, E., *The Letter to the Romans*, 1959.
Buck, C. H., Jr., "The Collection for the Saints," *Harvard Theological Review*, Vol. XLII, 1950.
————, "Dikaiosune Theou," *Journal of Biblical Literature*, Vol. LXXXII, 1964.
Burton, E. D., *Epistle to the Galatians*, 1921.
Caird, C. B., "Chronology of the N. T.," *Interpreter's Dictionary of the Bible*, Vol. I, 1962.
Crownfield, F. R., "The Singular Problem of the Dual Galatians," *Journal of Biblical Literature*, Vol. LXIV, 1945.
Daube, D., "The Interpretation of a Generic Singular in Galatians 3:16," *Jewish Quarterly Review*, Vol. XXXV, 1944.
Davies, W. D., *Paul and Rabbinic Judaism*, 1948.
Dodd, C. H., *The Epistle of Paul to the Romans*, 1932.
————, *New Testament Studies*, 1953.
Duncan, G. S., *Epistle of Paul to the Galatians*, 1934.
Goguel, M., *The Birth of Christianity*, trans. H. C. Snape, 1953.
Higgins, A. J. B., ed., *New Testament Essays*, 1959.
Johnson, S., "Paul and the Manual of Discipline," *Journal of Biblical Literature*, Vol. XLVIII, 1955.
Käsemann, E., *New Testament Questions of Today*, trans. W. J. Montague, 1960.
Knox, J., *Chapters in a Life of Paul*, 1950.
Knox, W. L., *St. Paul and the Church at Jerusalem*, 1925.
Lake, K., *The Earlier Epistles of St. Paul*, 1919.
Leenhardt, F. J., *The Epistle to the Romans*, trans. H. Knight, 1960.
Lightfoot, J. B., *Saint Paul's Epistle to the Galatians*, 1905.
Morrison, C. D., *The Powers That Be*, 1960.
Nock, A. D., *St. Paul*, 1938.
Nygren, A., *Commentary on Romans*, trans. C. C. Rasmussen, 1949.
Ogg, G., *The Chronology of the Life of Paul*, 1968.

Ramsay, W. M., *A Historical Commentary on St. Paul's Epistle to the Galatians*, 1900.
———, *St. Paul the Traveller and Roman Citizen*, 1896.
Reumann, J., "The Gospel of the Righteousness of God," *Interpretation*, Vol. XX, 1966.
Richardson, A., "Salvation," *Interpreter's Dictionary of the Bible*, Vol. IV, 1962.
Ridderbos, H. N., *The Epistle of Paul to the Churches of Galatia*, 1953.
Ropes, J. H., *The Singular Problem of the Epistle to the Galatians*, 1929.
Russell, D. S., *The Method and Message of Jewish Apocalyptic*, 1964.
Sanders, J. T., "Pauls' Autobiographical Statements in Galatians 1–2," *Journal of Biblical Literature*, Vol. LXXXV, 1966.
Scott, C. A. A., *Christianity According to St. Paul*, 1927.
Smith, M., "Pauline Problems," *Harvard Theological Review*, 1957.
Snaith, N. H., *The Distinctive Ideas of the Old Testament*, 1944.
Taylor, G. M., "The Function of 'Pistis Christou' in Galatians," *Journal of Biblical Literature*, Vol. LXXXV, 1966.
Wikenhauser, *New Testament Introduction*, trans. J. Cunningham, 1963.

17. Beare, F. W., *A Commentary on the Epistle to the Philippians*, 1959.
Bruce, F. F., *Epistle to the Colossians*, 1957.
———, "St. Paul at Rome," *Bulletin of the John Rylands Library* 48 (1966).
Dibelius, M., and Kümmel, W. G., *Paul*, trans. F. Clark, 1953.
Dodd, C. H., *New Testament Studies*, 1953.
Duncan, G. S., *St. Paul's Ephesian Ministry*, 1929.
Goodspeed, E. J., *An Introduction to the New Testament*, 1937.
———, *New Solutions to New Testament Problems*, 1927.
Harrison, P. N., "The Pastoral Epistles and Duncan's Ephesian Theory," *New Testament Studies*, Vol. II, 1956.
Hunter, A. M., *Interpreting the New Testament 1900–1950*, 1951.
Käsemann, E., "A Critical Analysis of Philippians 2:5–11," *Journal for Theology and Church*, Vol. V, 1968.
———, *Essays on New Testament Themes*, trans. W. J. Montague, 1960.
Knox, J., *Philemon among the Letters of Paul*, 1935.
Lightfoot, J. B., *Colossians and Philemon*, 1875.
Lohse, E., "Pauline Theology in the Letter to the Colossians," *New Testament Studies*, Vol. XV, 1969.
Martin, R. P., *Carmen Christi*, 1967.
Michael, J. H., *The Epistle of Paul to the Philippians*, 1927.
Mitton, C. L., *The Epistle to the Ephesians*, 1951.
Moule, C. F. D., *The Epistles of Paul the Apostle to the Colossians and to Philemon*, 1957.
Preiss, T., *Life in Christ*, trans. H. Knight, 1952.
Robinson, J. M., "A Formal Analysis of Colossians 1:15–20," *Journal of Biblical Literature*, Vol. LXXVI, 1956.
Sanders, A., "Dissenting Deities and Philippians 2:1–11," *Journal of Biblical Literature*, Vol. LXXXVIII, 1969.
Sanders, E. P., "Literary Dependence in Colossians," *Journal of Biblical Literature*, Vol. LXXXV, 1966.
Synge F. C., *Philippians and Colossians*, 1951.
Talbert, C. H., "The Problem of Pre-existence in Philippians 2:6–11," *Journal of Biblical Literature*, Vol. LXXXVI, 1967.
van Unnik, *Newly Discovered Gnostic Writings*, trans. H. H. Hoskins, 1960.

18. Brandon, S. G. F., *The Fall of Jerusalem and the Christian Church*, 1951.
Carrington, P., *Early Christian Church*, Vol. I, 1957.
Cullmann, O., *The Christology of the New Testament*, 1959.
Danielou, J., *The Dead Sea Scrolls and Primitive Christianity*, trans. S. Attanasio, 1958.
Dix, G., *Jew and Greek: A Study in the Primitive Church*, 1953.
Elliott-Binns, L. E., *Galilean Christianity*, 1956.
Grant, R. M., *A Historical Introduction to the New Testament*, 1963.
Gwatkin, H. M., *Early Church History to A. D. 313*, Vol. I, 1909.
Kee, H. C. and Young, F. W., *Understanding the New Testament*, 1957.
Klassen, W., and Snyder, G. F., eds., *Current Issues in New Testament Interpretation*, 1962.

Lake, K., *Apostolic Fathers* (2 vols.), 1913.

Merrill, E. T., *Essays in Early Christian History*, 1924.

Munck, J., "Jewish-Christianity in Post-Apostolic Times," *New Testament Studies*, Vol. VI, 1960.

Reicke, B., *The New Testament Era*, trans. D. E. Green, 1968.

Richardson, C., *Early Christian Fathers*, 1953.

Shepherd, M. H., Jr., "The Post-Apostolic Age," *Interpreter's Bible*, Vol. VII.

Smith, M., "The Report About Peter in 1 Clement v. 4," *New Testament Studies*, Vol. VII, 1960.

Stauffer, E., *Christ and Caesar*, trans. K. and R. Smith, 1955.

Stevenson, J., *A New Eusebius*, 1957.

Weiss, J., *History of Primitive Christianity*, trans and ed., F. C. Grant, 1937; reprinted, *Earliest Christianity*, 1959.

Willoughby, H. R., ed., *The Study of the Bible Today and Tomorrow*, 1947.

19.   Barrett, C. K., *The Pastoral Epistles*, 1963.

Cross, F. L., ed., *Studies in Ephesians*, 1956.

Duncan, G. S., *St. Paul's Ephesian Ministry*, 1929.

Easton, B. S., *The Pastoral Epistles*, 1947.

Goodspeed, E., *Christianity Goes to Press*, 1940.

Goodspeed, E. J., *An Introduction to the New Testament*, 1937.

———, *The Key to Ephesians*, 1956.

———, *The Meaning of Ephesians*, 1933.

Grayston, K., and Herdan, G., "The Authorship of the Pastorals in the Light of Statistical Linguistics," *New Testament Studies*, Vol. VI, 1959.

Guthrie, D., *The Pastoral Epistles*, 1957.

Harrison, P. N., "The Pastoral Epistles and Duncan's Ephesian Theory," *New Testament Studies*, Vol. VII, 1956.

———, *The Problem of the Pastoral Epistles*, 1921.

Hennecke, E. and Schneemelcher, W., *New Testament Apocrypha*, Vol. II, 1963.

Hort, F. J. A., *Prolegommena to St. Paul's Epistles to the Romans and Ephesians*, 1895.

Johnston, G., "Ephesians," *Interpreter's Dictionary of the Bible*, Vol. II, 1962.

Kelly, J. N. D., *The Pastoral Epistles*, 1963.

Knox, J., *Marcion and the New Testament*, 1942.

Moule, C. F. D., "The Problem of the Pastoral Epistles," *Bulletin of the John Rylands Library*, 47 (1965).

Murphy-O'Connor, J., ed., *Paul and Qumran*, 1968.

Robinson, J. A., *St. Paul's Epistle to the Ephesians*, 1909.

Schweizer, E., *Lordship and Discipleship*, 1960.

Scott, C. A. A., *Christianity According to St. Paul*, 1927.

Scott, E. F., *The Pastoral Epistles*, 1937.

Wikenhauser, *New Testament Introduction*, trans. J. Cunningham, 1963.

Wilson, R. McL., *Gnosis and the New Testament*, 1968.

20.   Beare, F. W., *The First Epistle of Peter*, 2d rev., 1958.

Beker, J. C., "Second Letter of Peter," *Interpreter's Dictionary of the Bible*, Vol. III, 1962.

———, "Letter of Jude," *Interpreter's Dictionary of the Bible*, Vol. II, 1962.

Bristol, L. O., "Primitive Christian Preaching and the Epistle to the Hebrews," *Journal of Biblical Literature*, Vol. LXVIII, 1949.

Bruce, A. B., *The Epistle to the Hebrews*, 1899.

Bruce, F. F., *The Epistle to the Hebrews*, 1964.

———, "Recent Contributions to the Understanding of Hebrews," *Expository Times*, Vol. LXXX, 1965.

Cranfield, C. E. B., "The Message of James," *Scottish Journal of Theology*, Vol. XVIII, 1965.

Danielou, J., *The Dead Sea Scrolls and Primitive Christianity*, trans. S. Attanasio, 1958.

Davies, W. D., and Daube, D., eds., *The Background of the New Testament and Its Eschatology*, 1956.

Dibelius, M., *A Fresh Approach to the New Testament and Early Christian Literature*, 1936.

Elliott-Binns, L. E., *Galilean Christianity*, 1956.

Enslin, M. S., *Christian Beginnings*, 1938.

Filson, F. V., "The Epistle to the Hebrews," *Journal of Bible and Religion*, Vol. XXII, 1954.

————, *Yesterday: A Study of Hebrews in the Light of Chapter 13*, 1967.

Fuller, R. H. and Wright, G. E., *The Book of the Acts of God*, 1957.

Goodspeed, E. J., *An Introduction to the New Testament*, 1937.

Gaster, T. H., *The Dead Sea Scriptures in English Translation*, 1956.

Heard, R. G., *An Introduction to the New Testament*, 1950.

Hunter, A. M., *Interpreting the New Testament 1900–1950*, 1951.

James, M. R., trans., *Apocryphal New Testament*, 1924.

Käsemann, E., *Essays on New Testament Themes*, trans. W. J. Montague, 1960.

Lake, K., *An Introduction to the New Testament*, 1937.

Manley, G. T., "Babylon on the Nile," *Evangelical Quarterly*, Vol. XVI, 1944.

Manson, T. W., ed., *A Companion to the Bible*, 1946.

————, "The Problem of the Epistle to the Hebrews," *Bulletin of the John Rylands Library*, 32 (1949).

Manson, W., *The Epistle to the Hebrews*, 1951.

Mitton, C. L., "The Relationship Between 1 Peter and Ephesians," *Journal of Theological Studies*, Vol. I, n. s. (1950).

Moffatt, J., *The Epistle to the Hebrews*, 1924.

————, *The General Epistles*, 1928.

Moule, C. F. D., "The Nature and Purpose of 1 Peter," *New Testament Studies*, Vol. III, 1956.

Nairne, A., *The Epistle of Priesthood*, 1917.

Reicke, B., *Epistles of James, Peter and Jude*, 1964.

Sanday, W., and Headlam, A. C., *The Epistle to the Romans*, 5th ed., 1902.

Schubert, K., *The Dead Sea Community*, trans. J. W. Doberstein, 1959.

Scott, E. F., *The Epistle to the Hebrews*, 1922.

————, *The Literature of the New Testament*, 1932.

Selwyn, E. G., *The First Epistle of St. Peter*, 2d. ed., 1947.

Streeter, B. H., *The Primitive Church*, 1930.

Swetnam, J., "On the Literary Genre of the 'Epistle' to the Hebrews," *Novum Testamentum* XI (1969).

Talbert, C. H., "II Peter and the Delay of the Parousia," *Vigiliae Christianae*, Vol. XX, 1966.

Tasker, R. V. G., *The General Epistle of James*, 1956.

————, *The Gospel in the Epistle to the Hebrews*, 1950.

van Unnik, W. C., "First Letter of Peter," *Interpreter's Dictionary of the Bible*, Vol. III, 1962.

————, "The Teaching of Good Works in 1 Peter," *New Testament Studies* Vol. I, 1955.

Wand, J. W. C., *The General Epistles of St. Peter and St. Jude*, 1934.

Westcott, B. F., *The Epistle to the Hebrews*, 3d. ed., 1906.

21. Barclay, W., *Letters to the Seven Churches*, 1957.

Barrett, *The Gospel According to St. John*, 1955.

Bernard, J. H., *The Gospel of John*, 1928.

Bowman, J. W., "Book of Revelation," *Interpreter's Dictionary of the Bible*, Vol. IV, 1962.

Caird, C. B., "Letters of John," *Interpreter's Dictionary of the Bible*, Vol. II, 1962.

————, *The Revelation of St. John the Divine*, 1966.

Charles, R. H., *The Revelation of St. John* (2 vols.), 1920.

Dodd, C. H., *The Johannine Epistles*, 1946.

Farrar, A. M., *A Rebirth of Images*, 1949.

Fuller, R. H., and Wright, G. E., *The Book of the Acts of God*, 1957.

Heard, R. G., *An Introduction to the New Testament*, 1950.

Kallas, J., "The Apocalypse—An Apocalyptic Book?" *Journal of Biblical Literature*, Vol. LXXXVI, 1967.

Kiddle, M., *The Revelation of St. John*, 1940.

Klassen, W., "Vengeance in the Apocalypse of John," *Catholic Biblical Quarterly*, Vol. XXVIII, 1966.

Lake, K., *An Introduction to the New Testament*, 1937.

Mowry, L., "Revelation 4–5 and Early Liturgical Usage," *Journal of Biblical Literature*, Vol. LXXI, 1952.

Preston, R. H., and Hanson, A. T., *The Revelation of St. John the Divine*, 1949.

Scott, E. F., *The Book of Revelation*, 1941.

Wilson, R. McL., *Gnosis and the New Testament*, 1968.

22. Bacon, B. W., *The Gospel of the Hellenists*, 1933.

Barrett, C. K., *The Gospel According to St. John*, 1955.

Beare, F. W., "The Risen Jesus Bestows the Spirit," *Canadian Journal of Theology*, Vol. IV, 1958.

Black, M., *An Aramaic Approach to the Gospels and Acts*, 2d. ed., 1954.

Burrows, M., *The Dead Sea Scrolls,* 1955.

Brooke, A. E., *The Johannine Epistles,* 1948.

Brown, R. E., *The Gospel According to John, Anchor Bible* Vol. XXIX, 1966; and Vol. XXIXA, 1970.

————, "The Paraclete in the Fourth Gospel," *New Testament Studies,* Vol. XIII, 1967.

Caird, C. B., "John, Letters of," *Interpreter's Dictionary of the Bible,* Vol. II, 1962.

Colwell, E. C., *John Defends the Gospel,* 1936.

————, and Titus, E., *The Gospel of the Spirit,* 1953.

Cross, F. M., Jr., *The Ancient Library of Qumran and Modern Biblical Studies,* rev. ed., 1961.

Cullmann, O., "A New Approach to the Interpretation of the Fourth Gospel," *Expository Times,* Vol. LXXI, 1959.

Davies, W. D., *Invitation to the New Testament,* 1966.

————, and Daube, D., *The Background of the New Testament and Its Eschatology,* 1956.

Dodd, C. H., "The First Epistle of John and the Fourth Gospel," *Bulletin of the John Rylands Library* 21 (1937).

————, *The Interpretation of the Fourth Gospel,* 1953.

————, *Historical Tradition in the Fourth Gospel,* 1963.

Fortna, R., *The Gospel of Signs: A Reconstruction of the Narrative Source Underlying the Fourth Gospel,* 1969.

Gardner-Smith, P. N., *St. John and the Synoptics,* 1938.

Goodwin, C., "How Did John Treat His Sources?" *Journal of Biblical Literature,* Vol. LXXIII, 1954.

Grant, R. M., *Gnosticism and Early Christianity,* 1959.

Hahn, F., *Mission in the New Testament,* trans. F. Clarke, 1965.

Howard, W. F., *Christianity According to St. John,* 1946.

————, "The Common Authorship of the Johannine Gospel and Epistles," *Journal of Theological Studies,* Vol. LVIII, 1947.

————, *The Fourth Gospel in Recent Criticism and Interpretation,* rev. C. K. Barrett, 4th ed., 1955.

Hunter, A. M., *Interpreting the New Testament 1900–1950,* 1951.

————, "Recent Trends in Johannine Studies," *Expository Times,* Vol. LXXI, 1960.

Käsemann, E., *The Testament of Jesus,* trans. G. Krodel, 1968.

Klassen, W., and Snyder, G. F., eds., *Current Issues in New Testament Interpretation,* 1962.

Manson, T. W., "The Gospel of John," *Bulletin of the John Rylands Library,* 30 (1947).

Martyn, J. L., *History and Theology in the Fourth Gospel,* 1968.

Neill, S., *The Interpretation of the New Testament 1861–1961,* 1964.

The New Testament in the Apostolic Fathers, Oxford Society of Historical Theology, 1905.

Price, J. L., "The Search for the Theology of the Fourth Evangelist," *Journal of the American Academy of Religion,* Vol. XXXV, 1967.

Robinson, J. A. T., "The Destination and Purpose of St. John's Gospel," *New Testament Studies,* Vol. VI, 1960.

————, *Twelve New Testament Studies,* 1962.

Sanders, J. N., *The Fourth Gospel in the Early Church,* 1943.

Schnackenburg, R., *The Gospel According to St. John,* trans. K. Smyth, 1968.

Schweitzer, A., *The Mysticism of Paul the Apostle,* trans. W. Montgomery, 1931.

Schweizer, E., "Orthodox Proclamation," *Interpretation,* Vol. VIII, 1954.

Smith, D. M., Jr., *The Composition and Order of the Fourth Gospel,* 1966.

Stendahl, K., ed., *The Scrolls and the New Testament,* 1957.

Strachan, R. H., *The Fourth Gospel,* 3rd. ed., 1941.

Teeple, H., "Qumran and the Origin of the Fourth Gospel," *Novum Testamentum* IV, 1960.

Titus, E., *The Message of the Fourth Gospel,* 1957.

Westcott, B. F., *The Gospel According to John,* 1903.

INDEX

Abba, 316f
Abraham, 226, 423ff., 438
Achaia, 392
Acra, the, 39f
Acts of the Apostles, 20f., 24, 95–111, 116–136,
    140–156, 225f., 354–379, 422, 488, 522
Adam, 226
Adam-Christ typology, 439
Additions to Esther, 51
Aelia Capitolina, 47
Against Apion, 55
Against Flaccus, 56
Agape, 490
Age to Come, 147, 274, 279, 296, 304, 315, 564
Agrapha, 244f
Albinus, procurator, 46
Alexander Janneus, 40ff., 53, 69
Alexander the Great, 31, 34f., 330f
Alexandria, 35, 36, 50, 55, 137, 153,
    195, 337, 348, 350, 554, 588
Alogi, 575
'amme ha-ares, 77, 149, 156, 284f., 297
Ananias, 359
Ananias, the high priest, 376
Ancyra, 418
Angels, 70, 72, 542
Annas, 480
Anthony, 451
Antichrist, 567
Anti-Marcionite Prologue, 100, 215
Antigonus, 35
Antigonid dynasty, 35
Antioch in Syria, 35, 137, 152–154, 177, 195,
    211, 225, 332, 352, 355, 423, 482, 489, 588
Antiochus III, 37
Antiochus IV ("Epiphanes"), 31, 37, 39, 82
Antipater, 41ff
Antiquities of the Jews, 55, 241
Antitheses of *Matthew,* 286–289
Apatheia, 342
Aphrodite, 400
Apocalyptic-type sayings, 168, 181f., 228f
Apocalyptic writings, 56f., 75, 81–89,
    119f., 126, 142, 181f., 553ff., 557
Apocrypha, 50f., 70
Apocryphal gospels, 168, 244ff
Apollo, 59, 331, 333
Apollos, 144f., 372, 399
Apostacy, 485, 510
Apostles, 119, 140–144, 277, 399, 487f., 503, 545
Apostolicity, 488f
Appian Way, 353
Apuleius, 338

Aquila, 372
Arabia, 359f
Aramaic, 49, 103f., 117, 126, 127, 149, 187,
    209f., 264, 293, 316, 577
Archelaus, 44
Areatas, King, 360
Aristarchus, 461
Aristobulus II, 41
Armageddon, 564
Artemis, 329, 331, 372
Asia, Roman province of, 464
Asklepius, 344
Assumption of Moses, 51, 86
Astrology, 340
Athens, 337, 369f., 388
Atonement, 409f
Attis, 336f
Augustus, 137, 139, 333, 340, 415

Babylon, 35, 49, 524, 563f
Babylonian Exile, 67, 79
Babylonian Talmud, 49
Bacchus—*see* Dionysus
Baptism, 118, 131ff., 144–146, 163, 226, 257,
    272f., 350, 372, 440, 491, 513, 522, 525f., 593
Barnabas, 154, 355, 359f., 362, 366, 419, 423
Bar nasha, 125, 264, 303f
Barth, Karl, 12, 235f
1 Baruch, 50, 81
2 Baruch, 51, 87f, 433
3 Baruch, 51
Basilides, Gospel of, 246
Beelzebub controversy, 181
Bel and the Dragon, 51
Bernice, 378
Beroea, 369
Bethlehem, 301
Biblicism, 6
Bishops, 487–490, 503, 507
Bithynia, 479, 490
Body of Christ, 212, 403f., 408, 468f., 502
Body-Soul Dualism—*see* Dualism.
Book of Adam and Eve, 51
Book of Daily Prayers, 50
Bornkamm, Günther, 237f
Bousset, Wilhelm, 56f
Bread, 146–148, 162f., 403
Brutus, 451
Bultmann, Rudolf, 12ff., 166, 236ff, 265, 581–584

Cadbury, H. J., 20
Caesar Augustus, 43f, 451
Caesarea, 92, 93, 221f., 351, 376, 450, 453

Caesarea Philippi, 302
Cairo-Damascus Document—see Fragments of a Zadokite Work
CD—see Fragments of a Zadokite Work
Calendar—see Jewish Calendar
Caligula—see Gaius
Calvin, John, 527
Cana, 529
Canon, NT, 3f
Capernaum, 61, 231
Cappadocia, 418
Cassius, 451
Castor, 333
Catholic Epistles, 25, 520–547, 565–570
Cenchreae, 371, 427f
Cerinthus, 484, 575
Charles, R. H., 50f
Chenoboskion Manuscripts, 246; see Nag Hammadi
Chislev, 65
Chrism, 569
Christ, 115, 117, 119f., 124, 153, 198f., 211ff., 236f.; see Messiah, Christology
Christ Party at Corinth, 396, 399
Christians, first use of the name, 153
Christology, 123–131, 211ff., 238, 242, 457f., 467ff., 483f., 497f., 501f., 567
Chronology of New Testament Era, 21ff., 164, 195, 210f., 246–251, 310, 314, 384f., 392, 418–421, 427–430, 453ff., 508
Chrysippus, 341
Church, 50, 107ff., 123f., 131f., 135f., 140–156, 160f., 169ff., 181, 206, 208f., 211–215, 228ff., 362f., 424, 429f., 456f., 468f., 480ff., 482–491, 502ff., 510f., 598
Cicero, 341
Cilicia, 153
Cilician Gates, 34
Circumcision, 37, 46f., 63, 349f., 364ff., 366, 396, 423–426, 458
Claudius, 23, 44, 381, 414
Claudius Lysias, 374ff
Cleanthes, 341
Clement of Alexandria, 200, 245, 527, 575
Clement of Rome, 483, 485, 488, 528
1 Clement, 477f., 527f., 535, 570
Codex Sinaiticus, 573
Collingwood, R. G., 237
Colossae, 461, 463ff., 486
Colossians, 21, 450, 459f., 463–470, 497–500
Community consciousness, 135f
Community meals, 146–148, 162f., 403f
Confession, 120
Conflation, 205
Conflict stories, 180f., 284–288, 313
Contemplative Life, The, 56
Conversion of Paul, 357–360, 421f
Conzelmann, Hans, 237
Coponius, 44
Corinth, 365, 370f., 373, 383, 388, 392–411, 418, 427f., 451, 488, 543, 570

Corinthian correspondence, 392–411, 445, 497
1 Corinthians, 21, 126, 397–405, 409, 427, 454, 487, 497
2 Corinthians, 21, 126, 405–411, 451, 456
Cornelius, 97, 144, 154, 365
Crispus, 371
Criterion of coherence, 239f
Criterion of dissimilarity, 239f
Criterion of multiple or cross-sectional attestation, 239f
Crucifixion, 118, 161f., 248f., 319, 358, 407f., 506, 599
Cup of Blessing, 64
Cyprus, 152, 360f
Cybele, 336f., 448
Cybele-Attis mysteries, 336f

Damaris, 370
Damascus, 138, 357, 359f., 369
Daniel, 82, 84, 126, 263f., 304f
David, 79f
Davidic Messiah, 80, 88, 117f., 312
Day of Atonement, 65
Day of the Lord, the, 79ff., 119, 388ff., 391f
Deacons, 487ff., 507
Dead Sea Scrolls, 52ff., 57, 60, 72–76, 149, 180, 586
Dead Sea Sect—see Qumran Community
Decius, 480
Delos, 337
Demeter, 332f., 336
Demetrius, 372
Democritus, 341
Demons, 70, 281, 401ff., 425
Demythologizing, 13f
Derbe, 362, 419
De Rerum Natura, 341
Deuteronomy, 128
Diana, 333
Diaspora, 50, 77, 149f., 348ff., 397
Dibelius, Martin, 105, 166
Didache, 164, 209, 488, 490f., 541
Dilthey, Wilhelm, 237
Dio Cassius, 478
Dionysiac mystery religion, 332
Dionysius, 370
Dionysius of Alexandria, 554
Dionysus, 327, 332f., 336, 592
Diotrephes, 566, 569
Disciples, 94, 102, 145, 171, 196ff., 204, 211, 277, 285
Dispersion—see Diaspora
Divorce, 285
Docetism, 484, 567, 569
Dodd, C. H., 240, 258ff., 265, 294f., 441
Domitian, 336, 478f., 523, 549f., 554ff
Domitilla, 478
Dualism, 332, 389, 400f., 426

Easter, 125, 162
Ebeling, Gerhard, 14, 237
Ebionites, 481, 484

Ecclesiasticus, 51, 79f
Edict of Cyrus, 36
Editorial Framework Hypothesis, 189; *see Mark*
Egnatian Way, 407, 451
Egypt, 35ff., 46, 337f
Egyptians, Gospel of the, 246
Eighteen Benedictions, 50
Elder, the, 570, 580
Elders, 140, 142, 362f., 487f., 507
Elect Lady, The 566f
Election, 78, 119
Elusinian mystery religion, 332
Embassy to Gaius, 56
Emperor Cult, 333, 336, 479
Ending of *Mark*, 199f
1 Enoch, 51, 542f
2 Enoch, 51
Epaphras, 462, 464
Epaphroditus, 451, 453f., 456, 458
Ephesians, 21, 348, 450, 459f., 488, 496–504, 521
Ephesus, 352, 372ff., 392, 407, 418, 427f., 450f., 453ff., 461, 479, 498f., 554, 556, 575, 588
Epictetus, 341
Epicureanism, 340f., 369
Epicurus, 341
"Epiphanes"—*see* Antiochus IV
Epiphanius, 480f., 575
Erasmus, 497
Eschatology, 75, 78–89, 97, 110, 119–121, 153, 163, 180, 181f., 196f., 211f., 228ff., 256–266, 270–274, 279, 282, 290, 294, 305, 386, 389f., 391f., 409, 431ff., 445, 481, 487, 514f., 533f., 546f., 592f
1 Esdras, 51
2 Esdras, 51, 87f
Essenes, 54, 56f., 68, 72–76, 135f., 141f., 148, 149, 156, 180, 530
Ethical Teaching in Ephesians, 504
Ethical Teaching in Pastorals, 510f
Ethical Teaching of Jesus—*see* Teaching of Jesus
Ethical Teaching of Paul, 389f., 399, 400–404, 444, 459, 469f
Ethiopian eunuch, 154
Euangelion, 121
Eucharist, 158, 403, 490, 593
Eusebius, 200, 209, 245, 478, 521, 527, 535, 570, 575
Evangelists, 503
Every Good Man Is Free, 56
Existentialist theology, 237ff
Expiation, 437f
Ezekiel, 79, 264, 564
4 Ezra, 51, 87f., 433, 479

Faith, 120, 364, 366, 424f., 429f., 434f., 438, 459, 506, 536, 538ff
Feast of Booths, 40
Feast of Tabernacles, 65
Feast of Unleavened Bread, 65
Feast of Weeks, 65
Felix, procurator, 46, 55, 376f

Festivals, 37
Festus, procurator, 46, 377f
Filial piety, 63
Flavius Clemens, 478
Foods laws, 364f., 423, 425
Food offered to idols, 365, 401ff
Forgiveness, 119f., 146, 228, 292
Form Criticism, 104, 165–173
Fourth Gospel—*see John, The Gospel According to*
Fragments of a Zadokite Work, 51, 54, 72, 74, 84f
Fragment hypothesis, 506, 508
Fuchs, Ernst, 237
Fulfillment of the Scriptures, 117ff., 121ff., 123–129, 160f., 179f., 191, 211ff., 229f., 311–319, 369, 377, 379, 533f
Fundamentalism, 6

Gaius, 565, 569
Gaius (Caligula), Emperor, 44, 54, 91, 93, 336, 338
Galatae, 418
Galatia, 392, 418ff., 454
Galatians, 21, 358ff., 363–366, 416–426, 438f., 445
Galilee, 43ff., 55, 61, 143, 152, 158, 193, 195, 223f., 226f., 231f., 276–297, 321
Galli, 337
Gallio, 370, 383
Gamaliel, 68, 102, 155, 480
Gemarah, 349
Genealogies, 180, 203, 211, 226
Genesis Apocryphon, 52f
Gentile Question, 363–366
Gentiles, 108f., 122, 153f., 156, 195, 224f., 226, 227, 349f., 361, 442, 481f., 502f
Georgius Monachus, 553
Geschichte, 13
Gessius Florus, procurator, 46
Gethsemane, 301, 316f
Gnosis, 345, 347f., 397, 511, 545, 569
Gnostic redeemer myth, 347f., 467
Gnosticism, 345–348, 545ff., 567, 575, 586ff
God-fearers, 108, 227, 349
Goodspeed, Edgar, 499f., 504
Gospel, 121–123, 195, 363, 421, 431ff., 538, 563
Great Mother—*see* Cybele
Greek, 50, 153, 187f., 201, 210, 224, 521f., 527
Greek City-States, 331f
Greek mystery religions, 332

Habakkuk, 434
Habakkuk, Commentary on (IQp Hab), 52f., 84f., 434
Haburah, 315
Hades, 332
Hadrian, 46f., 68, 138, 481
Haggadah, 48f., 68, 402
Halakah, 48, 68
Hanukkah, 39, 65
Harnack, Adolf von, 386
Hasideans (Hasidim), 39f., 69
Hasmoneans, 39ff., 43f., 54, 69, 84, 86

Healing, 134f
Hebrew, 50
Hebrews, the, 148-150
Hebrews, The Letter to the, 24, 126, 152, 243, 483, 496, 519, 527-534
Heidegger, Martin, 13, 237
Hellenistic Age, 35
Hellenists, 116, 140, 143, 148-150, 156
Heracles, 31
Hercules, 333
Hermeneutical problem, 5, 9-15
Hermes, 331, 362
Hermes Trismegistus, 344f
Hermetica, the, 344f., 348, 350, 586
Herod the Great, 32, 41ff., 59, 64, 66, 273f., 333
Herod Agrippa I, 44, 91ff., 137ff., 143, 154-156, 299, 351, 414, 553
Herod Agrippa II, 44f., 54, 378
Herod Antipas, 44f., 231, 296
Herodias, 44
Hezekiah's "bandits," 43
Hierapolis, 464
Higher criticism, 7, 8
Hillel, 68, 87, 285, 287f
Hillel the Elder, 48
Hirelings, 62f
Historical criticism, 6f
Historie, 12f
History, Paul's theology of, 423f., 442f
Holy Spirit, 97, 108, 119f., 131-136, 144-146, 153f., 225-230, 355, 361, 363, 366, 397, 400, 426, 483, 488, 491, 514, 575, 597, 599
Horus, 337
Hume, David, 11
Hymenaeus, 514
Hyrcanus II, 41, 43

I-type sayings of Jesus, 168, 287ff
Iconium, 361f., 419
Idumea, 41, 44
Ignatius, 210, 481, 482ff., 485f., 489f., 575, 588
Interim-ethik, 258, 260
Irenaeus, 99f., 186f., 194, 200, 215, 346, 484, 521, 552, 570, 574f
Isaiah, 79, 128, 129, 211f., 226, 273, 293, 308f., 379, 432
Isaiah Scroll (IQ Is^a), 52f
Isaiah Scroll, Incomplete (IQ Is^b), 52f
Isaiah Scroll of St. Mark's Monastery—*see Isaiah Scroll* (IQ Is^a)
Ishmael ben Elisha, 68
Isis, 328, 337ff

James, the brother of Jesus, 102, 140, 142ff., 360, 365, 396, 480
James, The Letter of, 25, 513, 534-540
James, the son of Zebedee, 154-156, 553
Jamnia, 46, 57, 87
Jason, 388
Jeremiah, 79, 211
Jericho, 43
Jerome, 543, 552

Jerusalem, 34, 36f., 40, 46f., 54, 59, 79, 81, 87f., 92, 143, 150f., 152-156, 161, 181f., 193, 203, 210, 221, 224, 230, 233, 310ff., 355, 373f., 392, 396, 419f., 421ff., 480ff
Jerusalem Collection, 373, 410f., 427
Jerusalem Conference, 363-366, 419f., 422f
Jerusalem Talmud—see Palestine Talmud
Jesus, 26, 121, 134f., 136, 145f., 146-148, 155, 157ff., 160-323, 358f., 378, 555, 571, 574-600
Jesus Christ, 195
Jesus the Son of Sirach—*see Wisdom of Jesus the Son of Sirach*
Jews, 108f., 149ff., 153, 154-156, 181, 195, 213, 225ff., 336, 361, 368f., 379, 442f., 479, 480ff., 502f
Jewish Calendar, 64f
Jewish War, the, 55
Johanan ben Zakkai, 46, 68
John the Son of Zebedee, 150, 152ff., 552-555, 574f., 577-588
John the Baptist, 118, 145f., 159, 163, 180, 226, 270-274, 590
John the Elder, 554, 565f
John, the Gospel according to, 25, 152, 243f., 348, 481, 483, 488, 496, 555, 570, 571-600
John, The First Letter of, 25, 483, 556, 567-570
John, The Second Letter of, 25, 566f
John, The Third Letter of, 25, 565f
John Hyrcanus, 40, 59, 69, 71
John Mark, 194, 366
Jonathan, 40
Joseph, 180
Joseph ben Tobias, 39
Josephus, Flavius, 34, 44ff., 54f., 68f., 72-76, 102, 241, 271, 349
Joshua-Jason, 37f
Jubilees, 51, 70, 83, 542
Judaism, 62-89, 108f., 156, 181, 336, 348ff., 358f., 465, 478, 586
Judaizers, 364, 396f., 408, 420ff
Judas Aristobulus, 40
Judas the Galilean, 45, 76
Judas the Gaulanite—*see* Judas the Galilean
Judas Iscariot, 299, 317
Judas Maccabee, 39, 43, 76
Jude, the Letter of, 25, 486, 541ff., 545, 556
Judea, 35, 44, 143, 152, 269, 309f., 355, 392, 454, 475
Judgement, 119, 145f., 564
Judith, 50, 70, 80f
Julius Caesar, 41, 333, 451
Juno, 333
Jupiter, 332f., 478f
Justification, 437f
Justin Martyr, 215, 245, 481, 543, 575

Käsemann, Ernst, 237
Keltai—*see* Galatae
Kerygma, 121-123, 130, 142f., 145f., 152, 161, 163, 164, 178, 189f., 191, 236f., 399f., 404, 416, 434, 457, 469, 483ff., 512, 514, 533f., 536, 540, 543, 547

Kerygmatic Outline hypothesis, 189f.; see Mark
Kiddush, 64, 315
King of the Jews, 211
Kingdom of God, 196, 206, 238, 251–260, 276, 288f., 296ff., 305ff., 315, 593
Kingdom of Heaven, 214, 256; see Kingdom of God
Kittim, the, 53, 85
Knox, John, 460f
Koine, 35
Kore, 332f., 336

L—see Special Luke
Lake, Kirsopp, 386
Lamb, the, 562f
Laodicea, 464, 479, 556
Laodiceans, Letter to the, 464
Last Supper, 146–148, 162f., 313–316
Latin, 195, 451
Law, 364ff., 371, 374f., 396f., 423ff., 434f., 440f., 459, 465, 498, 506, 540
Laying on of hands, 132, 153
Lazarus, 595
Legends, 167
Letter of Aristeas, 50f., 350
Letter of Jeremiah, 51
Lietzmann, Hans, 264
Life of Josephus, 55
Literary Criticism, 7f
Logos, 341, 589f
Lord, 119f., 126f., 230, 336
Lord's Day, the, 490, 560
Lord's Supper, 403f., 490
Lower criticism, 7
Lucretius, 341
Luke, the Gospel according to, 24, 105f., 107, 185, 215–230, 378f
Luke, 100f., 105–107, 116, 215f., 223ff., 363, 365, 461
Luke's Great Omission, 216
Luther, Martin, 535
Lycaonia, 418
Lycus River, 464
Lydia, 366
Lysias—see Claudius Lysias
Lystra, 316f., 366, 419

M—see Special Matthew
Maccabean dynasty—see Hasmoneans
1 Maccabees, 51, 80
2 Maccabees, 51
4 Maccabees, 51, 350
Macedonia, 366–369, 388, 392, 405, 427, 451
Magic, 340, 372
Manson, T. W., 240
Manual of Discipline (IQS), 52f., 83f., 128
Maranatha, 126f
Marcion, 100, 428, 505, 554
Marcus Aurelius, 341
Mariamne, 43
Mark the Evangelist, 194, 215
Mark, Gospel according to, 24, 184, 187–200, 552f

Markan hypothesis, 188f
Marriage, 62, 73, 401, 502
Mars, 333
Martyrdom of Isaiah, 51
Martyrs, 150ff., 196–199, 562, 563
Martyria, 121, 130f
Mary Magdalene, 600
Mattathias, 39, 86
Matthew, the apostle and disciple, 201
Matthew, the Evangelist, 201, 210
Matthew, the Gospel according to, 24, 185, 200–215, 481, 485
Meander River, 464
Melchizedek, 533
Menelaus, 39
Messiah, 79–89, 99, 123ff., 145f., 146–148, 161, 163, 180, 198, 211ff., 226, 275f., 302ff., 358
Messiah of Aaron, 83
Messianic Hope, 79ff
Messianic Kingdom, 564
Messianic Secret motif in Mark, 190f., 198, 303
Methodology, 17–27
Micah, 79, 211
Midrashim, 48f
Midrash Rabbah, 49
Miletus, 374
Ministry of Jesus, 160–164, 170ff., 188–191, 203, 206, 224, 226ff., 247f., 577
Miracles, 102
Miracle Stories, 167, 180, 277–282
Mishnah, the, 48ff., 349
Missionary Journeys, 355, 360–363, 366–371, 372–374, 419f., 451
Mithra, 339f., 449
Modein, 39
Mount Zion, 153
Moore, G. F. 56f
Moses, 73, 214
Mosaic Law, 37
Muratorian Canon, 100
Mystai, 332
Mysterion, 332, 469
Mystery religions, 147f., 331f., 348, 399, 405, 466
Mysticism, 343ff
Myths, 167

Nabateans, 41, 360, 413
Nag Hammadi, 245ff., 346, 521, 587
Nahum, Commentary on (4Qp Nahum), 53
Nationalism, 86, 125, 151, 227f., 276, 312
Nativity Stories, 225f., 247, 321ff
Nature, arguments from, 362f., 369, 435f
Nazarenes, 481
Nazareth, 44f., 226f
Nazarite Vows, 374
Nero, 23, 24, 46, 196f., 336, 381, 477f., 556
New Covenant, 74, 211, 214, 408
New Israel, 211, 213, 277, 424
New Jerusalem, 83, 87f., 565
New Law, 214
Nicodemus, 596

Nicolaitans, 486, 556
Niebuhr, Richard R., 14
Nisan, 65
Non-Christian References to Jesus, 241f
Non-Synoptic References to Jesus in *NT*, 242ff
Normative Judaism, 56f
North Galatian Theory, 418–421

Octavian, 33, 43, 451
Old Testament, 37, 50, 99, 141, 149–152, 161f.,
    179f., 202ff., 209, 211ff., 275, 283, 321f., 350,
    363, 423f., 432ff., 458, 482f., 563ff., 589, 591
Olympian Zeus, 37
Onesimus, 460, 462f
Onesiphorus, 514
Onias III, 37
Oral Law, 68, 70, 72, 283, 349
Orders, Church, 48
Origen, 200, 245, 527, 535, 554
Orphic Mystery Religion, 332
Osiris, 337f
Oxyrhynchus Papyri, 245f

Pairs, 68
Pais—see Servant of God
Palestine Talmud, 49
Pannenberg, Wolfhart, 14
Papias, 187, 245, 521, 553, 569f., 580
Papias Tradition, the, 187, 194, 200, 209f
Parables, 165, 167f., 181, 238, 255, 269, 289–296
Paraclete, 597
Parousia, 110, 227, 546
Passion, the, 161–163, 166, 178f., 197f., 203,
    219–221, 228f., 310–319, 595–600
Passover, 50, 64f., 158, 310, 314f
Pastoral Letters, the, 25, 481, 488f., 505–515
Pastors, 503
Paul, 20, 23, 97, 100f., 105ff., 110, 116, 121f.,
    132, 145, 147f., 152, 154, 161, 200, 212, 215,
    225, 230, 242f., 354–379, 483, 496–500, 521,
    526, 527f., 539f., 580
Pella, 46, 480
Pentecost, 65, 97, 131–134, 143, 230
Perea, 44f
Persecution of Christians, 23ff., 152, 154–156,
    196–199, 357f., 368f., 388, 477–480, 522f., 526
Persephone—*see* Kore
Persian Empire, 34f
Pesher, 68, 180, 209, 211f
Pessinus, 418
Peter, 23, 97, 100f., 116, 128, 132, 140–144, 150,
    152–155, 186f., 194, 200, 215, 221, 302ff.,
    317, 360f., 365f., 378, 396, 399, 423, 520–524,
    600
Peter, the First Letter of, 24, 478, 496, 520–527
Peter, the Second Letter of, 25, 483, 486, 496, 521,
    541, 543–547
Peter, the Gospel of, 246
Pharisees, 40f., 46, 54, 57, 68, 69–71, 74, 77,
    135, 143, 155, 167, 180f., 213, 283–286, 291,
    313, 358f., 375f., 481

Philemon, the Letter to, 21, 450, 459–463
Philemon, 461ff
Philetus, 514
Philip, the Apostle, 152f., 222, 355
Philip, the Gospel of, 246
Philip of Macedon, 34
Philip, son of Herod the Great, 44
Philip of Side, 553
Philippi, 366, 368, 451, 453ff
Philippians, 21, 450–459
Philo Judaeus, 55f., 72–76, 349f., 533
Phoebe, 427f
Phoenicia, 152
Phrygia, 418, 454
Phrygians, 362, 392
Pirke Aboth, 51
Pisidia, 418
Pisidian Antioch, 361, 419f
Platonism, 341f., 344, 350, 533f
Pleroma, 347, 465
Pliny the Younger, 242, 479, 490
Pluto—*see* Hades
Pollux, 333
Polycarp, 521, 541, 569, 575
Pompey, 41
Pontius Pilate, 93, 299
Posidonius, 341f., 344, 350
Post-Bultmannian, 237f
Prayer of Azariah, 51
Prayer of Manasseh, 51
Preaching—*see* Kerygma
Predestination, 74
Preface to *Luke-Acts*, 95
Pre-Gnosticism, 346ff., 350, 397, 400, 425, 465f.,
    484, 485f., 502f., 507, 510f., 542
Priests, 37, 40f., 45, 64ff., 67f., 79, 141, 143,
    154, 313f
Priority of *Mark*, 173ff., 187
Priscilla, 372
Prison (or Captivity) Epistles, 21
Procurators, 44ff., 155
Promised Land, 151
Pronouncement stories of the Gospels, 166f
Prophecy, 74
Prophet like Moses, 128f
Prophetic-type sayings, 168
Prophets, 487f., 503
Proselytes, 349
Protoevangelium of James, 246
Proto-Gnosticism, 345
Proto-*Luke* hypothesis, 223f
Providence, 69, 74, 161f., 342, 458
Province Hypothesis—*see* South Galatian
    Theory
Psalms, 97, 126, 273, 312, 432
Psalms of Solomon, 51, 84, 433
Pseudepigrapha, 51, 57, 70
Psychological hermeneutic, 12
Ptolmaic Kingdom, 35ff., 337
Ptolemy Lagi, 31, 35

Publicans, 45

Q—Quelle, 173, 175–178, 180, 202f., 209f., 217, 223, 305
IQH—*see Thanksgiving Hymns*
IQp Hab—*see Habakkuk, commentary on*
IQ Isᵃ—*see Isaiah Scroll*
IQ Isᵇ—*see Isaiah Scroll, incomplete*
IQM—*see War of the Sons*
4QpNahum—*see Nahum, commentary on*
IQS—*see Manual of Discipline*
Quest of the Historical Jesus, 235–251
Quirinius, Governor of Syria, 45
Quirinius, War god, 333
Qumran Community, 32, 41, 43, 52ff., 60, 68f., 72–76, 128f., 139, 141ff., 149, 209, 211f., 270ff., 279, 288, 315, 481, 563, 586f

Rabbi, 67, 282f
Rabbi Judah the Patriarch, 48
Rabbinic Literature, 47–50
Ramsay, Sir William, 418f
Ranke, Leopold von, 11
Realized Eschatology, 258ff
Reconciliation, 409f
Redaction criticism, 130
Redemption, 437f
Repentance, 120, 291f., 485
Resurrection, 70ff., 82, 84ff., 113, 118f., 122, 161–163, 229f., 319ff., 337ff., 376, 388f., 404f., 514, 595–600
Revelation to John, the, 24, 184, 478f., 486, 551, 553–565, 570, 572
Revisionist historians, 5f
Righteousness of God, 430, 431ff., 459
Ritual Defilement, 285f
Roman Empire, 35, 41, 477–480
Roman Law, 162, 368f., 371, 374–378, 424f., 438f
Roman Religion, 332–336
Romans, Paul's Letter to the, 21, 125, 126, 373, 409, 424, 426–445, 521
Rome, 153, 194f., 196, 378f., 451, 453ff., 461, 464, 473ff., 488f., 516, 523f., 528f., 563
Rule of the Community—see A Manual of Discipline

Sabbath, 37, 39, 48, 63f., 167, 284, 349
Sadducees, 45f., 71f., 154f., 276, 313, 376
Saints, the, 119
Salome Alexandra, 41
Salvation, 119ff., 146, 163, 226, 228, 332, 344, 363, 364f., 409f., 431ff., 513
Samaria, 44, 139, 152f., 227f., 333, 355
Samaritans, 149, 151, 152f., 156, 221f., 227f., 481, 571
Sanhedrin, 43, 45, 66f., 155, 313f., 318, 375f., 480
Sarapis, 337f
Sardis, 556
Satan, 196f

Savior, 226, 336, 479, 483, 512
Sayings Source—*see Q*
Schleiermacher, Friedrich, 12
School of St. Matthew, 209
Schweitzer, Albert, 20f., 235, 257f., 264f., 294
Schweizer, Eduard, 266, 582
Scribes, 36, 67f., 282f
Sebaste, 139, 333
Second Coming of Christ—*see Parousia*
Seleucid Kingdom, 35, 37ff., 40
Seleucus, 31, 35f
Seneca, 341
Sepphoris, 44f
Septuagint, 37, 50f., 108, 349f., 521, 529, 533
Sergius Paulus, 361
Servant of God, 129, 309
Setting in Life, 169
Seven Seals, the, 562
Seven Visions, the, 563f
Seventy, the, 227
Shammai, 68, 285
Sheol, 70
Shepherd of Hermas, 485, 527, 535
Sibylline Oracles, 51, 336
Sicarii, 46
Signs and Wonders, 132–135, 163, 365, 591–595
Silas, 366–370
Silvanus, 386, 520, 522; *see* Silas
Simeon, 225f
Similitudes of Enoch, 84f., 263
Simon, 40
Simon, son of Mattathias, 39
Simon ben Kosibah, 47
Sin, 120, 145f., 332, 437, 439
Sinners, 284f., 291
Smyrna, 479, 556
Son of David, 124f., 180, 211, 303
Son of God, 127f., 196, 198f., 226, 264, 316f., 336, 593f
Son of Man, 24, 84f., 88, 125f., 197, 261–266, 303–309
Sopherim, 67
Sosthenes, 371
South Galatian Theory, 418–421
Spain, 427ff., 454f
Speaking in Tongues, 133, 403f
Special *Luke,* 217–222
Special *Matthew,* 203–206
Speeches in *Acts,* 95, 104f., 116–121, 361, 369f., 377f., 454
Spermatikoi Logoi, 342
Spirit, 341
Spirits, 70, 72, 279, 281, 425, 465
Stephen, 128, 150–152, 155, 357, 376, 529
Stoic diatribe, 343, 350, 537
Stoicheia, 465, 468
Stoicism, 340–344, 350, 369, 537f., 546
Story of Ahikar, 51
Suetonius, 23
Sulla, 337